CONNECTIONS: A HISTORY OF PSYCHOLOGY AS A SCIENCE

Michael G. Livingston

Big Star Dawn, LLC

For Anne and Sophia,

I love you more than all the stars in the heavens ♥ *thats adorable*

CONTENTS

PREFACE

The scholarly study of the history of psychology has transformed our understanding of psychology in the last 30 years with exciting and surprisingly relevant new insights. Yet these exciting new insights do not seem to infiltrate the history of psychology courses. Students often find these courses dull and divorced from their understanding of contemporary psychology. Part of the fault rests with the history of psychology textbooks. These texts tend to focus solely on the philosophical roots of the field (an invaluable area of study to understand modern psychology, but not the history of modern psychology itself) or on the lives of great psychologists and their ideas. What is generally neglected is first the contemporary history of the field which would connect history to the current knowledge of students and second the historical context in which important psychologists lived and worked.

Connections: A History of Psychology as a Science focuses on the contemporary history of the field from its founding in 1879 to developments in the 1990s. The book examines important psychologists and their ideas in a broad context. Twenty-two percent of the text reviews the philosophical and historical roots of modern psychology, material that is crucial for an understanding of contemporary psychology. Thirty-four percent of the text is devoted to the history of psychology from 1879 to 1949, the age of the founders and great schools of psychology. Finally, the remaining forty-six percent is devoted to the history of the field from 1950 to the 1990s, a period when psychology experienced rapid expansion and specialization during a time that is generally known as that of big science. By placing the significant figures and their ideas in historical context, Connections: A History of Psychology as a Science allows students to see broad historical patterns and connect the history of psychology with the political, social, and cultural history of the times. More importantly, the text will allow the student to connect the history of psychology to the present-day field of psychology and to their own lives. The result is a history of psychology which I believe will be at once interesting and relevant to students and the general reader. Connections: A History of Psychology as a Science is a fresh approach to the history of psychology.

I am deeply thankful to my colleagues and students for their support over the years as this history text evolved. I would especially like to thank: Alyse Carpenter, Jean Collins, Anne Radolinski, John Radolinski, Anne Rasset, Candace Wilhelm, Maximilian Wilhelm, and Richard Wielkiewicz. It goes without saying that all errors of fact and interpretation are mine and mine alone.

PART I: THE PRE-HISTORY OF MODERN PSYCHOLOGY

"A science ignorant of its founders does not know how far it has traveled or in what direction; it, too, is lost."

ALVIN W. GOULDNER, (1958), P. 8.

No one living today knows for sure when humans first asked questions about human nature. We do know that for millennia the world's major religions have dealt with such questions. Starting with the ancient Greeks, questions about human nature also came within the purview of philosophy. In the 1700s, the specialized branch of philosophy dealing with questions of human nature became known as psychology (Lapointe, 1970).

Modern psychology emerged as a separate scientific field in the 1870s in central Europe and the eastern United States. This psychology was called "the New Psychology" to distinguish it from the older religious and philosophical ideas about human nature. The New Psychology was based on the use of scientific research methods and the empirical investigation of psychological questions, questions that had for centuries been the intellectual property of philosophy and religion. Religion and philosophy answered questions about human nature with casual observation and speculation. The New Psychology answered questions about human nature with systematic observation and experimentation. The New Psychology is now simply called psychology or, more accurately, modern psychology.

Connections: A History of Psychology as a Science is divided into three parts. Part I, consisting of chapters 1, 2, and 3, surveys the pre-history of psychology: the history of psychology before it became a science. Chapter 1 discusses why history is important, some basic concepts and ideas essential to an historical understanding of psychology, and previews what lies ahead in the book. Chapter 2 surveys some of the important concepts and ideas developed during modern psychology's long pre-history, including ideas from Greek and

Renaissance philosophers and from the founders of science. These ideas still play a very important role in the thinking of present day psychologists and we cannot understand the field without knowing something of this historical legacy. Chapter 3 examines more closely the developments in the 1800s that gave birth to the science of psychology: developments in biology, philosophy, medicine, and statistics.

Part II explores in detail the early history of modern psychology, the period from the 1870s to the 1940s. This period is sometimes referred to as the age of schools because it was dominated by broad approaches to psychology as a science known as schools. The most important of these schools are covered in chapters 4 through 8. Chapter 4 introduces the founder of European psychology, Wilhelm Wundt, and his students. European psychology was a science of consciousness. Chapter 5 introduces the founder of American psychology, William James, and the other Americans who developed a psychology related to, but distinct from, European psychology. American psychology eventually came to be called functionalism, for it was a science of the function of consciousness and behavior. Chapter 6 introduces the third founder of modern psychology, Sigmund Freud, and his unique approach to psychology called psychoanalysis. Psychoanalysis was both a science of the unconscious and a set of techniques, a therapy, for treating mental illness. While Freud's school of psychology remained vibrant through World War II, Wundt and James' psychologies were supplanted by two new schools. In the U.S., behaviorism, the psychology of behavior, replaced functionalism as the dominant school. In Europe, Gestalt psychology, the psychology of systems, replaced the psychology of consciousness. The history of behaviorism is presented in Chapter 7. The history of Gestalt psychology is presented in Chapter 8.

Part III examines the contemporary history of psychology, the period from the 1950s to the 1990s, by focusing on the history of various subfields within psychology. After World War II the field of psychology expanded at an exponential rate. Along with this expansion came a dramatic increase in the number of psychologists engaged in research and practice, the amount of research carried out, and the increasing focus of psychologists on subfields within the larger field of psychology. At the same time, the great schools of psychology lost their influence. The contemporary history of psychology is an age of what can be considered big science and diversification. The best way to examine this history of big science and diversification is through a linked history of selected subfields in modern psychology. Chapter 9 examines the history of physiological psychology and perception. Chapter 10 looks at the history of cognitive psychology. Chapter 11 focuses on the history of developmental psychology. Chapter 12 looks at the linked history of social psychology and personality psychology. Chapter 13 examines the history of clinical psychology and psychotherapy. Chapter 14 looks at the history of selected areas within applied psychology. The text ends with Chapter 15, which highlights some common themes and some of the lessons of the history of psychology.

History can be a complicated and confusing subject to those who do not have a strong background in the area. It is often hard to keep the names and dates straight, let alone the ideas and events. History seems to be "just one damn thing after another" (a quip that has been attributed to both the historian Arnold Toynbee and to the industrialist Henry Ford). It is important to know key people, dates, and ideas, and these are stressed and repeated in the text. However, it is also important to look for the patterns and the general themes. Knowledge of the patterns and general themes will in fact help you remember the key people, dates, and ideas.

Dates occurring before the birth of Christ are designated by BCE (before the Common Era). Dates occurring after the birth of Christ are designated by CE (the Common Era) or more often simply written without a designation. Finally, I use the American English spelling of all words except in direct quotes.

Around the same time that modern psychology was born, the detective story as a literary genre was created. The person most responsible for the popularity of the genre in the English-speaking world was Sir Arthur Conan Doyle (1859-1930), the creator of Sherlock Holmes. Holmes has become the prototype of the modern detective who combines logic with the search for and examination of evidence. It is no accident that the detective story was created when criminology was trying to apply scientific methods to criminal investigations (Mandel, 1984) in the late 1800s, the same time scholars began to apply scientific methods to the understanding of psychological questions.

Historians sometimes think of themselves as detectives (Winks, 1969). You are also a detective; as you read what is ahead, you will start an investigation to solve the mystery of why, and how, the psychology that you have learned has become what it is. At the start of each case Sherlock Holmes would say to his sidekick "Come Watson, the game is afoot." Indeed, it is.

References

Gouldner, A.W. (1958). Introduction. In E.   Durkeim, *Socialism*. New York: Collier Books.

Lapointe, F.H. (1970). Origin and evolution of the term "psychology." *American Psychologist, 25*, 640-646.

Mandel, E. (1984). *Delightful murder: A social history of the crime story.* Minneapolis, MN: University of Minnesota Press.

Winks, R.W. (1969). *The historian as detective.* New York: Harper & Row.

CHAPTER 1: APPROACHES TO HISTORY

"The past is never dead. It is not even past."

WILLIAM FAULKNER (1951)

own sake. Let us examine each of these issues.

An internal history looks at the people and ideas separated from the broader society and culture while an external history de-emphasizes the people and ideas and focuses on the broader social forces that shape the field. One advantage to internal histories is that the content of the field, extremely important in science, can be explored in detail. History of science that does not examine the theories and experiments of science is impoverished and bare. An advantage of external histories is that broader patterns that shape a field are made visible. Internal histories often cannot reveal the broader external patterns that shape science. To recognize patterns in the past you need both internal histories and external histories.

This text provides a balance between an internal and external account. The advantage of this approach is that historical patterns are seen more clearly. The disadvantage is that some important people and ideas are omitted or given less time and attention than they deserve.

A troublesome danger is that an internal history can be used to portray the present as the best of all possible worlds, as the end product of a series of progressive steps culminating in the present. This is called Whig history (Butterfield, 1931/1965), named after the Whigs, the British political party in the 1700 and 1800s that championed the idea of political progress and improvement. Whig history assumes progress and ignores the features of the past and present that suggest otherwise.

The kind of history you write, the kind of story you tell about the past, is shaped by certain assumptions about the past. These assumptions are often called theories of history and are part of your metahistory, but they are not the theories you would find in the physical sciences or psychology. Rather, theories of history can be conceptualized as guiding assumptions or heuristics.

One of these theories of history is the Great Men Theory, associated with the work of Thomas Carlyle (1785-1881). Carlyle believed that the past is created by the actions of great men. "*Universal History, the history of what man has accomplished in this world, is at bottom the History of the Great Men who have worked here. They were the leaders of men, these great ones; the modellers, patterns, and in a wide sense creators, of whatsoever the general mass of men contrived to do or attain; all things that we see standing accomplished in the world are properly the outer ma-*

terial result, the practical realisation and embodiment, of Thoughts that dwelt in the Great Men sent into the world" (Carlyle,1841/1963, p. 1).

A second theory of history is associated with the German philosopher, Georg Wilhelm Freidrich Hegel (1770-1831). Hegel argued that the past is created by the spirit (*Geist* in German) of the historical age or times (*Zeit* in German). Hegel's Zeitgeist Theory stresses that the spirit of the historical epoch unfolds over time and shapes people and events. (Hegel, 1837/1953). Thus, great men and past events are the consequence of the zeitgeist, not the cause of it.

A third theory of history was developed by the philosopher and political analyst, Karl Marx (1818-1883). Marx argues that people make history, in the sense of the past and present, but within the constraints of material conditions; some of these material conditions are themselves the product of past human actions. Marx further emphasizes that while individuals matter, groups of people usually have far more influence than single people. The officer corps and soldiers, their equipment, training and tactics, for instance, are more important than a single general. Marx calls his theory of history historical materialism.

The Marxist theory of history is a synthesis of the Great Men theory of Carlyle and the Zeitgeist theory of Hegel. It is a synthesis that emphasizes material conditions as opposed to the general spirit of the time. The kernel of this theory is contained in a famous passage from Marx (1869/1934): *"Men make their own history, but they do not make it just as they please; they do not make it under circumstances chosen by themselves, but under circumstances directly encountered, given, and transmitted from the past. The tradition of all dead generations weighs like a nightmare on the brain of the living"* (p. 10). According to Marx, all of us make history, but not everyone makes history equally. History is contingent upon human actions and constrained by the material conditions inherited from the past. Progress is not inevitable, but it is a possibility.

Theories of history are important because they encourage us to look at certain features of the past and ignore others. This is both good and bad. It is bad when it leads us to see what we already believe, a powerful tendency in human thinking known as the confirmation bias. This bias operates in our everyday thinking and shapes the thinking of both scientists and historians

(Faust, 1984). Only careful examination of evidence and use of tested research methods can help us overcome it.

On a deeper level, some philosophers of science such as Sandra Harding (1986; 1991) and Helen Longino (1990) have argued for standpoint epistemology, the position that where one is in a social structure (rich vs. poor, male vs. female, white vs. black) has a powerful influence on both how science is carried out and on how histories of science are written.

Recent work in the history of psychology highlights the danger of confirmation bias and the relevance of standpoint epistemology. Historical studies of psychology in the 1980s (Scarborough & Furumoto, 1987; Stevens & Gardner, 1982a; Stevens & Gardner, 1982b) showed that women had experienced a double marginalization. The first marginalization was that they were often prevented from entering the field of psychology (often through denial of the opportunity to go to college or graduate school) or were discriminated against when they did get into the field (for example, by being denied jobs). The second marginalization was that they have been omitted from the histories of psychology when they were successful in overcoming the first marginalization. The history of psychology shows a continuing effort over time to overcome this double marginalization. Women were not the only groups affected by this double marginalization; minorities also experienced it (Guthrie, 1976).

Another crucial historiographic issue is a problem that should be familiar to all students of psychology: What is cause and what is effect in human behavior? The historian's task is to tease out the independent variables (the causes) from the dependent variables (the effects) in complex situations for which the data may not be adequate (Shermer, 2002), and cause and effect form a complex web over time. The need to untangle cause from effect requires careful attention to different kinds of evidence and to the quality of that evidence. It is for this reason that historians are obsessed with evidence and the evaluation of evidence.

How historians tell their tales is not just influenced by the kind of tale they wish to tell (the type of history), by whether they take an internal or external approach, or by their theory of history. It is also determined by whether they are interested in the study of the past for what it tells us about the present, called presentism, as opposed to the study of the past on its own terms, called historicism (Stocking, 1965). Stocking (1965) notes that practicing behavioral scientists tend to prefer presentist histories—they want their history to be useful to the current problems they face. Practicing historians, on the other hand, tend to prefer historicist histories—they want a history that explicates the past in its own terms.

The history of psychology has a strong tendency toward presentism, and presentist histories have a strong tendency toward Whig histories. Stocking (1965) has summed it up well: *"Precisely because in the history of the behavioral sciences there are legitimate and compelling reasons for studying 'the past for the sake of the present,' it is all the more important to keep in mind the pitfalls of a presentist approach. And beyond this I would argue that the utilities we are seeking in the present are in fact best realized by an approach which is in practice if not in impulse `affective' and `historicist'"* (p. 217). The best presentist history, Stocking correctly argues, is strongly historicist.

The History Of Psychology And The Philosophy Of Science

Psychologists and historians of psychology continue to be greatly influenced by philosophers, especially philosophers of science. These philosophers have given psychologists a number of concepts and raised several important issues that psychologists struggle with, such as, what is a science? Or, how do we know what is true? And finally, a question that critics often raise—is psychology a science?

One of the most influential of the philosophers of science was Karl Popper (1902-1994). Popper was interested in the logic of science and how scientists apply logic in the search for scientific truths. Popper (1959/1968) suggested that scientists proceed by making conjectures about the nature of a phenomenon. These conjectures are then tested empirically. The purpose of these empirical tests is to kill-off the conjecture. If you have not killed it off, it has gained some support, or to use Popper's term, corroboration. For a hypothesis or theory to be scientific according to Popper, we must be able to disprove it (Popper called this disconfirmation). Such is the principle of falsifiability: something is not scientific unless it can be disconfirmed or disproved. The more precise a theory's predictions, the easier it is to disprove. The easier a theory is to disprove, the more scientific the theory. Theories that are hard to disprove, that make predictions that are hard to disconfirm, or that predict something after it has already occurred (called postdiction) are not scientific. Popper's view of the logic of science is nicely expressed in the quip *"The great tragedy of science—the slaying of a beautiful theory by an ugly fact"* (Huxley, 1870/1894).

Departing dramatically from Popper's approach, the American philosopher and historian Thomas Kuhn (1922-1996) argued that there are two types of science, normal science that exists within a well-established scientific paradigm (a model way of thinking about and studying the world), and scientific revolutions (Kuhn, 1962). Scientific revolutions introduce a new paradigm into the field, one that eventually supplants the existing paradigm. Scientific revolutions (called paradigm shifts by Kuhn) occur when anomalies start to build up. Anomalies are empirical findings that do not make sense or that contradict the existing paradigm. Often anomalies are ignored by scientists, but they cause some scientists to question the dominant paradigm (Kuhn, 1962).

A third influential philosopher of science is Imre Lakatos (1922-1974). Lakatos built upon and modified the work of Popper and Kuhn in an effort to integrate the two very different accounts of science. Lakatos (1970) developed the concept of research programs to supplant the concept of a paradigm. Lakatos argued that research programs have two kinds of assumptions, making up a hard core and a protective belt. The hard core assumptions are never questioned; their truth is assumed. The protective belt consists of secondary assumptions that are tested, questioned, and, if necessary, altered. In addition, research programs can be either progressive or degenerative. Progressive research programs produce new discoveries, new technologies, and lead to the investigation of new problems or to the investigation of old problems in new ways. A degenerative research program is one in which the discoveries are fewer and fewer and little headway is made on the same old problems. When a research program degenerates sufficiently, one or more new research programs will supplant it, creating a problem shift, which according to Lakatos, is a focus on a new set of problems with a new set of assumptions.

The philosophy of science has raised interesting questions for psychology and the history of psychology. The most provocative of these questions is whether or not psychology is a science. Popper's work suggests that at least large sections of psychology, such as psychoanalysis, personality psychology, and clinical psychology, are not scientific because the theories of these areas are not easy to falsify. Kuhn's work suggests that psychology may not have an overriding paradigm; in Kuhn's terms psychology is pre-paradigmatic. Some psychologists argue that psychology has a paradigm, while others argue that it does not. Lakatos' work suggests that psychology had a progressive research program in behaviorism (see Chapter 7) until it started to degenerate in the 1950s and was replaced by cognitivism (see Chapter 10).

Popper, Kuhn, and Lakatos use the physical sciences as their conceptual and historical models of what science should be or really is. Your choice of models has a strong effect on how you answer the question: Is psychology a science? If you select physics, chemistry or astronomy as your model, then the answer is "no." If you select biology, then the answer is "yes, maybe." Biology became an empirical field early in the 1600s. A key turning point was the publication of William Harvey's (1578-1657) work on the heart and the circulation of blood in 1628. Yet it was not until 231 years later, with the publication of the Charles Darwin's (1809-1882) masterpiece *The Origin of Species* in 1859, that biology could be said to have acquired a paradigm. This paradigm was consolidated in the early 1900s, when knowledge of genetics was integrated into the theory to form the modern synthesis. An analogy with biology suggests that paradigms are not the defining feature of science, but are a consequence of a successful historical development as a science. Sometimes, as in the case of biology, success comes after hundreds of years of careful, hard work.

Without a doubt, psychologists and historians of psychology have been greatly influenced by philosophy. Wolman (1971) noted many philosophers have developed their ideas from "yesterday's psychology." Likening psychologists to "a man who owns a gold mine and borrows his own money" (p. 884), Wolman argues that it is time to develop philosophical ideas on the basis of current psychological knowledge; it is time for psychologists to develop their own philosophy of science. This philosophy of science must be suited to the needs of psychological research.

Central to the concerns of Popper, Kuhn, and Lakatos is the question of what separates or distinguishes science and scientific claims to truth from non-science and non-scientific claims to truth. This is called the demarcation problem. Psychologists care about the demarcation problem because we claim that what we are doing is science and that what we find has value because it is scientific. If psychology (or other fields that claim to be science) cannot be demarcated (separated from) non-science, then psychology has no special claim or status.

The great physicist Isaac Newton (1642-1727) studied alchemy. Alchemy, which in the 1600s was a traditional form of chemistry that sought ways to turn base metals into gold and to create a chemical potion that would extend human life, is not considered scientific now. Was alchemy scientific in the 1600s? Could it have been a legitimate science in the 1600s but not a legitimate science in the 1900s? This latter question itself suggests that what qualifies as science changes with the historical epoch and that there is no universal answer to the demarcation problem. Other questions also arise. What, for instance, is the relationship between Newton's laws of physics and his work in alchemy?

In psychology, William James (1842-1910) studied parapsychology (what is commonly called ESP or extra-sensory perception) and tried to communicate with spirits. This is an area not considered scientific now, but was it then? What is the relationship between William James' work in emotions, perception, and religion, and his study of parapsychology? The history of psychology is filled with "occult doubles" (Leahey & Leahey, 1983), non-scientific ideas that were considered scientific by many at the time they were promulgated. We will come back to the demarcation problem again and again in the history of psychology.

Why And How Psychologists Study History

Psychologists study the history of their field in order to achieve a deeper, more integrated understanding of the concepts, methods, and ideas of the field. History is considered such an important area of psychology that it is required in 64% of undergraduate programs, offered as a course in 84% of undergraduate programs, and taught in 91% of Ph.D. and Psy.D. programs (Fuchs & Viney, 2002). Two journals are devoted to the history of the field (*The History of Psychology* and *The Journal of the History of the Behavioral Sciences*) and a division of the American Psychological Association (Division 26) is dedicated to the history of psychology.

The study of the history of psychology furnishes a psychologist with a perspective on the field (Boring, 1950), helping she or he to distinguish between the new and the merely repackaged, the substantial and the merely fashionable (Allport, 1964). The perspective is also a kind of preventive medicine in that it helps individuals to avoid psychology's previous mistakes (Watson, 1966). Is it any wonder then that so many psychology programs offer history of psychology?

How, precisely, psychologists study the history of their field is a question that requires a longer answer. Put another way, how do historians of psychology practice their craft?

The Historian's Craft

Historians are like detectives, assembling information about the past as a detective assembles evidence. The most significant type of evidence is the primary source. The primary source can be an eyewitness account of participants, original texts, or physical evidence from the period. Kragh (1987) provides a long list of primary sources, including: letters, diaries and laboratory journals, notebooks, rough drafts of scientific work, reports and accounts from scientific institutions, published scientific articles and books, textbooks, exam papers and lecture notes, autobiographies and memoirs, films and photographs, television programs, interviews and questionnaires, newspapers or non-scientific books, and buildings or apparatuses. Many of these primary sources are found in archives, collections of historical documents often housed in libraries or museums. Hence, they are commonly referred to as archival sources.

In addition to primary sources, historians use secondary sources. Think of the difference between primary sources and secondary sources as similar to the difference between knowing something firsthand because you experienced it yourself and knowing something secondhand because someone told you about it. Some common examples of secondary sources include memorial volumes and obituaries, biographies, retrospective reflections, and other history textbooks (Kragh, 1987).

One sometimes neglected primary source in the history of science, especially for histories of the recent past, are oral histories. Oral histories "collect spoken memories and personal commentaries of historical significance through recorded interviews" (Ritchie, 1995, p.1). They are a valuable source of information about the past from the point of view of participants reflecting on their prior participation. The interview may be considered a primary source; the historian's synthesis of these interviews into a single narrative is a secondary source. Oral history has been used to study a variety of topics, including the experience of everyday people during the Great Depression, immigrants, and Holocaust survivors.

One especially popular kind of secondary source in the history of science is the biography. Biographies as an approach to the history of science have several advantages. Biographies make possible an "integrated perspective on science" (Kragh, 1987, p. 171) and also foster an in-depth understanding of an individual and his or her work. Some biographies combine psychology with history. These works are known as psychobiographies. Examples include Erik Erikson's (1958) study of Martin Luther and, more recently, John Bowlby's (1992) study of Charles Darwin.

While biographies have advantages, they also have disadvantages. The biography does not permit you to make historical or psychological generalizations. The biographer has a tendency to treat the subject as a hero or saint, glorifying their actions and personality. When this happens, the biography becomes a hagiography --an uncritical and inaccurate portrayal, literally the "story of a saint." Hagiographies were originally stories of the lives of the saints in the Catholic Church and were traditionally written as propaganda pieces.

A second valuable secondary source is the prosopography. Prosopography is a biography of a group of people. The most famous prosopography was carried out by Francis Galton (1822-1911), Charles Darwin's cousin who we will meet again in Chapter 3. Galton carried out a prosopographic study of gifted individuals in his work, *Hereditary Genius* (1869). A more recent example of a prosopographic study is that of Frank Sulloway. Sulloway (1997), in developing and testing his theory of birth-order and personality, examined scientists' birth order and their receptivity to new theories.

Prosopography as a method of historical research is similar to a longitudinal research design in psychology. Longitudinal studies follow a group of individuals through time and can be thought of as prospective prosopographic studies. For instance, the longitudinal study of gifted and talented children carried out over the last 80 years (Terman & Oden, 1947; Holahan, Sears, & Cronbach, 1995) and the study of talented art students over their adult life (Getzels & Csikszentmihalyi, 1976) are both psychological studies and historical studies; they are prospective prosopographic studies.

A third valuable secondary source is the replication of classic experiments in the history of a field, an endeavor known as experimental history of science. This method cannot be generalized to other kinds of history, but can be used in the history of science where key experiments can be replicated under conditions as close as possible to the original conditions. This form of replication is useful as it can enhance our understanding of the research reports of classic experiments and can also assist the historian in determining whether the experiment was actually carried out.

Finally, historians can employ statistical methods and quantification, just as psychologists do, to analyze large sets of data. This is known as quantitative history. Quantitative historical studies of science often focus on two areas: communication patterns among scientists and the growth of science or a field within science (Kragh, 1987, p. 182). The latter is often based on statistical analysis of publications or citation patterns.

The historian must often discover and assemble primary and secondary source material to tell her or his story, but the job does not stop there. An essential part of the historian's craft is evaluating the source material, a difficult task requiring judgment and skill. Errors can creep into a history from the primary and secondary sources themselves as well as the biases and prejudices of the historian. With respect to the former, it is imperative that historians have access to and understand the primary sources. Errors may occur when historians rely too heavily on secondary sources. While all historians must rely somewhat on secondary sources, a careless or uncritical reliance results in the reproduction of errors. Historians, it seems, need to know what they are talking about and rely as much as possible on primary sources (Henle, 1986). After all, *one does not gain in knowledge if what one knows is wrong*" (Henle, 1986, p. xix).

It is not enough for historians to attend carefully to the evidence. They must guard against a powerful bias in human thinking, the confirmation bias, our tendency to look for facts and interpret evidence in a way that confirms what we already think. Confirmation bias is the psychological mechanism by which political and personal bias enters historical narratives. Historians need to be mindful of the bias and guard against it by testing their ideas against the evidence and, especially by seeking out evidence that would disprove what they think. In this respect, historians are similar to scientists who must struggle against the same tendency to view evidence in such a way that one's pre-existing beliefs are confirmed. Historical reasoning, like scientific reasoning, has its limits (Faust, 1984).

Can History Be A Science?

Some historians of science have argued that history, as a study of the past and our accounts of the past, can be a science. This argument is especially made by historians of biology, such as Michael T. Ghiselin (1984) and Michael Shermer (2002). Ghiselin, a biologist and biographer of Darwin, and Shermer, a psychologist, historian of science, and biographer of Alfred Russell Wallace (1823-1913), have both been deeply influenced by the theory of evolution. Darwin worked on problems of what happened in the past, including geology, evolution, and biogeography. In studying these historical phenomena, he created a science of historical subjects. Nor was he the first to do so. Before Darwin, Sir Charles Lyell developed modern geology as an historical science.

Many professional historians would shudder at the thought of history as science. The inadequacy of data concerning the past, the biases, the distortions, the gaps in the record, and other factors makes it impossible to ever know the truth of what happened in the sense that chemists or physicists believe they can know the truth of the physical world. Professional historians are indeed correct; enormous gaps exist in the evidence and many times the data are inadequate.

Darwin was well aware of the problems with missing and inadequate data and the challenges that this posed for developing a science of historical subjects. These problems are not insurmountable, however. By testing a theory with as many different kinds of evidence and carefully evaluating each piece of evidence, you can slowly develop a science of historical subjects, including a science of human history. Ghiselin notes that while Darwin was "willing to entertain any hypothesis, he subjected each one to the most demanding tests" (Ghiselin, 1984, p. 237). In short: the problems with evidence make the science of historical subjects a difficult pursuit, but not an impossible one.

The History Of The History Of Psychology

All fields have a history, including history itself. The notion of historical narratives of the past based on evidence began with the ancient Greeks. The Greeks viewed eyewitnesses as the only reliable source of knowledge about the past and thus restricted their histories to what we would call contemporary history. They produced some of the first great historical works, including Herodotus' history of the Persian Wars and Thucydides' history of the Peloponnesian War between Athens and Sparta. Herodotus, in fact, is often called the "father of history."

The history of science was also developed by the ancient Greeks. Although the original historical accounts have been lost, we still have access to the histories developed in the late Roman Empire that included histories of Greek science and mathematics. When science was re-born in its present, modern form in the 1500s and 1600s, it included historical descriptions of previous work by ancient Greek and Roman scientists. Early modern scientists placed their work in an historical context, viewing history as a kind of taking stock of what had been achieved and what was still to be answered (Kragh, 1987). This is still done in all the sciences where research reports begin with a literature review going over the history of the problem or area of research, and with research reviews that sum up an entire body of studies.

History of psychology also has its own history. Almost from the inception of the new psychology, psychologists (but usually not historians, who seemed uninterested in the field until relatively recently) wrote histories of the field. Many of these histories focused on the intellectual pre-history of the field, the history of the ideas and philosophical works that were psychology's starting point. The classic example of this approach is the work of E.G. Boring, whose *History of Experimental Psychology* was first published in 1929 and whose second revised edition was published in 1950 (Boring, 1950). Boring's work has in many ways become the model for subsequent histories of the field. It is an internal history that devotes extensive coverage to the intellectual prehistory of the field. A second influential history of psychology was Edna Heidbreder's (1933) *Seven Psychologies*, which examined the history of seven different psychological schools.

Boring's history in particular was considered the standard work in the field until the mid-1960s when history of psychology started a period of growth and attracted the attention not only of working psychologists but of professional historians. Notable developments in the 1960s included the publication of new historical surveys of the field, biographies and autobiographies, and the establishment of archives housing the papers and correspondence of psychologists.

History, like truth, can never be impartial. These early histories were shaped by the concerns of their authors, as all histories, including this one, must. Take the case of Boring's 1929 classic. At the time of its writing, Boring was preoccupied with two political struggles within the field. On the one hand, he tried to resist the increasingly practical direction of psychology, a direction that had accelerated dramatically with the U.S. entrance into World War I (a topic I return to again in Chapter 7). On the other hand, he sought to increase psychology's separation from and, in some instances, subordination to, philosophy. "As he himself acknowledged, *the History of Experimental Psychology* was written partly to show his philosophical brethren that philosophy had had an important role in psychology's development, a role that had served its purpose and had become anachronistic and obtrusive" (O'Donnell, 1979, p. 291).

Questions And Themes

What is the nature of human nature? Are we the product of our environment or of our biology? Are we born good or born evil? Do we possess freedom or is our life determined? How do we perceive the world? How do we know the world? What is the relationship between our bodies and our awareness of ourselves? Is there a purpose in life? How do people grow and change? How are people the same or different? What is human happiness? How do you live "the good life"? What is normal and what is abnormal human behavior?

These fundamental questions can be answered through art (painting, poetry, theater, film, music, and novels), religion, and philosophy as well as psychology. What distinguishes psychology from these other human endeavors is its epistemology—how it approaches the fundamental questions.

While psychology deals with the big questions throughout its past and present, any historical account of psychology's past will tend to emphasize certain themes over others. The themes emphasized in this text are:

1) Everything is connected to everything else;
2) Psychology is shaped by the broader society and culture;
3) Psychology shapes the broader society and culture;
4) Psychology is an eminently practical field;
5) Psychological "truth" must be carefully proven.

The first theme is eloquently captured by the epigraph from historian William Manchester that opens this chapter. Everything is indeed connected to everything else. Sometimes the connections are direct, but often they are distant and subtle. The concept is a staple of much historical work. Understanding history requires knowing the connections between people and events. Knowing connections is a prerequisite for recognizing historical patterns.

The second theme, that psychology is shaped by the broader culture and society, emphasizes context. Just as a person's behavior is shaped by the environment (or their context) so the field of psychology is shaped by its environment. While this may seem obvious, the way that the broader culture and society shapes the field is often invisible in the present. It is only (or mostly) through the study of history that we can identify how the environment has shaped psychology.

While it is true that society shapes psychology, it is also true that psychology has profoundly shaped modern society. This is the third theme. Many students enter the field of psychology because of their interest in people—in helping people or understanding them. What they do not realize is that psychology has had a profound influence on society. The way business is conducted, the way parents raise their children, the way we think about ourselves and our problems, have all been shaped by psychology

The fourth theme is a variant of the third theme—psychology is an eminently practical field. Part of the influence that psychology has had on society is through the practical technologies that psychology has produced. These technologies include such things as therapy techniques to help people solve their personal problems, psychological testing that helps schools diagnose and educate children, and public opinion polls that help politicians know what their constituency thinks. Psychology also has helped with the design of effective machines (called human factors engineering) and with the creation of effective public policies or programs. Psychology is a science, but part of that science is a set of technologies. And like all technologies, they can be used for good or evil.

The fifth theme that runs through the text is that psychological "truth" must be carefully evaluated. Psychology deals with topics of utmost importance to people in areas where people have strong preconceived notions. It is easy to use psychology to justify your beliefs, and it is easy for your beliefs to bias your research or your interpretation of the research. Prejudice and bigotry often wrap themselves in the cloak of scientific respectability.

While prejudice and bigotry sometimes pass themselves off as science, and we will explore several historical examples in the text. It is more common still for unsupported ideas, or ideas that have only weak support, to be accepted as true because they accord with our preconceptions or assumptions. Our preconceptions and shared assumptions are not examined as closely as they should be. There is much that is not known, and some things that are believed to be true are not.

These five themes, that everything is connected to everything else, psychology is shaped by its broader societal context, that psychology shapes the broader society, that psychology is eminently practical and that claims to psychological truth must be carefully evaluated, will start to appear in Chapter 4 when we begin the actual history of psychology, and some themes will be emphasized in certain chapters more than the others. To understand the past of our field, keep in mind the themes that underlie the history.

You have now completed your basic training as an historical detective. The investigation will begin in an unlikely place: ancient Greece, circa 500 BCE.

References

Allport, G.W. (1964). The open system in personality theory. In H.M. Ruiten-beek (Ed.), *Varieties of personality theory* (pp. 149-166). New York: E.P. Dutton.

Bowlby, J. (1991). *Charles Darwin: A new life.* New York: Norton.

Boring, E.G. (1950). *A history of experimental psychology*, 2nd ed. New York: Appleton-Century-Crofts.

Burckhardt, J. (1979). *Reflections on history.* Indianapolis: Liberty Press.

Butterfield, H. (1931/1965). *The Whig interpretation of history.* New York: W. W. Norton & Co.

Carlyle, T. (1841/1963). *On heroes, hero-worship and the heroic in history.* London: Oxford University Press.

Dawson, C. (1951). The problem of metahistory. *History Today, 1*(6), 9-12.

Diamond, J. (2005). *Collapse: How societies choose to fail or succeed.* New York: Viking Press.

Erikson, E. (1958). *Young man Luther: A study in psychoanalysis and history* (Austin Riggs Monographs No. 4). New York: Norton.

Faust, D. (1984). *The limits of scientific reason.* Minneapolis: University of Minnesota Press.

Fuchs, A. H., & Viney, W. (2002). The course in the history of psychology: Present status and future concerns. *History of Psychology, 5*, 3-15.

Galton, F. (1869). *Hereditary genius: An inquiry into its laws and consequences.* London: Macmillan.

Getzels, J.W., & Csikszentmihalyi, M. (1976). *The creative vision*. New York: John Wiley & Sons.

Ghiselin, M.T. (1984). *The triumph of the darwinian method*. Chicago: University of Chicago Press.

Guthrie, R.V. (1976). *Even the rat was white: A historical view of psychology*. New York: Harper & Row.

Harding, S. (1986). *The science question in feminism*. Ithaca, NY: Cornell University Press.

Harding, S. (1991). *Whose science? Whose knowledge?* Ithaca, NY: Cornell University Press.

Hegel, G.W.F. (1837/1953). *Reason in history: A general introduction to the philosophy of history*. Indianapolis: Bobbs-Merrill.

Heidbreder, E. (1933). *Seven psychologies*. Englewood Cliffs, NJ: Prentice-Hall.

Henle, M. (1986). *1879 and all that*. New York: Columbia University Press.

Holahan, C. K., Sears, R.R., & Cronbach, L.J. (1995). *The gifted group in later maturity*. Stanford: Stanford University Press.

Huxley, T.H. (1870/1894). Biogenesis and abiogenesis. In *Collected essays*, Vol. 8.

Kragh, H. (1987). *An introduction to the historiography of science*. Cambridge: Cambridge University Press.

Kuhn, T. S. (1962). *The structure of scientific revolutions*. Chicago and London: University of Chicago Press.

Lakatos, I. (1970). Falsification and the methodology of scientific research programmes. In I. Lakatos and A. Musgrave, *Criticism and the growth of knowledge.* Cambridge: Cambridge University Press.

Lapointe, F.H. (1970). Origin and evolution of the term "psychology." *American Psychologists, 25,* 640-646.

Leahey, T.H., & Leahey, G.E. (1983). *Psychology's occult doubles: Psychology and the problem of pseudoscience.* Chicago: Nelson-Hall.

Longino, H. (1990). *Science as social knowledge.* Princeton, NJ: Princeton University Press.

Manchester, W. (1992). *A world lit only by fire. The medieval mind and the renaissance: Portrait of an age.* Boston: Little, Brown and Company.

Marx, K. (1869/1934). *The eighteenth brumaire of Louis Bonaparte.* Moscow: Progress Publisher.

McNeill, J. R. (2000). *Something new under the sun: An environmental history of the twentieth-century world.* New York: W.W. Norton & Co.

O'Donnell, J.M. (1979). The crisis of experimentalism in the 1920s: E.G. Boring and his uses of history. *American Psychologist, 34*(4), 289-295.

Popper, K.R. (1959/1968). *The logic of scientific discovery.* New York: Harper & Row.

Raphelson, A.C. (1982). The history course as the capstone of the psychology curriculum. *Journal of the History of the Behavioral Sciences, 18*(3), 279-285.

Ritchie, D.A. (1995). *Doing oral history.* New York: Simon & Schuster Macmillan.

Scarborough, E. & Furumoto, L. (1987). *Untold lives: The first generation of American women psychologists*. New York: Columbia University Press.

Shermer, M. (2002). *In Darwin's shadow: The life and science of Alfred Russel Wallace*. Oxford: Oxford University Press.

Stevens, G. & Gardner, S. (1982a). *The women of psychology, Vol. I: Pioneers and innovators*. Cambridge, MA: Schenkman Publishing.

Stevens, G. & Gardner, S. (1982b). *The women of psychology, Vol. II: Expansion and refinement*. Cambridge, MA: Schenkman Publishing.

Stocking Jr., G. W. (1965). On the limits of "presentism" and "historicism" in the historiography of the behavioral sciences. *Journal of the History of the Behavioral Sciences, 1*, 211-218.

Sulloway, F.J. (1997). *Born to rebel: Birth order, family dynamics, and creative lives*. New York: Vintage.

Tainter, J.A. (1990). *The collapse of complex societies*. Cambrigde, England: Cambridge University Press.

Terman, L.M., & Oden, D.H. (1947). *Gifted child grows up: Twenty-five years follow-up of a group* (Genetic Studies of Genius). Stanford: Stanford University Press.

Turchin, P., & Nefedov, S.A. (2009). *Secular cycles*. Princeton, NJ: Princeton University Press.

Watson, R.I. (1966). The role and use of history in the psychology curriculum. *Journal of the History of the Behavioral Sciences, 2*(1), 64-69.

Wolman, B.B. (1971). Does psychology need its own philosophy of science? *American Psychologist, 26*, 877-886.

CHAPTER 2: PHILOSOPHICAL AND SCIENTIFIC FOUNDATIONS

Psychology has a long past, yet its real history is short. For thousands of years it has existed and has been growing older; but in the earlier part of this period it cannot boast of any continuous progress toward a riper and richer development. In the fourth century before our era that giant thinker, Aristotle, built it up into an edifice comparing very favorably with other science of that time. But this edifice stood without undergoing any noteworthy changes or extensions, well into the eighteenth or even the nineteenth century. Only in recent times do we find an advance, at first slow but later increasing in rapidity, in the development of psychology.

HERMANN EBBINGHAUS (1908/1973), P. 3.

The moment you are born, you receive an enormous inheritance from the past, a body of wealth almost unimaginable. Without this inheritance you would be born into a world without human language and tools, without domesticated plants and animals, without buildings and roads and airplanes. From the moment you are born, you enter a world that provides a rich legacy of the past to all who currently live. Humans could no more survive without this legacy than a naked and toolless person could survive on an arctic island.

As you grow and become educated, you master some of this legacy. You learn to speak and to write a language, sometimes several. You learn about religion, philosophy, and art. You learn to drive a car, use a phone, and play the guitar. None of us, no matter how smart we are or how long we live, can master every element of this enormous inheritance we have been given. But collectively, we can master much of it. One way of coping with the enormous legacy is to become a specialist, to master that part of the past related to some specific field. As a student of psychology, that is what you are doing by studying the history of psychology

Modern psychology has a long pre-history or past, as one of the founders of modern psychology Hermann Ebbinghaus wrote. We have inherited a rich legacy from the past that shapes the field. Before we actually explore the history of modern psychology we must understand something of the legacy of the past. Our journey begins with the ancient Greeks.

The Contributions Of The Greeks—Classical Philosophy

Around 600 BCE in what is now Greece, Southern Italy, and Turkey, an enormous cultural flowering took place that has given much to our civilization. This flowering of the ancient Greek civilization is typically broken into two time periods: the classical period from around 600 BCE to the conquest of the Greek City States by Alexander the Great (356-323 BCE); and the Hellenistic period from the time of Alexander the Great through the conquest by the Romans until approximately the division of the Roman Empire into an Eastern Empire and a Western Empire. The Classical Period (also called the Hellenic Period) is the period of the Greek City States. The Hellenistic Period is the period of large multicultural empires that were influenced by, and spread, Greek culture.

Nothing comes from nothing. The Classic Greek culture built upon an early Greek culture, the Mycenaean, which flourished from 1400 to 1200 BCE. The Mycenae Greeks fought the Trojan War around approximately 1200 BCE. The Mycenae culture in turn built upon the Minoan culture of Crete, a culture that flourished from 2200 to 1500 BCE. The Minoan culture is believed to have collapsed as a result of the volcanic explosion that disrupted trade routes and agricultural production. Eventually the Minoans were invaded by the Mycenae Greeks, who adopted a number of Minoan technologies.

The Mycenaean culture went into a long dark age and re-emerged around 600 BCE, having adopted the Hebrew Alphabet by adding vowels to it and standardizing the order of the letters. The development of the Greek Alphabet and the emergence of literacy precipitated the long flowering of Greek culture. Two classics of world literature, the *Iliad* and the *Odyssey*, by Homer, were written down (based most likely on oral epic poems) hundreds of years after the Trojan War at the beginning of the classical period. From the writing of the *Iliad* and the *Odyssey* to the conquest of the Greeks by the Romans in 197 BCE, the Greeks experience a period of almost 500 years of explosive change and innovation (Cahill, 2003).

The Greeks made numerous advances and innovations, some of which we have inherited. One of their most important, in terms of their political and economic success, was the structure of their army. Prior to the Greeks, armies were more like gangs of individuals. The classic Greeks were constantly at war, with each other and with outsiders, and their armies were tightly coordinated, highly disciplined killing machines. Greek soldiers were heavily armored in bronze and fought in a tight formation called a phalanx. War was an art. With battles carefully planned beforehand and with the site carefully selected, war became a skilled craft for the Greeks (Cahill, 2003).

The Greek alphabet and the development of warfare were just the starting point. The Greeks went on to make a number of innovations in politics (inventing trial by jury and democracy), art (creating a life-like realistic style in sculpture), theater (they invented western theater and produced the first dramas and comedies), mathematics (refining and developing the Egyptian invention of geometry for example) and astronomy (Cahill, 2003). They also pioneered the writing of history, with Herodotus writing a history of the Persian Wars and, in the next generation, Thucydides writing a history of the Peloponnesian Wars between Athens and Sparta. But the Greeks' most important innovations, for the history of psychology, were the creation of philosophy and science.

The Greek philosophers produced a rich corpus of ideas and theories. For psychology, four fundamental philosophical concepts have had the greatest impact: idealism, empiricism, skepticism, and materialism. Each of these philosophical concepts was the product of numerous Greek, and later Roman, philosophers. But each is also associated with one towering figure: idealism with Plato; Empiricism with Aristotle; skepticism with Pyrrho; and materialism with Epicurus.

The Power Of Idealism

In philosophical terms, idealism is the view that spirit and mind are fundamental aspects of the universe. Idealism is the opposite of the philosophical view of common sense realism, the idea that what we perceive exists. Instead the idealist would argue that there is a reality beyond and above our simple perceptions. Idealism is also opposed to materialism, the idea that matter is the fundamental aspect of the universe. The term "idealism" was not used to describe this philosophical notion until the 1700s, when it was first used by Leibniz (who you will meet later in this chapter), but the idea itself has been around far longer (Acton, 1967). The philosophical term "idealism" has little to do with the non-philosophical modern usage of someone who lives by her or his ideals or who embraces high ideals.

The first complete expression of idealism, in the philosophical sense, was developed by the philosopher known as Plato (427-347 BCE). I say "known as" because in fact Plato was his nickname (meaning "broad-shouldered") and not his real name. Plato got his name because of his very broad and muscular shoulders. As a youth, he was a follower of Socrates and a champion athlete. He later founded a school of philosophy in Athens called the Academy, the word still used to describe the world of higher education today. Some of Plato's works are purportedly a presentation of Socrates' ideas, and other works represent Plato's own philosophical views. Plato's idealism is contained in his theory of forms, which represents his own ideas and not those of Socrates (Hunt, 1993).

According to Plato, everything we perceive in the world is a manifestation of a pure form or idea that exists in the abstract. This abstract existence is a reality beyond our perceptions of reality. Beyond every circle or square we perceive is a pure form or idea of circle and square. Our perceptions of these geometric shapes are faulty copies of the pure idea; faulty copies that result from the interaction of matter with the pure form or idea. Each form or idea had an essence that characterized it and the faulty copies of the pure form also are characterized by the essence. Thus, Plato not only developed the philosophical concept of idealism, but he argued for essentialism, the notion that all objects in a set share a common and defining essence.

Plato's idealism is perhaps best illustrated in his allegory of the cave. In the allegory of the cave, people are chained to the wall of a cave and can only look at the wall opposite them. Behind them is the opening to the cave and a road where individuals pass, and beyond the road is a fire blazing, that casts shadows of the people traveling on the road. The prisoners in the cave see only the shadows cast from the real world above, not the real world itself. These shadows make up the prisoners' world. Were one to escape, Plato wrote, and make his way to the surface, he would not be able to perceive the objects around him without first going through a period of adjustment. For Plato, the prisoners represent humanity and the shadows represent the world that we know through our senses. The upper world of real objects makes up the world of platonic forms or ideas, the reality beyond the reality of our faulty senses (Hunt, 1993).

How can we know the real world of forms if not through our senses? According to Plato, we know the forms through a process of thinking and reasoning, and through introspection that recovers knowledge from your previous existence. Plato, you see, assumed that the soul was immortal and that we could know the truth by remembering (through introspection) the forms that we experienced before we were born when our souls dwelled among the pure forms. Another way of perceiving the true forms is through mathematics, a description of the reality beyond the "reality" of our sense impressions. Plato's idealism thus also entailed rationalism (you learn the truth through reason) and nativism (you have inborn knowledge) as well as essentialism. These four related concepts, idealism, rationalism, nativism, and essentialism have exerted a powerful hold over western thinking. For example, the Christian idea of the soul and everlasting life owes much to Plato. The Jews at the time of Jesus believed, for example, that you would die and come back to life on the day of resurrection, not that your soul would live forever in heaven. Plato has cast a long shadow indeed.

The Influence Of Empiricism

Empiricism is the notion that experience is the source of knowledge (Hamlyn, 1967). The individual often considered the founder of this perspective is Aristotle (384-322 BCE). Aristotle was the son of the court physician to Amyntas II, the king of Macedonia. His father died when he was very young, and he was sent to Athens where he studied at Plato's Academy. Upon Plato's death in 347 BCE, Aristotle left Athens, spending time in Assos and on the island of Lesbos, where he conducted a number of biological studies. In 342 BCE, Aristotle was appointed tutor to the son of Philip II of Macedonia, the future Alexander the Great. After three years as a tutor, Aristotle spent another five years at Stagira, finally returning to Athens in 335 BCE to found the Lyceum, his school of philosophy. After Alexander's death in 323 BCE Aristotle had to flee Athens; he was in danger from the anti-Macedonian faction within Athens. He died on the island of Euboea the next year (Kerford, 1967; Robinson, 1995).

Aristotle and his followers left a vast body of work, and it is difficult to distinguish Aristotle's own work from the later additions of his students. It is also the case that his work evolved and changed. In his early period, he embraced Plato's philosophy. But over time he moved away from Plato's idealism to embrace empiricism and to develop, with his students, the first sciences. Aristotle's work contains many texts on biology, including classification of plants and animals (taxonomy), botany, and zoology. His writings also contain an extensive treatment of rhetoric, the art of persuasion, as well as the first complete text of psychology. This psychology text, known as *De Anima* in Latin, and *De Psyche* in Greek, contains chapters that you would find in many modern Psychology texts, including memory, perception, and thinking (Kerford, 1967). It was this work, which is considered the first work on psychology, that led Ebbinghaus to write that psychology has a long past.

The Impact Of Skepticism

Skepticism is the questioning of knowledge claims—it asks, in short, how do you know what you claim to know? The Greek philosopher considered the founder of skepticism is Pyrrho of Elis (360-270 BCE). Pyrrho left no writings —what we know of Pyrrho comes from the two different approaches to skepticism developed by the Greeks. The first approach was developed by philosophers in Plato's Academy following Plato's death. This skepticism, known as Academic Skepticism, rejected Plato's theory of forms and said that we cannot know anything that goes on beyond our immediate experience. The best information we can obtain, they further argued, can tell us only what is probable. Nothing is 100% certain, but some claims are more probable than others. The arguments of the Academic skeptics were preserved in the writings of Cicero, the Roman writer (Popkin, 1972).

A second approach was developed by a group of physicians associated with the school of medicine in Alexandria (Egypt). This approach, known as Pyrrhonian Skepticism, developed a set of arguments that undermined the certainty of belief. The Pyrrhonians were especially interested in undermining the claims of dogmatic philosophers—those who like Plato claimed certain knowledge. The skeptics preferred to suspend judgment about that which they had no immediate knowledge (Popkin, 1972).

The vast majority of the work of the skeptics was lost or destroyed with the fall of the Roman Empire in the west, except for two collections of skeptical arguments by one of the last skeptic philosophers, Sextus Empiricus. These collections are essentially powerful arguments against the belief in anything for which there is not observable evidence (Popkin, 1972).

Skepticism, academic and Pyrrhonian, was to have a profound influence on the rise of modern science and the Renaissance. Skepticism, as we shall see, is an important, some would say crucial, element of modern science and of scientific method (Popkin, 1979).

The Specter Of Materialism

The philosophical notion of materialism has little to do with our current usage of materialism as the pursuit of material goods. Rather, the philosophical notion of materialism is the idea "everything that is, is material" (Campbell, 1967).

Materialist philosophy has a long ancestry in Greek philosophy, starting with Thales, who tried to explain the world in terms of fundamental substances, and continues with the work of the great materialist Democritus. But the most influential materialist philosopher was Epicurus (341-270 BCE). Epicurus was born on the island of Samos and moved to Athens in middle age. In Athens he started the philosophical school, "The Garden," where he taught his views on materialism and how to lead a good life. Many of Epicurus' views on materialism were taken from Democritus, but Epicurus also made a number of criticisms and modifications in Democritus' ideas. For instance, Epicurus emphasized both the role of chance and the role of contingency (something could not happen unless something else has happened first). His emphasis on contingency led him to espouse a theory of evolution, arguing that life evolved from matter and that one species evolves from another. He also argued that the stars are suns, like our own sun, that worlds exist beyond our own circling these distant suns, and that space and time are boundless. As a materialist, Epicurus rejected the idea of gods and an afterlife, and stressed human freedom within material constraints. He also opposed reductionism and attempted to resolve psychological questions about how humans perceive and reason (Foster, 2000;

Epicurus was ADVANCED

De Lacy, 1967).

Epicurus was born shortly after the death of Plato and shortly before Aristotle founded his famous school, the Lyceum, in Athens. He lived most of his life in the aftermath of Alexander the Great's death, when Alexander's generals fought for control of the vast empire he had created. Living in a time of religious doubt and social turmoil, Epicurus devoted considerable time to developing his philosophy of how we should live our lives. He is an exemplar of a graceful-life philosopher that emerged in the Hellenistic world. These graceful-life philosophers tried to provide answers to the question: how do you live a meaningful and happy life in an unjust world often filled with pain and suffering? The starting point of Epicurus' ethics is his materialism—the realization that death is the end (there is no afterlife or otherworldly heaven or hell) and that religions are superstitious beliefs. Epicurus emphasized the importance of friendship and of maximizing pleasure and minimizing pain, but he rejected simple hedonism and advocated what he considered higher pleasures, such as good conversation and friendship, the appreciation of beauty, and thinking (Foster, 2000).

Much of what we know about Epicurus comes from the works of his follower the Roman poet and philosopher Lucretius (b. 99 BCE). Lucretius' major work was entitled *De rerum natura.* (in English, *On the nature of things*). *On the nature of things* was to have, as we shall see, an enormous influence on the Renaissance and the birth of modern science. His philosophy also has had a great influence on political and social thought up to our own day (Popkin, 1979).

The Scientific Spirit—Greek And Islamic Science

The naturalistic attitudes of the Greek philosophers and their insatiable curiosity about the world resulted in one of their greatest achievements—the invention of science. Greek science combined the four philosophical strands we have discussed: idealism, empiricism, materialism, and skepticism. Greek scientists looked at the world in order to fathom the reality behind the appearance. They tested their ideas against empirical observations. They sought naturalistic material explanations of the world. And they questioned and criticized each other's ideas and evidence. They worked in astronomy, medicine, biology, physics, and chemistry (Lindberg, 1992).

Perhaps their greatest achievements came in the field of astronomy. One of the early greats in this field was Hipparchus, born in what is now Turkey. Among his achievements he calculated the length of the year to within six and a half minutes, discovered that the world wobbles on its axis as it spins, and developed a star catalogue showing the position of constellations in the heavens. He also developed a system of coordinates to plot the positions of stars and a system to rank their brightness (Chang, 2005).

Recently some of Hipparchus' work was rediscovered. The discovery came when it was recognized that the Farnese Atlas, a statue of Atlas holding the heavens on his shoulder in the Naples Museum, was actually a pictorial representation of the lost star catalogue. The globe, showing 41 constellations (for example, the constellation Taurus is represented by a bull, the constellation Cygnus by a swan, etc.) accurately shows the positions of the stars in 125 BCE. While the statue itself dates from 150 CE, it was a copy of an earlier statue and the sculptor would have had access to copies of Hipparchus' star catalogue (Chang, 2005).

Another significant Greek astronomer was Aristarchus of Samos (310-230 BCE). Unlike many of his contemporaries, he developed a heliocentric model of the solar system in which the sun is the center of the system and the earth and the other planets revolve around the sun. Aristarchus also argued that the earth rotates on its axis (Lindberg, 1992).

In addition to astronomy, perhaps the greatest of Greek sciences was medicine, another of the important and unique contributions of the Greeks to western culture. The father of Greek medicine was the pre-Socratic Hippocrates (birth date unknown), for whom the Hippocratic Oath is named. The Hippocratics (the physician-followers of Hippocrates) adopted an empirical approach to medicine that was to dominate western and Islamic medical practice for over 2000 years (Hunt, 1993).

Most of what we know about Hippocrates comes from the great Hippocratic physician Galen (130-200 CE). Galen was a Greek born in Asia Minor during the height of the Roman Empire. He carried out dissections on human cadavers and vivisection on animals. He stressed the importance of carrying out dissections as often as possible and required his students to do so, even though the practice was falling out of favor with the rise of Christianity. Later, human dissection was to disappear almost entirely under Christianity and Islam (Islam prohibits dissection). Galen insisted that physicians be well-educated, arguing that "the best doctor is also a philosopher." Galen practiced medical experimentation and is credited with making a number of discoveries, but because we know so little about the medical practice of his time, we can't be sure which of the discoveries were his and which have been mistakenly attributed to him. We do know that he used the human pulse to diagnose illness (a practice still done today), argued that blood runs through the veins (not air as many believed), discovered heart valves, that urine was formed in the kidneys, that rabies was spread by dog bites, and that tuberculosis was contagious. He mistakenly held that the heart had only two chambers and that humans have a five-lobed liver. Some of his mistakes were made because he generalized the results of dissection on animals to humans. Dogs, for instance, have a five-lobed liver (Hunt, 1993; Lindberg, 1992).

The Roman Empire started to decline around 200 CE, but continued in the west until the final fall of Rome in 476 CE. In the East, the empire became, under Constantine the Great, the Byzantine Empire. Adopting Christianity as the official religion and with its capital at Constantinople (now called Istanbul), the Byzantine Empire lasted until it was conquered by the Ottoman Turks in 1453 CE (Norwich, 1997). After 200 CE, the influence of the Classical and Hellenistic Greeks declined sharply. The first flowering of western culture had faded and wilted. Over the next 1800 years the legacy of the Greeks would persist, influencing all subsequent western and middle-eastern cultures. In particular, the concepts of idealism, empiricism, materialism, and skepticism would combine and evolve in fascinating ways during the second great flowering, the Renaissance.

What I like to call the "in-between times", the time in Western European history between the demise of the Roman Empire and the Renaissance, has been called the Middle Ages. This has often been portrayed as a primitive and backward period, and in some ways and in some places in Europe, it was. But the characterization of the times between the fall of the Roman Empire and the Renaissance as a "Dark Age" ignores the changes that were occurring in Christian Western Europe and in the civilizations of Eastern Europe and non-Christian Western Europe. I am of course talking about the Byzantine Empire in the east and the Islamic kingdom of al-Andalus in the west, in present day Spain and Portugal.

Islamic forces invaded Spain in 711 CE, crossing the Straits of Morocco, and defeating the Visigoths, the barbarians who had invaded and conquered the Roman province of Hispania. The Visigoths converted to Christianity after they invaded Spain and built their capital at Toledo, the site of an earlier Roman city. The Islamic forces conquered most (but not all) of what is now Spain and Portugal as well as the Mediterranean coast of France, establishing their provincial capital at Cordoba, also a city originally built by the Romans and later occupied by the Visigoths (Menocal, 2002).

In 750 CE the Umayyads, the ruling dynasty of the vast Islamic empire that stretched from Portugal and Morocco to present-day Pakistan in the East and including all of North Africa and the Middle East (with the exception of Asia Minor, controlled by the Byzantine Empire at the time), was overthrown in their capital of Damascus by the Abbasids. The sole surviving member of the Umayyad dynasty was the grandson of the Caliph (the supreme ruler of the Islamic Empire), Abd al-Rahman. Abd al-Rahman fled west with his mother, a Berber from Morocco, across the desert of North Africa. Arriving in al-Andalus in 755, he assembled an army of Berbers and Syrians loyal to his and his mother's families and ousted the Emir (governor) of al-Andalus in a battle outside the walls of Cordoba in May 756 CE. Establishing himself as Emir, Abd al-Rahman founded a dynasty that ruled al-Andalus until it collapsed in violent civil war between 1009 and 1032 (Menocal, 2002).

Meanwhile back in the Islamic heartland, the new Abbasid rulers moved the capital of the House of Islam (as they called the Islamic Empire) from Damascus to Baghdad. They did nothing against the new Emir, apparently willing to tolerate the sole survivor at the very margins of the empire, possibly assuming that he would fade into oblivion. But Abd al-Rahman was a survivor and set out to establish a vibrant and dynamic culture.

The Islamic expansion that led to the vast empire ruled by the Umayyads and later the Abbasids was built on the cultural richness of the peoples and cultures they conquered and assimilated. This cultural and material spolia (the leftover remains of a collapsed civilization) was preserved, revived, and diffused throughout the Islamic Empire. Integrating material and ideas from the Greeks and Romans, from the Christians, Jews and Persians, they created a rich and cosmopolitan society (Menocal, 2002).

Nowhere was this dynamic mixture better exemplified than in al-Andalus. The Umayyads created a society based on *convivencia*, the living together in mutual respect of Christians, Jews, and Muslims. They preserved and commented on much of Greek philosophy and science, made substantial advances in medicine and mathematics and created, for the second time in the history of the world, a science. The Jewish people had been treated as slaves by the Christianized Visigoths. Under Umayyad rule they experienced prosperity and a cultural renaissance. Likewise, the Christians enjoyed substantial religious freedom and economic prosperity (Menocal, 2002).

The Greek philosopher that most interested the Muslims was Aristotle. The three most prominent philosophers from the House of Islam were all physicians: Ibn Sina (980-1037 CE), known in the west by his Latinized name of Avicenna, Ibn Rushd (1126-1198), known by his Latinized name of Averroes, and Moses ben Maimon (1135-1204), known by his Latinized name of Maimonides. Avicenna and Averroes were Muslims; Maimonides was Jewish. The three developed and refined Aristotle's philosophy and tried to reconcile Aristotle with their respective religions, incorporating elements of empiricism and skepticism. Maimonides, for instance, rejected astrology as false even though it is mentioned in both the Talmud and the Bible. They also made a number of medical advances. Avicenna used music to treat depressed patients (and thus can be considered the inventor of music therapy). Averroes discovered that the retina (not the lens of the eye, as was believed) is the part of the eye sensitive to light. He also argued that there is no conflict between religion and philosophy. Maimonides studied psychosomatic illness and described the relationship between behavior and mental health. The medical practice of all three was limited, however, by the Islamic prohibition on human dissection. Many of Galen's errors persisted as a consequence and the Islamic physicians did not follow Galen's advice to perform extensive human dissections.

Another important advance that contributed to Islamic science was the development of mathematics. The Arabs used Arabic numerals (which we use today), along with the concept of zero instead of the difficult-to-use Roman Numerals. The Arabs also invented algebra (from the Arabic al-jebr).

Alchemy (from the Arabic words al-kimiya, meaning the art of transmutation) was practiced by the ancient Greeks and by the Chinese at least as early as 400 BCE (Levere, 2001). (I restrict my discussion to the western alchemic tradition, as Chinese alchemy had no impact on the west). Greek alchemy, like Greek science in general, was both a foundation for later science and quite different from modern science in that it included concepts and ideas we no longer consider scientific.

As with other elements of other Greek sciences, the Arabs incorporated and developed Greek Alchemy. The principal center of Greek alchemy in the Hellenistic world was Alexandria (Egypt). In Alexandria the science of the Greeks mixed with the practices of the Egyptians and with the most important technologies of the time, including metallurgy, fermentation, and distillation. When the Arabs conquered Egypt, they fell heir to a vast quantity of Greek texts containing what some historians have called the Alexandrian Heritage. These texts were translated first in Damascus by the Umyyads and later in Baghdad by the Abbasids. Building on this corpus of translated works, Islamic alchemists developed a number of techniques and theories. The two most prominent of these Islamic alchemists were Jabir ibn Hayyan (known as Geber in Western Europe) and Al Razi (864-925 CE). Works attributed to Jabir may have been written by his followers, as was often the case with Aristotle (Hill, 1993; Turner, 1995).

Islamic alchemists made substantial advances in distillation, the extraction of oils for perfumes and scents, the production of soaps, dyes, and colored inks, as well as advances in the use of reagents and the production of metal alloys (Hill, 1993). Islamic swords became the best in the world for many hundreds of years. The swords of Toledo (of Islamic manufacture) were prized in the Middle Ages and are still used in the U.S. Marine Corps by officers. Along with other elements of Greek culture, alchemy also entered Christian Western Europe through al-Andalus (Lindberg, 1992).

When the emirate of al-Andalus broke-up in 1032, it was replaced by a series of smaller kingdoms similar, in some respects, to the Greek city-states of the classic Greek period. These kingdoms were called *taifas*; some were ruled by Muslim kings, others by Christian kings. The traditions of *convivencia* and Islamic culture lived on in many of these *taifas* and spread into Christian Europe

(Menocal, 2002).

One of the two most important figures in this spread of classic and Arab culture into Christian Western Europe was the Dominican monk Albertus Magnus (1200-1280). Albertus was later made a saint by the Catholic Church. He read Aristotle and the Muslim and Jewish commentaries on Aristotle and re-introduced Aristotle's work to Christian Western Europe at a time when the Catholic Church considered Aristotle to be a heretic. Influenced by Aristotle's empiricism, Albertus also made direct observations of nature, making a number of contributions to botany. In addition, Albertus wrote about and practiced alchemy.

A student of Albertus Magnus at the University of Paris and another Dominican, Thomas Aquinas (1225-1274) integrated the philosophy of Aristotle into Catholic traditions. Aquinas was also, like his teacher, a devotee of alchemy. His integration tried to reconcile faith and reason while integrating Aristotle's philosophy into Christian thought. Aquinas, later sainted as well by the Catholic Church for his contributions, re-introduced empiricism and an emphasis on reasoning back into the Catholic Church. While the church later treated Aristotle's ideas as dogma (not open to questioning or test), Aristotle's emphasis on thinking and empiricism could not be denied. This internal tension within the Church's Aristotelian theology generated conflicts over the next several hundred years. The genie of classical philosophy and science, so to speak, had been let out of the bottle.

The Renaissance, Capitalism, And The Birth Of Modern Science

The Renaissance was a period of dynamic cultural, political, and economic change that began in the late 1300s in Italy and then spread throughout Europe. The period was marked by dramatic changes in art, architecture, and literature, as well as changes in politics and economics and extended through the 1500s. The beginnings of the Renaissance in Italy were marked by such works as Dante's (1265-1321) *Divine Comedy*, one of the first literary works in Italian as opposed to Latin, and the sculpture of Donatello (1386-1466). Soon thereafter, such Italian artists as Leonardo da Vinci (1452-1519) and Michelangelo (1475-1564) were producing such masterpieces of world art as The Last Supper (1497) and the Mona Lisa (1504) (both painted by da Vinci) and the statue of David (by Michelangelo) made between 1501 and 1504.

The Renaissance was also a time of transformation in politics and economics. New political forms emerged, such as the strong city-state in Italy and the beginnings of strong, centralized nation states in England and Spain. In England the strong nation state was built by Henry VIII (1491-1547), a product of a Renaissance education and himself a "Renaissance Man," the term applied to someone of broad learning and interests. Henry VIII was versatile in several languages and was a composer of music. Under his rule, a strong centralized bureaucracy was built that substantially increased the power of the king over the power of the aristocracy. Henry also broke with the Catholic Church, establishing the Church of England under his control, further strengthening the English Monarchy. Similar developments occurred in Spain under the Catholic Monarchs Ferdinand and Isabel, in France, and in Central Europe under the Hapsburgs.

Simultaneously with the emergence of these new political forms was the emergence of a new economic system—mercantile capitalism. Beginning in the Italian city states, this mercantile capitalism (capitalism based on trade) produced enormous profits which paid for the great art works of the Renaissance, as well as fueled the general intellectual flowering of which the art masterpieces were just a part (Wood, 1999).

Mercantile capitalism provoked a feverish quest for new trade routes and new overseas outposts. Spain and Portugal, and soon after England and France, sought new trade routes to the East. Trade with the East along overland routes was controlled by the Italian merchants, thus blocking the nations to the west. Portugal and Spain took the lead in finding alternative routes by sea, thus initiating an age of European discovery and colonization. The most dramatic and perhaps the most important discovery historically was the arrival in 1492 of Christopher Columbus in the Western Hemisphere, thus opening North, Central, and South America to trade and colonization. Columbus did not "discover" the New World in the sense of finding something new, as it had been settled by humans tens of thousands of years before. Nor was Columbus the first European to reach the Western Hemisphere. That feat was accomplished by the Vikings who explored the Canadian coast and set up a temporary colony in Newfoundland some five hundred years before. Instead it was an opening of a period of intense interaction between Europe and the Western Hemisphere that profoundly changed the world.

A wave of massive exploration and colonization followed Columbus's first voyage. By the 1520s the colonization and exploration had accelerated. Hernando Cortez (1460-1521) and his conquistadores were in Mexico conquering the Aztec Empire (1519-1521) and claiming all of Mexico for Spain, Ponce de Leon (1461-1521) had conquered Puerto Rico and explored Florida, and Ferdinand Magellan (1480-1521) set out to circle the globe by ship. Magellan did not live to the end of his expedition, which circled the globe between 1519 and 1522. Like so many of his contemporary explorers and conquistadores, he died in the act.

The exploration and colonization of the New World brought enormous wealth to the European nation states and to their merchants. It also exposed the Europeans to new cultures and new food crops. Much of the agricultural riches of the New World were either shipped to Europe as a product (such as tobacco) or transplanted into Europe as crops (such as corn and tomatoes). This Columbian Exchange (the exchange of plants and animals between the Western Hemisphere and Europe) changed both hemispheres dramatically.

The Renaissance And The Re-Discovery Of Classical Civilization

Central to the Renaissance was the rediscovery and dissemination of classical texts. The dissemination of the texts was greatly accelerated by the invention (in the West, for China had invented a similar process many years earlier) of the printing press in 1453 by Johannes Gutenberg. More than any other invention of its time, the printing press transformed the culture of Europe and altered world history. Soon after its invention, all sorts of books in Latin and in the vernacular (the common language of a country or region, such as Italian, French, German, English, and Spanish) were being published and read widely. Now the ideas of the Greeks and Romans became available to those who did not read Latin or who were not specialized scholars within the Catholic Church.

Also, in 1453 Constantinople fell to the Ottoman Turks, ending once and for all the Roman Empire in the East, known for hundreds and hundreds of years as the Byzantine Empire. The decline and fall of Byzantium lead to an influx of scholars and educated people to the west (Norwich, 1997). For example, the works of the skeptics were introduced into Western Europe, most likely from the Byzantine Empire, around 1441 when the work of Sextus Empiricus and Cicero became available (Popkin, 1967).

The re-introduction of skepticism into European thought created an intellectual crisis, called the Pyrrhonian Crisis at the time (after Pyrrho). Skepticism was an important element of the thought of Desiderius Erasmus (1466-1536), the Dutch humanist who sought to reform the corruption of the Catholic Church. An ordained priest, Erasmus advocated tolerance, was a strong opponent of superstitious beliefs, and also advocated education for women (Popkin, 1979). Erasmus wrote his greatest work, *In Praise of Folly*, in 1512 while he stayed with his friend Sir Thomas More. More was also a Renaissance scholar as well as an advisor to the king of England, Henry VIII. More also advocated for the education of women in his Renaissance novel about a perfect society which he named *Utopia*. More was later executed by Henry VIII for opposing Henry's break with Catholicism.

Much of Erasmus's criticisms were directed against the unbelievably corrupt Catholic Church of that age. In an effort to silence Erasmus with a bribe, the Catholic Church offered to make Erasmus a Cardinal. When he turned them down, the church placed his books on the index of forbidden books. This did little to stop people from reading the work, which was a best-seller and reprinted over 40 times during his lifetime alone.

Another influential skeptic, and the person who helped spread the influence of extreme skepticism in Europe, was the French essayist Michel de Montaigne (1533-1592). Montaigne's essays undermined the belief in indisputable knowledge, especially religious knowledge. In the essay *Apology for Raymond Sebond*, Montaigne argues that the only plausible basis for religious belief is faith (Popkin, 1979).

While the major thrust of the skeptical criticism was against religion, it soon spread to other knowledge claims. Erasmus, for instance, criticized mistakes made in ancient texts by the Greeks and Romans. The criticism soon spread to the accepted ancient science and philosophy of the Greeks that was still taught in the medieval universities.

One of the first of the ancient sciences to be affected was medicine. In 1543 (the date now accepted as the birthdate of modern medicine) Vesa-

[handwritten margin note: maybe we aren't advancing exponentially and I just didn't know my history]

46

lius (1514-1564) published the first modern textbook on human anatomy: *De Humanis Corporis Fabrica*, usually called simply *De Fabrica*. Vesalius was an accomplished classicist, fluent and well-read in Greek and Latin. His aim was to rediscover the ancient knowledge of Galen by doing what Galen did—extensive dissections. Vesalius performed his dissections and autopsies in front of his students and had them gather close around so they could observe more carefully. He transformed medical education and created accurate medical textbooks. In the process of his work, he also discovered and corrected some of Galen's errors, such as Galen's belief in the two-chambered heart. The petrified dogma of Greek science was being overturned by the return to the Greek empirical approach.

The works of Epicurus were made available mostly through editions of Lucretius' work *On the Nature of Things*. Lucretius' work was re-discovered in 1417 by the famed Italian humanist and book hunter Poggio Bracciolini and circulated in hand-copied editions throughout Italy (Greenblatt, 2011). It was printed for the first time in 1473. Over the next 150 years it went through some 30 editions (Foster, 2000). Soon after its publication, the work started to influence such philosophers as Francis Bacon (1561-1626), an early advocate of the scientific method who argued that "knowledge is power," a sentiment shared by many Renaissance thinkers.

Combined, the intellectual ferment generated by the re-introduction (in some cases) and the spread (in all cases) of ancient Greek and Roman philosophy, combined with the other changes in politics and economics, created the conditions for the birth (for the third time) of science. This "new science," as it was called at the time to distinguish it from the older sciences of the Greeks and Arabs, built upon ancient science and philosophy but also went beyond it. The starting point for the new science, as it was for Greek science, was astronomy.

The New Astronomy

During the one thousand years between the decline in classic Greek thought and the Renaissance, much of ancient Greek philosophy and science had been lost and much of what was left become a rigid, unquestioned dogma. So, while you had the substance of Aristotelian science, for example, you did not have the empirical approach that drove Aristotle's work, as well as so many of the other Greek scholars.

One element of Greek science that was preserved and turned into dogma, was the astronomical theory of Ptolemy (85-165 CE). Ptolemy, combining earlier models of planetary motion developed by Greeks such as Plato and Aristotle with the most accurate observations of the paths of the planets in the heavens, created a complex model of the solar system in which the earth was stationary and in the center of the system and the sun and planets moved around the earth in complex circular orbits with epicycles around the main circular orbits. This model, while complex, was highly accurate in predicting the orbits of planets in the heavens and was preserved throughout the middle ages.

The intellectual turmoil brought about by the rediscovery and dissemination of classical works, as well as the dramatic changes in politics and economics, led to a questioning of the accepted explanations that had been preserved throughout the middle ages.

The most thoughtful and revolutionary questioning of the Ptolemaic system was produced by the Polish priest and mathematician Nicolaus Copernicus (1473-1543). Copernicus developed a heliocentric (or sun-centered) model of the solar system that was much simpler than the Ptolemaic system as early as 1515. The model was not published until his death in 1543. The book that he had written, *The Revolutions of the Heavenly Spheres*, was dedicated to the pope (a common tactic of those who wanted to avoid censorship and persecution by the Catholic Inquisition) and addressed a problem the church was concerned with, namely the creation of a new calendar. But the work was a revolutionary attack on the basic assumptions of the church that the earth was at the center of the solar system and the sun and planets moved around a stationary earth. Copernicus's book contained considerable mathematics and was not accessible to the average reader, so it escaped immediately being placed on the church's list of banned books (Margolis, 2002).

While Copernicus introduced a new theory into astronomy, the Danish astronomer Tycho Brahe (1546-1601) introduced new instruments (the telescope had not been invented yet) and a new spirit of observation. Born into a noble family, Tycho Brahe was educated at the University of Copenhagen and the University of Leipzig (which, as we shall see later, was the birth place of the "new" psychology). He traveled around Europe, visiting various universities and in 1566 lost part of his nose in a sword duel in Wittenberg. From that time on, he wore a gold and silver artificial nose to cover the gap in his face (Ferguson, 2002).

In 1570 he returned to Denmark and in 1572 discovered a new star in the constellation of Cassiopeia. He persuaded the king to found an observatory, situated on the island of Hven near Copenhagen. The observatory, Uraniburg, became a leading center for astronomy in Europe. Tycho designed and built a number of observatory instruments which he would periodically check and re-calibrate. He and his students carefully observed the stars and planets on a continuous basis (instead of intermittently as many of the ancients did) and made a number of new discoveries of stellar and planetary movements, as well as the most accurate observations that had ever been made. Tycho also owned a printing press at Uraniburg and produced a number of books on astronomy (Ferguson, 2002).

In 1597 Tycho had a falling out with the king and left Denmark with his family, books, and astronomical and alchemic instruments. (Like many of the early scientists, Tycho practiced alchemy.) Traveling south, he and his family were eventually welcomed in Prague by Emperor Rudolph II. At the time, Prague was an important intellectual center and Tycho set up an observatory there to continue his work (Ferguson, 2002).

Tycho was a committed Aristotelian dedicated to careful observation and empirical studies of astronomy. As an Aristotelian, he found it extremely difficult to accept Copernicus' theory that placed the sun in the center of the solar system. Copernicus's theory violates Aristotelian physics which holds that the Earth is at rest. Tycho died in 1601 in Prague. He revitalized astronomy as a science and made a number of discoveries never before known by the ancient astronomers of Greece, Rome, and the Islamic world.

One of the converts to Copernicus' heliocentric theory of the solar system was Johannes Kepler (1571-1630). Born in present day Germany, Kepler first studied to be a Lutheran minister but later switched to mathematics and astronomy. Like Copernicus, Kepler was a Platonist who believed that the real world exists behind the world of appearances (philosophical idealism) and

[handwritten margin note: Aristotle already defined science that long ago]

could be described mathematically (Ferguson, 2002).

Kepler worked as a school teacher and mathematician in Graz, a Catholic, German-speaking area of the Holy Roman Empire. While working in Graz he published his first book in 1596, *Mysterium comographicum*, a strong defense of the Copernican theory. This book was apparently read by Galileo, and the two started a long correspondence. During the Counter-Reformation Kepler was in danger because he was not Catholic (nor was he accepted by the Lutheran faith although he had been raised Lutheran), so in 1600 he got a ride to Prague and arranged a meeting with Tycho. Tycho hired Kepler to calculate the orbits of planets based on his detailed observation data. These data were closely guarded by Tycho (and later by his family after his death) but Kepler had been given access to the data on Mars before Tycho's death. After Tycho's death, Kepler apparently got access to the data on the other planets through less than legal means. Kepler also was appointed Imperial Mathematician, the post that Tycho had held (Ferguson, 2002; Gingerich, 1993).

Kepler discovered, using Tycho's highly precise data, that the orbit of Mars is not circular as Copernicus had argued, but elliptical. This discovery eliminated the need in Copernicus' theory of epicycles (small circles around the main orbit) which were features of both the heliocentric and geocentric models of the solar system. Kepler published his results in 1609 in *Astronomia Nova* (New Astronomy). This work contains Kepler's first and second laws (Ferguson, 2002; Gingerich, 1993).

In 1612 Lutherans were forced to flee Prague and Kepler moved to Linz, on the Danube River. After moving to Linz, he had to defend his mother against charges of witchcraft. In 1619 he published *Harmonices mundi*, a work based on all of Tycho's data and containing Kepler's third law. In 1621 he published a systematic account of the heliocentric theory. In addition to these many achievements, Kepler completed tables used to calculate the positions of the planets on any date in the past or future, suggested that the sun rotates on its axis, examined binocular vision and the retinal image, designed glasses for both nearsightedness and farsightedness, and described the principles underlying the working of telescopes. Two of his minor but interesting achievements: he invented the word satellite and he calculated the year of Jesus' birth (Ferguson, 2002; Gingerich, 1993).

Together, Copernicus, Tycho, and Kepler created a new astronomy that rivaled and surpassed that of both the Greeks and the Arabs. Combining the idealism and mathematical descriptions of Plato with the empiricism of Aristotle, they transformed our understanding of the cosmos and started an intellectual tradition that has given us our first real glimpse of the galaxy. But such a radical scientific revolution (to use Thomas Kuhn's term) had far-reaching implications. Some of those implications affected religion and philosophy. More immediately, the new astronomy affected the understanding of physics here on Earth, leading within a short time to the birth of a new physics.

The New Physics: Galileo

Galileo Galilei (1564-1642) was a talented mathematician and astronomer who was appointed professor of mathematics at the University of Pisa in 1589 at the age of 25. He became a popular and respected teacher at Pisa. In his lectures he began to advocate for the empirical testing of hypotheses about the physical world, including advocating the use of inclined planes as a way of slowing down the rate of ball descent so that their speed could be more easily measured. In 1592, after the death of his father, he took a position at the University of Padua, one of the leading universities of the time, at three times the salary he earned at Pisa. At Padua, he taught geometry and Ptolemaic astronomy to medical students. By this time Galileo had become a convert to the Copernican system (he stated this in a private letter to Kepler in 1598, two years before Kepler met Tycho in Prague) and rejected Aristotelian physics and astronomy. Between 1602 and 1604, he worked out his law of falling bodies and discovered that a projectile follows a parabolic path. Crucial to these discoveries were a series of experiments he carried out with inclined planes and pendulums. He did not publish these results until 1639 as *Discourses and mathematical demonstrations concerning the two new sciences* (Sobel, 2000).

Galileo publicly argued against Aristotle in a series of lectures in 1604 when he discussed the appearance of a new star (the Kepler Supernova). His arguments were based on estimates of the distance of the star from the Earth, using parallax. Aristotle had argued (as had many of the ancient Greeks) that the changes in the heavens occurred in the lunar regions close to the Earth, not further out where the heavens were unchanging. By showing that the new star was further away than the moon, he disproved Aristotle. By looking at the predictions made by Aristotle's theory and testing those predictions empirically, Galileo pioneered the basic logic of the modern scientific method (Sobel, 2000).

In 1609 Galileo learned from a friend and fellow mathematician in Venice of the invention of the telescope by a Dutch lens maker. Realizing how important such a device would be to sailors and astronomers, he set about learning how to grind lenses so that he could build his own telescope. His first one used available lenses and had a magnification of four. Using lenses he ground himself and his knowledge of mathematics, he improved the telescopes until they had a magnification of 9 or 10. Giving a demonstration to the Venetian Senate (Venice at the time was a city state with a republican form of government where only the well-to-do could vote), he impressed them so much he got a large raise (in exchange for giving them rights to manufacture the telescope, which Galileo did not own anyway) (Sobel, 2000).

Almost immediately, Galileo used his telescopes to make astronomical observations. In December of 1609 and January 1610, he made a series of discoveries: he discovered mountains on the moon, that the Milky Way was made up of many tiny stars invisible to the unaided eye, and that Jupiter was orbited by four smaller moons. Galileo named these moons the Medicean Stars, after Cosimo de Medici, the Grand Duke of Tuscany (These moons are now known as the Galilean Moons, after their discoverer). Galileo also sent the Grand Duke a telescope. Galileo published a report of his discoveries and of the telescope in May 1610 in a short book entitled (in English) *Starry messenger* (Sobel, 2000).

In June of 1610, Galileo was appointed Chief Mathematician at the University of Pisa. He had no teaching duties and a very large salary. He now devoted himself almost entirely to research. In July of 1610 he observed that Saturn was a large orb accompanied by two smaller orbs on each side that would vanish periodically. Galileo's telescope was not powerful enough to distinguish the rings of Saturn. He later discovered the phases of Venus (1610) and sunspots (1612).

Galileo was now treated as a celebrity by almost everyone, including the Catholic Church. While the Catholic Church condemned the Copernican theory in 1616, Galileo was not personally affected. He was forbidden to teach the Copernican theory, but since he was discreet about his views and he did not teach anymore, he thought he was not at risk. While being discrete, he was never silent. In 1616 he wrote the *Letter to the Grand Duchess*, in which he attacked Aristotle and his followers and argued for a non-literal view of the Bible because a literal interpretation would contradict the facts of the material world as proven by science. In the *Letter*, Galileo adopted a stance that had earlier been adapted by the Islamic scientists of al-Andalus: Avicenna, Averroes and Maimonides (Sobel, 2000).

In spite of Galileo's achievements and his friendship with Pope Urban VIII (who became pope in 1623), he got in trouble with the Catholic Church. After publishing *The Assayer* in 1623, a description of the new scientific methods and mathematics as applied to physics and astronomy, he started work in 1624 on his *Dialogue concerning the two chief systems of the world—Ptolemaic and Copernican*. The book is a brilliant defense of the Copernican system and a harsh attack on the Ptolemaic system, but not everything Galileo said was correct. In particular, Galileo had rejected Kepler's theory that the moon caused the tides. Instead, Galileo argued that the tides provided evidence of the rotation of the earth. Not completed until 1630, the book provoked an immediate response from the Inquisition, which banned the sale of the book and ordered Galileo to stand trial. Unable to travel to Rome for his trial because of failing health, Galileo was not actually tried until 1633. He was found guilty of heresy and sentenced to life in prison. Because of Galileo's status and friendship with influential members of the Vatican, he was confined to house arrest, under guard by officers of the Inquisition (Sobel, 2000).

Galileo spent his time under house arrest working on his last and greatest work, the *Discourses and mathematical demonstrations concerning the two new sciences*. The *Discourses* expanded on work he had started in 1590 and developed in 1602-1604 on experiments with motion of bodies through space. The book was smuggled out of Galileo's home and published in Holland (a more tolerant country at the time) in 1638 (Sobel, 2000).

The works of Galileo in physics and astronomy insured the triumph of the new astronomy and created a new (non-Aristotelian) physics. Galileo created modern physics, based on experimental methods and mathematical models of physical phenomena. Like Kepler and Copernicus, Galileo had a strong streak of *a guy before copernicus thought sun was at center, then copernicus, then galileo. progress could've been so much faster*

Platonic Idealism in him. While rejecting the content of Aristotle's thought, as made dogma by the Catholic and Protestant churches of the time, he embraced the spirit of Aristotle's empiricism.

There was now a powerful and seductive model of how to do science. For the third time in human history, a society had developed science as a cultural practice and institution. The new physics, the model of this new science, drew upon the contributions of the Greeks and Arabs, but far exceeded them. A new epoch in human history had begun.

The New Biology

Within a short time, the spirit of the new astronomy and the new physics spread to other fields. William Harvey (1578-1657) was an English physician who had studied medicine at the University of Padua after graduating from Cambridge University in 1597. Padua was considered the leading medical school in the world at that time. As a medical student, Harvey would have listened to lectures on geometry and astronomy by none other than Galileo himself. He also studied with the well-known anatomist, Hieronymus Fabricius. Harvey received his medical degree from the University of Padua in 1602 and returned to London where he began a successful career as a physician. He worked as a doctor at London's St. Bartholomew's Hospital (which we shall run across again in Chapter 13 on the history of clinical psychology), lectured for many years at the Royal College of Physicians, became physician to King James I and, after James death, physician to his son Charles I.

Harvey developed a theory that the blood circulated in the body and that the heart acted as a pump moving the blood through the body. He presented his theory in his lectures starting in 1616 and carried out a number of very detailed studies of humans and animals to support the theory. The results of these studies were published by him in Germany in a 72-page monograph (written in Latin as was common still in scientific articles and books) entitled *Exercitatio Anatomica de Motu Cordis et Sanguinis in Animalibus,* or in English, *Anatomical Essay on the Motion of the Heart and Blood in Animals.*

His monograph caused many to turn on Harvey. He lost patients and was attacked by other physicians and the popular press of his day. The reason is that he had overturned the accepted authority on blood and circulation who

another person attacked bc ppl are afraid of change

had dominated medicine for the previous 1400 years—Galen (130-201 CE). Galen taught that the body created new blood as it used up old blood. As Harvey's work was confirmed by the studies and observations of other physicians, his fame spread throughout Europe. In addition to his work on circulation of blood, he also published in 1651 the results of his studies of embryology in his *Essay on the Generation of Animals*.

Harvey was the first to adopt a modern scientific method to the study of medical and biological problems. He carefully observed, carried out systematic observations, and tested his ideas against facts. He also took steps to minimize his own biases and superstitions. Harvey's work inspired generations of scientists who carried out work in biology and medicine, but there persisted a strong countertrend against a scientific biology and medicine. This countertrend was especially strong in the English-speaking world and was buttressed by the failure of the new science of biology and medicine to produce practical and effective therapies (Shryock, 1936).

While Harvey was the first, he was by no means the only important contributor to the new biology. Following in the generation after Harvey was Robert Hooke (1635-1708), often considered to be London's Leonardo da Vinci. Hooke was a true "Renaissance Man" who contributed to a number of fields. He was also Isaac Newton's (who I discuss in the next section) main scientific rival, and the bitter feud between the two helps to account for Hooke's obscurity. Newton was a politically powerful and influential rival who was also vindictive toward Hooke (Jardine, 2004).

Hooke invented the universal joint, used in every automobile in the world today. He invented the iris diaphragm used in cameras and the balance spring used in watches and clocks. He also made improvements to a number of meteorological instruments. After the Great London Fire of 1666, he surveyed the city and participated in its re-building. He also worked with Robert Boyle on the physics of gases, as well as carried out his own work on combustion and elasticity (Jardine, 2004).

Hooke's main work in biology was *Micrographia*, published in 1665. While Hooke did not invent the microscope, he built the first compound microscope, the most advanced in its day, which included illumination and an iris diaphragm. He used the microscope to carry out a series of observations on plants, animals and fossils at the microscopic level. In the process, he coined the term "cell" to describe the basic component parts of plants and animals and founded the field of microbiology (Jardine, 2004).

Micrographia contains detailed descriptions of his observations along with magnificent drawings of bird feathers, insects, and microscopic organisms. The book became a best-seller but also generated a great deal of ridicule—critics viewed the subject matter as trivial (Jardine, 2004).

Critics who made fun of Hooke's work missed the many achievements of the book, one of which was Hook's analysis of fossils. He examined fossils under the microscope and compared them to living creatures. Comparing petrified wood to rotten oak under the microscope, he noted how plants and animals could become fossils through the action of mineralized water. Prior to Hooke, most everyone accepted Aristotle's explanation of fossils as formed and grown within the earth. Hooke, by showing that fossils were formed from living plants and animals (some now extinct or no longer found in the area, such as sea shells found on mountain tops), set the stage for a revolution in geology and biology (Jardine, 2004).

In 1678 Hooke confirmed the discovery of Anton Leeuwenhoek of bacteria and protozoa. In spite of his distinguished career as one of the greatest scientists in his era, Hooke died alone and in poverty. Unhappy in life, he was almost forgotten in death. His work, however, transformed the world and helped to create the new biology pioneered by Harvey (Jardine, 2004).

From Alchemy To Chemistry

Alchemy was practiced by most of the originators of the modern scientific revolution. Tycho Brahe and Kepler, for example were both practicing alchemists who devoted considerable time to alchemic research. Another practicing alchemist was Robert Boyle (1627-1691), sometimes considered the father of modern chemistry. Boyle performed carefully controlled experiments (he would even record the place, weather, and time of his experiments) and wrote up his experiments in careful detail (Levere, 2001; Brock, 1992).

Boyle's first major scientific work was *The Spring and Weight of Air*, published in 1660. Boyle (working with Robert Hooke, who actually invented the pump with Boyle) developed a vacuum pump and used it to carry out a series of experiments showing that air is necessary for the conduction of sound, for fire, and for life. In a second edition of this work, published in 1662, Boyle described experiments leading to the discovery of the pressure-volume inverse relationship, now known as Boyle's Law. (Levere, 2001; Brock, 1992). Many of these experiments were also carried out in collaboration with Hooke, who also invented the apparatus need to perform the experiments.

In 1661 Boyle published his most important work, *The Sceptical Chymist*. This book attacks what Boyle viewed as faulty reasoning and poor experimentation in Aristotelian chemistry (alchemy). Boyle firmly believed in the importance of breaking matter down into its simplest elements (a program of research followed by chemists after him) but he rejected the current models as not being truly empirical. He referred to his approach as empirical philosophy. Nowadays we call it the scientific method. He insisted that studies be carefully controlled, public, and reproducible, rejecting the secrecy that accompanied alchemy (Levere, 2001; Brock, 1992).

development of scientific method

Boyle was an active member of the Royal Society, a group of eminent scientists and mathematicians that were formally recognized by the new king shortly after the restoration. The group started out as an informal "invisible college," a term used by the participants that likened their group to the close-knit colleges that made up Oxford and Cambridge. (They were invisible because they had no buildings or campus). The group started meeting weekly in 1645 (in London or Oxford) and Boyle joined the group in 1654. In addition to his connections with the leading scientists and mathematicians of his time through the Royal Society, Boyle was close friends with Isaac Newton, had worked with Robert Hooke, and had as his research assistant at one time John Locke, who we shall meet soon.

The Newtonian Revolution And The Unification Of Physics

The work of the new astronomy and the new physics culminated in a unified view of the physical universe developed by Isaac Newton (1642-1727). Newton graduated from Cambridge University in 1665 and was appointed to a chair at Cambridge in 1669. As a student Newton studied the philosophy of Descartes, Gassendi, and Hobbes. He also studied the work of Galileo and Kepler as well as a great number of works in mathematics, such as Euclid's

Geometry and Descartes' *La Geometrie*. The next 18 years of his life, from 1669 to 1687, were a period of enormous creativity for Newton. He carried out work in optics, mathematics (inventing Calculus), mechanics and gravitation. His main work on gravitation and mechanics were published in 1687 (but completed many years before) in *Philosophiae Naturalis Principia Mathematica* (Mathematical Principles of Natural Philosophy, more generally referred to as the *Principia*). In *Principia* Newton identifies and explains the movement of planets, comets, and moons as a function of gravity. Later in the work he develops a theory of fluids, how they move and how things move through them (this is known as fluid mechanics). As a result of this work he was able to calculate the speed of sound through air. In the last part of the *Principia* Newton demonstrated how the orbits of the planets correspond to his prediction, showed how comets obey the same mathematical laws, demonstrated how tides were the result of the gravitational pull of the sun and moon, and calculated the relative masses of different planets and moons in the solar system (Cohen, 1985).

Newton was very conscious of his debt to other scientists. In an exchange with Hooke, his bitter rival, Newton wrote "If I have seen further, it is by standing on ye shoulders of giants." Given that Hooke was a very short person, this is both an acknowledgement of Newton's intellectual debt to others, and a not-so-subtle insult. Newton was both very sensitive to criticism and extremely vindictive to his opponents. Often, he would not publish his work until after critics had died. Sometimes he would carry out protracted vendettas against his opponents, such as Hooke and Leibniz.

After 1687 Newton turned his attention to politics. He was elected to Parliament twice from Cambridge on the basis of his strong defense of intellectual freedom against the monarchy's attacks on the universities. He was appointed warden of the royal mint in 1696 and master of the mint in 1699, a job he devoted considerable time to, developing new ways to produce coinage and to foil counterfeiters. He was elected president of the Royal Society in 1703 and was re-elected every year until his death. He became the first scientist to be knighted in England in 1705. In addition to his work in mathematics and physics, he studied alchemy intensely for over 40 years and wrote extensively on religion and history.

Newton's work introduced a scientific paradigm (in the sense that Thomas

Kuhn described it) into physics that was to dominate the field for over 200 years, until the development of the theory of relativity and quantum mechanics (Cohen, 1985). This paradigm led to steady and often spectacular progress in physics. The paradigm also profoundly shaped the general culture, resulting in a Newtonian world view. What are the elements of that world view?

The Newtonian universe is clock-like, governed by natural laws that can be described by mathematics. This universe is highly predictable and understandable, albeit imperfectly. The beauties of the universe are a testament to God's creation but run without the intervention of God. While Newton was deeply, though somewhat unconventionally, religious, his theory fostered the popularity of deism and materialism. Lastly, the Newtonian universe could be understood only through science, a way of knowing based on the modern scientific method developed by Galileo more than anyone else.

Contributions From Post-Renaissance Philosophy

I have traced the development of the Renaissance and the birth of modern science through the 1700s. The general intellectual, political, and economic changes brought about by the Renaissance, the birth of the nation-state and capitalism also had a profound effect on philosophy and religion. In particular, the Renaissance and the birth of science had a jarring effect on the accepted philosophy of the times (a highly Christianized version of selected Classic philosophy combined with religious doctrine) leading to the birth of modern philosophy with Rene Descartes.

Religion too was affected, with the Protestant Reformation and the Catholic Counter-Reformation occurring against a backdrop of bloody religious wars. The starting point for both the rebirth of philosophy and the Reformation and Counter-Reformation was the Crisis of Skepticism.

Skepticism And Religion

The Protestant Reformation is usually dated to 1517, the year the Catholic priest and theologian Martin Luther nailed his Ninety-Five Theses to a church door in Wittenburg, Germany. At first the Vatican ignored Luther's challenge as just another minor protest movement, but soon the protests spread and developed into a full-fledged split with the Catholic Church, resulting in a number of protestant Christian denominations.

Skepticism raises the question posed by the Greek philosophers: how do you know this (whatever "this" may be) is true? How do you judge what is true? —this is the problem of the criterion of truth. The arguments of Erasmus and the skeptics undermined the received authority of the Catholic Church. This was not the prime force in the Reformation, however, which was fueled by the incredible corruption of the Catholic Church at the time and the practice of taxing believers (through the selling of indulgences—essentially buying forgiveness for your sins) that was draining considerable wealth away from northern Europe to Rome. Still, skepticism did play a role in both the break with the Catholic Church and the protestant theologies that developed in response (Popkin, 1979).

There were three possible responses to skepticism—the first was fideism, the notion that faith is necessary for accepting the truth of a proposition. Fideism has several variants, ranging from the complete denial of any role for reason and evidence, to the view that faith is primary and reason and evidence, while important, are ultimately secondary. Fideism characterizes much of Protestant Christianity to this day (Popkin, 1979).

The second response to skepticism is a middle way, or mitigated skepticism, which incorporates a careful examination of evidence and criticisms of one's reasoning, without casting all knowledge into doubt. Mitigated skepticism is compatible with, and indeed fosters, a scientific attitude—an attitude that leads you to not take anything at face value and to ask the question: where is the evidence for this? Mitigated skepticism became an essential element in the creation of modern science, just as it had been an important element in Greek and Islamic science (Popkin, 1979).

The third response is to use skepticism to cast doubt on skepticism itself, thus affirming (weakly) one's beliefs in the face of skeptical attacks (Popkin, 1979). This approach was taken by Augustine (354-430 CE) who argued that doubting entails thinking and thinking means you exist and are alive. Augustine thus used skepticism to undermine skepticism, an approach that was to be used almost 1200 years later by another individual who was trying to defend religion from skeptical doubts: Rene Descartes.

Descartes And Dualism

Rene Descartes (1596-1650) was born in France and was educated at the elite Jesuit school La Fleche. He was an excellent student and especially good at mathematics. Descartes did not like to be bothered and so moved dozens of times. He also spent large amounts of time lying in bed thinking. Both habits proved enormously productive in Descartes' case. One of his first great achievements was the integration of geometry and algebra into analytic geometry, inspired by his realization when he was lying in bed watching a fly that the fly's location could be described with three numbers, representing the distance from the two walls and the ceiling (Grene, 1985).

Descartes, who corresponded with Galileo and knew Gassendi and Hobbes (see below), was concerned by the collapse of philosophical knowledge in the face of skepticism. He decided to defeat skepticism, as Augustine had done, by using skepticism. He set out to doubt everything, until he could not doubt anything else. Like Augustine (who Descartes had studied at La Fleche), he arrived at the same conclusion—he could not doubt his own awareness of doubting, or as he wrote, *cogito, ergo sum,* I think, therefore I am. From this starting point he went on to discover other universal truths in the form of innate ideas, such as the idea of infinity, the axioms of geometry, and the existence of God. Because God exists, and he would not deceive us, we can trust our knowledge of the senses (Grene, 1985; Williams, 1967).

To Descartes' skeptical contemporaries and to moderns familiar with non-Euclidian geometry, Descartes' defeat of skepticism by using skepticism seems flimsy at best. While he is most famous for his attack on skepticism, his contributions to the development of a nativistic philosophical psychology are perhaps more important. Descartes argued that mind and body are two different kinds of substances. The body can be treated like a machine and understood scientifically. The mind cannot be understood scientifically and is endowed by God with powers of perception and cognition that go beyond the mechanical. Thus, his mind-body dualism (known as Cartesian Dualism) is an effort to reconcile a scientific understanding of the material with a spiritual understanding of the psychological. It is a defense of religion against materialism (Popkin, 1979).

How far we've come...

At the same time that Descartes tried to defend humans from the materialistic implications of the new physics and astronomy, he offered a materialistic analysis of the body. Bodies were automata—nothing more than machines without the god-given mind or soul. Descartes also treated animals as automata, arguing that they did not have minds or souls. Descartes offered a mechanistic explanation of perception in terms of the physical energies of the stimulus setting off a physical response in the nerves and brain, what nowadays we would call a neural impulse, resulting in sensations. These sensations had to be interpreted by the mind, the presence of God in each of us. Descartes emphasized simultaneously a mechanical analysis of the body and a non-mechanical analysis of consciousness, perception, and cognition (Williams, 1967).

Descartes' arguments for mind-body dualism and for the existence of innate ideas, as well as his efforts to stave off skepticism and reconcile a spiritual worldview with a mechanical understanding of humans, were not appreciated by everyone. The Catholic Church banned his works, while at the same time he achieved considerable fame and influence within Europe. Descartes' work earned him the title of the father of modern philosophy, as he not only integrated and adopted classic ideas, but went beyond them to offer a creative synthesis (Williams, 1967).

The Cartesian solution was not accepted by everyone. One of the strongest opponents of Descartes on the continent was Pierre Gassendi (1592-1655). Gassendi received a doctorate in theology in 1614 and was ordained a priest in 1616. After ordination he began work as a philosophy professor at Aix. His first book, *Exercitationes Paradoxicae Adversus Aristoteleos*, published in 1624, attacked Aristotelianism and introduced Gassendi's mitigated skepticism (Popkin, 1967). In addition to embracing mitigated skepticism between the extreme skepticism of Sextus Empiricus and dogmatic, unquestioned beliefs, he embraced Epicurean philosophy (or at least a version of it that was compatible with Christianity).

In addition to his work in philosophy, Gassendi carried out a number of studies in astronomy and physics. He worked as well for a time as the philosophy teacher to the young Molière, who later became one of France's most important playwrights (Popkin, 1967; Popkin 1979).

After Descartes published his *Meditations*, Mersenne, a mutual friend of both men, asked Gassendi to expand his criticisms into a larger work. The result was Gassendi's *Disquisitio Metaphysica*, published in 1644—a massive attack on Descartes' philosophy and especially his dogmatic conclusions (Grene, 1985; Popkin, 1979).

The British Empiricists

The reaction to Descartes was also negative in Great Britain. Thomas Hobbes (1588-1679), a friend of Gassendi and an acquaintance of Descartes, developed a materialist and empiricist theory of knowledge to rival Descartes and complement Gassendi.

Hobbes graduated from Oxford in 1608 and found work as a tutor to the son of the Earl of Devonshire. This gave Hobbes the opportunity to meet important people, travel, and use the earl's library. Hobbes accompanied the earl on a visit to the Continent in 1610. Educated circles on the Continent were abuzz from Galileo's discoveries and Kepler's publication of the first two laws of planetary motion. Hobbes also served for a time as the secretary to the British philosopher Francis Bacon, who espoused an inductive, Aristotelian approach to science (Peters, 1967).

Hobbes' first major work was a translation of Thucydides from Greek into English in 1628. At that time he also warned of a looming civil war between King and Parliament, a prophecy that was to tragically come true in the following decades. Hobbes was a staunch foe of democracy, an institution he viewed as a great evil, and defended the rule of kings in a number of his works (Peters, 1967).

Hobbes spent the years 1634-1637 on the Continent and met with Galileo in Italy. Although Hobbes was a friend of both Descartes and Gassendi, he was much closer to Gassendi personally and philosophically. Hobbes developed a mechanistic psychology influenced by Galileo's approach to physics. He also defended the monarchy on psychological grounds, arguing that humans need to be governed by a strong, despotic hand to curb their natural passions. This argument was circulated in manuscript form under the title *The Elements of Law* in 1640, during the short parliament. When the long parliament later impeached the Earl of Strafford in late 1640, Hobbes saw the writing on the wall and fled to France, priding himself later as being 'the first to flee.' While

63

in France, Hobbes worked on optics and became involved in an often heated exchange with Descartes over the latter's masterpiece, *The Meditations* (Peters, 1967).

Hobbes was planning on retiring in 1646 to the south of France when he got an offer he could not refuse: he was asked to be the private tutor for Charles II, who had just gone into exile in France. Hobbes published his political masterpiece *The Leviathan*, in 1651, two years after Charles I was executed and during the political turmoil that ended when Cromwell became Lord Protector in 1653. Hobbes' book was both enormously controversial and also influential among the conservative factions in English society. With the restoration of the monarchy in 1660, Hobbes, then 78, was granted a pension and free access to the new king, his former pupil (Peters, 1967).

Hobbes was both a materialist and an atheist who was feared and loathed by many in England. In 1665 plague swept through England and in 1666 the Great Fire destroyed London. Many blamed the presence of atheists for these disasters and a bill was passed in Parliament for the suppression of atheists. Hobbes was investigated by Parliament, but the investigation was dropped, most likely because of the intervention of the king. In his mid-80s, Hobbes did a verse translation of both the *Iliad* and the *Odyssey* (Peters, 1967).

Hobbes' psychology was mechanistic and materialistic. As for the nature of sensation he argued that external objects in the world directly, or through a medium (such as sound waves through air), pressed on the senses. This pressure was then conveyed by the nerves to the brain and heart. Sensations are a form of mechanical motion that have the character of the external object. Hobbes explained recognition as a result of the sense organs retaining some previous motions. He explained selective attention, the fact that it is hard for humans to pay attention to several things at once, also in mechanical terms. He went on to explain a variety of psychological phenomena, such as memory, imagination, thinking, dreaming, and emotions, all in materialistic and mechanistic terms (Peters, 1967).

Hobbes' philosophical psychology was important for two reasons. First, it was an explanation entirely devoid of theological concepts and references to God. In this sense it was, like the work of Kepler and Galileo, entirely naturalistic. This should not be surprising, given Hobbes' atheism. Following from his atheism, Hobbes also rejected the idea of innate ideas. Hobbes rejected nativism and embraced empiricism, the idea that all thinking comes from experience. Second, shorn of the language we now find archaic, his ideas are surprisingly modern.

While Thomas Hobbes is considered the first of the British Empiricists, the ideas of the Empiricists were really developed by John Locke (1632-1704). Locke was 10 when the English Revolution broke out and growing up during the revolution was to have a significant impact on his interests and ideas. Locke was 17 when Charles I was executed at Whitehall Castle, close to Locke's school. Most likely he witnessed the execution. In 1652 Locke got a scholarship to study at Oxford. His first published work was a poem in honor of Oliver Cromwell. Locke went on to earn his bachelor's, master's, and doctorate degree at Oxford (Hunt, 1993; Robinson, 1986).

While at Oxford, Locke became the student and research assistant of Robert Boyle. Later they became close friends. Locke also became a member of the Royal Society and in 1689 Locke and Newton met and started a life-long association (Like Boyle and Newton, Locke was a deeply religious person and much of the Locke-Newton correspondence is about theological issues). Locke carried out studies in chemistry and meteorology, as well as published a book on money and interest, but he would have been a mere footnote in history were it not for the publication, at the age of 60, of his *An Essay Concerning Human Understanding*. The essay was a masterpiece. After its publication Locke went on to publish other works on education and politics. Locke's ideas on politics and education were to have a profound effect, including influencing the U.S. constitution, but here we will focus on his psychological ideas (Hunt, 1993; Robinson, 1986).

Like Hobbes, Locke rejected Descartes' nativism and offered an empiricist theory of psychology. While not rejecting mind-body dualism, as Hobbes had done, Locke argued that the mind was a blank slate (a *tabula rasa*) and that knowledge and thinking are a consequence of experience. Ideas, the basic building blocks of mental life, come from our sensations or reflections on prior sensations. Ideas can be either simple or complex (amalgams of simple ideas) and complex ideas emerge through the process of association. Understanding the law of association is essential to understanding complex ideas. Finally, all ideas entail pleasure or pain. The mixture of pleasure and pain defines the more complex emotions that we experience such as love and hate. In an argument reminiscent of Epicurus, Gassendi and Hobbes, Locke argued that that which causes pleasure is good and that which causes pain is bad (Hunt, 1993; Robinson, 1986).

Locke's philosophical psychology was more developed and refined than Hobbes' and was to have a profound influence on later philosophy and on modern psychology. It developed into the British school of empiricism and later British Associationism, an outgrowth of British empiricism. Locke stands, along with Descartes, as one of the two most influential philosophers in the history of modern psychology.

The third British Empiricist was George Berkeley (for whom Berkeley, California is named). Berkeley (1685-1753) was born in Ireland and graduated from Trinity College, Dublin. At the time Ireland was controlled by Great Britain, so while Berkeley is Irish he is considered a British Empiricist. Berkeley eventually became an Anglican Bishop in Ireland.

Berkeley, like Boyle, Newton, and Locke, was deeply religious. But unlike them Berkeley opposed materialism and felt that the works of Descartes, Hobbes, Newton, and Locke, had done much to undermine religion. He proposed a radical subjectivism based on his theory of perception. All that was real, Berkeley argued, was what was perceived. External reality exists, Berkeley argued, because it is perceived by God, the ultimate perceiver. Berkeley did accept the empiricist philosophical psychology of Locke, especially the idea of associationism, but he also expanded Locke's work with a theory of depth perception and size constancy. Berkeley published his theory in 1709 (when he was 24) under the title *An Essay Toward a New Theory of Vision* (Hunt, 1993; Robinson, 1986).

Leibniz, Nativism, And The Defense Of Dualism

Gottfried Wilhelm von Leibniz (1646-1716) was born into an academic family in Leipzig, Germany, where his father was a professor. He received his bachelor's degree from Leipzig and his doctorate in law from the University of Altdorf (he transferred to Altdorf after being denied his doctorate at Leipzig). Instead of taking a university post, Leibniz practiced law, worked as a librarian, and worked as a political advisor and a diplomat.

Leibniz had broad interests and talents. He sought his whole life to re-unify Christianity. He also worked to unify all human knowledge into a single conceptual framework. He did work in alchemy (he was the secretary of the Nuremberg alchemy society for a time), mathematics, and physics, as well as law and poetry—a great deal of which he wrote.

Leibniz's greatest success was in mathematics, where he invented a calculating machine capable of addition, subtraction, multiplication and division. As an aside, he also advocated the use of binary number systems, like those now used in computers, as simpler and more effective. His greatest achievement was the development, independently from Newton, of calculus.

Leibniz's importance within psychology comes from his criticism of British Empiricism and the development of his own philosophical psychology. Leibniz argued that experience cannot lead to ideas unless the potential to have ideas is already present. In this, he used an analogy with his calculating machine. Ideas are not material, but the brain and sensations are—the material cannot cause the immaterial. The brain is like the workings of his calculating machine; the ideas are like the calculations the machine performs. Experience causes an idea to be realized, but the potential must be innate. Leibniz dramatically expanded the notion of nativism, a notion that was to have a significant impact on our thinking about the relationship between the brain and experience. In defending this strong version of nativism, he also championed a strong version of mind-body dualism: the functioning of the brain is not the same as ideas, feelings, and consciousness.

Leibniz also argued for the existence of unconscious perception, that is, perception outside of our awareness. These "little perceptions" accumulate and have an impact on awareness, a process he called apperception. Leibniz's notion of the unconscious was, as we shall see, to have an enormous impact on modern psychology.

Leibniz is infamous for other ideas, such as the idea of monads, but these other ideas had almost no impact on modern psychology and need not concern us here.

The Persistence Of Materialism

Julien Offray De La Mettrie (1709-1751) was a French philosopher and physician who generated more than his share of controversy with his attacks on Descartes and Leibniz, and his advocacy of a comprehensive materialist view of humans. De La Mettrie published his first philosophical work after working for several years as a military surgeon during the War of Austrian Succession. In the *Natural History of the Soul* (1745), in which De La Mettrie attacked the dualism of Descartes and Liebniz, De La Mettrie argues that the soul depends on the central nervous system, especially the brain, and could be studied by the scientist. This book was immediately banned by the French censors and De La Mettrie fled to Holland, a country noted for its tolerance (Vartian, 1967).

While in Holland, De La Mettrie wrote and published *Man a Machine* (De La Mettrie, 1748/1961). Written in a popular and engaging style, *Man a Machine* was more explicitly materialist than his first work. Here De La Mattrie argued, as in his first book, that states of the soul depend on states of the body. The individual is a "living machine" whose thinking and behavior are the consequence of physiological processes. De La Mettrie made extensive use of medical data and the latest physiological discoveries to buttress his arguments. He also argued for an experimental-inductive approach to psychology, as opposed to the then-dominant philosophical and un-empirical approach. In addition, he made arguments in favor of atheism, an attack on his religious critics (Vartian, 1967).

Man a Machine was so provocative that even the normally tolerant Dutch condemned him. Forced to flee yet again, De La Mettrie found refuge in Berlin, under the protection of Prussian king Frederick the Great. Frederick made De La Mettrie a member of the Royal Academy of Science and appointed him a royal physician. In Berlin De La Mettrie published several works, including his *Discourse on Happiness* (1750). In the *Discourse* he argues that happiness is the optimum state of pleasure in the man-machine. Happiness is not grounded in ethics but in pleasure. The book further added to De La Mettrie's controversial reputation. When he died the next year of over-eating, his critics used his fate as an example of the dangers of materialism and atheism (Vartian, 1967).

In spite of the herculean efforts made to attack and suppress his work before and after his death, De La Mettrie's ideas exerted a strong influence on physiology and biology over the 150 years after his death.

Philosophical Psychology

The battle between idealism and materialism, between nativism and empiricism raged on in the 1700s. The Scottish philosopher David Hume (1711-1776) took up the battle against idealism and nativism. As you would expect, Hume was a skeptic who doubted religion. Impressed with the achievements of the natural sciences, especially the work of Newton, he sought to introduce the scientific method into what was then called moral philosophy and what we would call the social sciences. For Hume, this new science of man was essentially psychological and all of the natural sciences rest upon a psychological foundation. The new science was also inductive (following Bacon) and not hypothetico-deductive, following Galileo and Newton (Hunt, 1993; Robinson, 1986). Hume laid out his basic arguments for the new science in his *Treatise of Human Nature, Being an Attempt to Introduce the Experimental Method of Reasoning into Moral Subjects,* published in two volumes in 1739 and 1740. The title clearly indicates Hume's aim. The book was a failure and he published a revised, abbreviated version in 1748 under the title *An Enquiry Concerning Human Understanding.* The *Enquiry* was very successful. In it Hume combined the empiricism of Hobbes, Locke, and Berkeley with Newtonian science, as Hume understood it. In so doing, he established a full-blown, highly developed philosophical psychology (Hunt, 1993; Robinson, 1986). This philosophical psychology was called British Associationism; it emphasized learning and the association of ideas and perceptions.

Hume's last work, *Dialogue Concerning Natural Religion*, was not published until three years after his death. Hume gave the work to his close friend Adam Smith. Smith, a Scottish philosopher is best known as the father of economics. In 1776 Smith published *The Wealth of Nation,* the work that started modern economics.

While Hume's philosophy represented an extension of British empiricism, it was not the only important philosophical approach in Britain in the 1700s. Thomas Reid (1710-1796) was the most prominent of the Scottish common sense philosophers. Reid and the other common sense philosophers rejected Hume's skepticism and championed a realist view of the world. Arguing that objects perceived in the world are real, you must distinguish between the real object, the act of perceiving, and the perceiver. Reid also argued that perceptions are not compounds of simple sensations, as the British empiricists had argued, and that we have certain innate ideas and mental faculties. Our mind is not, as Locke argued, a *tabula rasa* (Brody, 1969).

Fundamental to the debate between Hume and Reid over the question of empiricism versus nativism was the question of God. Reid, and other nativists starting with Descartes, postulated that God made humans and implanted in us certain true ideas about the world. One of those true, common sense ideas according to Reid was that God exists. Hume, a doubter or atheist (it is unclear which), rejected the notion of nativism—there was no God to implant true ideas in humans' brains (Brody, 1969).

Reid's common sense realism evolved, in the work of his student Dugald Stewart (1753-1828), into a theory of psychology based on philosophical speculation. Stewart incorporated many of the empiricist and associationist ideas into Reid's work. This synthesis, published by Stewart in 1792 in his work *Philosophy of the Human Mind*, has a structure similar to a psychology text (and Aristotle's *De Anima*) with chapters on attention, memory, learning, and dreaming. This philosophical psychology was referred to as faculty psychology because it emphasized different human faculties such as memory and attention. Faculty Psychology was generally compatible with and supportive of Christian beliefs (both Catholic and Protestant) and became very influential throughout the English-speaking world in the 1800s.

The Legacy Of The Past

This account of the four hundred year span from 1400 to almost 1800 is highly selective and omits many important events and people. It is a selective account that emphasizes the important elements of psychology's long past or pre-history: the people who have bequeathed to modern psychology some of its fundamental ideas and approaches. Perhaps the most important part of this legacy is the idea of a scientific view of the world. This scientific view of the world, blending elements of Platonic Idealism, Aristotelian Empiricism, Academic and Pyrrhonian Skepticism, and Epicurean Materialism, sought to explain the reality behind our naïve sense impression, describing that reality with mathematics and supporting their ideas with carefully collected empirical evidence. In addition to the model of scientific understanding and the scientific method, the basic philosophical ideas of the Greeks on the world and human nature, and their elaborations and refinements from 1400 to 1800, provide most of the fundamental concepts and hypotheses on human nature that were to shape the emergence and early history of modern psychology.

We have traveled on a 2,400 year journey through history and now must slow down as we approach the birth of modern psychology in 1879. The people, events, and ideas of the late 1700s and of the 1800s are crucial to an understanding of what psychology is, where it came from, and where it may be going.

References

Acton, H. B. (1967). Idealism. In Edwards (1967b), pp. 110-118.

Brock, W.H. (1992). *The Norton history of chemistry*. New York: W. W. Norton.
Brody, B. (1969). Introduction. In T. Reid (1813,1814,1815/1969). Essays on the intellectual powers of man. Cambridge, MA: M.I.T. Press.

Cahill, T. (2003). *Sailing the wine dark seas: Why the Greeks matter*. New York: Anchor Books, A division of Random House.

Campbell, K. (1967). Materialism. In Edwards (1967d), pp. 179-188.

Chang, K. (2005). Visions of ancient night sky were hiding in plain sight for centuries. *New York Times*, January 18, 2005, p. D3.

Cohen, I.B. (1985). *Revolution in science*. Cambridge, MA: Belknap Press of Harvard University Press.

De La Mettrie, J.O. (1748/1961). *Man A machine*. La Salle, IL: Open Court Publishing Company.

De Lacy, P.H. (1967). Epicurus. In Edwards (1967b), pp. 3-5.
Ebbinghaus, H. (1908/1973). *Psychology: An elementary text-book*. Boston: D.C. Heath.

Edwards, P. (ed.) (1967a). *The encyclopedia of philosophy*, Vol. 1. New York: Macmillan Publishing & The Free Press.

Edwards, P. (ed.) (1967b). *The encyclopedia of philosophy*, Vol. 3. New York: Macmillan Publishing & The Free Press.

Edwards, P. (ed.) (1967c). *The encyclopedia of philosophy*, Vol. 4. New York: Macmillan Publishing & The Free Press.

French in 1813. Bell was to work as a surgeon a second time for the British as they fought the French in the Battle of Waterloo. During the battle Bell was reported to have operated on the wounded non-stop to the point of exhaustion.

Bell carried out systematic dissections on animals to explore the structure of the brain and published his findings in 1811 (he only made 100 copies). In *An Idea for a New Anatomy of the Brain*, Bell argued that there are two types of nerves: sensory nerves that carry information from the body and motor nerves that carry information from the spinal cord to the muscles. Bell showed that the ventral nerves of the spine are motor nerves. Bell thus became the first to fully support the hypothesis advanced by both Galen and Descartes, that there are two types of nerves, one for the senses and one for the muscles. Bell also described in this book the functions of the cerebellum. In 1822 the French physiologist Francois Magendie (1783-1855), having heard of Bell's discoveries from one of Bell's assistants, confirmed the existence of the ventral nerves as being motor nerves and, in addition, supported Bell's hypothesis that the dorsal nerves of the spine are sensory. This led to a conflict between the two men, that was later resolved when the two scientists agreed to refer to their joint discovery as the Bell-Magendie Law (Young, 1970).

During his lifetime, Bell made a number of discoveries about the nervous system. He discovered that lesions in the seventh cranial nerve cause facial paralysis (Bell's Palsy) and discovered the functioning of the exterior respiratory nerve (called Bell's Nerve). He also wrote books on surgical techniques, diseases of the urethra, prostate, and rectum, and on gunshot wounds. In 1836, at the age of 62, he returned to Edinburgh to become professor of surgery at his alma mater and to devote time to fly-fishing.

Johannes Müller And The Doctrine Of Specific Nerve Energies

Johannes Müller (1801-1858) was the greatest physiologist on the continent in the first half of the 19th century. He was born in Koblenz, Germany and received his doctorate from the University of Bonn in 1822, at the age of 21. He taught at the University of Bonn until 1833 when he took the new chair of physiology at the University of Berlin. An enormously gifted anatomist and experimentalist, he was also a talented teacher who was worshiped by his students, many of whom went on to be the leading physiologists of the next 50 years (Young, 1970).

Müller was born at a time when the small and independent German principalities were being transformed as a result of the French Revolution and Napoleonic Wars. France and England were the leading economic powers in the world at the start of the French Revolution. France, followed closely by England, was the leading center of science in the world, due in part to the kind of training French scientists received in the French universities. In response, Germany started to consolidate politically under the powerful Prussian kingdom and the Germans transformed their university system, making it, in a short time, the best university system in the world. Accompanied by an expansion of elementary and secondary education, German universities soon became important centers for the sciences. This success in turn fueled Germany's rise as a world power that would soon rival France and Great Britain (Hobsbawm, 1996).

In 1826 Müller published two books on vision, one on illusions, misperceptions, and subjective visual experiences, the second on the comparative physiology of human and animal perceptual systems. A few years later, in 1830, Müller confirmed the Bell-Magendie Law with a series of experiments on frogs and published two more books, this time on endocrinology. Müller is best known for the development of the Doctrine of Specific Nerve Energies (an idea he credited to Bell, for whom Müller had enormous respect). The doctrine states that there are five types of sensory nerves. Each nerve responds in a characteristic way, no matter how it is stimulated physically. Thus, we see light or shapes as a result of pressing on the eyeball or by a blow to the back of the head (which physically stimulates the visual cortex). In addition, the nerves do not send copies of the external object to the brain, but signals (Young, 1970).

Müller's doctrine was to prove wrong in its details, as his students later showed. The neural impulse is the same, no matter what kind of sensory nerve is involved—what makes a difference is the part of the brain into which the signal feeds. But while he was wrong in detail, he was on the right path.

Müller made substantial progress in physiology, especially the understanding of the physiology of perception. But his work also raised a number of philosophical problems: How did the brain transform the signals into our subjective experience? Do we not perceive the world, instead of just the sensations

82

of the world? For Müller, these were not especially troublesome questions, as he was a Kantian (see below) who believed that we had innate knowledge of the world. Müller was not just a great empiricist, like Galen or Aristotle. He was also a Cartesian who believed in innate knowledge, the presence of God in each of us. He espoused the philosophy of vitalism—that humans and animals have a vital spirit (given to them by the deity) that make perception and life itself possible. While Müller rejected materialism, many of his students would not. Müller, however, never let his philosophical disagreements with his students interfere with being a stimulating and nurturing teacher who did everything he could to encourage his students and help them be successful (Hunt, 1993). And successful they were. Herman von Helmholtz (1821-1894) became the leading physiologist (and physicist) of the second half of the century. Emil Du Bois-Reymond (1818-1896) succeeded Müller at Berlin and did important work on the physiology of electric eels. Ernst Brücke (1819-1892) taught at the University of Vienna and was Sigmund Freud's teacher and advisor. These three, among others, were convinced materialists who sought to vanish vitalistic ideas from biology. They formed a blood brotherhood (swearing an oath using their blood) to that end (Young, 1970).

Müller suffered from depression. His first recorded prolonged depression occurred shortly after his appointment at Bonn. A second one occurred when he was 39, a third when he was 47 during the Revolution of 1848 (he was opposed to the revolution and dismayed at what was happening). Finally, he committed suicide in 1858 during his fourth major depression (Hunt, 1993).

Helmholtz And The Brain As Machine

Herman von Helmholtz (1821-1894) was born in Potsdam, Germany. His family did not have money for him to go to college, so he enrolled in a scholarship program with the German Army. In exchange for his education in medicine and surgery, Helmholtz would serve for 8 years as a doctor in the German military. He attended college in Berlin, and in his second year of college, at the age of 18, Helmholtz started doing research with Müller, ultimately writing his doctoral dissertation under Müller's direction. Under the German university system, all recipients of a doctorate must do a dissertation consisting of original work. In the U.S. university system original research is required for the

Ph.D. and a few other doctorates, but not for doctorates in medicine, law, dentistry, and pharmacy. After graduation Helmholtz served five years of his eight-year stint as a military surgeon. He was given an early honorable discharge because of the scientific papers he published while serving in the army. After being discharged he started on a long academic career where he steadily rose in fame as he contributed to advances in physiology, physics, and mathematics (Watson, 1978). Our concerns are with his work in physiology, most of which he carried out early in his academic career.

In 1848 Helmholtz carried out a series of experiments on the speed of the neural impulse. Whereas Müller, like most vitalists, physiologists, and philosophers at the time, argued that the neural impulse was almost instantaneous; Helmholtz showed that it wasn't. Building on the work of Du Bois-Reymond, who had shown that electrical activity in nerves could be measured during the contractions of human muscles, Helmholtz dissected a muscle and nerve in a frog's leg. When he stimulated the frog's nerve, the muscle contracted. The time between the stimulation of the nerve and the muscle contraction (the latency period) was the time, Helmholtz reasoned, that the neural impulse took to travel the distance from the point of stimulation to the muscle. Using the length of the nerve, Helmholtz calculated that the speed of the neural impulse was approximately 25 meters per second (about 83 feet per second). The speed of sound (at sea level in dry air) is approximately 340 meters per second. The nerve impulse is thus considerably slower than sound, far short of instantaneous (Watson, 1978; Young, 1970).

Helmholtz extended his research to human subjects by applying stimulation to their leg and then having the subjects press a button when they felt it. The subjects took longer to report the stimulation when it was applied to their toes, for instance, than when it was applied to their thighs.

Helmholtz's work was not accepted and appreciated at first (partly because of the highly technical nature of the research reports), but it profoundly challenged vitalist conceptions of the brain and nervous system. The nervous system could now be thought of strictly as a machine, albeit a complex one, without a vital essence or spirit.

Shortly after conducting his studies on the speed of the neural impulse, Helmholtz invented the ophthalmoscope, a device used today to examine the retina of the eye. He now turned his attention to the neurophysiology of vision. Building on an earlier theory by Thomas Young, Helmholtz tried to show how we perceive color, given that there is a stark difference between the nature of light and our perception of the world. The resulting theory is commonly referred to as the trichromatic theory of color vision. Helmholtz showed that there are three different color receptor cells in the retina: one for red, one for green, and one for blue-violet. If all are stimulated at once, we see white. If the red and green are stimulated equally, we see yellow. Helmoltz's theory (which is the basis for our modern understanding of color vision) explained the different types of color blindness and why different physical frequencies of light can produce the same subjective experience of color. Helmholtz later went on to explore the neurophysiology of hearing, making significant discoveries in how hearing works (Watson, 1978; Young, 1970).

Helmholtz was surprised by how inaccurate the senses were in detecting the physical world. He postulated that the brain had to build a model of the world based on this limited sense data through a process of unconscious inference. In his general approach he followed the British Empiricists, especially Locke and Berkeley. The concept of unconscious inference was originally Leibniz's and was later developed by Herbart, whom you shall meet later in this chapter.

In 1856 Helmholtz published his masterpiece on vision, the *Handbook of Physiological Optics*. He continued to research and publish in the areas of neural physiology even though he suffered a number of personal tragedies (the death of his father in 1858 and his wife in 1859, leaving him with two young children —he remarried in 1861). Around 1866 his research began to focus on physics, especially the areas of thermodynamics, electrodynamics, and the mathematics of non-Euclidian space. He continued his interests in neurophysiology but did little research relevant to the history of psychology. An avid musician and mountain climber, Helmholtz was elevated to the nobility (hence the von before his last name) in 1882 for his contributions to science. In 1893 he visited the Chicago World's Fair and his friend William James at Harvard. On the return trip he suffered a bad fall on a ship and died the next year in 1894 (Watson, 1978).

Brain Localization

At the same time that Bell, Müller, and Müller's students were making such enormous progress in neurophysiology of the senses, another group of medical doctors and physiologists were making strides in exploring the brain itself. The first of these was Franz Joseph Gall (1758-1828). Gall was born in Germany and received his medical doctorate in Vienna in 1785, where he set up a successful medical practice. Gall is best known for his development, along with his student and research collaborator Johann Spurzheim, of phrenology, the popular unscientific doctrine that personality and intellectual abilities could be determined from measuring the skull. While phrenology was rejected by many scientists at the time, it was an extension of one of Gall's more valuable ideas: the idea of brain localization. Gall argued that the various functions, such as speech, are localized in various parts of the brain. He studied the brains of humans and animals to try to develop a functional anatomy of the brain. In the process of his work he discovered that the gray matter of the brain contains cell bodies and the white matter contains cell fibers, called axons. Besides a number of discoveries concerning the hierarchical structure of the brain structures, Gall and Spurzheim pioneered a new approach to brain dissection. Instead of slicing the brain into small sections, they dissected the brain following the brain's own structure. Gall's harshest critic, Pierre Flourens, who we shall meet in a moment, eventually praised Gall as the "author of the true anatomy of the brain" (Young, 1970).

Gall's doctrine offended religious authorities and vitalist medical doctors alike. In 1801 the Austrian Emperor prohibited Gall from lecturing because his materialistic and fatalistic doctrines threatened religion and morality; the Catholic Church banned his books. Gall left Vienna in 1805 with Spurzheim, settling in Paris in 1807 after touring Europe. Widely popular later in the century among ordinary people (especially in the United States), Gall's ideas were unpopular at the time in France. Napoleon, for example, detested the fact that Gall was German and a materialist. Gall's doctrines generated enormous controversy among scientists as well, especially the doctrine of phrenology. In 1816 Magendie (later famous for the Bell-Magendie Law) invited Spurzheim to examine the brain of the great French philosopher and mathematician Laplace, whose brain Magendie had preserved. Before Spurzheim's arrival, Magendie switched Laplace's brain with the brain of a severely mentally retarded

times of context [handwritten marginalia]

spicy!!! - also nested

person. Spurzheim praised the brain of the mentally retarded person as that of a great man. Magendie published the demonstration as a way of undermining phrenology.

The most sustained attack on Gall's theory of brain localization came from Pierre Flourens (1794-1867). Flourens was a gifted neurosurgeon. He carried out a number of experiments in which he used ablation (the systematic and often very precise destruction of brain tissue) on animals who were then tested for behavioral responses after recovery from surgery. In 1823 he published his masterpiece *Experimental Research on the Properties and Functions of the Nervous System in Vertebrates*. Flourens systematically ablated more and more of the cerebellum and removed the cerebral cortex from a number of animals. Removal of the cerebral cortex left only reflex actions, such as the dilation of the pupils of the eye when exposed to light, but resulted in functional blindness and a total lack of voluntary action. The destruction of the cerebellum resulted in a lack of coordination of motor activity such as walking, flying, and standing upright. Systematic destruction of the medulla oblongata showed that the medulla controlled respiration and heart rate. Destruction of this "vital knot" as Flourens called it, resulted in death. He also noted that slight destruction of brain tissue results in a temporary loss of function that is later recovered (Young, 1970).

Would this be allowed today?

On the basis of his work, Flourens developed the doctrine of equipotentiality and mass action. It is the cerebral cortex as a whole, he argued, that acts as an interconnected system determining perception, cognition, volition, and other psychological functions. The doctrine directly contradicts Gall's theory of cerebral localization.

In 1843 Flourens directly attacked phrenology in his book *An Examination of Phrenology*. Flourens criticized phrenology on logical and empirical grounds, using his own research on brain functioning and on the skull, which showed that the thickness of the skull varies and does not correspond to the underlying brain structures. Flourens disproved phrenology (although his disproof did nothing to hurt the popularity phrenology enjoyed) but not the doctrine of cerebral localization, which was to be revived by physicians studying disorders in patients with brain damage (Young, 1970).

Gall was one of the first to note the relationship between head injuries and speech loss. In one patient Gall examined, a soldier with a sword wound to the ear behind his left eye, Gall noted that the soldier could not remember names of friends or common objects. The debates among the scientific followers of Gall, who argued for localization of speech while rejecting the wilder claims of phrenology that had been disproved by Flourens, continued into the 1860s. When Paul Broca (1824-1880) performed an autopsy on the brain of one of his patients (known as Tan because he would answer "tan, tan" to any question) who had developed paralysis of the right side of his body. Medical examination showed that Tan had normal speech organs, could solve math problems, and seemed to understand what was said to him. After Tan's death, Broca's autopsy showed that Tan had a cavity in his brain the size of a small egg in the left frontal lobe. The autopsy of a later patient who had lost his speech showed destruction in the same area of the brain. Broca's report and presentation of the two brains, as well as his later studies on expressive aphasics, established a localized organ for speech production now known as Broca's area. Broca also showed that the speech area was only in the left frontal lobe (Young, 1970).

Broca's findings were followed by a number of others showing some localization of specific functions. In 1874 the German physician Carl Wernicke (1848-1905) showed that a second kind of aphasia associated with the ability to produce only nonsense speech is associated with damage to an area in the left temporal lobe. This aphasia is now referred to as Wernicke's Aphasia. Wernicke went on to correlate a number of behavioral disorders with damage to specific parts of the nervous system and brain (Young, 1970).

By the mid-1870s, neurophysiologists had made great progress in understanding the structure and functioning of the brain in both humans and animals. In physiology, vitalism was dead as a scientific belief and materialism was triumphant. The progress in neurophysiology, much of it the product of work on the continent, was not the only significant development in biology.

Across the channel in England, a radical biological theory had been proposed. This theory, which was to unify biology into a single science in the same way that Newton's work had unified physics into a single science, was proposed by the most reluctant of revolutionaries—Charles R. Darwin.

Darwin And Evolution

Unlike the New Physics which achieved dramatic, even stunning, success in a short time by the standards of history, the New Biology proceeded slowly through observation and experimentation to accumulate a body of knowledge. The two groups that practiced the new biology were physician-researchers like Bell, Müller, Helmholtz, Gall, and Flourens, and naturalists who carried out studies of plants, insects, and animals. Some of these naturalists were practical business people interested in improving agriculture, while others were wealthy gentleman or preachers interested in the natural world. In England, Erasmus Darwin was an example of a naturalist who was also a medical doctor. By the time Erasmus Darwin's grandson Charles Darwin was born (1809), the new biologists had been working for almost 200 years, but they did not have a unifying paradigm as did physics. Their unifying paradigm was to evolve out of the work of Charles Darwin.

Darwin's Early Life → movie

Charles Darwin (1809-1882) was born at his father's estate in Shrewsbury. His father Robert W. Darwin was a successful physician; Charles's grandfather was the legendary Erasmus Darwin. Robert Darwin had married Susannah Wedgwood, the daughter of Josiah Wedgwood, the industrialist who transformed the manufacture of pottery and ceramics. Susannah Wedgwood Darwin died in 1817 when Charles was eight. Charles' father Robert had high expectations for his son, expectations that were often disappointed. The elder Darwin once wrote to his young son, "You care for nothing but shooting, dogs, and rat catching, and you will be a disgrace to yourself and your family." Young Charles spent a great deal of time collecting bugs, rocks and minerals, and hunting. Charles was an expert shot and an excellent rider as a young teenager (Clark, 1984).

In 1825, at the age of 16, Robert sent his son to Edinburgh to study medicine, following the family tradition. Charles did not do well there. He couldn't stand human dissection, liked to collect sea creatures in the Firth of Forth near the university, and spent a great deal of time hunting and drinking. He dropped out after a year. His father, not surprisingly, was very disappointed in his son, and sent him back to college in 1827, this time to Cambridge University, to study to be a minister (Clark, 1984).

Something happened to Charles Darwin at Cambridge: he fell in love with natural history. At the time, natural history included what we now call biology as well as geology. He spent time with the great botanist John Henslow collecting plants. Upon graduation Darwin was called by his classmates "The man who walks with Henslow". Charles also studied geology with Adam Segdwick, the great creationist geologist, and read texts on geology as well as William Paley's *View of the Evidence of Christianity*. Paley (1743-1805) was a leading theologian of the time, a proponent of natural theology which argues for the existence of God and the truth of Christianity from the scientific facts. Paley had taught at Cambridge and his intellectual influence was still strong when Darwin attended almost 25 years after Paley's death.

Darwin graduated with a B.A in April of 1831 and spent the summer doing research with Sedgwick, intent on taking a position as a minister in a rural parish after the summer research project ended. Then fate intervened. Captain Robert FitzRoy, the young commander of H.M.S. Beagle, was looking for a gentleman naturalist. The naturalist's job was a kind of science officer. Darwin was to manage the scientific equipment and microscope, gather sea creatures, fossils, bugs, and plants and animals, and bring back the specimens to England. The gentleman part of the job was to dine with the captain and be his companion. It was important that the captain, especially one like FitzRoy, could talk with someone of his own social standing while on the long sea voyages. FitzRoy had served as First Mate for a captain who had committed suicide off the coast of South America, leaving FitzRoy to bring the ship and crew back to England. Fitzroy almost rejected Darwin for the job, as he believed in phrenology and did not like the look of Darwin. But Darwin came highly recommend by his teachers at Cambridge, and the two got along very well. Then another obstacle came up. Robert Darwin did not want his son to go—he wanted him to settle down and start a career. Charles turned to his uncle Josiah, who interceded on Charles' behalf. With the support of Josiah Wedgwood, Charles got his father's blessing to go. The Beagle, with Charles Darwin on board, departed on December 27, 1831 on a voyage that was to last five years (Clarke, 1984).

The Voyage Of The Beagle

The Beagle took Darwin to South America where it sent expeditions into orous plants, climbing plants, and earthworms. All of these books, in addition to being valuable contributions to our understanding of plants and animals, furnished additional evidence for the theory of evolution. In addition to his scientific works, Darwin wrote an autobiography and a biography of his grandfather Erasmus. Both his own autobiography and the biography of his grandfather were edited by his family members (with Charles Darwin's full support and knowledge) so as to minimize the negative or controversial effects that the works might have (Clark, 1984; also see Ghiselin, 1984).

Darwin died April 19, 1882 and was buried at Westminster Abbey near Isaac Newton. During his life he had won the Royal Medal, the Copley Medal, and been knighted for his contributions to science. His pallbearers included his friends Hooker, Huxley, and Wallace, as well as the president of the Royal Society and the U.S. ambassador to Great Britain (Clark, 1984).

The Theory And Its Implications

What was the theory of natural selection and why was it so controversial?

The theory of evolution by natural selection is both complex and simple. It can be divided into five basic components:

1. Evolution—Species change over time.
2. Descent with modification—groups of descendants share common ancestors; there is a branching pattern to the descent.
3. Gradualism—Change is slow in geological terms; over long periods evolution accounts for new species.
4. Multiplication of species—evolution produces both new species and an increasing number of species.
5. Natural Selection—One of the mechanisms for evolution is natural selection, which has five steps. First, populations tend to increase indefinitely in a geometric ratio. Second, in the natural world populations stabilize at a certain level. Third, there is a struggle for existence within a species and between species, as well as in the face of the natural world, and not all organisms produced survive. Fourth, species show variation. Fifth, in the struggle for existence those variations that are better suited to the environment are more likely to survive (and in turn, leave behind more offspring) than those less suited to the environment, a phenomenon known as differential reproductive success (Mayr, 1982).

The theory was profoundly disturbing to Darwin's contemporaries and remains so today. Indeed, it is one of the five or six most disturbing theories in the history of science (Sherman, 2002), perhaps the single most disturbing. The theory is both materialistic (the explanation for the origins of species is solely in natural, material terms) and is an invisible hand explanation. An invisible hand explanation is not teleological, i.e., there is no purpose to the functioning of the system and no being is consciously guiding it. Invisible hand explanations were developed by Adam Smith in his masterful work on economics, *The Wealth of Nations*, which was originally published in 1776. As an aside, Darwin read Smith's work when he was developing his theory (as well as the work of the economist Thomas Malthus, who postulated that human populations grow geometrically and that there is a struggle for existence) and acknowledged being influenced by the idea of invisible hand explanations.

"Nothing in biology makes sense except in the light of evolution" (Dobzhansky, 1973, p. 125). Once Darwin and Wallace introduced the theory with extensive studies showing its validity, many biologists, such as Huxley, were stunned that no one had seen before what Darwin and Wallace had seen. Darwin's theory integrated the study of biology in the same way that Newton's theory integrated physics—the theory provided a unifying paradigm, a law of nature that offered a scientific explanation of the many observations naturalists were making, an explanation that leads to new discoveries and new problems.

Darwin's theory has a number of broader cultural consequences, in addition to being a powerful explanation of speciation. Natural selection undermines essentialism and the idea of Platonic types. Species are no longer conceptualized as having an essence, but are ever-changing without any fixed characteristics. The challenge to essentialism undermines a number of religious beliefs, including the belief in the soul and life after death. Natural selection replaces the static model of creationism with a dynamic model of evolution, again undermining a number of religious beliefs, such as the literal truth of the Genesis story of creation. Additionally, it undermines the idea of intelligent design (that humans and other life-forms were designed by a supreme being) and replaces it with "design" by natural selection. Natural selection undermines the idea that God or gods are needed for speciation; instead, speciation is a natural process that occurs without divine intervention. From here it is but a short victions. Marx and Engels embraced the theory for the same reason that the educated public rejected it—because of its radical cultural implications. Marx wrote to Darwin later in life offering to dedicate the second volume of *Capital* to him; Darwin politely declined (Foster, 2000).

The reaction of the general public was much more complex. Many came to embrace a doctrine of Social Darwinism, a doctrine that Darwin rejected. Social Darwinism was really the product of the social philosopher Herbert Spencer. Spencer argued that in society the strong survive and it is survival of the fittest, a phrase Spencer, not Darwin coined. (Darwin did not use the phrase in the first edition of *The Origins*, but added it to later editions). Social Darwinism was used to justify the enormous wealth and power of the industrial capitalists (after all, as the most successful they were the fittest in society) and to argue against efforts to aid the poor and oppressed. The power of Darwin's theory of natural selection gave a great deal of status and believability to the idea of Social Darwinism (Hofstadter, 1959).

Many individuals, both Biblical literalists and those who were not literalists or not religious, became aware of the radical implications of the theory. As a consequence, opposition to the theory spread outside of the community of biologists and the community of the well-educated to the general public in both Europe and the United States. People who had never read Darwin's work or who were incapable of judging the evidence and arguments for and against the theory, were strongly, even passionately, opposed to it. This situation continues to this day in many parts of the U.S., less so in Europe.

Darwin: The Reluctant Revolutionary

Charles Darwin had, like his distinguished grandfather, a talent for friendship. Darwin's wife and children loved him deeply. His close friends considered him both an intellectual giant and the perfect Victorian gentleman. Darwin was a man of enormous intellectual integrity who, at the same time, was uncomfortable with the radical implications of his theory. Within the environment of the Victorian gentleman, he was radical, favoring extension of voting rights and the abolition of slavery while opposing the abuses of colonial rule; he did not, however, wish to oppose his society in general. Darwin was first and foremost a thoroughgoing empiricist who did not believe in anything which he could not understand or for which there was no evidence, but he did not want to create controversy or upset the social order in which he held a favored position. He purposely delayed publication of his theory, fearing the kind of negative general reaction that had tarnished his grandfather's fame. When he published *The Origin* he avoided all mention of human evolution save one ("light would be thrown on the origin of man and his history") because a more developed discussion of human evolution would have been injurious to the success of the book and to the reception of the theory. Darwin had a personal reason to minimize the radical implications of his theory as well—his wife Emma and a number of his children were devoted Christians who did not like the theory or its implications (Clark, 1984).

Darwin was a reluctant, ambivalent revolutionary who felt that his materialist theory of evolution by means of natural selection was as close as he could get to the truth of the natural world. Yet he was uncomfortable with the broader cultural implications of the theory. He had no doubts, by the time he died, of the general truth of the theory for the biological world.

The Darwinian Revolution And The Unification Of Biology

Darwin's theory provided a powerful, unifying framework for the study of botany and zoology, comparative anatomy and physiology, paleontology, and comparative animal behavior. It opened new lines of research and investigation, such as the study of ecology and the study of human evolution, and provided a powerful impetus to a scientific psychology. It was incomplete, however, and not completely successful until biologists figured out the mechanisms of heredity, leading to the grand synthesis in the early and mid-1900s. The study of the molecular and cellular basis of evolution, as well as the selection mechanisms, continue to this day and there remain a number of unresolved issues, such as the disagreement between gradualists (like Darwin) and the punctuated-equilibrium position (advocated by Darwin's cousin Francis Galton). The theory of evolution by natural selection and the theory of evolution by sexual selection rank Darwin next to Newton and Einstein as one of the three most important scientists of all time. Opposition to the theory continues to this day because of the radical implications for other areas of knowledge.

Since its inception, the theory has had a lasting effect on the history of psychology, as we shall see in the chapters ahead. But the theory is so radical in its implications and so far-reaching that the assimilation of the theory into psychology has been slow and partial at best (Ghiselin, 1973).

Psychiatry And Medicine

The late 1700s and the 1800s were a time of significant advances in medicine, the result of slow and often uneven progress in the new biology. The period saw the development of experimental medicine and two different approaches to psychiatry, the branch of medicine that deals with emotional and behavioral problems. The two approaches to psychiatry lack convenient names. The first approach may be termed the biopsychosocial approach, an approach that holds that psychiatric illnesses can be due to biological problems such as disease or brain trauma, psychological problems such as abuse or stress, social problems such as discrimination and stigma, or some combination of these three problems. The second approach may be termed the biological approach, an approach that holds that psychiatric illnesses are due to biological problems, such as chemical imbalances, viruses, or brain traumas. The history of psychiatry has alternated between these two approaches (Shorter, 1997). The history of these two views begins with the colorful figure of Franz Anton Mesmer.

Hypnotism

Franz Anton Mesmer (1734-1815) was born in Germany and received his medical degree from the University of Vienna. His dissertation was on the effects of the planets' gravitational fields on humans. Shortly after receiving his doctorate he met a priest who had used magnets to cure patients. This practice fit in well with Mesmer's theory (as magnetism and gravity were related in his view). Mesmer then used magnets to cure patients of illnesses, achieving notable success in some cases. He discovered that he did not need actual magnets to achieve results, arguing that all creatures have innate magnetic properties, what he called animal magnetism (Gauld, 1992). Others began referring to his techniques as Mesmerism.

Mesmer's use of magnets soon led him into conflict with Catholic priests *could there be a naturalistic explanation of God*

who used exorcism to dispel demon possession. In a well-publicized conflict with the famed exorcist and priest Johann Gassner (1727-1779), Mesmer showed that animal magnetism could explain the success of exorcism. By providing a naturalistic explanation of super-natural phenomena, Mesmer achieved considerable scientific fame (Gauld, 1992).

He soon was embroiled in more controversy when his claim to have cured a young pianist's blindness was shown to be faked. He then fled Vienna for Paris where he found great success and attracted influential supporters such as Queen Marie Antoinette. Because of the demand for treatment, Mesmer started to treat patients in groups (Gauld, 1992).

Mesmer's success in Paris, like his success in Vienna, generated controversy. Both the Catholic Church and the medical establishment criticized his methods and theory. In 1784 a scientific commission was appointed to investigate Mesmer's theory. Leading scientists, including the chemist Antoine Lavoiser and the physicist and diplomat (representing the American revolutionaries) Benjamin Franklin, were appointed to the commission. Franklin chaired the commission which carried out a series of experiments to test Mesmer's claims. The commission found no evidence that magnetism influenced illness and concluded that animal magnetism was mystical, not scientific. The commission's report ended Mesmer's career, although his methods were still used by his followers and developed over the next 100 years, principally by surgeons and psychiatrists (Gauld, 1992).

Mesmer had, of course, discovered hypnotism. His followers soon made a number of discoveries. Marquis de Puysequr (1751-1825) discovered that patients could be put into a sleep-like state (Mesmer's patients often had violent fits), showed amnesia about what happened during the trance, and were highly suggestible. This suggestibility made them very susceptible to the hypnotist's commands during the trance (hence the power of stage hypnotists to make people do silly things on stage) and to carry out suggestions after they woke up from the trance, now called posthypnotic suggestion. British physicians experimented with hypnotism as a way of minimizing pain during surgery and in the post-operative period. Meanwhile, French physicians found that while all people are susceptible to hypnotism, some are more easily hypnotizable than others, and that certain psychiatric illnesses could be treated using hypnosis

(Gauld, 1992).

Philippe Pinel And The Birth Of The Therapeutic Asylum

The study and development of hypnotism was not the only advance in psychiatry during the early and mid-1800s. Insane asylums had been around for centuries, a product of the middle ages and Renaissance. These asylums were little more than prisons, with the inhabitants kept in chains in filthy cells. The most famous of these asylums was in London, the Bethlehem Royal Hospital, founded in 1547. In the accent of Londoners, the name Bethlehem came to be pronounced Bedlam, now a synonym for chaos and disorder.

The two major insane asylums in Paris were Bicêtre (for men) and Salpêtriére (for women). Four years after the start of the French Revolution the revolutionary government asked Philippe Pinel (1745-1826), a supporter of the revolution and a medical doctor, to take over Bicêtre in 1793. Pinel achieved almost instant fame when he ordered the prisoners freed from their chains. Two years later, Pinel was also named director of Salpêtriére, where he again ordered the removal of all chains. In the place of chains, Pinel ordered the use of the straitjacket to confine more dangerous patients. The less dangerous patients were allowed to be free (Shorter, 1997).

Pinel's real fame comes from the publication of his textbook on psychiatry in 1801 on the treatment of mental illness (called alienation). The medical doctors who followed Pinel's general approach soon become known as alienists, people who treat mental alienation. Pinel argued that the asylum could be structured so that it healed the insane, not just imprisoned them. Two elements were crucial to this cure. The first was a relationship of trust between the doctor and the patient that permitted them to talk about the patient's problems, even the patient's most intimate thoughts and feelings. This talking cure was the first modern version of psychotherapy (and the basis of Freud's later development of psychoanalysis). The second element was to have a healthy environment for the patient, with fresh air, healthy food, exercise, and meaningful activities (Shorter, 1997).

Pinel's moral treatment, as it came to be called, was part of an influential international current. Others who contributed to this current were William Tuke, who founded a private asylum in 1796 in York, England, based on many of the same principles Pinel advocated. Vincenzio Chiarugi developed guidelines for human treatment of the insane in Italian asylums, and Johann Reil, a German neuroanatomist, developed a number of Chiarugi's ideas and applied them to German insane asylums. Reil also coined the term "psychiatry" in 1808 (Shorter, 1997).

Pinel's talking cure, essentially psychotherapy, was based on the idea that psychiatric illness or alienation could be caused by biological, psychological, or social factors. He is thus the essential founder of the biopsychosocial approach, an approach that emphasizes psychotherapy and the therapeutic asylum (Shorter, 1997).

The idea of the therapeutic asylum spread steadily and won a number of adherents among physicians. The number of asylums grew steadily into the 1840s, mostly treating a relatively small number of patients in humane conditions in Europe and the U.S. Then in the 1850s the number of patients started to grow exponentially; the asylums were flooded with extreme cases that did not respond to treatment and the asylums again became, to all intents and purposes, warehouses for the insane no better than the prisons (Shorter, 1997). What caused this flood of mentally ill patients that drowned the first therapeutic asylums?

The Collapse Of The Asylum

Two simultaneous factors combined to doom the biopsychosocial approach and the therapeutic asylum: one was the spread of industrial capitalism, the other was the spread of a virulent sexually transmitted disease, the AIDS of the 1800s: neurosyphilis.

As industrial capitalism grew and spread, coming to be the dominant economic organization in the last half of the 1800s, so too did problems caused by the factory system. One of these problems was the brutal working conditions and harsh living conditions of factory workers. Thrown together in the growing industrial centers with poor housing, contaminated water and air, and subjected to brutal 12-hour days, the new factory workers turned to drugs, chiefly alcohol, as an escape. Alcohol abuse (as distinct from alcohol use) rose beyond any previously known limits and was linked to a variety of social and domestic problems such as child abuse and wife abuse. As alcohol abuse rose, so too did the brain damage associated with chronic alcoholism, leading to increasing numbers of patients in asylums (Shorter, 1997).

In addition to the overconsumption of alcohol, the new factories produced environmental toxins, some of which caused brain damage (Foster, 1999; Engels, 1845/1984). One example was the mercury poisoning suffered by hatters —the workers who made hats in hat factories. The hatters used mercurous nitrate and worked in poorly ventilated factories. The prolonged exposure to mercury vapors caused a number of neurological problems including blurred vision, shakes and trembling of the limbs, and speech problems. The hatters literally went mad, a phrase common in England by the 1830s and used in Lewis Carroll's *Alice in Wonderland* published in 1865. Mercury was not outlawed in the manufacture of hats in the U.S. until 1941, as a result of sustained efforts by unions, and is still a substantial source of environmental neurotoxins in the world. In the U.S. most mercury poisoning comes from fish that accumulate large concentrations of mercury in their bodies, mercury produced in coal-fired power plants and carried in air particles where it enters lakes and streams

In addition to the flood of the insane caused by alcohol overconsumption and environmental pollution, a new sexually transmitted disease spread throughout Europe and the Americas. Neurosyphilis is an infection of the central nervous system that develops approximately 10 to 15 years after the initial infection. Known in the 1800s as the disease of the century and rivaling the frequency of AIDS in this century (Shorter, 1997), neurosyphilis was spread during the Napoleonic Wars fought in the early 1800s.

The first symptoms of neurosyphilis are psychiatric in nature, including manic behavior and delusions of grandeur. As the disease progresses, symptoms include an unusual gait, pain the in the abdomen, senility, and paralysis. During the height of the disease, at least 20% of Americans and Europeans were infected with the disease and at least 6% of all Europeans and Americans died from the disease, most likely many more, but statistics were generally only kept on the wealthy and middle class patients (Shorter, 1997). These rates are higher than the less than one-half of 1% of Americans and Europeans who now are infected with the HIV and are similar to the rates for sub-Sahara Africa, where the AIDS epidemic has reached ghastly proportions. The combination of neurosphilis, chronic alcohol abuse, and environmental neurotoxins doomed the efforts of the psychiatrists to treat mental illness with therapy in an asylum. An alternative to the talking cure developed in the form of biological psychiatry.

Griesinger And The Birth Of Biological Psychiatry

The biological approach to psychiatry was not new; in fact, it had developed around the same time as the biopsychosocial approach. One of the best known of the early advocates of the biological approach was the American physician and revolutionary Benjamin Rush. Rush was a signer of the Declaration of Independence and worked (without pay) as a physician for the Continental Army, treating the sick and wounded at Valley Forge and after a number of important battles. Rush argued that mental illness was caused by organic problems in the brain, not by social or psychological causes (Shorter, 1997).

Rush's view, while widespread, was not the dominant view in the early 1800s. It was not until Wilhelm Griesinger (1817-1868) was appointed as professor of psychiatry at the University of Berlin that this changed. One of the failings of the proponents of the biopsychosocial approach was that they were not interested in medical education and research and focused their attention on management of asylums. As a consequence, few taught in medical schools, where psychiatry was a neglected specialty. Griesinger received his medical degree from the University of Tubingen, where he studied internal medicine and psychiatry. At the age of 28 he published a textbook of psychiatry, but spent most of his career in internal medicine, being given the position of professor of internal medicine at the University of Zurich in 1860. In 1861 Griesinger published a second, substantially revised edition of his psychiatric text. This edition incorporated much of the latest scholarly research on the brain and nervous system and advanced the view that psychiatric illnesses were brain diseases. This second edition was hugely successful and the most influential book on psychiatry for at least the next 30 years (Shorter, 1997).

Soon after, in 1865, Griesinger was offered the post of professor of psychiatry at the University of Berlin, which quickly became one of the leading medical schools in the world, rivaling the University of Vienna and the Scottish universities. Griesinger dramatically changed psychiatric education, emphasizing medical examination of patients, diagnosis, and the application of the latest scientific findings. He used real patients in his lectures and soon was a popular and influential teacher. In addition to medical students, practicing psychiatrists would often attend his courses. In 1867 Griesinger founded a new scientific journal, the *Archive for Psychiatry and Nervous Diseases*, to supplant the main journal of the biopsychosocial approach that was read by alienists and asylum psychiatrists, the *Journal of General Psychiatry*. The *Archive* advocated the "new" view that psychiatric illnesses were diseases of the brain. Griesinger died the next year at the age of 51 when his appendix burst. In spite of his early death, his impact on psychiatry was profound. Griesinger laid the intellectual, educational, and scholarly basis for a new biological psychiatry that was to dominate medicine into the next century (Shorter, 1997).

Statistics And Psychological Measurement

Statistics and measurement theory form an integral part of modern psychology, as every psychology major who has taken statistics and research methods knows. Statistics was first formalized as a mathematical theory by Blaise Pascal and Pierre Fermat in 1654. The two mathematicians had been presented with a gambling problem and in their correspondence concerning the problem developed some of the basics of probability theory. The Dutch mathematician Christian Huygens (a teacher of Leibniz, the co-developer of calculus) learned of the correspondence and followed it up in 1657 with the publication of his work on gambling entitled *De Ratiociniis in Ludo Aleae* (On reasoning in games of chance). Statistics continued to be popular into the 1700s because of its connection to gambling. In the late 1600s and early 1700s advances were made in statistics by Jakob Bernoulli (1654-1705) and Abraham de Moivre (1667-1754), but both of these mathematicians confined their work to applications of statistics to games. This changed in the early 1800s, with the work of A-M Legendre, C.F. Gauss, and P.S. Laplace. These three mathematicians, especially Laplace, applied statistics to a number of different problems and developed many new techniques (Stigler, 1986).

Quetelet

Another important founder of statistics was Adolph Quetelet (1796-1874).

He was born in Belgium at the time the industrial revolution was spreading from Britain to the Low Countries (Belgium and the Netherlands). He received his doctorate in mathematics from the University of Ghent (in Belgium) in 1819. He taught mathematics in Brussels until 1823 when he went to Paris to study astronomy and statistics, where he studied with Laplace (the mathematician whose brain had been preserved by Magendie). In 1833 Quetelet established an observatory in Belgium, sponsored by the government, where he worked on a variety of data sets (Stigler, 1986). Quetelet extended statistical methods beyond their use in astronomy to record average values for observations and standard or averaged errors of measurement. He found that a variety of human characteristics, such as weight, height, and chest circumference all corresponded to a normal distribution with a central or average value. He developed improvements in census taking, collected and analyzed statistics on crime, and developed a measure of obesity, known (and still used today) as the Body Mass Index (BMI), also called the Quetelet Index. In 1853, Quetelet organized the first international conference devoted to statistics, and helped form the Statistical Society of London as well as the Statistical Section of the British Association for the Advancement of Science (Stigler, 1986).

Quetelet thought that statistics could be used to discover the physical and psychological (he called them "moral") characteristics of human beings. He called his new science social mechanics and developed it in two books filled with statistical analysis of social behavior, one published in 1835 and the second in 1846. These books not only stimulated great interest in statistics, but generated debates over free will: was human behavior a result of free will, or, as suggested by the regularity of the statistical data, was it governed by certain laws and regularities (Stigler, 1986)?

Psychophysics

Psychophysics is the study of the relationship between physical sensations and perceptions. Psychophysics is an important forerunner of the new psychology and was soon, with the birth of the new psychology in 1879, to become an important part of the field. Psychophysics grew out of the work of Ernst Heinrich Weber (1795-1878), who was born in Wittenberg, Germany, and attended medical school at the University of Leipzig, where he received his doctorate in 1815. He spent the rest of his career as a professor at Leipzig, where he retired in 1871 (Watson, 1978).

Weber was interested as a physiologist in the sense of touch, an area that was not extensively studied. Weber showed that the sense of touch is actually a combination of a number of senses, including a sense of pressure, of pain, and of temperature. He developed a technique for measuring the sensitivity of the skin by applying pressure at two points on the skin near each other at the same time. When the pressure is applied so that the person feels two points as opposed to one, Weber said that you reached the two-point threshold. The two-point threshold is different in different parts of the body. The lips, for instance, have a smaller threshold (i.e., you can feel two points when they are closer together) than the back, which has the largest two-point threshold in the body, approximately 60 millimeters (Watson, 1978).

In addition to touch, Weber was interested in kinesthesis, the sense in our muscles. In a set of very important experiments on our ability to discriminate different weights, Weber had his subjects lift a standard weight and then left a test weight and judge whether the test weight was lighter, heavier, or the same weight. On the basis of this study, Weber was able to determine the smallest difference that could be detected from the standard, an amount he called the just noticeable difference or jnd. Weber discovered that the jnd was not a fixed weight, but a constant fraction of the standard. Thus, we do not perceive absolute differences in weights, but relative differences (Watson, 1978). This relationship is known as Weber's law, so named by Gustav Fechner, whom we meet next.

Gustav Theodor Fechner (1801-1887) graduated with his medical degree from the University of Leipzig in 1822, seven years after Weber. Working for a number of years as a translator, guest lecturer, and private tutor, Fechner wrote tirelessly and carried out studies in physics, especially electricity. In 1834 he finally secured a position at Leipzig, his interests slowly developing in the area of vision. In 1840 Fechner suffered a severe episode of depression that lasted for several years. After recovering, his interests shifted away from physics toward philosophy. In particular, Fechner rejected materialism, which he called the "night view" of the universe, and embraced the notions of mind and spirit. Fechner believed that the mind and body must be connected and set out to explore that connection. His starting point was the work of his colleague, Ernst Weber. Fechner expressed Weber's discovery mathematically and created a field of study called psychophysics, with the publication in 1860 of his master-piece, *The Elements of Psychophysics.*

Even as a physicist, Fechner was uncomfortable with materialism and wrote a number of works (both serious and satirical) under the pen name Dr. Mises. Fechner used his pen name to champion his spiritual and mystical views, as well as to ridicule the views of materialists. He carried out empirical studies of parapsychology and spiritual phenomena, as did Alfred Russel Wallace, the co-discoverer of evolution, and William James, whom we will meet soon (Hunt, 1993; Watson, 1978).

In his *Elements of Psychophysics,* Fechner applied rigorous experimental methods and statistical analysis to studies of sensation and perception. In doing so, he sought to elucidate the relationship between the physical world and the psychological world or, in the terms of his times, between the mind and the body. Fechner demonstrated that a science of psychology was pos-sible and he developed a number of methods for studying perception (Watson, 1978)

Fechner went on to create a second field of study, in addition to psychophys-ics, that of experimental esthetics, the experimental study of what we find beautiful and what we do not find beautiful. He did this by analyzing people's reactions to thousands of paintings. Fechner died at the age of 87 after a long and enormously productive career. He was eulogized by Wilhelm Wundt, Fechner's friend and colleague at the University of Leipzig, and the founder of modern psychology (Watson, 1978).

Discussions of the work of Weber and Fechner are usually included along with the work of other neurophysiologists such as Müller and Helmholtz. While a description of their work could appropriately be placed there, that would cloud their major contributions. They both showed the power of statis-tical analysis and mathematical models for understanding psychological phe-nomena. This was the last step that was needed to be taken for psychology to be a science similar to the sciences of physics, chemistry, and biology.

Galton And Regression To The Mean

Francis Galton (1822-1911), known as Frank to his friends and relatives, was a grandson of Erasmus Darwin and a cousin of Charles Darwin. He, like Charles Darwin, had two grandfathers that were members of the Lunar Society. His paternal grandfather was Samuel Galton Junior. His father Samuel Tertius married Erasmus Darwin's daughter Violetta. Francis Galton was the youngest of seven children and his father was a wealthy banker. Galton was a gifted child, learning to read and write by the age of 30 months and reading Shakespeare for fun at the age of seven. He was sent off to boarding school where he was miserable and did poorly. At the age of 16 his father took him out of school and he served an apprenticeship at Birmingham General Hospital, in preparation for being sent off to medical school (Gillham, 2001).

Galton was not happy with medicine as a career, and his older cousin Charles Darwin, who had just returned from his four-year travels around the world, intervened with Galton's father, persuading him to let Francis transfer to Cambridge, where he could study mathematics. He graduated in 1843, but was disappointed that he did not graduate with honors. While the highly competitive Galton loved mathematics, he was not especially talented at it (Gillham, 2001).

Galton's life changed dramatically shortly after graduation with the unexpected death of his father. The death of Galton's father left the young Francis a very wealthy man. He could now do exactly what he wanted for the rest of his life. Galton now spent six years sowing his wild oats, a time he referred to later as his "fallow years". Galton loved to travel and visited Egypt, the Sudan, and the Middle East. He returned to England to party and socialize with his friends. In 1849 he grew unhappy with his aimless life, and consulted a phrenologist. He also learned of David Livingstone's discoveries in Central Africa, discoveries that aroused his interest. He approached his cousin Charles for advice, and his cousin Captain Douglas Galton, already famous as an engineer. (Douglas Galton later went on to do important work in sanitation engineering, building water and sewer systems.) Francis Galton conceived of an expedition of discovery to Africa, and was urged by his cousins to get the backing of the Royal Geographic Society. Introduced by an old college friend, Galton talked with the vice-president of the Royal Geographic Society and got the society's support. Sponsored by his cousins, Francis was elected a member of the society and he prepared to travel to Africa, funding the expedition entirely from his own wealth, but with the advice and guidance of the explorers and geographers of the Royal Geographic Society. The voyage to Cape Town, South Africa, took 86 days. Galton spent the time reading and learning to use a sextant so he could make careful maps of the territory he was to explore. Galton spent two years, from 1850 to 1852, traveling through South Africa and exploring the area of what is now the country of Namibia. He encountered a number of problems and had many adventures. He sent a number of papers back to London to be read at the Royal Geographic Society; the papers were well-written and contained careful maps and measurements. Upon his return to Great Britain he was an instant celebrity. Trying to escape the publicity he traveled to Norway, and then vacationed with his family at Dover, where one of his sisters took care of him. At Dover he worked on a popular account of his travels, published in 1853 as *Tropical South Africa*. Galton's book was well received by reviewers and sold well; Darwin wrote Galton a letter telling him how much he enjoyed and admired the book. The same year Galton was awarded the Founder's Medal from the Royal Geographic Society for the precision of his maps and measurements. Galton had set a new standard for exploration and geography. Later that year Galton married Louisa Butler, a woman he had met and fallen madly in love with in Dover (Gillham, 2001).

Frank and Loui (as Francis called her) honeymooned in Switzerland and Italy. Galton was never again to go on an expedition of discovery, but he and his wife were frequent travelers in Europe. Galton contributed a section to *Hints for Travelers*, a popular guide for explorers published by the society. He published the *Art of Travel* in 1855, a practical guide for travelers and explorers in all parts of the world, based on his own experiences in Africa and material he gathered from other explorers. In addition to his successful books, Galton worked on a number of inventions, which he called Galton's toys. These toys included the periscope, a rotary steam engine, the quincunx (a device that illustrates how random variation can produce a normal distribution) and an improvement in the telegraph. In addition to his toys, Galton developed modern weather maps in this period (Gillham, 2001).

Galton's life changed when his cousin and friend Charles Darwin (Galton frequently went to Down House to join Darwin for lunch) published the *Origin of*

Species in 1859. The publication of Darwin's revolutionary work caused Galton to enter a third period of his adult life, the first period being his wild years and the second being his years as explorer, geographer, and travel writer: his third period was to focus on the application of evolutionary theory to humans and explorations of heritability and variation (Gillham, 2001).

Galton studied the work of Quetelet, work made known to Galton through a mathematician friend, a few years after reading Darwin's book. He made use of published lists and biographies of eminent and influential men (no women were listed in any of his sources) in an effort to estimate the frequency of highly talented and eminent men. The first product of his new interests were articles in 1865 in *Macmillan's Magazine*. The magazine was a broadly read, high-quality magazine that included famous poets, novelists, and scientists among its writers. Galton estimated that eminence was rare, occurring approximately in one out of very 3,000 to 4,000 people. In addition, Galton cited evidence that talent and eminence were passed on from parents to children (Gillham, 2001).

These articles were part of a larger project that culminated in the publication of Galton's book, *Hereditary Genius,* published in 1869. This was Galton's first major work on human inheritance. In it he tried to demonstrate, using statistical analysis of biographical data from university examinations, biographies, and lists of talented and eminent people, that human talent was normally distributed (forming a bell curve) and the truly talented were statistically rare, accounting for about 1 in 4,000 people. He further argued that this talent was inherited. Yet Galton was still mindful of the potential effects of the environment. To address the possibility of environmental influences, Galton compared the eminence of sons adopted by eminent men to biological sons of eminent men. The biological sons had a much higher likelihood of being eminent than the adopted sons. Galton's procedure is the basis for the now frequently used adoption studies. In addition, Galton found that the probability of a descendent being eminent declines as the offspring become more distantly related (Gillham, 2001).

Following the publication of *Hereditary Genius*, Galton started two ongoing research programs, one focused on the measurement of human characteristics and their variability, the other on inheritance. His next book, *English Men of Science: Their Nature and Nurture* (Galton coined the phrase Nature vs. Nurture to describe the relative effects of inheritance and environment), was published in 1875. In Galton's studies he noted that very talented men have children who are a bit less talented. The same tendency toward regression to the mean, as he called it, occurred with most human characteristics, such as height and weight. In addition, Galton developed a way to graphically display data for two variables from the same subject, a chart now called the scatterplot and seen in every introductory statistic text in the world (Stigler, 1986).

Galton continued his work through the 1880s, making important contributions to both the study of inheritance and statistics, and we shall return to his work in the next chapter as it occurred concurrently with the new psychology and had a direct impact on what was happening. Galton's work on the statistical description of human characteristics and the application of statistics to questions of heredity paved the way for the new psychology in 1879.

Philosophy in the 1800s

The neurophysiologists, naturalists, physician, and statisticians of the 1800s were not the narrow specialists that their present-day counterparts often are. They had broad interests and broad views. In particular, they were all interested in philosophy and philosophical questions. What was true of other scientists was also true of the founders of psychology, as we shall see in the next two chapters. Modern psychology developed in three locations and strongly drew upon the philosophical works from the 1800s. To understand these influences, we need to start with one of the most important philosophers of the last 250 years: Immanuel Kant.

The Influence Of Immanuel Kant

Immanuel Kant (1724-1804) developed a number of philosophical ideas that were to dominate the 1800s. Much of his work was a reaction to Hume's analysis. Kant was born in Prussia (in what is now Germany) and educated at the University of Konigsberg. In addition to being a philosopher, he also carried out scientific work and is best known for his hypothesis on the evolution of the solar system, a hypothesis that essentially proved correct. Kant's influence in philosophy comes from his two major works, the *Critique of Pure Reason* published in 1781, and the *Critique of Practical Reason* published in 1788. In these works and several others Kant explored questions of perception and knowledge, human ethics, and metaphysics (Watson, 1978).

It was his philosophy of perception and human knowledge that most shaped the new psychology 75 years after his death. Kant argued that sensory data alone could not account for our knowledge of the external world. We have to add, Kant argued, something to our sensory experience. That added element is our innate knowledge. Kant called this *a priori* thought, a Latin phrase meaning "coming before." Examples of such innate, *a priori* concepts include time, space, cause and effect, negation, and reality. The ability of the mind to think and to perceive, according to Kant, depends on the presence of these innate categories (Watson, 1978).

In ethics, Kant rejected the hedonism found in the British philosophers such as Hume and argued for human free will and the importance of the categorical imperative—a universal principle that should govern all ethical behavior, according to Kant. The categorical imperative asserts that you should never do anything that you would not want to see elevated to a universal rule. For instance, killing is sometimes justified. If elevated to a universal rule, this would produce a violent and immoral world. The categorical imperative, according to Kant, is the basis for the various versions of the Golden Rule found in several religions (do unto others as you would have them do unto you, love thy neighbor as thyself, etc.).

Kant argued that the only basis for psychology, an understanding of consciousness, was introspection, and introspection could never be scientific. Consciousness is always changing and is therefore difficult to study reliably. The act of introspection also changes the consciousness observed. Finally, scientific laws could only be formulated, according to Kant, mathematically. Consciousness could not be expressed in mathematical laws; hence it could never be a science. His argument that psychology could never be a science was to have a negative effect on the development of the new psychology, and his critique of introspectionism was later to influence the rise of behaviorism (Watson, 1978).

The Philosophical Psychology Of Johann Friedrich Herbart

Johann Friedrich Herbart (1776-1841) was born in Germany and, after attending a number of universities and working in Switzerland as a tutor, finally got his doctorate in 1802 from the University of Gottingen. From 1802 to 1809 he worked as an instructor at Gottingen, and then took the position formerly held by Kant at the University of Konigsberg (Watson, 1978).

Herbart introduced a number of concepts that were to prove very important in the following century. The most important of these ideas was the unconscious. Herbart argued that no idea is ever really destroyed, rather each competes for consciousness: some ideas lose the struggle for existence by sinking into the unconscious. Another of his important concepts was the idea of the sensory threshold or "limen," which is the border between consciousness and the unconscious. His final important concept was that of the apperceptive mass, the assembly of compatible ideas in consciousness (Herbart borrowed the idea of the apperceptive mass from Liebniz and developed the idea further).

Herbart, while following Kant's thinking on a number of issues, argued that psychology could be a science in the sense that perception and cognition could be described mathematically. He published his main efforts in *Psychology as a Science* in 1824. This work shaped the new psychology, especially the studies of perception by Weber and Fechner that we have discussed above (Watson, 1978).

Utilitarianism: Jeremy Bentham And James Mill

The associationism of Locke, Berkeley, and Hume was transformed in the late 1700s into what is perhaps the most important philosophical idea developed in Great Britain: the philosophy of Utilitarianism. The major proponents of utilitarianism were Jeremy Bentham, James Mill, and John Stuart Mill.

Jeremy Bentham (1748-1832) was the son of a wealthy family and was educated at Oxford. When he was 20 he read a political essay by Joseph Priestley, the radical cleric and chemist who was a member of the Lunar Society. In the essay Priestly used the expression "the greatest happiness for the greatest number." This provoked the development of Bentham's own thinking about philosophy.

The result of Bentham's thinking was the idea of utility as a fundamental moral principle. He applied this principle in his first book on law, arguing that laws should promote the general happiness of the population—that is, the greatest happiness for the greatest number. Bentham developed this idea more fully and applied it to ethics in his second book, *Introduction to the Principles of Morals* (published privately in 1780 in an abridged version and published in its entirety in 1789). Bentham rejected natural law arguments, the idea that people have inherent human rights as a consequence of just being human, and substituted utilitarianism in its place. The American Declaration of Independence, the French Revolution's Declaration of the Rights of Man, and many religiously-based systems of ethics are based on natural law arguments. While Bentham rejected the moral basis of both the American and French declarations, he supported both revolutions.

Bentham argued that individuals are the best judges of what makes them happy and what gives them pain. In general he argued against government interference in the behavior of individuals. He also argued that governments had three general obligations to their citizens. The first obligation is to prevent people from suffering unnecessarily by insuring a minimum level of income for all and to provide for the safety of people and their property. The second obligation of government to citizens is to encourage material prosperity. The third obligation is to encourage the equality of means to happiness. This is related to his notion of marginal utility, that an extra $100 will bring much more happiness to a starving person than to a billionaire. He argued for progressive taxation on this basis and redistribution from the rich to the poor, since an extra $100 will diminish the happiness of a billionaire only slightly while it will increase the happiness of a poor person greatly. Bentham argued that governments should be careful to balance this redistribution with concerns for increasing the general welfare, as progressive taxation also may stifle initiative and harm economic prosperity, thus decreasing overall happiness.

It should be obvious at this point that Bentham was not just a philosopher but also an economist who helped introduce into economics the idea of the utility function and marginal utility. He was a close friend of the economist David Ricardo, the most important economist in the generation of economists that followed Adam Smith, and of several important politicians. In addition to his work in economics, Bentham was a political activist and educator. Bentham founded the University College London in 1826, still an important British university, so that Catholics, Jews, and religious non-conformists could get a university education. These three groups were excluded from British universities during the 1800s.

Bentham developed an unusual idea for a model prison, the Panopticon, which he campaigned for during the early 1790s. The panopticon was a tower in which the prison cells were on the outside wall with windows, and a central chamber in the middle of the tower provided windows into each cell so that all prisoners could be seen by the guards or prison officials without being able to see them. While never built, it was an idea that anticipated modern video surveillance of prisons, offices, and shopping centers, as well as the modern interrogation rooms with two-way mirrors or video surveillance.

Bentham's psychology was based on hedonism, the idea that individuals seek to maximize pleasure (or reward) and minimize pain (or punishment). This idea was to be developed by his followers and to have a lasting effect, especially on American psychology.

A close friend of Bentham and Ricardo was James Mill (1773-1836). James Mill was born the son of a cobbler and was sent to the University of Edinburgh with the financial support of a local wealthy gentleman. At Edinburgh Mill studied with Dugald Stewart, a friend and collaborator of both Adam Smith and Thomas Reid. At the time Mill studied with him, Stewart was one of the leading representatives of the common sense school. After graduating, Mill worked for a short time as a preacher, then as a traveling tutor, finally moving from Scotland to London in 1802, where he worked as a journalist and met Bentham and Ricardo. James Mill became an economist, philosopher, and historian. As a philosopher he followed Bentham's teachings; as an economist he followed Ricardo's teachings. In 1817 he published his *History of India*, which established his reputation as an historian and landed him a job as an executive of the East India Company, the large British Corporation that administered India for the British government.

Unlike Bentham, Mill opposed almost all government intervention in people's lives, especially progressive and redistributive taxation. The exception to his opposition to government intervention was his advocacy of education. Without education, John Mill argued, people would not be able to maximize their own pleasure and minimize their own pain. People need education so that they can make the right choices and figure out what is in their long-term best interest.

The Utilitarianism Of John Stuart Mill

James Mill is often overshadowed by his son, John Stuart Mill (1806-1873). Named after the man who had paid for his father's college education (Sir John Stuart), Mill was educated by his father, with the advice and guidance of Bentham, and was a child prodigy. By the age of three, he knew Greek, by 12 he was a skilled logician and knew Latin. By the age of 16 he was a well-trained economist. And by the age of 20, he experienced a period of major depression accompanied by anxiety disorders. On recovering from his depression, Mill embraced the emotional and aesthetic aspects of life, reading poetry and novels, and enjoying art and friendship.

In 1830 John Stuart Mill met Harriet Taylor, a married woman who was an invalid. Harriet's husband was very tolerant of their close and apparently non-sexual relationship, and the two collaborated and co-authored a number of works together (Mill was a prolific writer of both scholarly and popular books, essays, and reviews). Mill married Harriet Taylor in 1851, a few years after the death of her husband. The two were very happy together until her death in 1858, in Avignon, France. From 1858 to his death in 1873, John Stuart Mill spent part of every year in Avignon to be close to her grave. He died in France at the age of 67.

John Stuart Mill made major contributions to philosophy, economics, and political theory, worked as an executive in the East India Company (under his father James Mill), and served as a Liberal member of parliament from 1865 to 1868. His first major philosophical book was *System of Logic, Ratiocinative and Inductive* (1843), which deals both with logic and with scientific method. His best known work during his lifetime was his *Principles of Political Economy* (1848), a synthesis and elaboration of Adam Smith's thinking and the work of David Ricardo. In 1859 he published the essay *On Liberty*, a work strongly shaped by his recently deceased wife, and a work on parliamentary reform. The fundamental idea of *On Liberty* is that no one has the right to coerce another person through legal means or public opinion, except in self-defense. This is a powerful argument against paternalistic laws, such as those against smoking or drug use, designed to save people from themselves. Mill's argument, for instance, would mean the legalization of drugs, but would also imply harsh penalties for driving while under the influence of drugs. Mill's argument has become a classic libertarian argument for human freedom from the coercion of the majority. *On Liberty* was one of two highly controversial short works he published during his lifetime.

In 1863, Mill published his greatest philosophical work, *Utilitarianism*. Utilitarianism is a synthesis of the thinking of Bentham and John Stuart Mill's father, with the work of the British Empiricists such as Hume. In the book, which is devoted to an application of utilitarianism to ethics, Mill criticizes Kant's ethics and argues that ethics should be guided by utility: the greatest good for the greatest number, with "good" being understood to be not just simple pleasures but intellectual, aesthetic, and moral pleasures as well. As a student of the history of psychology, you should note the striking similarity that Mill's ethics has to the ethics of the materialist followers of Epicurus.

John Stuart Mill's last major work was published in 1869, *On the Subjection of Women*. Like his essay on human liberty, this work was highly controversial and, again like his essay on liberty, it was deeply influenced by the thinking of his deceased wife. In this essay, Mill shows that any argument that seeks to deny women equal rights and opportunities is baseless. Along with Mary Wollstonecraft's *On the Vindication of the Rights of Women*, Mill's work is one of the foundational texts of feminism.

Mill kept several texts to be published after his death, including his *Autobiography* (1873), which contains the description of his education and nervous breakdown, and *Three Essays on Religion* (1874). In the essays he argued that it was impossible for the universe to be governed by an all-powerful and loving god, and argued for an agnostic position on religion and deism. Again, note the similarities with the materialistic doctrines of Epicurus.

John Stuart Mill had a powerful influence on politics, economics, and philosophy, but little direct influence on what was to become the new psychology. The influence on the new psychology was to come through Mill's friend and protégé, Alexander Bain.

The Philosophical Psychology Of Alexander Bain

Alexander Bain (1818-1903) was born and educated in Scotland. After graduating from college he moved to London where he became friends with John Stuart Mill. Bain worked as a journalist and writer (he wrote biographies of both James Mill and John Stuart Mill). It was not until the publication of his two-volume work in psychology that his academic reputation as a philosopher was established. The first volume was entitled *The Senses and the Intellect* (1855) and the second volume was entitled *The Emotions and the Will* (1859). In 1860 he was appointed to a position at the University of Aberdeen, his alma mater. He went on to found the first scholarly journal devoted to psychology, *Mind*, in 1876 (Reed, 1997).

Bain did not carry out psychological research, but he did integrate the current work in neurophysiology with philosophical explanations of psychological processes. His efforts to ground explanations of psychology in detailed neurophysiological processes was crucial to the development of modern psychology and is still important to more biologically-oriented psychologists. Bain was interested in learning and thinking, emotions, and intentional behavior, what was called at the time volition (or will). He explained learning and thinking on the basis of laws of association developed by British philosophers and explained how voluntary behavior (as opposed to reflexive behavior which was also extensively studied at the time) is shaped by hedonism, the desire to seek reinforcement and avoid punishment. Bain described an early version of operant conditioning, later investigated by E.L. Thorndike and B.F. Skinner in greater detail. Bain also linked emotions with intentional behavior or will—intentional behavior, what we choose to do, is shaped by our emotions. Thus voluntary behavior is not so much free choice as behavior controlled not by the environment but by feelings (Reed, 1997).

Bain's philosophical psychology takes us beyond Herbart's philosophical psychology and brings us to the very edge of modern psychology. All that was missing was for Bain to carry out his own research to test and develop his psychological hypotheses. Bain's work was to have a powerful effect on the first generation of psychologists, especially those in the U.S.

Franz Brentano's Act Psychology

Franz Brentano (1838-1917) was born in Germany and received his doctorate in philosophy from the University of Tubingen. He was ordained as a priest (although he later left the priesthood and married) and taught first at the University of Wurzburg in Germany. In 1874 he moved to the University of Vienna where he taught philosophy and published his major work, *Psychology from an Empirical Standpoint* (Watson, 1978). As we shall see later, Brentano was Freud's philosophy professor at the University of Vienna.

Brentano argued that mental processes have a function or purpose. Mental processes (thinking, feeling, judging, perceiving, etc.) also possess intentionality: that is, they are about something: I remember my first day at college; I judge a political candidate; I love my family. Thus mental processes are both functional and intentional (Watson, 1978).

Brentano's second major contribution regarded method. Brentano felt that one could discover the intentions and functions of mental processes through a process of introspection into meaningful experience. By examining your own thoughts, feelings, memories, and perceptions, you could discover the true nature of mental processes. Brentano rejected rigorous scientific research for a kind of phenomenological introspection that was to become the hallmark of Freud's self-analysis (Watson, 1978).

Out Of Chaos

Modern psychology, the "New Psychology" as it was called when it was clearly established in 1879, could not have developed were it not for the rise of industrial capitalism, and the industrial and political revolutions that occurred between 1789 and 1879. Concurrent with this dual revolution was the rise and expansion of research-oriented universities, the expansion of higher education, and the phenomenal growth of chemistry, biology, including physiology and evolutionary theory, medicine, statistics and philosophy. Out of this chaos, as Mary Shelley would have noted, came the creative synthesis that was the new, scientific, psychology.

Viewed broadly from the outside, the fields that gave rise to the new psychology were clearly shaped by the broader culture. But they also shaped the broader culture in a profound way—the empiricism and mitigated skepticism of science shaped many people's lives and personal beliefs, and helped shape the economic development of the period. Throughout the period we have examined, the conflict between materialism and idealism, and between belief and skepticism, convulsed society and the people in it. The progress of the sciences, especially neurophysiology and the theory of evolution, in turn was a powerful spur to materialism.

Science depends on the creative genius and hard work of the scholars themselves. The history of this period is one of impressive achievements and discoveries that transformed our understanding of the world and ourselves, perhaps forever.

When Was Psychology Born?

It is far harder to determine when a new science is born then to determine when a baby is born. In general, the birth dates of a science are reasonable judgments made by historians. These judgments are subject to disagreement however, and are ultimately a matter of convention: that is, we simply agree to declare a science to be born at a particular date.

The consensus for the birth date of modern psychology is 1879, the year that Wilhelm Wundt, who you will get to know very well in the next chapter, established his lab for graduate students in psychology at the University of Leipzig. This was first suggested by the historian of psychology, E.G. Boring, who was a follower of Wundt's approach to psychology. But the decision to list Wundt as the founder is somewhat arbitrary upon close examination. William James had used lab equipment to demonstrate psychological phenomena several years before 1879. In addition, a reasonable argument can be made for selecting 1860 as the founding year, for that was the year in which Fechner published his *Elements*. Some historians of psychology (Reed, 1997) want to push the starting date back even further to 1848.

Whichever year you select, and ultimately it is a selection, it is clear that by 1879, at the latest, a new science had been born. The year 1879 marks a point that we can say, unequivocally, that a new science has come into existence. History is a contingent process. Two places had the preconditions necessary for the development of scientific psychology before any other places on the planet: Germany and the eastern seaboard of the United States.

Why Did It Take So Long?

In his germinal work on the history and philosophy of science, Kuhn(1962/1970) argued that science proceeds through a process of scientific revolution to normal science to scientific revolution, with a revolution taking place when one scientific paradigm supplants another. Paradigms are powerful explanatory theories and models that allow scientists to continue the process of discovery and research within the paradigms' broad parameters. Kuhn calls this continuing process normal science.

Kuhn developed his ideas using the history of physics, especially the work of Newton, as a model (Kuhn, 1962/1970). Subsequent critics have called attention to the existence of pre-paradigmatic sciences: science without a paradigm. The science of psychology is one example of a science without a paradigm. Here I am explicitly defining science as the use of careful observation and experimentation to discover facts and causal relationships. Given this definition, we can ask: how long did it take, historically, for the different sciences to achieve a paradigm? For this we need to have a date when a science was born (somewhat a matter of convention) and when the paradigm emerged. This is further complicated by the fact that science emerged three times in the history of the west, first in ancient Greece, second in the Arab world in the early middle ages, and a third time in Renaissance Europe. We will look at the rebirth of science, that is to say modern science, in the Renaissance and post-Renaissance period.

The easiest way to compare the dates is to look at a simple table. In table 2.1, I have the conventionally accepted date of birth (DOB) when fields become empirical sciences, the date that the first paradigm emerged (DOP), the time between the birth and emergence of the paradigm (Time to Paradigm), and the age of the science as of 2020.

Table 2.1

Science	DOB	DOP	Time to Paradigm	Age
Astronomy	1543	1687	144	477
Physics	1638	1687	49	382
Chemistry	1661	1783	122	359
Biology	1628	1859	231	392
Psychology	1879	--	--	141

Given how long it takes for a paradigm to emerge after the birth of a science, it is not surprising that psychology does not yet have a paradigm. We will leave aside for a moment the question of whether or not a social science could ever have a paradigm. What is perhaps more striking is that psychology as a science emerged very late. While there are a number of reasons for this lateness, especially the arguments of many important philosophers, it was the advances in biology (the theory of evolution and discoveries in neurophysiology) that pushed philosophical psychology towards science. In a sense then, philosophy and biology are the parent fields of psychology. Both fields are still closely connected intellectually to psychology to this day.

References

Clarke, R.W. (1984). *The survival of Charles Darwin: A biography of a man and an idea.* New York: Avon Books.

Darwin, C. (1859/1958). *The origin of species, by means of natural selection or the preservation of favoured races in the struggle for life.* New York: Mentor.

Dobzhansky, T. (1973). Nothing in biology makes sense except in the light of evolution. *The American Biology Teacher, 35,* 125-129.

Engels, F. (1845/1984). *The condition of the working class in England.* Chicago: Academy Chicago Publishers.

Foster, J.B. (1999). *The vulnerable planet: A short economic history of the environment* (Rev. ed.). New York: Monthly Review Press.
Foster, J.B. (2000). *Marx's ecology: Materialism and nature.* New York: Monthly Review Press.

Gauld, A. (1992). *A history of hypnotism.* Cambridge: Cambridge University Press.

Ghiselin, M.T. (1973). Darwin and evolutionary psychology. *Science, 179,* 964-968.

Ghiselin, M.T. (1984). *The triumph of the darwinian method.* Chicago: University of Chicago Press.

Gillham, N.W. (2001). *A life of Sir Francis Galton: From african exploration to the birth of eugenics.* Oxford: Oxford University Press.

Goya Y Lucientes, F. (1967). *The disasters of war.* New York: Dover Publications.

Hobsbawn, E.J. (1979). *The age of capital, 1848-1875.* New York: Mentor.

Hobsbawm, E. J. (1996). *The age of revolution, 1789-1848.* New York: Vintage Books.

Hofstadter, R. (1959). *Social darwinism in american thought* (Rev. Ed.). New York: George Brazille.

Hull, D.L. (1973). *Darwin and his critics: The reception of Darwin's theory of evolution by the scientific community*. Chicago: University of Chicago Press.

Hunt, M. (1993). *The story of psychology*. New York: Doubleday.

King-Hele, D. (1999). *Erasmus Darwin: A life of unequalled achievement*. London: Giles de la Mare Publishers.

Kuhn, T.S. (1962/1970). *The structure of scientific revolutions* (2nd edition). Chicago, IL: University of Chicago Press.

Marx, K. & Engels, F. (1848/1998). *The communist manifesto: A modern edition*, with an Introduction by E.J. Hobsbawm. New York: Verso.

Mayr, E. (1982). *The growth of biological thought: Diversity, evolution, and inheritance*. Cambridge, MA: The Belknap Pres of Harvard University Press.

Moorehead, A. (1971). *Darwin and the Beagle*. New York: Penguin Books.

Reed, E.S. (1997). *From soul to mind: The emergence of psychology from Erasmus Darwin to William James*. New Haven, CT: Yale University Press.

Shelley, M.W. (1818/1996). *Frankenstein; or, the modern Prometheus*. New York: W.W. Norton and Company.

Shermer, M. (2002). *In Darwin's shadow: The life and science of Alfred Russel Wallace*. New York: Oxford University Press.

Shorter, E. (1997). *A history of psychiatry: From the era of the asylum to the age of prozac*. New York: John Wiley & Sons.

Stigler, S.M. (1986). *The history of statistics: The measurement of uncertainty before 1900*. Cambridge, MA: The Belknap Press of Harvard University Press.

Uglow, J. (2002). *The lunar men: Five friends whose curiosity changed the world*. New York: Farrar, Straus and Giroux.

Watson, R.I. (1978). *The great psychologists*, 4th edition. New York: J.B. Lippincott Company.

Wood, E.M. (1999). *The origins of capitalism.* New York: Monthly Review Press.

Young, R.M. (1970). *Mind, brain and adaptation in the nineteenth century.* Oxford: Claredon Press.

PART II: MODERN PSYCHOLOGY FROM 1879 TO 1949: THE AGE OF SCHOOLS

Modern psychology was born out of the developments in sciences and society during the long 19th century that stretched from the French Revolution in 1789 to the First World War in 1914. By 1879 a distinct and new approach to understanding humans had been born, christened at birth as the New Psychology by both the scientists who created it and the broader public that observed its birth and infancy.

The New Psychology was born almost simultaneously in two distinct regions: the German-speaking part of Europe and the Northeastern United States. The reasons why it was born at these places are explored in Chapter 4 and Chapter 5.

Two individuals more than any others, one a German and the other an American, can be considered the founders of the new field: Wilhelm Wundt and William James. Had these two not lived, the New Psychology would still have been born, but it would not have enjoyed the enormous success and influence it achieved in such a short time. Wundt and James had very different personalities, but their psychologies shared some important characteristics. Both were emphatically empirical—embracing the mitigated skepticism and careful analysis of evidence that characterizes all of the sciences. Both also were deeply idealistic in the philosophical sense—responding to the materialism of their age with efforts to empirically demonstrate the existence of mind and soul.

While there was fairly extensive interchange between the psychologists of Europe and the psychologists of America, two very different psychological schools developed. A school, in this sense of the term, means a group of scholars who share a common definition of their field, have many of the same assumptions about their field, use similar methods, and study similar problems. Wundt's school of psychology lacks an accepted historical name, although it is sometimes called voluntarism. James' school of psychology eventually came to be known as functionalism. We will explore the differences and similarities of these two schools shortly; for now, keep in mind that both were defined by an interest in consciousness.

Twenty years after the birth of the first two schools, a third school of psychology was born: psychoanalysis. Psychoanalysis is associated closely with the name of its founder, Sigmund Freud, and is typically considered to have been started in 1900 with the publication of Freud's germinal work, The Interpretation of Dreams. Freud's contributions to psychology were substantial and he is often considered the third founder of psychology and is without a doubt the most well-known psychologist of the last 100 years. The irony, or at least one of many historical ironies that surround psychoanalysis, is that Freud sought to create a separate science. Indeed, the school of psychoanalysis was different in important ways from the first two schools. First, psychoanalysis emphasized the unconscious—not the conscious. Second, psychoanalysis rejected the rigorous scientific empiricism of Wundt and James, embracing instead philosophical introspectionism and case studies. Finally, in another irony, Freud rejected the dualism of Wundt and James (which permitted the belief in the spiritual) for a thorough-going materialism and atheism. Psychoanalysis attracted intense interest from the functionalists in the United States, but was ignored by many European psychologists. Freud's rejection of rigorous empiricism proved to be a key difference between his school and the first two schools. This is why I often refer to psychoanalysis as the renegade school. We examine the history of psychoanalysis in Chapter 6 and follow psychoanalysis from its inception up to the start of World War II, when much of the psychoanalytic establishment in Continental Europe had either been pushed into exile or killed.

The long 19th century ended in a violent convulsion of war and revolution: the Great War, which we now call World War I, the Russian Revolution, the Mexican Revolution, and the unsuccessful revolutions in Germany and Italy. In the United States, the government carried out a wave of political repression against labor unions, socialists, and anarchists; women won the right to vote in 1920 after a 60 year struggle, and prohibition began. Two new schools emerged out of the ferment and chaos: behaviorism in the United States and Gestalt psychology in Germany. Both behaviorism and Gestalt psychology challenged the previous schools (and each other). Both also tried to resolve, in very different ways, the intellectual crisis generated by the end of the old order and the start of a new order. Chapter 7 traces the rise of behaviorism in the period immediately before World War I and its later development up through World War II. In Chapter 8 we will examine the birth of Gestalt psychology in the period immediately before World War I and follow its growth of and eventual destruction by the Nazis in Hitler's Germany.

After World War I the planet was devastated by a world-wide depression now known as the Great Depression, the rise of fascism in Europe, the unthinkable violence of the Holocaust, and a second great world war, ending with the dropping of two atomic bombs on Japan by the United States. The modern world, the world you now live in, was born. The history of psychology during this post-World War II era is presented in Part III. To understand the drama of the last 70 years of psychology's history, you must understand how the stage was set in the pre-World War II period; we must understand psychology's childhood and adolescence—the age of schools.

The Social And Economic Forces That Shaped The New Psychology

A number of broad social and economic forces shaped the emergence of psychology as a science in the latter half of the long 19th century. Here I wish to just highlight some of the most important forces so you can understand some of the hows and whys of psychology's early development. These broad social and economic forces include industrial capitalism and the formation of the modern class structure, sexism and the exploitation of women, and the caste systems that existed in various countries, in particular the racial caste system in the US and the anti-semitic caste system of Europe.

The rise of industrial capitalism at the start of the long 19th century transformed the basis of the production of goods and products in the core capitalist states of Western Europe and the US. This permitted relatively small groups of workers to produce massive numbers of products for less money. These products were often of equal and in some cases superior quality to locally produced products. As a result, the wealth of the core capitalist states started to increase at a much faster rate than the wealth of other countries. Europe and the US got rich; their populations exploded, and their political and military power allowed them to dominate the world. This lead to the establishment of the first essentially planetary civilization. While substantial differences in language and cultures existed, the entire planet was united under a single economic and technological regime—capitalism.

One of the first and most important commodities under the emerging industrial capitalism was cotton. The need for massive amounts of cotton to feed the factories of England produced an increase in slavery, especially in the US where it was dying out after the American Revolution. As a result, slave-owners in the Eastern US started to sell slaves and force-march them to newly developed cotton (and indigo) producing areas. These areas had been stolen from Native Americans, or the indigenous peoples were killed by the advancing cotton producers. The absolute number of slaves in the new cotton producing areas (the states of Georgia, Mississippi, Alabama, Louisiana, Texas, and large parts of the states that are contiguous with these states) increased drastically. For instance, in 1800, early in the long 19th century, there were 100,000 slaves living the area now made up of Mississippi and Louisiana. By 1840 there were 250,000. By 1860, on the eve of the civil war, there were 750,000 slaves (Dunbar-Ortiz, 2018).

Cotton and slavery were so central to the industrial revolution and the resulting wealth that it is not hyperbole to say that modern capitalism was created from the blood of slaves. In fact, the historical record is now clear (cf., Baptist, 2014; Beckert, 2014).

The rise of industrial capitalism produced modern colonialism. The creation of vast empires at the end of the 1400s began with the arrival of Columbus in 1492 and the development of agrarian capitalism. The development of industrial capitalism set off a new upsurge in foreign conquest, especially in Africa and Asia. These newly conquered areas became integrated into the world capitalist system through trade, investment, and resource extraction. When droughts lowered production of food crops, millions died in China, India, Africa, and South America between 1860 and 1890. They died not because there was not enough food, but because the food that existed was being exported to the rich capitalist countries while the local governments allied with the core capitalist countries (in some cases such as India the local governments were the colonial administrations) did little to intervene. These massive deaths have been called the "Late Victorian Holocausts" and were the first major mass deaths since the black plague in the Middle Ages (Davis, 2001).

Finally, the status of women also changed. Always and everywhere the subordinate gender, the rise of industrial capitalism brought women and children into the factories in huge numbers. Women and children were paid a fraction, often less than 50%, of what the men were paid. Often they were better able to operate the machines that required fine motor skills. The result for the children, women, and men in the factories (called by the British poet William Blake "the dark satanic mills") was a short and brutal existence in a living hell. In some industries, such as the textile industry, over half the work force was made up of women (Foster & Clark, 2018). These brutal conditions were not a secret. Indeed, some of the first sociological studies to take place (sociology as a social science was born several decades before psychology) were studies of factory conditions. One of the most famous was done by Friedrich Engels (Engels, 1845/1984). Engels later went on to found communism with Karl Marx, in response to the strife and misery created by the industrial revolution.

Such was the historic time and place into which Psychology was born as a science. These social forces not just set the stage, but shaped the growth of the new science in often subtle, and not so subtle, ways.

References

Baptist, E. E. (2014). *The half has ever been told: Slavery and the making of American Capitalism.* New York: Basic Books.

Beckert, S. (2014). *Empire of cotton: A global history.* New York: Vintage Books.

Davis, M. (2001). *Late Victorian Holocausts: El niño famines and the making of the Third World.* London: Verso Books.

Dunbar-Ortiz, R. (2018). Settler capitalism and the Second Amendment. Monthly Review, 68(8), 26-32.

Engels, F. (1845/1984). The conditions of the Working Class in England. Chicago, IL: Academy Chicago Publishers.

Foster, J. B., & Clark, B. (2018), Women, Nature, and Capital in the Industrial Revolution. Monthly Review, 68(8), 1-24.

CHAPTER 4: WILHELM WUNDT AND EXPERIMENTAL PSYCHOLOGY

It seems to me that perhaps the time has come for psychology to begin to be a science —some measurements have already been made in the region lying between the physical changes in the nerves and the appearance of consciousness (in the shape of sense perceptions), and more may come of it. ...Helmholtz and a man named Wundt at Heidelberg are working on it.

LETTER FROM WILLIAM JAMES TO THOMAS W. WARD, NOVEMBER 1867 (H. JAMES, 1920, PP. 118-119).

By the late 1860s knowledgeable observers of the scientific scene such as William James knew that something important was happening around them. Developments in physiology, medicine, biology, and statistics now made it possible to investigate empirically and scientifically questions formerly the exclusive property of philosophy and religion. This awareness of a new beginning for psychology, a new psychology as scientists later called it, excited some of the finest intellects in Germany and the U.S. But before we can turn to the founders and the first generation that followed them, we must briefly review some of the general conditions of the 1870s in Germany and ask two questions: Why this time? Why these places?

The Time Has Come For Psychology To Begin To Be A Science

The university system in Germany was substantially changed after the Napoleonic Wars. Using the French university as their starting point, German principalities, and later the unified German State (unified in 1871 by Otto von Bismark) constructed a unique, open, and dynamic system of higher education which stressed science and technology. For example, King Frederick William III supported the University of Berlin in 1809 believing that the way to economic and political recovery was through science and education. The German system embraced freedom of teaching (Lehrfreiheit) and freedom of learning

(Lernfreiheit). Freedom of teaching meant that professors could choose the topics they taught, how they taught, and what they presented without any interference from outsiders. Freedom of learning meant that students did not take a test at the end of each course but only at the end of their studies. Detailed knowledge of this or that lecture was not important—understanding, insight, and application were. Students were also encouraged to, and most did, take classes at several universities and sought out the most interesting professors. Students did not just listen and take notes, they questioned, argued, and discussed with their professors. Professors often converted lecture notes into books and students took a wide variety of courses. As a consequence of the German system with its freedom of learning and teaching, Germany produced a large number of scientists in the 1800; and the universities fueled Germany's scientific and economic rise to pre-eminence (Dobson & Bruce, 1972). The U.S. system of higher education lagged considerably behind that of Europe until after the U.S. Civil War. The changes in the U.S. system that created the institutional conditions for the birth of the new psychology in the U.S. will be described in the next chapter.

Wilhelm Wundt And The Founding Of Psychology In 1879

Sciences are not created by single individuals but by communities of scholars working within an institutional, intellectual, and cultural context. Still, not all members of the community are equal. Some are pioneers and some have more influence than others. The first and most influential of the early pioneers is considered by many to be the father of psychology as a science, Wilhelm Wundt.

Wundt's Early Life

Wilhelm Wundt (1832-1920) was born near Mannheim, Germany into an intellectual middle class family. His father was a Lutheran minister. His paternal grandfather had been a professor of history at the University of Heidelberg and two of his maternal uncles were medical doctors and professors of physiology. Wundt grew up essentially as an only child; his brother was eight years older than him and was away at school for most of Wundt's childhood (Fancher, 1990).

psychology to the fields of linguistics and psycholinguistics, anthropology, and cross-cultural psychology, but these contributions were not as significant to the history of psychology as his experimental work and his general theory.

Wundt's experimental psychology focused on consciousness; the processes and contents of which we are aware. This emphasis on perceptual processes and cognitive processes of which we are aware severely limited the subject matter to which experimental procedures were applied and the questions that could be asked. Many other members of the first generation of European psychology would reject this narrow emphasis, as we shall see below.

The Impact Of Wilhelm Wundt

Wundt was one of the rare people in the history of psychology who made significant contributions as a researcher, theorist, teacher, and institution builder. As a researcher he pioneered work in the study of attention, perception, emotions, and language. As a theorist he constructed a philosophically sophisticated theory of human cognition and emotions. As a teacher, Wundt supervised 186 Ph.D. dissertations between 1876 and 1920 (not all of them in psychology, however). He wrote significant college textbooks that were translated into several languages and used throughout the world, taught numerous undergraduate classes, and worked with many post-doctoral students. As an institution builder, Wundt started a scientific journal, created the first graduate program in psychology, and founded the first advanced research laboratory.

Given Wundt's impact on the history of psychology, why is it that so few psychology students in the U.S. have heard of him? The reasons for the general unfamiliarity with Wundt and his role are interesting and tell us much about the history of the new psychology.

Theoretical differences between Wundt and many Americans help explain our ignorance of his role. For instance, the Americans stressed evolutionary theory more than did Wundt, who placed more relative emphasis on neurophysiology. Additionally, Wundt and James viewed choice and free will very differently. This certainly had an impact on Wundt's fate in the U.S. Wundt also fell victim to the anti-German hysteria that swept the U.S. around World War I. Some of his former students became experts on the so-called evils of German culture and the "weaknesses" of Wundt's psychology. The pre-eminent

American historian of psychology E.G. Boring was especially guilty of this kind of character assassination (Blumenthal, 2001). Still later, both Wundt's system of psychology and the functionalist approach advocated by James were pushed aside when positivism became fashionable as "the" guiding approach to science (Danziger, 1979). Later psychologists also distorted and maligned Wundt's work as a way of justifying their own contributions, especially to show how current psychology had "advanced" over the backward understanding of previous theorists. Many psychologists in the post-World War I period criticized Wundt's method as unscientific introspection, a criticism that was also applied to Freud, but in Freud's case it was actually applicable (Danziger, 1980). Finally, G. Stanley Hall, whom we shall meet shortly, blamed the decline of psychology in America in the 1900s on Wundt's influence (Rieber, 2001). For all of the above reasons, Wundt is practically the unknown father of modern psychology.

The First Generation Of European Psychologists

Wundt's impact in Europe was almost instantaneous. Within a very short time a generation of psychologists sprang up. Many were German, but not all as the New Psychology spread to all the countries of Europe. Many, but not all, of this first generation, had studied directly with Wundt.

Külpe And The Experimental Study Of Thinking

Oswald Külpe (1862-1915) was a German born in Latvia at a time when Latvia was under the control of the Russian Tsar. He received his Ph.D. from Wundt at Leipzig in 1887 where he stayed as a lecturer and as Wundt's chief assistant until 1894, when he was appointed to a professorship at the University of Würzburg. Külpe spent the next 15 years at Würzburg, carrying out a number of experimental studies and training a number of Ph.D.s in psychology. In 1909 he left Würzburg for the University of Berlin and his interests shifted to philosophy.

Külpe had established a psychology laboratory at Würzburg that by 1896 rivaled Wundt's. Külpe believed that higher thinking processes could be studied using Wundt's methods. The typical study in Külpe's lab involved a subject who performed some complex task involving thinking, memory, or judgment and was then asked to introspect and report on his thought processes. One of the discoveries using this approach was that, contrary to what Wundt claimed, some thinking did not involve images. This claim that there was "imageless thought" in some instances generated a controversy between the two labs and pitted Külpe against his former teacher and mentor (Watson, 1978). Külpe and his students became known as the Würzburg School, although it is not a school in the sense that we are using the term here.

The Würzburg School developed a number of important ideas. Of these the most well- known is the concept of mental set. How an individual solves a problem, they discovered, is often determined by unconscious prior expectations. These unconscious prior expectations, which they called a mental set, shapes how the individual goes about solving a problem after it is presented (Watson, 1978).

One of Külpe's most prominent students was Karl Bühler (1879-1963). Bühler, who grew up in a poor family, graduated from medical school in 1903. After studying philosophy he moved to Würzburg to study complex thinking under Külpe. Bühler moved to the University of Berlin in 1909 with Külpe, and after Külpe's unexpected death in 1915 at the age of 54, Bühler took over supervision of a number of his graduate students.

Ebbinghaus And The Experimental Study Of Memory

Hermann Ebbinghaus (1850-1909) was born near Bonn; his father was a wealthy business owner. He studied at several universities before earning his Ph.D. in philosophy at the University of Bonn in 1873. After completing his dissertation, Ebbinghaus spent three years traveling in England and France. During his travels he happened upon a copy of Fechner's *Elements of Psychophysics*, which he immediately purchased and read. In a flash of insight, he realized that the philosophical problems which concerned him as a philosopher could be studied scientifically. Ebbinghaus began a series of studies of his own memory shortly after returning from his travels to his home in Berlin. The studies, began in 1879 and published in 1885 (Ebbinghaus, 1885/1964) demonstrated that higher mental processes (which Wundt argued could not be studied using experimental techniques) could indeed be studied scientifically. In the process of carrying out his studies he developed a number of research techniques that are still used in psychology and discovered a number of facts about human memory.

In particular, he is noted for four achievements in his study of his own memory. First, he developed objective measures of memory, such as recall rates and savings method (how much less time it takes to re-learn material that you once could recall but now cannot). Second, he used standardized material such as nonsense syllables or trigrams (*e.g.*, MQR) and stanzas of a poem to test memory (Hilgard, 1963). Third, he discovered that retention increases with frequency of repetition, while forgetting of what was learned seems to occur naturally over time, more being forgotten at first and the rate of forgetting decreasing after an initial period of forgetting. This is now known as the Ebbinghaus Forgetting Curve (Ebbinghaus, 1885/1963). Fourth, he applied statistical analysis, including analysis of standard errors, and mathematical models to the data he discovered (Hilgard, 1963).

Scientists immediately recognized Ebbingaus' work as important. It was reviewed in 1885 in the journal *Mind* where it received praised as significant. William James discussed it approvingly five years later in his *Principles of Psychology* (Hilgard, 1963). A year after publishing his book, Ebbinghaus was made an assistant professor at the University of Berlin where he already worked as a private tutor. Ebbinghaus immediately set up a psychological laboratory modeled on Wundt's lab in Leipzig, but smaller in scale. In 1890 he founded a psychology journal to compete with Wundt's. He was not promoted to full professor, however, because he did not publish a great deal of research, and so Ebbinghaus left the University of Berlin when Carl Stumpf was recruited from the University of Munich to be professor of psychology at Berlin. Ebbinghaus took a less prestigious job at the smaller University of Breslau in 1894, where a second period of productivity began (Watson, 1978).

At the University of Breslau he was asked to develop a short, easy-to-administer test that would show when students feel most fatigued during the school day. Ebbinghaus developed three tests and compared them. The first test was rapid addition and multiplication, the second, memory for a sequence of digits, and the third, a sentence completion test in which a student was given a sentence with a missing syllable or word and had to fill in what was missing. Ebbinghaus' data did not answer the original question about fatigue, but it did show that the better a student did in school, the better their performance on the quick sentence completion task. The fact that good, average, and poor students could be readily distinguished on the basis of a very simple test illustrated, according to Ebbinghaus, that intelligence combines information (Watson, 1978). Ebbinghaus' sentence completion test inspired research by Alfred Binet, whom you shall meet in a few moments, leading to the development of the IQ test. Ebbinghaus also published two highly successful psychology texts, the first in 1902 and the second in 1908, that soon rivaled Wundt's textbooks as standard college texts in the German speaking world. In 1905 he left Breslau for a better position at the University of Halle, where he died suddenly from pneumonia in 1909 at the age of 59 (Watson, 1978).

Binet And The Experimental Study Of Intelligence

Alfred Binet (1857-1911) was born into an intellectual and prosperous family. His father was a successful physician, as were both his grandfathers. Binet's parents separated when he was young and he was raised by his mother, an artist. At age 15, Binet and his mother moved to Paris. He entered college in 1872 and graduated with a law degree in 1878. He never practiced, however, and seemed to have had little interest in law (Siegler, 1994).

He next briefly tried medical school but dropped out, horrified at the gruesome nature of the operating room. Without a career but independently wealthy, he started reading extensively in the French national library to pass the time. Apparently by accident he discovered works on the new psychology and his interest was fired. Binet read Fechner's and Weber's work on the two-point threshold and around 1880 he started to carry out experiments and publish articles in Ribot's *Revue Philosophique.* Binet's first studies were highly flawed, as he had no training in research design, and garnered him considerable criticism from other scientists. After four years as a "library psychologist," as he called himself, Binet secured a job with Charcot, one of France's leading psychiatrists, at the Salpêtrière in Paris (Fancher, 1990).

Binet worked for Charcot from 1883 to 1890 as an unpaid researcher. He supported himself with his personal wealth. Binet was an enthusiastic proponent of Charcot and argued, harking back to Mesmer's discredited work on animal magnetism, that magnets could influence the hypnotic state. His published experiments and co-authored book on the subject were discredited because of their very flawed experimental studies. Binet left Charcot's laboratory in 1890 after a string of 20, often embarrassingly flawed, published papers and three books. The experience was not wasted however. He had learned a great deal about experimental design and closely observed the growth and development of his own two daughters, whom he loved deeply. Binet's one lasting contribution from his time with Charcot was a paper on sexual fetishism, a term Binet coined (Fancher, 1990).

Binet spent over a year looking for a new position. By accident he met the director of the new Laboratory for Physiological Psychology of the Sorbonne, Henri Beaunis. Binet, then 34 years old, was shy and introverted. He mustered his courage and offered his services free to Beaunis; the budget of the new laboratory was limited, so Beaunis accepted Binet's offer and made him an unpaid researcher. This started an enormously productive period in which Binet produced a series of high quality studies and books, soon becoming France's leading experimental psychologist. In 1894 he succeeded Beaunis as the director of the Laboratory of Physiological Psychology and the following year he started the *L'Annee Psychologique*, which soon replaced Ribot's journal as the leading source of the new psychology. Binet worked at the Laboratory until his death at age 54 in 1911, always unpaid (Fancher, 1990).

Binet's work at the Laboratory of Physiological Psychology was extensive, high- quality, and diverse. In all, he published over 200 research articles, reviews, and books in the 21 years he spent at the Laboratory. One of the areas he became most well-known for (before, that is, his development of the intelligence test which we shall discuss soon) was work on suggestibility in adults and children (which today fall under the rubric of social conformity and children's memory distortions due to suggestion). Using some experiments similar to those later used by Solomon Ash, he showed that children's memories were highly suggestible and that adults often conform (unknowingly) to the judgments of others or to preconceived opinions (Siegler, 1994).

Binet also studied memory for prose, the cognition of expert chess players, and expert human calculators. In addition to psychology, Binet was interested in the theater and studied the thinking of playwrights, directors, and actors, and wrote four plays himself; all four of which were performed in Paris theaters

(Siegler, 1994).

Around 1895 Binet became interested in individual differences in intelligence, a fact that impressed him when he studied his own daughters, both of whom were bright even though they appeared to think in very different ways. Unhappy with the tests developed by Galton, he started to develop and test short, easy-to-administer tests of memory, judgment, imagination, and personality. He used his then teenage daughters as test subjects for many of these tests. He published the results of his work in 1903, in a book for which no English translation exists. This was not a problem for most of the founding American psychologists who were multilingual. The title of Binet's book could be translated into English as *The Experimental Study of Intelligence* (Fancher, 1990).

Binet was unhappy with the results of his studies. No combination of short tests seemed to match the depth and richness of a detailed and extensive clinical case study. Yet the work prepared the ground for Binet's most well-known achievement, the intelligence test (Fancher, 1990).

In 1904 the French Minister of Public Instruction appointed a committee to make recommendations about "subnormal" children, that is, children who did not seem to do well in school. The committee, to which Binet belonged, recommended that the subnormal children be placed in special schools where they could get additional instruction and help. This created a new problem: How can you identify these children before the fact? Binet immediately set out to solve this problem by creating a standard test of intelligence that could identify subnormal children. Working with Theodore Simon and testing a large number of Parisian school children, they developed a scale in 1908 and immediately set out to revise and improve it through more research and testing. The revision, published in 1911 and known as the Binet-Simon test, proved to be highly effective in identifying children and generated considerable interest in other countries.

The Binet-Simon scale did not take into account the chronological age of the child, a problem soon solved in 1911 by William Stern (1871-1938), who developed a way of scoring the tests based on dividing the child's mental age (as given by their test score) by their chronological age to get their Intelligence Quotient or IQ. The resulting ratio is multiplied by 100 to eliminate the decimal point (Watson, 1978).

Stern received his Ph.D. from the University of Berlin in 1893, where he studied with Ebbinghaus. Stern joined Ebbinghaus on the faculty of the University of Breslau in 1897 and stayed until 1916. It was at Breslau that Ebbinghaus developed the sentence completion task later used as part of the IQ test, and it was at Breslau that Stern developed the formula of IQ.

Binet's work was translated into English in 1916 (Binet & Simon, 1916/1983) and dramatically affected American psychology. Lewis Terman (1877-1956) of Stanford University soon modified the test for use in the U.S. In 1916 Terman published the revision as the Stanford-Binet, the most widely-used intelligence test in the U.S. for several decades and the "father" of all other intelligence tests used in the U.S. today (Fancher, 1990).

Binet's death in 1911 at the age of 54 was a tragic loss to the New Psychology. In much of his work, he emphasized the variability of thinking and intelligence. He no doubt would have continued his creative and productive research career.

Titchener: Wundt's "American Disciple"

Edward Bradford Titchener (1867-1927) was born in England and received his undergraduate degree at Oxford where he studied philosophy and classics, but also worked as a research assistant in physiology. Interested in psychology and unhappy with the little psychology that was taught at Oxford, Titchener traveled to Leipzig to do graduate work with Wundt. Titchener studied with Wundt in Liepzig from 1890 to 1892. Among his friends were over a half dozen American students and Külpe, who then worked as Wundt's chief assistant (Watson, 1978).

Titchener returned to Oxford in 1892 before traveling to the U.S., where he had accepted a job at Cornell University as an assistant professor and director of the psychology laboratory. Titchener was enormously productive and hardworking. Between 1893 and 1900 he wrote 62 articles, set up his laboratory and directed a number of doctoral dissertations (Watson, 1978).

Titchener was not a social and outgoing person. While he maintained close friendships with colleagues from his Leipzig days, he never integrated into American culture or formed new relationships. He was elected to the American Psychological Association (APA) in 1892 soon after he arrived in the U.S. and shortly after the APA was formed. He left the APA because of a dispute and in 1904 formed his own group, the "Experimentalists" (Watson, 1978). The Experimentalists proved to be an important organization and network for experimental psychologists. Many young researchers advanced because of connections formed through the group. Significantly for all of psychology, the group explicitly excluded women and became a powerful mechanism for limiting the participation of women in the field (Scarborough & Furumoto, 1987). The fact that Titchener taught at Cornell, one of the few private universities that permitted women to earn a Ph.D. (the public universities such as the University of Michigan and the University of California were much more open to women), created another barrier to women.

Titchener was considered by many to be Wundt's representative in the U.S., Wundt's "American Disciple." Calling Titchener "Wundt's American Disciple" is doubly ironic in that not only was Titchener not American, he differed significantly from Wundt on a number of issues. For a long time, Wundt was not well-understood by historians of psychology because the historians did not use primary sources (Wundt's own writing) but used secondary sources based on Titchener's writing (Blumenthal, 1975). Titchener called his approach structuralist, because he wanted to emphasize the structural elements of consciousness, a minority approach within American psychology. American historians of psychology thus mistakenly assumed that Wundt's approach was structuralist.

Titchener did make a substantial contribution, however, because of his emphasis on the importance of experimental investigation. Not as interested in philosophy as many early psychologists, Titchener believed that only through experimental investigation could we discover the truth. This experimental investigation was "hard discipline" imposed on researchers; a discipline that could destroy their prior beliefs and cherished hypotheses. Unlike Wundt, Titchener placed no limits on the uses of experimental method. Titchener's emphasis on the value of experimental research, along with the 56 Ph.D.s he graduated between 1894 and 1927, his four books, and his translations of the work of Wundt and Külpe, made a lasting contribution to psychology. Many of his graduate students became prominent psychologists in the field (Tweney,

1987).

Before concluding our discussion of the first European psychologists, we should ask ourselves why Europe and why the late 1800s. Simply put, the advanced economies of Europe, especially Germany, and the sophisticated university system that encouraged freedom of teaching and freedom of learning, which we now call academic freedom, made the birth of the New Psychology possible. At roughly the same time other social sciences were born, including sociology, anthropology, and linguistics .

References

Binet, A. & Simon, T. (1916/1983). *The development of intelligence in children.* Salem, NH: Ayer Publishing.

Blumenthal, A. L. (1975). A reappraisal of Wilhelm Wundt. *American Psychologist, 30,* 1081-1088.

Blumenthal, A.L. (2001). A Wundt primer: The operating characteristics of consciousness. In R.W. Rieber & D. K. Robinson (eds.) *Wilhem Wundt In history: The making of scientific psychology.* New York: Plenum, pp. 121-144.

Boring, E. G. (1950). *A history of experimental psychology* (2nd edition). New York: Appleton Century Crofts.
Danziger, K. (1979). The positivist repudiation of Wundt. *Journal of the History of the Behavioral Sciences, 15,* 205-230.

Danziger, K. (1980). The history of introspection reconsidered. *Journal of the History of the Behavioral Sciences, 16,* 241-262.

Diamond, S. (2001). Wundt before Leipzig. In R.W. Rieber & D. K. Robinson (eds.) *Whilhelm Wundt in history: The making of scientific psychology,* pp. 1-68.

Dobson, V. & Bruce, D. (1972). The german university and the development of experimental psychology. *Journal of the History of the Behavioral Sciences, 8*(2), 204-207.

Ebbinghaus, H. (1885/1964). *Memory: A contribution to experimental psychology.* New York: Dover Press.

Fancher, R. E. (1990). *Pioneers of psychology,* 2nd ed. New York: W. W. Norton & Company.

Haupt, E.J. (2001). Laboratories for experimental psychology: Gottingen's ascendency over Leipzig in the 1890s. In R.W. Rieber & D. K. Robinson (eds.) *Wilhelm Wundt in history: The making of scientific psychology.* New York: Plenum.

Hilgard, E.R. (1963). Introduction to Dover Edition. In H. Ebbinghaus, *Memory: A contribution to experimental psychology.* New York: Dover..

Hobsbawm, E.J. (1975). *The age of capital: 1848-1875.* New York: Charles Scribner's Sons.

James, H. (1920). *The letters of William James,* Vol. 1. Boston: Atlantic Monthly Press.

Rieber, R.W. (2001). Wundt and the Americans: From flirtation to abandonment. In R.W. Rieber & D. K. Robinson (eds.) *Wilhelm Wundt In history: The making of scientific psychology.* New York: Plenum.

Rieber, R.W. & Robinson, D.K. (eds.)(2001). *Wilhelm Wundt In history: The making of scientific psychology.* New York: Plenum.

Scarborough, E. & Furumoto, L. (1987). *Untold lives: The first generation of American women psychologists.* New York: Columbia University Press.

Scott, W.D. (1903). *The theory of advertising.* Boston: Small Maynard.

Siegler, R.S. (1994). The Other Alfred Binet. In Parke, Ornstein, Rieser, and Zahn-Waxler (eds.), *A century of developmental psychology.* Washington, DC: American Psychological Association, pp. 175-202.

Tweney, R.D. (1987). Programmatic research in experimental psychology: E.B. Titchener's laboratory investigations, 1891-1927. In M.G. Ash & W.R. Woodward (Eds.) *Psychology in twentieth-century thought and society.* Cambridge: Cambridge University Press.

Watson, R.I. (1978). *The great psychologists* (4th ed.). New York: J.B. Lippencott.

Wolf, T.H. (1973). *Alfred Binet.* Chicago, IL: University of Chicago Press.

CHAPTER 5: WILLIAM JAMES AND AMERICAN FUNCTIONALISM

When we talk of 'psychology as a natural science,' we must assume that that means a sort of psychology that stands at last on solid ground. It means just the reverse; it means a psychology particularly fragile, and into which the waters of metaphysical criticism leak at every joint, a psychology all of whose elementary assumptions and data must be reconsidered in wider connections and translated into other terms. It is, in short, a phrase of diffidence, and not of arrogance; and it is strange indeed to hear people talk triumphantly of 'the New Psychology,' and write 'Histories of Psychology,' when into the real elements and forces which the word covers not the first glimpse of clear insight exists. A string of raw facts; a little gossip and wrangle about opinions; a little classification and generalization on the mere descriptive level; a strong prejudice that we have states of mind, and that our brain conditions them; but not a single law in the sense which physics shows us laws, not a single proposition from which any consequences can be causally be deduced. We don't even know the terms between which the elementary laws would obtain if we had them. This is no science, it is only the hope of a science. The matter of science is with us.

JAMES (1892/1985), PP. 334-335.

We explored the intellectual context that gave birth to the New Psychology in Chapter 3 and at the start of Chapter 4 briefly explored the institutional context that gave birth to the first school of psychology In Europe. The eastern seaboard of the U.S. was the second place that saw the birth of the New Psychology, almost simultaneously with its birth in Europe. Again we must ask, why the eastern U.S., and why at almost the same historical moment?

The Institutional Context Of American Psychology

The U.S. system of higher education was behind that of Europe, especially Germany, until around the time of the U.S. Civil War. After the Civil War the U.S. entered a period of rapid growth and improvement in higher education that drove U.S. economic development and its emergence as a world power. From 1849 to 1875, for instance, 18 new universities were founded worldwide and five of the 18 were founded in the U.S. American universities became noted for the training of engineers who could apply the science and technology developed in Europe (Hobsbawm, 1975).

do we have this today?

Three factors were crucial to the expansion and improvement of U.S. higher education: the support of the federal government; the leadership of reforming college presidents; and the patronage of wealthy businessmen. The federal support came from the passage in 1862 of the Morrill Land Grant College Act of 1862. Passed by the radical Republicans who took control of Congress during the Civil War, the act provided for a grant of land to colleges and universities to be used or sold to support higher education. The act required that colleges or universities who received the grants teach subjects related to agriculture and the "mechanical arts" (engineering, agronomy, geology, chemistry, and physics) as well as other scientific and classic subjects. By the end of the 1870s the Morrill Act had benefited 40 established and new universities, including the great land grant universities of the Midwest (Bruce, 1987).

In addition to the impact of the Morrill Act, the quality of American higher education after the Civil War dramatically improved through the importation and modification of the German university model by two important leaders of reform in education: Charles W. Eliot and Daniel Coit Gilman. Eliot, who became president of Harvard University, and Gilman, who became president of the new Johns Hopkins University, created the modern American university and in doing so helped create the institutional infrastructure for the sciences and the social sciences.

Charles W. Eliot (1834-1926) was born into a prominent Boston family. His father, a Harvard graduate, was a state legislator, mayor of Boston, and a member of the U.S. Congress. His mother was from a wealthy and prominent Boston merchant family. Eliot graduated from Harvard in 1853 and became a tutor there in 1854 in mathematics and chemistry. Eliot became known as an innovator because of his use of written exams and laboratory activities (Bledstein, 1976). In 1858 he received a five-year contract as an assistant professor in the Lawrence Scientific School of Harvard. The contract came at an important time in his life as his father had lost most of the family fortune in the financial panic of 1857. All that Eliot had left was his own salary and an inheritance from his maternal grandfather.

Eliot's employment at the Lawrence Scientific School put him at the right place at the right time. The school was an important early experiment in American higher education. Set up within Harvard as a specialized school for science and engineering, the school was organized in the spring of 1848 with a large donation from a Massachusetts industrialist. Harvard hired Louis Agassiz to teach at the Lawrence School. Agassiz (1807-1873) was famous as both a biologist and a geologist—he was the person who discovered evidence for the Ice Age in Europe. Agassiz came to the U.S. permanently because of the closure of his university in the wake of the 1848 revolution. With the defeat of the revolution, many liberal strongholds such as universities were closed or professors were fired.

Agassiz's first wife died of tuberculosis in 1848 and he re-married in 1850. His second wife, Elizabeth Cabot Cary, was from a prominent Boston family. Soon after they married, Elizabeth Agassiz started a school for girls. She was to become the first president of Radcliff College (Menand, 2001).

Agassiz was the most important opponent of Darwin's theory of evolution in the U.S. This put him at odds with the other world class biologist at Harvard, Asa Gray. Gray was the most important botanist in the U.S. and a friend of Charles Darwin. Gray became one of the leading proponents of evolution in the U.S. (Menand, 2001).

Agassiz was not just a prominent scientist; he was an important leader and organizer of American science. Agassiz formed a small intellectual club which was to eventually be called the Lazzaroni. The Lazzaroni, which included Harvard mathematician Benjamin Peirce (1809-1880) and Benjamin Franklin's great grandson Alexander D. Bache (1806-1867), were instrumental in promoting and organizing science in the U.S. It was through their efforts that the Smithsonian, the American Association for the Advancement of Science, and the National Academy of Sciences were formed. They also persuaded congress to sponsor a number of military-scientific expeditions in geology and biology. Peirce became the head of the U.S. Coast Survey, the government agency that supported astronomy and geological exploration in the U.S., and mapped most of the country's coast (Bruce, 1987).

Eliot did well as an assistant professor at the Lawrence Scientific School, he published studies in applied chemistry on impurities in metals, and worked at improving the curriculum and structure of the school. But it was apparently not enough. In 1863 when his contract as an assistant professor ended he was not re-hired. A number of his friends urged him to leave the academy and go into business, were he could recover his family's fortune, and Eliot received at least one very well-paying job offer, but he declined it. Instead, he did something seemingly foolhardy: he borrowed some money, took all of his grandfather's inheritance, and went to Europe for two years to study European higher education. Eliot spent the two years carefully studying all aspects of higher education in Europe, including the role of higher education in economic development. He then returned to Boston and took a job as professor of chemistry at the newly-formed Massachusetts Institute of Technology, a school founded to train engineers and scientists for American industry (Bledstein, 1976).

In 1869 Eliot published a two-part essay in the Atlantic Monthly, one of the leading magazines of the time, on higher education. His essay, "The New Education," presented Eliot's ideas about higher education and argued that there is a strong link between higher education and economic development and prosperity. Eliot's ideas had a powerful effect on many leading Americans, including a number of business executives. Shortly after, Harvard appointed Eliot their new president at age 35 where he served from 1869 to 1909. Eliot reformed both undergraduate education and graduate education at Harvard. His reforms later became models for the rest of the U.S. He gave undergraduates more freedom by broadening the undergraduate curriculum to include many more majors and a system of electives. He urged the adoption of standardized (and later national) college entrance examinations. He increased the Harvard faculty from 60 to 600 and increased the Harvard endowment from 2.25 million to 20 million. In 1872 he established graduate degrees (the M.A. and the Ph.D., based on the European models), and in 1890 established a separate graduate school. He also reformed the teaching and the curriculum of the professional schools in law, divinity, and medicine, initiated the concepts of sabbaticals for faculty members, and exchange programs with foreign universities (Bledstein, 1976).

Eliot is the most important reformer of higher education in the U.S. in the last 150 years, but he was not the only significant person. Almost equally important was Daniel Coit Gilman (1831-1908), born into a wealthy Connecticut business family and educated at Yale, graduating in 1852. While at Yale, Gilman was a student of James D. Dana, one of Agassiz's Lazzaroni. After a year of graduate study at Harvard, he served as a U.S. attaché in St. Petersburg from 1853 to 1855. He then returned to Yale where he worked with Dana to draw up plans for the Sheffield Scientific School, a department within Yale similar to the Lawrence Scientific School. Gilman remained at Yale until 1872 as a professor of geography, librarian, and administrator. He had been offered the presidencies of several universities but refused. He finally left Yale in 1872 after competing for the job of president of Yale and losing. He moved west, to become president of the recently founded University of California, in Berkeley, California. After two frustrating years at the University of California, he was offered and accepted the job of president of the newly founded Johns Hopkins University in 1874. Gilman spent much of 1875 looking for the best faculty in the U.S. and Europe for his new university, which opened in Baltimore in 1876 (Bledstein, 1976). The genesis for Johns Hopkins came from the will of the Baltimore business magnate Johns Hopkins, who had died in 1873 leaving his fortune to be used in the establishment of a university (Bruce, 1987).

While Gilman had worked in St. Petersburg as an attaché he had the opportunity to travel in Europe and spent time studying, much like Eliot was to do a decade later, the European university system, especially the universities in Germany. As president of Johns Hopkins he rejected "partisan and sectarian" hiring (that is, hiring people on the basis of religious affiliation or political beliefs) and hired solely on the basis of scientific achievement (Bruce, 1987). This non-partisan (non-religious and non-political) stance generated controversy from the very beginning. The opening ceremonies at Johns Hopkins were criticized for not opening and closing with a prayer. But that was not the least of it: T. H. Huxley, known as "Darwin's Bulldog" and the person who coined the word agnostic, was invited by Gilman to give a special opening lecture. Gilman was trying to recruit the best biology department in the country, one that would equal if not rival the biology departments at the best European universities. Many local leaders and citizens considered the university to be a center of godless materialism (O'Donnell, 1985).

Johns Hopkins was a specialized graduate school modeled after the great German research universities. Graduate students were given fellowships to study toward their masters and doctoral degrees, i.e., they were paid to be graduate students. Research was emphasized, teaching was de-emphasized. Of the first cohort of 59 graduate students at Johns Hopkins, 34 were in the hard sciences and 2 were in engineering, a clear majority for science and engineering. By 1890, research had become an important function of all major U.S. universities (Bruce, 1987).

Combining the intellectual advances that occurred from the late 1700s to the mid-1800s with the institutional structure of the German and American University systems was like pouring gasoline on a fire. The resulting explosive growth of science and technology in Germany and the U.S. drove both nations to economic pre-eminence and the status of world powers. Part of that explosive growth was the creation of new fields of science and social science. The New Psychology in Germany and the U.S. was part of this explosive growth. Not surprisingly, given the more advanced status of Germany, it occurred first there, and almost immediately after, in the U.S. We now turn to the father of American psychology, William James, and the other founders of American psychology

William James

William James (1842-1910) was the most influential and pre-eminent of a group of fascinating and creative individuals that made up the first generation of American psychologists. Most of the members of the first generation, the founding fathers and mothers (for there were indeed a number of important women in the group) shared the general characteristics of scientific innovators that have been described by historians and psychologists (Shermer, 2002; Sulloway, 1996). They were all hard-working, conscientious, and open to experience. Almost all came from intellectual middle-class or upper-class families and were highly educated. Many came from the same region of the U.S, the northeast, where higher education was concentrated (and where the few colleges that allowed women to be students before 1900 were to be found).

The founders of American psychology also shared a second important characteristic that distinguished them from European Psychology and later gave the school of American psychology its name: Functionalism. This shared characteristic was that they were influenced, greatly, by Darwin and the theory of evolution by natural selection. This influence was integrated into the concern with empirical scientific methods and physiology, as well as the focus on consciousness that characterized the German New Psychology. The influence of Darwin played out in a number of ways. First, it led to a focus on individual variation and questions of nature versus nurture. Second, it led to an examination of the adaptive significance of consciousness. Third, the Darwinian influence led to an interest in behavior as well as consciousness. Finally, the Darwinian influence led the Americans away from a strict focus on perception and cognition, to a broader focus which included practical applications of psychology to real life problems. It will not surprise you, then, when you discover that the Functionalists developed such sub-fields of psychology as psychometrics, educational psychology, child and developmental psychology, personality psychology, social psychology, and, perhaps most surprising of all to those who do not know the history of psychology, clinical psychology.

While it was a group of extraordinary individuals that really created American Psychology, one person in the group stands out above the rest as *primus inter pares*, the first among equals. That person, generally considered the father of American psychology, is William James.

The Development Of William James

William James was born into a wealthy and eccentric American family in 1842 in New York City. His grandfather had invested in the Erie Canal and made a substantial fortune. His father, Henry James, Sr., had grappled with anxiety disorders and depression, experiencing an acute crisis in 1844 when William was two years old. The elder James resolved his emotional problems by embracing the philosophy of the Swedish mystic Emmanuel Swedenborg (1688-1772). Henry James, Sr. would go on to write a number of books on religious and philosophical themes and became an advocate of the Swedenborgian philosophy. Henry James, Sr. also spent considerable time giving his children (five in all, with William James being the oldest) an education. He took his children in and out of private schools in Europe and the U.S., alternating with private tutors. His children got a highly unorthodox, yet very stimulating education (Fancher, 1990).

William James was followed by his brother Henry James, Jr. (the American novelist), Garth Wilkinson (known as Wilky), Robertson (called Bob by his family) and Alice. Of the two oldest siblings, it is often said that William wrote psychology like a novelist and Henry wrote novels like a psychologist. Both were masters of prose; both were keen observers of human beings. Alice (1848-1892) was highly gifted as a thinker and writer as well, but grew up in a household that was thoroughly sexist and she was constrained by the sexism of her time. She died tragically at the age of 44 of breast cancer, but not before profoundly changing her siblings' ideas about women (For a moving account of Alice's life, see the biography by Jean Strouse (Strouse, 1980)). Her diary, which was sent to her three surviving brothers upon her death, was also published in an edited version in 1934 and in a complete version in 1964, both times to critical literary acclaim (Strouse, 1980).

Henry James, Sr. was a member of the New England intellectual elite. Ralph Waldo Emerson often dined at his home, as did many of the leading writers and scientists in New England. He was also an avid abolitionist. The James children often visited the Emerson's and knew John Brown's daughter (John Brown was the radical abolitionist who tried to start a slave uprising by seizing the U.S. Armory at Harpers Ferry), who lived with the Emerson family. When the Civil War started it was natural for all of the James boys to join the Army. Henry James Sr. forbid his two oldest sons from joining—Wilky and Bob joined immediately. Wilky first served with the 44th Massachusetts Regiment and in 1863 transferred as an adjutant (a staff officer who aids the commanding officer of a unit) to Colonel Robert Gould Shaw of the 54th Massachusetts Regiment, a unit made up of free Blacks from throughout the entire U.S. The unit was commanded by white officers and fought with unequalled heroism during the war. (Col. Shaw and the 54th Massachusetts are portrayed in the 1989 movie *Glory*, which won three Academy Awards and starred Matthew Broderick, Denzel Washington, and Morgan Freeman.) On July 18 the regiment was ordered to attack the Confederate stronghold at Fort Wagner (South Carolina). Fifty percent of the unit, including Shaw, were killed in the attack. Wilky was next to Shaw when the latter was shot; Wilky was also seriously injured at the same time and was to have physical and emotional problems the rest of his life. Bob had joined the 55th Massachusetts Regiment (also made up of Black troops commanded by White officers) at the age of 17. Bob did not like military service and wrote his family frequently about his desire to resign (Strouse, 1980).

William James had wanted to be a painter (he had considerable artistic talent as revealed in his surviving sketches) but his father was totally opposed to such a career. In 1861 William was sent to Harvard to study chemistry at the new Lawrence Scientific School, where he studied under Charles Eliot, later to be president of Harvard. Soon William's interests shifted to neurophysiology, especially the work of Müller, Helmholtz (remember that Helmholtz had discovered the speed of the neural impulse in 1850), and du Bois-Reymond. In 1864 his interests shifted somewhat again and he enrolled in Harvard Medical School (Fancher, 1990).

When James switched from chemistry to biology he also changed advisors. His new advisor was Louis Agassiz, the famed naturalist and one of America's leading scientists. Agassiz was a creationist and when James first met him in 1861 the distinguished Harvard professor was involved in a heated conflict with Charles Darwin over evolution. Even after switching to the medical school, James remained deeply interested in physiology and biology. When Agassiz organized an expedition to the Amazon in 1865 to search for evidence to refute evolutionary theory, James volunteered to go as a research assistant. James did not stay for the entire expedition. He was seasick during the entire voyage and soon contracted smallpox in the jungle. He returned home with a bad back and eye difficulties caused by the smallpox. (Menand, 2001).

James' trip to the Amazon convinced him that he was not a good field biologist. But perhaps his trip was doomed from the start, for he had become a convert to Darwin's theory before he left with Agassiz for Brazil. In 1865 before he left he published his first two articles, both reviews, of works by T.H. Huxley and Alfred Russel Wallace. Both reviews were sympathetic. James took Darwin's work very seriously, and both his psychology and later his philosophy strongly reflected the influence of Darwin. He liked the ideas but recoiled at the materialism inherent in the theory. Much of his work in psychology and philosophy was to be a working out of the implications of Darwin's work while attempting to refute its materialism (Menand, 2001).

James became depressed after returning from Brazil and contemplated suicide. Part of the problem was that his family had taken up residence in Cambridge and insisted that he live with them. In April of 1867 he succeeded in convincing his father to permit him to take time off from medical school to travel to Europe for his health and to study German science. William's health improved in Europe after taking "cures" at several spas, and he had a chance to meet a number of leading scientists. During his 18 months in Europe, he also read an important article by Wilhelm Wundt on physiological psychology, leading James to write the letter used at the start of Chapter 4. James returned from Europe and finished his medical school education in 1869, but he remained depressed. The materialistic neurophysiology of Germany both impressed him and caused him to despair. The mechanistic world view seemed to have no place for free will, God, or a spiritual dimension (Fancher, 1990).

William James' emotional crisis came to a head in 1870, when he again considered killing himself instead of facing a life without meaning. The turning point came when he, according to his later accounts, read an essay on free will. The next day, he decided that as his first act of free will, he would believe in free will. Thus began a slow process whereby James cured himself of his emotional disorders (although he was never totally cured) and found purpose in his life. He tried to change his attitude toward life, became more optimistic, and sought to live fully with awareness every day (Fancher, 1990).

William James' process of self-therapy was helped along by a job offer from Charles Eliot in 1872 to teach physiology at Harvard. So began a 35-year teaching career at Harvard where James was to be in turn a professor of physiology, a professor of psychology, and a professor of philosophy. James' process of self-therapy was also helped along when he fell in love with Alice Gibbons, whom he courted for two years and finally married in 1878. In typical William James fashion, he saw both the pros and cons of marriage and could not make up his mind whether he loved her or not. He did love her, but they often had terrific shouting matches during their long marriage. James often left to get away from her, and as soon as he was away he would miss her terribly and want to return. Alice gave him enormous emotional support and stability, as well as raised their six children (Menand, 2001).

James, like a number of other early American psychologists, systematically experimented with drugs. This drug experimentation was an important part of his thinking on psychology and religion, and probably began in 1874. That same year he published an unsigned article in the *Atlantic Monthly* in which he reviewed a book on the use of nitrous oxide to gain philosophical and religious insight. Nitrous oxide, also known as laughing gas, had been discovered by a member of the Lunar Society, the chemist Joseph Priestly, in 1772 and was used as a recreational drug until the middle of the 1880s. In 1846, ether was found to be an effective anesthetic in dentistry. Shortly afterwards, nitrous oxide was also found to be effective. Modern surgery was born and nitrous oxide became an important medical tool but its recreational use did not disappear (Tymoczko, 1996).

James systematically experimented with nitrous oxide on himself. He wrote about his experiences as he "got high." He often found that he could not understand what he had written while high, but the revelations proved crucial to the development of his thinking in a number of areas (we will discuss these ideas soon). He published his results or discussed them in print several times in his life, including in an article in *Psychological Review* (James, 1898) and in his masterpiece on the psychology of religion (James, 1902). James concluded that rational consciousness was just one kind of human consciousness, and that in fact humans are capable of altered states of consciousness which are as important to understand as the normal, rational consciousness so prized by western science and philosophy. His experiments with nitrous oxide illustrate James' great openness to experience and his empiricism free of preconceptions about the truth or falsity of religious beliefs, the paranormal, and the mystical (Tymoczko, 1996).

James was a well-liked and charismatic figure. He avoided the formal conservative suits of his fellow college professors and dressed with flair and color. He often could be seen in animated conversations with his students walking to and from class. He often taught or entertained his students at his home or in the Harvard library, where he would sometimes hold classes next to a fireplace. He was liked by his students and he treated them as intellectual equals on a shared journey of discovery. He had a number of students who went on to be famous psychologists, philosophers, politicians (such as President Teddy Roosevelt, who adopted a philosophy of life strikingly similar to that of his teacher) and writers. James was interested in what his students thought, and collected written course evaluations decades before that practice became standard procedure in American colleges. He also constantly sought out the practical applications from psychology and philosophy, a hallmark of his approach to both fields. When Gertrude Stein (who was later a respected poet and patron of the arts) was in his class, she took one look at her final exam and wrote "Dear Professor James, I am sorry but really I do not feel like an examination paper in philosophy today," and left the room. James wrote back "Dear Miss Stein, I understand perfectly how you feel; I often feel like that myself," and gave her the highest grade in class (Fancher, 1990). Stein went on to do graduate work with James and carried out an important study of automatic behavior and mindlessness. She left without finishing her Ph.D. to pursue her writing career.

James And The Birth Of American Psychology

In early 1872, shortly before he was asked to teach at Harvard and two years after the depths of his emotional crisis, James and a group of his young friends formed a discussion group similar in many ways to the Lunar Society. Such groups were common at the time in the U.S. among intellectuals. William James' father had been a member, along with Emerson, of one such group. Agassiz had founded another such group that fostered the advancement of science in the U.S., the Lazzaroni described earlier in the chapter. James' group of young intellectuals called themselves the Metaphysical Club, and the club's members were destined to change American history. Besides William James, the group included the young lawyer and hero of the civil war, Oliver Wendell Holmes, Jr., Charles S. Peirce, and Chauncey Wright as well as several other young lawyers. Holmes was the son of the poet and novelist Oliver Wendell Holmes, Sr., who in addition to his literary achievements was a physician and Dean of the Harvard Medical School. Oliver Wendell Holmes, Jr. later went on to be a successful law professor and legal scholar, becoming in his later years one of the greatest jurists to serve on the U.S. Supreme Court. Charles S. Peirce (pronounced "purse") was the son of the Harvard mathematician and astronomer Benjamin Peirce. Benjamin Peirce was also a leading member of the Lazzaroni. C.S. Peirce made substantial contributions to logic and mathematics, as well as contributions to research methods in psychology and to philosophy. Peirce lacked his father's propriety, however, and frequently scandalized society by seducing women and cheating on his wife. He also became a drug addict and nearly died of malnutrition before being rescued and brought back to the U.S. by James. Chauncey Wright was the central figure in the group, a chain-smoking mathematician who had been educated at Harvard by Benjamin Peirce. Wright was known as the Cambridge Socrates. Wright lived for conversation and was enormously well-read. He was, however, without ambition. He worked intensely for three months out of the year as a mathematician for the U.S. government and then spent the remaining nine months talking and drinking, for he was, in addition to a chain smoker, an alcoholic who frequently suffered from depression. Wright had grasped Darwin's work early on and was a consistent advocate of the evolutionary point of view (Menand, 2001).

William James later gave Peirce and Wright the credit for developing the philosophy of pragmatism, a philosophy that was to be the first significant American contribution to philosophy (Menand, 2001). The central idea of pragmatism is that the truth of a concept is to be judged by its consequences —useful ideas are true; useless ideas are false. Pragmatism also, at least in the hands of William James, led to a tolerance of divergent points of view and a belief in a "multiverse" of truths; as opposed to a single truth, many truths existed (Menand, 2001).

William James' interest in physiology started to shift, in part because of his knowledge and exposure to the work of the German physiologists, especially Wundt, and in part because of the stimulus of the Metaphysical Club. In 1875 James offered his first course in psychology, on the relationship between physiology and psychology. He also started a small laboratory for teaching purposes. In 1876, G. Stanley Hall arrived as the first graduate student in psychology in the U.S. Hall received his Ph.D. two years later in 1878 with James as his advisor. Also in 1878, James signed a contract for a textbook on the New Psychology, a book that was finally completed and published in 1890. Before the book was published in 1890, James was recognized as the father of the New Psychology in America for his many articles, classes, and his training of graduate students (Fancher, 1990).

James' Psychology

interesting bc of his free will beliefs

From its inception, James' psychology differed from Wundt's in important ways. First, James' theory placed greater emphasis on evolution. While both Wundt and James combined neurophysiology and evolutionary biology in their theories, they gave different weight to the two components. As a consequence, James was not only interested in consciousness but in the functions of consciousness and of behaviors. The concern with function flows from both evolutionary theory and from the philosophy of pragmatism, which is itself influenced by evolutionary theory. James and Wundt also had very different views on free will (James believed in it; Wundt believed we make choices but that those choices are determined by our emotional states) and they differed in the all- important theory of emotions. James developed a theory rooted in Darwin's work now known as the James-Lange Theory (the Danish psychologist Carl Lange developed a theory similar to James a year after James published his theory in the U.S.). James argued that emotions are embodied and the product of evolution. They serve important functions (here he agrees with Wundt that emotions are an important part of a dynamic psychology). Finally, we do not perceive a stimulus, have an emotional response, then have a physical-bodily reaction. Instead we perceive a stimulus, have a bodily response, and perceiving the bodily response, have an emotion. The emotion, in other words, is the perception of our bodily responses to a stimulus.

Because of the influence of Darwin's work, James and his students were also interested in the psychology of animals. Finally, James was interested in the practical application of psychology to human problems and encouraged this interest in his students.

James' work gave American psychology a distinct set of problems and concerns. In addition, James developed a number of concepts that were and are important—one was the notion of the self-concept, later developed by one of his students. Another unique Jamesian concept is the stream of consciousness: consciousness is like an ever-moving and ever-changing stream. Thus from its inception, the New Psychology in America represented a distinct school from that of German psychology under Wundt.

In the early 1890s James' interests shifted again toward philosophy. He did however continue to carry out research on parapsychology (extra-sensory perception) and religion. In 1902 he published the results of his work on the psychology of religion (James, 1902/1961) and is usually credited with having developed the psychological study of religion. His research on ESP and parapsychology made James the father of parapsychology and the first real ghost hunter (Blum, 2006). James search for ghosts and proof of life after death was motivated by his deep commitment to empiricism and his efforts to create a psychology of human experience

The First Generation Of American Psychologists

The first generation of American psychologists were a brilliant and idiosyncratic group. Most came from middle-class intellectual backgrounds and most studied in both the U.S. and Europe. Unlike Wundt and James, who were trained in medicine and physiology, the first generation studied a variety of areas as undergraduates (especially philosophy), received Ph.D.s in psychology from the newly established labs and graduate programs, and studied in Europe at some point in their university education. Like James, many often spoke two, three, or four languages. From the beginning, they were deeply influenced by the work of Darwin as well. Not all of the first generation were native-born Americans. A few were immigrants trained in Europe. We now turn to a discussion of the lives and work of some of the most outstanding members of the first generation. The very first was G. Stanley Hall, the first American Ph.D. in psychology.

G. Stanley Hall And The Study Of Human Development

G. Stanley Hall (1844-1924) was born in Massachusetts. His father was a successful farmer and school teacher who also served in the state legislature and his mother had also been a school teacher. Both parents emphasized education and were very religious. He graduated from Williams College in 1867 and then went to Union Theological Seminary in New York to study for the ministry. But something happened on the way to the pulpit—Hall read Darwin and was won over to the theory. When he gave his first practice sermon to the students and faculty at Union, the president of the seminary went down on his knees and prayed for Hall's soul. Hall soon dropped out and borrowed money so that he could study in Germany where he spent a year and a half studying philosophy and physiology. Among the people he met was Du Bois-Reymond, one of the four great materialist physiologists of the age (Fancher, 1990).

Hall returned to the U.S. in 1871 where he landed a job as an instructor of philosophy and religion at Antioch College in Ohio. While at Antioch he read Wundt's book on physiological psychology, a work that turned his interests to the emerging New Psychology. He left Antioch in 1876 intending to study with Wundt in Leipzig but only made it as far as Harvard, where he got a job as an instructor in English and became James' first graduate student in psychology. Finishing his Ph.D. in 1878 (while working full time as an instructor), he borrowed money and finally made it to Leipzig where he was a postgraduate student (now called a postdoc for post-doctoral fellow) of Wundt's (Fancher, 1990).

Hall returned to Boston in 1880 without a full-time job. He was invited, however, by Harvard president Charles Eliot to give a series of special Saturday lectures on education. These lectures were a success and gained Hall the attention of Daniel Coit Gilman, who was looking for faculty in philosophy and psychology at Johns Hopkins (Fancher, 1990). At this point in Hall's career, he had published a number of respected articles. In addition to his doctoral dissertation which was published in 1878 (Hall, 1878), he published two articles on the teaching of philosophy in American colleges (Hall, 1876; Hall, 1879). He also had strong recommendations from both Wundt and James. James had told Gilman that Hall was the only person in the country, other than himself, who could teach the New Psychology (White, 2002).

Hall was appointed to a half-time position at Johns Hopkins in philosophy in 1881. He was one of three half-time lecturers in philosophy. The other two were C.S. Peirce, one of the members of the Metaphysical Club, who taught logic and psychology, and the brilliant philosopher George S. Morris. Gilman wanted a "safe" philosophy professor, a person who was sufficiently religious that Gilman could use the appointment as a shield for the biology department, which was thought to be unabashedly materialist (White, 2002). Of the three, Hall was the least controversial, or at least he appeared to be so. Morris was not religiously orthodox. Peirce was not religiously orthodox and his life was filled with scandal. He had, for instance, been banned from the Harvard campus by Harvard President Eliot and divorced his first wife, a religious feminist who believed that adultery should be punished with life imprisonment or death.

Given Peirce's frequent cheating on his wife, the marriage was not a happy one. Peirce was soon to be fired by Johns Hopkins, the first of three psychologists to be fired for immorality over the next 40 years (Menand, 2001). Only Hall was both religious and free from scandal. When Gilman finally appointed a full time professor of philosophy and psychology in 1884, it was G. Stanley Hall. The appointment of Hall is generally considered to be the first professorship of psychology in the U.S. Shortly after taking the full time position at Johns Hopkins, Hall founded the first American psychology laboratory (White, 2002).

Gilman was not disappointed in his choice. Hall believed that materialism shows a lack of education; that psychology shows that there is an identity of thought and matter, which is evidence of the divine. He argued, in one of his first lectures on the new psychology, that the field was deeply and fundamentally religious—specifically Christian, and that psychology was vital to the future of religion in the U.S. Hall called the new psychology "Christian to its root and center" (White, 2002). Hall was not posturing. He was deeply concerned with religious issues and would research religious questions (like his graduate school teacher William James) throughout his career. He also, like James, took evolution seriously while at the same time defended religion from materialism.

At Johns Hopkins, Hall developed a three-year program of study in psychology which included the study of sensation, perception, memory, attention, and learning. Students also studied animal instincts, child development, altered states of consciousness such as hypnosis, and psychopathology such as paranoia and hysteria. He attracted a number of graduate students who were to emerge soon as leaders in the new field as well (White, 2002).

In 1888 Hall was offered the job of president of Clark University in Massachusetts. Clark, which was still being built, was founded by Jonas Clark. Modeled after Johns Hopkins, Clark University was to have graduate programs in psychology, chemistry, physics, biology, and mathematics. The university opened in 1889 and Hall was not only president of the university but professor of psychology (White, 2002). It was at Clark that Hall founded another laboratory of psychology in the U.S., the fifth such lab. The second, third and fourth labs founded in the U.S. were all started by Hall's Johns Hopkins students the previous year. Hall brought with him as the lab director an 1888 Ph.D. from

Hopkins, and one of Hall's former graduate students, E.C. Sanford (Hilgard, 1987).

In addition to running Clark University, Hall carried out an extensive program of research. He refined and used Galton's questionnaire method to collect data on children and adolescents. He was the first to study adolescents as a separate group and was also, later in his life, the first to study the elderly as a special population. He was interested in the study of sex and gave lectures (for men only) on the topic. He also followed closely developments in European psychology and was one of the first to introduce the works of Freud and Jung into the U.S. As part of this effort, he invited Freud, Jung, and Wundt (who could not attend) to a special conference to mark the 20th anniversary of Clark University in 1909.

The audience at the 1909 Clark Conference was made up of a distinguished gathering of psychologists. Besides James, Hall, Tichener, Cattell, Baldwin, and Stern, Freud attended as a major speaker. With Freud was Swiss psychiatrist Carl Jung, the English psychoanalyst Ernest Jones, and the American psychiatrist A.A. Brill. In addition, the anthropologist Franz Boas and a host of other significant psychologists and psychiatrists were present. Besides these luminaries, the audience was filled with fascinating figures, among them the feared anarchist Emma Goldman. Goldman had first heard Freud lecture in 1896 in Vienna. For Goldman, Freud's work explored the oppression of women and the importance of sexuality, both important ideas in her own life and political philosophy where she championed the rights of women, free love, and birth control. "Red Emma," as she was sometimes referred to in the press, was one of the most feared people in America during the first decades of the 20th century (Goldman, 1930).

Hall's teacher William James supported women, although not always with the courage of his convictions. Hall's attitude toward women was more paradoxical. Hall, like many who embraced evolutionary theory, used it as a defense of the inherently different nature of men and women. Women were "the mother of the species" while men were the competitors and creators. This attitude was little different from Henry James, Sr., and was typical of the time period. Hall argued that the psychological differences between men and women existed at all stages of development. One consequence of his position was that he strongly opposed the move to coeducation that had gained considerable ground in the country. By 1900 almost all public high schools were coeducational. The presence of women in college and graduate school was still controversial and rejected by many. Hall wrote a number of articles against coeducation and published them in the mainstream press. Hall did allow women to enroll as graduate students, mostly in the department of education where they were trained as teachers. He also allowed a small number of women in as graduate students in a limited number of other departments, in part because of a desire to avoid public criticism, especially from feminists (both women and men). It appears that Hall was never exposed in the classroom to women or men who espoused feminism. The students he selected to study at Clark (Hall was responsible for selecting graduate students) tended to share his views on the traditional roles of women. Feminists, then, went elsewhere. Still, Hall was responsible for educating a number of women in the graduate programs at Clark (Diehl, 1986), an irony given that he was among the group of male psychologists (along with Titchener and others) who fought so hard to exclude women.

Mary Whiton Calkins And The Study Of Personality

Mary Whiton Calkins (1863-1930) was born in Hartford, Connecticut and grew up in Buffalo, New York. She was the oldest of five children. Like most of the first generation of psychologists, she came from a middle-class family that placed a high value on education. Her father was a minister who had received his undergraduate degree from Yale University, had done post-graduate work for a year at the Union Theological Seminary and then had studied for two years at the University of Halle, in Germany. Mary's mother had little formal education (as was very typical of middle-class females born before the U.S. civil war) but was an intelligent and accomplished woman. She accompanied her husband to Germany during the latter's graduate study and both she and her husband spoke excellent German. When Mary was born, they decided to speak only German in the house. As a consequence, Mary Whiton Calkins grew up bilingual, speaking fluent German as well as English before she started college (Scarborough & Furumoto, 1987).

Calkins' father took a job in Newton, Massachusetts in 1881. After completing high school in Newton, near Boston, Mary Calkins attended Smith College in Northhampton, Massachusetts, from 1881 to 1885. Smith, founded in 1871, was one of a small number of colleges open to women and, like the others, was an all-women institution. Calkins thrived at Smith, graduating with a degree in classical languages, in spite of the tragedy that occurred in her first year: her sister Maud died from rheumatic heart disease. While at Smith, Calkins took a course in psychology, that is, the old philosophical psychology (Scarborough & Furumoto, 1987).

After graduation, Calkins' father took her and her three surviving siblings (all boys) to Europe for a year to enrich their education. Immediately upon returning Calkins was offered a job teaching Greek at Wellesley College, located near Boston. Wellesley, which had been founded in 1870 as an all-women college, also had an all-women faculty. The founders of Wellesley had difficulty finding qualified scholars (not surprising since women had only recently been able to enter college and were not yet permitted to attend graduate school). As a response, Wellesley found highly talented women with promise as college teachers and scholars and helped them acquire higher education. Calkins was one such highly talented and promising woman. After teaching Greek at Wellesley, Calkins was recruited to teach the New Psychology that was being introduced into the college curriculum (Scarborough & Furumoto, 1987).

So began Calkins' search for graduate training. She initially considered study in Germany, given her fluency in German and the significance of a German Ph.D. in psychology. She rejected it though, because of the restrictions and prejudice encountered by women in German Universities. German universities of the time were even more hostile toward women than American universities. She also approached Yale and the University of Michigan. Both schools allowed women to study there and had graduate programs in psychology, but both were far from her home (where she was deeply involved with the care of her invalid mother) and lacked, at the time, laboratory facilities. Finally, her search focused on Clark University where G. Stanley Hall was both president of the university and professor of psychology, and Harvard University, which had a vibrant department under the leadership of William James. While both universities offered the Ph.D. in psychology and had advanced laboratory facilities, there was one problem: Neither school permitted women to study at the undergraduate or graduate levels. Calkins began a struggle to break down the barriers to her and, by extension, to other women (Scarborough & Furumoto, 1987).

Calkins first proposed attending the Harvard Annex, an unofficial program in which women received classes taught by Harvard professors (the same classes that the men received). The Annex was a program organized by Boston feminists who were agitating for higher education for women. The Annex later evolved into Radcliff College. After meeting with Josiah Royce, professor of philosophy, and William James, they suggested that she enroll in Harvard proper to study psychology and philosophy. It is unknown who actually came up with the idea (Royce, James, or Calkins herself), but both Royce and James were extremely enthusiastic about the proposal. So began a long process of lobbying by Joyce, James, and Calkins's father the Reverend Wolcott Calkins. The Reverend Calkins even met with the President of Harvard, Charles Eliot. Two of Calkins' brothers were students at Harvard at the time. Eliot was adamantly opposed to women in higher education, as was the Harvard Corporation and the Harvard Board of Overseers, to whom Eliot reported. After much lobbying and a petition to the Corporation, Calkins was denied the right to enroll at Harvard. The arguments and persuasive powers of Royce, James, and the Rev. Calkins had some impact however. Mary Calkins was allowed to "attend gratuitously their course" during the coming academic year, with the understanding that "by accepting this privilege, Miss Calkins does not become a student of the University entitled to registration" (Scarborough & Furumoto, 1987, pp. 33 & 35).

Calkins began her study at Harvard in the fall of 1890. James had just finished his masterpiece, the *Principles of Psychology*, and was organizing a graduate seminar using the book as his text. Four other students were in the seminar, all of whom were of course male and all of whom dropped out (for reasons lost in the mists of history). Calkins was James' only student in the seminar. Together they went through the *Principles* in front of a library fireplace, where James held the seminar (Scarborough & Furumoto, 1987). At James' suggestion, Calkins also studied as a private student of E.C. Sanford (1859-1924). Sanford had recently taken his Ph.D. at Johns Hopkins and followed Hall to Clark University. Clark did not allow women graduate students at that time but did allow them to take private instruction from professors. Sanford lacked the sexist attitudes of Harvard's Eliot and of Clark's Hall. Calkins remembered him years later as a caring teacher with enormous knowledge of experimental procedure who devoted considerable time to his students. Sanford was to become a strong advocate of Calkins and helped her establish the psychology lab at Wellesley College. Together, the two conducted a study of dreams, which they presented at the first APA meeting in December 1892. Calkins had to commute 40 miles to work with Sanford at Clark, a substantial commute at that time. During her year of study with James and Sanford, Calkins also carried out a pioneering study of association and learning, which James urged her to publish (Scarborough & Furumoto, 1987).

After a year of study Calkins returned to Wellesley to begin her career as a psychology professor. She did not feel adequately prepared though, and continued her efforts to get the Ph.D. Royce urged her to study at Cornell, a university that not only admitted women to their graduate school, but gave them financial support in the form of fellowships as well. Sanford urged her to study in Europe and noted that Hugo Münsterberg, a former student of Wundt's and a professor at the University of Freiburg, regularly included women among his students, a significant break from the previously sexist European practices and the practice at places like Clark and Johns Hopkins. James, mysteriously, urged Calkins not to make a decision until later. Then in April 1892 James wrote to Calkins giving her the news, James had recruited Münsterberg to teach at Harvard (Münsterberg's life and contributions are described below). Calkins and Münsterberg shared many interests and she became good friends with he and his wife. Münsterberg, like James, Royce, and Sanford, became her advocate and friend. While teaching full time, Calkins worked in Münsterberg's lab at Harvard. Then in 1894-1895 she took a leave to study and work full time at Harvard, where she carried out original work in human memory. Meanwhile, Münsterberg had begun a campaign to get Calkins the right to be admitted as a Harvard Ph.D. candidate. Describing her as the best student he had ever worked with at Harvard, he pressed the administration to admit her. President Eliot and the Harvard Corporation refused, although caving in to growing pressure they had decided a few months prior to Münsterberg's request to admit women to graduate courses, but not allow them to receive a degree. The year before, Harvard had been forced to make another concession to women's education and had converted the unofficial Harvard Annex into Radcliffe College for women. Women and men were not in the same classes at the new Radcliffe, but the courses were taught by the same professors (Scarborough & Furumoto, 1987).

Calkins made the next move. In April 1895, when Münsterberg's three-year contract with Harvard was about to end (he returned to Germany for a time and then came back to Harvard for the rest of his life), she requested that she take an unofficial Ph.D. oral examination equivalent to the official oral examination for the Ph.D. She had by this time completed the equivalent of all of the requirements for the doctorate. Her published studies more than equaled the usual Ph.D. doctoral dissertation. The department was enthusiastic about the proposal. She took the exam in May and did an outstanding job, described by James as "the most brilliant examination for the Ph.D. we have had at Harvard" (cited in Scarborough & Furumoto, 1987, p. 46). James was also reported to have said at the conclusion of the exam, "Now Santayana, go hang yourself." Santayana was a young philosophy professor who, up to that time, had enjoyed the distinction of having given the most brilliant examination for a Ph.D. at Harvard (Scarborough & Furumoto, 1987).

Harvard refused to grant Calkins her degree. She returned to Wellesley without a Ph.D. to begin her long and successful career as a professor of psychology and later philosophy. Seven years later, in 1902, Harvard tried to make up for its bigotry and discrimination. The university offered Calkins and three other women who had completed all of the work for their degree, but not the degree itself, a consolation prize, a Ph.D. from Radcliffe. Two of the women accepted; two, including Calkins, refused on the grounds that accepting would be acquiescing to Harvard's sexist practices. Women graduate students who completed their doctoral work at Harvard were not given a Harvard Ph.D. until 1963 (Scarborough & Furumoto, 1987).

In addition to her work on dreams, learning, and memory, Calkins developed a psychology of the self, building on James's work on the self in *The Principles,* developed a laboratory for Introductory Psychology students, and wrote several psychology textbooks (Calkins, 1930). It is her psychology of the self that is of most interest to the historian of psychology, also called by Calkins "Per-

TRIPLE
MARGINALIZATION

sonalistic Psychology." The psychology of the self was the real starting point for personality psychology.

Beginning in 1900, Calkins tried to broaden and re-define psychology as "the science of the self, or person, as related to its environment, physical and social" (Calkins, 1930/1961, p. 42). Self-psychology consists of three basic components: the self, the object, and the relationship of the self to the object. Calkins conceptualized self-psychology as a broadening of the functionalist approach to consciousness, one that could encompass much of psychoanalysis (with which she was very familiar) and supersede the criticisms of functionalist research raised by behaviorists. Self-psychology also incorporates Gestalt Psychology, and thus, she argues, represents an overarching synthesis (Calkins, 1930/1961).

Calkins was very discrete about her politics. In 1913 (at the age of 50) she rejected the label of feminist. Feminism, for Calkins, implied a rejection of marriage. She argued that women need not reject marriage "with a good man that loves you and that you love in turn" for a career. A few years later in a newspaper interview during a visit to the University of California at Berkeley she acknowledged that she was a suffragist but again rejected the label of feminist (Scarborough & Furumoto, 1987). But Calkins' statements cannot be taken at face value. In 1888, two years before she started graduate study at Harvard, she published a small empirical study of profit sharing (Calkins, 1888), a position strongly advocated by the socialist followers of Saint-Simon. Profit sharing, along with social security insurance, full legal rights (including voting rights) and higher education open to all people with talent, were positions advocated by the socialist followers of Saint-Simone. These socialists sought to distinguish themselves from Marxists and Anarchists, many of whom rejected marriage. Calkins' statements are consistent with the political views of a socialist feminist at the start of the 1900s.

Whatever Calkins' politics, she broke down barriers for women and served as a role model and inspiration for her students and other women across the country. The development of her research program and theory were hindered, nevertheless, by her position at a primarily undergraduate teaching institution. Had she the laboratory space and graduate students of her colleagues at Johns Hopkins, Cornell, or Harvard, her impact on psychology would have

had to be careful

been even greater than it was. The primary limitation, in Calkins' own view, was a consequence of the need to balance a difficult career as a scholar with the equally important social obligations of family. This balancing act was difficult for all women, given their social roles as caregivers, but was even more difficult for married women (Scarborough & Furumoto, 1987). Calkins never married, but she did spend most of her adult life caring for her invalid mother and later her father. Calkins knew personally the difficulty of balancing work and family. That she was a success at both illustrates her enormous talent and ability.

Later in her career Calkins' work shifted away from psychology toward philosophy. Like Wundt, James, and Külpe before her, and Baldwin and Dewey (whom we shall meet shortly) after her, Calkins viewed philosophy and psychology as related—each field informing the other. For instance, she was interested in the intellectual roots of the new psychology and revised an English translation of De La Mettrie's *Man the Machine* in 1912 (De La Mettrie, 1912/1961). The preface points out that the historical and philosophical notes are from a Master's thesis on De La Mettrie by Gertrude Bussey (one of Calkins' students) who also did the first translated version. The preface also thanks "Professor George Santayana, of Harvard University" for his valued assistance. Santayana, recall, was the brilliant philosophy colleague of William James who was bested, in James' view, by Calkins' final oral examination. Calkins' career in philosophy was as distinguished as her career in psychology. In 1905 she was the first woman to be president of the American Psychological Association. In 1918 she was the first woman to be president of the American Philosophical Association. Approximately half of Calkins' scholarly output, which included four books and over 100 articles, is devoted to philosophy (Scarborough & Furumoto, 1987).

James McKeen Cattell and Mental Testing

James McKeen Cattell (1860-1944) was born into a wealthy and successful Pennsylvania family. His father was a Presbyterian minister and college professor who became president of Lafayette College (located in Pennsylvania) soon after James McKeen Cattell was born. His mother was a member of the wealthy McKeen family. He graduated with highest honors from Lafayette College and also received a master's degree in English (his undergraduate major) from

Lafayette. While studying for his master's degree he spent a year in Germany studying at the University of Leipzig. At Leipzig, Cattell met Wundt and immediately fell in love with the new psychology. When he returned to the U.S. in 1882 he entered Johns Hopkins to study the new psychology under the recently hired G. Stanley Hall—who had received his Ph.D. in turn with William James, and then had been Wundt's first American student. After a year at Johns Hopkins, Cattell returned to Leipzig to work with Wundt, earning his Ph.D. in 1886 and becoming the first of Wundt's American Ph.D.s. Cattell also has the distinction of introducing the newly invented typewriter to Wundt, who soon became a skilled typist, increasing his production of books and articles. From Leipzig, Cattell went to England where Francis Galton secured for him a position at Cambridge University. Cattell had meet Galton briefly while traveling through England to Germany in 1884, when he also visited Galton's laboratory. While working with Wundt he had read a great deal of Galton's research and was very impressed with Galton's approach to measurement, which, using Galton's term, he called psychometry. Cattell's year as a Cambridge professor was very productive and fulfilling. He ran a laboratory similar to Galton's that focused on mental testing, he wrote book reviews, taught, and began work on a book on mental testing and measurement—a book he never completed (Gilham, 2001).

Cattell was athletic and a sports enthusiast. He played college football as an undergraduate and was the manager of his college baseball team. In Europe he joined a dueling club and became good at sword fighting, perhaps the only sport he never really liked. He also became an avid tennis player in Europe and would often play against a fellow student of Wundt's, James Mark Baldwin. Later in life, his regular opponent was Edward Thorndike. (We shall meet both Baldwin and Thorndike soon, as they were important psychologists.) Cattell also took up golf in Europe, another sport he played avidly for most of his life (Sokal, 1971).

In addition to Cattell's passion for sports, he systematically experimented with drugs while at Johns Hopkins and during his time in Europe. Besides alcohol, caffeine and tobacco, he was a heavy user of hashish. While in Europe he embraced socialism, a political creed he never abandoned (Sokal, 1971; 1981).

Upon returning to the U.S. in 1887 he taught as a lecturer at Bryn Mawr

College and then in 1888 he became Professor of Psychology at the University of Pennsylvania. In 1891 he moved to Columbia University where he was head of the Department of Psychology, Anthropology, and Philosophy. Like Hall, Cattell was not just a scientist but an institution builder. He went on to be a co-founder (with James Mark Baldwin) and editor of *Psychological Review* from 1894 to 1903. He was the editor and publisher of the (still to this day) very prestigious journal *Science* from 1894 to 1944. He was president of the APA in 1895 and founded the Psychological Corporation in 1921.

Cattell's major contributions, in addition to his work as an editor and publisher, came from his research on mental testing (a term he coined) and from his teaching. He taught a large number of graduate students (as well as collaborated with his colleagues Thorndike and Woodworth). Cattell also carried out studies of scientific achievement and eminence, modeled somewhat after the studies of his mentor Francis Galton. Cattell's work as a researcher in psychology was severely hampered by the political persecution he experienced immediately prior to and during World War I (Watson, 1978).

Prior to World War I, Cattell had earned the enmity of the president and trustees of Columbia University for his outspoken defense of academic freedom. In 1913 Cattell authored a book on higher education in the U.S. entitled *University Control* (Cattell, 1913), in which he called for the curtailment of the power and privileges of college presidents and trustees. This was one of the first proposals calling for the shared governance of the university, with autonomy of the professors over curriculum, hiring, and promotion of faculty. Cattell described the university as an association or community of scholars. The trustees tried to fire him but backed down because of faculty protests. Cattell was not alone in calling for faculty governance of the university; There were widespread actions at the time to win faculty control over hiring and dismissals at Columbia (Gruber, 1975).

On October 1, 1917, at the start of the new academic year, Cattell was fired by the trustees. The reasons for Cattell's dismissal, according the trustees, included treason and sedition. The actions that provoked these charges occurred in August of 1917, when Cattell wrote members of the U.S congress urging them to respect the rights of conscripts (people who are drafted into the military) to refuse combat on moral grounds, individuals we would call conscientious objectors. Cattell did not use official Columbia University stationary for this; he used personal stationary that had his work address on it. Such was the nature of Cattell's treason: the exercise of his constitutional right to petition his government. Cattell's firing followed the trustees' interrogation of the historian Charles Beard for his defense of a speaker who criticized the U.S. government and the interrogation by the trustees of two younger faculty who had spoken out against military training at meetings of students (Gruber, 1975).

Cattell did not need his job (and was denied the pension he had earned from his many years at Columbia). He had inherited money and made a good bit of his own from his publishing company, magazines, and journals. He was active however in the formation of the American Association of University Professors (the AAUP) in 1915, along with his Psychology Department colleague John Dewey. The AAUP became the leading defender of academic freedom, shared governance, and tenure in the U.S., all ideas and proposals articulated by Cattell (Gruber, 1975). Cattell remained active in psychology and science until his death in 1944.

Lightner Witmer And The Emergence Of Clinical Psychology

Lightner Witmer (1867-1956) followed a pattern among the early psychologists that should surprise no one at this point. The son of an intellectual, middle-class family, he was the oldest of three children. Witmer's father was a pharmacist and a graduate of the Philadelphia College of Pharmacy. Not much is known of Witmer's mother. Witmer and his two siblings all graduated from the University of Pennsylvania. Witmer began his graduate education in psychology with Cattell at the University of Pennsylvania and later went to the University of Leipzig to finish his Ph.D. with Wundt. Witmer's brother earned his MD at the University of Pennsylvania while his sister earned her MD at the Women's Medical College in Philadelphia (McReynolds, 1987). Needless to say, it was very unusual at the time for a family to produce two MDs and a Ph.D., especially given the fact that one of them was a woman.

Witmer earned his Ph.D. with Wundt in 1892 with a dissertation on aesthetic judgements. He also studied with Külpe and others at Leipzig. After finishing his degree he returned immediately to take up the position of psychology professor vacated by Cattell when the later had left for Columbia University (the University of Pennsylvania held the job for Witmer while he finished his degree). Upon taking up his duties at the University of Pennsylvania, Witmer became a founding member of the new APA and hosted the organization's first meeting at the University of Pennsylvania (McReynolds, 1987).

Witmer's interest started to shift toward the application of psychology in 1894 when he began teaching courses in psychology for teachers. Early in 1896 one of the students in his class presented him with a case of a 14-year-old boy with problems in spelling. Witmer began working with the boy, the first instance of a psychologist working with an individual in order to help the individual with his or her problems. Now Witmer's thinking started to change dramatically. By mid-1896 he was giving a special course on methods of dealing with individuals with handicaps or behavioral problems. In late 1896 he published a germinal paper on applying psychology to practical problems (Witmer, 1896) and at the end of the year he presented at the annual APA meeting a paper where he used the term "psychological clinic." In all, Witmer treated an estimated 24 individuals (most of whom were children) in 1896. Witmer also began supervising graduate students interested in working with people in psychological clinics (McReynolds, 1987).

It was in his APA paper (the abstract of his paper was published the next year, cf. Witmer, 1897) that Witmer outlined the structure of his psychological clinic and of clinical psychology (not yet so named) as a field. The purpose of clinical psychology is to apply psychological principles to therapy, rehabilitation, and education. As an aside, Witmer and his graduate students went on to be founders of school psychology and speech therapy. The psychologist would use psychological tests to help diagnosis and plan the program of treatment (O'Donnell, 1985).

In 1907 Witmer founded the journal *The Psychological Clinic*, a journal which both defined and named the new field. This journal was the major clinical journal in the U.S. until it was discontinued in 1935 (McReynolds, 1987). Witmer's efforts to develop a specialty within psychology devoted to helping individuals was joined by many of his graduate students and by other early functionalists such as Lewis Terman and Henry Goddard, both of whom we shall meet in later chapters.

Like Cattell and Dewey, whom you shall meet soon, Witmer became involved in the battles over academic freedom that occurred as the U.S. approached World War I. In Witmer's case, he was not the object of the attack, but a major defender of his colleague Scott Nearing, in what became known as the Nearing Case at the University of Pennsylvania. Nearing was a popular and highly praised economist at the University of Pennsylvania's Wharton School. Nearing was also roundly condemned by leaders in business for his controversial stands—he opposed child labor and corporate crime. In June of 1915 Nearing's contract was not renewed by decision of the board of trustees of the university (many of whom were business executives who made money using child labor or who had been criticized by Nearing for their corporate crimes). Students, faculty colleagues, and graduates of the Wharton School all rallied around Nearing. Witmer, who did not agree with some of Nearing's positions on issues and who did not approve of his "methods" (Nearing often spoke to church and community groups), nevertheless threw himself into the case. When Witmer first heard of the firing on campus, he burst out, "I don't give a damn for Nearing. He and I disagree in almost everything, but this is my fight. If they can do that to him they can do it to any of us. It's time to act" (McReynolds, 1997, p. 185). Witmer published a number of carefully reasoned, factual, and impassioned articles on the Nearing Case, and quickly produced a book on the case (Witmer, 1915). The interference of the trustees in the freedom of the faculty to research and teach what the scholars themselves judged to be important topics in their fields was a grave threat to the quality of the university, the quality of education, and the existence of science. Witmer, who could have easily done little or nothing, was passionate in his defense of Nearing. The issues involved went beyond Scott Nearing himself, to the very existence of modern science and the modern university.

E. L. Thorndike: Animal Learning And Educational Psychology

Edward Lee Thorndike (1874-1947) was born in Massachusetts and went to college at Wesleyan College in Connecticut, graduating in 1895. Thorndike was a brilliant student at Wesleyan, as well as editor of the student newspaper and a college tennis champion. He did not like his only psychology course in college and so had no interest in the subject until he read James' *Principles of Psychology* while preparing for an optional examination for an academic prize (which he won). After graduation he enrolled at Harvard to study English and French literature, but took one of William James' psychology classes in his first semester. The next semester Thorndike took two more psychology courses and changed his field of study to psychology. James became both his advisor and his friend (Fancher, 1990).

While at Harvard, Thorndike attended a lecture by C. Lloyd Morgan (1852-1936), a biologist who studied animal behavior. Starting with Darwin's work, biologists had a strong interest in animal behavior as an area of biology tied to the theory of evolution by natural and sexual selection. The first great researcher in this area was George Romanes (1848-1894), a friend of Darwin's. Romanes' work was based on often unsystematic observation, and was soon criticized by Morgan, who sought a more rigorous study of animal behavior based on systematic observation and experimentation. At Harvard, Morgan discussed his experimental work with chickens. Thorndike seized on the topic of animal learning and proposed to use chickens as his subjects. James strongly supported his young friend, even though he had no personal experience with animal research. Thorndike first kept his chickens in his room, until his landlady kicked him out. James sought lab space for him at Harvard, but to no avail. James then offered Thorndike "lab space" in the basement of James' home, where Thorndike completed his experiments. (Fancher, 1990).

Thorndike left Harvard (with James' support) after finishing his master's degree to study at Columbia with Cattell. Thorndike's decision was motivated by Columbia's strong experimental program coupled with James' shift away from psychology toward philosophy. His decision was also motivated by his failed love life—Thorndike had proposed marriage to a woman from a nearby town and been rejected. Cattell soon found space for Thorndike's chickens (he had kept them in his New York City apartment) at Columbia. Thorndike finished his Ph.D. in 16 months, performing a series of path-breaking experiments on learning in cats (which I will discuss shortly), publishing his results in a special supplement to *Psychological Review* (Thorndike, 1898), as well as presenting them to the New York Academy of Sciences and the annual APA meeting. After completing his Ph.D. Thorndike took a job at a women's college in Cleveland and married the woman who had rejected him while he was at Harvard. After a year in Cleveland he took a position at Columbia, where he remained for the rest of his career (Fancher, 1990).

Thorndike carried out a number of important studies in his career, many of them on learning in humans and animals, on education, and on psychometrics and intelligence. He was elected president of the APA in 1921 and in a poll conducted among psychologists in 1921 was considered the leading psychologist of his generation (Fancher, 1990).

Thorndike discovered the basics of what we now call operant conditioning (and what he called connectionism) from his work with cats. The cats had to escape from a box of Thorndike's design called a puzzle box. The cats learned only by trial and error. Most of the cats' behaviors failed to open the box. These behaviors were weakened. Behaviors that opened the box seemed to be strengthened. This he called the law of effect; the effect of an action causes the connection between a stimulus and response to be either strengthened or weakened. Thorndike also discovered that the more often the connection between a stimulus and response was made, the stronger the connection. (Thorndike, 1898). Thorndike's work was immediately recognized as an important study in animal learning and the comparative study of animal behavior (an area that came to be called comparative psychology), and a study important for education.

Soon after returning to Columbia, Thorndike carried out another series of studies with his graduate school classmate Robert Session Woodworth (1869-1962). Woodworth had been born in Massachusetts and educated at Amherst College. Like Thorndike, he was inspired by James' *Principles* and went to graduate school at Harvard to study with James in 1897. He left after receiving his master's degree to get his Ph.D. under Cattell at Columbia in 1899. After teaching physiology at New York Hospital and studying with the one of the leading physiologists of the day, Charles Sherrington, in England, Woodworth took a position at Columbia in 1903 where he worked for the rest of his career.

Thorndike and Woodworth studied over 8,000 New York City high school students to test one of the most widespread educational theories of their day. Most educators believed that the study of a topic such as mathematics or language would increase a student's intelligence or "mental muscle." This theory was prominently defended by the philosophical psychology, especially faculty psychology of the Scottish school. Thorndike and Woodworth found very little benefit in the study of a subject for "mental muscle." Instead, students gained knowledge and skills specific to an area, with limited transfer to other fields (Thorndike & Woodworth, 1901). The study by Thorndike and Woodworth was just the first of many to examine the transfer of training problem in humans and other animals, and in educational psychology. Thorndike, who studied a number of animal species such as monkeys, can be considered the discoverer of operant conditioning (a discovery usually erroneously attributed to a later psychologist, B.F. Skinner, whom you shall meet in chapter 7). He is also the founder of educational psychology, and he influenced millions of children worldwide through his work on the psychology of teaching and learning with his many books on the subject (*e.g.*, Thorndike, 1906).

Margaret Floy Washburn And Comparative Psychology

Margaret Floy Washburn (1871-1939) was the most successful of the early women psychologists, and along with Calkins and Christine Ladd-Franklin (1847-1930), was one of the most important psychologists of her day. Washburn was born and grew up in New York City, the only daughter of intellectual, middle-class parents. Her father was an avid reader and businessman. Her mother had graduated from high school (a rare feat at the time) and her mother's sister had been in the first class at Vassar and later became a medical doctor. Like her aunt, Washburn attended Vassar, graduating in 1892. Washburn, like all of the founders, had broad intellectual interests. In college her passions were poetry and philosophy. By her senior year, she had also developed a deep interest in science. The natural combination of her interests, it seemed to Washburn, was the New Psychology (Scarborough & Furumoto, 1987).

Washburn immediately sought entrance into Columbia University's graduate program, a plan that was enthusiastically supported by her parents. She was refused entrance and spent the fall semester of 1892 translating one of Wundt's articles on scientific methods. (Again, like so many of the founders, Washburn was multilingual; she later translated one of Wundt's books.) Columbia refused her admittance as a graduate student but did allow her to audit classes. At Columbia she studied with Cattell, who treated her with a status equal to his male graduate students and encouraged her efforts. In later years, Washburn would remember Cattell, with "affectionate gratitude," as her "first teacher." Cattell advised Washburn to study at Cornell, where she would be granted status as a regular graduate student. Washburn took her mentor's advice and transferred to Cornell (Scarborough & Furumoto, 1987).

Washburn received her Ph.D. in 1894, after only two years of study. Her advisor was Titchener, newly arrived from Germany. Unfortunately, Washburn did not like Titchener; he apparently did not treat her very well. He was, however, impressed with her doctoral dissertation and sent it to Wundt for publication. She joined the APA in 1894, one of only three women in the organization, and was elected president of the APA in 1921, the second woman to hold that post. During the nine years after graduating from Cornell, Washburn held a variety of posts. She taught first at Wells College, a women's college near Cornell, for six years while continuing to collaborate with Cornell faculty. In 1900 she became dean of women students at Cornell and also taught courses in social psychology and animal psychology. She also was asked by a Cornell professor of philosophy to marry him, but she declined; she did not want to give up her career. In 1902, tired of her work as an administrator, she took a position as an assistant professor at the University of Cininnati. Then in 1903, Washburn was offered a job at Vassar (Scarborough & Furumoto, 1987).

Washburn's years at Vassar were marked by enormous professional success and intellectual achievement. In addition to being president of the APA in 1921 she was a frequent member of APA committees, often as chair of the committee. She was elected to the National Academy of Sciences in 1931, only the second woman to be so honored. Washburn achieved all of this in spite of the limitations on psychologists at small liberal arts colleges: heavy teaching loads and work with undergraduates, lack of resources for research, lack of graduate students and colleagues with expertise in certain specialties. Washburn was a respected and effective teacher, but she was also perceived as aloof perhaps because she sought to avoid interpersonal obligations (outside of her family) and concentrate on her work (Scarborough & Furumoto, 1987).

Washburn's major achievement was in the area of comparative psychology. As mentioned in the section on Thorndike, comparative psychology grew out of Darwin's theory of evolution and his research on animal behavior, was de-

So interconnected

veloped by Darwin's friend George Romanes, and transformed into a rigorous area of research by C. Lloyd Morgan. In 1908 she published a synthesis of experimental and observational research on animal behavior, from simple organisms such as the amoeba, through invertebrates, vertebrates, and ending with mammals, entitled *The Animal Mind* (Washburn, 1908).

In *The Animal Mind* Washburn integrates experimental research across a number of species: research on sensory discrimination (vision, hearing, smell), the orientation to gravity, movement, learning and attention. Washburn was interested in the evolution of mind and consciousness, what we would now think of as the evolution of perception, learning, and movement (Washburn, 1908). Washburn's book went through a number of editions, the last being in 1936, and had a significant impact on the field. In addition to her own studies and the masterpiece on comparative psychology, Washburn carried out published studies with her undergraduate students and contributed frequently to edited volumes (Scarborough & Furumoto, 1987).

In spite of her success and standing within the field, Washburn continued to face marginalization and a double standard throughout her entire career. Known for her wit and irony, Washburn often joked about her situation. She also was not afraid to complain. In 1911, before John B. Watson founded behaviorism, which we shall explore in detail in Chapter 7, she noted that Watson was irresponsible, his work was careless, and that he had given her considerable trouble by bungling the preparation of a literature review for the *Journal of Animal Behavior*. In 1911 Watson was already a highly successful comparative psychologist, a professor at Johns Hopkins University and editor of *Psychological Review*. Washburn referred to herself and her colleague C.H. Turner as "inferior." Turner, who was one of the first African American Ph.D.s in Psychology and a talented comparative psychologist, had done considerable work for the journal while Watson had done little. Washburn, writing ironically, did not consider either she or Turner to be inferior, but it angered her that they were treated as such. Turner had difficulty finding work and spent much of his career teaching high school. Had either Washburn or Turner been white men, they would have held high-ranking positions at major research universities. (Scarborough & Furumoto, 1987). Both Washburn's experience and Turner's experience illustrate the double marginalization of women and African Americans.

Charles Henry Turner (1867-1923) was born in the immediate aftermath of the Civil War in Cincinnati, Ohio. He received his Ph.D. from the University of Chicago (the same school as Watson) in zoology, although his specialty was comparative psychology. Turner spent most of his professional career teaching at a high school in St. Louis. In addition to discovering several species of animals, doing some of the early studies of crayfish and bird brain anatomy, and developing a number of research techniques, he carried out studies of ant behavior, color vision in honey bees, and wasp predation. He also was the first to prove that insects can hear and distinguish pitch and that cockroaches can learn by trial and error (Abramson, 2002). Compared to Turner, Watson's achievements as a comparative psychologist (described in Chapter 7) pale. Yet it was Watson who was a full professor at Johns Hopkins and editor of *Psychological Review* (and later president of the APA), not someone else. This irked Washburn; historians do not know how Turner felt about the situation. Both Washburn and Turner were marginalized twice, once while living when they were treated as "professional inferiors," to use Washburn's phrase, and a second time by being neglected in most history of psychology texts. How Watson came to hold the position that he did is tied to the life and fate of another important functionalist, James Mark Baldwin, to whom we now turn.

James Mark Baldwin: The Study Of Cognitive Development

James Mark Baldwin (1861-1934) was one of the most creative and eloquent of the first generation of American psychologists, yet at the peak of his success his career in the U.S. ended abruptly in scandal, and his contribution to the field was marginalized for decades by historians afraid of the stench of scandal surrounding him. Baldwin was born in Columbia, South Carolina, the only one of the founding generation to come from the southern U.S. Little is known of his childhood or parents, who were originally from Connecticut. In 1881 he enrolled in Princeton University where he studied languages and philosophy (like so many of the first generation, he too was multilingual, speaking French, German, and Spanish). While at Princeton, Baldwin excelled, taking a number of academic honors, serving as the managing editor of a literary magazine and, upon graduation in 1884, winning a prestigious fellowship to study in Germany for an entire year (Wozniak, 2001).

While an undergraduate Baldwin took classes from and was influenced by James McCosh, the president of Princeton. McCosh was the last great advocate of Scottish realism, the philosophical psychology that was first developed by Thomas Reid. McCosh did not feel that science and religion were incompatible. (Princeton was a Presbyterian college under the control of the church; Princeton's primary mission was to educate people to be Presbyterian ministers and missionaries.) McCosh introduced Wundt's new psychology to his students as well as Darwin's theory of evolution (Wozniak, 2001).

After graduating from Princeton Baldwin spent an enormously stimulating year in Europe. He spent three semesters there and enrolled in a different university each semester. After spending the summer after graduation in Germany to improve his German, he studied first at Leipzig with Wundt (he attended Wundt's lectures and served as a subject in Wundt's lab), a semester in Berlin where he studied philosophy, and a semester at Freiburg. Upon returning to the U.S. in 1885 he started working at Princeton as an instructor in French and German. He also began graduate studies at Princeton's Theological Seminary. Baldwin spent two years at Princeton as a graduate student and instructor. While there he completed his first paper in psychology and translated Ribot's *German Psychology of To-day*, the first intellectual history of the new psychology that showed the influence of Kant, Herbart, and Fechner on Wundt's work (Wozniak, 2001). Ribot, who we met in the previous chapter, was the founder of the new psychology in France and one of Binet's influences.

After spending two years at Princeton, Baldwin left for Lake Forest University in 1887 where he took a position as a professor of philosophy. He spent two years at Lake Forest, during which he finished his dissertation under McCosh's supervision, got married, and published his first book on psychology, marking his definitive transition to experimental psychology. This work established Baldwin's reputation and secured him a better job at the University of Toronto in 1889. At Toronto, Baldwin established the first experimental psychology lab in Canada and carried out a series of experimental studies on infant reaching. The establishment of the psychology lab secured Baldwin's position in history as one of the parents of Canadian Psychology. His studies of infant reaching were inspired by the birth of his two daughters, born in 1889 and

1891 (Wozniak, 2001). Carefully controlled and quantitative, these studies set a high standard for experimental rigor and established, more than any other work, the experimental study of cognitive development (Cairns, 1994). In 1892 Baldwin was one of the founding members of the APA. While at Toronto he also traveled to France to study and observe Charcot's work, along with the work of Janet and Bernheim.

By this time Baldwin was a rising star in the new psychology, a scientist who combined rigorous research methods, sophisticated theory, and an elegant writing style second only to William James. He was next offered a post at his alma mater, returning to Princeton in 1893 to a named chair in psychology. At Princeton he established an experimental psychology laboratory. Baldwin, who stayed at Princeton until 1903, now entered his period of greatest productivity and influence as a psychologist (Wozniak, 2001).

During Baldwin's years at Princeton he co-founded in 1894 the journal *Psychological Review* with James McKeen Cattell and served as president of the APA (in 1897, at the age of 36). He also produced his three greatest works in psychology, works that integrated the findings of experimental psychology with philosophy and biology to produce the first full-blown theories in the field. The first of these works was *Mental Development in the Child and the Race* (Baldwin, 1895). *Mental Development* was Baldwin's first complete application of evolutionary theory to psychology, his book focused on the cognitive development of the individual as a process of growth and adaptation. "Race," in Baldwin's work, referred to cross-cultural comparisons (Wozniak, 2001). This work was to go through a number of editions and was translated into a several languages; it had a major impact on the thinking of both Jean Piaget and Lev Vygotsky (Cairns, 1994)..

Baldwin extended this theory immediately to encompass social relations and the development of the social self in *Social and Ethical Interpretations in Mental Development* (Baldwin, 1897). At this point in his career Baldwin turned away from empirical research and shifted his focus increasingly to philosophy. He became the editor of the *Dictionary of Philosophy and Psychology*, a work that contained contributions from all of the major philosophers and psychologists of his day. While this consumed much of his time, he did produce one more great work of psychology at Princeton, his *Development and Evolution* (Baldwin,

1902).

In 1903 Baldwin left Princeton to become chair of the philosophy and psychology at Johns Hopkins University. At Johns Hopkins Baldwin founded and was the main editor of another important psychological journal, *Psychological Bulletin*. He also sought to recruit some of the top young psychologists of the day to re-build the Johns Hopkins program in psychology. One of the young stars he recruited in 1907 was John Watson of the University of Chicago. Baldwin produced the first two volumes of what was to become a four-volume work on the development of cognition and experience, entitled *Thought and Things* (Baldwin, 1906; Baldwin, 1908). These works were difficult, philosophically sophisticated, and did not have much of an impact on the field because of Baldwin's sudden fall from grace (Wozniak, 2001).

In 1908, Baldwin was arrested in a police raid on a Baltimore house of prostitution. In order to contain the scandal, the president of Johns Hopkins fired him immediately. Baldwin thus became the second psychologist at Johns Hopkins University to be fired for immoral behavior. Before leaving Baldwin walked into Watson's office and told him he was now the editor of *Psychological Bulletin* and the head of the department. Watson's career took a giant leap forward while Baldwin left the country in disgrace. From being considered second only to William James, he was now *persona non grata*.

Baldwin did not give up doing what he did best. From 1908 to 1912 he divided his time between Mexico, where he taught at the National Autonomous University of Mexico (UNAM) in Mexico City, and Paris. In 1912 he moved permanently to Europe (Wozniak, 2001). He produced four more books on psychology in this period, *Darwin and the Humanities* (Baldwin, 1909), *The Individual and Society* (Baldwin, 1911a), and the last two volumes of *Thought and Things* (Baldwin, 1911b; Baldwin, 1915).

In 1915, when Baldwin was 56, he turned his attention to politics. Alarmed by what he perceived to be the growing threat of Germany, he campaigned for U.S. involvement in the Great War. In 1916 he authored a "Message from Americans Abroad" that was circulated within the U.S., wrote a book on American Neutrality, and gave an invited lecture at Oxford criticizing German political ideology. He also survived a German U-boat attack when he traveled from France to England on a passenger ship. During the war he worked in a number of relief efforts for the French and was awarded the Legion of Honor, one of the highest medals given by the French government, for his service (Wozniak, 2001). Other than a memoir and an autobiography, he produced little after the Great War.

Like other founders before him, Baldwin shifted from psychology to philosophy as his career matured. But he was also, in many ways, the successor to James as the leader of American psychology. A stylish writer, a sophisticated thinker, and a skilled researcher, he seemed to have all of the talents needed for greatness. While still influential in Europe after the scandal that destroyed his career, he and his work were shunned by American psychologists. At the same time he was virtually obliterated from the history of the field, only to be recognized again in the 1980s (Cairns, 1994). Without a doubt, the loss of one of the foremost leaders in the field was a blow to the New Psychology in the U.S.

Hugo Münsterberg And Applied Psychology

Hugo Münsterberg (1863-1916) was born in Gdansk, now part of Poland but at the time part of Germany. After receiving his Ph.D. with Wundt in 1885, Münsterberg took a position at the University of Freiberg, where he established a psychology laboratory and where he earned a reputation as a rising star and gifted teacher. He became one of the leading American psychologists after being recruited to Harvard by William James in 1892, at the age of 29, where he was Calkins' major advisor. After three years at Harvard, Münsterberg returned to Germany from 1895 to 1897. He then returned to Harvard for the rest of his life as he was recruited there to take charge of the psychology laboratory (Hilgard, 1987).

Münsterberg is often considered a social reactionary who valued a highly stratified society in which women "knew their place" (Hilgard, 1897), but this is a gross oversimplification. Münsterberg was part of a small group that supported women in psychology (the group also included William James and E.C. Sanford). Calkins referred to Münsterberg as one of her three great teachers, along with James and Sanford, and remembered him with great affection (Calkins, 1930). In her autobiography she interrupts her narrative to tell a story of a meeting of the APA executive committee in 1905 at Harvard. Calkins was at the time the President of the APA and Münsterberg, the host of the meeting, was a member of the committee (he had served as president of the APA in 1899). The committee had scheduled a lunch meeting at the Harvard Union, but the group was denied entrance by the "burly head waiter" because women were not allowed in the main dining room. Calkins noted "it was almost by main force that Professor Münsterberg gained his point and the Committee its lunch" (Calkins, 1930, p. 34). At the time few men dared to publicly break society's rules and treat women as equal human beings.

Münsterberg was enormously influential in the U.S., not only as a researcher, teacher, and popular public lecturer, but also as a pioneer in applying psychology to real world problems. Beginning around 1900, Münsterberg sought to apply psychology to the legal system, medicine, business, and clinical practice. For his wide-ranging contributions he is often considered the father of applied psychology.

Münsterberg was instrumental in developing forensic psychology, the application of psychology to crime and legal questions. His work in this field culminated in his book *On the Witness Stand* (Münsterberg, 1908), in which he argued that psychology was important for evaluating eyewitness testimony, false confessions, and evidence. In writing *On the Witness Stand*, Münsterberg drew on the work of Binet on suggestibility and William Stern on eyewitness testimony.

Münsterberg is also the co-founder of industrial psychology, along with Walter Dill Scott of Northwestern University. Like Münsterberg, Scott was a student of Wundt's and received his Ph.D. at Leipzig. Scott applied psychology to advertising (Scott, 1903) and began a vibrant area of psychological research in persuasion and advertising. Münsterberg focused instead on production (Münsterberg, 1913). He divided the psychology of industrial production into three areas: the best possible worker, the best possible work, and the best possible effect. These three areas embraced such areas as personnel selection, vocational guidance, on-the-job training, and man-machine problems. Münsterberg also carried out path-breaking studies of switchboard operators and accidents among street car drivers (Hilgard, 1987). In addition to his creation of forensic psychology and his co-creation of industrial psychology, Münsterberg also made contributions to clinical psychology (Münsterberg, 1909a) and educational psychology (Münsterberg, 1909b).

Toward the end of his life, Münsterberg became unpopular for his position on World War I. Münsterberg, like a large number of Americans, opposed the war. Many at Harvard and in the halls of the U.S. Congress however were staunchly pro-English, and Münsterberg was branded a "pro-German" sympathizer whom some suspected of being a spy. There were threats against his life, and many of his colleagues shunned him. (Spillman & Spillman, 1993).

Münsterberg was not circumspect with his views. He perceived a great wave of anti-German hysteria sweeping the country, fueled by a propaganda campaign carried out by influential American leaders. He laid out his criticisms of this campaign and for "fair play" in *The War and America* (Münsterberg, 1914). Here, he pulled no punches. One of the leaders of the anti-German campaign was Charles W. Eliot, the former president of Harvard and Münsterberg's former boss. Münsterberg put faith in President Wilson. Little did he know, that while Wilson was claiming to keep us out of war, he was secretly maneuvering to bring the U.S. into the conflict on the side of the British (Karp, 2003). On May 7, 1915, Germany attacked and sunk the British passenger liner Lusitania. Of the over 1,200 killed on board, 128 were American. As the pro-war hysteria built, Münsterberg found himself increasingly isolated at Harvard.

Münsterberg, a man who had dined at the White House and had befriended President Theodore Roosevelt and President William Howard Taft, a man who had been visited by German royalty and who had been decorated by Kaiser Wilhelm II, had fallen far indeed (Hilgard, 1987). In 1916 at the age of 53 he died of a cerebral hemorrhage as he began a Saturday lecture at Radcliffe (Spillman & Spillman, 1993).

William McDougal and Social Psychology

William McDougal (1871-1938) was born in England, educated at Cambridge, and went on to be one of the founders of the new psychology in Great Britain. He came to the U.S. in 1920 to take a professorship at Harvard, effectively taking Münsterberg's position. (Harvard had difficulty replacing Münsterberg with an American.) McDougal became one of the leading opponents of behaviorism, of which we shall learn much more in Chapter 7. He was deeply influenced by Darwinian ideas and American psychology, and can be considered a functionalist. With the publication of *An Introduction to Social*

Psychology (McDougal, 1908) he became a leader in the field of social psychology. McDougal's social psychology emphasized the role of motivation and drives in social behavior.

John Dewey And The Chicago Functionalists

John Dewey (1859-1952) was born in Burlington, Vermont and grew up there. After graduating from the University of Vermont he worked for three years as a high school teacher. In 1882 he started graduate school at Johns Hopkins University where he studied with G. Stanley Hall, C.S. Peirce (of the Metaphysical Club—holding one of his few academic jobs) and the brilliant American philosopher George S. Morris. After earning his Ph.D. in 1884 he taught at the University of Michigan for 10 years and then in 1894 left for the University of Chicago. At Chicago he was a close collaborator with Jane Addams and founded an experimental school based on his psychological theories of education, cognition, and development. He moved one more time, in 1905, to Columbia University, where he stayed until his retirement (Watson, 1978). Most of Dewey's work in psychology took place while he was at Michigan and Chicago. After moving to Columbia the focus of his work shifted to philosophy. Following a path that had been blazed by James, Külpe, Calkins, and Baldwin, among others, he became one of the most influential American philosophers of the 20th century (Menand, 2001).

Perhaps Dewey's greatest work in psychology was a theoretical article on the reflex arc concept (Dewey, 1896). The term reflex arc may sound strange to modern students, but the concept should not be foreign. The idea of stimulus-response (that a stimulus in the environment produces a series of reactions in the nervous system leading to a behavior) is rooted in the work of Descartes and was to be fundamental to behaviorism and other mechanistic theories (such as information processing accounts of cognition). Dewey argued that this concept made no sense and could not explain anything. Instead, any real explanation had to posit an active, thinking organism that sought out information and interpreted the world. Dewey's work represented a significant theoretical advance for functionalism.

At the University of Michigan and the University of Chicago Dewey worked with a group of talented psychologists. One of the most prominent was James

Rowland Angell, a graduate student of Dewey's at Michigan and later a colleague at the University of Chicago. Angell was the son of James Burrill Angell who, besides being a prominent professor of modern languages, was president of the University of Vermont and later the University of Michigan. Like Cattell and other early psychologists, Angell was an avid athlete (Angell, 1961).

Angell was to become a president of the APA and he gave American psychology its name: functionalism. In his presidential address to the APA (Angell, 1907) he extended the basis of American psychology by giving it a coherent theoretical basis. James was overjoyed. Later Angell was to criticize the rise of behaviorism and the efforts by behaviorists to exclude consciousness from the study of psychology (Angell, 1913). In this he opposed one of his former students, John B. Watson. Watson was one of five of Angell's students who served as president of the APA (Angell, 1961). The mature functionalism of Dewey, Angell, and others was often called the Chicago School.

The Institutionalization And Spread Of The New Psychology

From the first psychology courses and labs in Germany and the U.S., the field experienced rapid growth in the number of undergraduate students, Ph.D.s, laboratories and programs. Along with this growth came the organization of professional associations such as the American Psychological Association in 1892 and the increase in communication through scientific journals and conferences. This rapid growth (illustrated in Figure 5.1) could not have occurred unless the institutional context for the new psychology was not primed and ready. That institutional context was the growth of universities, and the role that universities were coming to play in the economic advancement of first Germany and the U.S., and later the other advanced economies of Europe and North America.

The New Psychology also grew rapidly, I would argue, because it served a number of important societal needs, including the need to understand and manage humans in a complex society. The explosive growth of the New Psychology showed that both the time was ripe and the need was great. If Wundt and James had never been born, someone else would have, around the same time or perhaps shortly later, founded the New Psychology. This is not to deprecate the brilliance and hard work of the first generation. The contributions made by the first generation could not have been made by less talented, less thoughtful individuals. They shaped psychology over the last century, a psychology that is now global in terms of its institutional reach.

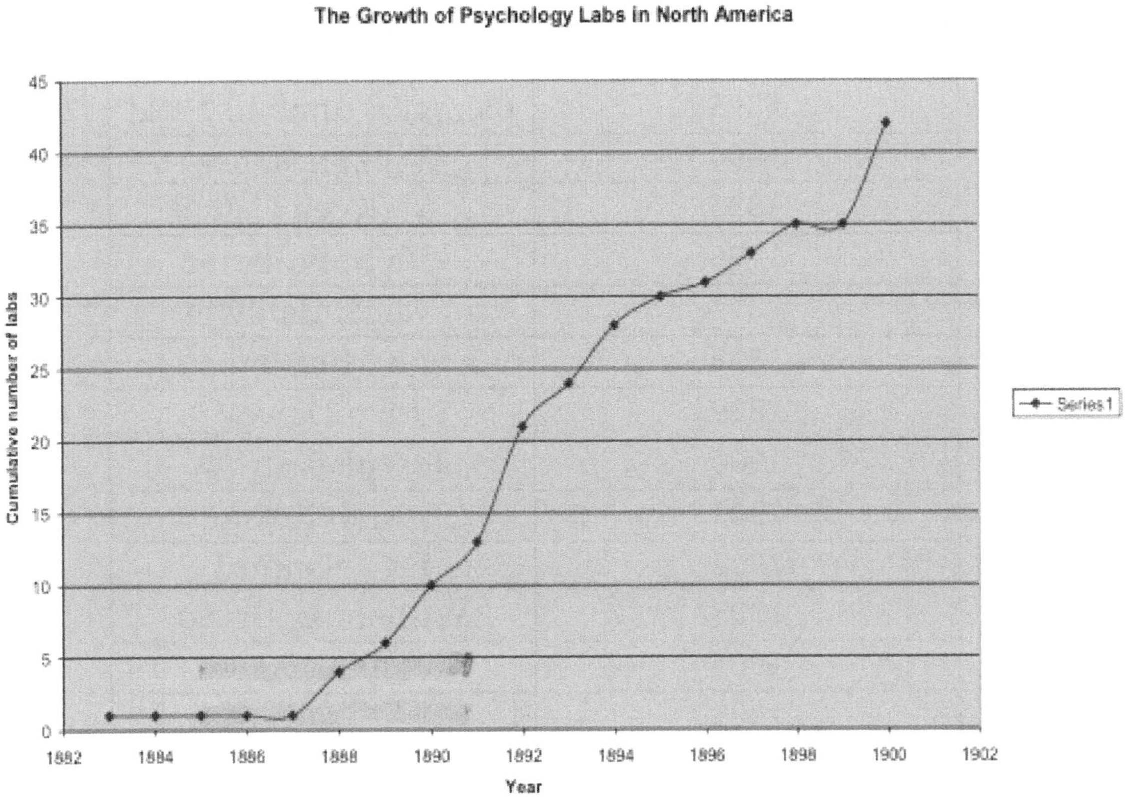

The Growth of Psychology Labs in North America

Figure 5.1 The Growth Of Psychology Laboratories In North America, 1882-1902.

(Data are taken from Hilgard, 1987, who provides a comprehensive list of American psychology laboratories from 1883 to 1900).

Finally, Table 5.1 lists the presidents of the APA, from 1892 to 1919. The presidency of the APA is an indicator of leadership among the first generation. Note in Table 5.1 that William James is the only person to have served twice as president of the APA

Table 5.1: The Presidents Of The American Psychological Association, 1892 To 1919

Date of Presidency	President
1892	G. Stanley Hall
1893	George Trumbull Ladd
1894	William James
1895	J. McKeen Cattell
1896	G.S. Fullerton
1897	J.M. Baldwin
1898	Hugo Munsterberg
1899	John Dewey
1900	Joseph Jastrow
1901	Josiah Royce
1902	E.C. Sanford
1903	William L. Bryan
1904	William James
1905	Mary W. Calkins
1906	James R. Angell
1907	Henry R. Marshall
1908	George M. Stratton
1909	Charles H. Judd
1910	Walter B. Pillsbury
1911	Carl E. Seashore
1912	Edward L. Thorndike
1913	Howard C. Warren
1914	R.S. Woodworth
1915	John B. Watson
1916	Raymond Dodge
1917	Robert M. Yerkes
1918	J.W. Baird
1919	Walter Dill Scott

By the end of World War I, Wundt's vision of psychology and his influence had been eclipsed. In the U.S., Wundt was essentially "abandoned" by psychologists who had taken his initial methods and ideas and expanded and enriched them with diverse topics, theories, and methods (Rieber, 2001). In Europe also, Wundt had been eclipsed. The new psychology in Great Britain was strongly influenced by British philosophy, the theory of evolution, and American psychology. The new psychology in France was shaped by Binet's work, which in turn drew from British philosophy and the work of Charcot and French psychiatry. Even in Germany, Wundt's laboratory was surpassed by the psychology laboratory at the University of Gottingen in the 1890s (Haupt, 2001), and by the different theories and research areas of psychologists at Wurzburg, Berlin, and other German Universities.

But this is an oversimplification. The New Psychology, including its institutional structures of journals, institutes and academic departments, its methods, theories, and discoveries, were innovations that traveled back and forth, west to the U.S. and east to Europe, in rapid succession. Innovation fueled further innovation; new methods, theories, and discoveries fueling further methodological and theoretical advances and discoveries. American psychologists were especially open to this process, but so were most European psychologists outside of Wundt's direct influence. Further, this process of rapid back-and-forth spread of innovations took place within a network of individuals who were connected to one another professionally and personally.

so connected

Psychology's Political And Moral Heritage

By now you should be aware of a curious fact: the founding generation of American psychologists was highly political, although there is no simple way to classify their politics. At least three, James, Hall, and Dewey, came from families that were active abolitionists (opposed to slavery) at a time when most whites supported slavery in the U.S. James, Cattell and Münsterberg were anti-war activists. William James was one of the leaders of the Anti-Imperialist League (along with other prominent Americans such as Mark Twain and Jane Addams, the founder of Hull House in Chicago). The Anti-Imperialist League opposed the Spanish-American War of 1898, in which the U.S. fought Spain for control of the colonies that were breaking free of Spain. The U.S. took control of Puerto Rico, Guam, Cuba, and the Philippines. The U.S. conquest of the Philippines was especially brutal, as the U.S. Army had to fight a popular independence movement (Beisner, 1968). Münsterberg and Cattell opposed World War I, and both suffered as a consequence (Münsterberg literally dying from the stress and Cattell being fired for writing a letter to congress). Three were prominent proponents of academic freedom (Cattell, Witmer, and Dewey) and were active in the formation of the oldest, and still most important organization of academics in the U.S., the American Association of University Professors (the AAUP). Two were prominent education reformers: John Dewey and E.L. Thorndike. And some were feminists (Dewey), supporters of women's suffrage (Washburn and Calkins) or highly sympathetic to women's right to education (James, Sanford, and Münsterberg). C.H. Turner, one of the first black psychologists, was a life-long advocate for civil rights for minorities. Finally, there is some evidence, cited above, that Mary Whiton Calkins was a socialist, at least when she was young.

John Dewey was perhaps the most politically engaged of the founding generation. In addition to his involvement in academic freedom, education reform, and women's rights, he was also a founder of the American Civil Liberties Union (the ACLU), which is still one of the leading defenders of civil liberties in the U.S., a founding member of the National Association for the Advancement of Colored Peoples (the NAACP), and a founder of the New York City Teachers Union.

Not all members of the first generation were on the left (although it appears that the majority of them were). Baldwin was pro-war and worked tirelessly to bring the U.S. into World War I. Hall held traditional sex-role stereotypes and tried to keep women out of the profession. And many of the first generation, like the majority of their educated peers, were racist and anti-Semitic.

Collectively, the best generalization is perhaps that they were all very involved with the political and social world around. They did not just seek to create a new science; they sought to create a new world. Wow!!!

Psychologists claim that theirs is an objective, disinterested science yet at the same time psychologists have had a strong concern for the welfare of *why i'm here :)*

individuals and of society from the very inception of the field (Pickens & Dewsbury, 2002). This concern manifested itself in the high level of political involvement, often liberal or radical, just discussed. The concern for the welfare of individuals was also clearly expressed in the development of the many applied applications of psychology pioneered by American psychologists, such as educational psychology, industrial psychology, and of course clinical psychology. This concern with the well-being of others' also manifested itself in the writing of utopias for mass audiences.

Sir Thomas More (1478-1535), Renaissance scholar, political advisor to King Henry VIII, and friend of the great Renaissance humanist Erasmus wrote the most famous utopian novel, called *Utopia,* in 1516. *Utopia*, a term which More derived from the Greek *topos* (place), *ou* (not) and *eu* (well), was a description of a perfect society that did not exist. Since More's work, many authors have written utopias and anti-utopias, also called dystopias. Utopian and dystopian novels are especially popular in science fiction. Interestingly, psychologists have had a strong penchant for writing utopias based on psychological principles. Three of the founders of psychology wrote important utopias: G. Stanley Hall (Hall, 1920), Hugo Münsterberg (Münsterberg, 1916), and William McDougal (McDougal, 1921).

The founders were not the only psychologists to write utopias. Later on, the behaviorists John B. Watson (Watson, 1929) and B.F. Skinner (Skinner, 1948) wrote utopias. Skinner's was especially popular. These utopias reveal a great deal about the social and cultural context of psychology, as historian of psychology Jill Morawski (Morawski, 1982) has shown. Psychology has a moral heritage, a strong ongoing concern for the welfare of individuals and groups. Yet this moral concern often reflects the assumptions and values of the broader society. In all cases however, psychologists see themselves as capable of playing a unique role in the improvement of human welfare. In all cases, psychology is believed to be indispensable for the common good. The idea that psychology could be an instrument of oppression or a source of problems rarely enters the minds of psychologists, at least until relatively recently in the field's history

World War I: The End of the Long Nineteenth Century

World War I was a pivotal event in the history of the New Psychology. It was the end of the long nineteenth century. The twentieth century had arrived at last, but what kind of world it would produce was not at all clear until another 30 years of historical change and trauma were to pass. But before we can continue the historical narrative, we must backtrack to the last decades of the 1800s and return to Europe, but not to Germany. Instead we must go to the Austro-Hungarian Empire at the end of the 1800s where yet a third school of psychology was about to be born—the psychoanalysis of Sigmund Freud.

References

Abramson, C.I. (2002). *Selected papers and biography of Charles Henry Turner (1867-1923): Pioneer in the comparative animal behavior movement.* Lewiston, NY: Edwin Mellen.

Allport, G. (1961/1985). Introduction to *Psychology: The briefer course.* Notre Dame, IN: University of Notre Dame Press.

Angell, J. R. (1907). The province of functional psychology. *Psychological Review, 14,* 61-91.

Angell, J.R. (1913). Behavior as a category of psychology. *Psychological Review, 20,* 255-270.

Angell, J.R. (1961). Autobiography. In C. Murchison (Ed.), *A history of psychology in autobiography,* Vol. 3. New York: Russell & Russell.

Baldwin, J.M. (1895). *Mental development in the child and the race: Methods and processes.* New York: Macmillan.

Baldwin, J.M. (1897). *Social and ethical interpretations in mental development: A study in social psychology.* New York: Macmillan.

Baldwin, J.M. (ed.) (1901-1905). *Dictionary of philosophy and psychology.* New York: Macmillan.

Baldwin, J.M. (1902). *Development and evolution.* New York: Macmillan.

Baldwin, J.M (1906). *Thought and things: A study in the development and meaning of thought, or genetic logic I. functional logic, or genetic theory of knowledge.* New York: Macmillan.

Baldwin, J.M. (1908). *Thought and things: A study of the development and meaning of thought. Or genetic logic II. Experimental logic, or genetic theory of thought.* London: Swan Sonnenschein.

Baldwin, J.M. (1909). *Darwin and the humanities.* Baltimore: Review Publishing.

Baldwin, J.M. (1911a). *The individual and society. Or psychology and sociology.*

Boston: Badger.

Baldwin, J.M. (1911b). *Thought and things: A study of the development and* meaning *of thought. Or genetic logic III. Interest and art being real logic. I Genetic epistemology.* London: George Allen.

Baldwin, J.M. (1915). *Genetic theory of reality. Being the outcome of genetic logic as issuing in aesthetic theory of reality called pancalism.* New York: Putnam.

Beisner, R.L. (1968). *Twelve against empire: The anti-imperialists, 1898-1900.* New York: McGraw-Hill.

Bledstein, B.J. (1976). *The culture of professionalism: The middle class and the development of higher education in America.* New York: Norton.

Blum, D. (2006). *Ghost hunters: William James and the search for scientific proof of life after death.* New York: Penguin Books.
Boring, E. G. (1950). *A history of experimental psychology* (2nd edition). New York: Appleton Century Crofts.

Bruce, R.V. (1987). *The launching of modern american science: 1846-1876.* Ithaca, NY: Cornell University Press.

Cahan, E.D. (1994). John Dewey and Human Development. In Parke, Ornstein, Rieser, and Zahn-Waxler (eds.), *A century of developmental psychology.* Washington, DC: American Psychological Association, pp. 145-167.

Cairns, R.B. (1994). The Making of a Developmental Science: The Contributions and Intellectual Heritage of James Mark Baldwin. In Parke, Ornstein, Rieser, and Zahn-Waxler (eds.), *A century of developmental psychology.* Washington, DC: American Psychological Association, pp. 127-143.

Calkins, M.W. (1888). *Sharing the profits.* Boston: Gunn & Company.

Calkins, M.W. (1930/1961). Mary Whiton Calkins. In Murchison (ed.) *A history of psychology in autobiography*, Vol. 1, pp. 31-62.

Cattell, J.M (1913). *University control.* New York: Science Publishers.

De La Mettrie, J. O. (1912/1961). *Man a machine.* La Salle, IL: Open Court Publishing.

Dewey, J. (1896). The reflex arc concept in psychology. *Psychological Review, 3*(4), 357-370.

Diehl, L.A. (1986). The paradox of G. Stanley Hall: Foe of coeducation and educator of women. *American Psychologist, 41*(8), 868-878.

Fancher, R. E. (1990). *Pioneers of psychology,* 2nd ed. New York: W. W. Norton & Company.

Gillham, N.W. (2001). *A life of Sir Francis Galton: From African exploration to the birth of eugenics.* New York: Oxford University Press.

Goldman, E. (1930). *Living my life.* New York: Dover.

Gruber, C.S. (1975). *Mars and Minerva: World War I and the uses of higher learning in America.* Baton Rouge: Louisiana State University.

Hall, G.S. (1876). College instruction in philosophy. *The Nation, 23,* 180.

Hall, G.S. (1878). The muscular perception of space. *Mind, 3,* 433-450.

Hall, G.S. (1879). Philosophy in the United States. *Mind, 4,* 89-105.

Hall, G.S. (1920). The fall of Atlantis. In *Recreations of a psychologist,* by G. Stanley Hall. New York: Appleton.
Hilgard, E.R. (1987). *Psychology in America: A historical survey.* San Diego, CA: Harcourt Brace Jovanovich.

Hobsbawm, E.J. (1975). *The age of capital: 1848-1875.* New York: Charles Scribner's Sons.

Horley, J. (2001). After "The Baltimore Affair": James Mark Baldwin's life and work, 1908-1934. *History of Psychology, 4*(1), 24-33.

James, W. (1890/1983). *The principles of psychology.* Cambridge, MA: Harvard University Press

James, W. (1892/1985). *Psychology: The briefer course.* Notre Dame, IN: University of Notre Dame Press.

James, W. (1902/1961). *The varieties of religious experience.* New York: Macmillan Publishing Company.

Karp, W. (2003). *The politics of war.* New York: Franklin Square Press.

McDougal, W. (1921). *National welfare and national decay.* London: Methuen.

McReynolds, P. (1987). Lightner Witmer: Little-known founder of clinical psychology. *American Psychologist, 42,* 849-858.

McReynolds, P. (1997). *Lightner Witmer: His life and times.* Washington, DC: American Psychological Association.
Menand, L. (2001). *The Metaphysical Club: A story of ideas in America.* London: HarperCollins.

Miller, G. A. (1983). Introduction to William James' *The principles of psychology.* Cambridge, MA: Harvard University Press.

Morawski, J.G. (1982). Assessing Psychology's moral heritage through our neglected utopias. *American Psychologist, 37,* 1082-1095.

Münsterberg, H. (1908). *On the witness stand: essays on psychology and crime.* New York: Doubleday Page.

Münsterberg, H. (1909a). *Psychotherapy.* New York: Moffat Yard.

Münsterberg, H. (1909b). *Psychology and the teacher.* New York: Appleton.

Münsterberg, H. (1913). *Psychology and industrial efficiency.* Boston: Houghton Mifflin.

Münsterberg, H. (1914). *The war and America.* New York: Appleton.

Münsterberg, H. (1916). *Tomorrow: Letters to a friend in Germany.* New York: Appleton.

Murchison, C. (1930/1961). *A history of psychology in autobiography,* Vol. 1. New York: Russell & Russell.
O'Donnell, J.M. (1985). *The origins of behaviorism: American psychology,*

1870-1920. New York: New York University Press.

Parke, R.D., Ornstein, P.A., Rieser, J.J., & Zahn-Waxler, C. (eds) (1994). *A century of developmental psychology.* Washington, D.C.: American Psychological Association.

Scarborough, E. & Furumoto, L. (1987). *Untold lives: The first generation of American women psychologists.* New York: Columbia University Press.

Scott, W.D. (1903). *The theory of advertising.* Boston: Small Maynard.

Shermer, M. (2002). *In Darwin's shadow: The life and science of Alfred Russel Wallace.* Oxford: Oxford University Press.

Skinner, B.F. (1948). *Walden two.* New York: Macmillan.

Sokal, M.M. (1971). The unpublished autobiography of James McKeen Cattell. *American Psychologist, 26,* 626-635.

Sokal, M.M. (1981). *An education in psychology: James McKeen Cattell's journal and letters from Germany and England, 1880-1888.* Cambridge, MA: MIT Press.

Spillman, J. & Spillman, L. (1993). The rise and fall of Hugo Münsterberg. *Journal of the History of the Behavioral Sciences, 29,* 322-338.
Strouse, J. (1980). *Alice James: A biography.* Boston: Houghton Mifflin Company.

Sulloway, F. (1996). *Born to rebel: Birth order, family dynamics, and creative lives.* New York: Pantheon.

Thorndike, E.L. (1898). Animal intelligence: An experimental study of the associative process in animals. *Psychological Review*, Monograph Supplement, *2*(8).

Thorndike, E.L. (1906). *The principles of teaching.* New York: A. G. Seiler.

Thorndike, E.L. & Woodworth, R.S. (1901). The Influence of improvement in one mental function upon the efficiency of other mental functions. *Psychological Review, 8,* 247-261, 384-395, 556-564.

Tweney, R.D. (1987). Programmatic research in experimental psychology: E.B.

Titchener's laboratory investigations, 1891-1927. In M.G. Ash & W.R. Woodward (Eds.) *Psychology in twentieth-century thought and society*. Cambridge: Cambridge University Press.

Tymoczko, D. (May 1996). The nitrous oxide philosopher. *The Atlantic Monthly*, pp. 93-101.

Washburn, M.F. (1908). *The animal mind: A text-book of comparative psychology*. New York: Macmillan.

Watson, J.B. (1929). Should a child have more than one mother? *Liberty Magazine*, 31-35.
Watson, R.I. (1978). *The great psychologists* (4th ed.). New York: J.B. Lippencott.

White, S.H. (2002). G. Stanley Hall: From philosophy to developmental psychology. In W.E. Pickren & D.A. Dewsbury (Eds.) *Evolving perspectives on the history of psychology*. Washington, DC: American Psychological Association.

Witmer, L. (1896). Practical work in psychology. *Pediatrics, 2*, 462-471.

Witmer, L. (1897). The organization of practical work in psychology. *Psychological Review, 4*, 116-117.

Witmer, L. (1915). *The Nearing Case*. New York: B.W. Huebsch.

Wozniak, R. H. (2001). Introduction, in *Selected works of James Mark Baldwin*. Bristol:Thoemmes Continuum, pp. v-xxxi.

CHAPTER 6: FREUD AND PSYCHOANALYSIS

You are probably aware that our cures are brought about through the fixation of the libido prevailing in the unconscious (transference), and that this transference is most readily obtained in hysteria. Transference provides the impulse necessary for understanding and translating the language of the ucs. [unconscious];where it is lacking, the patient does not make the effort or does not listen when we submit our translation to him. Essentially, one might say, the cure is effected by love.

SIGMUND FREUD TO CARL G. JUNG, DECEMBER 6, 1906 (MCGUIRE, 1974, PP. 12-13).

The simultaneous birth of the New Psychology in both Germany and the United States was not a coincidence. What quickly become two schools of psychology was soon augmented by a third school: Psychoanalysis. The creation of Sigmund Freud and his disciples, psychoanalysis was touted by Freud as a "new science," distinct from the New Psychology. Questions of the distinctiveness of psychoanalysis will be addressed shortly and in the final section of this chapter. Historically, Freud's work was embraced by a large number of psychologists as a school within the New Psychology. The work of Freud and his followers shaped the New Psychology as well as the public's views of both psychology and human nature. For these reasons, I consider the history of psychoanalysis as part of the history of psychology. Some treat psychoanalysis as a separate field from psychology and write internal histories of psychoanalysis, while others, with considerable justification given the impact that Freud had on certain branches of medicine (such as psychiatry and the study of psychosomatic illness), consider psychoanalysis to be part of the history of psychiatry (Shorter, 1997). Still, most psychologists consider him one of the most important figures in the history of our field. For instance, the great historian of psychology E.G. Boring listed Freud as one of the four most influential individuals in the history and pre-history of the field. The other three were Darwin, Helmholtz, and James (Boring, 1950). Over 50 years after Boring, psychologists still consider Freud one of the three most influential figures in the history of the field (Haggbloom, 2002).

The Renegade School

No approach to psychology has generated as much controversy or criticism as psychoanalysis. Psychoanalysis has been criticized as unscientific (Dawes, 1994) and pseudoscientific (Crews, 1998). Many of the criticisms relate to Freud's rejection of the careful experimental and observational methods being developed within the New Psychology. Freud did not reject scientific methods in other areas (before developing psychoanalysis he was a successful brain researcher); nor did he reject empiricism. Psychoanalysis was based on a different kind of empiricism, the empirical evidence generated by self-reflection and the clinical cases seen by Freud and his followers. This rejection of the accepted scientific practices in the New Psychology made Freud a renegade, the outlaw bad boy of the new psychology. William James, for example, knew of Freud's work from the mid-1890s onward and met him in 1909 at the Clark University Conference. James wrote that Freud's ideas "can't fail to throw light on human nature, but I confess he made on me personally the impression of a man obsessed with fixed ideas" (Hale, 1971, p. 19).

Freud's renegade status also resulted from the institutional context of psychoanalysis. Unlike the American and German schools of psychology which developed in universities, psychoanalysis developed outside of universities (the institutional context of the New Psychology) and outside of mental hospitals (the institutional context of psychiatry). Instead, the original institutional context of psychoanalysis was the office of the analyst in his or her private practice. The patient came to the office for the "talking cure," a treatment for emotional problems that were untreatable by existing methods within psychiatry. Psychoanalysis was both the therapy procedures used in the talking cure, as well as the theory of psychology that Freud and his followers built based on introspection, self-analysis, and the experience of therapy. The theory emphasized the role of the unconscious and can most accurately be considered a psychology of the unconscious.

Fin-De-Siècle Vienna

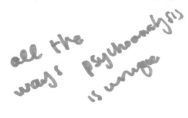

While the office of the psychoanalyst, often just called the analyst for short, was the institutional context of psychoanalysis, the city of Vienna and the Austro-Hungarian, or Hapsburg, Empire was the political and social context that gave birth to and shaped psychoanalysis. Vienna was the capital of the Hapsburg Empire, a multi-ethnic empire that included all of present-day Austria, Slovakia, Czech Republic, Hungary, Croatia, Serbia, Bosnia, Bulgaria, and Romania. Considered one of the six great powers of the world in the 19th century (the others being England, France, Germany, Russia, and the Ottoman Empire), the Hapsburg empire was in decline, falling behind England, Germany and France every day, and was soon to be surpassed by the U.S. All of the contradictions and conflicts of the long 19th century and the multiethnic Hapsburg Empire were played out in its capital and greatest city, Vienna.

The long 19th century had flowered and ripened and now seemed to be rotting to the intellectuals of the Hapsburg Empire. The age of empire was, it seemed, descending into chaos. Out of the chaos emerged many of the achievements associated with the first part of the 20th century and the last part of the 19th: the modern architecture of Adolph Loos, the philosophy of the Vienna Circle and of Ludwig Wittgenstein, the modern music of Arnold Schonberg, the modern paintings of Gustav Klimt and Oscar Kokoschka, and the school of psychology called psychoanalysis—meaning literally the analysis of the soul. In addition to the artistic, philosophical and scientific outpourings from turn-of-the- century Vienna, political and social movements grew like plants in a hot house. Hitler's fascism was born on the streets of Vienna. Herzl declared the program of Zionism there. And a unique form of socialism took root there, known as Austrian Marxism (Janik & Toulmin, 1973; Schorske, 1981).

It is a puzzle to the historian, and historians love puzzles, as to why Vienna in the last decade of the 1800s and the first two decades of the 1900s was such a center of human creativity. It was the fourth largest city in Europe, the capital of a diverse multiethnic nation with a vibrant café culture, a history of music and art, and an excellent university. All of these factors were of course important. It was also, however, the times. The acceleration of history and the end of an age were acutely felt by many. Some were willing to break with the past and create a bold new future. A spirit of personal and intellectual exploration pervaded the time and place, Vienna was a hothouse where new ideas, movements, and styles were born and bred. Out of this hothouse came psychoanalysis (Schorske, 1981).

Psychoanalysis

Freud used the term psychoanalysis in three interrelated senses: first, it was the therapeutic techniques he developed which form the basis for much of modern psychotherapy; second, it was a theory of psychology which applied to both normal and neurotic individuals, which he developed in conjunction with psychotherapy; and third, psychoanalysis refers to the movement Freud organized. The tight organization of this movement made psychoanalysis the most clearly defined of the first schools. Its lack of scientific methods also made it the most prone to splits and rivalries more characteristic of political movements than of science. In order to understand the history of psychoanalysis, we must understand it in all three senses (the therapeutic techniques, the theory, and the movement). Each of these three dimensions of psychoanalysis is closely tied to Freud's life and thought.

Freud's Life Before Psychoanalysis

Sigmund Freud (1856-1939) was born in Freiburg in the province of Moravia. His father, Jacob, was a merchant and his mother, Amalia, was Jacob's third wife (the previous two had died). Sigmund's mother was from Vienna and was only 20 when she married Jacob, who was 20 years her senior. Sigmund had older brothers from Jacob's previous marriages. He was the oldest of Amalia's seven children; Sigmund had five full sisters and one full brother (Gay, 1988).

At the age of four, the Freud family moved to Vienna after a brief move to Leipzig. Sigmund was the favorite child and was recognized by his parents as gifted. While the family lived a crowded apartment in the Leopoldstadt, the traditional Jewish neighborhood of Vienna, Sigmund was given his own small private room in which he could do his homework and read. The Habsburg Empire, in response to pressures that had emerged in the 1848 revolutions that swept Europe, slowly moved away from the autocratic monarchy that had existed for hundreds of years. The empire initiated limited reforms in the 1860s, including greater freedoms for Jews. The Jewish residents of Vienna still faced considerable prejudice and restrictions (the word anti-Semitism had not yet been coined), as did most citizens of the Empire. While political parties developed and freedom of the press spread, only about 6% of adult males could vote by the mid-1870s when Freud started his university studies. Still, the 1860s and 1870s were times of opportunity for the Jewish citizens of the Empire. They could at last attend university and enter the professions of law and medicine (Gay, 1988). Later on Jews would be allowed access to other professions, such as university teaching and journalism, but at the time Freud started college, these professions were closed to him by law.

Sigmund was a talented and hardworking student in his gymnasium, the college-preparatory high school from which all university students in the German-speaking world were required to have graduated. He graduated first in his class. As a high school student he developed a deep love of books; reading and collecting books were his chief hobbies (Gay, 1988). In his last year at the gymnasium he changed his career plans from law to medicine, in part after reading about Darwin's work which he later said "strongly attracted" him (Sulloway, 1983).

Freud started college in the fall of 1873 at the University of Vienna. In May of 1873 a stock market crash in the Empire lead to widespread bankruptcies and bank failures. The harsh economic consequences of the failure were blamed on the Jews (who in fact had absolutely nothing to do with it given their general poverty and exclusion from society; they suffered as everyone else in the Empire). Those who had complained earlier of a "Jewish Invasion" of Vienna now launched anti-Semitic attacks on Jews in the press. Given the outpouring of hate, Sigmund became more conscious of his identity as a Jew and the barriers in society to his career ambitions (Gay, 1988).

At the time Freud started at the University of Vienna, the university was the finest in the Empire and one of the best in the world. The normal course of study for a medical student lasted five years. Freud, however, took eight years to graduate. It was not the case, as sometimes happens with American students, that he changed majors and failed to complete classes. Freud was not really very interested in practicing medicine: He wanted to be a scientist who studied biology. In his first year he enrolled in an elective course with Carl Claus, one of the leading experts on evolutionary theory in the German-speaking world. He also enrolled in classes with Ernst Brücke (1819-1892), one of the leading neurophysiologists in Europe and one of the band of materialists, along with Helmholtz, that had sworn to banish vitalism from biology (see Chapter 3). Brücke soon became Freud's advisor and friend. Freud referred to him as a father figure and named one of his sons after him—Freud had a habit of naming his children after people he admired deeply, as we shall see. Freud soon began carrying out research under both Claus's and Brücke's direction. From 1876 to 1882 (while still a student) he published six scientific papers. Two of the papers dealt with the neuroanatomy of a species of primitive fish, one detailed the gonadal structure of the eel (eels are bisexual, changing from females to males during their life-cycle), one was a study of the nerve cells of the crayfish, and one of the papers detailed a new procedure for staining nerve cells for examination under the microscope (Sulloway, 1983). Freud's record of scientific achievement as a student established his reputation as an enormously promising scientist.

In addition to his medical school courses and his work in the labs of Claus and Brücke, Freud took three and a half years of elective courses with the philosopher Franz Brentano (see Chapter 3). Brentano published his major work, *Psychology from an Empirical Standpoint,* in 1874 soon after Freud started college. Brentano emphasized that psychology had to be dynamic: that is it had to emphasize motivation, that there was a distinction between objective reality and subjective reality, and there was an unconscious that operated in human thinking. All of these ideas would later be developed and elaborated by Freud in his work (Fancher, 1990; Sulloway, 1983).

In spite of Freud's enormous success as a young scientist, his prospects for a decent job were not good. In addition to the existing barriers to Jews, Brücke had two able research assistants who were slightly older than Freud. Finally, young scientists made little money and Freud was anxious to marry his fiancée, Martha Bernays. In 1882 Brücke took Freud aside and pointed out the financial problems he would face. Reluctantly, Freud took up the practice of medicine. This was not the end of his research in neurophysiology, however. He continued to carry out research and publish over the next 15 years on staining techniques for neurons, the structure of the medulla oblongata, the structure of nerve cells in crayfish, cerebral paralysis in children, and aphasia. In addition, he translated works on hypnotism from French to German by such leading psychiatrists as Jean Martin Charcot (1825-1893) and Hippolyte Bernheim (1840-1919). Freud was by the age of 40 (in 1896) a respected, if somewhat controversial, researcher.

The controversy stemmed not from his work in neurophysiology, but from his experiments with cocaine. Freud discovered (but was scooped by one of his colleagues) that cocaine can be used as topical anesthesia in eye surgery. He then went on to study other possible uses of cocaine. In the process he used it himself regularly and prescribed it to others. Freud never became addicted to cocaine himself, although he used it on a regular basis for over 10 years (it is a little-known fact that not all cocaine users become addicted) but several of the people for whom he prescribed it for did in fact become addicts (Sulloway, 1983).

Freud's research activities were in addition to his full time job as a physician and lecturer at the University of Vienna. Starting in 1882 he spent three years working intensely at Vienna General Hospital, the best hospital in the Empire. During his residency he spent three months in the surgery unit, six months in internal medicine, five months in psychiatry, three months each in dermatology and ophthalmology, and 14 months in nervous diseases. During this time he worked with Theodore Meynert (1833-1892) who was considered the greatest psychiatrist and brain anatomist in the Empire. Meynert was so impressed with Freud that he invited him to carry out research in his lab, which Freud did from 1883 to 1886. Freud's record of achievement led to his nomination as an assistant professor in the medical school in 1885, a nomination that was supported by both Brücke and Meynert. During this time Freud also became famous as a diagnostician—he could pinpoint areas of the brain that had been damaged by stroke or accidents based on the symptoms of the patient (Sulloway, 1983).

In 1885 Freud won a prestigious fellowship to study in Paris with Jean Martin Charcot. Freud spent 20 weeks on the fellowship from the winter of 1885 to the spring of 1886. Most of this time was spent with Charcot in Paris (Alfred Binet was at the time working for Charcot). Charcot was the one of the leading neurologists in Europe and one of the major proponents of hypnotism, which he used to treat hysteria (see Chapter 3). Freud was deeply impressed with Charcot. Like Freud, Charcot was multilingual and spoke German, English,

Spanish, and Italian, in addition to French. Like Freud, Charcot was very well-read. Freud fell under Charcot's spell and later named his first-born son after him. Freud was not able to carry out his research in Paris; the facilities were not as advanced as in Vienna and he had little personal contact with Charcot, who had students from all over Europe vying for his attention. So as a way to work directly with Charcot, Freud proposed to translate his works into German from French. Charcot liked the idea and the German edition (translated by Freud) of Charcot's book, *New Lectures on the Diseases of the Nervous System, Particularly on Hysteria*, appeared in 1886 slightly before the French edition reached the bookstores (Sulloway, 1983).

Freud returned to Vienna a convert to Charcot's theory of hysteria and to the use of hypnotism. When he began his private practice shortly afterwards in nervous diseases, he used hypnotism in addition to the other commonly used remedies at the time: bed rest, hot baths, and shock treatments. Freud's support for Charcot's theories also alienated some of his support in Vienna. The Viennese medical establishment was skeptical of some of Charcot's work, and with good reason. As it turned out, some of Charcot's dramatic demonstrations were the result of the influence of hypnosis on the suggestible patients (Sulloway, 1983).

It was as a practicing neurologist that Freud, in conjunction with his friend and mentor Josef Breuer, developed the "talking cure," the basis for much of subsequent psychotherapy. Josef Breuer (1842-1925) was fourteen years Freud's senior. Like Freud, he was from a Jewish family, had been educated at the University of Vienna, and was a student of Ernest Brücke. In fact, the two had met in Brücke's lab in 1877. Breuer was in general medical practice and saw a variety of patients. During the first 10 years after getting his medical degree he was a part-time assistant professor (a Privatdozent) at the University of Vienna, but after failing to be promoted he devoted full time to private practice (Sulloway, 1983).

Like Freud, Breuer was a highly accomplished researcher. He published around 20 scientific papers in his lifetime; the papers reported on his careful and clever scientific studies. Among the papers were two important discoveries: the first was the discovery, along with one of his teachers, the famous Ewald Hering, of the mechanism that controls breathing via the vagus nerve.

This mechanism is now known as the Hering-Breuer Reflex. His second discovery (along with the physicist and physiologist Ernst Mach, for whom the speed of sound is named and the chemist A. Crum Brown) was of the function of the semicircular canals in the ear in controlling balance and posture. Breuer was such a skilled and respected physician that many of the scientists and physicians in Vienna went to him as their personal or family physician, including Brücke himself. Breuer was also respected for his insightful mind and fascinating conversation. He had a lengthy correspondence with Franz Brentano and others. Breuer was also widely respected as a warm and generous person. He referred many clients to Freud and even loaned Freud money when he was starting his private practice (Sulloway, 1983).

Freud began using hypnotism in the mid to late 1880s with his patients, in part at the urging of Breuer. Breuer had treated a case of hysteria (he did not see many of these cases, unlike Freud who frequently treated hysteric patients in his practice) from December 1880 to June 1882. This case, named the case of Anna O. in Breuer's later published account, is one of the most famous clinical case studies in the history of psychology. Anna O., whose real name was Bertha Pappenheim, presented a number of hysterical symptoms, including intermittent paralysis of various parts of her body, disturbed vision and movement, delirium, and multiple personalities. She would at times lose her ability to speak German and much of the therapy was carried out in English (like Freud, Breuer was also multilingual). When her hysteria was at its worst, Anna O. would have hallucinations about events that had happened to her exactly one year earlier, a fact Breuer corroborated using the diary of Anna's mother (Sulloway, 1983).

To treat her, Breuer would place Anna O. in a hypnotic trance each day and have her recount her hallucinations. Bringing to consciousness her hallucinations helped to relieve, temporarily, her symptoms. Because the relief of symptoms was based on her talking about what had happened to her, Anna O. dubbed it "the talking-cure." Breuer called the process of bringing the thoughts and memories to consciousness catharsis, after the Greek concept of catharsis or relief of emotions (Sulloway, 1983).

Anna O.'s cure was never complete (she suffered some symptoms for a number of years after treatment ended) but she made substantial progress and was able to function reasonably well. Later on in the late 1880s she became an important leader of the women's movement and one of the founders of the field of social work. She worked with orphans and unwed mothers and led struggles against prostitution and white slavery (Sulloway, 1983).

Freud, who had a large number of patients suffering from hysteria, adopted Breuer's talking cure, and with experience started to modify and experiment with it. He discovered that he did not need to hypnotize patients; he could place his hands on the patient's head to induce catharsis. Later, he would dispense altogether with hypnosis and replace it with free association in which the patient talks about whatever enters awareness in conjunction with dreams, actions, or memories (Sulloway, 1983).

Breuer and Freud collaborated on a book published in 1895, *Studies on Hysteria* (Breuer & Freud, 1895). Breuer wrote the introductory chapter and reported the case of Anna O. Freud contributed four case studies and the concluding chapter on treatment of hysteria. Hysterics, they argued, suffer from reminiscences and many of these reminiscences are linked to earlier psychological traumas. Hysteria is a kind of short-circuit in the brain, caused by these traumas, that leads to the intrusion of unpleasant memories into normal consciousness from the unconscious. Their theory of hysteria was influenced by current work in hysteria and by earlier work by Herbart, Fechner, and the materialist approach to physiology. The idea that earlier psychological traumas lead to later psychological problems became known as the Trauma Paradigm. The book was very well received and integrated detailed, gripping case studies with a physiological theory of hysteria and a new treatment approach (Sulloway, 1983).

The development of the talking cure by Breuer and Freud was not so much an invention as a re-invention. The original talking cure had been developed by Pinel and others in the late 1700s and early 1800s, as described in Chapter 3. While most of psychiatry and neurology had embraced a biological approach, and this was certainly the approach in which both Freud and Breuer had been trained, some residue of what had been called moral treatment still existed, especially in France. This approach had also integrated the use of hypnotism into clinical practice and was familiar to Charcot and others. Freud and Breuer re-invented a biopsychosocial approach to treating mental illness; an approach that integrated biology with the psychological history and development of the individual (Shorter, 1997). This approach was in opposition to a strictly biological approach to mental illness, an approach that while popular, especially among the public, had a number of weaknesses (as most practicing psychiatrists knew). Breuer and Freud re-established the biopsychosocial approach and advanced it by integrating detailed case studies, an advancement in treatment, and a psychophysiological model: the trauma paradigm.

The Roots Of Psychoanalysis In Biology And Medicine

Around the time that Breuer and Freud's book on hysteria was published, Freud broke his relationship with his mentor. While Breuer continued to give critical support to Freud and hold affection for his younger protégé his entire life, Freud ignored him (although in his writings Freud often gave credit to Breuer for the essential re-discovery of the talking cure and its cathartic effects). Freud would avoid going places where he might run into his old friend and if they met by chance on the street, Freud would lower his head and ignore the older man's greetings. While the reasons for the break are complex (and would later be distorted by Freud and his followers to make Freud look more original and heroic), the main issue was Freud's exclusive emphasis on the sexual nature of the early traumas that led to hysteria. Breuer and others argued that while some cases could be linked to sexual abuse, incest, or rape, not all cases had a sexual cause. While Breuer was very explicit about the role of sexual factors as a cause of hysteria in print and in public presentations, he was more cautious as a scientist and less willing to make radical claims, as was Freud who considered himself less a scientist and more a bold conqueror. Simply put, compared to Breuer's generous and critical nature, Freud was a fanatic about his ideas (Sulloway, 1983).

At the same time that *Studies on Hysteria* appeared in 1895, Freud was embarked on an ambitious theoretical project which he called psychology for neurologists. Later titled the *Project for a Scientific Psychology*, the draft manuscript was an attempt to elaborate a neurophysiological theory of neurosis, a problem Freud referred to as the choice of neurosis (that is, why does a patient have one symptom or neurosis as opposed to another), the role of sexual feelings in neurosis, and the problem of repression, that is, why certain memories, experiences, and emotions are kept out of consciousness or lost to consciousness (Sulloway, 1983). Freud never published the manuscript and destroyed all of his personal copies. An incomplete draft was preserved by Freud's friend and intellectual collaborator Wilhelm Fleiss and was later published after Freud's death (Freud, 1895/1956).

Wilhelm Fleiss (1858-1928) along with Breuer, was Freud's most important early collaborator. Freud corresponded with Fleiss from 1887 to 1902. Their close, some would say intimate, collaboration began around the time of Freud's break with Breuer in 1895 and lasted until the publication of Freud's *Interpretation of Dreams* in 1900. Fleiss lived in Berlin and was a physician who specialized in nose and throat disorders. Fleiss was also a researcher who had a deep interest in sex and biological cycles, what are now called biorhythms. While his work and relationship with Freud was later minimized or dismissed (indeed, many Freudians later characterized Fleiss as something of a nutcase), Fleiss had a significant impact on Freud, both as a sounding board for Freud's ideas and as a source of ideas and analysis. They exchanged letters frequently, shared drafts of their manuscripts with each other, and frequently meet face to face in what Freud liked to call their "congresses" to discuss ideas (Sulloway, 1983).

Fleiss was also interested in the relationship of the nose and smell with sexuality. He hypothesized that smell was linked to sexuality in humans, an evolutionary left-over from the role of smell in sexual behavior in many mammalian species. Fleiss' hypotheses were later to be partially supported with the discovery of pheromones in humans and the synchronization of ovulation in women who live together, due to pheromone signals (Sulloway, 1983).

Fleiss was a proponent of the idea of childhood sexuality and the bisexual nature of humans (and other animal species). Fleiss had amassed substantial support for the presence of spontaneous sexual behaviors in infants (as had other sexologists of the time, as we shall discover shortly) which he published in 1897, but which Freud read in draft form before that date. Fleiss also advocated the idea of bisexuality, following Darwin and other biologists. Using the phylogenetic principle accepted at the time that ontogeny recapitulates phylogeny (development "repeats" evolutionary history), Fleiss argued that originally humans are born with undifferentiated sexual desires, which develop later on into heterosexual adult passions. If the process of development is distorted, the individual could become homosexual or develop a variety of sexual neurosis. The notion of bisexuality is not so odd if you realize that during prenatal development humans have both male and female reproductive organs, as do other mammalian species. Finally, Fleiss advocated the concept of the id, the unconscious part of the mind that contains biological instincts and repressed sexual passions (Sulloway, 1983).

Freud and Fleiss both were extremely knowledgeable about sexology and the work of the leading sexologists of the time. Sexologists study human sexual development and behavior, including the development of heterosexuality and homosexuality, sexual disorders such as frigidity and impotence, and sexual neurosis such as sadomasochism and fetishes. The pre-eminent sexologist of the time was Richard von Krafft-Ebing (1840-1902). Krafft-Ebing had selected psychiatry as his medical specialization while taking a medical school course with Wilhelm Griesinger, the founder of the modern biological approach to psychiatry. Krafft-Ebing's detailed study of sexual pathology, *Psychopathia Sexualis*, was published in 1886. In 1889 Krafft-Ebing moved to Vienna to join the medical school faculty at the University of Vienna. There he was on very good terms with his younger colleague Sigmund Freud, to whom Krafft-Ebing frequently gave autographed copies of all of his works. Freud read these works carefully. Krafft-Ebing was also one of Freud's strongest supporters for promotion to associate (Extraordinary) professor (Sulloway, 1983).

In addition to Krafft-Ebing's work, Freud carefully read the work of psychiatrist and sexologist Albert Moll (1862-1939) who, like Freud, had studied with Charcot and Bernheim and knew Binet and Meynert. Freud also studied the works of and corresponded with Havelock Ellis (1859-1939). In addition to Krafft-Ebing and Moll, Ellis was the third of the three great sexologists of the last half of the 19th century and the first half of the 20th century (Sulloway, 1983).

The *Project for a Scientific Psychology* was abandoned: Freud felt that too little was known about the structure and function of the brain to develop a theory of neurosis that would also integrate the phenomena of repression and the significance of sex. In turning away from a neurophysiological theory (he in fact incorporated a number of physiological concepts in his work throughout the rest of his life), he did not abandon biology. Instead, he turned to Darwin's *amazing how important this was*

theory of evolution, especially the notion of the past as key to understanding the present and the fact of ontogeny recapitulating phylogeny, to develop a comprehensive psychological theory that would integrate the research on sex and sexual instincts (called libido by the sexologists), the unconscious, and the development and cause of neurosis into a single theory. Noting the similarities between hallucinations, hysterical symptoms, and dreaming, Freud argued that the analysis of dreams and other behaviors can provide therapists and scientists with data about the individual's unconscious, especially about the events or developments that produced the neurosis. He began to ask subjects to report on their dreams and analyze their own dreams using free association. He also began a self-analysis using his own dreams and free association in the summer and fall of 1897 (Sulloway, 1983).

In a period of a few years, Freud synthesized a new psychological theory of both normal and neurotic functioning using ideas from neurophysiology, evolutionary biology, the sexologists, and his own clinical treatment of neurosis. This synthesis was worked out in a series of books. The first of these was *The Interpretation of Dreams* (1900), followed soon after by *The Psychopathology of Everyday Life* (1901), *Jokes and their Relation to the Unconscious* (1905a), and *Three Essays on the Theory of Sexuality* (1905b) and several important case studies. A new school of psychology was born: one that emphasized the unconscious, that was inspired by evolutionary and neurophysiological concepts, and was connected to a unique form of clinical treatment of neurotic patients. While the theory changed and evolved over time, in part as a result of Freud's collaborators and critics, the basic structure of the theory remained unchanged (Sulloway, 1983).

The Structure Of Psychoanalysis   3 parts

Psychoanalysis as Freud developed it consisted of three interrelated fields: the psychotherapy practices that Freud developed to treat neurosis; the psychological theory of human nature he developed in conjunction with the therapy practices; and an organized movement dedicated to advancing and developing the practice and theory.

While Freud later set down guidelines for the therapist (called the analyst by Freud) to follow, his own treatment practices were very flexible and he violated most of his guidelines at one time or another. The patient was treated four or five times a week, usually for 55 minutes. Patients arrived at Freud's home (his offices were located in his family's apartment) at Bergasse 19 in a middle class neighborhood of Vienna near the university. They sat on a couch with Freud out of view in a stuffed chair that sat off to the side of the couch. There was no compelling reason for this arrangement. The couch was so patients could recline in a relaxed state and Freud was out of view because he could not stand people looking at him all day. Freud would sometimes analyze people for several years, but it was also the case that he would analyze people for very short periods. Freud would learn a great deal about his patients' personal histories and symptoms before starting the process of therapy. During analysis patients would free associate to dreams, to slips of the tongue or to their own actions. From time to time Freud would interpret these, but often it was the patient who did the interpretation. Sometimes Freud said little; other times he would say a great deal. Sometimes he would give his patients a book *CBT!* to read or make suggestions about articles to read. He would also give them advice about major decisions they were making (*e.g.*, whom to marry, whether they should get a divorce or have an affair) or practical concerns, such as how to use birth control. Sometimes he told patients about his own life. Sometimes he invited patients to a family dinner or to meetings of the psychoanalytic society. On occasion Freud would analyze both members of a couple. He even analyzed his daughter Anna.

Many of Freud's actions as a therapist would be considered unethical today. *wouldn't be possibly not* Unlike modern therapists, Freud was only slightly interested in relieving his patients' suffering. Instead, Freud's approach was intellectual—he wanted his patients to discover the truth about themselves and gain insight into why they acted, felt, and thought the way they did. While he tried to relieve their symptoms and suffering, the primary goal was self-understanding (Roazen, 1975).

Freud emphasized several important dynamics that occur during treatment. First, the patient often transfers feelings they had for someone else onto the analyst during treatment. This transference can be used by an analyst to help the patient explore unconscious motivation. Likewise, Freud warned of the problem of counter-transference. Counter-transference occurs when the analyst or therapist transfers his or her own feelings for someone else onto the patient. In addition to transference and counter-transference, the patient will often show resistance to the effort to understand his or her unconscious motivations. This resistance also has meaning and can be used to help the patient gain greater insight. For Freud, transference, counter-transference, resistance, dreams, behavioral or verbal slips (parapraxis), and symptoms all had meaning and could be used by the analyst and patient to gain an understanding of the unconscious (Sulloway, 1983).

A Cure Through Love—The Practice Of Psychotherapy

Writing to Carl Jung in 1906, Freud said that psychoanalysis (meaning psychotherapy) was essentially "a cure through love." This remark shows how far Freud had come in the development of therapeutic technique. Freud did not explicitly publish on his new technique until he produced a series of papers from 1911 to 1915. While his close collaborators knew about the technique and many hints appear in his case studies of the Rat Man and Little Hans, these papers represent his first full statement of technique and how it had evolved.

Freud traces the history of technique in his paper on "Remembering, Repeating, and Working Through" (Freud, 1914/1958) through three stages. The first stage was that of the talking cure developed by Freud and Breuer. This stage consisted of the use of hypnosis, suggestion, and catharsis (venting). The second stage developed from 1895 to 1905 when Freud published the disastrous Dora case (Dora herself was treated in 1900). This stage consisted of the use of free association, dream analysis, and interpretations by the therapist. Freud sought to uncover the unconscious thoughts and desires that produced the neurosis. The third stage emphasized the relationship between the patient and the therapist. Here, dream interpretation and free association were used as a somewhat limited tool. The therapist provided interpretations, but generally only as possibilities when the patient was close to discovering the truth for themselves (but still having trouble because of resistance). Most of the interpretations focused on the resistance that the patient experiences, the problems faced during self-exploration.

Freud did not publish the papers on technique in a logical order, but instead published them as he more or less finished them. It thus helps to think about them in their logical order, not their chronological order. The first paper in logical order is "Recommendations to physicians practicing psycho-analysis" (Freud 1912/1958). This is the basic introduction ("for dummies" so to speak) of what to do in therapy. The paper includes pieces of basic advice such as you should not take notes during a session and you should not disclose too much about yourself to your clients.

The second paper in logical order is "On the beginning of treatment" (Freud, 1913/1958). This paper is a mix of practical advice, such as how to talk about money and appointment times, and general guidelines such as where do the patient and therapist begin, when do you end treatment, and the importance of rapport between client and therapist. — relationshy

The third paper in logical order is "Remembering, repeating, and working-through (Freud, 1914/1958).

The fourth paper in logical order is "Observations on transference-love (Freud, 1915/1958).

The fifth paper in logical order is "The handling of dream-interpretation in psycho-analysis" (Freud, 1911/1958).

The sixth and final paper in logical order is a theoretical analysis of transference entitled "The dynamics of transference" (Freud, 1912/1958).

Freud's technique continued to evolve and he would return to some of the concepts later in his career. The new approach to therapy that he had developed did signal a turn in Freud's interest, away from a focus on the dynamics of desire to the dynamics of relationships: within this new focus, the concepts of transference and the unconscious relationship prototypes such as the father imago would hold pride of place.

So much for the practice of psychoanalysis. If Freud's only achievement had been to re-discover (along with Breuer) and develop psychotherapy he would be justly remembered as the father of psychotherapy. But Freud developed a psychological theory as well. Crucial to his theory was the use of therapeutic techniques such as free association, dream analysis, and the analysis of parapraxis to explore the instinctual unconscious which, following Fleiss, he called the id. Freud integrated a great deal of the work of the sexologists into his theory and clinical practice. Many of his patients' problems were associated with, in Freud's view, sex. Freud's theory and clinical practice rested on certain general principles he adopted from the evolutionary biology and neurophysiology of the time. It is for this reason that some historians (e.g., Sulloway, 1983) call Freud a crypto-biologist (a "hidden" or secret biologist) and Ernest Jones called Freud the Darwin of the mind (Sulloway, 1983).

The three basic biological assumptions that guided Freud's work were the idea of psychophysical energy (instinctual energy that drives personality and development), Lamarckian evolution (the idea that acquired characteristics could be transmitted through heredity or that past experiences could be preserved in the unconscious), and the biogenetic principle, the idea that we develop over time, that past developments shape the present, and that in our psychological development we re-capitulate our evolutionary history. It is because of these three guiding assumptions that Freud placed such emphasis on instincts, especially sexual instincts, on the role of early experience, and on psychological development. It was also because of these three guiding assumptions that Freud sought to explain both the development of mental illness and normal, healthy human development (Sulloway, 1983).

The Development Of Psychoanalytic Theory

Psychoanalytic theory was never a static and finished system. Freud responded to the ideas of his critics and his followers, and his thinking changed as a result of his own experience. But he insulated his theory from empirical refutation. Instead of carefully controlled experiments or observations, the proof of the theory was in the understanding of the analyst. This kind of empiricism (the empiricism of individual experience and personal introspection) was borrowed from Freud's philosophy professor Franz Brentano. It was a rejection of the experimental research Freud had carried out during the first part of his professional life. He also insulated his ideas from criticism by arguing that only those who had gone through therapy could judge the truth of his ideas (Hale, 1971). Freud sought to protect his ideas from real empirical investigation. In addition, he and his followers treated critics harshly by "psychoanalyzing" them (without having them in therapy) and demonstrating their mental illness, envy, and psychological problems. Thus, not only were empirical tests of Freud's ideas forbidden and only those who had undergone analysis considered legitimate commentators on the theory, but critics were portrayed as mentally ill and in need of therapy (Szasz, 1990).

sassy

230

Psychoanalysis And Karl Popper's Philosophy Of Science

Unbeknownst to most psychologists, the great philosopher of science Karl Popper (1902-1994) was influenced by psychoanalysis. The influence was negative: Popper reacted against psychoanalysis which he viewed as unscientific and irrational because no evidence of any kind could be used to disprove it. Popper's connection with psychoanalysis was personal and intimate.

We met Karl Popper in Chapter 1. He is one of the three or four most influential philosophers of science in the 20th century. Born in Vienna of Jewish parents, Popper grew up in Fin-de-Siècle Vienna and was 12 years old when World War I started. The war radicalized Popper and his generation and by the end of the war he was an anti-war socialist active in the politics of Red Vienna. The socialists were attempting to create a new society, a model of revolution without violence, and the theories of Adler (see below) and Freud played an important role in their politics and their debates. Popper knew Alfred Adler personally, spent considerable time at his home, and worked in one of his clinics. Popper liked Adler and thought he was kind, warm, and socially responsible. He read several of Adler's books (given to him by Adler himself) and accepted some of it, but he disagreed with other elements of Adler's thinking and after interrogating Adler closely, Popper seems to have broken off his relationships with Adler and his family (Hacohen, 2000).

Popper also read Freud's work and accepted some of it, such as the reality of the unconsciousness and the latent content of dreams. Further, Popper's family was connected to Freud in several ways. They were close family friends with some of Freud's early followers and were related to Joseph Breuer. Popper's father had a number of Freud's books in their original editions on his shelves and the Popper family vacationed with some of Freud's relatives. In spite of these close connections to Freud and the acceptance of some of his ideas, Popper was also critical of Freud's work. Freud could interpret a clinical case as an example of Freudian theory and Adler could interpret the same case as an example of Adlerian theory. Neither theory could be disproved. Neither theory could make predictions, only postdictions (after the fact explanations). Popper did not yet in the early 1920s articulate the idea of falsifiability as the demarcation between science and dogma, but his experience moved him in that direction (Hacohen, 2000).

Ater graduating from college Popper started graduate school at the University of Vienna, all the while remaining active in social reform and politics. His Ph.D. was in philosophy and psychology. His advisor was Karl Bühler, who had come to Vienna from Berlin where he had taken over for Oswald Külpe. Bühler had studied with Külpe at Würzburg. Popper's thesis, "On the Methodological Problem of Cognitive Psychology" examined the epistemology of different schools of psychology, including behaviorism and Gestalt Psychology. He defended his thesis in 1928. Popper's work in psychology set the stage for his later innovations in philosophy, innovations grounded in his understanding of psychology and his rejection of psychoanalysis (Hacohen, 2000).

The Psychoanalytic Movement

Psychoanalysis developed not only as a system of concepts and a therapeutic practice, it developed as an organized group with its own journals, training institutes, conferences, and national and international organizations. The story of these developments is also an important part of the history of psychoanalysis, and part of the reason for its success.

The organized psychoanalytic movement began modestly in the fall of 1902, when at the suggestion of Wilhelm Stekel, one of Freud's medical colleagues who had also been a patient, a group started to meet at Freud's home every Wednesday night to learn about psychoanalysis. Originally called the Wednesday Psychological Society, Freud invited others to join, including Alfred Adler. The discussions were lively and generally included the presentation of a paper. Following the presentation, coffee and cakes were served along with cigars and cigarettes, and a 15 minute social break. Then the discussion, often very animated, of the paper took place. The group grew and by 1906 had 17 members and an average attendance of 12. In 1907 they hired a secretary to keep minutes of their discussions and in 1908 formally constituted the group as the Vienna Psychoanalytic Society (Gay, 1988).

Freud had steadily gained a number of adherents not only in Vienna but throughout Europe and the United States. In 1908 the first International Congress of Psychoanalysis met in 1908 in Salzburg. Individuals from Vienna, Berlin, Zurich, Budapest, London, and New York attended and heard papers by

Freud, Jung, Adler, Ferenczi, and others. The first psychoanalytic journal was started at this congress with Carl Jung, a rising star in psychiatry and a new adherent to psychoanalysis as the editor. Freud next received an invitation to speak at the 20th anniversary celebration at Clark University, which he attended in 1909. His series of talks at Clark (see Chapter 5 and below) were both an honor and a significant achievement. The next international congress took place in 1910, at which an international organization was proposed, The International Psychoanalytic Association (IPA) was formed shortly afterwards with Jung as its first president (Gay, 1988).

caused

The IPA was essentially Freud's idea, and in getting the proposal accepted he antagonized a number of his followers. Freud had insisted that the presidency go to Jung, in part because he did not want psychoanalysis to be considered a "Jewish Science." Freud essentially named Jung as his successor in the movement. This antagonized a number of Freud's long-term supporters, including Stekel and Adler. Freud tried to placate his Viennese followers by resigning as the presiding officer of the Vienna Psychoanalytic Society and naming Adler in his stead. He also proposed a second journal, a monthly, to be edited by Adler and Stekel in Vienna (Gay, 1988).

The formation of the IPA started a series of events that culminated in a split between Adler and Freud in February of 1911. Twenty-five percent of the Vienna Psychoanalytic society left with Adler immediately; others were to follow. Adler developed psychoanalysis (both therapeutic practice and theory) in ways opposed by Freud, and called his variant of psychoanalysis Individual Psychology (which we will discuss later in the chapter).

The first split in the movement generated enormous hostility. And it was soon followed by a second split. Personal and theoretical differences between Freud and Jung had been growing. Near the end of 1912, Jung systematically presented his differences with Freud in a lecture series at Fordham University, in the U.S. The most important difference between Adler and Jung on the one hand, and Freud on the other, was the extent to which neurosis stemmed from current psychological or personal problems as opposed to childhood problems. Both Jung and Adler shifted emphasis away from childhood sexual conflicts (without ever totally abandoning them) as a cause for mental illness toward the present (Sulloway, 1983).

In 1912 Freud took the step of forming a secret committee to respond to the critics of psychoanalysis and control the movement he had created. The committee was composed of Freud and his closest supporters: Ernest Jones, Otto Rank, Karl Abraham, Sandor Ferenczi, and Hanns Sachs. In 1919 Freud added Max Eitingon as well. The existence of the committee was kept secret until 1927. Freud presented each member of the secret committee with a specially made gold ring mounted with a carved Greek gemstone from his collection of antiquities. From 1912 onward there were no more large scale defections from his movement, although numerous individuals left Freud's movement or were expelled (Sulloway, 1983; Gay, 1988).

Freud Comes To America

In September of 1909 Freud traveled to the U.S. to receive an honorary degree from Clark University for his contributions to the New Psychology. The president of Clark was G. Stanley Hall, one of the leading American psychologists. Hall wanted to organize a significant event to mark Clark's 20th anniversary as a university. He invited both Freud and Wundt, but Wundt was not able to attend because of a prior commitment—Wundt was to be a keynote speaker at the 500th anniversary of Leipzig University.

This was Freud's first and only visit to the U.S., but he was not a stranger to American psychologists and psychiatrists. While his work was virtually unknown to the U.S. public at large, as are most contemporary scientists and scholars, his work was well known to American psychologists and psychiatrists. In fact, American psychologists welcomed Freud's work more than any other group of psychologists (Hale, 1971). Part of the receptivity to Freud stemmed from the shared Darwinian heritage that shaped both Freudian Psychoanalysis (which the Americans considered part of the New Psychology) and American psychology. Part of the receptivity stemmed from the Americans' interest in the practical application of psychology. Those that opposed the application of the New Psychology, such as Titchener, were hostile to Freud. Those who favored the application of psychology such as James, Münsterberg, and Hall, were friendly to Freud's work (Hale, 1971).

Freud sailed from Europe with Jung and Ferenczi. The three amused themselves during the eight day voyage by analyzing each other's dreams. On the trip, Freud was pleased to discover his cabin steward reading a copy of *The Psychopathology of Everyday Life*. The three visitors from Europe spent a week in New York City with Ernest Jones, one of Freud's key followers in England who was teaching in Canada at the time, and A.A. Brill, a New York psychiatrist who was also a prominent advocate for Freud's work. After the week in New York the five traveled to Clark where Freud gave five lectures on psychoanalysis (Gay, 1988).

The lectures were composed by Freud during his morning walks with Ferenczi each day. He gave his lectures in German (almost the entire audience of psychologists and psychiatrists spoke German, so this was not a problem for them) and Hall later published an English translation as articles in the *American Journal of Psychology*, which he edited in book form as *Five Introductory Lectures on Psychoanalysis*. The lectures and discussions were also summarized in several major newspapers. Freud covered a range of topics, including dream interpretation and free association, therapy techniques, the unconscious, and sexual repression. He criticized restrictive sexual morals that produce a variety of neurotic symptoms and reviewed the evidence of infant and childhood sexuality. In general, his remarks were very well-received and generated interesting questions from the audience (Hale, 1971). At the 1909 Clark University conference many (but not all) of the distinguished guests posed for a group photograph. The photograph is a unique historical document showing the largest gathering of the founders of psychology in one place at one time (See figure 6.1).

James was dying of heart disease at the time of the conference but made the trip expressly to meet Freud, whose work he had been following carefully since 1894. James and Freud took a walk around campus to talk about psychology, but at one point James had to stop because of chest pains. Freud later commented on how much he admired James' courage in the face of death (Hale, 1971).

James was not entirely enthusiastic. Writing to Mary Whiton Calkins he expressed his hope that Freud would push his ideas to the limit so as to enrich functional psychology. He also voiced his suspicion that Freud was a regular hallucine (a person who suffers from hallucinations). To a colleague in Europe, James expressed a similar assessment of Freud's work, adding that Freud impressed him as "a man obsessed with fixed ideas." Part of James discomfort came from Freud's materialism, a materialism that excluded moral responsibility and freedom (Hale, 1971).

Others were much more enthusiastic. G. Stanley Hall and James Mark Baldwin had for some years argued that the repressive sexual morals of America were a cause of psychological and social problems. In Freud they found a champion. Psychiatrists were likewise impressed with the hope of psychoanalysis. Prior to Freud's visit, one of the leading psychiatrists in the U.S. had concluded in a major paper that psychiatric treatment based on the biological model was "simply a pile of rubbish" (Hale, 1971). Finally, James Jackson Putnam, America's leading neurologist and a professor at Harvard Medical School was convinced of the value of psychoanalysis and helped to found the American Psychoanalytic Association in 1911 (Hale, 1971).

After Freud's visit in 1909, his influence among American psychiatrists and clinical psychologists grew considerably. He also started to acquire a mass following among educated Americans. Freud had arrived.

Psychoanalysis And The Hero Myth: The Selling Of Sigmund Freud

Freud was many things: a traditional European gentleman, a very well educated and hardworking medical doctor and researcher, a charming conversationalist and gifted public speaker, a talented writer with a highly intelligent mind. But he was also vain and extraordinarily ambitious, and very intolerant of criticism of his ideas. These characteristics blend together in his development of psychoanalysis. One consequence of this blend is that Freud formed a secular (as opposed to religious) cult around himself to further his ideas and his career. This cult had several important mechanisms of control. First was the secret committee that dominated the psychoanalytic establishment and responded to Freud's critics. Second was the claim that the truth of psychoanalysis could only be judged in therapy by experienced psychoanalysts or their patients. Third was the attack on critics by portraying them as mentally ill (Sulloway, 1983; Szasz, 1990).

The three characteristics outlined above mark the sociological characteristics of a secular cult within science. There were also numerous psychological characteristics of a cult. Freud's followers always referred to him as

"The Professor" and celebrated his birthday. They frequently sent him gifts and almost all of them placed a photo of Freud in their home or office. Characteristic of a cult, they also exaggerated outside criticism and glorified their leader portraying him as a unique genius with special insights (Sulloway, 1983).

Part of Freud's control over his followers came from his enormous charm and intelligence. But that is not the whole story. Many also relied on Freud for their livelihood. Freud referred clients to them and they would often not be able to survive without those referrals. Freud also had treated many of them as his patients, or had his closest followers treat them as patients. Freud knew secrets about his followers that gave him enormous control over their lives. Freud would sometimes treat husband and wife separately, and get confidential information about his followers from their psychoanalysts (who were in treatment with Freud). Freud even approved marriages, divorces, and affairs of his followers (Sulloway, 1983; Roazen, 1975). All of these actions, clearly unethical for a therapist, constitute cult-like behavior. It is no wonder that a relatively large number of Freud's closest followers committed suicide rather than break openly with "The Professor."

One of the chief objectives of the secular cult surrounding Freud was the promotion of Freud and his ideas. This has led to a number of myths (false ideas commonly accepted as historic truths) in Freudian scholarship. Sulloway (1983) has documented 26 such myths and outlined their function. This list of 26 myths excludes specific cases of factual distortions, omissions, or biases which permeate Freudian hagiographies. Perhaps the greatest of these hagiographies (because it is also filled with extensive factual material as well) is Ernest Jones' three volume biography of Freud (Jones, 1953; Jones, 1955; Jones, 1957).

An interesting example of both these myths and factual distortions is provided by the case of Karl Kraus. Kraus was an influential writer, actor, and social critic who published a small but widely read magazine in Vienna, *Die Fackel* (The Torch). Freud and Kraus had corresponded with each other and had read each other's work. In 1910 a member of the Vienna Psychoanalytic Society presented a paper on Kraus and his mental illness. The Freudians claim that Kraus attacked them afterwards because he was upset by the paper. As

Szasz (1990) and others have shown, the paper on Kraus was actually an attempt to portray a critic as mentally ill. Kraus had first criticized psychoanalysis in 1908, criticizing both the theory of dream interpretations (one can never prove or disprove a Freudian interpretation) and Freud's use of case histories. Kraus especially opposed the psychoanalysis of great writers and artists, such as Leonardo Da Vinci, on the basis of secondary and incomplete information. Kraus viewed these as little more than character assassinations. Kraus eventually criticized Freud for other issues as well—for instance, Freud praised the Italian fascist Benito Mussolini (and sent him a gift) while Kraus was an early and fierce critic of both Mussolini and Hitler; Freud favored forced commitment of patients (sending them to a mental hospital without their consent) while Kraus opposed all forced commitment of patients; and Freud at first favored Germany and the Austro-Hungarian Empire's actions in World War I while Kraus opposed the war. All of the criticisms raised by Kraus were answered with psychoanalytic character assassination, both during Kraus's lifetime and after his death, in standard historical accounts by Freudians (Szasz, 1990). Freud and his followers did not care who they slandered or attacked, as long as it furthered their cause or prevented real or imagined damage to it.

The Great War And Red Vienna

On June 28th, 1914, Archduke Ferdinand of the Austro-Hungarian Empire was assassinated by a Serbian separatist. This was the match that started the fire of World War I, called the Great War by contemporaries, for no one had ever seen or imagined such a horrible conflict. Military and political leaders of the powerful European nations had been fearing or hoping for the war for several years, but when it came they were not prepared for the consequences. Within a month of the assassination, on July 28, the empire declared war on Serbia. On August 1, Germany (the empire's primary supporter) declared war on Russia (Serbia's primary backer). On August 3, Germany declared war on France (Russia's primary backer) and on August 4, Great Britain declared war on Germany (Britain was France's primary backer). The war soon stalled, with troops involved in long and bloody trench warfare in France and Belgium. Casualties mounted quickly from the use of modern weapons (machine guns and long range artillery) as well as the use of poison gas. At first the war generated enthusiastic mass support, but when the realities of war penetrated the euphoria, people quickly became disillusioned. One of the first signs of trouble was the massive Christmas Day rebellion (so-called by military historians) when on Christmas 1914 German, French, and English troops spontaneously stopped fighting, exchanged photos and names, played soccer, and sang Christmas carols together. More social breakdowns (from the point of view of the military and government leaders) were to follow.

Psychologists and psychoanalysts joined their respective government's war efforts. The war and its impact on American psychology will be discussed in the next chapter. Here we focus on the impact of the war and its aftermath on psychoanalysis. Two of Freud's three sons, Ernst and Martin, joined the military. A number of Freud's closest supporters also joined. Sandor Ferenczi, for instance, served in the Hungarian army (Gay, 1988) and Karl Abraham served as the chief psychiatrist with the German 20th Army Corps (Danto, 2005). Many worked with soldiers who had been physically or psychologically injured in the war. While Freud himself was 58 at the start of the war and was considered too old to serve, the experience of the war was to change both the practice and theory of psychoanalysis.

Around 1916, the military commands of several nations endorsed the use of psychoanalysis to treat what at the time was called "war neuroses" and what we now call Post-Traumatic Stress Disorder (PTSD). Abraham and others started to develop brief therapies, designed to get soldiers back to the front as soon as possible or to relieve their major symptoms (Danto, 2005).

During the Great War, revolution broke out in Russia as dissatisfaction with the war and the repressive policies of the Tsar produced widespread rebellion. During the revolution the Bolsheviks, under the leadership of Lenin and Trotsky, seized power. Renaming themselves the Communist Party of the U.S.S.R, they negotiated peace with Germany and took themselves out of the war. At approximately the same time (April 6, 1917) the U.S. entered the Great War on the side of Great Britain and France, after a long, covert effort by U.S. President Woodrow Wilson, to win over the American people (Karp, 1979).

The entry of the U.S. into the conflict turned the tide and spelled defeat for Germany and the Austro-Hungarian Empire. The ruler of Germany, Kaiser

Wilhelm II, abdicated the German throne on November 9, 1918 and a truce (the Armistice) was declared November 11. Austria (the Austro-Hungarian Empire no longer existed and had splintered into a number of different countries) declared itself a republic on November 12 with Vienna as its capital. The Austrian Republic was declared by a coalition of Austrian political forces, ranging from communist to very conservative pro-Monarchists. The future of the republic was unclear. Nor was the situation any clearer in other parts of central Europe. In Bavaria and Hungary, soviet republics were declared modeled after the soviets (councils) that formed the basis of the Russian revolution. In Germany and Italy revolutions broke out led by workers and intellectuals sympathetic to the Russian example. Within a year, the revolutions in Germany and Italy, and the Soviet Republics in Hungary and Bavaria were crushed, but the political future was still uncertain.

Austria was governed by a conservative political party, but Vienna was controlled by the socialists who had to struggle against both the conservatives on their right and Communist Party on their left. They carried out a series of economic and cultural reforms to turn Vienna into a "socialist experiment" which became known as Red Vienna. Within Red Vienna, the ideas of both Freud and Adler competed for popular support (Gruber, 1991).

Post-War Psychoanalysis

Freud's own thinking shifted as a consequence of the war. He became more pessimistic about human nature and began to examine the role of other instinctual drives besides sex as motives for human action, shifting focus to aggression. He also moved in a direction already suggested by followers or former followers: he began to pay more attention to the role of the ego and personality structure (Sulloway, 1983; Danto, 2005).

In the midst of the chaos near the end of the war, Freud and his followers organized an international congress to chart the future of the movement (and Freud always referred to psychoanalysis as a movement). The congress was held in Budapest on September 28, 1918 as the war was winding down. The previous international congress had been held in Munich in 1913, before the outbreak of war. The congress was much smaller than the one in Munich, with only 42 participants, mostly from the Central Powers. Official representatives of the German, Austrian, and Hungarian government were also present—governments were interested in the use of psychoanalysis for the treatment of veterans suffering from war neurosis (Gay, 1988).

Before the war Freud had argued that patients do not appreciate psychoanalysis unless they are charged a reasonable fee. Even at that time however, Freud had made a practice of treating 20% of his clients free or for nominal fees. The war and its consequent deprivations on the home front caused a shift in Freud's thinking. 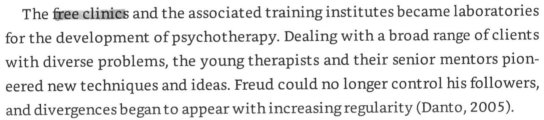 He now argued that psychoanalysis should be given free to those who need it or that the analysts should adopt a flexible fee approach, with the patient paying what he or she could afford. He also argued for the use of lay (*i.e.,* non-medically trained) analysts in conjunction with free treatment. Freud had encouraged a number of non-medical doctors to practice psychoanalysis before war, including his young protégé Otto Rank, who had a Ph.D. in literature. At the congress Freud called for the establishment of free clinics throughout Europe, in conjunction with training institutes for the training of additional medical and lay analysts. Free clinics were soon established in Berlin, Frankfurt, Vienna, and Budapest (Danto, 2005).

The free clinics and the associated training institutes became laboratories for the development of psychotherapy. Dealing with a broad range of clients with diverse problems, the young therapists and their senior mentors pioneered new techniques and ideas. Freud could no longer control his followers, and divergences began to appear with increasing regularity (Danto, 2005).

Freud also faced a string of personal tragedies. In 1920 his beloved daughter Sophie died from influenza, which swept through Europe at the close of the war, as well as his close friend Anton von Freund. In 1923, Sophie's son, a grandson whom Freud also loved a great deal, died; it was the same year one of Freud's favorite nieces committed suicide at the age of 23. Also in 1923, Freud was diagnosed with cancer. Freud turned increasingly to his youngest daughter Anna for support. She became both his closest collaborator and his caretaker. Freud's later work, focusing on Thanatos (the death instinct), aggression, and suicide also reflect his experiences at the time (Gay, 1988).

Freud's cancer went into remission from 1923 to 1936. In spite of his age (he turned 70 in 1926) and personal losses he remained active and worked regularly seeing patients, lecturing, and writing. He produced more in his 60s and 70s, in fact, than most people produce in a lifetime. His energy for psychotherapy diminished however and instead of the active, flexible approach he had used for much of his career as an analyst, he became increasingly passive during the therapy sessions (Roazen, 1975; Sulloway, 1983; Gay, 1988).

After the Great War Freud and psychoanalysis had achieved considerable respect within psychiatry and psychology, as well as growing public popularity. Freud became a household name, although most did not understand psychoanalysis. In 1930 he received the Goethe Prize, a significant German literary award, for his work. He was nominated a number of times for the Nobel Prize, but was passed over each time. This was a bitter disappointment to Freud, who had always coveted the Nobel Prize in Medicine (Gay, 1988).

Freud On Homosexuality: His Mature View

Throughout Freud's work, we see a series of overlapping interests. He would be interested in one topic for a long time, then shift to a new interest. For example, from 1895 to 1909 one of his interests was "the dynamics of desire" (Edmundson, 2007, p. 7). It was during this period that Freud developed his ideas on sexual abuse, libido, psychosexual development, and homosexuality (Freud, 1896/1989; Freud, 1905b).

While Freud's interest shifted away from the dynamics of desire after 1909, he never totally abandoned his interest in this topic and continued to revise his thinking. His views on homosexuality illustrate this quite clearly. By 1935 Freud no longer considered homosexuality an inversion (a specific kind of mental illness) but instead considered homosexuality a variant of healthy adult sexuality. This is clear from a letter he wrote, in English, to an American women who had written him about therapy for her homosexual son. Freud wrote:

"I gather from your letter that your son is a homosexual. I am most impressed by the fact that you do not mention this term yourself in your information about him. May I ask you why you avoid it? Homosexuality is assuredly no advantage, but it is nothing to be ashamed of, no vice, no degradation, it cannot be classified as an illness; we consider it a variation of the sexual function, produced by a certain arrest of sexual development. Many highly respectable individuals of ancient and modern times have been homosexuals, several of the greatest men among them (Plato, Mich-

elangelo, Leonardo da Vinci, etc.). It is a great injustice to persecute homosexuality as a crime—and a cruelty, too. If you do not believe me, read the books of Havelock Ellis"

(GAY, 1988, P. 610).

Freud goes on to argue that he cannot change the woman's son into a heterosexual through therapy, but he can help him achieve "harmony, peace of mind, and full efficiency" (Gay, 1988, p. 610).

Here Freud does not abandon his view that sexuality (both normal and perverted, both heterosexual and homosexual) results from a biopsychosocial process (Freud, 1905b). Homosexuality for Freud is not strictly biological, but then neither is heterosexuality. Homosexuality is a variant, not a choice, not a vice, not a disease, and not a degradation.

Freud And The Nazis—The Last Days

Throughout the 1930s, as the right gained control step by step in both Germany and Austria, Freud's followers started to flee. Many eventually immigrated to England and the U.S., while Freud simply refused to consider leaving (Roazen, 1975). The rise of fascism took place gradually. After the Great War and the defeat of the Communist uprising, the Germans established a democratic republic, known as the Weimar Republic. The republic was divided by intense social conflicts, but also opened up opportunities to many previously excluded groups, such as Jews, women, and homosexuals. Within this environment, a strong fascist movement led by Adolph Hitler gained popular support. After the depression of 1929 devastated the country, the Nazis (Hitler's political party) won seats in the German Parliament. In 1933 Hitler was appointed Chancellor (essentially a prime minister in a parliamentary system). Later that year the Nazis set fire to the parliament building (the Reichstag Fire) to provoke a political crisis. They blamed the fire on communists and socialists and established a one-party dictatorship. From 1934 to 1936 they passed an increasingly severe set of laws that denied people their political rights, increased Nazi control over the state, and targeted specific groups for repression. One of the main groups targeted were Jewish people. Similar events were taking place in Austria and in 1938, the Nazi party in Austria arranged for a vote on the question of the annexation of Austria by Germany, the Anschluss. Later that year, Germany and the German Nazi party took control of Austria.

When the Nazis established a one party dictatorship in Germany in 1934 they started burning books; Freud's books were burned in public bonfires in Berlin (Roazen, 1975). While many of Freud's followers started to leave central Europe, Freud himself resisted. There was still a large group in Vienna when the Nazis annexed the country (really an invasion welcomed by many of the right-wing Austrians). Influential friends immediately came to Vienna to protect Freud and his circle. Still, Freud did not want to leave. It was only after his daughter and collaborator Anna was taken into custody by the Gestapo that he agreed to leave. Through ransoms and political pressure, most got out, including Anna. Only one analyst was killed by the Nazis in Vienna. The others escaped, including Freud's wife and remaining children. Freud's four sisters all died at the hands of the Nazis (Roazen, 1975).

When Freud left continental Europe for England he took his art collection, consisting mostly of antiquities he had collected over the years, his books and much of the family furniture. Many of his personal papers and correspondence were destroyed by him during packing, although his daughter and others were able to save some of the personal papers (Roazen, 1975). This was the third time that Freud had systematically destroyed his personal papers, diaries, and correspondence. The first two times, in 1885 and 1907, he did so to cripple the work of future historians seeking to understand his work and to help create an image of himself as a genius and hero (Sulloway, 1983).

Freud and his family fled to London, where they settled (the home is now a museum). He was already suffering from cancer which had returned in 1936 and again in 1938. By the time Freud arrived in London he was in intense pain. Until the very end he refused almost all pain killers, including aspirin. In February 1939 his doctors declared his condition incurable. After undergoing numerous operations, including operations that left a large hole in his face, and radiation treatment, Freud prepared himself for death. He continued to see patients until the end of July. He also continued to read and write letters, but he stopped working on his last manuscript in September 1938. Visitors reported that he had become forgetful and lost his sharp intelligence. He and his doctors agreed that when Freud could not stand the pain anymore, the doctors would help Freud commit suicide. On September 21, 1939 he put the last book he was reading aside and spoke with his personal physician about their agreement. The doctor gave Freud opiates, promising Freud that he would respect his right to euthanasia. Freud took the opiates on the evening of September 22 and fell into a deep sleep. On September 23, 1939, he died. Freud left his library and antiquities to his daughter Anna and left the rest of his estate in a trust for his wife. Following his wishes, he was cremated and buried in London (Roazen, 1975).

Neo-Analytic Thought: Freud's Disciples And Apostates

Freud developed a third school of psychology; at times his followers even used the term Freudian Psychology to describe it. His school of psychology was not static and a number of significant members broke with him to found their own variants of psychoanalysis. While there are differences, we need to emphasize also the similarities—all of the followers and apostates (those who broke with Freud to start their own schools) shared the basic features of the talking cure, the genesis of modern psychotherapy. They also shared Freud's belief in the unconscious and they shared, some more than others, certain biological assumptions from Freud's theory. For that reason we can consider them variants of Freud's psychoanalysis, or as they are sometimes referred to, as neo-analytic psychology. It is a mistake, however, to reduce these psychologists to supporting actors in Freud's life story, as is often done in traditional histories of psychoanalysis. Each had a life before and after Freud. Each made significant contributions to psychology.

Alfred Adler And Individual Psychology

Alfred Adler (1870-1937) was born near Vienna, the second child in a family of seven children. He was a confident and outgoing child who loved to sing. When Alfred was four, a younger brother died of diphtheria and a year later Alfred himself almost died of pneumonia. As a consequence of these experiences, he decided at a young age to become a medical doctor. Later his parents sent him to the same gymnasium that Freud had attended. He was unhappy there and switched to a different school were he did better academically. After graduation in 1888 he enrolled at the University of Vienna to study medicine. Unlike Freud, who had also studied medicine at the University of Vienna, Adler was not interested in research and wanted to become a physician to help people. He took mostly required courses and never attended any of Freud's lectures, which were not required. He did however take a course from Krafft-Ebing on neurological disorders and read Krafft-Ebing's book on sexual deviation. After passing his first medical exams Adler served as a physician in the Austrian military for six months, and then worked at a free clinic for the poor in Vienna. He passed his second round of medical exams in 1894 and was awarded his MD in 1895, after which he continued to work at the free clinic and served another stint as an army physician.

nice guy [handwritten margin note]

In 1897 Adler feel deeply in love with a Jewish immigrant from Russia, Raissa Epstein. Raissa and Alfred were married in a traditional Jewish ceremony in December 1897. Raissa was a socialist and a feminist who would have considerable impact on Alfred and his work. Their relationship was sometimes stormy. She insisted, for instance, that Alfred do some of the child care, totally atypical of a Viennese man. Raissa also resented that she and other women had to stay at home while their husbands spent every evening at the cafes with male friends. Over the years they spent time apart. But Alfred slowly changed his actions at home. He started helping with the child care and permitted Raissa to work outside of the home as a translator. She was skilled at her job and had studied biology at the University of Zurich before moving to Vienna.

context [handwritten margin note]

When Alfred and Raissa married he was still poor and struggling with his career. In 1898 he opened a clinic in the Leopoldstadt neighborhood of Vienna. Many of his first patients came from a nearby Prater amusement park or from tailors and cobblers who experienced a variety of industrial illnesses. These workers suffered from illnesses related to unhealthy working conditions (cloth dust, airless workrooms) and depression. Adler's experience treating these patients and his research into their working conditions formed the basis for his first book, *The Health Book for the Tailoring Trade*. In this work Adler argued for model factories, improved worker housing, and fixed maximum working hours as measures that would substantially improve the physical and emotional health of workers.

Adler's work was leading him in two directions; the first was toward health education and public health policy, the second was toward psychiatry and mental illness. His growing interest in the second led him to attend Freud's lectures at the University of Vienna in 1899 and to read the *Interpretation of Dreams* when it was published in 1900. The two met in 1902 when Adler became a founder (and later a leading member) of the Wednesday Psychological Society, later re-named the Vienna Psychoanalytic Society. From Freud, Adler learned the fundamentals of psychoanalysis as a therapy technique.

Adler started to contribute papers to the Wednesday Psychological Society and from these papers grew his differences with Freud. His first major psychological monograph, *The Study of Organ Inferiority*, was published in 1907. This work, praised at first by Freud, suggested that sex is not the primary drive but that a number of drives are more or less equally important, including the drive toward aggression and the drive to overcome feelings of inferiority. Differences between Freud and Adler increased, as Freud viewed Adler's work as a threat to his concepts.

The differences between Freud and Adler were not just professional, but also political. In 1907, Raissa brought home two new friends recently escaped from Russia: Natalia Sedova Trotsky and Leon Trotsky. Leon Trotsky had been a leader of the St. Petersburg Soviet (Workers Council) and a key figure in the failed 1905 Russian revolution. He escaped prison camp and fled to Vienna, where he continued his political work. The Adlers and Trotskys took their children to the park together and Leon and Alfred frequently played chess together. Leon Trotsky later returned to Russia where he became one of the key leaders of the second Russian revolution and the founder of the Red Army. Adler became a confirmed Marxist under the influence of his wife and friends (he met Raissa at a socialist political meeting, suggesting that he had already become a socialist in college) and a feminist. Freud, on the other hand, was a liberal and a traditionalist. Freud was especially upset by Adler's interest in Marxism.

Their growing differences were exacerbated by Freud's proposals for the International Psychoanalytic Association (IPA). Soon after its founding Adler and Freud broke publicly in early 1911 (see above). Adler soon started his own group, organized around a weekly discussion group in his home that included Raissa. Initially calling themselves the Society for Free Psychoanalytic Study, Adler re-named the group the Society for Individual Psychology to reflect changes in his approach. Adler's theory is still called Individual Psychology to this day. Shortly after his break from Freud, Adler published *The Neurotic Constitution*, a book that influenced clinical psychology and psychiatry everywhere. In this work Adler argued that the drive toward mastery (being competent) is fundamental, that human beings have goals and that these goals differ from individual to individual, and that we all develop ideas ("guiding fictions" Adler called them) that give our life meaning. In addition, Adler was developing a number of important therapeutic techniques. Early on, he broke with Freud's practice of having the patient lie on a coach with the analyst in a chair out of sight. Adler faced his patients and both sat in comfortable chairs. Around the time of his break with Freud he started to assign his patients homework, asking that they act for a week "as if" they were the kind of person they wanted to be. Such homework assignments were a dramatic innovation in clinical practice. Other such techniques were to be developed by Jung and other neo-analysts once they broke with Freud.

CBT

G. Stanley Hall was familiar with Adler's work and started to correspond with him after Freud and Adler broke. Hall started to publicize Adler's ideas within the U.S., just as he publicized the work of Freud and Jung. Around this time Hall also broke with Freud over the question of the primacy of sex in neurosis and child development. Freud perceived the criticism of supporters such as Hall and the defections of Adler and Jung as threats to the success of himself and his ideas. He responded by writing a "history" of psychoanalysis that presented his side of the controversy and attacked his critics. He referred to the history as "the bomb" and not only presented a biased account of the history of psychoanalysis, but included character assassinations of Adler and Jung.

Adler had learned from Freud much about promoting and disseminating ideas in psychology. Adler's books include material from literature, religion, and philosophy, in addition to psychology. His weekly meetings of the Society for Individual Psychology were patterned after the Vienna Psychoanalytic Society. Adler started a journal as well to publish and develop the ideas of the society.

The Great War disrupted Adler's work, as he and many of his followers were drafted into the army. At the same time, Adler, who had applied for a teach-

how these men became who they are context

ing position at the university, learned that he was rejected for the job. To make matters worse, his wife and children who had been visiting Russia were trapped by events and could not return to Vienna for some time.

Adler hated military duty during the war and loathed the way soldiers in the hospital were treated by the military command. But he also started to develop and modify his ideas. During the war his influence continued to spread with the translation and publication of his work in the U.S. and other countries.

With the end of the war and the proclamation of the Austrian Republic in November of 1918, Adler's position in society changed dramatically. Raissa and Alfred became involved with the Social Democratic Party, soon to win control of Vienna and create Red Vienna. At the same time they also broke with Trotsky, their old friend, and criticized the violence of the Russian Revolution. Adler became a frequent teacher at the People's Institute (an educational institute for the working class of Vienna). A warm, engaging speaker known for his brilliance and charm, he became actively involved with training teachers (and later parents) in how to deal with problem children.

In 1920 he published an explication of his theory and by 1923 he became a regular lecturer in Europe and the U.S. International conferences for Individual Psychology were organized in 1922 and 1925. In 1929, Adler made the decision to move to the U.S. Raissa refused to leave and so the couple spent most of the next six years apart, save for summer visits that Adler fit into his work schedule. (Like Freud, Adler was an extreme workaholic, often working 12 to 18 hours a day). Adler's lectures were popular and his book *Understanding Human Nature* (a presentation of his theories for the public) became a best seller in the U.S. His success made him a very well-to-do person. Unlike Freud, he did not create a cult around himself, permitted dissent, and did not criticize people who disagreed with him. While he is not as well-known as Freud, his contributions were substantial.

In addition to the innovations in therapeutic practice that have been discussed previously, Adler developed a number of important ideas. He stressed that therapy was a kind of re-education and that prevention was as important (if not more important) than a cure. He and his collaborators developed a number of child-rearing techniques, such as the practice of logical consequences which have proven very effective. He and his collaborators also pioneered parent education classes.

In addition to the ideas of the inferiority complex and the drive for competence, Adler developed ideas about the role of birth order in the development of personality and the role of social interest in mental health.

Adler's health began to decline (he suffered from heart disease) and the political situation in Germany and Austria was worsening. When the socialists in Vienna were suppressed in 1934 by pro-Nazi Austrians, Raissa was put in jail for a short time. Fearing for her life, Albert finally persuaded her to come to the U.S. Adler's health continued to decline but he would not stop working long hours, and on an international speaking tour he died suddenly of a heart attack in Aberdeen, Scotland, on May 28, 1937, at the age of 67. Raissa outlived her husband by 25 years and several of their children became successful and influential psychotherapists.

Adler's death was reported worldwide, and many mourned his passing. One exception was Freud. When one of Freud's followers wrote to "the Professor" about how he was moved by the news of Alder's death, Freud wrote back: "I don't understand your sympathy for Adler. For a Jew boy out of a Viennese suburb a death in Aberdeen is an unheard-of career in itself and proof of how far he had got on. The world really rewarded him richly for his service in having contradicted psychoanalysis" (quoted in Roazen, 1975, p. 209). Freud, it seems, never forgave those who competed with him for influence or disagreed with his ideas. It is perhaps Adler who has the last laugh however: while Adler's name is less well-known to students of psychology, his influence has been, one could argue, as great as that of Freud's. Certainly some of Adler's concepts such as birth order, the inferiority complex, and his ideas on child rearing and parent education, have proven fruitful. In addition, modern psychotherapy is much closer to Adler's work than it is to Freud's. Finally, Adler influenced a number of clinical psychologists, including Viktor Frankl, who survived the concentration camps and went on to develop logotherapy, Carl Rogers, the developer of client-centered therapy and an innovator in the field of clinical psychology (we shall learn more about Rogers in Chapter 13 on the history of clinical psychology after World War II), and Abraham Maslow, one of the founders of humanistic psychology (also described in Chapter 13).

Carl G. Jung

Carl Gustav Jung (1875-1961) was born in Switzerland. His father was a minister and his grandfather, after whom he was named, was a famous medical school professor at the University of Basel. At the age of 11 he moved from the rural area where he had grown up to the town of Basel to attend school. Jung was often sick as a child; there is some evidence that his illnesses were psychosomatic, a result of the conflicts between his parents and his mother's emotional problems. He was also a very bright and studious child who read a great deal. One of Jung's first interests was religion, but he was very skeptical of the established religions and rarely attended his father's services. He had many questions and doubts about religion and read widely in search of answers. By the time he graduated from secondary school he was first in his class. He had read extensively works by Greek and German philosophers. The philosopher that influenced him the most was Schopenhauer (Hall & Nordby, 1973).

After graduation, Jung was uncertain which area of study to pursue. He was interested in comparative religion, philosophy, science, and archeology. Limited funds prevented him from going to any school other than the University of Basel, which did not have a program in archeology. Relatives discouraged him from studying religion, so he finally settled on science. After beginning college he realized that he could study medicine, an area that appealed to him because of his personal experiences with illness (Hall & Nordby, 1973).

Jung's father died suddenly a year after he started college, leaving his family in poverty. Jung got financial support from a well-to-do uncle and worked at the college to finish his studies and help support his family. He could not decide what area to specialize in but finally selected psychiatry after reading one of Krafft-Ebing's books on the field. During college, Jung carried out experiments with a medium who claimed to channel another person. He also continued to read extensively in medical school. For his doctoral dissertation (medical doctors in the German system are required to carry out a piece of original research, the doctoral dissertation; in the U.S. system medical doctors are not required to complete a doctoral dissertation, only Ph.D.s are required to do so) he wrote up the results of his studies of the medium (Hall & Nordby, 1973).

When Jung selected psychiatry as his field, psychiatry was not well respected. He was successful however in getting a job at one of the most important mental hospitals in Europe, the Burgholzli Mental Hospital in Zurich. Jung began work in December of 1900. The director of the hospital was Eugen Bleuler, a psychiatrist famous for his treatments of psychotics and for his discovery of schizophrenia. Jung had read *Studies on Hysteria* in medical school and read *The Interpretation of Dreams* when it was published in 1900. Jung thrived at the Burgholzli and in 1905 he was appointed lecturer in psychiatry at the University of Zurich. He also developed a private practice, using many of the techniques of psychoanalysis (Hall & Nordby, 1973).

Jung followed Freud's work closely from 1900 onward. He also carried out his own studies of the severely mentally ill at the hospital, studying the content of their symptoms and developing and testing a word association test designed to uncover the presence of unconscious mental complexes in the patient. The research on the word association tests won Jung wide respect within the psychiatric profession. He also published his first book on schizophrenia, *The Psychology of Dementia Praecox* (Jung, 1907/1953) which proposed an essentially Freudian theory of schizophrenia. Jung sent Freud a copy of the book and they had started corresponding in 1906. After reading the book, Freud invited Jung to visit him in Vienna (Hall & Nordby, 1973).

When they first met the two talked for 13 hours straight. Afterwards, they wrote to each other every week. Freud was ecstatic to have acquired a non-Jewish follower of such standing in the field of psychiatry. Freud referred to Jung as his heir and as the crown prince of psychoanalysis. While Freud and Jung had a number of important differences, Freud felt he could win Jung over to his ideas. The two shared many common interests: archeology, comparative religion, philosophy, and biology. Like Freud, Jung was multilingual, conversant in English, French, Latin, and Greek, as well as his native German. Later in life, Jung added Swahili to his list of languages. But the two also had many differences. Jung was not just fascinated with religion; he believed it was an important element in human life, whereas Freud argued that religion was a neurotic illusion. The two also disagreed on the nature of the unconscious, the role of biology in psychology, and the significance of childhood sexuality. Jung de-emphasized the role of biology and minimized the significance of childhood sexuality. These differences later produced strains between the two, although their differences were also personal as well as philosophical (Hall & Nordby, 1973; Sulloway, 1983; Storr, 1973).

As already discussed, Jung traveled with Freud and Ferenczi for seven weeks in 1909 on the trip to Clark University. While Freud was the featured speaker, Jung also gave a series of lectures. When the International Psychoanalytic Association was formed in 1910, Jung became its first president at Freud's insistence. Their differences were soon to come to a head, however. In November 1911, Jung's colleague (and lover, for although married in 1903 with a family that eventually included four daughters and a son, Jung had a series of lovers and mistresses his whole life, as we shall see shortly) Sabina Spielrein gave a paper to the Vienna Psychoanalytic Society that concerned and upset Freud, because of its biological assumptions that were different from his own (Sulloway, 1983). Seeing an impending break, Freud prepared a defense of his views against Jung, which he published as *Totem and Taboo* (Freud, 1912c), a response to Jung's *Psychology of the Unconscious* (Jung, 1917/1953), which was originally published in 1912 as well. Jung also presented his critique of Freud's work in his 1912 lectures at Fordham University in the U.S.

Jung was 37 in 1912 when he broke with Freud. The break plunged Jung into mental turmoil, which Jung described as a state of confusion and inner uncertainty (Hall & Nordby, 1973). At the time he had trouble reading, writing, and working. He resigned his professorship at the University of Zurich. But Jung had learned well from his master and when he started to recover he took steps to further his ideas and set up a cult around himself, just as Freud had done, although the cult was not secular but religious--a pagan religious cult. (Noll, 1997).

The story of Jung's cult and associated pagan religion starts during the period of Freud and Jung's collaboration and involves one of the many fascinating individuals attracted to psychoanalysis: Otto Gross. Otto Gross was the son of Hans Gross, the founder of modern criminology, a lawyer and professor of criminal law, and the founder of the first modern crime lab. Hans Gross was famous throughout the world and was a paragon of law and order. Hans' son Otto was equally as brilliant and trained as a psychiatrist. He was also a political anarchist who advocated free love and took cocaine, morphine, and opium. In 1902, he was admitted to the Burgholzli for drug addiction. It is not known if Jung treated him at the time. After completing treatment, Otto Gross returned to his old habits and habitats. In 1904 he began to study psychoanalysis and in 1907 he published a book comparing Freud's concepts of manic-depression with those of Emil Kraepelin, one of the leading biological psychiatrists of his day (Noll, 1997). (Kraepelin had both an M.D. and a Ph.D. His Ph.D. was earned in psychology from Wilhelm Wundt). Freud was impressed with the book and hoped to make Gross, both a non-Jew and the son of one of the most famous lawyers in Europe, one of his followers (Noll, 1997).

Otto Gross introduced psychoanalysis to the pre-World War I counter-culture. Every period of capitalism has produced a counter-culture. The U.S. counter-culture of the 1950s and early 1960s (the Beats) and the U.S. counter-culture of the 1960s and early 1970s were not unique historical developments. One of the centers of the counter-cultural movement in central Europe before World War I was the neighborhood of Schwabing in Munich, where artists, writers, drug users, nudists and anarchists gathered. Otto Gross was an expert on the German philosopher Nietzsche, whom he could quote at length. Gross conducted psychoanalytic sessions for artists and writers at public cafes. Many of the writers found psychoanalysis to be both a helpful form of therapy and a stimulus to their creativity. Soon Gross had developed a large following (Noll, 1997).

Freud did not approve of the counter-culture, nor did Otto's father Hans Gross. And it was not just the drug use and the artists that they disapproved of--Otto Gross advocated free love, sexual freedom cut loose from all conventional morality, as a cure for psychological neuroses, an aid to human creativity, and a revolt against a repressive society. He had numerous lovers, some of whom went temporarily insane and at least one whom he coaxed to suicide. He had children by different women (in one case, by two sisters, one of whom later married the writer D.H. Lawrence) and was considered by some as the most dangerous man in Europe (Noll, 1997).

Otto's father Hans and Otto's wife (for he was married during this entire time) conspired to have him forcibly committed, with Freud's help. Freud recruited Jung to treat Gross and together Freud and Jung persuaded Gross to enter treatment for drug addiction. Freud hoped to save Gross for the cause. Gross arrived in Zurich for treatment in May of 1908. Within a short time Jung was holding around-the-clock therapy sessions with Gross, but it was not Jung treating Gross—the two took turns analyzing each other. On June 17 Gross escaped from the hospital and was soon back in Munich using drugs. Jung, however, was changed for good (Noll, 1997).

After the mutual therapy session Jung believed, like Gross, that free and guiltless sexual relationships would make one more creative and psychologically healthy, and would put one in touch with the divine. After this point, Jung practiced *de facto* polygamy, often having sexual relations, some of long duration, with a number of women. He also encouraged his patients to do so, as well as therapists he trained. His first lover was his patient and later collaborator Sabina Spielrein, who in 1911 delivered the paper to the Vienna Psychoanalytic Society that had so upset Freud. At the same time he was having an affair with Speilrein and carrying on sexual relations with his wife, he started a long-term affair with his former patient and research assistant Antonia (Toni) Wolff. Wolff is often known as Jung's second wife, because of the length and intensity of his relationship with her, but she was not his only second "wife", and sometimes he had several at one time, in addition to shorter affairs (Noll, 1997).

Jung's embrace of polygamy soon merged with his study of religion and his own self-analysis. He came to believe he was an Aryan Christ, a non-Christian pagan god who was in touch with the spiritual world through the collective unconscious. In conjunction with his belief in direct contact with the spiritual world, he believed that he, and potentially everyone, had past lives and multiple components of their personality in their unconscious. Analysis, for Jung, became a therapy and a religion (Noll, 1997).

Jung kept his religion secret, sharing it only with his followers and patients. To the public at large he presented his ideas in the guise of psychology, often hinting at but never explicitly stating his true beliefs. He also, like Freud, engaged in deception and character assassination to further his career and cult. He typically erased former lovers and colleagues from the historical record (both Gross and Spielrein suffered this fate) and published an influential autobiography entitled *Memories, Dreams, and Reflections* (Jung, 1961) which contains as much propaganda as it does autobiography. And just as Freud sought to control the historical record by controlling sources, a number of important documents had not been released to the public (Noll, 1997). The most important of these documents, Jung's *Red Book,* was only published in 2009, a major new source of historians of psychology (Jung, 2009).

Freud generated many hypotheses from his underlying biological meta-theory. In a parallel fashion Jung generated many concepts and hypotheses from his underlying pagan religion: among these important concepts we find the notion of the collective unconscious, psychological types, and individuation.

Otto Rank

Otto Rank (1884-1939) was born into a working-class family in Vienna. His parents separated when he was young and he started work to help support the family. Like many workers, he went to the young Alfred Adler for medical services. While Rank had little formal education he read voraciously and became interested in Freud's ideas. While undergoing an examination by Adler he started to discuss Freud's works. Adler must have been impressed, for he offered to introduce the two, an offer Rank quickly accepted. Freud and Rank met in 1906, when Rank was 22 (Roazen, 1975).

Freud soon became Rank's mentor and protector. He hired Rank as the secretary of the Vienna Psychoanalytic Society and encouraged him to go to college. Freud delegated to Rank the task of revising *The Interpretation of Dreams*. In all, Rank revised four editions of Freud's greatest work and was Freud's research assistant for many other works. With Freud's emotional and financial support, Rank finished his Ph.D. in 1912. Rank also edited or co-edited important psychoanalytic journals and was the youngest member of the secret committee formed in 1912 to protect and further the psychoanalytic movement (Roazen, 1975).

Freud treated Rank like his own son and the close relationship the two shared led to jealousy among Freud's other followers and even among his own children. Rank was erudite and a specialist in mythology and literature. He was charming and highly intelligent, and he waited on Freud hand and foot, lighting his cigars, bringing him a glass of water, and even managing Freud's finances (Roazen, 1975).

Rank's relationship with Freud changed as a consequence of World War I. Rank was drafted and sent to Poland to edit the army's official journal. While in Poland he fell in love and married. He was also separated from Freud for long periods for the first time in his adult life. After the war he returned to Freud and Rank's wife was treated as one of Freud's own daughter-in-laws. Rank also began to treat patients, becoming one of the first lay (non-medically trained) analysts (Roazen, 1975).

As a result of his own clinical practice and life experiences, Rank started to develop his own ideas which deviated from fundamental ideas of psycho-analysis. The break became evident in late 1923 when Rank published his *The Trauma of Birth* (Rank, 1924/1973). Initially Freud praised the book, but later turned against Rank. Rank emphasized the relationship with the mother as being important, not just the relationship with the father, and stressed the role of emotional support for the client by the therapist during therapy (Roazen, 1975).

The differences between Freud and Rank were soon exploited by other members of the committee who sought to protect Freud's work from heresies. Freud, who was first diagnosed with cancer in 1923, tried to keep Rank as a follower and was deeply hurt by the differences with his once "favorite son." Rank went to Paris in 1924, became depressed, and returned to Freud to be treated for depression. Soon Freud reported that Rank's neuroses had been cured and that Rank was once again a loyal follower. But when Rank traveled to America in 1925 the differences re-emerged. Rank returned to Vienna one final time to pay his respects to Freud in 1926, and then never came back. Their break was complete (Roazen, 1975).

Rank now divided his time between Paris and New York and saw patients in both places. He also separated from his wife, who stayed in Paris (and stayed a follower of Freud's) in 1935 when Rank moved permanently to the U.S. They were formally divorced in 1939, shortly before Rank re-married. In Paris and New York Rank started to emphasize short term therapy, in contrast to Freudian analysis which often lasted four or five years. He also worked to set up the School of Social Work at the University of Pennsylvania. He died in 1939, at the age of 55, a few months after Freud died, from an allergic reaction to medicine he was given for a throat infection (Roazen, 1975). Immediately upon his death, Freud's loyal followers, especially Jones and Brill, started to slander him. In spite of the sustained public relations campaign against Rank and his work, he had a significant influence on the psychology of creativity, on social work, and on the development of psychotherapy (Lieberman, 1985).

Women And Psychoanalysis

Freud had highly competitive relationships with men. If one was not totally for him, one was against him. With women, Freud's relationships were very different. Women found Freud enormously charming and they were attracted to him emotionally and sexually. Freud, for his part, did not find them threatening, and was more tolerant of disagreement with women. Throughout his career Freud collected women as helpers and supporters during the process of analyzing them, yet another example of his unethical behavior.

While Freud's charisma with women was substantial, he did not seem to understand them. In a famous quote, contained in a letter to Princess Marie Bonaparte, one of his many women followers and a person who, risking her own freedom, flew to Vienna after the Nazi annexation to help Freud leave the country safely, Freud wrote "The great question that has never been answered and which I have not yet been able to answer, despite my thirty years of research into the feminine soul, is 'What does a woman want?'" (Jones, 1955). More significantly, Freud's theory was based on his own, and his society's biases regarding women.

It is perhaps because of Freud's non-competitive attitudes toward women that so many of them became central figures in psychoanalysis. And given their experience *qua* women, it should come as no surprise that they also sought to revise the theory as well as the practice of psychoanalysis.

Melanie Klein

Melanie Klein (1882-1960) gave up her plans to be a medical doctor when she became engaged at the age of 17 and married the day after she turned 21. She was prone to depression and was unhappy in her marriage. She soon had two children (a third was born in 1914) and was in and out of sanatoriums for depression. In 1909 she and her family moved to Budapest when her husband was transferred there for his work and in 1912 she entered psychoanalysis with Sandor Ferenczi, one of Freud's inner circle. With the start of the Great War in 1914 both her therapist and her husband were drafted into the military. To make her life even more difficult, her mother, whom she had depended on for many years to help raise the children, died (Sayers, 1991).

The year 1914 was really a turning point in Melanie Klein's life, although she only realized that in retrospect. Her husband was injured in the war in 1916 and became an invalid. He lost his job as well and finally found work in Sweden in 1919 after the war ended. The communist revolution in Hungary at the end of the Great War led to the opening of university posts to Jews. Ferenczi became the first university professor of psychoanalysis. Then, the counter-revolution crushed the regime and Ferenczi was dismissed from his post. The new government was violently anti-Semitic (both Ferenczi and Klein were Jewish). During this time, Klein had read a great deal about psychoanalysis and had analyzed her own children to help them deal with their emotional problems (Sayers, 1991).

Klein gave her first paper on psychoanalysis in 1919, the year she joined the Hungarian Psychoanalytic Society. She soon moved to Berlin where she was analyzed by Karl Abraham and became a member of the Berlin Psychoanalytic Society. Klein developed the practice of child psychoanalysis in competition with Anna Freud. The two competing approaches differed in both their theory and practice. Klein emphasized the importance of the child's fantasies and the role of transference by the child to the therapist. In 1926, shortly after the break-up of her marriage and the death of Abraham, she accepted a job in London. She was invited by Jones who both wanted to increase the strength of psychoanalysis in England and sought a therapist for his own children. This set up a long-standing division among British psychoanalysts between the supporters of Klein and the supporters of Anna Freud. This division was sharpened with the arrival of Anna Freud in London in 1939 (Sayers, 1991).

Klein developed what is known as the object-relations approach to psychoanalysis. This approach emphasizes the importance of relationships, especially the first relationship with the mother, for the later psychological health of the individual. The child's first relationship forms an unconscious mental model of what a relationship should be. Like her main rival Anna Freud, Klein was to have a significant impact on both developmental psychology and the practice of child clinical psychology in the post-World War II period.

Karen Horney

Karen Horney (1885-1952) was born in Hamburg, Germany of a Dutch mother and a Norwegian father. By the start of high school she had decided on being a doctor, and with the support of her mother, enrolled in a high school that would prepare her for university. Around the age of 18 (in 1903) she began a life-long pattern of having sexual relationships with men, all of whom she had trouble staying faithful to. In 1904 her parents separated and she and her mother had to survive by doing odd jobs and taking in boarders. In 1906 she started college, studying medicine. In 1909 she married Oskar Horney, one of her lovers, whom she had met at university, and took his last name. The couple moved to Berlin for his work and she transferred to the University of Berlin to continue her studies. At the University she went into psychoanalysis with Karl Abraham, one of Freud's inner circle, for depression and unspecified sexual difficulties. Horney had her first child, a daughter, in 1910 (she had two more daughters later). She enjoyed being a mother but, according to her daughters, was a distant and impulsive mother. Horney sent her girls to a number of experimental schools and had them psychoanalyzed by Melanie Klein. Her husband, meantime, had become very wealthy through his work. Horney started seeing patients in 1912, after finishing medical school, and rose steadily in the Berlin Psychoanalytic Society, becoming its secretary in 1915. She began giving lectures to physicians on psychoanalysis in 1917 (Sayers, 1991).

When Freud called for the establishment of free clinics that would provide psychoanalysis to everyone, the first such clinic was founded in Berlin. Horney became its first woman member and later, with the formation of the Berlin Psychoanalytic Institute (dedicated to teaching and research in psychoanalysis), she became the first women instructor at the Institute. Horney soon developed a critique of Freud's account of female development, a critique that had broad implications for both Freud's theory and the practice of therapy (Sayers, 1991).

Horney's major criticism was that Freud's theory did not take into consideration the role of the social environment in psychological development, especially the impact that gender roles and gender discrimination play in the development of boys and girls. Many of Freud's concepts, she argued, were examples of Freud passing off his own experiences as a male in a male-dominated culture as biological truths. Horney's critique had a significant impact on feminist thought and psychology in the post-World War II era. Her first and most influential book, *The Neurotic Personality of Our Time* (Horney, 1937), summarized her criticism of psychoanalysis and showed the role of social factors in the development of mental illness.

In 1930, Horney moved to the United States after the Great Depression, which affected not just the United States but all of Europe, destroyed her husband's fortune. Settling first in Chicago where she worked with the new-found Chicago Psychoanalytic Institute, she moved to New York in 1934. Her marriage, which fell apart in the late 1920's, ended in divorce in the mid-1930s. During the remainder of her life she continued to teach, write, and work as a practicing psychoanalyst, developing a feminist psychoanalytic theory that was to influence substantially both modern feminism and modern clinical psychology (Sayers, 1991). We will return to her contributions when we examine the history of clinical psychology in the post-World War II period.

Anna Freud

Anna Freud (1895-1982) was Freud's youngest child. She was not as pretty as her sisters and often felt neglected by her mother. She was assertive and intellectual, which delighted her father, but he did not allow her to get the kind of high school education that would have permitted her to go to college. Instead, Freud sent her to a finishing school. Anna was interested in many of her father's ideas and pleaded with him to let her go to America with him in 1909—he did not allow it. She studied to become a teacher and work in a day care center for poor children before the Great War. In 1914, right before the war, her father allowed her to visit England. He also interfered with her relationships with men (something he was to do his entire life); Ernst Jones was interested in her but Freud was convinced that it was only because Jones wanted to get closer to Freud himself (Sayers, 1991).

During the Great War, Anna attended her father's Saturday lectures on psychoanalysis and entered analysis with him in 1918. She also briefly considered going to college to become a doctor but, again, her father dissuaded her. By 1920 she had given up teaching and was working as a translator for the various psychoanalytic journals, as well as preparing to be a psychoanalyst. She became a member of the Vienna Psychoanalytic Society in 1922. Her paper reiterated her father's positions on female sexual development, specifically, that females have fantasies of being beaten (Sayers, 1991).

When Freud developed cancer in 1923, Anna became his secretary and caregiver. She also started to act as his representative and spokesperson. She started to develop her own ideas as a result of her experience as a therapist working mostly with children. Anna Freud's work made her, along with Melanie Klein with whom she came into conflict over therapeutic technique, the mother of child psychotherapy. In her work she stressed the need to gain rapport with the child and the significance of using dolls and other toys to facilitate communication between child and therapist. In addition to analyzing children's dreams, she analyzed their daydreams and their drawings. By 1926 she was lecturing on child psychoanalysis and began to train analysts in Vienna, Prague, and Berlin (Sayers, 1991).

Anna Freud's first book, *The Ego and the Mechanisms of Defense* (1937), was published in 1936 in German and given to her father as a gift for his 80th birthday. Publication of the work in English was delayed by Jones, who was jealous of Anna's influence on her father and, according to the elder Freud, still upset about being rejected by Anna in 1914. Her work was a major development in psychoanalysis and shifted attention to the adaptive role of the ego and the psychological defense mechanisms that individuals use to deal with their negative emotions. She also started an experimental school based on psychoanalytic principles. She hired Peter Blos (later to become a famous authority on adolescence) and Erik Erikson, a young artist who was one of her patients, to teach at the school. Erikson, who we shall meet again in the chapter on the history of developmental psychology, was sometimes annoyed at Anna for knitting during their therapy sessions (Anna always did some form of needle work while seeing patients). She later gave Erikson a sweater for his newborn baby, thus changing his annoyance to respect (Sayers, 1991).

The elder Freud was reluctant to leave Vienna, even after the Nazi annexation. He was finally persuaded to leave after Anna was taken into custody and interrogated by the Gestapo. Anna helped her father move, in the process saving a number of his letters and papers that he was eager to destroy. He had previously destroyed his papers and letters on two previous occasions. Once settled in London, Anna was Freud's constant caregiver, until the very end of his life (Gay, 1988).

World War II soon engulfed Great Britain. With Sigmund Freud's death Anna was now free from her duties as caretaker and nurse to her father. Anna now entered a highly productive phase of her professional life. She became the leading figure in the psychoanalytic movement and helped to establish the Freud Museum in England and the Freud Archives. During the war she became director of two nurseries for war orphans. After the war she continued her work with children who were refugees of German concentration camps. Her observations of the effects of maternal separation on children (called separation anxiety) led her to argue that the child's first relationship with the mother forms the pattern for all subsequent relationships. After the war, she continued to make contributions to child psychotherapy as well as to the application of psychology to legal issues such as child custody (Sayers, 1991). We will return to some of her post-World War II contributions to psychology in later chapters.

The Political And Cultural Context Of Psychoanalysis

Psychoanalysis developed as the renegade school of the new psychology in part because of the political and cultural context in which it developed. One of the important factors was the anti-Semitism that pervaded European and American culture. This anti-Semitism made it difficult for Jewish physicians to achieve the kind of academic and professional success that non-Jews of equal ability could achieve. The appeal of psychoanalysis was that it provided the outsider (Jews and women) with a way to be insiders. Freud was aware that this was one of the appeals of psychoanalysis and he and his followers often magnified the opposition and resistance to their thinking while portraying themselves as heroes struggling against fierce resistance. This hero myth, invented to promote the success of psychoanalysis and of Freud's work, should not obscure the fact that anti-Semitism and discrimination against Jewish professionals was real and ubiquitous in Germany and the Austro-Hungarian Empire. When that discrimination lessened during the years of Red Vienna and the Weimar Republic, psychoanalysis exploded in influence and popularity.

A second element of the political and cultural context that bears repeating is the high level of sexual repression in both the U.S. and Europe at the end of the 1800s. Freud's work was part of a broader movement, both by sexologists and by counter-cultural dissidents, to liberalize the sexual mores that produced, as Freud and others demonstrated, high rates of mental illness and emotional anguish, especially among women. Freud's theory was, and was perceived as, radical and liberating in the context of the time. He stated loudly and clearly what his contemporary sexologists whispered in medical jargon.

A third element of the political and cultural context was the cultural reverberations caused by the Darwinian Revolution. Freud's work, a direct effort to come to grips with Darwin in the sphere of psychology, was merely one of many such attempts to work through the significance of evolution for human life and culture.

A fourth and related element is the widespread materialism and atheism of 19th century intellectual life. This materialism was embraced by Freud against the beliefs of the American and European masses and provided an alternative world view.

Finally, the sense of political and moral decay that pervaded the end of the long 19th century produced an intense search for new meanings and new ideas. Psychoanalysis was part and parcel of that search, offering both a new world view and a method for healing the emotional pain felt by so many.

The Achievements Of Psychoanalysis

Freud, his followers, and his apostates accomplished much. They invented and developed the craft of psychotherapy more than any other group of people in history. Clinical psychologists, psychiatrists, social workers, and religious ministers and their millions of patients owe much to this development of the craft of the psychotherapy. Freud and his followers also tried to ground psychological theory in biology, an attempt that was both admirable and offers lessons for psychology to this day. In addition to therapeutic techniques, they developed a number of hypotheses, some of which have proven useful and significant to our understanding of psychology. Perhaps the most important of these concepts is the notion of the unconscious itself, but certainly others are significant, such as the influence of birth order, personality types, defense mechanisms, attachment, and ego psychology. To sum up the contributions to human culture of Freud and his followers is difficult and controversial. Here is my list: First, they invented and developed psychotherapy. In this, Freud can be rightfully considered the father of psychotherapy. Second, Freud was one of the three fathers of psychology, along with Wundt and James. Third, Freud was a significant political theorist. Fourth, Freud and his followers were significant literary critics. Fifth, Freud and his followers (or former followers) inspired many writers and artists. Sixth, Freud was a significant social reformer, working to promote sex education, fight sexual and physical abuse, foster high quality childrearing, and treat soldiers who suffered from what we now call PTSD.

Freud, especially, and his followers also rejected empiricism and the scientific methods that could have tested and evaluated his ideas. In his pursuit of fame and influence, Freud turned his back on what made the new psychology "new." Freud promoted himself ruthlessly, not concerned with whom he hurt or how many people he manipulated to achieve his goals. In this, Jung followed his teacher, although perhaps not to the same extent. Freud also manipulated public images and created myths, lying and covering up inconvenient truths. Freud's legacy is thus mixed and remains controversial to this day.

Shortly after Freud's death, the poet W.H. Auden (Auden, 1940) published "In Memory of Sigmund Freud." In the poem Auden notes that "only hate was happy" at the death, highlighting the enormous impact of Freud as an advocate for people. Auden ends his poem with a magnificent tribute to Freud the humanist who wanted us to love each other, but also ourselves:

> One rational voice is dumb. Over his grave
> the household of Impulse mourns one dearly loved:
> sad is Eros, builder of cities,
> and weeping anarchic Aphrodite.

Should The History Of Psychology Be Rated X?

Stephen Brush (1974) once suggested, perhaps tongue-in-cheek, that the history of science should be rated X because it is not suitable for young people —the real history of science destroys college students' illusions about how scientists do science. Certainly Brush's argument applies to psychology—the psychologists you have met so far frequently had emotional problems, many used drugs, some were self-centered, and acted immorally. They were often also ambitious, jealous, and highly competitive. Some, like Freud and Jung, furthered their ambitions by forming cults, carrying out sustained public relations campaigns, and promoting themselves as geniuses at every turn. Many also tried to shape the historical record in their favor.

At the same time, the history of psychology shows that the contributors were also very hard working, well educated, and intelligent. They tended to have broad intellectual interests and rich experiences. And, importantly, they pursued their intellectual passions with dogged tenacity. None of this should come as a surprise to students who are familiar with the psychology of creativity.

What relationship does the personality or behavior of a psychologist have to do with the validity of her or his work? Popper argued that we must distinguish between the context of discovery (the factors that have led you to hypothesize some law of nature or to discover some fact) and the context of collaboration (the evidence that a law of nature or fact is indeed true). Because you may find a psychologist morally repugnant does not mean that the discoveries or ideas are wrong or useless. Likewise, because a theory is useful or a proposed fact is true does not mean the discoverer is a saint. Every great scientist, whether physicist, biologist, or psychologist, is also only human. The study of the history of psychology helps you appreciate both the achievements of the past, and the humanness of those who built the discipline.

every science has "rated x" history,
that doesn't mean it shouldn't be
taught

References

Auden, W.H. (1940). *Another time.* New York: Random House.

Boring, E. G. (1950). *A history of experimental psychology*, 2nd edition. New York: Appleton-Century-Crofts.

Breuer, J., & Freud, S. (1895). *Studies in hysteria.* In *Standard editions*, Vol. 2. London: Hogarth Press.

Brush, S. G. (1974). Should the history of science be rated X? *Science, 183,* 1164-1172.

Crews, F.C. (Ed.). (1998). *Unauthorized Freud: Doubters confront a legend.* New York: Viking.

Danto, E.A. (2005). *Freud's free clinics: Psychoanalysis and social justice, 1918-1938.* New York: Columbia University Press.

Dawes, R.M. (1994). *House of cards: Psychology and psychotherapy built on* myth. New York: Free Press.

Edmundson, M. (2007). *The death of Sigmund Freud: The legacy of his last days.* New York: Bloomsbury.

Fancher, R.E. (1990). *Pioneers in psychology*, 2nd edition. New York: W.W. Norton.

Freud, A. (1937). *The ego and mechanisms of defense.* New York: International Universities Press.

Freud, S. (1895/1956). *Project for a scientific psychology.* In J. Strachey (Ed.), *The standard edition of the complete psychological works of Sigmund Freud, Vol. 1.* London: Hogarth Press, pp. 281-397.

Freud, S. (1896/1989). The aetiology of hysteria. In P. Gay (Ed.), *The Freud reader* (pp. 97-111). New York: W.W. Norton

Freud, S. (1900). *The interpretation of dreams*. In J. Strachey (Ed.), *The standard edition of the complete psychological works of Sigmund Freud, Vol. 4 & 5*. London: Hogarth Press.

Freud, S. (1901). *The psychopathology of everyday life*. In J. Strachey (Ed.), *The standard edition of the complete psychological works of Sigmund Freud, Vol. 6*. London: Hogarth Press.

Freud, S. (1905a). *Jokes and their relation to the unconscious*. In J. Strachey (Ed.), *The standard edition of the complete psychological works of Sigmund Freud, Vol. 8*. London: Hogarth Press.

Freud, S. (1905b). *Three essays on the theory of sexuality*.. In J. Strachey (Ed.), *The standard edition of the complete psychological works of Sigmund Freud, Vol. 7*. London: Hogarth Press, pp. 125-243.

Freud, S. (1910/1989). 'Wild' psycho-analysis. In P. Gay (Ed.), *The Freud reader* (pp. 351-356). New York: W.W. Norton.

Freud, S. (1911/1958). The handling of dream-interpretation in psycho-analysis. In J. Strachey (Ed.), *The standard edition of the complete psychological works of Sigmund Freud, Vol. XII*, (pp. 89-96). London: Hogarth Press.

Freud, S. (1912a/1958). The dynamics of transference. In J. Strachey (Ed.), *The standard edition of the complete psychological works of Sigmund Freud, Vol. XII*, (pp. 97-108). London: Hogarth Press.

Freud, S. (1912b/1958). Recommendations to physicians practicing psycho-analysis. In J. Strachey (Ed.), *The standard edition of the complete psychological works of Sigmund Freud, Vol. XII*, (pp. 109-120). London: Hogarth Press.

Freud, S. (1912c). *Totem and taboo*. In J. Strachey (Ed.). *The standard edition of the complete psychologicl works of Sigmund Freud, Vol. 13*. London: Hogarth Press, pp.1-161.

Freud, S. (1913/1958). On the beginning of treatment (Further recommendations on the technique of Psycho-analysis I). In J. Strachey (Ed.), *The standard edition of the complete psychological works of Sigmund Freud, Vol. XII*, (pp. 121-144). London: Hogarth Press.

Freud, S. (1914/1958). Remembering, repeating, and working through (Further recommendations on the technique of psycho-analysis II). In J. Strachey (Ed.), *The standard edition of the completepsychological works of Sigmund Freud, Vol. XII*, (pp. 145-156). London: Hogarth Press.

Freud, S. (1915/1958). Observations on transference-love (Further recommendations on
the technique of psycho-analysis III). In J. Strachey (Ed.), *The standard edition of the complete psychological works of Sigmund Freud, Vol. XII*, (pp. 157-171). London: Hogarth Press.

Gay, P. (1988). *Freud: A life for our time*. New York: Anchor Books/Doubleday.

Gay, P. (1989). *The Freud reader*. New York: W.W. Norton & Comp.
Gruber, H. (1991). *Red Vienna: Experiment in working-class culture, 1919-1934*. New York: Oxford University Press.

Hacohen, M.C. (2000). *Karl Popper—The formative years, 1902-1945*. Cambridge: Cambridge University Press.

Haggbloom, S.J., Warnick, R., Warnick, J.E., Jones, V.K., Yarbrough, G.L., Russell, T.M., Borecky, C.M., McGahhey, R., Powell III, J.L., Beavers, J., & Monte, E. (2002). The 100 most eminent psychologists of the 20th century. *Review of General Psychology, 6*(2), 139-125.

Hale, N.G. (1971). *Freud and the Americans*, Vol. 1. New York: Oxford University Press.

Hall, C.S. & Nordby, V.J. (1973). *A primer of Jungian psychology*. New York: Mentor.

Horney, K. (1937). *The neurotic personality of our time.* New York: Norton.

Janik, A. & Toulmin, S. (1973). *Wittgenstein's Vienna.* New York: Simon and Schuster.

Jones, E. (1953). *The life and work of Sigmund Freud, Vol. 1: The formative years and the great discoveries, 1856-1900.* New York: Basic Books.

Jones, E. (1955). *The life and work of Sigmund Freud, Vol. 2: Years of maturity, 1901-1919.* New York: Basic Books.

Jones, E. (1957). *The life and work of Sigmund Freud, Vol. 3: The last phase, 1919-1939.* New York: Basic Books.

Jung, C.G. (1907/1953). *The psychology of dementia praecox.* In C.G. Jung (1953), *Collected works, 3*, 3-151. New York: Pantheon Books.

Jung, C.G. (1917/1953). *The psychology of the unconscious.* In C.G. Jung (1953), *Collected works, 7*, 3-117. New York: Pantheon Books.

Jung, C.G. (1961). *Memories, dreams, and reflections.* New York: Vintage Books.
Jung, C. G. (2009). *The red book: Liber novus.* Edited by Sonu Shamdasani. New York: W.W. Norton & Company.

Karp, W. (1979). *The politics of war: The story of two wars which altered forever the political life of the American republic.* New York: Harper & Row.

Lieberman, E. J. (1985). *Acts of will: The life and work of Otto Rank.* New York: The

Free Press.

McGuire, W., ed. (1974). *The Freud/Jung letters: The correspondence between Sigmund Freud and C.G. Jung.* Translated by R. Manheim & R.F.C. Hull. Princeton, NJ: Princeton University Press.

Noll, R. (1997). *The aryan Christ: The secret life of Carl Jung.* New York: Random House.

Rank, O. (1924/1973). *The trauma of birth.* New York: Harper Torchbooks.

Roazen, P. (1975). *Freud and his followers.* New York: Alfred A. Knopf.

Sayers, J. (1991). *Mothers of psychoanalysis: Helene Deutsch, Karen Horney, Anna Freud, Melanie Klein.* New York: W.W. Norton.

Schorske, C.E. (1981). *Fin-de-siècle Vienna: Politics and culture.* New York: Vintage.

Shorter, E. (1997). *A history of psychiatry: From the age of the asylum to the age of prozac.* New York: John Wiley & Sons.

Storr, A. (1973). *C.G. Jung.* New York: Viking Press.

Sulloway, F.J. (1983). *Freud: Biologist of the mind.* New York: Basic Books.

Szasz, T. (1990) *Anti-Freud: Karl Kraus' criticism of psychoanalysis and psychiatry.* Syracuse, NY: Syracuse University Press.

CHAPTER 7: BEHAVIORISM

The Second Coming

Turning and turning in the widening gyre
The falcon cannot hear the falconer;
Things fall apart, the centre cannot hold;
Mere anarchy is loosed upon the world,
The blood-dimmed tide is loosed and everywhere
The ceremony of innocence is drowned;
The best lack all conviction, while the worst
Are full of passionate intensity.
Surely some revelation is at hand;
Surely the Second Coming is at hand.
The Second Coming! Hardly are those words out
When a vast image out of Spiritus Mundi
Troubles my sight; somewhere in sands of the des ert
A shape with lion body and the head of a man,
A gaze blank and pitiless as the sun,
Is moving its slow thighs, while all about it
Reel shadows of the indignant desert birds.
The darkness drops again; but now I know
That twenty centuries of stony sleep
Were vexed to a nightmare by a rocking cradle,
And what rough beast, its hour come round at last,
Slouches towards Bethlehem to be born?

WILLIAM BUTLER YEATS (1920)

Things Fall Apart: Revolution And Counter-Revolution In Psychology

As the long nineteenth century drew to a close, the world was convulsed in war, revolution, and counter-revolution. These dramatic events played out not just on the stage of world and national politics, but in social and intellectual spheres. Yeats' poem, used as the epigraph for this chapter, was written in 1919 and published the following year. Composed in the immediate aftermath of World War I and during the Russian Revolution and using symbolism of the apocalypse and the second coming, the poem reflects both the despair and hope of the new age: an age of revolution and counter-revolution.

context of the time

In psychology, revolution and counter-revolution played out in the rise of two schools that simultaneously built upon and opposed the first three schools. These new schools have been referred to by historians as behaviorism and Gestalt psychology. Behaviorism arose in the U.S. and Gestalt psychology arose in Germany at approximately the same time on the eve of World War I.

Behaviorism and Gestalt psychology share a common demographic factor—both were the creation of the second generation of psychologists. If one conceptualizes the first generation as those who received their doctorates (either Ph.D. or M.D.) from 1870 to 1900 (Wundt and James, as the founders of the discipline, fall slightly prior to this time frame), the second generation would be those who received their doctorates from 1901 to 1930. The first or founding generation established the contours of the field; the second generation developed within those contours. In both the U.S. and Europe, the second generation differed from the first, both in terms of their backgrounds and in terms of their approach to psychology.

Behaviorism constituted a revolution against the first three schools. All revolutions grew out of existing social and intellectual conditions and no revolution is completely different from the proceeding ancient regime. Behaviorism grew out of functionalism and shared many of its characteristics, while at the same time rejecting consciousness (and the unconscious) as the subject matter of psychology. Like psychoanalysis and unlike functionalism and volunteerism, behaviorism was reductionistic and mechanistic. Gestalt psychology was a counter-revolution against mechanism and reductionism. Consciousness, or more precisely experience, remained the subject matter of psychology, but it was experience that could not be reduced to its elements or explained in a mechanistic fashion. Behaviorism and Gestalt psychology were in direct conflict with each other and both shaped psychology profoundly from the end of World War I until the 1950s.

Behaviorism: The Rejection Of Consciousness

Behaviorism arose in America as a distinct school (a theory, set of preferred methods, and favored problems) in opposition to pre-existing German and American psychology. The opposition should not be exaggerated though; behaviorism shared many characteristics with the established approaches in the U.S. and Europe. Furthermore, the field of U.S. psychology changed slowly in response to the behaviorist school (and not just in response to behaviorism, but to other social forces that shaped behaviorism as well as the rest of psychology).

The defining feature of behaviorism was a re-definition of what a science of psychology should study. American and European psychologists from the two "old" schools (leaving aside psychoanalysis for the moment) emphasized that psychology studied consciousness and experience. This emphasis was broad and included the study of perception, cognition, social psychology, developmental psychology, personality, and abnormal psychology, as well as the application of psychology to real-world problems such as psychotherapy and testing. Behavior (of humans and non-human animals) was part of this broad emphasis. In short, these schools covered most of the areas associated with present day psychology.

Freudian psychology emphasized the unconscious, but here again the emphasis was broad and included not just abnormal psychology and developmental psychology, but the psychology of creativity, religion, human sexuality, and psychotherapy. Behaviorism rejected the previous emphasis of psychology. For the behaviorist, the science of psychology needed to focus exclusively on the study of behavior.

There are three interrelated reasons why behaviorism came to dominate the science of psychology in the U.S. First, the study of consciousness was closely associated, both in the mind of the public and intellectually, with its German roots. The anti-German hysteria that swept the U.S. starting in 1914 made an "American" alternative to "Germanic" science attractive. Second, around the turn of the century positivism and materialism become more popular (in part as a consequence of the success of the hard sciences and advances in technology). The new psychology, with its anti-materialist assumptions and concerns, now appeared in the light of this new intellectual fashion to be unscientific. Third, psychology was experiencing considerable societal pressure to be less philosophical and more practical (O'Donnell, 1985). This anti-philosophy, pro-practicality trend was linked to the continuing professionalization of psychology within the dynamic capitalist economy of the U.S.

In addition to the three external (in the sense that they existed outside of the field of psychology) pressures I have just outlined, an internal factor also contributed to the rise of behaviorism. The use of some forms of introspectionism produced contradictory results, resulting in tangled debates on the nature of thinking (*e.g.*, if thought was based on images or if it was imageless) and experience.

More than any other person, John B. Watson (1878-1958) was responsible for articulating and popularizing the school of behaviorism in the U.S. But before we can introduce Watson and examine the part he played in the development of behaviorism, we must set the historical stage.

The Roots Of Behaviorism In Functionalism

Behaviorism developed in the context of functionalism. The functionalists were concerned with both the practical application of psychology (as described in Chapter 5) and the use of empirical methods to investigate questions. In addition, because functionalism was shaped by evolutionary theory, it concerned itself not just with humans but also with non-human animals. Non-human animals were studied in their own right (in comparative psychology) and as a way to discover general psychological principles. The two most important functionalists, in terms of laying the foundation for later behaviorism, were E.L. Thorndike and Margaret Floy Washburn.

Thorndike, as discussed in Chapter 5, used rigorously designed experiments to test hypotheses regarding learning and animal intelligence. These experiments led him to formulate the basic laws of operant or instrumental conditioning. The same year that Thorndike published his path-breaking studies of instrumental learning, Willard S. Small began a series of studies on the white rat and maze learning which he published in 1900 and 1901 (Small, 1900; Small, 1901). Animal research proved enormously useful to the development of educational psychology and many of the comparative psychologists, such as Thorndike himself, later went on to work in school systems as educational psychologists or as researchers in the area of educational psychology (O'Donnell, 1985).

This is not to say that comparative psychology was a numerically significant subfield within American psychology. It was a small specialty, both in the number of active researchers and in terms of journal articles published. In 1908, for example, only six animal experiments were published, representing 4.1 percent of the total number of published articles. In 1910, the APA contained 218 members, 187 of whom had contributed to psychology (the APA at the time also included philosophers interested in the implications of psychology for philosophy). Nineteen of the 187 psychologists listed comparative psychology as one of their concerns, but only six of the 187 (3 percent) were active in comparative research (O'Donnell, 1985).

Within the field of comparative psychology conflict soon developed between the older researchers who examined animal psychology so as to make inferences about animal consciousness (the evolution of consciousness being an important concern of functionalist psychology) and the newer generation that excluded consciousness because is was an unneeded inference that violated Morgan's Canon. The leading member of the older generation was Washburn and the leading member of the younger generation was John B. Watson. Washburn did not just dislike Watson because of his sexism and racism (see Chapter 5) but because he embraced a different focus as to the subject matter of comparative psychology.

An important strategy of the younger generation of comparative psychologists who came under criticism was to argue that the proper focus of psychology was not consciousness but behavior. These criticisms came not only from psychologists but from university administrators who did not see any need to fund animal research and from sectors of the public who opposed the inhumane use of animals in research, especially vivisection (O'Donnell, 1985). The rhetorical strategy of arguing that the proper study of psychology was behavior was quietly pursued at first by Watson and a few other members of the younger generation of comparative psychologists. The emphasis on behavior was to resonate with the broader public immediately after World War I.

Continuing Influence Of Physiology

Physiology, especially neurophysiology, was not just influential in the period leading up to the birth of the New Psychology. Physiology continued to influence psychology, an influence that I would argue continues to this day. Nowhere is the ongoing influence of physiology more clearly seen than in the rise and success of behaviorism. Work in physiology provided basic concepts and inspiration to the behaviorist school.

One of the first influences on behaviorism was the materialist German-American physiologist Jacques Loeb (1859-1924), who emigrated to the U.S. from Germany in 1892. Loeb had studied at several German universities and received his M.D. in 1884 from the University of Strasburg. From 1884 to 1886, Loeb worked at the University of Würzburg where, in addition to his physiological research, he carried out studies in psychology and developed studies of tropism (response of plants or animals to physical stimuli). Loeb was Jewish; academic advancement was blocked to him. So from 1889 to 1891 he worked as an independent scholar, taking part-time jobs at different universities. He also met, fell in love with, and married an American woman. Married to an American woman and lacking a professional job, he decided to immigrate to the U.S. Loeb soon found permanent employment at the newly founded University of Chicago, where he worked from 1892 to 1903. After the University of Chicago, Loeb worked at the University of California and the Rockefeller Institute of Medicine in New York City (Wozniak, 1997).

Loeb's most influential work (in terms of its impact upon psychology) was *Comparative Physiology of the Brain and Comparative Psychology* (Loeb, 1900). Combining studies of neurophysiology and animal behavior, the work exerted a strong influence on a young generation of comparative psychologists, especially Watson, who studied with Loeb at the University of Chicago and wanted to do his dissertation with Loeb. Watson's advisor dissuaded him from doing so because Loeb was considered controversial. Nevertheless, Loeb's work exerted a strong influence on Watson and on other early behaviorists such as Robert Yerkes (1876-1956) and directly inspired Watson's behaviorism (Wozniak, 1997).

A second major figure from physiology was Ivan Petrovich Pavlov

(1849-1936). Pavlov was a Russian who won the Nobel Prize in 1904 for his work on digestion. Pavlov's parents were poor but educated. His father was an orthodox priest and his mother the daughter of an orthodox priest (priests can marry in the Russian Orthodox Church). He won a scholarship to study at the University of St. Petersburg and worked as a laboratory researcher to help fund his graduate education. Pavlov focused his research on the study of digestion and adopted the mechanistic and materialist philosophy that dominated physiology at that time in Germany. He received his M.D. in 1883 (Fancher, 1990).

After receiving his medical degree Pavlov spent two years studying at German universities as a post-doctoral researcher, first in Breslau and then in Leipzig. Thus Pavlov and Wundt were together at the University of Leipzig at the same time and Pavlov was there shortly after the birth of the new psychology. At Leipzig Pavlov worked with Carl Ludwig (1816-1895), one of the materialists who had sworn an oath to destroy vitalism with Helmholtz, Brücke, and Du Bois-Reymond. After returning to Russia, Pavlov worked hard and established a very productive laboratory, steadily rising in stature. In 1890 he became a professor at the Medical Military Academy of St. Petersburg and in 1891 he was asked to organize a department of physiology at the newly formed Russian Institute of Experimental Medicine (Kimble, 1991a).

Pavlov began his work on reflexes in 1902 when he fortuitously discovered that his experimental animals (he was using dogs) would salivate when the animal keepers would enter the room. He began a systematic study of this reflex and first presented his studies in his 1904 Nobel Lecture. A summary of Pavlov's research was published in the U.S. in 1909 (Yerkes & Morgulis, 1909) and a more comprehensive summary of his work was published in English in 1927 (Pavlov, 1927/1960). While the work of Pavlov did not exert a great influence on Watson's theory (Watson was far more influenced by Loeb and one of Pavlov's contemporaries, Vladimir M. Bechterev), Pavlov's work did inspire Watson's most famous experiment on the conditioning of a fear response in infants (Cohen, 1979). The real influence of Pavlov was to be felt in the decades after the publication of his work in English in the 1920s.

A third influential figure from physiology was Vladimir M. Bechterev (1857-1927) a Russian contemporary of Pavlov's. Bechterev extended Pavlov's work in two directions—first to muscle reflexes and second to human beings. Watson and his student Karl S. Lashley (1890-1959) learned of Bechterev's work in 1914 or 1915 and began research using his concepts soon after. Lashley developed a removable tube that fit into the human cheek to collect saliva and Watson began a series of experiments that measured muscle reflexes in humans when they received a slight shock in the finger or toe (Fancher, 1990).

The influence of physiology was not direct but mediated by a particular approach to psychology known as behaviorism. After functionalism, behaviorism is perhaps the most significant school of psychology to emerge from the U.S. The person most responsible for the promotion of behaviorism in the U.S. was the controversial and influential chair of the Johns Hopkins University Department of Psychology, John B. Watson. We cannot understand behaviorism without understanding Watson, his aims, and his achievements.

John B. Watson—Scientific Revolutionary Or Salesman?

John B. Watson (1878-1958) was born in Greenville, South Carolina. His parents were poor and his mother was a devout fundamentalist Christian who was strict with her children. Watson was close to his father, who taught him a number of trades such as carpentry. His parents were in some ways extreme opposites: while his mother was a devout member of her church, his father was interested mostly in drinking, swearing, and chasing women. When Watson turned 13 his father left home never to return (Cohen, 1979).

After his father's departure Watson was rebellious in school and often mocked his teachers. He frequently fought with his classmates until they started to bleed. And he and his friends engaged in what was then called "nigger fighting;" they would attack innocent blacks after school and beat them up. Watson was arrested at least twice as a teenager, once for beating a black man and once for firing a gun in Greenville (Cohen, 1979).

Watson was perhaps one of the least likely people to go to college, but go to college he did. He seems to have been desperate to escape life in the south and saw education as a way out. He somehow persuaded the president of Furman University (a Baptist college located in Greenville) to admit him. Watson lived at home and worked his way through college, trying to avoid the religious courses. He studied languages, history, math, science, philosophy, and the new psychology. He learned German so that he could read Wundt. By college Watson had already rejected religion and discovered his interest in women. While in college he reportedly had an affair with an older woman and a relationship with one of the three female students at Furman (Cohen, 1979).

Watson did very well in college but his natural rebelliousness would sometimes sabotage his success. In his senior year, his mentor and advisor said that he would flunk anyone who turned in his paper backwards. Watson proceeded to turn his 16 page final paper backwards, and was flunked. This forced Watson to spend another year at Furman. He took additional courses so that he could get a Master of Arts degree, finally graduating in 1899 (Cohen, 1979).

Upon graduation Watson took a low-level (for someone with an M.A. degree) job as a teacher in a one-room school house near Greenville. He stayed in the area because his mother was very sick. As a teacher Watson was very successful and innovative. He also kept rats as pets in the classroom and trained them. He was, as his former students attest, a skilled animal trainer. When Watson's mother died in July of 1900, Watson was eager to move on. He persuaded the president of Furman to write him a letter of recommendation to the University of Chicago and to Princeton, the two schools he applied to for his Ph.D. By September, Watson was a student at the University of Chicago. His former mentor from Furman was now on the faculty there, as was John Dewey, the person with whom Watson had gone to study (Cohen, 1979).

Watson arrived in Chicago near the end of August with no place to live and only $50 to his name. Watson had, since his first year as an undergraduate, been an incredibly hard worker. He did not find philosophy interesting and soon switched to psychology, studying under James R. Angell. Angell was Watson's mentor at Chicago, a veritable father figure. But while Watson respected Angell, he admired the scientific approach of one of his other teachers more— Jacques Loeb. Angell thought Loeb too controversial, however, and persuaded Watson to do research with another member of the faculty. Still Watson was attracted to the materialist and mechanistic approach of Loeb and he voiced criticism of the typical research on humans that involved introspection (Cohen, 1979).

Because of Watson's dissatisfaction with human research, his skill with animals, and his admiration for Loeb's work, he gravitated naturally toward comparative and physiological psychology. The starting point for his own work was Thorndike's *Animal Intelligence* (Thorndike, 1898) and Small's work with rats (Small, 1900; Small, 1901). Watson began his own studies in the autumn of 1901. He worked feverishly (he had an enormous ability to work long and hard, almost compulsively, with little sleep—an ability he maintained until late middle age) on studies of learning in rats, building complex mazes and elaborate apparatuses for the rats. Watson compared the learning of rats on different tasks and compared rats at different developmental stages to one another. After he had carefully described the performance of rats on different tasks and at different developmental stages, he proceeded to dissect the rat brains to compare similarities and differences in brain structure. This attempt to carefully examine learning, performance, and corresponding brain structures was to be path-breaking (Cohen, 1979).

Before completing his dissertation, Watson suffered a nervous breakdown, developing severe depression, insomnia, and phobias in late 1902. Watson was to be prone to depression his whole life, but this first major breakdown had many causes. In addition to his long hours of work on his dissertation, his need to work to support himself outside the lab, and his emerging intellectual differences with his mentor, Watson's relationship with his girlfriend (of which historians know little) ended in a break-up. Watson dealt with his depression by going on vacation to get away from his environment (a practice he was to recommend later in his life as an alternative to suicide). Watson vacationed with friends in Michigan for a month. When he returned to Chicago he was rested and seemingly recovered from his depression (Cohen, 1979).

Watson completed his dissertation in 1903 and became the youngest person ever to get a Ph.D. from the University of Chicago at that time. His dissertation was published as *Animal Education* (Watson, 1903), a name that is an obvious allusion to Thorndike's work. His work was well-received in professional journals and such intellectual magazines such as *The Nation* but was harshly criticized by animal rights activists. Angell recommended Watson for a job at the University of Chicago and so Watson stayed at Chicago instead of taking some of his other job offers. He plunged into his new responsibilities as a teacher and researcher. He also soon fell in love with one of his students, the daughter of a wealthy Chicago family, and in opposition to her family they married. Watson stayed at Chicago until 1908. While there Watson continued to carry out research on learning in rats (including the effects of destroying various sense modalities such as smell, sight, and touch from whiskers, on the rats' ability to traverse a maze), bird behavior in the wild (studies he carried out in the Tortugas off the Florida coast), bird migration, and primate behavior. Also while at Chicago, Watson developed a close relationship with two colleagues, the young comparative psychologist Robert Yerkes, and a graduate student in biology Karl Lashley. He was to work or correspond closely with both of these researchers as they developed the school of behaviorism (Cohen, 1979).

Always worried about money, Watson could not resist a lucrative offer from Johns Hopkins University that included a promotion in rank and a large raise; thus, Watson started at Johns Hopkins in 1908. Dramatically, in his first semester there, James Mark Baldwin, the chair of the department and a leading functionalist, had to resign because of a sex scandal (see Chapter 5). Watson became chair of the department and inherited Baldwin's editorship of the *Psychological Review*. Now holding a prominent and powerful position in the field, Watson began to develop and publicize his behaviorist views on psychology (Cohen, 1979).

Psychology As The Behaviorist Views It

Watson first presented his ideas, developed in collaboration with Yerkes and Lashley, in a series of lectures at Columbia University in early 1913. These lectures were soon published in *Psychological Review* (Watson, 1913) under the title *Psychology as the Behaviorist Views It*. Apparently, editorship has its privileges. The next year he published a work on comparative psychology from the behaviorist perspective (Watson, 1914). Watson's work as a comparative psychologist, editor, and theorist were recognized in 1914 with his election as President of the APA. While this election did not signal the acceptance of his ideas, as many often claim, it did acknowledge his standing within the profession (Cohen, 1979).

Watson's 1913 paper on behaviorism presents the fundamental postulates of the behaviorist school—the goal of psychology is the prediction and control of behavior, the methods must be objective and exclude introspectionism, and there is no distinction between humans and other animals. Watson's paper was essentially critical of the three existing schools and provoked negative responses from most of the leading psychologists, including Angell, Cattell, Woodworth, and Thorndike (Clifford, 1984).

In 1914 Watson carried out experiments on conditioning with Lashley and read a French translation of Bekhterev's work. Yerkes had introduced Pavlov's work to the U.S. in 1909. Now Watson had what he needed for a positive research program—the work of Thorndike on learning, and the work of Bechterev and Pavlov on reflexes, provided him with the mechanisms he needed to explain behavior.

In 1915, Watson (Watson, 1916) proposed in his APA presidential address that the conditioned reflex could be a fundamental building block for behaviorism (the talk was published the following year). Watson suggested that conditioning could explain the development of emotional reactions and certain psychiatric disorders, elevating conditioning's importance as a basic explanatory mechanism of psychology. Soon Watson was focusing his research on children, carrying out extensive observational studies at the Phipps Clinic in Baltimore. He also began collaborating with psychiatrists in his studies of children. Watson felt that the study of children and animals would advance the behaviorist school (Cohen, 1979). Watson's research projects were soon to be interrupted by World War I.

American Psychology Goes To War

While the Great War in Europe began in 1914, the U.S. did not get involved until April 6, 1917 when President Wilson signed the declaration of war. The American Psychological Association quickly formed a committee to advise the association on how psychology could best serve the war effort. Psychologists who opposed the war (such as Cattell) were excluded from this effort for obvious reasons. The committee concluded that the most useful task for psychologists was to develop screening tests for the large number of recruits entering the armed forces.

A number of psychologists were given leave from their jobs and joined the military, most as officers. Robert Yerkes, the behaviorist collaborator of Watson, was commissioned a Major and directed a group of psychologist that developed the Army Alpha and the Army Beta tests. These tests (which we shall discuss in Chapter 14) were given to over 1.7 million recruits and fostered the development of subsequent mental ability tests such as the Scholastic Aptitude Test, known to most as the SAT (Hunt, 1993).

Watson, too, joined the army and was commissioned a Major in August 1917. Watson's job was to develop tests that would identify potential pilots. He soon perfected a number of behavioral tests that simulated actual flight conditions as tools for selecting and screening candidates, and he also worked on the military use of homing pigeons and was sent to Europe to study British pilots. Watson did not tolerate incompetence, however, and he found a number of U.S. officers to be incompetent. One issue was the validity of a rotation test used to select pilots. Watson's research showed the test to be invalid. Furthermore, some people who "flunked" the invalid test were made pilots anyway if they had connections. Watson's conflicts with his superiors got him assigned to a combat position in late 1918. The war ended just as Watson was to be sent to the front. Major Watson was delighted to return to his job at Johns Hopkins (Cohen, 1979).

As a whole, the war proved very beneficial to psychology, convincing many of the practical benefits that psychology afforded. Commenting on the war, Cattell remarked that it "put psychology on the map" and Hall concluded that the war reinforced the trend toward applied psychology (Hunt, 1993).

The Fall Of John B. Watson And The Rise Of Behaviorism

Watson returned from the war at the apex of his career as a psychologist. He then planned an ambitious series of studies to revolutionize the field and completed important work on the conditioning of emotional responses in an infant, the now famous Little Albert study (Watson & Rayner, 1920) which was little more than a demonstration (Harris, 1979). He also published the mature statement of his position (Watson, 1919).

Watson valued careful observation of complex behavior in natural environments almost as much as he valued careful experimentation. He carried out large numbers of observations on infant and child development, which he incorporated into his 1919 book (Watson, 1919), a work arguing that careful observation was as important as careful experimentation. Observation and experimentation go hand in hand, Watson argued. Field observations suggest what needed to be studied experimentally. Experimental results must be brought back to the field. Watson also argued that an individual's personal history shapes his or her behavior. He discusses a broad range of psychological subjects, including personality, work, and emotions, as well as mental health (Watson, 1919).

The other significant work that Watson produced immediately after the war was a study of emotional conditioning in an infant, a study he conducted with a young graduate student, Rosalie Rayner, whom he met in the fall of 1919. Watson and Rayner conditioned a small child, Albert, to fear a rat, an animal that the child had not previously shown any fear toward. They also demonstrated that this fear generalized to similar objects in the child's environment, such as a rabbit and a sealskin coat. The fear did not generalize to distinctly different items, such as a block (Watson & Rayner, 1920). The study became a fundamental demonstration of Watson's approach and is often cited in introductory psychology texts, as well as more advanced texts on behavioral therapy, and is considered a classic study in the field (Harris, 1979). For many years the identity of Little Albert, as he was described in the study, was unknown. In a triumph of historical research, Beck, Levinson, and Irons (2009) discovered the true identity of Albert: Douglas Merritte (1919-1925), the child of an unwed mother who died at the age of six, most probably from meningitis (Beck, Levinson, & Irons, 2009).

Watson had a long history of marital infidelity. He frequently slept with other women and cheated on his wife, Mary, when he was away at conferences or meetings and when he was in the military. His wife put up with his affairs as long as she felt sure he would not leave her. This changed in 1920 however, when Watson began an affair with Rosalie Rayner, his graduate assistant. He seemed to be deeply in love with her and was public about their affair, being seen around Baltimore in public places together. Mary discovered one of Rosalie's love letters to Watson and, after talking to her lawyer, devised a plan to obtain Watson's other letters to his lover. Watson's wife arranged to attend dinner at the Rayners' home (Rosalie lived with her parents) and during dinner Mary Watson complained of feeling sick and needing to rest. She rested in Rosalie's room, which she searched carefully, and discovered a large number of John Watson's very passionate letters to Rosalie. Mary also realized that the affair was more serious than she had expected and that Watson was thinking of leaving her for the younger woman. The Watsons separated in April of 1920, but Mary continued her efforts to get her husband to end his affair. Among her efforts, she approached the Rayners and told them of the affair. They arranged to send their daughter to Europe to be away from Watson, hoping that this would end the relationship (Cohen, 1979).

During the summer, one of Mary's brothers tried blackmailing the Rayners with the stolen love letters, to no avail. Watson became worried that the university would fire him, but claimed to some of his colleagues that he was too influential to be fired. Watson became worried that a series of experiments he was carrying out on the effects of alcohol on performance (prohibition went into effect on January 16, 1920 at midnight) would generate controversy. Still, there was no sign from the administration that the growing scandal had altered Watson's status within the university. Then, suddenly on September 29 the head of the Phipps Clinic wrote a private and confidential letter to the president of the university. The next day, the president of Johns Hopkins summoned Watson to his office and fired him. Watson was devastated and left the university immediately for New York. He was immediately abandoned by almost all of his former friends except for Lashley, Titchener, William Thomas (a sociologist who himself had been fired from the University of Chicago for a sex scandal), and the psychiatrist Leslie Hohlman. Thomas lived in New York and let the unemployed Watson live at his house. Thomas also gave Watson money and spent considerable time listening to the distressed Watson talk about his problems. Thomas also introduced Watson to employees of the J. Walter Thompson Advertising Agency, where he would soon work. The divorce hearing took place in November of 1920 and was reported in the media as a scandal in December. In January 1921, Watson married Rosalie Rayner at a small private ceremony in New York. Her separation had not diminished her love for Watson in the least. Her parents were furious (Cohen, 1979).

Did Watson Conduct Sex Experiments?

A story that has circulated among psychologists for many years (I first heard it from a behaviorist in the 1980s) was that Watson was not fired from Johns Hopkins simply for having an affair with his student and wanting to leave his wife, both scandalous enough at the time for a college professor, but that there was another reason—he and Rosalie had been carrying out experiments, using each other as subjects, on the physiology of sexual responses. The claim that John Watson and Rosalie Rayner were conducting sex experiments was articulated in print by McConnell (1982), a prominent behaviorist and Magoun (1981), but has been denied by Buckley (1989), the author of an important biography of Watson. Buckley has written "the contention that Mary Ickes Watson found records of sexual experiments that she used as evidence in her divorce suit is simply not true" (Buckley, 1989, p. 212). Buckley's argument rests on the complete court transcripts, which contain no mention of such experiments and no criticisms of Watson's work as a scientist. This is not McConnell's claim, nor is it Magoun's. The argument is not that Mary Watson used this information in the trial; the argument is that Watson and Rayner carried out sex experiments and Mary Watson discovered them and used the information to get at her husband (but not at the trial).

Let us consider the evidence, all of which is circumstantial.

First, Watson read Freud's work starting in 1910 and was interested in it and sympathetic to some of Freud's claims. Watson's main criticism of Freud was that Freud focused on the awareness of sexuality, not on sexual behavior, which should be the real focus of psychological research (Cohen, 1979).

Second, Watson began carrying out studies on sex immediately after the end of the Great War. One of these studies, which he carried out with Karl Lashley (Watson & Lashley, 1920), was on the effects of two anti-venereal disease films produced by the army on sexual behaviors and attitudes. Essentially arguing for abstinence and moral restraint, the films were intended to reduce the number of soldiers who frequented prostitutes. Watson and Lashley found that the films did not increase the audience's knowledge of VD nor did they change the audience's sexual behaviors. The study made use of questionnaires and examined the impact of film showings in three communities, and included a detailed analysis of the film itself (Cohen, 1979). Another study, carried out again with Lashley (Watson & Lashley, 1919), examined doctors' attitudes toward sex and the kind of advice doctors gave to patients. The study showed that few doctors were comfortable or qualified to give advice on sex and sexually transmitted diseases. Based on his studies, Watson increasingly argued that sexual behavior had to be studied by psychologists (Cohen, 1979).

Third, a small box of physiological recording instruments that could be used to measure blood flow in the penis or clitoris was discovered at Johns Hopkins in the 1940s.

Fourth, Watson was not fired because of his divorce and the ensuing public scandal—he was in fact fired long before the divorce took place. Sometime between September 20 and September 28, 1920, secret information was revealed to the administration about Watson. This information led to Watson's firing. At the same time, Watson's many friends and allies seemed to abandon him suddenly. The president of the university called Watson in and demanded his resignation. Watson resigned on the spot (Cohen, 1979).

Finally, Johns Hopkins had considerable motive to keep the records of the studies secret or in fact to destroy them. More than just an affair with a student —the study of sex would have generated enormous public opposition, as it did decades later with other sex researchers.

So, Watson had motive (both scientific and personal), means, and opportunity. Will we ever find definitive evidence of what happened? At this point it is unlikely. The most balanced and comprehensive evaluation of the evidence was provided by Benjamin, Whitaker, Ramsey, and Zeve (2009), who conclude that the evidence is inconclusive. Benjamin et al. hope that the story is finally eliminated from textbooks and lecture notes, but this, I fear, is the wrong conclusion. A mystery unsolved is still a mystery. Somewhere in some diary or personal correspondence, or perhaps in the archives of Johns Hopkins University, conclusive evidence may still be hidden.

After The Fall

Watson began working for the J. Walter Thompson Advertising Agency in 1920. Reluctant to give up an important part of his life, Watson continued working as a psychologist while working full time as an influential advertising executive. He wrote frequently for popular magazines and was often interviewed by the press and on radio. Indeed, Watson became the first pop psychologist in the U.S., a role which many now occupy (e.g., Dr. Phil). He also continued to teach, working in the evenings and weekends at the New School for Social Research in New York City, where he started in the fall of 1922 (Cohen,

1979). He also invited other psychologists to give talks to his students, including William MacDougal, the prominent social psychologist and functionalist. The guest lecture by MacDougall led to a series of public debates between the two men on their respective positions. The most famous of these debates took place at the Psychology Club in Washington D.C. on February 5, 1924 and was later published (Watson & MacDougal, 1929) as *The Battle of Behaviorism*.

While teaching at the New School, Watson also worked with Mary Cover Jones, a friend of Rosalie's who was doing graduate work in psychology at Columbia University. Watson wrote a grant to fund a nursery school for children and designed a number of observational and experimental studies of children at the nursery. One of the studies, a follow-up to the Little Albert experiment, was an effort to remove fear from a young child, Peter (Jones, 1924). Jones' work provided one of the basic procedures for behaviorally removing phobias, a procedure that was to be developed later as a fundamental technique of behavioral therapy. Thus, Jones and Watson can be considered the founders of behavioral therapy (Cohen, 1979).

Watson modified his lectures and speeches and published them as a popular account of his theory in *Behaviorism* (Watson, 1925; Watson, 1930). Both editions sold well and did much to popularize his theory. They also were more dogmatic and strident in tone than his earlier mature statement of his theory (Watson, 1919). Finally, in 1928 Watson published *Psychological Care of the Infant and Child* (Watson, 1928). This was an influential childrearing book for parents and sold well. Childrearing manuals had become widespread and influential in the earlier years of the 1900s (Hulbert, 2003), a phenomenon linked to the rise of child psychology (see Chapter 11).

Watson was increasingly frustrated by his inability to carry out basic scientific research. The demands of his career as an advertising executive, his work as a popular writer on psychology, and his family all made it difficult for him. By 1930, when Watson turned 52, his incredible ability for hard work started to decline. He cut back on public appearances and media interviews, and stopped writing (except for a few short pieces such as an autobiographical essay and an unpublished article on suicide). When Rosalie died suddenly and tragically in 1936 of dysentery, Watson withdrew into his advertising job and personal life on his Connecticut estate. He was 58 and very wealthy, but the one person he had really loved in his entire life had died. The APA, an organization that he had once served as president, honored him in 1957 with a gold medal, the organization's highest honor, for his contributions to psychology. The citation read: "To John B. Watson whose work has been one of the vital determinants of the form and substance of modern psychology. He initiated a revolution in psychological thought and his writings have been a point of departure for continuing lines of fruitful research." Watson went to the convention in New York with his children and friends (Karl Lashley, one of the few psychologists who had not abandoned him, joined him in New York). When the time came to accept the medal, though, Watson sent his son in his stead. After 38 years of professional ostracism, Watson still felt wounded. He died the next year at age 80 (Cohen, 1979).

What was Watson's contribution to psychology? Baars (1986) has argued that both theory and metatheory are important in psychology. Watson not only introduced a new school of psychology, a particular theory and view of psychology, he introduced a new metatheory. The school of behaviorism that Watson founded is often called Watsonian behaviorism (or later, radical behaviorism). There were few Watsonian behaviorists in American psychology after Watson. Certainly Lashley was one, as was Yerkes, along with a handful of other researchers in the 1920s. In the 1930s a new generation of Watsonian Behaviorists, none of whom knew Watson personally, would arise. The foremost of these Watsonians would be B.F. Skinner, whom we will introduce shortly.

Watson also helped alter the metatheory of psychology. A metatheory, according to Baars (1986) is a viewpoint about how one does a science. This viewpoint includes a definition of the subject of the science along with general epistemological commitments about how one does research and develops theory. Baars has distinguished three metatheories in the history of modern psychology: introspectionism or the psychology of consciousness, behaviorism, and cognitivism. Cognitivism developed in the 1950s and 1960s in what is called the Cognitive Revolution (discussed in Chapter 10). Introspectionism as a metatheory defined psychology as the study of consciousness or experience and was not reductionistic or mechanistic. Behaviorism defined psychology as the study of behavior and was highly reductionistic and mechanistic (Baars, 1986).

Watsonian behaviorism developed a distinct school within psychology as well as changed the metatheory of the field. Watson's considerable skills as a researcher and theorist were not by themselves enough to alter the metatheory of modern psychology. At least two other factors were at play; First, Watson was a highly skilled salesperson who publicized his views on psychology to the public. His promotion of behaviorism altered the public's perception of psychology as a science and influenced many young college students and educated laypeople.

While the development of behaviorism as a school owed much to the continuing influence of biology on psychology, the success of the behaviorism as a metatheory owed much to the continuing influence of philosophy on psychology. One of the influences came out of Freud's Vienna—the philosophy of Logical Positivism. The second influence came from the ideas of operationalism, presented by the physicist Percy W. Bridgman and championed by Harvard psychologist S.S. Stevens (1906-1973).

Logical positivism was developed by a group of philosophers in Vienna in the early years of the 20th century. Known later as the Vienna Circle, a group of philosophers based in Vienna in the years between the two world wars, these philosophers sought to rid modern philosophy of a number of puzzles by applying methods that had been used successfully in the sciences. These methods included logic and the definition of words by reference to operations performed by the scientist. Logical positivism also rejected a large number of terms as meaningless. Associated with a number of physicists, the logical positivists attracted considerable status as clear thinking philosophers. Ludwig Wittgenstein's early work *Tractatus Logico-Philosophicus* (Wittgenstein, 1922), written while Wittgenstein was a soldier in the trenches of World War I, was an important starting point for the Vienna Circle, although he was not a member of the group. A number of British philosophers, including the mathematician Bertrand Russell, were also sympathetic to and held views similar to the Vienna Circle (Janik & Toulmin, 1973). In the U.S., one of the leading representatives of the Vienna Circle was Herbert Feigl, a long time faculty member at the University of Minnesota who had fled Europe and later became a close friend of B.F. Skinner's (Weiner, 1996).

Besides logical positivism, the other philosophical influence on psychology's metatheory came from Bridgman's *The Logic of Modern Physics* (Bridgman, 1927). Bridgman, who taught at Harvard and had won the Noble Prize in Physics, argued that all concepts and terms that could not be precisely defined in terms of operations performed to measure them should be discarded as vacuous or as pseudo-problems. Ever desperate for status, many psychologists embraced the concept of operationalism as a way to make psychology a rigorous science. One of the chief proponents of operationalism was S.S. Stevens, an experimental psychologist at Harvard in the 30s, 40s, and 50s (Stevens, 1935a; Stevens, 1935b). Few psychologists could resist the two pressures, the one from the public's understanding of psychology as the study of behavior and the other from philosophy. While many psychologists (including the majority who had been trained before 1920) remained essentially functionalists, the metatheory of the field shifted. Psychology by the end of the 1920s was now the study of behavior, not consciousness, and it was increasingly reductionistic and mechanistic. The behavioristic metatheory was to dominate psychology from the 1920s to the late 1950s, almost as long as the introspectionist metatheory dominated the field.

The Varieties Of Behaviorism After Watson

It is a mistake to conceive of behaviorism as a monolithic approach to psychology. While Watson was successful in changing the general direction and emphasis in the field, there were many variants, some of which retained elements of earlier functionalist school or incorporated elements of competing schools, such as psychoanalysis or Gestalt psychology. The most famous of the behaviorists, however, was also the most Watsonian, B.F. Skinner.

The Radical Behaviorism of B.F. Skinner

The leading proponent of behaviorism (as a distinct school of psychology as opposed to the metatheory) in the years following Watson's forced retirement from the field was B. F. Skinner (1904-1990). Skinner, known to most as Fred, was born in Susquehanna, Pennsylvania. His parents had not gone to college but his father had read law while working as an apprentice in a law firm and later passed the bar exam. The Skinner family was middle class, but just barely, and his parents wanted Fred to get a college education and study law. Around the time Skinner started college his father got a lucrative job as an attorney for a railroad company and Skinner's family joined the upper middle class. Fred was a talented young man who worked hard. He wrote stories and poems and got some of them published. He was accepted at Hamilton College, a liberal arts college in New York. He was the first person in his extended family ever to attend a liberal arts college. During his first year in college, Skinner's only brother died. While at college Skinner felt like a "hick" compared to many of the other students. He was not successful at extra-curricular activities and spent a great deal of time writing and reading. He befriended some of his teachers, including the dean of the college, who treated Skinner like a son (Wiener, 1996).

Skinner steadily gained confidence as a student and loved the intellectual environment the college provided. He met the poet Robert Frost while a senior and Frost complemented Skinner on one of the young man's published poems. This strengthened Skinner's desire to be a writer, and after graduation he persuaded his father to support him for a year so that he could write a novel. The year, described by Skinner as his "Dark Year" was largely unproductive. Skinner had trouble writing and had little to say. He eventually stopped trying and spent time living in New York City (where he frequented the counter-cultural scene in Greenwich Village) and Europe. In frustration, Skinner's father suggested that they write a law book on workmen's compensation issues, an area in which the senior Skinner had developed considerable expertise. The two co-authored the book, with B.F. Skinner doing most of the writing based on his father's ideas and research. The book was a modest success and B.F. Skinner's share of the royalties helped support him in graduate school (Wiener, 1996).

During Skinner's Dark Year, he read an essay by Bertrand Russell that praised Watson's work. Skinner immediately read Watson and then Pavlov and Loeb. He became excited about the ideas of psychology as a science of behavior (he had little or no exposure to psychology in college) and applied to Harvard Graduate School to study psychology. Skinner's parents did not really know what a psychologist did but they were happy that he was no longer wasting his life and that he was studying at a prestigious university. Skinner started graduate school in 1928 and finished his Ph.D. in three years (in 1931), an impressive achievement for someone with no previous education in psychology (Wiener,

1996).

Skinner was initially intimidated at Harvard, again feeling like a "hick" but he soon fell in love with the stimulating environment. He worked very hard and socialized little. During his two years off to write he had numerous sexual relationships, a practice he was to resume after getting his Ph.D. But while working on his degree he was single- minded. His only real friend was Fred Keller, a fellow graduate student who shared his commitment to behaviorism. Keller and Skinner were to remain lifelong friends with an unshakable commitment to Watsonian behaviorism (later Skinnerian or radical behaviorism). Keller went on to be the chair of the Psychology Department at Columbia University. Fred Keller was also perhaps the only person who called Skinner by his first name, Burrhus (Wiener, 1996).

While at Harvard, Skinner demonstrated a high level of skill as a maker of laboratory equipment and as a researcher. He also was a strident and dogmatic behaviorist, frequently clashing with his advisor, the famous E.G. Boring. Boring, known as Garry to his friends, respected Skinner for his intellect and skill, considering Skinner one of the best graduate students of his generation. They also disagreed strongly about the subject matter and approach of psychology. Skinner was more of a Watsonian than Watson in graduate school, criticizing Watson's book *Behaviorism* for spending too much time on mental subjects and too little time on behavior. In addition to Boring, Skinner was also a student of S.S. Stevens and Percy W. Bridgman who taught at Harvard while Skinner was a student there. Skinner also clashed frequently with the psychoanalytically oriented member of the faculty, Henry Murray (Wiener, 1996), who you will meet again in Chapter 12.

Skinner's doctoral dissertation illustrates both his self-confidence as a psychologist and his behaviorist views. Boring rejected the first draft of Skinner's thesis and submitted a detailed critique calling for a large number of changes. Boring was especially upset with Skinner's weak understanding of the literature and poorly organized literature review. Skinner ignored Boring and submitted his thesis for publication. It was accepted; Boring was now outflanked. He continued to request changes in the thesis but was essentially ignored by Skinner. Boring, who respected Skinner's hard work and talent, relented. Skinner passed his final oral examination without any problems (Wiener, 1996).

Skinner spent five more years at Harvard carrying out his research. For three of those years he was a Junior Fellow, a prestigious appointment for a young scholar and one that allowed him to do exactly what he wanted to do. Skinner later worked at the University of Minnesota from 1936 to 1945 (a period of enormous productivity for him) and at Indiana University from 1945 to 1948, before returning to Harvard in 1948 where he remained until his retirement. Shortly after starting his job at the University of Minnesota, Skinner married and soon was the father of two daughters (Wiener, 1996).

Skinner's closest friend at Minnesota was the logical positivist Herbert Feigl. Lashley was also a member of the faculty for a time as well. Skinner developed into a talented teacher and often taught honors students. He taught a variety of courses, including courses on the psychology of literature (Skinner was enormously well read in fiction, reading novels and plays in both English and French). His primary focus however, was on his research. He was a skillful designer and builder of experimental apparatuses, just as Watson had been. Skinner was also very hard-working and productive, as well as a skilled writer. These characteristics were essential to his success as a scientist, success he began to enjoy at Minnesota (Wiener, 1996).

Skinner's animal subject of choice was the pigeon, not the rat. He tended to avoid studies with large numbers of subjects and instead focused on studies with small numbers of animals that he would then replicate. He also tended to avoid the typical statistical inference tests used by psychologists, adopting instead the graphic display of data, his most well-known graphic display being the cumulative record of a response.

Skinner's first book, *The Behavior of Organisms* (Skinner, 1938) was based on his research at Harvard. While it did not sell widely at first, it did present the fundamentals of Skinner's approach to operant conditioning (the conditioning of behavior through environmental contingencies of reinforcement and punishment). The following year he published a description of the experimental apparatus that has become known as the Skinner Box, a pen or cage in which the experimenter can control the reinforcements and punishments of an animal (Skinner, 1939).

In addition to *The Behavior of Organisms*, Skinner's most important scientific works are *Schedules of Reinforcement* (Skinner & Ferster, 1957) in which he describes research on the effects of different reinforcement schedules on behavior, and *Verbal Behavior* (Skinner, 1957), which attempts a behaviorist analysis of language. In addition, Skinner produced important work on superstition (Skinner, 1948a), education (Skinner, 1968), and teaching machines (Skinner, 1958; Skinner 1961a; Skinner, 1961b), the forerunners of current computer based instruction. Finally, Skinner wrote an Introductory Psychology college textbook (Skinner, 1953) that presented psychology from a strictly behaviorist perspective. This was a somewhat idiosyncratic approach, as most beginning college texts try to present a broad survey of the field that covers contributions from all schools. The text did cover a broad range of topics (emotions, thinking, self-control, the self, and social behavior), but from a behaviorist perspective, and bears some resemblance to Watson's *Behaviorism* (Watson, 1925/1970).

Throughout Skinner's career he also wrote for broader audiences, much like Watson and Freud did. For instance, he wrote an article on Gertrude Stein's poetry in the *Atlantic Monthly* early in his career (Skinner, 1934), an article in the *Ladies Home Journal* on the baby tender (Skinner, 1945), an article on animal training in *Scientific American* (Skinner, 1951), and articles in *Psychology Today* (Skinner, 1969) and *The New York Times* (1972b). But Skinner did not just write for broader audiences on occasion: two of his major works were written for mass audiences, *Walden Two* (Skinner, 1948b) and his most controversial work, *Beyond Freedom and Dignity* (Skinner, 1971). Both books became bestsellers and contributed substantially to Skinner's standing as a scientist. Indeed, both books made him the most famous psychologist since Freud (Wiener, 1996). *Beyond Freedom and Dignity* become a Book of the Month Club selection and was serialized in both *Psychology Today* and *The New York Post* (see Skinner, 1972a for the publication history). *Walden Two* is a utopian novel about a community based on behaviorist principles. In addition to being a best-seller, the novel was the basis for a number of communes organized in the 1960s. *Beyond Freedom and Dignity* is an application of behaviorism to politics and political theory. In this work Skinner argues that humans are controlled by their environment, that we are not autonomous entities with free will. The environment is largely of our own making, however, and we can re-make the

connects to our previous discussion

environment so that humans are happier, more productive, and more satisfied with life. Skinner especially argues against the role of punishment in society (government, family, school) and in favor of reinforcing desired behavior. Skinner's contribution to political theory makes him one of the leading libertarian anarchists of the last 100 years.

In all, Skinner's skill as a researcher and writer, his productivity, and his cultivation of a mass audience helped to make him the most influential of all the behaviorists. It was also the case, however, that he often obscured the source of his ideas. In *Beyond Freedom and Dignity* he noted that individuals are given greater credit for their achievements when we do not know the causes of those achievements. So too with intellectual achievements. Skinner often failed to cite previous research that he was using as the basis for his own work, a behavior pattern apparent to Boring in Skinner's doctoral dissertation (see above). Early in Skinner's career he was often caught doing this, when for instance reviewers of *The Behavior of Organisms* (Skinner, 1938) noted that Skinner did not cite Thorndike's work, which was the basis for Skinner's work. In 1939 Skinner wrote to Thorndike to apologize for not citing the latter's work, and to offer excuses (Clifford, 1984). As with Freud, self-promotion benefited Skinner's career and public reputation.

The Neo-Behaviorism Of Clark Hull And Edwin Guthrie

Watson was certainly successful in changing the public perception of psychology and in developing an influential approach. But many psychologists, while influenced by Watson, retained strong functionalist characteristics. One prominent example of this blending of behaviorism and functionalism is Clark Hull (1884-1952) who was one of the leading psychologists of the 1920s, 30s, and 40s. He explicitly considered himself a functionalist (Kimble, 1991b; see especially Hull, 1929) while many historians of psychology describe him as a behaviorist or neo-behaviorist (Hergenhahn, 2005; Hothersall, 2004; Schultz & Schultz, 2004). While he himself rejected the label of behaviorist, in the Watsonian and Skinnerian sense, he did embrace behaviorism as a metatheory: he was clearly mechanistic in his approach and he emphasized the study of behavior.

Hull was born in a log cabin in upstate New York and his family moved to Michigan when he was around four years old. He studied in a one-room school house until he was 16, when he passed the teacher's exam and became a teacher. Hull soon decided to attend college to study mining engineering. He enrolled in Alma College in Michigan to begin his studies. While at Alma he contracted typhoid fever, almost died from contaminated food, and then contracted poliomyelitis, which resulted in the need to use a leg brace for the rest of his life (Hull himself designed and built his first leg brace). His polio also forced him to change his career plans to something less physically demanding (Kimble, 1991b).

Hull's illness forced him to drop out of college for a time and return home to teach again in a one room school house. He got married, read all of William James' *Principles of Psychology* as preparation for his new major, and after two years returned to college, this time to the University of Michigan, to study psychology. He and his wife were broke after he graduated from Michigan so he worked again as a teacher for a year before starting graduate school at the University of Wisconsin (Kimble, 1991b).

In graduate school Hull concentrated his research on what he called the evolution of concepts, what is now often referred to as concept formation. Inventing a machine to present Chinese ideographs and using the basic approach of Ebbinghaus, Hull showed that we learn concepts slowly (Hull, 1920). After finishing his Ph.D. in 1918 Hull taught at the University of Wisconsin where he carried out research on the effects of smoking on memory (Kimble, 1991b), aptitude testing (Hull, 1928) and experimental studies of hypnosis which he continued at Yale University where he moved in 1929 (Hull, 1933). Hull was recruited to Yale by James R. Angell, president of Yale University, who you will recall had been both a president of the APA and the former graduate school advisor to John Watson.

Although Hull started his career late in life (he was 34 when he got his Ph.D.) because of the hardships he encountered, he became a prominent and respected researcher. In addition to his rigorous and highly respected work on concept formation, aptitude testing, and hypnosis, he engaged in theoretical debates within psychology, including his functionalist interpretation of the conditioned reflex (Hull, 1929) and his functionalist interpretation of the Gestalt concept of fields of force (Hull, 1938). He also, as part of his work on aptitude testing, invented a working calculator that computed correlation co-efficients, a device that saved researchers an enormous amount of time in the pre-computer days when correlations had to be computed using only paper and pencil (Kimble, 1991b).

Hull's status as an expert experimentalist who made substantial contributions to a variety of areas resulted in his election in 1936 as president of the APA. In his presidential address (Hull, 1937) he presented his general learning theory, which was to be the focus of the rest of his career. Hull was clearly a functionalist, as shown not just in his own statements but in his theoretical contributions, but he, like his contemporaries, showed the influence of both physiology and behaviorism on this thinking. He was also perhaps one of the more scientifically ambitious of American psychologists for he sought, much like the Gestalt psychologists, Watson, and Skinner, to create a general theory for psychology. The heart and soul of Hull's general theory was the process of learning, the mediating variables between the environment and behaviors.

Hull's focus on learning and his effort to build a logical and integrated theory of learning as a theoretical basis for psychology resulted in his most influential work, *Principles of Behavior* (Hull, 1943) and two later works (Hull, 1951; Hull, 1952). These works stimulated extensive research on simple learning (Kimble, 1991b) as well as more complex forms of learning, including social behavior.

Hull was more than anything else a functionalist psychologist who embraced rigorous experimental methods and a mechanistic view of the human being. Indeed, he considered himself a mechanist as well as a functionalist and thought of the human being as a complex robot or machine. In this sense he deviated from the early functionalists with their intense interest in spirituality and religion. In fact, at the University of Wisconsin Hull created controversy when he publicly challenged a prominent biologist who was lecturing on ESP. Hull's efforts at building an integrated and logical theory failed, but it was a magnificent failure, generating numerous experimental studies. His empirical work made substantial contributions to a number of areas, contributions that are still valued to this day (Kimble, 1991b).

Hull was not the only functionalist to embrace more rigorous experimentation and a focus on learning theory. Almost as significant was Edwin R.Guthrie (1886-1959). Guthrie was born into a middle class family in Lincoln, Nebraska, where his father sold pianos, bicycles, and furniture in his store. Guthrie was enormously gifted academically. In eighth grade he read Darwin's *Origin of Species* and *The Expression of Emotions in Man and Animals.* Guthrie graduated with honors from the University of Nebraska in 1907 with a degree in mathematics. He then worked as a high school math teacher while he worked on a master's degree in philosophy, which he earned in 1910. Guthrie then transferred to the University of Pennsylvania where he earned his Ph.D. in 1912. Guthrie was not able to find work as a college professor immediately and so worked as a high school math teacher again until he took a job at the University of Washington in 1914, where he spent the rest of his career (Prenzel-Guthrie, 1996).

The Purposive Behaviorism Of Edward C. Tolman

The three most influential experimental psychologists in the U.S. during the 1920s, 1930s, and 1940s, were Skinner, Hull, and Edward C. Tolman (1886-1959). Tolman often referred to his approach as that of purposive behaviorism, although it is clear that Tolman's work falls within the functionalist tradition while at the same time showing the influence of physiology, behaviorism, and Gestalt psychology on his empirical work and theorizing.

Unlike the other members of the second generation of American psychologists that we have examined (Watson, Yerkes, Skinner, Hull, and Guthrie), Tolman did not come from a working class or middle class background, but from the upper middle class or upper class. His father was president of a successful company in Massachusetts and a graduate of MIT. When he was growing up, his family valued equal rights for women and blacks, political reform, and pacifism (Gleitman, 1991). Tolman and his family came from the same cultural and intellectual background as many of the early functionalists, including James, Calkins, Hall, Cattell, Dewey, Washburn, and Thorndike.

Tolman graduated from MIT with a degree in engineering in 1911. His interests shifted away from engineering and toward philosophy and psychology in his senior year when he read a number of James' works. He enrolled the next year at Harvard in the combined philosophy and psychology department, taking courses with Yerkes (using Watson's just-published book on comparative psychology), Holt, and Langfield, and working as a researcher in Münsterberg's lab. At the end of his first year at Harvard Tolman went to Germany to improve his German and study with Kurt Koffka. He returned to Germany after World War I to study with Koffka a second time while he was a young faculty member at the University of California (Gleitman, 1991).

Tolman finished his Ph.D. in 1915. His thesis was an experimental study of memory. He took a job at Northwestern University in Chicago where he worked for three years before being fired in 1918. The reason given for his firing was the poor quality of his teaching, although Tolman believed that he was fired for his opposition to World War I and his publication of a pacifist statement in a student paper. In any case, Tolman was fortunate enough to be hired by the University of California where he was to work for 32 years (Gleitman, 1991) until being fired in 1950 for leading the faculty opposition to the signing of an anti-communist loyalty oath (Schrecker, 1986). As perhaps a partial atonement for its earlier repression of academic freedom, the University of California at Berkeley later named its psychology building Tolman Hall.

At the University of California Tolman produced a series of rigorous experimental studies in a variety of areas and contributed a number of important theoretical concepts. His contributions, like those of Hull and Guthrie, were recognized by his peers and he was elected President of the APA in 1937 (Innes, 1992a).

One set of studies focused on the inheritance of learning ability. These studies focused on the relative contribution of nature and nurture (biological factors and environmental factors) in animal learning. The nature vs. nurture question has always been an important one for functionalist psychologists, in part because of the influence of Darwin's work on their psychology. The studies that Tolman and his students carried out were focused on breeding maze-bright and maze-dull rats and measuring their performance. Many of these studies were carried out with Robert C. Tryon, a student and later colleague of Tolman's and one of the fathers of the field of behavioral genetics. Tyron's graduate student J. Hirsch became a leading figure in this field in the 1960s, and Tyron and Hirsch coined the name for the field. Hirsch later shifted to the fruit fly as a more advantageous research subject than the white rat (Innes, 1992b).

Tolman was also renowned for his non-reductionistic, cognitive behaviorism he described as purposive behaviorism. He showed experimentally that learning is different from performance in a famous study on latent learning

(learning without reinforcement) in which rats who had not been reinforced for learning a maze but merely permitted to roam the maze could perform as well as rats whose behavior had been consistently reinforced when the first group was given reinforcement (Tolman & Honzik, 1930). Tolman emphasized the role of cognition and purpose as intervening variables that must be studied in order to understand an organism's behavior (Tolman, 1928; Tolman, 1932) and studied cognitive maps in animals and humans (Tolman, 1948).

Like Skinner and Watson, Tolman also tried to influence the broader public. On the eve of World War II (Tolman, 1942) he published a psychological analysis of war, in the hopes that a greater understanding of war would help people avoid conflict in the future. Tolman was also a strong supporter of Gestalt psychologists in the U.S., especially his old friends Kurt Koffka, whom you shall meet in the next chapter, and Kurt Lewin, whom you shall meet in the next chapter and Chapter 12. Tolman was an active member of Lewin's Topology Group, described in Chapter 12 (Marrow, 1969).

Behaviorism, Racism, And Sexism

Behaviorism did not become the dominate school of psychology in the U.S. simply because it was more "scientific. Behaviorism reflected the increasing turn against radical social movements and radical social change that the Jamesians supported, albeit not universally or consistently, within the first generation. While we do not have evidence yet on all of the behaviorists, we know that Watson and his long-time collaborator Karl Lashley were deeply racist and supported Jim Crow laws in the south and throughout the country (Weidman, 1999; 2002). In fact, Lashley was also anti-Semitic; he supported Hitler and the Nazi program before World War II made such support unpopular in the U.S. (Weidman, 1999; 2002).

Hull was famous (or should we say infamous) for his anti-women prejudices, as will be described in Chapter 11, and Skinner was a notorious sexual predator. Only Tolman, of all the behaviorists, appeared to not be an extreme racist and sexist. Tolman was also not anti-semitic. He worked closely with a number of Jews in the Gestalt school of psychology and tried to find jobs for those fleeing Nazi persecution. The behaviorists are not the whole story however. We must also examine those that opposed them scientifically and politically, the Jamesian counterculture.

The Psychological Counterculture—The Legacy Of James.

Behaviorism as theory and metatheory rose to intellectual dominance in American psychology during a time of intense social conflict. The beginning of prohibition in 1920 produced the first substantial widespread organized crime in the U.S. and made cities the site of intense violence as federal and state authorities sought to stem the flow of alcohol in a war that could never be won. Prohibition produced a thriving business in increasingly potent illegal "booze" and speakeasies. The corruption that accompanied the illegal commerce in alcohol reached into congress and the White House as well (Behr, 1996). Prohibition did not end until December 5, 1933, after leading figures in both political parties abandoned efforts to control drinking in the face of their obvious failure and more pressing problems.

One of the most pressing problems was of course the Great Depression, which began in the U.S. with the stock market crash of 1929. By 1932, unemployment rose to 25 percent of the workforce, over 11 million people unemployed (Devine, Breen, Fredrickson, & Williams, 1987). But this was not the only crisis facing America: In 1930 a general drought hit the U.S., leading to massive dust storms that blackened the sky over much of the U.S. For several years to come, a region of the U.S. in the southern plains became a dust bowl, an area of widespread dust storms and soil erosion (Worster, 2004). The economic, social, and environmental crisis produced desperation among many groups of Americans. Veterans who had fought in the Great War marched on Washington in 1932, asking for their military bonus that had been promised to them, only to be attacked by U.S. troops (Dickson & Allen, 2004). Strikes, unionization drives, and homelessness marches spread during the mid-1930s. Finally, in Europe, fascism in Germany and Spain darkened the political air like the black soot from the dust bowl.

Not all psychologists embraced behaviorism, either as theory or metatheory. Some remained true to the original functionalism of James and shared the political concerns of the early functionalists. These psychologists formed a psychological counterculture that continued in the U.S. during the period dominated by behaviorism.

Three of the leading lights of this psychological counterculture were Gordon Allport (1897-1967), Gardner Murphy (1895-1979), and Lois Barclay Murphy (1902-2003). Each made substantial contributions (Allport to the study of personality and prejudice; Gardner Murphy to personality and history of psychology; Lois Barclay Murphy to child development and coping). Each also was active in a number of social struggles. Their significance is demonstrated by the fact that Allport was elected president of the APA in 1938 and Gardner Murphy was elected president of the APA in 1944. All were active in the Society for the Psychological Study of Social Issues (SPSSI), a group of psychologists dedicated to using psychological knowledge to fight against racism and fascism and in favor of labor unions (Pandora, 1997).

A significant element in this psychological counter-culture was the struggle against discrimination within psychology, specifically against the widespread anti-Semitism, racism, and sexism within the professional ranks. For example, the SPSSI sponsored studies of anti-Semitism and explored methods for countering racism. The anti-Semitism within the field (Winston, 1996; Winston, 1998) was no different from the general and widespread anti-Semitism in society at large in the U.S. (Michael, 2005). To fight against discrimination within the profession, the counter-culture also fought simultaneously against discrimination in society as a whole.

American Psychology Goes To War (Again)

With the advent of the Second World War American psychologists again joined the war effort. Tolman, after much soul-searching about his own pacifist beliefs, served in the Office of Strategic Services (OSS), the forerunner of the Central Intelligence Agency. Harvard's Henry Murray, with whom Skinner had clashed as a graduate student, served the OSS as director of psychological services. Skinner carried out research for the Pentagon and a large number of psychologists served as officers in the military. As was the case in World War I, the war benefited psychology a great deal, bringing research funds into the field and giving psychology status and employment opportunities they never before had. Two events that took place during the war: the passage of the G.I. Bill of Rights and the creation of the National Institute of Mental Health (which are described in the introduction to part III), spurred the growth of psychology and its applications.

In the 1950s many key behaviorists (broadly defined) died: Hull in 1952, Watson in 1958, Tolman and Guthrie in 1959. Behaviorism as a metatheory was still influential and the leading Watsonian behaviorist of his generation, B.F. Skinner, was nearing the height of his productivity (he remained productive through the 1980s as you will recall). But influences from within and without were soon to bring an abrupt transition to a new metatheory. This transition is known as the cognitive revolution and will be explored in detail in Chapter 10. But behaviorism did not die suddenly: it continued for years as the old behaviorists and their students remained active in research and teaching. This generalization is nicely illustrated with empirical data on the number of citations by year to articles published in cognitive, behavioral, psychoanalytic, and neuroscientific journals (Robins, Gosling, & Craik, 1999). What General Douglas MacArthur said of himself ("old soldiers never die, they just fade away") can also be applied to schools of psychology: old schools never die, they just fade away.

The Influence Of Psychoanalysis On Behaviorism

Behaviorism and psychoanalysis are often presented as diametrically opposed schools of psychology. In fact, psychoanalysis influenced behaviorism in subtle and numerous ways. First, both schools of psychology shared a materialist approach to human nature and both were anti-religious. Second, Watson was fascinated by psychoanalysis while at the same time rejecting the concept of the unconscious. Watson both helped popularize Freud's work in the U.S. and sought to explain Freud's central concepts in behaviorist terms by using such concepts as classical conditioning of emotional responses (Rilling 2007). Watson used Freud as an opponent with which to contrast behaviorism. He also began a program to empirically validate Freud's therapeutic techniques, including research on dreams and free association (Rilling, 2007). Third, B.F. Skinner, the other great radical behaviorist of the period, was deeply influenced by Freud, citing Freud more than any other author. Skinner sought psychoanalysis (and was turned down), used a number of Freudian concepts such as the unconscious control of behavior and selection of behavior by consequences, and explanations for metaphors (Overskeid, 2007). Fourth, behaviorist at Yale under Hull sought to integrate behaviorism with Freudian psychoanalysis (Dollard & Miller, 1950), a synthesis that was to influence a number of psychologists in the post-World War II period.

Given the many influences, behaviorism was shaped in dialogue with psychoanalysis. The conversation appears to have been one-way, however. There is very little historical evidence of behaviorism shaping psychoanalytic thought, either that of Freud or that of his followers.

The Triumph Of Methodological Behaviorism

While behaviorism as a school slowly faded in the 1950s and 1960s, one lasting impact of behaviorism has not changed: the triumph of methodological behaviorism. Methodological behaviorism consists of a number of related concepts relevant to the design of studies and the analysis of data and includes: 1) random assignment; 2) statistical significance testing; 3) use of control groups; 4) use of operational definitions; 5) development of psychometrics; and 6) random sampling. In order to appreciate these developments, we must briefly review pre-1916 statistical analysis and experimental design and trace the changes in analysis and design brought about under behaviorism.

Pre-1917 Statistics And Experimental Design

Statistical analysis and research design in the pre-Great War period was fairly sophisticated (Lovie, 1991). A standard research methods text was published by E.L.Thorndike (1904) and later revised in a second edition (Thorndike, 1913). This text was widely used by psychologists. Another important text by Kelly (1920) was a standard reference for most researchers. Psychologists were concerned with two important issues in their research: how to control for extraneous factors in an experiment and how to make inferences from their usually variable data.

Efforts to control for extraneous variables in experiments often employed matching of subjects in different conditions. Similar efforts were made in descriptive research to get representative samples of subjects. In addition to measures of central tendency, such as means and medians, researchers used measures of variability and effect size (although the term effect size had not yet been coined). The most common measure of variability was the Probable

Error (PE), the median of the unsigned variations from the central tendency. But the Mean Deviation (MV) and the Mean Square Deviation (similar to the standard deviation) were also used. The estimates of effect size were generally the differences between means divided by a measure of variability (usually the shared variability). The resulting ratios were used then as the basis of deciding whether or not the results of the study were worth considering. The ratio (or effect size) had to reach a critical value (Lovie, 1991). A relevant illustration of this use of effect sizes is found in G. Watson (1930), who examined happiness in adult education students by dividing the difference score of two groups by the standard deviation of the difference scores.

The Rise Of Quantification And Experimentation Under Behaviorism

Under behaviorism as the dominant metatheory, psychologists substantially transformed how they carried out research and analyzed data. The general outlines of this transformation are shown in several historical studies.

For example, in the area of abnormal and social psychology, Lissetz (1969) found very few experimental studies and few quantitative studies (experimental studies and descriptive studies that use quantitative analysis) in the 1910s and 1920s, with a steady rise in both categories in the 1930s and later (see Figure 7.1).

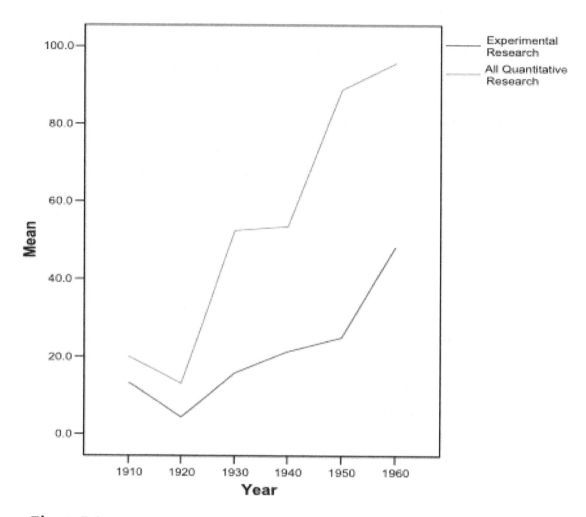

Figure 7.1

**The Rise In Quantification And Experimentation In Abnormal
& Social Psychology (Source: Lissetz, 1969)**

In a different analysis, Boring (1954) found that the number of articles using control groups (an excellent indicator of experimental design) increased steadily from 1916 to 1951 in the *Journal of Experimental Psychology.* Counting articles using control groups in 1916, 1933, and 1951, Boring found that the percentage of articles using control groups increased from zero in 1916, to 11% in 1933 and 52% in 1951.

The period of the 1930s witnessed a dramatic change in the use of statistics in psychology, a veritable statistical revolution. This revolution took place against the backdrop of a steady increase in quantification in most areas of psychology. The reasons for this increase in quantification will be explored below in the section on operational definitions. For the moment, let us turn to the statistical revolution.

Ronald Fisher And The Rise Of Statistical Significance Testing

One person has shaped how psychologists use statistical inference more than any other: Ronald A. Fisher (1890-1962). Fisher was sickly as a child and his eyesight was weak. He was forbidden to read by artificial light, and showed an early aptitude for astronomy and mathematics. During his secondary education at an elite private school in England, his math tutor would work with Fischer at night without paper, pencil, or visual aids. From his teens onward, he showed a powerful geometric insight that many think resulted from his unusual education in mathematics (Salsburg, 2001).

Fisher attended Cambridge University, starting in 1909, and achieved the title of wrangler, the highest mathematical distinction that an undergraduate at Cambridge can attain. After graduating from Cambridge he stayed an additional year to earn a master's degree in statistical mechanics and quantum theory. His first scientific paper was published while he was still an undergraduate, demonstrating that a complicated iterative formula was a straightforward result from a multidimensional geometric space (Salsburg, 2001).

After leaving Cambridge Fisher drifted from job to job for a time, working in an investment company, immigrating to Canada to farm, and returning to England to teach mathematics in several private schools. He was not a good teacher and was often short with his students. Then in 1919 Fisher's life, and the history of statistics, changed when he took a new job at the Rothamsted Agricultural Experimental Station north of London. The Rothamsted Station had been carrying out agricultural experiments (on the effects of fertilizer, rainfall, and other factors on crop productivity) since the 1830s. The results of these experiments had produced massive quantities of data, much of it confusing and most of it unpublished. Fisher's job was to run experiments at the station and to analyze data from current and previous experiments (Salsburg, 2001).

Fisher proceeded to revolutionize statistics in a series of publications (many in out-of-the way journals) in a few short years. Most of these publications were unknown to the majority of statisticians at first because of where they were published. Fisher had a conflict (perhaps the phrase bitter rivalry is more apt) with Karl Pearson (1857-1936), the editor of the journal *Biometrika* and a leading statistician (and follower of Galton). This personal conflict was to shape the history of statistics within the field of psychology, as we shall soon see (Salsburg, 2001).

Fisher rejected the statistical approach that had been pioneered by Pearson and developed statistical techniques superior to Pearson's. In a short period of time, he made mathematical advances in the area of correlation coefficients, developed the mathematics of Analysis of Variance and Analysis of Covariance, introduced the idea of degrees of freedom, generalized the procedure for t-tests, and introduced the use of p-values, associated with the Null Hypothesis Significance Test (NHST) procedure. Fisher also argued for the importance of random assignment to conditions as the best way to control extraneous variables (in place of matched group designs). The variety and power of these new techniques was breathtaking, and Fisher burst onto the scientific scene in 1925 with the publication of a book on statistical methods for non-mathematicians entitled *Statistical Methods for Research Workers* (Fisher, 1925). This book did not contain proofs of the techniques and mathematical theorems. Instead, it contained statistical tests for different types of data and research designs, along with convenient tables of deriving p-value (probability values for a test of the null hypothesis). In one place, researchers in agriculture, biology, and psychology now had a set of tools based on a sophisticated approach to statistics. The work was to go through multiple editions in many languages and shape a number of fields. In 1935 he was to extend this into the area of research design with the publication of a second seminal work, *The Design of Experiments* (Fisher, 1935), which included discussions of randomization, confounds, factorial designs, and other important topics. Questions of design were linked by Fisher to statistical procedures (Salsburg, 2001).

What was the fundamental difference between Pearson's approach to statistics and Fisher's? On one level, Fisher's mathematics were far more sophisticated, but this is not the basic difference between their two respective approaches. Pearson used statistics to describe characteristics of populations. These populations could be described in terms of distributions and Pearson described a number of types of skew distributions. Each distribution in turn could be described by four numbers: a measure of central tendency (*viz*, the mean), the standard deviation which indicates approximately how far on average the observations depart from the mean, how symmetrical the distribution is (called skew), and how far rare measurements are from the mean (called kurtosis). The significance of Pearson's approach must be appreciated in its historical context: prior to Darwin, scientists thought in terms of a clockwork universe in which variations from a central value represented error. Darwin's theory ushered in a new way of thinking which is still rejected by many, that of population thinking (as opposed to the essentialism that characterizes the clockwork universe). Pearson thought in terms of populations, and thinking in terms of populations led to the statistical revolution in 20th century science (Salsburg, 2001).

Pearson treated his data sets as the actual populations of interest. Fisher went two steps beyond Pearson. He treated every data set as an estimate of the underlying population. The estimate contains random error. Researchers need to make inferences from the data considered as estimates of the underlying reality to the population (the true state of the world). This innovation combined the population thinking of Darwin with the scientific world view of Newton, a potent combination indeed. Fisher then took another step. He used this approach to test possible models of the underlying world against the data and assign that model a probability—this is the p-value associated with the statistical significance test approach and the underlying model of reality has come to be called the null hypothesis. The differences between Pearson and Fisher were profound. It is not surprising that they did not like each other (Salsburg, 2001).

Criticism Of Statistical Significance: The Neyman-Pearson Approach

Just as Fisher's approach to statistical analysis had supplanted Karl Pearson's, soon Fisher's approach was supplanted. The dethronement of Fisher started with the meeting of Egon Pearson (1895-1980), Karl Pearson's son, and the Polish mathematician Jerzy Neyman (1894-1981). The Great War drove the young Neyman into Russia, where he studied mathematics at a provincial Russian university. He was largely self-taught in mathematics and after finishing his degree started work at the University of Warsaw. In the summer of 1928, Neyman spent the summer at the biometrical lab in London, where he befriended Egon Pearson and his wife. After Neyman returned to Warsaw, the two continued to correspond and they collaborated on three papers. The starting point for their joint work was the realization that Fisher's NHST procedure did not make sense. To understand this, ask yourself the question: "What does it mean to have a non-significant result in a significance test?" This simple question soon led the two young mathematicians to develop the concept of power analysis, the need to specify an alternative hypothesis to the null, and the need to consider the effect size as well as the significance level (called alpha) and the power (1-beta) when deciding upon the number of subjects needed for a study. Fisher had disdain for anyone who could not get statistically significant results most of the time because he knew that by increasing the sample size, even very small effects could be made to be statistically significant. The Neyman-Pearson approach to the NHST procedure is now the standard practice in biomedical research and is the recommended practice in psychological research (Salsburg, 2001).

Fisher's hatred of Karl Pearson transferred to Pearson's son Egon, and to Jerzy Neyman as well. Fisher spent the rest of his life attacking the Neyman-Pearson approach to significance testing. Most psychologists got their statistical significance testing procedures from Fisher and did not know about the problems with his approach, or with the solution developed by Neyman and Pearson in the early 1930s. For a number of years Fisher, Neyman, and Egon Pearson were colleagues at University College, London (the college founded by Jeremy Bentham, see Chapter 3). Neyman was consistently respectful and courteous to Fisher, who never missed an opportunity to attack his younger colleague (Salsburg, 2001).

Soon after completing the joint papers with Egon Pearson in 1933, Neyman went on to develop another important statistical technique, the confidence interval. He developed the technique for survey data as a way to compute an interval estimate from sample data that would capture the underlying population value. The interval would "capture" the underlying population value a percentage of times that the procedure was applied. For instance, the 95% confidence interval would include the true population value 95 times out of

100. In developing confidence intervals, Neyman was adopting both Fisher's frequentist definition of probability (probability is the number of times out of 100 that something is likely to occur) and building on the mathematics of hypothesis testing. Instead of indirectly examining the data against a hypothetical distribution (the null hypothesis) to tell us what the population value was not, Neyman used the data to tell us what the population value was (at a certain level of probability, of course). Neyman's procedures found immediate application in survey research and public opinion polling and is now widely used in biological and medical research (Salsburg, 2001).

The Triumph Of Sir Ronald Fisher

The British monarchy bestows knighthood on its most eminent scientists, for example Sir Isaac Newton and Sir Charles Darwin. Fisher's contributions to statistics and biology were so significant for science that he was knighted, hence becoming Sir Ronald. Recently the monarchy has extended this practice to artists, so now we have Sir Paul McCarthy and Sir Elton John as well.

In 1930, Fisher's work was just being introduced to the field of psychology. By 1940 this had changed, with the Fisherian approach to statistics and research design very widespread. By 1950, the revolution was complete. Statistics texts for psychologists would sometimes include a discussion of Type I and Type II errors, a concept developed by Neyman and Pearson, but only rarely a discussion of power or sample size (Lovie, 1991).

The dominance of Ronald Fisher is nicely illustrated in Guilford's (1950) widely used graduate textbook in statistics. Following Fisher's earlier work closely, Guilford confuses the concepts of significance and confidence and also assumes that a small p-value is a large effect size, and that a significant result is also reliable (it is not). These errors flow from Fisher's approach.

Several questions clamor for attention: Why did Fisher's approach win such widespread acceptance in such a short time? Why did the criticisms of that approach, and the reformulation of hypothesis testing by Neyman and Pearson, receive such scant attention for several decades? And why was the earlier approach to data analysis abandoned? Let me propose, as a set of hypotheses for future historians, some answers.

In 1900 as now, psychologists were faced with the difficult task of interpreting what the data tell us about the real world. Interpretation, a complex cognitive task, is made more difficult by the variability of the data. How do we know what is real and what is random error? Early psychologists examined central tendency and variability, and used a decision rule based on a critical value of an effect size to determine whether or not a result was "real." Not everyone was happy with the decision rule. For instance, Boring (1919) argued that there is a difference between mathematical (an effect size that reaches a critical value) and scientific significance. Small effects can have great practical and scientific importance, he pointed out. Still, psychologists had no alternative approach to analyzing their data and understanding its meaning.

Fisher provided an alternative decision rule, one that examined the variability of the data against a hypothetical mathematical model. Psychologists latched on to these procedures, both for their mathematical sophistication and for their appearance of scientific objectivity. The procedures responded to a genuine need of researchers and offered the appearance of scientific objectivity. Gone were the debates about whether this effect size was meaningful or not.

The resistance to the Neyman-Pearson reformulation stemmed in part from the ease of use that accompanied Fisher's statistical tests (he provided convenient tables) compared to the difficulty of using the Neyman-Pearson approach. Adoption of the later approach was also slowed by Fisher's harsh attacks on his younger colleagues, to be sure. But the difficult mathematical calculations associated with the reformulation also posed a real hurdle for most psychologists.

Many psychologists were also satisfied with the appearance of scientific objectivity. Gone was the widespread dissatisfaction with the earlier procedure. Now psychologists were satisfied that their results, being significant, were important and meaningful. The image is sometimes as important as the reality in science. I am not the first to suggest such a hypothesis. E.G. Boring (Boring, 1961) argued that psychologists are "insecure because of their unscientific heritage from philosophy and thus repeatedly insisting on the scientific validity of their new experimental psychology" (p. 254).

Operational Definitions And Quantification

One of the reasons (but not the only reason) for the increasing quantification during the 1920s and after was the effort to define the concepts and terms in an experiment more rigorously by giving concepts operational definitions. This effort flowed from the influence of philosophy, especially the work of Bridgman (Bridgman, 1927). This philosophy of science had its greatest impact through the work of S.S. Stevens, who had been a student of E.G. Boring and studied perception and psychophysics. He championed the concept of operational definition (*cf.*, Stevens, 1935a; Stevens, 1935b) which required that all theoretical terms in psychology be defined in terms of the operations used to measure them. A good operational definition needed to be specific, observable, and countable. This equivalence of the scientific with the countable side-stepped a number of conceptual problems in the field, such as if all interesting concepts can be measured and counted, what do the numbers and measurements really mean, and if the operational definitions are valid—that is, do they reflect real entities in the real psychological world? It also proved to be a powerful push toward quantification in research (Hornstein, 1988).

Operational definitions were not the only force pushing psychology toward greater quantification. Another force was the development of psychometrics: the principles of psychological measurement and test construction. This work was carried out especially by psychologists interested in measuring intellectual ability and attitudes. They developed a number of important statistical techniques, such as factor analysis and psychometric scaling, as well as many useful tests or commercial products that could be used in education and business (Hornstein, 1988). Together operational definitions and psychometrics provided improved research techniques and tools to psychologists, gave the appearance of a real science, and (in the case of psychometrics) provided useful products for society at large. Is it any wonder that the decades between 1920 and 1970 witnessed increasing quantification in psychology?

The Development Of Random Sampling

In the 1920s Fisher championed random assignment to experimental conditions as the most effective way to control for confounds. In the 1930s and 1940s, a related concept was introduced into descriptive survey research, the concept of random sampling. The concept of random sampling was developed by three groups in the 1930s who built upon each others work: Prasanta Chandra Mahalanobis of the Indian Statistical Institute, Jerzy Neyman in England, and Americans working in Washington, D.C. for the New Deal. Faced with the need to gather data in India, Mahalanobis rejected the use of extremely large samples (the common practice at the time was to try to get everyone counted in a census or survey) for smaller randomly selected samples. The statistics from the sample were likely wrong, but the population value could be captured using an interval estimate based on Neyman's development of the confidence interval. In a series of studies done at the Department of Commerce and the Department of Labor, U.S. government researchers showed that the random samples were far superior to (that is, more accurate) than large samples. In both India and the U.S., the work on random sampling extended to the development of economic indicators, the random sampling of key "signs" of economic performance. Among the first two economic indicators developed were a measure of the cost of goods to consumer, the Consumer Price Index, and the measure of unemployment (Salsburg, 2001). Several of the young American government researchers, including a young George Gallup, took the procedure of random sampling into the political arena where they conducted public opinion polls for political candidates and the news media.

Given the enduring legacy of behaviorism, it may be fair to say that we are all behaviorists now.

References

Baars B.J. (1986). *The cognitive revolution in psychology.* New York: Guilford Press.

Beck, H.P., Levinson, S., & Irons, G. (2009). Finding Little Albert. *American Psychologist, 64*(7), 605-614.

Behr, E. (1996). *Prohibition: Thirteen years that changed America.* New York: Arcade Publising.

Benjamin, L.T., Whitaker, J.L., Ramsey, R.M., & Zeve, D.R. (2007). John B. Watson's alleged sex research. *American Psychologist, 62*(2), 131-139.

Boring, E.G. (1919). Mathematical vs. scientific significance. *Psychological Bulletin, 16,* 335-339.

Boring, E.G. (1954). The nature and history of experimental control. *American Journal of Psychology, 67,* 573-589.

Boring, E.G. (1961). The beginning and growth of measurement in psychology. *ISIS, 52,* 238-257.

Bridgman, P.W. (1927). *The logic of modern physics.* New York: Macmillan.

Buckley, K.W. (1989). *Mechanical man: John Broadus Watson and the beginnings of behaviorism.* New York: Guilford Press.

Clifford, G.J. (1984). *Edward L. Thorndike: The sane positivist.* Middletown, CN: Wesleyan University Press.

Cohen, D. (1979). *J.B. Watson, the founder of behaviorism: A biography.* London: Routledge & Kegan Paul.

Devine, R.A., Breen, T.H., Fredrickson, G.M., & Williams, R.H. (1987). *America: Past and present* (2nd ed.). Glenview, IL: Scott, Foresman and Comp.

Dickson, P., & Allen, T.B. (2004). *The bonus army: An American epic.* New York: Walker & Comp.

Dollard, J., & Miller, N.E. (1950). *Personality and psychotherapy: An analysis in terms of learning, thinking, and culture.* New York: McGraw-Hill.

Fancher, R.E. (1990). *Pioneers of psychology* (2nd ed.). New York: W.W. Norton & Comp.

Fisher, R.A. (1925). *Statistical methods for research workers* (1st ed.). London: Oliver & Boyd.

Fisher, R.A. (1935). *The design of experiments* (1st ed.). London: Oliver & Boyd.

Gleitman, H. (1991). Edward Chace Tolman: A life of scientific and social purpose. In Kimble, Wertheimer, and White, *Portraits of pioneers in psychology.*

Guilford, J.P. (1950). *Fundamental statistics in psychology and education* (2nd ed.). New York: McGraw-Hill.

Harris, B. (1979). Whatever happened to Little Albert? *American Psychologist, 34*(2), 151-160.

Hergenhahn, B.R. (2005). *An introduction to the history of psychology,* (5th ed.). Belmont, CA: Thomson Wadsworth.

Hornstein, G.A. (1988). Quantifying psychological phenomena: Debates, dilemmas, and Implications. In
J.G. Morawski (1988), *The rise of experimentation in American psychology,* pp. 1-34.

Hothersall, D. (2004). *History of psychology* (4th ed.). New York: McGraw-Hill.

Hulbert, A. (2003). *Raising America: Experts, parents, and a century of advice about children.* New York: Alfred Knopf.

Hull, C. L (1920). Quantitative aspects of the evolution of concepts: An experimental study. *Psychological Monographs, 28,* 123.

Hull, C.L. (1928). *Aptitude testing.* Yonkers-on-Hudson, NY: World Book.

Hull, C.L.(1929). A functional interpretation of the conditioned reflex. *Psychological Review, 36,* 498-511.

Hull, C.L. (1933). *Hypnosis and suggestibility.* New York: Appleton-Century-

Crofts.

Hull, C.L. (1937). Mind, mechanism, and adaptive behavior. *Psychological Review, 44,* 1-32.

Hull, C.L. (1938). The goal-gradient hypothesis applied to some "field-force" problems in the behavior of young children. *Psychological Review, 45,* 271-299.

Hull, C.L. (1943). *Principles of behavior.* New York: Appleton.

Hull, C.L. (1951). *Essentials of behavior.* New Haven, CT: Yale University Press.

Hull, C.L. (1952). *A behavior system.* New Haven, CT: Yale University Press.

Hunt, M. (1993). *The story of psychology.* New York: Doubleday.

Innes, N.K. (1992a). Animal psychology in America revealed in APA presidential addresses. *Journal of Experimental Psychology: Animal Behavior Processes, 18*(1), 3-11.

Innes, N.K. (1992b). Tolman and Tryon: Early research on the inheritence of the ability to learn. *American Psychologist, 47*(2), 190-197.

Janik, A., & Toulmin, S. (1973). *Wittgenstein's Vienna.* New York: Simon & Schuster.

Jones, M.C. (1924). A laboratory study of fear: The case of Peter. *Pedagogical Seminary, 31,* 308-315.

Kelly, T. L. (1920). *Statistical methods.* New York: MacMillan.

Kimble, G. A. (1991a). The spirit of Ivan Petrovich Pavlov. In G.A. Kimble, M. Wertheimer, & C. White (Eds.), *Portraits of pioneers in Psychology,* Vol. 1, pp. 27-40.

Kimble, G. A. (1991b). Psychology from the standpoint of a mechanist: An appreciation of Clark L. Hull. In G.A. Kimble, M. Wertheimer, & C. White (Eds.), *Portraits of pioneers in psychology,* Vol. 1, pp. 209-225.

Kimble, G.A., Boneau, L.A., & Wertheimer, M. (1996). *Portraits of pioneers in psychology*, Vol. 2. Washington, DC: American Psychological Association & Hillsdale, NJ:Lawrence Erlbaum & Associates.

Kimble, G.A., Wertheimer, M., & White, C. (1991). *Portraits of pioneers in psychology*, Vol. 1. Washington, DC: American Psychological Association & Hillsdale, NJ: Lawrence Erlbaum & Associates.

Lissitz, R.W. (1969). A longitudinal study of the research methodology in *The Journal of Abnormal and Social Psychology, The Journal of Nervous and Mental Disease, and the American Journal of Psychiatry. Journal of the History of the Behavioral Sciences, 5*(3), 248-255.

Loeb, J. (1900). *Comparative physiology of the brain and comparative psychology.* New York: G.P. Putnam's Sons.

Lovie, A.D. (1991). A short history of statistics in twentieth century psychology. In Lovie, P, & Lovie, A.D., eds. (1991). *New developments in statistics for psychology and the social sciences*, Vol. 2.

Lovie, P, & Lovie, A.D., eds. (1991). *New developments in statistics for psychology and the social sciences*, Vol. 2. London: British Psychological Society & Routledge.

Magoun, H.W. (1981). John B.Watson and the study of human sexual behavior. *Journal of Sex Research, 17,* 368-378.

Marrow, A.J. (1969). *The practical theorist: The life and work of Kurt Lewin.* New York: Basic Books.

McConnell, J.V. (1982). *Understanding human behavior*, 4th ed. New York: Holt, Rinehart & Winston.

Michael, R. (2005). *A concise history of American anti-Semitism.* Lanham, Maryland: Rowman & Littlefield Publishers.

Morawski, J.G., ed. (1988). *The rise of experimentation in American psychology.* New Haven: Yale University Press.

O'Donnell, J.M. (1985). *The origins of behaviorism: American psychology, 1870-1920.* New York: New York University Press.

Overskeid, G. (2007). Looking for Skinner and finding Freud. *American Psychologist, 62*(6), 590-595.

Pandora, K. (1997). *Rebels within the ranks: Psychologists' critique of scientific authority and democratic realities in New Deal America.* Cambridge: Cambridge University Press.

Pavlov, I.P. (1927/1960). *Conditioned reflexes.* New York: Dover Publications.

Prenzel-Guthrie, P. (1996). Edwin Ray Guthrie: Pioneer learning theorist. In G.A. Kimble, L.A. Boneau, & M. Wertheimer (Eds.), *Portraits of pioneers in psychology,* Vol. 2, pp. 137-150.

Rilling, M. (2000). John Watson's paradoxical struggle to explain Freud. *American Psychologist, 55*(3), 301-312.

Robins, R.W., Gosling, S.D., & Craik, K.H. (1999). An empirical analysis of trends in psychology. *American Psychologist, 54*, 117-128.

Salsburg, D. (2001). *The lady tasting tea: How statistics revolutionized science in the twentieth century.* New York: Henry Holt and Company.

Schrecker, E.W. (1986). *No ivory tower: McCarthyism and the universities.* New York: Oxford University Press.

Schultz, D.P., & Schultz, S.E. (2004). *A history of modern psychology* (8th ed.). Belmont, CA: Thomson Wadsworth.

Skinner, B.F. (1934). Has Gertrude Stein a secret? *Atlantic Monthly, 153*, 50-57.

Skinner, B.F. (1938). *The behavior of organisms: An experimental analysis.* New York: Appleton-Century.
Skinner, B.F. (1939). An apparatus for the study of animal behavior. *Psychological Record, 3*, 166-176.

Skinner, B.F. (1945). The machine age comes to the nursery! Introducing the mechanical baby-tender. *Ladies Home Journal, 62* (October), 30-31, 135-136, 138.

Skinner, B.F. (1948a). "Superstition" in the pigeon. *Journal of Experimental Psychology, 38,* 168-172.

Skinner, B.F. (1948b). *Walden two.* New York: Macmillan.

Skinner, B.F. (1951). How to teach animals. *Scientific American, 185,* 26-29.

Skinner, B.F. (1953). *Science and human behavior.* New York: Macmillan

Skinner, B.F. (1957). *Verbal behavior.* New York: Appleton-Century-Crofts.

Skinner, B.F. (1958). Teaching machines. *Science, 128,* 969-977.

Skinner, B.F. (1961a). Why we need teaching machines. *Harvard Educational Review, 31,* 377-398.

Skinner, B.F. (1961b). Teaching machines. *Scientific American,* 205, 90-122.

Skinner, B.F. (1968). Teaching science in high school—what is wrong? *Science, 159,* 704-710.

Skinner, B.F. (1969). The machine that is man. *Psychology Today, 2*(April), 22-25, 60-63.

Skinner, B.F. (1971). *Beyond freedom and dignity.* New York: Knopf.

Skinner, B.F. (1972a). *Beyond freedom and dignity.* New York: Bantam/Vintage Books.

Skinner, B.F. (1972b). Freedom and dignity revisited. *The New York Times* (August 11), p. 29.

Skinner, B.F., & Ferster, C. (1957). *Schedules of reinforcement.* New York: Appleton-Century-Crofts.

Small, W.S. (1900). Experimental studies of the mental processes of the rat, I *American Journal of Psychology, 11,* 133-165.

Small, W.S. (1901). Experimental studies of the mental processes of the rat, II. *American Journal of Psychology, 12,* 205-239.

Stevens, S.S. (1935a). The operational basis of psychology. *American Journal of Psychology, 43*, 323-330.

Stevens, S.S. (1935b). The operational definition of psychological concepts. *Psychological Review, 42*, 517-527.

Thorndike, E.L. (1898). Animal intelligence [Monograph supplement] *Psychological Review, 2*(8).

Thorndike, E.L. (1904). *An introduction to the theory of mental and social measurements* (1st ed.). New York: Columbia University Teachers College.

Thorndike, E.L. (1913). *An introduction to the theory of mental and social measurements* (2nd ed.). New York: Columbia University Teachers College.

Tolman, E.C. (1928). Purposive behavior. *Psychological Review, 35*, 524-530.

Tolman, E.C. (1932). *Purposive behavior in animals and men*. New York: Naiburg.

Tolman, E.C. (1942). *Drives toward war*. New York: Appleton-Century-Crofts.

Tolman, E.C. (1948). Cognitive maps in rats and men. *Psychological Review, 55*, 189-208.

Tolman, E.C., & Honzik, C.H. (1930). Introduction and removal of rewards, and maze performance in rats. *University of California Publications in Psychology, 4*, 257-273.

Watson, G. (1930). Happiness among adult students of education. *Journal of Educational Psychology, 21*(2), 79-109.

Watson, J.B. (1903). *Animal education*. Chicago: University of Chicago Press.

Watson, J.B. (1913). Psychology as the behaviorist views it. *Psychological Review, 20*, 158-177.

Watson, J.B. (1914). *Behavior: An introduction to comparative Psychology*. New York: Holt.

Watson, J.B. (1916). The place of the conditioned reflex in psychology. *Psychological Review, 23*, 89-116.

Watson, J.B. (1919). *Psychology from the standpoint of a behaviorist.* Philadelphia: Lippincott.

Watson, J.B. (1925). *Behaviorism.* New York: Norton.

Watson, J.B. (1928). *Psychological care of the infant and child.* New York: Norton.

Watson, J.B. (1930). *Behaviorism,* (rev. ed.). New York: Norton.

Watson, J.B., & Lashley, K.S. (1919). A consensus of medical opinion upon questions relating to sex education and venereal disease campaigns. *Social Hygiene, 4,* 769-847.

Watson, J.B., & Lashley, K.S. (1920). The effects of a motion picture campaign on sexual hygiene. U.S. Interdepartmental Social Hygiene Board, pp. 1-88.

Watson, J.B., & MacDougall, W. (1929). *The battle of behaviorism: An exposition and an exposure.* New York: Norton.

Watson, J.B., & Rayner, R. (1920). Conditioned emotional reactions. *Journal of Experimental Psychology, 3,* 1-14.

Weidman, N.M. (1999). *Constructing scientific psychology: Karl Lashley's mind-brain debates.* Cambridge: Cambridge University Press.

Weidman, N.M. (2002). The depoliticization of Karl Lashley: A response to Dewsbury. *Journal of the History of the Behavioral Sciences, 38*(3), 247-253.

Wiener, D.N. (1996). *B.F. Skinner: Benign anarchist.* Needham Heights, MA: Allyn & Bacon.

Winston, A.S. (1996). "As his name indicates": R.S. Woodworth's letters of reference and employment for Jewish psychologists in the 1930s. *Journal of the History of the Behavioral Sciences, 32,* 30-43.

Winston, A.S. (1998). "The defects of his race": E.G. Boring and anti-semitism in american Psychology, 1923-1953. *History of Psychology, 1,* 27-51.

Wittgenstein, L. (1922). *Tractatus logico-philosophicus*. New York: Harcourt Brace.

Worster, D. (2004). *Dust bowl: The southern plains in the 1930s*. New York: Oxford University Press.

Wozniak, R. (1997). Jacques Loeb, comparative physiology of the brain, and Comparative Psychology. http://www.brynmawr.edu/Acads/Psych/rwozniak/loeb.html

Yerkes, R.M., & Morgulis, S. (1909). The method of Pavlov in animal psychology. *Psychological Review*, 6, 257-273.

CHAPTER 8: GESTALT PSYCHOLOGY

What is Gestalt theory and what does it intend? ...

The fundamental 'formula' of Gestalt theory might be expressed this way: There are wholes, the behavior of which is not determined by that of their individual elements, but where the part-processes are themselves determined by the intrinsic nature of the whole. It is the hope of Gestalt theory to determine the nature of such wholes.

With a formula such as this, one might close, for Gestalt theory is neither more nor less than this. It is not interested in puzzling out philosophic questions which such a formula might suggest. Gestalt theory has to do with concrete research; it is not only an outcome but a device; not only a theory about results but a means toward further discoveries. This is not merely the proposal of one or more problems but an attempt to see what is really taking place in science. This problem cannot be solved by listing possibilities for systematization, classification, and arrangement. If it is to be attacked at all, we must be guided by the spirit of the new method and by the concrete nature of things themselves which we are studying, and set ourselves to that which is really given by nature.

To repeat: the problem has not merely to do with scientific work—it is a fundamental problem of our times. Gestalt theory is not something suddenly and unexpectedly dropped upon us from above; it is, rather, a palpable convergence of problems ranging throughout the sciences and the various philosophical standpoints of modern times.

MAX WERTHEIMER (WERTHEIMER, 1924)

Gestalt Psychology: The Rejection Of Reductionism

While behaviorism was a revolution against the psychology of consciousness, so-called introspectionism, Gestalt psychology was a counter revolution —a revolution against behaviorism, reductionism, and mechanism in psychology. Gestalt psychology grew out of the Würzberg School and other currents in German psychology that emphasized the study of complex phenomena and rejected reductionism. Gestalt psychology built upon these currents to construct a non-reductionistic theory of consciousness that merged a phenomenological analysis of experience with a rigorous research methodology. In a very real sense, the Gestaltists merged the psychology of William James into the non-reductionistic German psychology of Külpe and others. To understand this counter-revolution, we must start with the three founders of Gestalt Psychology and their times.

The Three Founders: Max Wertheimer, Kurt Koffka, And Wolfgang Köhler

While the founding of Behaviorism is associated with a single person, John B. Watson, the founding of Gestalt Psychology is associated with a triumvirate of gifted German psychologists. While the three did not agree on everything, they worked together closely for many years, developing a comprehensive school of psychology that could have provided, but ultimately did not, an alternative metatheory to behaviorism. The three founders were Max Wertheimer (1880-1943), Kurt Koffka (1886-1941), and Wolfgang Köhler (1887-1967).

Max Wertheimer was born in Prague, the second child in a successful Jewish family. His father developed a number of accounting practices and methods for keeping track of inventory in warehouses, had written a successful accounting text, and in addition to being a successful business executive, operated a business school. His family also donated to a number of charities and his father was a respected philanthropist and community leader. Growing up, Max and his older brother were nurtured and loved in a richly intellectual household. The two brothers spoke German and Czech and in the German gymnasium they studied the typical college preparatory courses such as mathematics, Latin, Greek, history, and philosophy. Max also read a great deal, attended the theater often, and was an excellent violinist (King & Wertheimer, 2005).

Wertheimer began college at Charles University in Prague in 1898. Probably at the urging of his parents, he studied law. Given the freedom afforded the German university students, Wertheimer was able to study other subjects in addition to law, and took additional courses in psychology and philosophy. After five semesters of law school, Wertheimer changed programs to psychology and philosophy. In addition to the experimental and folk psychologies of Wundt, Wertheimer studied with the philosopher Christian von Ehrenfels. Ehrenfels had studied at the University of Vienna with Brentano and earned his doctorate under Brentano. Ehrenfels was a classmate of Sigmund Freud, although there is no evidence they were friends. Ehrenfels used Brentano's philosophical masterpiece, *Psychology from the Standpoint of an Empiricist*. In 1890, when Wertheimer was in his second year of college, Erhenfels published a significant paper on gestalt qualities that attacked the reductionistic and mechanistic approach of Wundtian psychology. Erhenfels argued that for many wholes, the whole is greater than the sum of its parts, that wholes possess properties or qualities independent of the separate parts. Furthermore, one could change and alter the parts, and still retain the same whole (King & Wertheimer, 2005).

After his shift to psychology Wertheimer retained a significant interest in certain aspects of the law, particularly the new field of criminology. Hans Gross, Europe's leading criminologist and the father of Otto Gross, whom we met in Chapter 7, urged Wertheimer to carry out experiments on lie detection, or the psychological diagnosis of criminal guilt. Working with a friend and classmate from law school, Wertheimer carried out a series of studies using reaction time in a word association task intended to distinguish between guilty subjects who confessed, innocent subjects, and guilty subjects who were lying about their guilt. A 41-page article summarizing the experiments was published in 1904 in Gross' journal. Wertheimer also collaborated with William Stern (see Chapter 4), a student and colleague of Ebbinghaus who was also studying forensic psychology at the time. The publication of Wertheimer's work led to a priority dispute between him and another young scholar who had independently developed a similar method—Carl Jung. Jung eventually acknowledged Wertheimer's priority in developing the technique, although there were some important differences in the approaches of the two researchers (King & Wertheimer, 2005).

As was typical of German students, Wertheimer studied at other German Universities. After spending eight semesters in Prague, he went to study psychology at the University of Berlin with Carl Stumpf in 1902. While in Berlin he frequented the theaters and concert halls, studied philosophy with Wilhelm Dilthey, and studied economics, literature, and music. After two years in Berlin, Wertheimer enrolled in the University of Würzberg in 1904 to study for his doctorate with Oswald Külpe (King & Wertheimer, 2005).

Wertheimer continued his studies of the psychological diagnosis of guilt at the University of Berlin and at Würzberg for his dissertation. He completed and defended his dissertation in December of 1904. Wertheimer was supported by his well-to-do family and continued his research on lie detection over the next several years. He also carried out studies on aphasia and the perception of music. His study of music perception made use of the indigenous music of Sri Lanka that had been recorded by European musicologists (King & Wertheimer, 2005).

In 1910 Wertheimer was traveling by train from Vienna to the Rhineland for vacation when he had an insight about apparent motion, a subject that had interested such significant people in the field as Helmholtz, Wundt, and James. He got off the train in Frankfort to use the lab facilities of a former teacher who now directed the Psychological Institute at the University of Frankfurt in order to test his idea. At Frankfurt, he met the two other individuals who were to be the founders of Gestalt Psychology: Wolfgang Köhler (1887-1967) and Kurt Koffka (1886-1941). Köhler had earned his Ph.D. from Stumpf at the University of Berlin in 1909 after studying physics with Max Planck, the founder of quantum mechanics. His early work was on hearing and in 1910 he was working at the University of Frankfurt. Koffka had also earned his Ph.D. from Stumpf at the University of Berlin in 1908 and had carried out research on imagery and thinking. Koffka had worked as an assistant to Külpe at Würzberg before joining Köhler at Frankfurt as an assistant (King & Wertheimer, 2005).

Wertheimer's former teacher loaned him a tachistoscope, a device that can project images for precise time intervals, and urged him to work with Köhler and Koffka. Together they (Wertheimer, Köhler, Koffka, and Koffka's wife who also served as a subject) discovered that if a shape is projected at one position, turned off, and projected at another position within 30 milliseconds or less, the subjects perceived two simultaneous events. If the images were projected at an interval greater than 200 milliseconds, two separate objects were perceived. If the interval between projections was approximately 60 milliseconds, a single moving object was perceived. They named this effect the phi phenomenon and it is experienced by anyone who has seen a movie. In a series of experiments Wertheimer eliminated a number of possible explanations for this phenomenon, concluding that we perceive motion as motion, not as a sum of two visual stimuli. The basis for a Gestalt psychology had been demonstrated empirically. Wertheimer published his results in a 1912 paper that formally marks the birth of Gestalt psychology. Of almost equal importance was a second paper he published in 1912 on the mathematical thinking of aboriginal peoples, which applied Gestalt concepts to the study of cognition (King & Wertheimer, 2005).

The three founders were soon intensely active in research on perception and cognition from the Gestalt perspective. Their activities were somewhat interrupted by the advent of the Great War. Köhler had been sent to Tenerife to study primate cognition and problem solving, while Wertheimer was drafted and carried out military research for the German government. Among his successful projects was an acoustic device for detecting ships, a device he patented and continued to receive royalties on until 1934. Koffka also worked on military research during the war (King & Wertheimer, 2005).

Koffka left the University of Frankfurt in 1911, shortly after completing the work with Wertheimer, taking a post at the University of Giessen, where he worked until 1927 with some time away during the war and for trips to the U.S and Great Britain after the war. Koffka spoke fluent English, having gone to the University of Edinburgh for a year before starting his formal undergraduate education at the University of Berlin (Harrower, 1983). Koffka's most productive period occurred after the end of the Great War when he focused on the study of perception and the study of child development. In 1922 he introduced Gestalt psychology into the U.S. (Koffka, 1922) in an article that used perception to illustrate Gestalt principles. Unfortunately, this led to a misconception that Gestalt psychology dealt only with perception (Watson, 1978).

Koffka's other major work in English in the 1920s was his *Growth of the Mind: An Introduction to Child Psychology* (Koffka, 1924/1959). This work presented a Gestalt analysis of perceptual development and learning, and detailed the Gestalt criticisms of other approaches, in particular behaviorism. In 1927 Koffka moved to the U.S. where he worked at Smith College until his death in 1941. At Smith he taught undergraduates and worked with scholars from around the world who came to work with him for short intervals. His primary research at Smith was on color vision (Watson, 1978).

Koffka was both modest and loyal, especially in terms of his loyalty to the theory of Gestalt psychology. In addition to his experimental and theoretical contributions, he became the spokesperson for Gestalt psychology in the English-speaking world and presented it as a systematic theory (Harrower, 1983). Koffka produced the only systematic statement of Gestalt psychology, *The Principles of Gestalt Psychology* (Koffka, 1935).

Was Köhler A Spy?

We have examined a number of historical mysteries regarding psychology so far, most recently the mystery surrounding John B. Watson's alleged sex experiments. Another historical mystery surrounds Wolfgang Köhler's activities during World War I while he was carrying out primate research on the Canary Islands. The mystery—was Köhler a spy for the German government during the war?

Köhler and his family arrived in Tenerife, one of the Canary Islands owned by Spain, in December of 1913 to take charge of a small primate research station established by Germany in 1912. When World War I broke out, he remained on the island conducting research that culminated in the work that established his international reputation as a psychologist and advanced the school of Gestalt psychology—*The Mentality of Apes* (Köhler, 1927).

Considerable mystery surrounds Köhler's time on Tenerife, a mystery that has been explored by Ronald Ley's delightful historical detective work, *A Whisper of Espionage* (Ley, 1990). Ley's book is significant not just for what he discovers about Köhler but as a first person account of the adventures and trials of historical research.

The detective story begins when Ley, on sabbatical, visits Tenerife on his way to London in January 1975. A long-time researcher in cognitive psychology, Ley had read Köhler's work as a graduate student and wanted to see if anything remained of the research station where the famous studies had been carried out. His search of the site soon led him to Manuel Gonzalez y Garcia, Köhler's animal caretaker and assistant. Gonzalez y Garcia was not only able to provide Ley with the locations (yes—the research station had been located at two different sites, having been forced to move during the war), but revealed that Köhler had been a spy for Germany (Ley, 1990).

Ley could not resist this puzzle and so began his work as a historical detective that was to take him several more times to Tenerife, as well as to archives in

London, West Germany, and East Germany. In the process, he also tracked down and interviewed Köhler's children and wife, as well as friends and co-workers. Ley never found a "smoking gun," absolutely incontrovertible proof that Köhler was a spy for Germany, but he did make a compelling case that Köhler in fact was spying for Germany while carrying out his studies (Ley, 1990).

Consider some of the facts that Ley presented:

1. Köhler, before being appointed to head the station, had no experience with animals. The rest of his life, he never worked in comparative psychology again.

2. Köhler had been trained as a physicist under the founder of quantum mechanics, Max Planck. He was knowledgeable about electronic equipment and could build, repair, and use radio equipment, a cutting-edge communication technology at the time and essential to the war.

3. The station was sponsored by the German government which often used scientific expeditions to further its political or economic interests. There are no apes on Tenerife and the animals had to be brought from the German colony of Cameron in Africa. It would have been far simpler to carry out the studies in Africa were the animals lived and Germany actually controlled the territory.

4. The historical evidence from both British archives and the German government's archives, as well as from German, Spanish, and British citizens who lived on Tenerife during the war, shows that Tenerife was an important center of German espionage. The island was used to observe the movement of British ships and report that movement, via radio, to German submarines. Köhler was a friend of the head of the German spy ring on the island.

5. Köhler lived in fear that the Spanish government (formally neutral during the war but with many members of the government siding with the Germans) or the British would endanger his family. His home was searched many times and the British forced the station to move during the war.

6. Köhler kept a secret radio transmitter in his home. Both locations for the primate research stations (where Köhler and his family lived) were ideal for radio transmission and observation of ships arriving and departing from the island.

7. Köhler left the island in haste with his family as soon as Germany lost the war.

8. Köhler claimed that he was stranded on the island, but as a reserve officer in the German army, had a duty to return to Germany. Other Germans who had reserve commissions did in fact return to Germany, although it was difficult and dangerous to do so. Köhler would have certainly tried to return, unless he had been asked (or ordered) to remain.

9. Köhler's work during the war was rewarded with a stipend to help him and his family after their return to Germany. In addition, he was soon appointed to serve as acting head of the Institute of Psychology at the University of Berlin for a year, then in 1921 was appointed to head the department at Gottingen, and after a year was appointed the permanent head of the Institute of Psychology at Berlin. Köhler become a full professor and head of the institute over his more senior colleagues Wertheimer and Koffka, at Germany's most prestigious university. The suspicious observer might think he was being rewarded for his valuable service during the war.

10. Finally, Köhler and his closest associates were very secretive about his activities during the war and Köhler often avoided talking about his actions in the war, including his important research with primates.

Ley's evidence is not conclusive, but is as good as much historical evidence can get. As Ley himself points out, the fact that Köhler was a spy during the war does not in any way diminish his work as a scientist. Furthermore, almost all psychologists served their governments during the war in Germany, the Austro-Hungarian Empire, Britain, and the U.S. Such ready service to the government's war efforts raises general questions however: What, for instance, is the general relationship of psychology to governmental (or corporate) power? What are the moral obligations of psychologists to their nation? These questions are as important now as they were before and during the Great War.

Köhler description of his primate studies (Köhler, 1927) established his international reputation. In 1922 Köhler was appointed the head of the psychology department at the University of Berlin, where he established the leading center of psychology in Germany and the center of Gestalt psychology. Other centers existed at the University of Frankfurt, where Wertheimer secured a position after some difficulty, and at Giessen, where Koffka taught. In addition to centers of Gestalt psychology at these three universities, Wertheimer, Koffka, and Köhler founded a scientific journal, the *Psychologische Forschung*, in

1921 (Ash, 1995).

The Basics Of Gestalt Theory

The basic idea of Gestalt psychology, which the founders named the fundamental formula, is that the whole is different from and greater than the sum of the parts; in fact, the structure of the whole gives the parts their significance. This point of view is in sharp contrast to the reductionism inherent in Wundt's volunteerism and American Functionalism and Behaviorism.

In addition to the phi phenomenon discussed above, the Gestalt psychologists described a number of other characteristics of perceptual phenomena—how we organize and perceive forms. These are sometimes called Gestalt laws, and include similarity (we group similar items into a whole), figure-ground relation (we focus our attention on one part of the field while the rest of the field provides the background), prägnanz, or the law of good form (we perceive the simplest shapes possible), and the law of closure (we tend to perceive enclosed shapes, even if they have gaps). These laws are illustrated in a number of well known gestalt stimuli such as the Necker Cube (by shifting your attention, the cube seems to move its orientation) and the Rubin vase (is it a vase or is it the profiles of two people facing each other).

Gestalt Theory Misunderstood

The reception of Gestalt psychology in the U.S. has been hampered historically by four misconceptions: misconceptions about isomorphism, learning, the extent of the theory, and a foolish equation of Gestalt psychology with Gestalt therapy.

In addition to the enormous bias American psychologists had against the fundamental formula of Gestalt psychology, American psychologists had great difficulty with two concepts from Gestalt theory: isomorphism and learning. The Gestalt theorists hypothesized that the phenomena of perception, summarized by the Gestalt laws, must have isomorphic process in the brain. This hypothesis guided much of their research in physiological psychology. The idea of isomorphism is not that we have pictures of the world in our head, rather there must be some functional correspondence with what we perceive and think with processes in the brain. Köhler in particular spent considerable time studying physiological psychology and perception, using the idea of iso-morphism as a heuristic (Henle, 1986). As we shall see in Chapter 9, this work in Gestalt psychology had a significant impact on two of the leading physio-logical psychologists of the last 100 years, Karl Lashley and Donald O. Hebb, al-though neither were Gestaltists.

A second concept that gave American psychologists much difficulty was the notion of learning. Gestalt psychologists have often been accused of being na-tivists when in fact they rejected nativism, just as they rejected trial and error learning as a major mechanism of learning. Instead, evolution has equipped us with abilities to perceive and structure the perceptual world. We learn to look and see, to listen and hear: this is different from learning a behavior because of reinforcement or punishment, as Skinner would argue (Henle, 1986). Tolman's work on learning without reinforcement supports the Gestalt viewpoint.

Gestalt psychology was often equated with studies of perception and cog-nition, areas that were not hot topics in the 1920s, 30s, and 40s in the U.S. be-cause of the domination of the behaviorist metatheory. It is true that Gestalt studies of perception and cognition were the most well-known works of the Gestalt psychologists. A part of this results from the use of these studies to il-lustrate the general gestalt ideas, part from the fact that Gestalt psychologists had made considerable progress in these areas. It ignores however the work of Gestalt psychologists in personality and social psychology (see Chapter 11) and in physiological psychology (see chapter 8). No understanding of Gestalt psychology as a comprehensive approach to psychology is possible without an awareness of work in these other areas.

Perhaps the most egregious misunderstanding is the confusion of Gestalt psychology with Gestalt Therapy. Gestalt Therapy, developed by Fritz Perls in the late 1940s through the 1970s, is an offshoot of psychoanalysis. While Perls' uses some general ideas from Gestalt psychology, such as the whole is greater than the sum of its parts, he essentially expropriated a few terms and the prestige of Gestalt psychology. This therapy approach achieved some fame in the 1960s and 1970s (e.g., Perls, 1971; Perls, 1972), but has almost absolutely nothing to do with Gestalt psychology, save a common first name (Henle, 1986).

The Rise Of Nazism And The Destruction Of Gestalt Psychology

With the January 30, 1933 assent to power of the Nazis, Jewish professors and non-Jewish professors who were critical of the regime were dismissed from their posts. No one was exempt; the dismissed professors included four Nobel Prize winners: Einstein, Haber, Franck, and Hertz. Köhler, who as a prominent Aryan scholar was safe, made a public stand against the dismissals. On April 28, 1933 he published the last openly anti-Nazi article to appear during the Nazi regime. Entitled *Conversations in Germany*, the article defended (albeit oftentimes in a mild fashion) the humanity of Jews and the value of their contributions to German culture. Köhler argued that "they [the people who refuse to join the Nazi Party] believe that only the quality of a human being should determine his worth, that intellectual achievement, character, and obvious contributions to German culture retain their significance whether a person is Jewish or not." (Henle, 1986, p. 228). Everyone, including Köhler, expected that the article would lead to his arrest. That night, Köhler and members of the institute played chamber music while they waited for the Nazis to arrive. That night was not the night (Henle, 1986).

The article generated a considerable response, with Köhler receiving a great deal of mail and the article circulating for several months. On November 3, 1933 the Nazis ordered all classes to begin with the Nazi salute. Köhler began his lecture to a class of 200 students, which also included a number of Nazi sympathizers as well as Nazi Brownshirts standing by the doors, with a caricature of the salute (Henle, 1986). He then proceeded to explain his actions:

Ladies and Gentlemen, I have just saluted you in the manner that the government has decreed. I could not see how to avoid it.

Still, I must say something about it. I am professor of philosophy in this university, and this circumstance obligates me to be candid with you, my students. A professor who wished to disguise his views by word or by action would have no place here. You could no longer respect him; he would no longer have anything to say to you about philosophy or important human affairs.

Therefore I say: the form of my salute was until recently the sign of very particular ideas in politics and elsewhere. If I want to be honest, and if I am to be respected by you, I must explain that, although I am prepared to give that salute, I do not share the ideology which it usually signifies or used to signify.

The National Socialists among you will particularly welcome this explanation. Nobility and purity of purpose among Germans are goals for which the National Socialists are working hard. I am no National Socialist. But out of the same need to act nobly and purely, I have told you what the German salute means in my case and what it does not mean. I know you will respect my motives. (Cited in Henle, 1986, p. 229).

Still the Nazis did not act against Köhler until early December when uniformed and plainclothes troops surrounded a classroom where Köhler was giving a colloquium. The Nazis checked everyone's identification cards as they left. Köhler did not interfere with the troops, but complained to the rector of the university later (Henle, 1986).

Köhler's criticisms of the German government may seem mild to us with historical hindsight. Yet his criticism was dangerous and could have resulted in his arrest on several occasions. He moderated his criticisms in order to protect and guard the integrity of the Institute of Psychology, his assistants and students, and the work being carried out at the institute (Henle, 1986).

While the rector of the university backed Köhler's demand for freedom from harassment, harassment continued. Troops tried to "inspect" his class again in February but Kohler refused to permit it. In April another inspection took place, this time resulting in a report urging the firing of two assistants and three employees, insulting Köhler, and recommending the re-organization of the Institute so that it could be better controlled. These recommendations were not based on any evidence, other than the smell of cigarette smoke and foreign language newspapers (which were not yet banned by the administration). The end was in sight for the institute, but not before Köhler made some final efforts to negotiate with the rector, who was backpedaling on his earlier promises. Students at the institute were questioned and threatened, staff members were fired by the university, and other staff members, siding with the Nazis, refused to obey Köhler. Köhler requested retirement but was refused. During the controversy Köhler went to the U.S. to give the William James lectures. While in the U.S. he received an official letter instructing him to sign a loyalty oath to Hitler. Meanwhile, a Nazi supporter was appointed to the institute to replace Kurt Lewin, who had been fired for being Jewish. Köhler refused to sign the oath, claiming that the law requiring loyalty oaths did not apply to him because he had asked to retire. He also asked that all of his assistants, who had been fired, be reinstated. He was turned down, and resigned (without his pension that he would have received had he retired). Gestalt psychology in Germany ended. The younger generation of Gestalt psychologists were scattered and effectively ended. The three founders and a few others such as Lewin were now in exile, mostly in the U.S. (Henle, 1986).

While the Gestalt school of psychology was effectively destroyed, psychology as a whole prospered under the Nazi regime. Of the 23 German universities with departments or institutes of psychology, the Nazis fired five chairs because of their Jewish background. Only one non-Jewish chair resigned in protest, and that was Köhler. The Nazis replaced these chairs with pro-Nazi heads. While the number of university students shrunk under the Nazi regime because the regime excluded non-Aryans and political opponents of the government, the number of psychology graduates increased. These students went into a number of professions opened by the Nazis, especially that of military psychology. The Nazis pushed the practical application and professionalization of psychology, while at the same time they destroyed Gestalt psychology and psychoanalysis as schools (Gueter, 1992).

Many of the students and researchers associated with Gestalt psychology perished or left the field, some turning to school psychology or medicine to make a living. Others were in exile in the U.S. By the end of the 1940s, Gestalt psychology was no longer a significant force within the field (Henle, 1986). Köhler lived on, continuing to write and research, as did some of the other students of Köhler, Koffka, and Wertheimer. Along with the other scientists expelled by the Nazis during their repressive regime, they enriched psychology and other scientific fields in Great Britain and the U.S. In part, these scientists helped fuel the post-World War II scientific and economic achievements of the U.S. They were, as two historians of science remarked, Hitler's unwitting gift to the English-speaking world (Medawar & Pyke, 2000).

The Globalization of Psychology in the 1920s, 30s, and 40s

From the three original centers (Germany, the Northeastern U.S., and the Austro-Hungarian Empire), psychology soon quickly spread to other parts of the world. Two of the first countries to develop thriving psychological establishments were Russia and Japan, both rapidly developing countries that were emerging as world powers in the late 1800s. The Moscow Psychological Society was founded in 1885 and the first laboratory of experimental psychology was founded a year later. The early research carried out there was strongly influenced by German psychology. At the same time, the work of Pavlov and his contemporaries such as Ivan Sechenov (1829-1905) and Bechterev exerted a strong materialist influence (Sahakian, 1975).

While Russian psychology was strongly influenced by Wundt, Japanese psychology was strongly influenced by American functionalism. The founders of the new psychology in Japan, Yujiro Motora (1858-1912) and Matatora Matsumoto (1865-1943), received Ph.D.s from Johns Hopkins and Yale, respectively. At Johns Hopkins Motora studied with and published research with G. Stanley Hall while Matsumoto studied with E. W. Scripture, one of the founders of American functionalism. Matsumoto also was very familiar with Wundt's work and applied psychology to a number of practical problems (Sahakian, 1975).

Soon after the Russian Revolution of 1917, Russian psychology was to experience a number of traumas because of the efforts by the government to control and manipulate science. The first post-revolutionary period strongly favored a Soviet form of behaviorism closely resembling Watsonian behaviorism in methods and concepts. This Soviet form of behaviorism was known as the reflex period. Between 1925 and 1936 a second school of psychology was favored, that of applied school psychology and testing known as the pedagogical period. Finally, in 1936 the government decreed that the basis of psychology was to be dialectical materialism, ushering in the dialectical period.

The greatest psychologists who applied dialectical materialism to psychology, Lev Vygotsky (1896-1934) and Alexander Luria (1902-1977) were not involved in this period. The former had died tragically at an early age and the latter was spied on by the secret police. The work of both was considered decadent and suspect because of their close ties with western science, especially the work of Jean Piaget and the Gestalt psychologists (Sahakian, 1975). It is only since the fall of the former Soviet Union that psychology is developing without the constraints of an official ideology in Russia.

Both behaviorism and Gestalt psychology were imported to and studied in Japan, shortly after they emerged in the U.S. and Germany. Behaviorism, while influential, was criticized on a number of grounds because of the strong influence of functionalism and Gestalt psychology. As a consequence, the purposive behaviorism of Tolman, a behaviorism that emphasized perception and cognition, found considerable favor in Japan. In addition, the Japanese developed their own version of psychotherapy based on Zen Buddhism, known as Morita Therapy after its founder, Shoma Morita (1874-1938) a psychiatrist and professor of psychiatry (Sahakian, 1975).

While psychology was well developed in industrialized countries such as Japan and the USSR by the 1930s, it had also spread to much of the rest of the world. For example, laboratories of experimental psychology were established in Argentina, the first in 1898 and the second in 1901 (Ardila, 1970). In 1916 Mexico established its first laboratory of experimental psychology. Other countries soon followed suit, establishing laboratories and training programs in selected universities. But the growth in psychology was slow and most of the work emphasized psychoanalytically oriented therapy and psychological testing. For example, by 1941 only approximately 100 Ph.D.s in psychology existed in all of Latin America (Marin, Kennedy, & Boyce, 1987), although a larger number of individuals had been trained as therapists or testers at the undergraduate level. These individuals generally referred to themselves, and were referred to by others, as psychologists.

While psychology had spread to most parts of the world by the 1940s, the level of development in different countries varied considerably. Europe and the U.S. were still the centers of the field, with important contributions being made in Japan and the USSR. The geographic spread of the field laid the basis for the dramatic worldwide growth in psychology that began in the 1950s.

World War 2 And The Fate Of The Second Schools

At the end of World War II Europe and the Soviet Union lay in ruins, as did Japan and much of China. The U.S. was poised to emerge as the leading superpower and most advanced economy in the world, rivaled only by the military and economic power of the Soviet Union. U.S. Psychology was now the center of world psychology, in terms of theory, institutional and educational structures, and application.

Psychology in the world had changed some since its inception in the 1870s, but the changes were perhaps not as great as is often assumed. Certainly the schools of functionalism, volunteerism, and psychoanalysis had been seemingly replaced by behaviorism, Gestalt psychology, and neo-analytic approaches. But this over-emphasizes theoretical differences and underemphasizes the basic continuity and similarity between psychology at the turn of the 20th century and psychology at mid-century. No better summary of this continuity exists than R.S. Woodworth's closing paragraphs in his 1951 survey of schools in psychology. Woodworth, you may recall, was a functionalist and colleague of Cattell's and Thorndike's at Columbia University. In 1931 he published a widely used survey of theoretical schools in Psychology. In the eighth edition of his text, published in 1951, he places the theoretical differences in their proper perspective.

The total field of psychology is very wide and diversified, and the possible applications of the science to human welfare are numerous. Some psychologists are drawn into one part of the field and some into another. Their diverse lines of work do not usually result in the formation of "schools," as was said in the introductory chapter, but to quite an extent the schools do represent different lines of work. The behaviorists are more interested in problems of learning, the Gestalt group more interested in problems of perception, the psychoanalysts more in motivation. The human individual, enmeshed in all of the problems, is what holds the specializing groups of psychologists together, and we may hope that the interrelations of problems will become increasingly evident with the general advance of the science. Already, rapprochements are becoming visible

(DASHIELL, 1939).

Another reason for the continued unity of psychology is found in the fact that only a minority of psychologists have become active adherents of any of the schools. Some may lean toward one school and some toward another, but on the whole the psychologists of the present time are proceeding on their way in the middle of the road. After all, there was a great deal in the psychology of 1900 against which there has been no revolt. Many of the results of the earlier research still hold good, and fresh research during the past half century has added many new results that have no direct connec-

tion with any of the schools. The psychologists of 1900 were on their way, and their way is our way, but we seem to be further ahead.

No worldwide census of psychologists has been attempted for fifteen years and more, and we do not know how numerous we are. Probably 10,000 would be a conservative estimate, a very large number in comparison with 1900, though very small in comparison with some contemporary scientific groups, as for example the chemists. If we could assemble all of these psychologists in a convention hall and ask the members of each school to stand and show themselves, a very large proportion of the entire group would remain seated. If, instead of mentioning the schools, we should ask the experimental psychologists to rise, the clinical psychologists, the social psychologists, the child psychologists, the educational psychologists, the industrial psychologists, and a few more such groups, we should soon have the entire convention on its feet. Anything like a cleavage into separate "psychologies" seems much more likely along such lines than along "school" lines. But for the present there seems to be a determination among psychologists to stick together in one inclusive group. Finally we may raise a question which has been hinted at more than once, especially in the early discussion of functional psychology. A broadly defined functional psychology starts with the question "What man does" and proceeds to the questions "How?" and "Why?" This we thought to be the underlying conception of psychology, coming down and persisting underneath even when the formal definitions were quite different. So broadly defined, we have said more than once, functional psychology scarcely deserves the name of a school because it would include so many psychologists who have not professed themselves. Now the question is whether our middle-of-the-roaders are not after all members of this broadly conceived functional school. If we had our convention assembled we could put the question to a vote. But if the middle-of-the-roaders are really functionalists, the question is then whether the same would not be true of all the schools. Are they not all functionalists at heart? Without calling them up one by one and pressing the question home, we can at least say that they have all made contributions to functional problems. Every school is good, though no one is good enough. No one of them has the full vision of the psychology of the future. One points to one alluring prospect, another to another. Every one has elements of vitality and is probably here to stay for a long time. Their negative pronouncements we can discount while we accept their positive contributions to psychology as a whole.

Woodworth's description of the majority of American psychologists as functionalist and eclectic (borrowing what they see as valuable from each school) is apt. American psychology never really became dominated by behaviorism, although behaviorism was the leading school in the U.S. from 1920 to 1950. Almost equally as influential in the U.S. was Gestalt psychology. In Europe, Gestalt psychology was the leading school but most European psychologists embraced an eclectic and practical psychology similar to American functionalism.

Woodworth also notes the importance of specialization within psychology: the real divisions within psychology did not exist between schools but between different specialties such as social, child, experimental, industrial, and clinical. The underlying unity of psychology exists not because of the dominance of this or that school, but because of the primary subject matter of the field, the human being, and the empirical approach to this subject matter. In this sense, psychology existed in a situation similar to the New Biology before the development of the theory of evolution and genetics.

References

Ardila, R. (1970). Landmarks in the history of Latin American psychology. *Journal of the History of the Behavioral Sciences, 6*(2), 140-146.

Ash, M.G. (1995). *Gestalt psychology in German culture, 1890-1967.* Cambridge: Cambridge University Press.

Dashiell, J.F. (1939). Some rapprochements in contemporary psychology. *Psychological Bulletin, 36,* 1-24.

Geuter, U. (1992). *The professionalization of psychology in Nazi Germany.* Cambridge: Cambridge University Press.

Harrower, M. (1983). *Kurt Koffka: An unwitting self-portrait.* Gainesville, FL: University Presses of Florida.

Henle, M. (1986). *1879 and all that.* New York: Columbia University Press.

King, D.B., & Wertheimer, M. (2005). *Max Wertheimer and gestalt theory.* New Brunswick, NJ: Transaction Publishers.

Koffka, K. (1922). Perception: An introduction to the gestalt-theorie. *Psychological Bulletin, 19,* 531-585.

Koffka, K. (1924/1959). *The growth of the mind: An introduction to child* psychology. Paterson, NJ: Littlefield, Adams & Company.

Koffka, K. (1935). *The principles of gestalt psychology.* New York: Harcourt Brace and Company.

Köhler, W. (1927). *The mentality of apes.* New York: Harcourt, Brace, & Company.

Ley, R. (1990). *A whisper of espionage.* Garden City Park, NY: Avery Publishing Group.

Marin, G., Kennedy, S., & Boyce, B.C. (1987). *Latin American psychology: A guide to research and training.* Washington, DC: American Psychological Association.

Medawar, J., & Pyke, D. (2000). *Hitler's gift: The true story of the scientists expelled by the Nazi regime*. New York: Arcade Publishing.

Perls, F. (1971). *Gestalt therapy verbatim*. New York: Bantam Books.

Perls, F. (1972). *In and out the garbage pail*. New York: Bantam Books.

Sahakian, W.S. (1975). *History and systems of psychology*. New York: John Wiley & Sons.

Watson, R.I. (1978). *The great psychologists* (4th ed.). New York: J.B. Lippincott Company.

Woodworth, R.S. (1951). *Contemporary schools of psychology* (8th ed.). London: Methuen Company, Ltd.

PART III: MODERN PSYCHOLOGY FROM 1950 TO THE 1990S:

Diversification And Big Science

From its inception as a distinct science and academic discipline in the 1870s, Psychology had grown dramatically. In the period following World War II this growth was to continue and accelerate, transforming the field in a number of ways. Perhaps the most obvious transformation was the increased specialization within psychology. Psychologists were more and more often trained within a special field where they concentrated their research, teaching, or professional activities. This increased specialization makes it virtually impossible to write a general history of psychology in the last half of the 20th century. Instead, one must write a history of the sub-fields and examine the links between the sub-fields as well as between the broader context and the historical development of psychology. This specialization and diversification began almost immediately after the founding of the new psychology, as shown in Chapters 4, 5, and 6, and continued between the two world wars, as shown in Chapters 7 and 8. Still, to do justice to the subfields, I will often take a step backwards into the early part of the 20th century before I can take two steps forward to the present.

In addition to the diversification of psychology, a second important transformation was the increase in the number of psychologists (defined narrowly as those holding doctorate degrees) worldwide. As noted in the last chapter, by 1950 there were perhaps 10,000 psychologists worldwide. By 2000, that number had increased 100-fold to approximately one million psychologists. While most of these psychologists work in developed countries, an increasing number are from, and work in, developing countries.

This growth in numbers is also related to the globalization of psychology. The history of the field from 1950 to the present includes the history of psychology in most countries of the world. Because of the confines of length, however, I will be forced to focus on the developments in the U.S. and Europe, with some attention to Japan and a select group of other countries.

In addition to the academic diversification, numerical growth, and global extension of psychology, three other changes need to be noted before we begin the history of different specialties: the shift from science to profession, the breakdown of the double marginalization of several groups, and the decline of the schools as influential forces.

Around 1950 a tipping point was reached: the number of applied psychologists, that is, those psychologists working in practical settings, exceeded the number of academic psychologists. By far and away, the majority of these applied psychologists worked as clinical psychologists. But psychologists worked in a variety of settings within government, business, the military, and non-profit sector. Psychology transformed from a science into a profession based on a science, so while there were still many psychologists carrying out psychological research (approximately one out of seven in the U.S. are college teachers and researchers at present), just as there are researchers in medical and dental schools, the majority of psychologists are not scientists but professionals, applying their expertise to the resolution of particular problems. The relationship of the science of psychology to the profession of psychology becomes an increasingly important part of our history.

Another important change was the breakdown of the double marginalization of "outsiders" such as women, Jews, African-Americans, and Hispanic-Americans. These excluded groups had contributed to the field from early in the history of the new psychology, overcoming numerous obstacles. But still in 1950s psychology was the province of white Christian (at least in upbringing) men. From 1950 to the present psychology has become more representative, with women and Jews making the greatest progress, and African-Americans and Hispano-Americans making the least. By the late 1990s, over half of all Ph.D. students in psychology were women. While breaking the color and religion barrier to psychology, these excluded groups also rediscovered the repressed role and untold stories of pioneering women, blacks, Jews, and Hispanics. The historical tales we tell often reflect not the past but our present.

Finally, all of these changes have produced the demise of schools within psychology. While, as I have argued, the use of schools as an analytic concept in the history of psychology exaggerates differences and minimizes commonalities within the field, schools did exist. In the post-World War II period these schools faded in significance as the practitioners within the field embraced whatever they found useful for dealing with the problems they faced. This practical and theoretical eclecticism was already evident in the 1930s and 1940s. While schools still had relevance among academic psychologists, more and more of them embraced mini-theories explaining a circumscribed problem while also adopting methodological behaviorism.

Within the U.S. the dramatic growth of psychology was impelled by events that took place in the 1930s and 1940s. The first of these events occurred in the summer of 1932 when 45,000 jobless veterans from the Great War marched, hitch-hiked, and hopped trains to Washington, D.C. to demand payment of a service bonus that they had been promised by the U.S. government. Known as the Bonus Army, the veterans set up well-organized camps (called by the press "shanty towns") in Washington and gathered peacefully at the Capital to request payment of their bonus. The bill granting their bonus passed the House of Representatives because of massive public support but was defeated in the senate because of the opposition of President Hoover. Hoover ordered the removal of the veterans and Army Chief of Staff Douglas MacArthur attacked the veterans on July 28, 1932. The vets, who were unarmed and peaceful, were evicted by troops using bayonets, tanks, and tear gas. When Franklin D. Roosevelt learned of the attack, he knew he would win the election (Dickson & Allen, 2004).

Once elected, Roosevelt, too, opposed payment of the bonus. The veterans did not win payment of a bonus until 1936 when public support became overwhelming. This was not the end of the bonus march however: When the U.S. entered World War II, the memory of the Great War veterans and their post-war plight was still fresh in most Americans' memories, and was especially sharp in the memories of the president. Seeking to avoid a similar crisis at the end of the Second World War, Roosevelt signed into law the G.I. Bill of Rights for returning veterans on June 22, 1944. The bill guaranteed free college (tuition and expenses plus a stipend for living expenses) to returning veterans for an eight-year period. The bill also included provisions for 52 weeks of unemployment benefits for veterans, loan guarantees for homes, farms, and businesses, and extensive construction of Veterans Administration hospitals (Dickson & Allen, 2004).

The Second World War involved millions of American women and men in military service. The U.S. involvement in the war began after the Japanese attack on Pearl Harbor, Hawaii (Hawaii was not yet a state) in December of 1941. After the war over eight million veterans took advantage of the G.I. Bill of Rights to go to college and buy homes, fueling a long and dramatic wave of economic prosperity in the U.S. In all, over 2.2 million had graduated from college, including approximately 450,000 engineers, 238,000 teachers, 90,000 scientists, and almost 90,000 doctors and dentists. The G.I. Bill of Rights dramatically increased the percentage of the U.S. population that had a college education (approximately 4.5% in 1945) to the current situation where approximately 25% of the U.S. population has a college degree (Dickson & Allen, 2004).

The G.I. Bill of Rights dramatically expanded U.S. higher education, but it was not the only consequence of the war. In 1946 Congress passed the National Mental Health Act which established the National Institute of Mental Health (NIMH). NIMH provided funds for research and graduate education in mental health related fields. Psychology was to benefit enormously from NIMH funding (Hilgard, 1987).

The Second World War produced numerous causalities and the facilities and tasks of the Veterans Administration expanded substantially. Some of the injured required psychological services and the VA became, after the war, a major source of employment and research funds for psychologists (Hilgard, 1987). War, it seems, was not only good for psychology in Germany, but in the U.S. as well.

These events are important in part because the destruction wrought by World War II devastated countries, higher education, and psychology outside of the U.S. so that the U.S. became the center of psychology in the world for decades after the Second World War. As a consequence, much of the story I tell of the history of the specialties will be the history of American psychology.

Let us now turn to the history of the different specialties within psychology from the 1950 to the present. We must start with a two specialties that are first among equals, for they emerged first in the New Psychology: Physiological

Psychology and the study of perception. As with the subsequent chapters, I will have to take a step back into the first half of the 20th century before I can take two steps forward to the present.

References

Dickson, P. & Allen, T.B. (2004). *The bonus army: An American epic*. New York: Walker & Company.

Hilgard, E.R. (1987). *Psychology in America: A historical survey*. San Diego, CA: Harcourt Brace Jovanovich.

CHAPTER 9: PHYSIOLOGICAL PSYCHOLOGY AND PERCEPTION

Psychology, or at least American psychology, is a second rate discipline. The main reason is that it does not stand in awe of its subject matter.

JAMES J. GIBSON (1972; AS CITED IN REED, 1988, P. 1).

Physiological psychology, the study of how the brain and nervous system influences thinking, feeling, consciousness, and behavior, and the study of perception, how we perceive the world around us, are two of the oldest subfields within the New Psychology. The initial work by Wundt and his students focused intensely on these two subfields. Both subfields clearly illustrate the connections of psychology to biology and philosophy. In this chapter we shall outline the rise and development of physiological psychology and the study of perception during the 20th century. We will also explore the implications of these two subfields for practical and philosophical questions. To begin, we need to return to neurophysiology at the end of the 1800s.

Cajal And Sherrington: Neurophysiology At The Turn Of The Century

The two most important figures in the history of neurophysiology are the Spanish scientist Santiago Ramon y Cajal (1852-1934) and the British scientist Sir. Charles S. Sherrington (1856-1952). Both scientists made significant contributions to neurophysiology and laid the foundations for the birth of neuroscience.

Ramon y Cajal (often just called Cajal in the same way that Tiger Woods is often just called Tiger) had originally wanted to be an artist. He was a talented painter and sketcher as a child. Ramon y Cajal's father was a surgeon who taught his son anatomy to improve his artwork. These early lessons in anatomy sparked Ramon y Cajal's interest and he eventually gave up art for anatomy and medicine, eventually focusing on brain anatomy. Ramon y Cajal was also a powerful writer whose poetic descriptions of cells and cell structures made the descriptions of tissue come alive (Kandel, 2006). In addition to his extensive publications on neurophysiology, he wrote science fiction (Ramon y Cajal, 1905/2001), an autobiography (Ramon y Cajal, 1937/1988), and a book of advice for young scientists (Ramon y Cajal, 1999). He was also a talented photographer as well as a painter (Otis, 2001).

Ramon y Cajal used a staining technique for neurons developed by the Italian neuroanatomist Camillo Golgi (with whom Ramon y Cajal shared the Nobel Prize in Medicine and Physiology in 1906) to explore the structure of the nervous system. Using this technique along with studying the brains of newborn animals (which are less developed) he developed what is called the neuronal doctrine, the basis of the advances in the last 100 years in our understanding of the brain (Kandel, 2006).

Before Ramon y Cajal's work, physiologists believed that the brain consisted of a single network of protoplasm. Given the technical limitations of the time, in terms of staining techniques and microscopes, this was a reasonable belief, given that the cells of the central nervous system seemed to be tangled together with no discernable breaks or gaps. Golgi, for instance, never accepted the neuronal doctrine and criticized Ramon y Cajal for decades in a bitter and often acrimonious fashion (Kandel, 2006).

Ramon y Cajal discovered that the nerve cell (called the Neuron by a German researcher) was made up of a cell body and two kinds of branches called dendrites and axons. The nerve cell was the basic unit of the brain, with the axon of one cell communicating with the dendrites of other cells at specialized regions. Soon after Ramon y Cajal's discovery, Sherrington named this region the "synapse". There are three types of neurons: motor neurons which connect to the muscles, sensory neurons which connect to the sensory organs such as the eye, and interneurons, which connect one neuron to another. The nerve cells form differentiated circuits because a given neuron will only have connections with certain other neurons. Ramon y Cajal also argued that the nerve signal travels in only one direction—from dendrites to axon—and that this makes it possible to trace neural circuits. Further, Ramon y Cajal hypothesized that there was a gap between the axon of one cell and the dendrites of other cells at the synapses, and that learning may take place through a process of growth or formation of synaptic connections in the brain. This hypothesis flowed from the fact, well known to Ramon y Cajal, that young organisms often had fewer neurons and fewer connections between neurons than older organisms (Kandel, 2006).

Ramon y Cajal's work raised questions that would take a century to answer: Is there a gap between axon and dendrite at the synapse? How does the nerve impulse travel along the axon? How does an impulse move from one neuron to the next? What are the circuits in the brain for memory, for perceptions, for anger, and for love? How do new circuits form and how do old circuits decay? Ramon y Cajal's achievements were recognized early on by other physiologists. Among the young physiologists who admired and appreciated the import of Ramon y Cajal's work was a talented young British physiologist, Charles Sherrington.

Sir Charles S. Sherrington (1856-1952) took a different approach from Ramon y Cajal; Sherrington studied the functioning of the central nervous system at the spinal cord level in decorticated animals (animals that had their cortex surgically removed). Sherrington was born in Britain and educated at Cambridge University (where he received his M.D. in 1885) and in Germany. He worked as a professor of physiology at Liverpool University from 1895 to 1913 and in London during most of the Great War. In 1917 he was made a Professor of Physiology at Oxford University where he stayed until he retired in 1936 (at the age of 80). He was knighted in 1922 for his work and received the Nobel Prize jointly with his Cambridge colleague E.D. Adrian in 1932 (Hilgard, 1987).

Sherrington's major work was *The Integrative Action of the Nervous System* (Sherrington, 1906), a book based on a series of lectures he gave at Yale University. In addition to introducing much of the standard terminology for the nervous system (such as the synapse), Sherrington showed that some neurons are excitatory (they cause another neuron to fire) and others are inhibitory (they prevent a neuron from firing). The inhibitory neurons prevent certain responses from occurring to stimuli and hence make possible the efficient and coordinated response to the world (Kandel, 2006). The work of Sherrington and Ramon y Cajal was immediately incorporated into psychology (Hilgard, 1987). It was on this stage of neurophysiology in the late 1800s and early 1900s that physiological psychology first entered as a distinct specialty within psychology.

how other psychologists influence new ones

Karl Lashley And The Search For The Engram

Physiological psychology emerged in the U.S. as a separate specialty within psychology in 1887, with a book by G.T. Ladd, (1842-1921) who worked at Yale University. Ladd's book was heavily influenced by the work of Wundt and James, and placed stress on neurophysiology. Two other influential early physiological psychologists in the U.S. were Robert Woodworth (1869-1962), whom we met in Chapter 8 as a historian of psychology, and Shepard Ivory Franz (1874-1933). Both received their Ph.D.s from Cattell at Columbia University in 1899. Woodworth went on to study with Sherrington and work in the New York City hospitals before returning to Columbia, where he taught for many years. In 1911 Woodworth revised Ladd's earlier work on physiological psychology (Thompson & Robinson, 1979).

Franz adopted the research methods of Thorndike and used them to measure the effects of brain lessons on behavior. He published his first study using this approach in 1902, around the time Watson was applying a similar approach. After taking several teaching positions, Franz worked at a U.S. government hospital from 1907-1924 where he also carried out research (Thompson & Robinson, 1979).

Karl Lashley (1890-1958) is considered by many to be the most important physiological psychologist in the twentieth century. We first met Lashley in Chapter 7, when he was a student and close collaborator of John B. Watson at Johns Hopkins University. After receiving his Ph.D. there (in genetics) he carried out research with both Watson and Franz. He later went to the University of Minnesota, the University of Chicago, and then in 1935 to Harvard (Thompson & Robinson, 1979).

Both Franz and Watson had pioneered what is known as the lesion-behavior approach to physiological psychology. The essence of this approach is to *ethics?* test for or train a particular behavior and then systematically cut (the cuts are known as lesions) or burn out (the burns are called ablations) parts of the brain to see how the behavior is affected. The lesion-behavior approach is an invaluable experimental complement to studies of behavior and brain injuries, the kind of descriptive studies that were so important in the nineteenth century to the progress of neurophysiology (see Chapter 3). Behaviorism and brain localization were complementary concepts: behaviorism assumed that the brain was a giant switch board based on stimulus-response circuits. Learning was assumed to occur when new circuits were formed in the brain. With the lesion-behavior approach, Lashley had a perfect technique to investigate the biological basis of behaviors (Thompson & Robinson, 1979).

Lashley devoted much of his work after Watson's fall from grace to the search for the location of memory in the brain; the place he called the engram. He carried out a series of careful studies using the lesion-behavior approach, culminating in a seminal monograph (Lashley, 1929) entitled *Brain Mechanisms and Intelligence*. In these studies he had trained rats on three progressively more difficult mazes, then he made lesions of different sizes and in different locations in the cerebral cortex. His finding was that it was not the location of the lesion that was important, but what the overall size of the lesion was, especially for the more difficult maze. This research resulted in Lashley's enunciation of two important concepts and his support for a third concept: the ideas of mass action, equipotentiality, and vicarious functioning. For Lashley, mass action was the idea that for complex behavior, the entire cortex was involved, that is, complex behaviors are distributed across many areas of the brain. The amount of area destroyed is more important than the specific area. Equipotentiality referred to the idea that even for localized functions, that which is lost when the entire area is removed may be unaffected if just a small area is destroyed. And vicarious functioning, an idea developed by Franz from working with hospital patients, referred to what we now call neuroplasticity. This means that something learned in one part of the brain can be relearned in a different part of the brain if the original area has been destroyed or damaged (Hilgard, 1987).

The same year Lashley published his seminal monograph, he was elected president of the APA. He continued teaching and carrying out research and was to shape physiological psychology more than any other researcher during the first 50 years of the 20th century. His other major contributions included his defense of the notion of biological instincts based on brain mechanisms (Lashley, 1938a) against his old teacher Watson and the radical behaviorists associated with Skinner, his studies of the role of the thalamus in emotions (Lashley, 1938b), and his argument against the reflex arc concept and switchboard model of the brain (Lashley, 1951). He also carried out pioneering studies of the neural basis of vision and in the fields of ethology and comparative psychology (Bruce, 1991). Perhaps as important as his research was his role as a teacher: he trained most of the leading physiological psychologists during the 1920s, 1930s, and 1940s in the U.S., including two that were to have a profound influence on the field: Donald Hebb and Roger Sperry (Hilgard, 1987).

Late in his career, Lashley acknowledged that he had not found the location of memory and learning. He wrote: "It [my research] has discovered nothing directly on the nature of the engram. I sometimes feel, in reviewing the localization of the memory trace, that the necessary conclusion is that learning is not possible" (Lashley, 1950, p. 478). Like all physiological psychologists, Lashley was limited by the research techniques available to him. At the time he started his research, the lesion-behavior method was the best that he had available. Because Lashley only destroyed the cortex in his rats, he did not reach into the lower parts of the brain that are so important to memory, as we will see below. In addition, maze-learning in rats was shown later to be a very poor measure of memory in rats because rats use a variety of senses and information to navigate a maze (Kandel, 2006).

Donald Hebb And Cell Assembles

The period from 1930 to 1950 was something of a dark age for physiological psychology, in spite of the brilliant but slow progress made by Lashley and his collaborators (Hilgard, 1987), as well as a number of important technical advances. However, Lashley himself was also partly to blame. In his APA presidential address he had cautioned psychologists against positing neurological models for behavior when so little was known about the actual functioning of the brain (Lashley, 1930). Perhaps a more important factor was the behaviorist metatheory that assumed that a science of psychology could be built without any "looking into the black box" of the mind and brain. Skinner (Skinner, 1938) was the most forceful advocate of this approach, while Tolman and his students rejected it, as we saw in Chapter 7.

The dark age for physiological psychology ended swiftly in 1949-1950, because of several important empirical advances and a major new theory developed by one of Lashley's students. The empirical advances included the re-

so much in the last 100 yrs. what's to come?

cording of nerve action potentials with cathode-ray tubes, a technology which was adopted widely in the 1930s (Thompson & Robinson, 1979), the discovery of the electroencephalogram (EEG) in 1929 and its use in the 1930s and 40s to study human and animal brain activity (Thompson & Robinson, 1979), and the development in the 1930s and 40s of implanted wires in the brain that could deliver electrical stimulation to the brains of conscious humans or animals (Delgado, 1969). The electron microscope, which was invented in Germany in 1932 and subsequently improved, was used in the 1950s to confirm Ramon y Cajals's hypothesis that a gap exists between the synapses of one neuron and the dendrites of another neuron. Finally, the ability to record impulses of single neurons by means of glass pipette (tiny hollow tubes) electrodes was developed in 1949 at the University of Chicago (Hilgard, 1987). All of these technological advances in instrumentation facilitated scientific advances. We shall see this pattern again—physiological psychology advances steadily along with advances in instrumentation, resulting in a new theoretical understanding of the brain being proposed approximately every 20 years.

A major theoretical approach was proposed by Donald O. Hebb (1904-1985) in 1949. Hebb was a Canadian born in Nova Scotia, educated at Dalhousie University and McGill University. Hebb attended graduate school part-time. He worked full time as a teacher and school principal after finishing his undergraduate degree. At McGill, Hebb carried out studies of conditioned reflexes with Babkin, a former student of Pavlov's and the discoverer of the Babkin reflex in children (Hilgard, 1987). At the age of 30, after finishing his master's degree, he left McGill to study with Lashley at the University of Chicago. When Lashley left for a position at Harvard the next year, Hebb went with him where, in 1936 he finished his Ph.D. in physiological psychology (Hilgard, 1987).

For the next several years Hebb did not have a permanent job, but he did continue to work with a series of prominent physiologists and carry out his own research. After graduating from Harvard he spent an extra year there with Lashley, then he spent two years (1937-1939) as a research fellow at the Neurological Institute of Montreal, where he worked with the gifted brain surgeon Wilder Penfield (1891-1976). After another three years as an assistant professor at Queens University in Ontario he spent five years at the Yerkes Primate Lab in Florida where Lashley carried out many of his studies (Hilgard, 1987).

Hebb's studies covered a wide variety of topics, from brain injuries in humans to the neurological basis of intelligence and the development of the brain under conditions of sensory deprivation. In his studies, Hebb had noted that it takes more brain tissue to establish intelligence than to retain it. He sought the neural basis for this and other facts but did not have the time to formulate a theory until after getting a permanent position at McGill University in 1947 (Hilgard, 1987).

Hebb's influential theoretical work, *The Organization of Behavior* (Hebb, 1949), integrated a great deal of previous research and contained important detailed discussions of such topics as emotional disturbances, perception, pain, and hunger. But it also introduced important new general concepts: the cell assembly, phase sequence, and central facilitation. These concepts were used throughout the book and stimulated intense interest in physiological psychology, thus ending the dark age when physiological psychology made steady progress but was generally neglected by the field of psychology as a whole (Hilgard, 1987).

Hebb's brief introduction to the concepts of cell assembly, phase sequence, and central facilitation is a model of clarity and shows his clean, compressed style of writing:

Any frequently repeated particular stimulation will lead to the slow development of a "cell-assembly," a diffuse structure comprising cells in the cortex and diencephalons (and also, perhaps, in the basal ganglia of the cerebrum), capable of acting briefly as a closed system, delivering facilitation to other such systems and usually having a specific motor facilitation. A series of such events constitute a "phase sequence"—the thought process. Each assembly may be aroused by a preceding assembly, by a sensory event, or—normally—by both. The central facilitation from one of these activities on the next is the prototype of "attention" (Hebb, 1949, p. XIX).

Hebb also argued that during sleep and infancy there are alternative organizations for the functioning of the brain, and that the organization of the brain is very delicate; if disturbed, the resulting disorganization results in emotional disturbance (if the disorganization is transitory) or neurosis or psychosis (if the disorganization is chronic).

Both Lashley and Hebb were influenced by Gestalt psychology (Thompson & Robinson, 1979). By the time of Hebb's theoretical masterpiece he had rejected the stimulus-response (or as Dewey much earlier had called it, the reflex arc) connection as the basis for learning. Hebb's work also marked a turning point in the history of physiological psychology. From 1949 onward the pace of research and discovery was to accelerate exponentially, a pattern we discussed in Chapter 1. This acceleration resulted in increased specialization and an increasing number of scientists active in the field.

The impact of Hebb's work was almost instantaneous. Hebb's friend David Krech (the two met at the University of Chicago when Krech was Lashley's post-doctoral fellow) began a series of studies on the chemical basis of the brain and on the effects of experience on brain growth. Krech (1909-1977) had been a doctoral student of Edward Tolman as well as a post-doctoral fellow of Lashley's. Early in his career he had shifted his focus to social psychology and in 1947 he was hired by the University of California at Berkeley to teach social psychology (Hilgard, 1987). Krech had left Swarthmore College where he was a colleague of Wolfgang Köhler; Köhler spent much of his time in the U.S. carrying out brain research based on Gestalt psychology and related to perception. At Berkeley Krech's interests again turned to physiological psychology under the influence of Tolman and Hebb. Krech worked with a team of three other principal investigators, the biochemist Melvin Calvin, the neuroanatomist Marian Diamond, and the young psychologist Mark Rosenzeig (1922-) who had taken a summer course with Hebb at Harvard graduate school and had read *The Organization of Behavior* in manuscript form before it was published (Hilgard, 1987). These four principal investigators and their associates discovered the first neurotransmitters (the chemical messengers that travel across the synaptic gap between axons and dendrites) in 1952 and the effects of enriched or impoverished experience on the growth of neural connections in 1960.

Roger Sperry And Split Brain Research

Another influential Lashley student was Roger Sperry. Sperry received his Ph.D. in zoology at the University of Chicago and then spent a year at Harvard as Lashley's post-doctoral fellow. When Lashley went to the Yerkes Primate lab in Florida, Sperry followed. Sperry later worked at the University of Chicago and the California Institute of Technology. It was at Chicago that Sperry supervised the first research in split brains in monkeys in 1961. "Split brains" are brains in which the corpus callosum, the structure that connects the left and right hemispheres of the cerebral cortex, is surgically severed. Cutting of the corpus callosum was used to successfully treat patients with severe epilepsy. Sperry and his colleagues also studied humans with split brains, discovering that they essentially have two different forms of consciousness, one associated with the left hemisphere that is essentially linguistic and the other consciousness, associated with the right hemisphere, that is nonverbal (Hilgard, 1987; Thompson & Robinson, 1979).

Cyborgs Are Us

Sperry's research on the split brain showed that consciousness rests on brain structures and that if you change the brain, you change consciousness. Even more disturbing, perhaps, was the work of Jose M. R. Delgado, a Spanish neurophysiologist who came to Yale University in 1950. Delgado's research explored the effects of electrically stimulating various parts of the brain by means of radio controlled neural implants. Throughout the 1950s and 60s Delgado was one of the leading researchers in this area. He even proposed that this technology could be used to cure humans of a number of mental diseases and enhance human evolution so that we could consciously create what he called a psychocivilized society (Delgado, 1969). What Delgado was advocating, of course, is a society of neurologically enhanced cyborgs.

Delgado inserted fine electrical wires into the brain so that they could stimulate specific brain regions. These wires were then attached to a miniaturized radio receiver and battery attached to the skull. The researcher could, by means of a remote control, send stimulation to the brain when desired. Delgado experimented with animals (mostly cats and monkeys, but he also used other animals) and also used the technique medically with humans. He showed that a number of behaviors, such as aggression, sleep and wakefulness, and pleasure and pain, could be induced through electrical stimulation (Delgado, 1969). Perhaps his most dramatic public demonstration of his work occurred in a bull ring in Spain in 1964. Delgado implanted a bull with one of his neural implants and then stepped into the ring with a matador's cape. As the bull charged, Delgado pressed a button on his remote control and instantly turned off the bull's angry charge (Slater, 2005).

Delgado described the limitations of technology, such as the imprecise knowledge about neural circuits and the inability to communicate with single neurons, but argued that some or all of these limitations could be overcome with the progress of the brain sciences (Delgado, 1969). Delgado has indeed been proven correct. We have made considerable progress in understanding neural circuits and the basic functioning of the brain since the late 1960s (see below). Some of the technological problems are also yielding to solutions. In 1995, for example, German scientists succeeded in connecting silicon chips (the basis of a computer) with neurons, so that the chip can cause the neuron to fire. Four years earlier, in 1991, the same team of German scientists built a chip that could be activated by a neuron (Browne, 1995). This work, while a long way from a complete computer-brain interface or an effective bionic limb controlled by the undamaged motor neurons in the body, is an important step in the direction of real "bionic" humans, often called cyborgs in science fiction novels and movies.

In the 1960s researchers in neural implants received considerable government funds for their research, but this came to an end in the mid-1970s as a result of Senate hearings that raised concerns about potential abuse of implants to control people. Interest in this area of research was renewed in 1987 when a French neurosurgeon discovered that electrical stimulation of the thalamus stopped a patient with Parkinson's disease from shaking. The Minneapolis-based firm Medtronic developed neural implants for Parkinson's that were approved by the FDA in the late 1990s. Over 30,000 of these devices are now used in patients across the globe and the procedure is known as Deep Brain Stimulation (DBS). As it turned out, the implants also altered emotional states in some patients, leading to research on the effects of neural implants on mental illness (Slater, 2005).

Between 2000 and 2004, around 100 implants were used on volunteer human subjects for severe cases of OCD (Obsessive-Compulsive Disorder) and depression. So far, results show that about half of the OCD patients have improved and over half of the patients with depression have improved. One of the major problems faced by doctors and medical researchers is that they cannot find a single location that yields consistent positive results. Patients also have to return to the doctor every month to have the levels of stimulation checked and adjusted (Slater, 2005). Since electronics have become considerably miniaturized since Delgado's early experiments, human subjects do not seem to be bothered by the implants. Much is not yet known about the impact of implants; they may induce long term change in brain chemistry and structure (Slater, 2005).

The ethical concerns that led to the de-funding of neural implant research in the 1970s have re-emerged. Who, as one of the leading researchers in the area asked, controls the "clicker" which controls the neural implant (Slater, 2005)? Can the technology be used to enhance the performance of soldiers and civilians? (For instance, neural implants could dramatically improve the ability of Air Force pilots.) What happens if some have access to it and others do not, intensifying the division between the haves and the have-nots? Finally, as with all medical treatments, is this technology safe and does it have unknown or unintended consequences? Will this technology lead to the enslavement of human beings? All of these issues have yet to be addressed in a broad political forum (Schulz, 2006). We may indeed be on the verge of a brave new cyborg world made up of bionic humans with brain implants and computer-brain interfaces.

Karl Pribram And The Holographic Brain

Following the approximate 20-year rule, another major theoretical integration occurred and was published in 1971 by Karl Pribram (1919-). Pribram received his M.D. degree in 1941 at the University of Chicago. He was a talented brain surgeon in private practice in Florida until lured into research by Lashley at the Yerkes Primate Lab where he worked with Lashley from 1946 to 1948. From 1948 to 1958 Pribram worked at Yale. He then moved to Stanford University for the remainder of his career. Pribram and his students published hundreds of experimental studies on the brain. He was the first to combine computer technology with surgical, anatomical, and electrical techniques. In addition, he contributed to the emergence of cognitive psychology (which we shall explore in the next chapter) as well (Hilgard, 1987).

In addition to his many empirical contributions, Pribram made major theoretical advances based on empirical work. He suggested that the brain was organized hierarchically in three layers with a core of homeostats that regulate the body, surrounded by a second layer consisting of the limbic system. The third layer consisted of the cortex which included the associative areas responsible for the integration of sensory and motor activity and for intentionality. Pribram also argued that the brain functioned like a hologram (a three-dimensional image produced by a laser) in that it could store information holographically. This later idea was perhaps his most controversial and provocative proposal (Hilgard, 1987).

A funny thing happened to physiological psychology on the way to the 21st century: It became something else. The name "physiological psychology" is used less frequently than before. In the late 1970s courses, textbooks and psychologists in this area were more likely to use the term biopsychology or psychobiology (Thompson & Robinson, 1979), a trend which continued in the 1980s and 1990s. Increasingly, psychologists formerly known as physiological psychologists now identify themselves as neuroscientists. Neuroscience is a field that includes neuroanatomy, neurophysiology, neurochemistry, genetics, and physiological psychology (Hilgard, 1987). The Society for Neuroscience was formed in 1970 and many of the early members had Ph.D.s from psychology programs (Thompson & Robinson, 1979). In the early 1970s neuroscience benefited from the financial support of the Alfred P. Sloan Foundation in New York, which provided the means to build institutional infrastructure (such as journals and conferences) and support research (Gardner, 1987). Neuroscience is now a growing discipline with its own departments in many universities. As we will see again in the history of cognitive psychology and developmental psychology, the role of outside financial support is crucial to a subfield's success.

The Biology Of Memory

Beginning in the early 1950s, physiological psychologists began to make substantial progress in finding the engram that had eluded Lashley for over 30 years. In their search, psychologists were to reject Lashley's concepts of mass action and equipotentiality. They were to find that the engram has a location; in fact it has several.

The crucial advances came with the detailed case study of a single patient, named H.M., over a 30-year period by Brenda Milner (1918-). Milner received her Ph.D. in 1952 after studying with Donald Hebb. She also carried out research with Wilder Penfield at McGill University in the 1950s. Her most famous set of studies were carried out on H.M.

H.M. was hit by a bicyclist as a child. His closed head trauma eventually developed into seizures that left him, in his mid-twenties, severely disabled. In desperation, his physician removed his hippocampus and part of the surface of both temporal lobes. After the surgery, H.M was free of seizures. He also had massive memory loss. Milner studied H.M. and tested his memory monthly for three decades. Out of H.M.'s tragedy came clues to the location of the engram (Kandel, 2006).

H.M. suffered no loss of his short term memory. His personality was not changed. He was kind and funny and intelligent. He also suffered from anterograde amnesia: the inability to convert any of his short term memories into long term memories. H.M. was forever young; he could not recognize himself in the mirror or recognize a photo of himself if it had been taken after his operation. He could not learn new explicit information or follow a long conversation. He simply could not form memories that lasted longer than a few minutes. His memory for the time before his operation was undamaged (Kandel, 2006).

Milner's work showed that short-term memory and long-term memory are distinct memory systems. Long-term memories are not stored in the hippocampus or temporal lobes, but they are processed there. Memory systems are located in different parts of the brain from perceptual and motor areas as well. Milner also showed that there are different kinds of long-term memories. H.M. could learn new skills, such as tracing a star in a mirror or solving the tower of Hanoi problem. But he could not remember ever having seen these problems before even after he had spent considerable time on them. This shows that implicit memory is a distinct system from explicit memory. Later researchers substantiated Milner's discoveries with experimental work on animals and humans. We have two kinds of long-term memories: explicit (also called declarative) memories and implicit (also called procedural) memories. Explicit memories are conscious. Implicit memories are unconscious (Kandel, 2006). Milner's productive career included many other studies of learning, memory, and brain function, and she is considered one of the founders of cognitive neuroscience.

In the 1970s and 1980s, Eric R. Kandel (1930-) and his colleagues uncovered the molecular and physiological basis for short-term and long-term memory. Kendal was born in Vienna into a middle-class Jewish family and he and his family fled Vienna in 1939. After growing up in New York and attending Harvard as an undergraduate and New York University Medical School, he specialized in psychiatry with the intention of becoming a psychoanalyst. He became fascinated with research in neurophysiology in the hopes that he could find the biological basis for Freud's ideas. After an enormously productive research career, in which he was also one of the leading figures in the new field of neuroscience, he won the Nobel Prize in 2000.

Kandel discovered that short-term memory depends on chemical changes at the synapses that lead a neuron that has fired several times in close proximity to increase the release of neurotransmitters, thus strengthening the short-term memory. This represents a functional change in the neurons involved in short term memory. If the memory is practiced again and again, the result is new synaptic growth. Every time you learn something (that is, you encode it into long-term memory) you change the neurocircuits in your brain, just as Ramon y Cajal had hypothesized (Kandal, 2006).

While "practice makes perfect" is the rule for changing short-term memories into long-term memories, highly salient emotional experiences can be converted to long-term memories almost immediately, since intense emotional states facilitate the formation of new synaptic growth. In addition to this work, Kandel also carried out pioneering work in the relationship between genetics and learning and the biology of procedural memory, such as classical conditioning (Kandel, 2006).

By the late 1980s, neuroscientists (a group that includes most physiological psychologists) had made substantial progress in solving the questions first raised by Ramon y Cajal, and investigated by Lashley, Hebb, and Pribram. Following our approximate twenty-year rule, a new theory of how the brain functions appeared. The author of the theory was another Nobel Prize winner in Medicine or Physiology who had turned to neuroscience: Gerald M. Edelman. His theory of how the mind emerges from the brain was based on an earlier biological theory, that of Charles Darwin.

A New Theory Of Physiological Psychology: Neural Darwinism

Gerald M. Edelman (1929-) received the Nobel Prize in 1972 for his discovery of how the immune system functions. After receiving the Nobel Prize he turned to neuroscience. Edelman takes psychology and philosophy seriously and integrates both into his biological theory of the mind in an effort to explain memory, perception, and consciousness. He lays out his theory in three major works, *Neural Darwinism: The Theory of Neuronal Group Selection* (Edelman, 1987), *Topobiology* (Edelman, 1988) and *The Remembered Present* (Edelman, 1989). Of these three, the third is the most accessible to the non-biologist. He has also published two popular accounts of this theory that expand on such topics as consciousness (Edelman, 1992; Edelman, 2004).

The key to Edelman's theory is the concept of selection, a concept he borrows from Darwin. Darwin showed that evolution was a blind process, a process that needed no designer or architect, where random variation was acted upon by the environment to select those individuals that had the characteristics that suited them to survive in a particular environment. This "survival of the fittest" was a process of chance variation and selection. Edelman argued that groups of neurons are selected by experience in a short- and long-term process discovered by Kandel and his co-workers. Our brains are molded by experience, and this interaction of experience and brain structure provides the basis of our consciousness. To highlight his debt to Darwin, Edelman calls his theory Neural Darwinism (Edelman, 1989; Edelman, 1992). Edelman thus provides a thoroughly materialist explanation of human consciousness that also addresses a number of philosophical issues and psychological questions (such as the development of mental illness). Edelman is the heir to Freud and follows in the tradition of Hebb and Pribram. His grand theory attempts to integrate existing research, puts forth new ideas that can be tested, and anchors the theory of the brain in psychology and philosophy.

The Study of Perception on the Eve of World War II

From the inception of the new psychology, the study of perception has been dominated by a general theory that is sometimes referred to as the classical theory. In the 1920s and 1930s Gestalt psychology arose as a challenge to the classical theory, a challenge that remained important until the 1960s when a second challenge to classical theory emerged: the ecological approach to perception developed by James and Eleanor Gibson and their colleagues (Hochberg, 1979).

The classical theory has dominated the study of perception within psychology since 1879; it also dominates common sense ideas about perception. What, then, is the classical theory?

The classical theory was formulated by Helmholtz between 1856 and 1866 with his three volume *Treatise on Physiological Optics* (cf. Helmholtz, 2005). The theory integrated the philosophical concepts of Descartes and the British empiricists with neural physiology. In a nutshell, people perceive stimuli that are impoverished--that is, they do not contain a lot of information. These stimuli, known as sensations, specify certain primary qualities such as color and shapes. These impoverished stimuli or sensations are then put together by the mind into complex perceptions, consisting of secondary qualities (qualities that do not exist in the world but exist in the mind that is making a model of the world). The distinction between primary and secondary qualities was made by Galileo and incorporated into the dualistic philosophy of Descartes. Helmholtz assumed that the impoverished stimuli were integrated by the nervous system in a process of unconscious inference. We learn to perceive, according to the classical theory, although considerable debate existed (and continues to exist) between the empiricists, who followed in the tradition of Locke and others who argued that the mind is essentially a blank slate and that the percepts are built up in a process of learning, and the nativists, who followed Kant who argued that certain concepts were innate in the mind and that these innate concepts formed the basis of our ability to perceive (Hochberg, 1979).

There are a number of conceptual and empirical problems associated with the classical theory. One is the question of what exactly is the stimulus. Is it the photons hitting the rods and cones in the eye? Is it the retinal image of an object (recall that the retinal image was discovered by Kepler and used by Descartes in his description of vision)? Furthermore—how can we perceive three-dimensional space from the two-dimensional stimuli? How can we perceive stable objects when the image of an object constantly changes shape as we or it moves in the environment? And how can learning to perceive occur without first knowing what it is we are perceiving (the nativist argument)? These problems are obvious to anyone who compares the classical theory of perception to the subjective experience, or phenomenology, of seeing, tasting, hearing, and touching.

The Gestalt psychologists were the first to seriously challenge the classical theory, although they accepted some of its assumptions. Some American functionalists were also dissatisfied with the classical theory, although the leading perceptual researchers in the U.S. in the early part of the 20th century, E.B. Titchener and some of his students such as E.G. Boring, in general supported the classical theory. The Gestalt psychologists viewed the study of perception as central to psychology (and philosophy). They argued that we do not perceive impoverished stimulus elements but higher order organization, or gestalts, and that this higher order organization actually gives meaning to the lower level elements. This concept was criticized as nativist by many psychologists (including present-day psychologists), but as the Gestalt psychologists pointed out, it is not nativist; it is anti-reductionistic. The criticisms and concerns about the classical theory and the competing Gestalt theory form the backdrop to the study of perception for most of the 20th century.

The study of perception was marginalized during the 1920s, 30s, and 40s in the U.S. with the advent of the behaviorist metatheory, but it did not die out, either among functionalists or Gestalt psychologists. Perceptual psychology, or more simply, perception, experienced a re-birth in the period immediately after World War II, similar to the rebirth experienced by physiological psychology. Most of this renewed interest and research focused on fixing or replacing the classical theory. With the acceleration of history in psychology following the Second World War, the number of researchers active in this area expanded dramatically, as did the progress made in this area. Two researchers dominated the field in the last 100 years, standing head and shoulders above the many other talented researchers. These two were not just partners in research, they were marital partners as well: James J. Gibson (1904-1979) and Eleanor J. Gibson (1910-2002), known to their friends and colleagues as Jimmy and Jackie.

A Revolutionary View Of Perception

The Gibsons made a large number of empirical discoveries and methodological contributions. They also developed two new theories of perception. The first was published in 1950 (J.J. Gibson, 1950) and was primarily the result of James Gibson's research during World War II for the Army Air Corps (which later became the Air Force). The second was a consequence of research and criticism of this theory which led to a new, more radical theory of perception (J.J. Gibson, 1966; E.J. Gibson, 1969; E. J. Gibson & Levin, 1975; J.J. Gibson, 1979). These theories will be described shortly, along with some of the empirical discoveries and methodological advances they supported. But first, who were James and Eleanor Gibson?

The Lives Of James And Eleanor Gibson

James J. Gibson was born in Ohio, the oldest of three sons. His family moved often when he was young and eventually settled in the Chicago area. After high school he attended Northwestern for a year, and then transferred to Princeton in 1922. Gibson found Princeton to be socially elitist and exclusionary but intellectually stimulating. He studied philosophy, psychology, geometry, and relativity theory with great enthusiasm. The psychology department at Princeton had a distinguished faculty, a mix of rising young stars and respected senior psychologists. The senior faculty included the psychologist and philosopher E.B. Holt, who had helped popularize Freud's ideas in the U.S. and had been a close friend and collaborator of William James, and Howard C. Warren, a co-founder of the *Journal of Experimental Psychology*. The junior faculty included Herbert Langfeld, who had studied perception and philosophy with Carl Stumpf in Berlin, and Leonard Carmichael, a young Harvard Ph.D. who had studied with Köhler and Wertheimer in Berlin in 1923. Gibson took Langfeld's course in experimental psychology during his senior year and was offered a graduate assistantship to study for his Ph.D. at Princeton. While studying for his Ph.D. Gibson worked and studied with all five aforementioned members of the psychology department and was deeply influenced by all of them (Reed, 1988).

While Gibson was influenced by functionalism and Gestalt theory, as well as the Jamesian philosophy of pragmatism and the new realism, he also was influenced by the spread of behaviorism. He sought to combine and reconcile these

stimulation (Reed, 1988).

The Mature Theory

The Gibsons did not stop developing their theory or carrying out empirical studies in the late 1960s. Eleanor Gibson applied the theory to the study of reading (Gibson & Levin, 1975) and James Gibson continued to develop the theory, introducing the concept of affordances. Information in stimulation specifies use values, what objects, people, and events afford the perceiver. The Gibsons thought that this concept, and their mature theory, provided a realist theory of values (values, that is, affordances, are real and exist in objects, people and events, even if and when we do not perceive those values). The mature theory, including discussion of various philosophical issues, was presented in James Gibson's last book, *The Ecological Theory of Visual Perception* (Gibson, 1979), published shortly after his death in 1979.

Eleanor Gibson continued developing the theory after her husband's death. She remained an active scholar and researcher until her death in 2002.

The Failure Of The Revolution?

The ecological theory of perception developed by the Gibsons has had a profound impact on both the concepts and methods used by perceptual psychologists, but the theory per se, which requires a rejection of the classical theory and its many philosophical assumptions, has not been accepted by many. Instead, the Gibsons have provided a powerful stimulus to others who try to revise the classical theory to account for the Gibsonian critique and the Gibsonian discoveries. The two major responses may be termed computational models of perception and neurophysiological models of perception. Both fall within the Helmholtzian tradition.

Computational models, sometimes called information processing models of perception, emphasize the process of unconscious inference that takes the impoverished stimuli and constructs a model of the world. Neurophysiological models explore the brain structures and processes that are involved in perception and the construction of cognitive maps, depth perception, and object constancies (Hochberg, 1979). These models have advanced considerably since Helmholtz's time. For instance, Torsten Wiesel and David Hubel won a

Nobel Prize for their discovery of neurons in the visual cortex that fire only at edges in a particular orientation. John O'Keefe discovered in 1971 that the hippocampus integrates a variety of sensory information into spatial maps. These spatial maps are located in the pyramidal cells of the hippocampus (Kandel, 2006). While the neurophysiological approach has made enormous progress, much is still not known. In addition, certain thorny philosophical issues remain. For instance, who "reads" the spatial maps? Still, we have come a long way since Helmholtz's initial work.

At this point in history, the neurophysiological and computational approaches to perception (which are compatible, indeed, complementary approaches) appear to have triumphed. As historians we can ask "why?" Let me suggest two answers. First, the cognitive metatheory that replaced the behaviorist metatheory certainly favored a computational approach. So perhaps the scientific debate between these two approaches was biased from the start. Certainly the general response (a lack of engagement and neglect) to the Gibsons' later books suggests this (Reed, 1988). But beyond this obvious bias in the debate lies the enormous success of physiological psychology cum neuroscience in discovering more and more about the working of the brain. Still, the Gibsons may have been on the right track—efforts at machine perception and at understanding how brains perceive the world will ultimately necessitate a description of the world that is being perceived, a description, as James Gibson would say, of the information in stimulation that must be picked up by the perceiving system. (See Kandel, Schwartz, & Jessel, 2000, p. 553 on neurons that respond to optic flow).

James Gibson had a deep respect for the history of his field. One of his former students reported how at the start of graduate school, Gibson took him to a room filled with old scientific articles and books and told him to "get out of date" in the literature (Reed, 1988). The Gibsons never made the mistake of thinking that the latest published article in an area represented the best work in a field. They both read broadly in a number of fields and over the history of philosophy and psychology. Advising psychologists to "get out of date" still strikes me as excellent advice.

The Gibsons also thought that psychologists were in awe of philosophy and neurophysiology, but not of psychology itself. This lack of awe made psychology a "second rate discipline." What did James Gibson mean by this? First he meant that psychologists too often accepted the assumptions of philosophy and neurophysiology as facts, when in the Gibsons' view they were assumptions to be tested. As a consequence of uncritical acceptance of what other disciplines claim about psychology, we can never really develop a true science of psychology (Reed, 1988). Whether or not you agree with the Gibsonian critique, their vision and their work shaped the history of psychology in the last half of the 20th century.

The Practical And Philosophical Significance Of Perception And Physiological Psychology

In the pragmatic tradition of American Functionalism, the study of perception and physiological psychology has enormous practical significance. James Gibson's work advanced the design of landing fields, pilot training and instrumentation, and led to the first flight simulators. Bill Purdy, one of the Gibson's graduate students who worked on the optic flow field, used his knowledge at General Electric to develop the first military flight simulators and the early video games that simulated flight and driving (Reed, 1998). The work of the Gibsons' has also influenced film techniques that give the viewer the sensation of movement (Reed, 1988).

The work in physiological psychology (now neuroscience) has already led to treatments for Parkinson's disease and OCD. And the applications of this research are just beginning. They may include genetically engineered enhanced intelligence (Kandler used a genetic manipulation to create genius mice that had superior memories to normal mice) or neural enhancements that permit paraplegics to walk and fighter pilots to control their crafts with their brain.

Also in the tradition of American functionalism, the work in perception and physiological psychology seeks to answer philosophical questions that go back over 500 years. What is perceived and how do we perceive? How do we learn and remember? What is the nature and basis of human consciousness? The findings of perceptual psychologists and neuroscientists can resolve the conflicts that have raged in philosophy for centuries. Psychology may make philosophy passé.

We may not like the answers. Freud talked about the three traumas that have shaken Western civilization: the discovery by Copernicus that the earth was not the center of the universe; the discovery by Darwin that humans (and other life forms) evolve over time; and Freud's discovery of the unconscious. The study of perception and neuroscience may give us a fourth trauma: a materialist explanation of perception, memory, and consciousness that leaves no room for the soul. We will have to wait to see how our culture responds to this impending trauma that may equal or surpass the first three.

Scary!

References

Browne, M.W. (1995). Neuron talks to Chip, and chip to Neuron. *The New York Times*, August 22, pp. B7, B9.

Bruce, D. (1991). Integrations of Lashley. In G. Kimble, M. Wertheimer, & C.L. White (Eds.), *Portrait of pioneers in psychology,* Vol. 1, pp. 307-323.

Delgado, J.M.R. (1969). *Physical control of the mind: Toward a psychocivilized society*. New York: Harper & Row.

Edelman, G. M. (1987). *Neural darwinism: The theory of neuronal group selection..* New York: Basic Books.

Edelman, G. M. (1988). *Topobiology*. New York: Basic Books.

Edelman, G.M. (1989). *The remembered present: A biological theory of consciousness..* New York: Basic Books.

Edelman, G.M. (1992). *Bright air, brilliant fire: On the matter of the mind*. New York: Basic Books.

Edelman, G. M. (2004). *Wider Than the sky: The phenomenal gift of consciousness*. New York: Basic Books.

Gardner, H. (1987). *The mind's new science: A history of the cognitive revolution*. New York: Basic Books.

Gibson, E.J. (1969). *Principles of perceptual learning and development*. New York: Appleton-Century-Crofts.

Gibson, E.J., & Levin, H. (1975). *The psychology of reading*. Cambridge,.MA: MIT Press.

Gibson, J.J. (1950). *The perception of the visual world.* Boston: Houghton Mifflin.

Gibson, J.J. (1960). The concept of the stimulus in psychology. *American Psychologist, 16,* 694-703.

Gibson, J.J. (1966). *The senses considered as perceptual Systems.* Boston: Houghton Mifflin.

Gibson, J.J. (1979). *The ecological approach to visual perception.* Boston: Houghton Mifflin.

Hearst, E., ed. (1979).*The first century of experimental psychology.* Hillsdale, NJ: Lawrence Erlbaum Associates.

Hebb, D.O. (1949). *Organization of behavior.* New York: John Wiley & Sons.

Helmholtz, H. (2005). *Treatise on physiological optics, Vol. III..* Edited by James P.C. Southall. Mineola, NY: Dover Publications.

Hilgard, E.R. (1987). *Psychology in America: A historical survey.* San Diego, CA: Harcourt Brace Jovanovich.

Hochberg, J. (1979). Sensation and perception. In E. Hearst, *The first century of experimental psychology,* pp. 89-142.

Jeffress, L.A. (Ed.). (1951). *Cerebral mechanisms in behavior: The Hixon Symposium.* New York: John Wiley.

Kandel, E. R. (2006). *In search of memory: The emergence of a new science of mind.* New York: W.W. Norton & Company.

Kandel, E. R., Schwartz, J.H., & Jessell, T.M. (2000). *Principles of neural science,* 4th ed. New York: McGraw-Hill.

Kimble, G.A., Wertheimer, M., & White, C.L. (Eds.). (1991). *Portraits of pioneers in psychology.* Washington, DC: American Psychological Association Hillsdale, NJ: Lawrence Erlbaum Associates.

Lashley, K.S. (1929). *Brain mechanisms and intelligence.* Chicago: University of Chicago Press.

Lashley, K.S. (1930). Basic neural mechanisms in behavior. *Psychological Review, 13,* 1-24.

Lashley, K.S. (1938a). The experimental analysis of instinctive behavior. *Psychological Review, 45,* 445-471.

Lashley, K.S. (1938b). The thalamus and emotion. *Psychological Review, 45,* 42-61.

Lashley, K.S. (1950). In search of the engram. *Symposium of the Society for Experimental Biology,* Vol 4, pp. 454-482. New York: Cambridge University Press.

Lashley, K.S. (1951). The problem of serial order in behavior. In L.A. Jeffress (Ed.), *Cerebral Mechanisms in Behavior,* pp. 112-136. New York: Wiley.

Otis, L. (2001). Introduction. In S. Ramon y Cajal *Vacation stories: Five science fiction tales,* pp. vii-xx.

Ramon y Cajal, S. (1937/1988). *Recollections of my life.* New York: Garland Publishing.

Ramon y Cajal, S. (1999). *Advice for a young investigator.* Translated by Neely Swanson and Larry W. Swanson. Cambridge, MA: MIT Press.

Ramon y Cajal, S. (1905/2001). *Vacation stories: Five science fiction tales.* Urbana and Chicago: University of Illinois Press.

Reed, E.S. (1988). *James J. Gibson and the psychology of perception.* New Haven: Yale University Press.

Schulz, K. (2006). Brave neuro world: The ethics of the new brain science. *The Nation*, January 9, pp. 11, 13-14, 16.

Sherrington, C. S. (1906). *The integrative action of the nervous system.* New York: Charles Scribner's Sons.

Skinner, B.F. (1938). *The behavior of organisms: An experimental analysis.* New York:Appleton-Century.

Slater, L. (2005). Who holds the clicker? *Mother Jones,* November, pp. 63-67, 90, 92.

Thompson, R.F., & Robinson, D.N. (1979). Physiological psychology. In E. Hearst, *The first century of experimental psychology,* pp. 407-454.

CHAPTER 10: COGNITION AND THE COGNITIVE REVOLUTION

You say you want a revolution
Well you know
We all want to change the world
You tell me that it's evolution
Well you know
We all want to change the world
But when you talk about destruction
Don't you know you can count me out.

JOHN LENNON (1971)

Cognition In The Age Of Behaviorism

Shortly after the birth of the New Psychology in 1879, psychologists in Europe and the U.S. soon developed an interest in the higher mental processes, what we now call cognition. William James' classic text (James, 1890/1983) included chapters on the stream of thought, consciousness, attention, memory, imagination, and reasoning. Later psychologists, as described in Chapters 4 and 5, extended the research on these topics. For instance, Külpe and Dewey studied thinking, Binet studied intelligence and problem solving, Ebbinghaus studied memory, Cattell studied mental testing, and Baldwin studied cognitive development. In the U.S. these topics became less important to the field in the 1920's as the focus of research shifted to questions framed by behaviorism.

In the history of modern psychology, behaviorism was an aberration, albeit an aberration that dominated one of the two centers of psychology worldwide. From 1920 to 1950, the heyday of behaviorism, a small number of researchers in the U.S. continued to study cognition; meanwhile the majority of studies in cognition took place in Europe, particularly in Germany, England, France, and Russia. These studies were carried out by European psychologists who were to have a significant impact on the last half of the 20th century.

Within the U.S., the dominance of behaviorism declined in the early 1950s, but nothing arose immediately to replace behaviorism. The return to questions of mental processes such as memory, attention, problem solving, creativity, and consciousness started to gain momentum in the 1950s and by 1960s a dramatic change was underway. This change, now called the cognitive revolution, was not perceived as a revolution by many of the participants at the time. In retrospect, the changes were dramatic. Before exploring these historic developments in the 1950s through the 1990s, let us step back and examine the study of cognition in the age of behaviorism, so that we can put the achievements of the last half century in their proper intellectual context. We will examine the work of researchers in Germany, England, France, and Russia, all of whom made substantial contributions to the study of cognition during the age of behaviorism.

Gestalt Studies Of Cognition

The Gestalt psychologists are best known for their work on perception. The three founders of Gestalt psychology, Max Wertheimer, Kurt Koffka, and Wolfgang Köhler, also spent considerable time studying higher mental processes as well. One of Wertheimer's first studies on thinking explored the relationship between logic and problem solving (Wertheimer, 1920). Wertheimer continued studies of problem solving and creativity throughout his career, many of which were published in English after his death in the book *Productive Thinking* (1945/1959).

Wertheimer distinguished between trial and error problem solving, problem solving based on procedures certain to provide the correct answer (what present day cognitive psychologists call algorithms), and productive thinking: thinking that exhibits insight or results in creative solutions. In *Productive Thinking* (Wertheimer, 1945/1959), he shows how insight and creative solutions emerge in both simple problems, such as finding the area of a parallelogram, and scientific discoveries by Galileo and Einstein (Wertheimer was a close personal friend of Einstein; When they both lived in Berlin they would hang out together a great deal). Wertheimer found many examples of productive thinking above and beyond the thinking associated with trial and error problem solving or algorithms. Thinking, according to Wertheimer, is characterized by perceiving the structure of the problem, understanding the relationships between different elements or parts of the problem, centering on crucial elements, and recognizing the problem gaps or missing pieces. Productive thinking was not piecemeal but "top down", flowing from perception of the problem gestalt. It was an active, intentional process.

Kurt Koffka studied thinking in infants and children (Koffka, 1924/1959) building upon earlier work in developmental psychology, including work on educational psychology by Thorndike (whom he criticizes a great deal but for whom he also has an enormous amount of respect) and the early work of Piaget, which he employs frequently. Watson and behaviorism are singled out for extensive criticism. A key notion in his work is the idea of cognitive structures (translated as configurations in an effort to avoid confusion with Titchener's structuralist ideas). Koffka argued that the child develops cognitively as his or her cognitive structure develops.

It is important to note that both Wertheimer's book on productive thinking and Koffka's book on cognitive development were re-published in the late 1950s in the U.S. as American psychologists re-focused their attention on thinking.

Of the three founders of Gestalt psychology, Köhler spent the least amount of time studying cognition. He did, however, produce one major study of primate cognition while he was on Tenerife during World War I (see Chapter 7). This work (Köhler, 1927) emphasized the role of insight in learning and problem solving among primates. One criticism leveled against Köhler's work by behaviorist was that the notion of insight was vague and that few experimental controls were used in his study.

Criticisms of the insight concept were addressed by one of Köhler's and Wertheimer's graduate students, Karl Duncker (1903-1940). After fleeing Germany, Duncker spent two years at Swarthmore College before committing suicide in despair over the fate of his family in Germany. His major study of problem solving was published in German in 1935 and translated into English posthumously in 1945 (Duncker, 1945). Like Wertheimer's book, it was to have a powerful effect on the cognitive revolution (Hilgard, 1987).

Duncker studied a variety of problems, both practical and logical. His most famous problem was how to radiate an inoperable tumor without damaging tissue. He had his subjects think out loud as they worked through the problems and then analyzed these records of problem solving (called protocols). Duncker found that problem solving moves from a general identification of what was needed to solve the problem to a more specific understanding of what was needed. Problem solutions were often the results of a serious of steps, each step forming a problem in itself and a solution that creates the basis for the next step. Duncker also identified a barrier to effective problem solving, which he called functional fixedness, the tendency to resist novel uses of objects or concepts. Functional fixedness keeps thinking and problem solving in a fixed path and prevents creative or original insights (Duncker, 1945). Duncker's work considerably advanced the understanding of problem solving and thinking, both methodologically and substantively. He also advanced the Gestalt work in cognition considerably.

Another student who made contributions to the Gestalt understanding of cognition was Bluma Zeigarnik (1900-1988). Zeigarnik was a woman from the Soviet Union who came to Berlin to study psychology. The Gestaltists had a large number of international students and, for the time period, an especially large number of women graduate students. Zeigarnik studied with Kurt Lewin, the junior colleague of Köhler and Wertheimer in Berlin who we shall meet again in Chapter 12. He was a giant in the field of social psychology and made significant contributions to developmental psychology. Lewin was a stimulating teacher who often continued discussions started in his classes in the Berlin cafés afterwards. He would sometime conduct informal experiments in the cafés to explore questions he and his students were discussing. One such informal experiment led to Zeigarnik's research (Marrow, 1969).

Lewin noticed that waiters in the cafes could recall a great deal of information about an order, until that order was filled. Once the order was filled, they seemed to forget it. Lewin theorized that the intention to carry out a task created tension as long as the goal was not yet achieved, and that these tensions influenced many aspects of behavior, such as memory. Zeigarnik tested this hypothesis by examining whether uncompleted tasks are recalled better than completed tasks. Her experiments indeed showed that we remember what we have not yet completed better than we remember what we have completed

(Zeigarnik, 1927), a fact about memory that is now called the Zeigarnik effect (Marrow, 1969).

After receiving her Ph.D. in Berlin in 1927, Zeigarnik returned to Russia where she collaborated with Lev Vygotsky and Alexander Luria. During World War II she worked alongside Luria in a military clinic devoted to the rehabilitation of brain injured soldiers. She later went on to develop techniques for diagnosing and treating a variety of mental illnesses. Her work in abnormal psychology, treatment, and diagnosis earned her the Lomonosov Prize (given in the Soviet Union) and the Kurt Lewin Award (given in the U.S.). She authored six scholarly books and over 120 scientific articles. Her work was translated into seven languages: English, German, Italian, Spanish, Portuguese, Polish, and Serbo-Croatian (Logvinenko & Sokolskaya, 1997). Zeigarnik was not only a coworker of Luria and a former student of Lewin, she was also their friend. Lewin, in turn, was also a friend of Luria's (Marrow, 1969).

Bartlett And Experimental Studies Of Memory

British psychologists were aware of developments in the U.S. and had easy access to American research, but they also maintained close ties with their colleagues in Continental Europe. British psychologists often appeared dumbfounded at the American's embrace of behaviorism and continued carrying out research influenced by American functionalism and European cognitive psychology.

One of the foremost British researchers on thinking and memory of the 1930s, 40s, and 50s was Frederick C. Bartlett (1886-1969). Bartlett (1932) carried out a series of studies that showed experimentally that pre-existing knowledge (which he called schema and we would call cognitive structure) and social processes had a potent effect on recall. On the basis of his studies Bartlett argued that recall was not a process of retrieving accurate information from memory, but it was a process of reconstructing on the basis of remembered features, social processes, and pre-existing schema, such as our understanding of what a story should be like. Bartlett continued carrying out research on memory and thinking and later published two works (Bartlett, 1951; Bartlett, 1958) on thinking that, as with the work of the Gestalt psychologists, fed the fires of revolution in the 1950s and 1960s.

Like most of the other influential psychologists we have discussed, Bartlett had a productive career and did work in several areas, including the application of psychological methods to anthropology, studies in cross-cultural psychology, and perception. During World War II he was a member of the Royal Air Force Flying Personnel Research Committee, where, like James Gibson (discussed in Chapter 9), Bartlett carried out research associated with the problems of flying. This work led to a number of advances in ergonomics (the design of tools and machines to fit human abilities and characteristics). He was knighted in 1948 for his contributions to science and to the war effort. In addition to his work, he directed the psychology lab at Cambridge University and was appointed the first professor of experimental psychology at Cambridge. He trained most of the important psychologists in Britain from the mid 1920s to the late 1950s (Sheehy, Chapman, & Conroy, 1997a). Bartlett was also a friend of Kurt Lewin's (Marrow, 1969).

Piaget And The Study Of Cognitive Development

Jean Piaget (1896-1980) was a child prodigy in biology, an unusual feat, given that most child prodigies are in areas that are well structured, such as mathematics, chess, or music. While in college he wrote a novel, majored in biology, and studied philosophy. After finishing his Ph.D. in biology, he switched his focus of attention to psychology in the hopes that the scientific study of children would resolve some of the key philosophical questions in the area of epistemology, the branch of philosophy concerned with questions of how we acquire knowledge of the world (Messerly, 1996). We shall return to Piaget and his impact in the next chapter, but for now a brief overview is needed, as his work helped stimulate the cognitive revolution.

Piaget's theory is one of the most complex and rich in psychology, on par with Freud's work. More than a theory however, Piaget's work represents a vast body of empirical studies, both experimental and observational, on children's cognitive development (Beilin, 1994). According to Beilin (1994), Piaget's research program can be divided into four stages. In the first stage, during the 1920s and early 1930s, Piaget was a master of observation and experimentation. He studied children's language and egocentricism (Piaget, 1923/1926), children's reasoning (Piaget, 1924/1928), conceptions of reality

(Piaget, 1923/1929), causality (1927/1930), and moral judgments (1932). In this first stage Piaget earned an international reputation and had a significant impact on European psychologists and on child psychologists in the U.S.

In the second stage of Piaget's research program during the 1930s, Piaget studied infancy, including his own infant children, and explored the relationship between children and the physical world of objects. He also continued to develop a theory of cognitive development based on biological and philosophical concepts that were congruent with his empirical findings. Like Bartlett, Piaget emphasized that thinking reflected cognitive structures. Unlike Bartlett, Piaget emphasized that these cognitive structures change and develop over time and that these changes represented adaptations to the world. Piaget also continued the development of stage theories of cognitive development, a practice he started in his early work and would continue throughout his career. Piaget's work in this second stage was not as well known in the U.S. because of the dominance within U.S. psychology of behaviorism and behaviorist topics. In fact, while he was producing a steady stream of books and empirical studies during this period, there was an 18-year gap in the translation of his works. After the publication of his book on moral reasoning in 1932, his next work did not appear in English until 1950.

Beginning in the late 1930s and early 1940s, Piaget entered his third stage, where he studied the development of logic, mathematics, and reasoning about the physical world. It was during this period that he developed his complete theory of cognitive development extending from infancy through adolescence. He also developed his mature theory of genetic (meaning developmental) epistemology based on biological concepts such as assimilation and accommodation of cognitive structures. It was this work from his third stage that started entering the U.S. in 1950 (see Piaget, 1950; 1962). A major stimulus to the cognitive revolution took place in 1963 when a young developmental psychologist, John Flavell, summarized 40 years of Piaget's studies and thinking for an English speaking audience in a book that was to both stimulate the cognitive revolution and dominate developmental psychology for the next 15 years (Flavell, 1963). The fourth stage of Piaget's research program began in the early 1970s (when Piaget himself was in his late 70s). From 1963 on, Piaget was one of the leaders of the cognitive revolution.

Russian Contributions: Vygotsky And Luria

Russian psychology (prior to the 1917 Russian Revolution) and later Soviet psychology (post-1917) were strongly dominated by a Russian version of behaviorism strongly influenced by the positivist and mechanistic work of Pavlov and others. An exception to this domination was the work of Lev Vygotsky (1896-1934) and his collaborators, among whom Alexander Luria (1902-1977) is perhaps the best known in the U.S. Vygotsky remains the most thoughtful proponent of Karl Marx's ideas and methods within psychology. It is precisely his use of Marxism that got him blacklisted by the Stalinist dictatorship in the mid-1930s. From the 1930 through the 1950s Vygotsky's colleagues continued applying his approach, running considerable risks to their lives and careers in the process (Kozulin, 1984).

Vygotsky also was deeply influenced by the work of both William James and Wihelm Wundt. He was very familiar with the research of Oswald Külpe and the Würzburg School and was influenced by both the Gestalt psychologists and the work of Piaget. In fact, much of Vygotsky's work was a kind of empirical and theoretical discussion with both the Gestaltists and with Piaget (Kozulin, 1984).

Vygotsky and his colleagues rejected the mechanism and positivism of behaviorism and instead embraced a psychology that examined higher mental processes, such as language, the production of art and science, thinking, and consciousness. In particular, Vygotsky argued that all of these higher mental processes must be understood developmentally and as a result of the interaction of social and cultural factors external to the individual and the person's lower mental processes, those characteristics which are more or less biologically based and which we share with other animals, such as classical and operant conditioning (Kozulin, 1984).

Vygotsky carried out research on children's language, arguing that egocentric speech (described by Piaget) was not a reflection of children's cognitive structure but a stage in the internalization of language, an internalization of a social product that gives children a tool for thinking which animals do not possess (Vygotsky, 1934/1962). Vygotsky and Luria (who was the principal investigator) studied the impact of literacy and industrialization on formerly illiterate farmers and nomads in what is now Uzbekistan (Luria, 1976). They discovered that literacy has a broad impact on how people think, classify, and conceive of the world. Industrial work also has an impact on thinking. Finally, Vygotsky and his colleagues applied their perspective to educational psychology with the concept of the zone of proximal development—learning, according to this concept, occurs when the child's level of cognitive development has laid the basis for the next step. You cannot learn things that are two steps beyond your level of cognitive development. Vygotsky died relatively young at 38 of tuberculosis in 1934. Shortly after his death he and his works were blacklisted by the Soviet government (Morss, 1997).

[handwritten margin note: crazy! do different language change cognition]

Taken together, the work of the Gestalt psychologists, of Bartlett, Piaget, and Vygotsky, provided a rich legacy of facts, methods, and concepts about thinking, problem solving, and memory. But it was not these influences by themselves that brought about the shift from behaviorism to cognitivism; It also required changes within American psychology, science, and culture. These changes occurred in the 1950s in a process that accelerated with both important new advances in our understanding of cognition and a re-discovery of previous work.

The 1950s: Seeds of Revolution

The 1950s are often assumed to be a time of conformity and complacency, when the good old days were indeed good. This assumption is both true and false. Europe was recovering from the massive devastation of the war and horror of the Holocaust. The U.S. was experiencing unprecedented economic growth. Yet at the same time in the U.S. there was widespread political repression sometimes referred to as McCarthyism (Schrecker, 1998). Universities were not spared the repression; indeed they were the frequent sites of repression (Schrecker, 1986). Many of the issues that dominated the 1960s (the struggle for civil rights for minorities and women, the Vietnam War, revolution in Cuba, and the drug and hippie counter-culture, were all born in the 1950s (Halberstam, 1993).

Within behaviorism all was not well. In 1950 Skinner published his attack on the mainstream behaviorism of Hull and Spence (Skinner, 1950). Skinner, always a master with provocative language, entitled his attack "Are theories of learning necessary?" Soon many prominent behaviorists such as Sigmund Koch were talking about the crisis in behaviorism. Skinner, who rejected all forms of theory and mentalism, did not think there was a crisis so much as the fact that too many behaviorists were too concerned with things in which they should not be interested. Still most behaviorists were unhappy (Baars, 1986). This un-happiness did not, however, lead immediately to the decline of the dominant behaviorist culture. Instead, a number of developments needed to take place before a new scientific culture superseded behaviorism. The first of these de-velopments came from engineering.

The Invention Of The Computer And Cybernetics

The first digital computer was built in 1937 by the Harvard mathematician and physicist Howard Aiken who worked collaboratively with IBM and the U.S. Army on the project. Using the decimal system to perform calculations, the Mark I, as it was dubbed, was eight feet high and 50 feet long. It had both electrical and mechanical parts. The Mark I was designed to perform ballistic calculations for the military. In 1940, Bell Labs produced their own computer using electrical relays and based on binary system to perform calculations. At the same time similar efforts to construct computers were taking place in Eng-land, led by the young mathematician Alan Turing, as well as in Germany. The military needs of World War II led to increased efforts at improving computer design and functioning. The Army's next big computer, ENIAC (Electronic Numerical Integrator and Calculator), was built during the war at the Univer-sity of Pennsylvania for ballistic calculations and for use in the atomic bomb project. Princeton mathematician John von Neumann, who worked on the atomic bomb project, developed the concept of the stored program, making computers easier to use and more flexible. Soon the concept of stored pro-grams developed into the idea of computer programming languages, making computers still more versatile (Noble, 1984).

The work on computers and electronics immediately before and during the war produced new inventions and new ways of thinking. At MIT the engineer Claude Shannon showed that Boolean algebra (binary-- based on ones and zeros) could be used to describe the functioning of electronic circuits. This insight enabled engineers to describe complex systems mathematically and linked logical operations with mechanistic operations. Turing showed mathematically that a digital thinking machine could be built. Finally, the engineer and mathematician Norbert Wiener developed the idea of cybernetics, the study of how information leads to adaptive or self-regulating systems (Noble, 1984).

Wiener published his most important statement of cybernetics in 1948 under the title *Cybernetics: Or Control and Communication in the Animal and the Machine* (Wiener, 1948). It was soon followed by an equally significant work by Shannon, *The Mathematical Theory of Communication* (Shannon & Weaver, 1949). In this work Shannon introduced the notion of information measurement, information processing, and the use of boxes and arrows as a tool for diagramming information processing systems. This work would soon have an impact on psychology (Hilgard, 1987).

Almost immediately with the advent of the computer, engineers, mathematicians, psychologists, and physiologists realized that there were strong parallels between thinking organisms with brains and thinking machines. A number of meetings were organized between 1946 and 1953 by the Macy Foundation that brought together psychologists, and neurophysiologists. The Macy Foundation meetings regularly included Gestalt psychologists Kurt Lewin and Wolfgang Köhler and mathematicians Norbert Wiener and John von Neumann. Others who attended included anthropologists Margaret Mead and Gregory Bateson, and child psychologist and psychoanalysist Erik Erikson (Baars, 1986).

In addition to the Macy Foundation meetings, the Hixon Fund at the California Institute of Technology organized an interdisciplinary meeting in 1948 on "Cerebral Mechanisms in Behavior." The proceedings of the symposium were published in 1951 (Jeffress, 1951). The Hixon Symposium opened with a paper by John von Neumann, the developer of the stored program, on a theory of automata (von Neumann, 1951) in which he argued that humans are essentially computing machines. Following this paper, the neurophysiologist and mathematician Warren McCulloch made a similar argument. This was followed by a brilliant presentation by Lashley, discussed in the previous chapter, on the problem of the serial order of behavior. Lashley's paper undercut the intellectual legitimacy of the behaviorist approach (Gardner, 1985). Von Neumann's presentation and McCulloch's presentation laid the basis for a new meta-theory in psychology, the cognitive meta-theory, in which the human being is an information processor (Baars, 1986). There were other presenters at the Hixon Symposium, including Wolfgang Köhler (Jeffress, 1951).

The Birth Of The Cognitive Revolution

While the intellectual seeds of the cognitive revolution were planted by the early 1950s, ideas by themselves do not change the history of psychology. What persuades psychologists are elegant experiments, new methods, and new empirical findings (Hilgard, 1987). All three were soon to appear on the scene, literally at the same time and place.

That time was September 10-12, 1956; the place was the Massachusetts Institute of Technology (MIT); the occasion was a Symposium on Information Theory. The second day, September 11, included a feature presentation by Allen Newell and Herbert Simon. Newell and Simon developed a software program called the Logic Theory Machine (generally referred to simply as the Logic Theorist) that was able to generate a complete proof of a mathematical theorem, a first in human history. The second featured presentation was by a young linguist named Noam Chomsky, who showed that other approaches to linguistics could not explain natural language but that his new approach, based on linguistic transformations, could. Another paper that day was presented by George A. Miller, on the capacity of human short term memory. Miller argued (using empirical evidence) that human short-term memory is limited to approximately seven items with a range of five to nine items. He called this capacity the magical number seven, plus or minus two (Gardner, 1985). Around the time of the symposium, Jerome Bruner and his colleagues published a lengthy study of thinking (Bruner, Goodnow, & Austin, 1956). Because of the importance of these four papers, I will discuss them in greater detail in a moment. But first, note that this date, like all such dates, is an historical convention. The cognitive revolution could be dated from the Hixon Symposium just as well, or to 1959-1960 when, as we shall soon see, a center for the study of cognition was established at Harvard.

Simon And Newell's The Logic Theorist

Herbert A. Simon (1916-2001) was a polymath, a person expert in many subjects. Simon read widely, taught himself a number of subjects, and showed strong interest in applied mathematics at an early age. He completed his bachelor's degree in economics at the University of Chicago in the same month that he turned 20, having skipped grades in school and earning college credit at the University of Chicago through examination, the practice of awarding a person college credit if they can perform well on a test of the subject, similar to our current AP exam system for high school students (Hilgard, 1987).

After graduating with his undergraduate degree in economics, Simon found a job evaluating the functioning and decision-making of municipal governments. He soon published his first book on this topic (Ridley & Simon, 1938) at the age of 22. Later Simon returned to the University of Chicago for his Ph.D. in political science, which he completed in 1943. His studies of public administration led ultimately to the publication of a ground breaking book in this field (Simon, 1947) which has gone into several editions. At the same time, he carried out work on the application of mathematics to economics and the process of decision making in business firms. It is for this early work in economics, public administration, and decision making in firms for which he won the Nobel Prize in Economics in 1978 (Hilgard, 1987).

Simon moved to the Carnegie Institute of Technology (now named Carnegie-Mellon University) in 1949 where his interests shifted away from economics and political science toward psychology and computer science (an area that, at the time, was not called computer science). Throughout his career, Simon had been known for his ability to work collaboratively and productively for many years with his colleagues. In 1952 Simon met Allen Newell (1927-1992) at the RAND Corporation, a think tank funded by government and corporate money (Baars, 1986; Gardner, 1985; Hilgard, 1987).

Working with John Clifford Shaw at RAND, the three worked toward converting computers from mere number-crunching machines into general symbol manipulation devices. The first problem they had to overcome was that the languages used to program computers, machine languages, were not easy for humans to use. What was needed, they thought, was a higher level language that could be used by humans to program the machines. They started to develop these information processing languages in 1955, laying the basis for all subsequent programming languages which are used today. In 1974, Newell and Simon shared the Turing Prize, (named after the British mathematician Alan Turing) from the Association for Computing Machinery for the development of programming languages (Baars, 1986; Gardner, 1985; Hilgard, 1987).

Over the Christmas vacation in 1955 Newell and Simon worked out the program for solving mathematical proofs that had been contained in Whitehead and Russell's *Principia Mathematica*. Named the Logic Theorist, the program ran on an early computer called the Johnniac, named after the Princeton mathematician John von Neumann (Simon had an impish sense of humor). The program was able to prove 38 of the first 52 theorems in *Principia*. Many were proved in less than one minute. A couple took much longer, 15 to 45 minutes. One proof was more elegant than the original, a fact that delighted Russell when he learned of it (Gardner, 1985). It was the Logic Theorist (Newell & Simon, 1956) that was demonstrated at the 1956 MIT conference that created such a stir. Not only did it help usher in the cognitive revolution in psychology, the program made the field of artificial intelligence a reality.

Newell and Simon were not content with a computer program that could prove theorems in symbolic logic as well as mathematicians could. They wanted to develop a computer program that could think like a person as the program solved a variety of problems. This required a more detailed knowledge of how humans solved problems. Newell and Simon soon took up protocol analysis and the thinking-out-loud techniques developed by the Gestalt psychologists to study such problems as the Tower of Hanoi puzzle and chess. Knowledge gained from protocol analysis was used to develop the first program that could play chess (Newell, Shaw, & Simon, 1958a) and to develop a theory of how humans went about solving problems (Newell, Shaw, & Simon, 1958b). Simon, Newell, and their colleagues went on to develop the General Problem Solver programs designed to solve a wide variety of tasks normally solved by thinking human beings. These programs all employed means-end analysis, which compares the current problem state with the general features of the desired outcome, a method discovered by Duncker (Gardner, 1985).

Simon was an outsider, not so much a psychologist as a Renaissance man who made important contributions to three fields (economics, psychology, and computer science). He was instrumental in bringing about the cognitive revolution in psychology and creating the field of artificial intelligence. Yet he and his collaborators seemed less intent on making a revolution than in solving important scientific problems. He continued making significant contributions to various fields through the rest of his long career. He did exactly what impresses psychologists: carried out elegant experiments, created new methods, and made new empirical discoveries. His most important methodological contribution was computer modeling of human cognitive processes, a method which many psychologists found liberated them from the confines of behaviorist experiments with animals.

pt 2.
psych
comp' suere

Noam Chomsky And The Theory Of Syntactical Structures

Noam Chomsky (1928-), like Herbert Simon, was an outsider who made contributions to several fields. Unlike Simon, Chomsky did appear intent on creating a cognitive revolution, or at least overthrowing behaviorism.

Chomsky received his bachelor's degree, master's degree, and Ph.D. from the University of Pennsylvania, studying logic, philosophy, and linguistics. His Ph.D. (1955) was in linguistics. He went from the University of Pennsylvania to Harvard where he was a member of the prestigious Society of Fellows (just as B.F. Skinner had been), which gave Chomsky the opportunity to develop his ideas. Around 1952 Chomsky realized that the behaviorist approach to language was inadequate and he began to develop in his classes at the University of Pennsylvania and Harvard an alternative approach. Around 1955 he and George Miller became close friends and Miller was very influenced by Chomsky's work. Because Chomsky's work was very different from mainstream approaches, he had a hard time publishing his research (Hilgard, 1987; Baars, 1986). After he finished his time as a Harvard Fellow, he took a job at MIT, where he has been ever since. MIT was one of the few places that would hire Chomsky given his, at the time, odd and controversial views on language and mind. MIT had no real social science programs and Chomsky was given great freedom there.

Chomsky's paper at the 1956 MIT conference was one of the first public presentations of Chomsky's theory (Chomsky, 1956). This was soon followed by a book (Chomsky, 1957) based on his class lectures, a book that presented the fundamental features of a non-behavioristic approach to linguistics. Then in

1959 he published a lengthy review (Chomsky, 1959) of Skinner's major work on verbal behavior (Skinner, 1957). Skinner's book is not well known now, but Chomsky's review, considered one of the most intellectually devastating in psychology's history, is still famous. In the review Chomsky showed how the behaviorist approach to language is inadequate to deal with real language. Only an approach based on cognitive structures would work. Chomsky published a revision and expansion of his theory in 1965 that was extremely influential in both linguistics and psychology (Chomsky, 1965).

Chomsky revolutionized linguistics and has continued to make significant contributions to linguistics. He is considered to be the most important linguist of the 20th century. Many of the other prominent linguists working today, although they may have rejected his approach, were his students or colleagues. Yet Chomsky is also known for his political analysis. He has published extensively in the area of politics and foreign policy and has been for a long time one of the most prominent critics of U.S. foreign policy, especially the war in Vietnam (Chomsky, 1969), U.S. policy towards Israel (Chomsky, 1983/1999), and the wars in the Persian Gulf and Iraq. He has also been a prominent critic of the U.S. media (Herman & Chomsky, 1988). These works have made Chomsky famous (or infamous) in many political circles. He is, as a consequence of his work in both linguistics and politics, the most well-known American college professor on the planet.

The Magical Number 7 Plus Or Minus 2

The leaders of the cognitive revolution came from within psychology as well as from without. Simon was a veritable Renaissance man whose work also included psychology while Chomsky came from linguistics. Perhaps the key leader within psychology was George A. Miller (1920-2012). Miller completed his undergraduate and master's degrees at the University of Alabama, then received his second master's degree and his Ph.D. from Harvard in 1946. During his graduate studies at Harvard he carried out classified military research on speech perception and communication. The specific topic of his doctoral thesis was classified and only some of his committee members were actually allowed to read his thesis (Baars, 1986). Miller's interest in language and communication, and the fact that he could not find an adequate textbook on the subject for a course he taught at Harvard, led him to write his first book on the topic in 1951 (Miller, 1951). Miller's first book was a behaviorist work, but he was to undergo a rapid transformation over the next few years away from behaviorism. He was noted as a skilled experimenter and had a strong mathematical background, and these, along with his interests in linguistics, made him especially knowledgeable about developments in linguistics and mathematics. In 1950 Miller left Harvard to spend a year at Princeton at the Institute for Advanced Studies where he studied mathematics. After his year at Princeton he spent several years at MIT before returning to Harvard in 1955 (Hilgard, 1987).

Miller was at the MIT conference along with Simon and Chomsky. His paper (Miller, 1956), published soon after the conference in *Psychological Review*, is considered a masterpiece of style and empirical argument. Miller was to gain a reputation for his graceful and engaging writing style, but it was his empirical arguments that persuaded a number of psychologists that mental phenomena could be studied rigorously. Miller also became one of the leading proponents of Chomsky's transformational grammar. He educated many psychologists on the significance and structure of Chomsky's theory (Baars, 1985).

A Study Of Thinking

Perhaps not as influential as Miller, Simon, and Chomsky, Jerome Bruner (1915-) was still one of the leading revolutionaries in the cognitive revolution. Educated at Duke as an undergraduate where he studied with William McDougall, Bruner went to Harvard for his Ph.D., where he studied social and personality psychology with Gordon Allport. Clearly a member of the psychology counter-culture that opposed behaviorism, Bruner worked with Rensis Likert (who played an important role in the history of social psychology) during the war. Bruner studied public moral and political propaganda. Before the end of the war, Bruner moved to Princeton to edit the journal *Public Opinion Quarterly* and to work with Hadley Cantril, another important social psychologist of the pre-war period (Hilgard, 1987). In this period Bruner also had connections to Gestalt psychology: One of his undergraduate professors had studied with Köhler in Germany (Hilgard, 1987) and Bruner joined Kurt Lewin's Topology Group (a group organized by Lewin to advance a Gestalt approach to social and personality psychology) in 1935, at the start of his graduate school education at Harvard.

After World War II, Bruner returned to Harvard as an instructor. His interests shifted somewhat to include the effects of motivation, experiences, and prior expectations on perception, studies that come to be called the New Look in perception. In the mid-1950s his attention shifted again, this time to thinking. Bruner completed his study of strategies used in problem solving (Bruner, Goodnow, & Austin, 1956) in 1955 shortly before he left for a yearlong sabbatical to work with Sir Charles Bartlett at Cambridge. Together Bruner and Bartlett organized a conference on cognition during the summer of 1955. While not as significant as the MIT conference a year later, the Cambridge University conference generated considerable excitement among the attendees (Hilgard, 1987). Bruner was to play a leading role as both researcher and political leader for the next 15 years of the cognitive revolution.

Simon, Chomsky, Miller, and Bruner were not the only researchers who created the cognitive revolution. Others carried out significant empirical studies and many young researchers soon took up the cognitive revolution. One other significant researcher who deserved special mention is Donald Broadbent.

Donald E. Broadbent (1926-1993) had planned to study engineering in college, but World War II interrupted his plans. Sent to the U.S. for pilot training (Broadbent was a pilot in the RAF), he discovered psychology, a subject that was not as well-known in England as it was in the U.S. His early interest, not surprising for a pilot, was in the problems people face when working with complicated technology. He took his undergraduate degree at Cambridge in 1949, where Sir Frederick Bartlett was chair of the department and Alan Turing was an influential figure. Broadbent's research was to show the influence of both of these figures throughout his career (Sheehy, Chapman, & Conroy, 1997b).

Upon completing his undergraduate degree Broadbent started work at the Applied Psychology Unit of Cambridge University. The Applied Psychology Unit had been founded by Bartlett during the war to study human-machine interactions. Broadbent's first research was on the effects of stress on human cognitive performance. He completed his Master's degree at Cambridge in 1951 and in 1958 become director of the Applied Psychology Unit. Broadbent did not receive his doctorate (a Sc.D., or doctorate of science) until 1965

1950. Between 1950 and 1962, nine of Piaget's books were translated and published in the U.S. (Flavell, 1963). Similar developments took place with the works by Gestalt psychologists: Both Wertheimer's classic on productive thinking and Koffka's work on cognitive development were republished in 1959 (Wertheimer, 1945/1959; Koffka, 1924/1959).

While the work of Bartlett was well-known to Bruner and some of the other leaders of the cognitive revolutions, and the works of the Gestalt psychologists and of Piaget swept through the U.S. in the 1950s and 1960s, the work of the Russians entered the U.S. a bit later. Vygotsky's major work *Thought and Language* (Vygotsky, 1934/1962) was published for the first time in English in 1962. In 1966 Luria's book *Higher Cortical Function in Man* (Luria, 1966) appeared and soon afterwards, a fascinating 30-year case study was published (Luria, 1968). Entitled *The Mind of a Mnemonist*, Luria's case study presented the research on S, a man with a near perfect memory. The forward to the book was written by Jerome Bruner. Many more of Vygotsky's articles and books appeared in the 1970s and 1980s (Morss, 1997) and Luria's research on the effects of literacy and industrialization appeared in 1976 (Luria, 1976).

The last significant psychologist to reenter the field was Wilhelm Wundt. Much of his work on attention, consciousness, and short-term memory, along with his considerable work on psycholinguistics, was reintroduced to American psychologists by Blumenthal in a book on psycholinguistics (Blumenthal, 1970), an interesting textbook on cognition (Blumenthal, 1977), and a series of historical studies on Wundt (*e.g.*, Blumenthal, 1975). Taken as a whole, the empirical work and theoretical concepts of these earlier researchers fueled the cognitive revolution and accelerated the progress that researchers were making. Many American psychologists had to relearn the value of history, and the value, as Gibson once observed, of getting out of date.

The Birth Of Cognitive Science

While the cognitive revolution in psychology was taking place, similar revolutions were taking place in linguistics, philosophy, and anthropology. Simultaneously, the cognitive revolution in psychology was closely linked to the development of a new field, artificial intelligence. Artificial intelligence seeks the creation of machines that think and behave intelligently, a goal that before the 1950s was pure science fiction.

The founding of artificial intelligence took place in the summer of 1956, a few months before the MIT conference that launched the cognitive revolution, at Dartmouth College in New Hampshire. It was a relatively small group of scholars that attended this working conference, including Herbert Simon and Allen Newell. Also attending was John McCarthy, a mathematician from Dartmouth who first created the term artificial intelligence. He later founded and directed the AI labs at MIT and Stanford. Marvin Minsky, considered the leader of the field of AI for a long time, came from Harvard, where he was a junior fellow (along with Chomsky). Minsky later served as director of the MIT AI lab (Gardner, 1985).

AI as a field expanded steadily in the 1960s and 1970s and produced some significant achievements. The optimistic hopes of some of its founders were not realized, however. Developments within AI have influenced cognitive psychology since the inception of the younger field.

Money has always been important in psychology since the end of the Second World War. This was especially true in the development of the cognitive revolution, which was heavily supported by corporate grant monies.

The support of grant monies also facilitated the evolution of a portion of cognitive psychology into cognitive science.

Criticism and Growth: The 1970s and 1980s

As the cognitive revolution seemed to sweep through psychology in the 1970s, critics appeared. Interestingly enough, these critics were often some of the leading revolutionaries themselves. Here we focus on two leading critics: Allen Newell and Ulric Neisser.

Newell was one of the first of the revolutionaries to criticize the course of the revolution. In a paper that is still important today as a critique of cognitive psychology, he asked the (rhetorical) question "Can you play 20 questions with nature and win?" His answer was that you could not, hence his title "You can't play 20 questions with nature and win." This elegant title captured his critique of cognitive research and theory that, in Newell's opinion, was piecemeal and fragmented. Instead of playing 20 questions, Newell argued for systematic series of studies that built models of entire, complex tasks, and that applied to many complex tasks (Newell, 1973).

Newell's criticisms were polite but significant. Soon a second prominent critic emerged: Ulric Neisser. Neisser joined the faculty at Cornell University in 1967, shortly after the publication of his book on cognitive psychology. At Cornell he met James Gibson and the two had a protracted series of debates about cognition and perception. These debates ultimately led Neisser to rethink his position on cognition, resulting in the first sustained critique of cognitive psychology from a non-behaviorist position (Neisser, 1976). The basis of Neisser's criticisms was the artificiality of cognitive psychology. Instead of studying cognition in the real and complex world, or making the laboratory reflect that real and complex world, cognitive psychology studied artificial cognition in artificial settings. His recommendation was to take a real world approach to cognition, studying complex tasks in and out of the lab that reflect what people really do when they think. Adopting Gibson's terminology, but not his philosophical assumptions, Neisser argued for an ecological approach to cognition.

Neither Newell nor Neisser (nor Bruner, who also emerged as a prominent critic) abandoned cognitive psychology and returned to behaviorism. Instead, they continued their research and theorizing in an effort to change the direction of the field. Their efforts soon bore fruit.

Studies Of Memory In The Real World

Neisser followed his own advice and carried out a number of studies on naturalistic, real world memory. In 1982 (Neisser, 1982) he reprinted his own studies, as well as contemporary and historical studies, that illustrated the ecological approach to cognition. Entitled *Memory Observed*, the book contained studies of expert witnesses, eyewitness testimony, forgetting in the real world, remembering to do things (prospective memory), literacy and memory, and mnemonists. The volume helped propel real-world memory into a more prominent research area (Neisser, 2003).

Perhaps the greatest student of real world memory is Elizabeth Loftus (1944-) Early in her career Loftus focused on the experimental study of eyewitness testimony (Loftus & Palmer, 1974) and soon became one of the nation's leading experts on the limits of eyewitness testimony. She demonstrated, using carefully controlled studies, that human memory is prone to distortion from leading questions and the effects of prior beliefs or information. By 1980, when she published a major textbook on memory (Loftus, 1980), she was an established expert on human memory.

Loftus watched with horror in the early 1990s as the therapists using recovered memory therapy began to "discover" numerous cased of repressed memories of sexual abuse, satanic ritual abuse, and UFO abductions. Based on her research into the suggestibility of everyday memory, she suspected that the memories had been implanted into the patients by the therapists through the latter's leading questions and suggestions. She started to carry out research in the area of recovered and repressed memory (Loftus, 1993), soon becoming a very controversial figure, vilified by clinicians and victim advocates because her research showed that most of the "recovered memories" could be created by the techniques used by therapists (Loftus, 2003). We shall return to the recovered memory controversy in the chapter on the history of clinical psychology and psychotherapy. While Loftus is now the leading expert of memory in the real world and the true heir of Neisser's approach to cognition, her work also demonstrates the power of the cognitive revolution to overturn widely held cultural beliefs even, or perhaps especially, beliefs held by other psychologists.

The Cuban revolutionary Ernesto "Che" Guevara once said that the job of the revolutionary is to make the revolution. The old cognitive revolutionaries never ceased making revolution. Neisser is a prime example. After championing the study of real-world memory, he went on to study memory and self-knowledge (Neisser, 1993) and memory and self-narrative (Neisser & Fivush, 1994), school achievement in minority children (Neisser, 1986), and the Flynn Effect, the fact that raw IQ scores have been rising steadily over the last 80 years in most developed countries (Niesser, 1998). None of these later works have had the impact of his work on real-world memory, but each has contributed to his overall efforts to transform cognitive psychology in a kind of permanent revolution.

Biases And Heuristics In Decision Making

Beginning in the 1970s, two Israeli psychologists who had received their

Ph.D.s from American universities began a path-breaking series of studies on biases and irrationalities in thinking. Daniel Kahneman (1934-) and Amos Tversky (1937-1996) showed that people do not think logically but instead think using heuristics (general rules for solving problems) that generally produce satisfactory solutions but can also lead to errors or illogical decision making (Gardner, 1987). These studies (contained in their edited volume, Kahneman, Slovic, & Tversky, 1982) further transformed the study of human thinking. No longer was the computer the dominant metaphor for human thinking. Now psychology had moved beyond that metaphor with specific descriptions of real people thinking about real problems.

Kahneman and Tversky's work soon produced a theory (called prospect theory) of how individuals evaluate economic decisions. In 2002 Kahneman was awarded the Nobel Prize in Economics (the Nobel is only awarded to the living) for the contributions that their research had made to that field, in spite of the fact that neither of them claimed to know much about economics.

The work on everyday cognition and cognitive biases were not the only developments in the 1970s, 80s, and 90s. There was also a substantial number of studies carried out in the field of social cognition (which is discussed in the chapter on social psychology), embodied cognition, and robotics. Taken as a whole, this work has had a far-reaching and transformative effect on modern society.

What Difference Did The Revolution Make?

The impact of the cognitive revolution can be divided, albeit somewhat arbitrarily, into two areas: first, the impact on psychology, and second, the impact on the broader culture.

Table 10.1

Nobel Prize Winners From Psychology

NAME	YEAR	NOBEL PRIZE	AREA OF PSYCH
Herbert Simon	1978	Economics	Cognitive
Robert Sperry	1981	Medicine/Physio	Physiological Psych
Daniel Kahneman	2002	Economics	Cognitive

NOTE: There is no Nobel Prize in Psychology

Within Psychology the cognitive revolution first replaced behaviorism as the metatheory; second, it returned American psychology to its early roots in functionalism and European psychology; and third, in the last thirty plus years, psychology made substantial empirical gains in our understanding of how humans think, remember, and decide. In the course of replacing behaviorism, returning American psychology to its roots, and discovering exciting new facts about human cognition, cognitive psychology transformed most other areas of the field and contributed to the development of new fields, such as Artificial Intelligence, Robotics, and Cognitive Neuroscience.

While the impact of the cognitive revolution within psychology and related fields is indisputable, the impact within society as a whole is less clear. Indeed, many of our common sense notions about memory, decision making, and problem solving seem to be shaped by computer metaphors or older ideas from psychoanalysis and philosophy, as the clash between Loftus and the recovered memory therapists illustrated. Perhaps we shall see the effects of the cognitive revolution unfold in our society over the next 30 years. In any event, we can safely conclude: the revolution made a difference.

Piaget, J. (1932). *The moral judgment of the child*. London: Kegan, Paul, Trench, & Trubner.

Piaget, J. (1950). *The psychology of intelligence*. London: Kegan, Paul, Trench, & Trubner.

Piaget, J. (1962). *Play, dreams, and imitation in childhood*. New York, NY: Norton.

Posner, M.I., & Shulman, G.L. (1979). Cognitive science. In E. Hearst (ed.), *The first century of experimental psychology*, pp. 371-405. Hillsdale, NJ: Lawrence Erlbaum Associates.

Ridley, C. E., & Simon, H.A. (1938). *Measuring municipal cctivities*. Chicago, IL: International City Managers Association.

Schrecker, E.W. (1986). *No ivory tower: McCarthyism and the universities.* New York, NY:Oxford University Press.

Schrecker, E. W. (1998). *Many are the crimes: McCarthyism in America.* Boston, MA: Little, Brown & Comp.

Selfridge, O.G., & Neisser, U. (1960). Pattern recognition by machine. *Scientific American, 203*, August, 60-68.

Shannon, C. E., & Weaver, W. (1949). *The mathematical theory of communication*. Urbana, IL: University of Illinois Press.

Sheehy, N. Chapman, A.J., & Conroy, W.A. (1997a). Bartlett, Frederick Charles. *Biographical dictionary of psychology* (pp. 50-51). London: Routledge.

Sheehy, N. Chapman, A.J., & Conroy, W.A. (1997b). Broadbent, Donald E. *Biographical dictionary of psychology* (pp. 95-97). London: Routledge.

Simon, H.A. (1947/1976). *Administrative behavior* (3rd ed.). New York, NY: Macmillan.

Skinner, B.F. (1950). Are theories of learning necessary? *Psychological Review, 57*, 193-216.

Skinner, B.F. (1953). *Science and human behavior*. New York, NY: Macmillan.

Skinner, B.F. (1957). *Verbal behavior*. New York, NY: Appleton-Century-Crofts.

Von Neumann, J. (1951). The general and logical theory of automata. In L.A. Jeffress (Ed.), *Cerebral mechanisms in behavior: The Hixon Symposium*. New York: Wiley.

Vygotsky, L.S. (1934/1962). *Thought and language*. Cambridge, MA: MIT Press.

Watson, J.B. (1924). *Behaviorism*. New York, NY: Norton.

Wertheimer, M. (1920). *Uber Schlussprozesse in productiven Denken*. Berlin: De Gruyter.

Wertheimer, M. (1945/1959). *Productive thinking* (enlarged edition). New York: Harper.

Wiener, N. (1948). *Cybernetics, or control and communication in the animal and the machine*. New York: John Wiley and Sons.

Zeigarnik, B. (1927). Das Behalten erledigter und underledigter Handlungen. *PsychologischeForschung, 9*, 1-85.

CHAPTER 11: DEVELOPMENTAL PSYCHOLOGY

For many years I have felt that no sound understanding of human or animal behavior can be had without reference to its beginnings, its course of development, and the factors by which that course is influenced. (Goodenough, 1945, p. vii)

Developmental psychology is the subfield of psychology that is concerned with origins, stability, and change. At certain points in history the field was fractured into smaller subfields, especially child psychology and gerontology. At other times it was a more coherent whole. Child psychology, adolescent psychology, adult development, and the study of aging and gerontology are all part of the larger whole—developmental psychology.

Developmental psychology is almost as old as the New Psychology itself. Growing out of the work of Wilhelm T. Preyer and G. Stanley Hall (see Chapter 5), developmental psychology was developed further by the work of James Mark Baldwin (whose tragic career and contributions are also discussed in Chapter 5). Hall emphasized development across the life-span, that is, from birth to old age. Others, such as Baldwin, emphasized infancy and childhood.

Almost from its very inception in the work of Hall and Preyer, developmental psychology was concerned with practical problems as well as scientific ones. Hall's book on adolescence, for instance, also provided advice to parents and teachers. This dual concern (science and application) emerged early in developmental psychology and has been an enduring characteristic of the field.

Child Psychology Between The World Wars

By 1910 there was a (very) small group of researchers concerned primarily with developmental psychology. Most of these researchers focused their time and energy on children. This trend was to increase throughout the 1920s, 30s, and 40s as interest in children waxed and interest in the elderly waned. In addition to this shift in interest, the field of developmental psychology was influenced by two strong forces emanating from other parts of psychology: behaviorism and psychoanalysis.

John B. Watson studied children during his time at Johns Hopkins University and later in New York City while he was also working as an advertising executive. Most of his Johns Hopkins studies of children were nursery school observations carried out between 1916 and 1919 as well a few demonstrations, the most famous of which is the Little Albert study in which Watson and his graduate student (soon-to-be wife) Rosalie Rayner demonstrated classical conditioning in an infant (Cohen, 1979; Watson & Raynor, 1920).

After his fall from academia in 1920, Watson continued his studies of children for another 10 years. The studies he carried out between 1920 and 1930 were done in collaboration with his wife. Watson and his wife made a number of observations on their own children between 1920 and 1930, and Watson argued repeatedly that psychologists need to spend more time observing and experimenting with children. He frequently argued that more was known about the development of monkeys than about the development of children. Ironically, Watson had been one of the key figures promoting the study of nonhuman primates and was in part responsible for this imbalance (Cohen, 1979).

In 1923 Watson succeeded in securing money from the Laura Spelman Rockefeller Foundation for a study of children. This money was used for observations and experiments carried out by Mary Cover Jones, who Watson supervised and for whom he acted as a mentor. Jones was a graduate student at Columbia and a friend of Rosalie Rayner (Cohen, 1979). One of the earliest products of the study was Jones' follow-up to the Little Albert study, a study of counter-conditioning (the removal of a formerly conditioned fear) in a child named Peter (Jones, 1924). We shall meet Mary Cover Jones again in Chapter 13 when we study the history of clinical psychology.

Watson was concerned with the practical applications of his work with children from the very beginning. In 1921 he and his wife (Watson & Watson, 1921) published a review of current knowledge about infants and children. They argued that very little was known about child development that could guide parents and doctors. Watson published some of the findings of his research in scholarly publications (Watson, 1926), but the main outlet was the popular manual for parents (Watson, 1928) entitled *Psychological Care of Infant and Child*.

Psychological Care of Infant and Child sold over 100,000 copies in its first few years, making it both widely read and influential. The advice to parents was often harsh (for instance, Watson was opposed to hugging and kissing children or to picking them up when they cried), based more on his overall behaviorist approach than on empirical data. While Watson had gathered data at Johns Hopkins and in New York, his claims far exceeded anything that could be justified by the rather meager data he had gathered. Watson's was not the first parenting manual: Hall and the pediatrician L. Emmett Holt had preceded him, as well as a few others. Indeed, Watson's manual was soon replaced by the works of Arnold Gesell, whom you shall meet soon (Hulbert, 2003). The eclipse of Watson's childrearing manual did not mean the end of the influence of behaviorism on developmental psychology. Behaviorism influenced the field for the next 30 years.

The second strong outside influence on developmental psychology was psychoanalysis. The works of Freud and his followers (especially Anna Freud and Melanie Klein) and the works of Carl Jung and Alfred Adler strongly influenced the field (see Chapter 6 for a discussion of these influences). Because much of this work was not empirical, the influence was less direct than the work of the behaviorists. This changed in the post-World War II period, as discussed below, when psychoanalytic ideas were tested and refined by empirically-oriented psychoanalysts and psychologists. To understand these later influences and the post-World War II history of developmental psychology, we must first review the important changes in the field that took place between the First and the Second World Wars.

The Child Study Movement And The Laura Spelman Rockefeller Foundation

As with both physiological psychology and cognitive psychology, developmental psychology, especially the child psychology subfield, benefited enormously from corporate sponsorship. The child study movement, originating in the 1890s, had led to an increased awareness of the plight of children. This movement sought to improve the conditions under which children developed into healthy adults. G. Stanley Hall was one of the key promoters of this movement among parents and educators (Smuts, 1985).

While Hall was successful in promoting the idea of child welfare among parents and teachers, he failed to generate sustained interest among psychologists. A 1918 survey of psychologists and psychiatrists found that only five researchers had a primary interest in child psychology (Smuts, 1985). Thus when Watson called for a focus on children and pointed out that there was more research being carried out on non-human primates than on children, he was right on target.

After World War I, there was a heightened awareness that the efforts to improve the lives of children far outstripped the knowledge about child development. Immediately after the war, corporate philanthropies shifted their monies toward basic research about children that could be used to guide the practical measures needed to improve children's lives. The most important of these corporate philanthropies was the Laura Spelman Rockefeller Memorial Fund (LSRM), set up with an endowment of $74 million by John D. Rockefeller, for his deceased wife, in 1918. In 1923, the fund shifted its focus from direct services to women and children toward funding of research that would produce knowledge (Smuts, 1985). Watson's own research on children in New York was supported by the fund, but that was a relatively small project for such a large philanthropy. Much more money went to three different projects: the creation and support of a series of research institutes, the launching of a series of major longitudinal studies, and the creation of research organizations and scientific journals. The LSRM fund monies were the largest but not the only funds that fueled the growth of child psychology. States (such as Iowa), universities, and other philanthropies also provided money.

The Institutes And Centers

As interest turned away from the war and toward children in 1920, the National Research Council (which was formed by the National Academy of Science in 1916 in response to possible war) formed a Committee on Child Welfare. This committee was charged with advising government agencies that dealt with children. The committee did not have a budget and so was inactive (Smuts, 1985). In 1925 the committee received funds from the LSRM Fund and was reorganized, and renamed, under the leadership of the respected experimentalist Robert S. Woodward. As the now active Committee on Child Development (CCD), the group sought to foster basic research in child development.

The committee's first publication, the annual *Child Development Abstracts and Bibliography*, began in 1927. The CCD also held biennial scientific conferences (the first in 1925, the second in 1927, and the third in 1929) and funded an award program to train child development researchers. As a consequence of the training program, the number of people studying children expanded rapidly. While the 1918 survey cited above showed only five people with a primary interest in child development, by 1927 a directory of researchers showed that there were 417 researchers listed as primarily interested in children. By 1931, the number had increased further to 627 (Smuts, 1985). Thus in 13 years the number had expanded 125-fold. Some of this expansion was due to the training of new researchers (in just one year, 1928, the CCD funded 130 people with scholarships or fellowships) and some of it was due to people moving into child development from other areas of psychology, medicine, or education. As has happened so often in the history of modern psychology, the science followed the money.

The LSRM Fund not only funded the CCD and its activities, but established and supported a series of research centers for the newly trained scientists to carry out research, teach, and disseminate new knowledge. The first such center had been established by the state of Iowa as a consequence of public pressure led by an Iowan housewife. This center, the Iowa Child Welfare Research Station, was established in 1918. In 1924, the LSRM Fund founded an institute of child development at Teacher's College, Columbia University (located in New York City) and provided monies to the Iowa Research Station. Over the next three years, the fund provided money for the founding of three more such institutes located at the University of Minnesota-Minneapolis (for a detailed history of the University of Minnesota institute, see Hartup, Johnson, & Weinberg, 2002), the University of California-Berkeley, and McGill University in Toronto, Canada. A clinic at Yale which studied children (founded by Arnold Gesell) was also funded. Two other such centers were also started by other philanthropies: the Merrill-Palmer Center in Detroit and the Fels Institute in Ohio (Smuts, 1985).

These institutes and centers, most closely associated with major universities, were to form the institutional backbone of developmental psychology through the 1940s. Most research on children was done in these institutes, most graduate students in developmental or child psychology were trained there, and a great deal of parent education and popular books and articles for parents came out of them.

The First Longitudinal Studies

The LSRM Fund also supported a series of longitudinal studies of children. A longitudinal study follows the same group of people (usually starting when they are very young) over a long period of time, testing, interviewing, and observing them on repeated occasions. While developmental psychologists realized the importance of longitudinal studies as early as 1899, practical problems prevented psychologists from carrying out such studies. Two of those practical problems were money and institutional support, but these problems were essentially overcome with grant monies and support from universities or the new institutes. A third practical problem was at the same time a scientific problem—how to reliably measure psychological characteristics over time. For intellectual ability, this problem seemed to have been solved by Lewis Terman in the U.S. with the development of the Stanford-Binet IQ test, a translation and modification of the test developed in France by Alfred Binet (Cairns & Cairns, 2006).

The first large-scale longitudinal study was initiated by Terman in 1921. Terman recruited 952 boys and girls between the ages of two and 14, all of whom had an IQ of 140 or above. Later the spouses and children of these subjects were added to the study, which continued until into the 1980s. As time passed, additional types of data, such as personality measures and social adaptations, were collected. Soon after the launching of Terman's study, other longitudinal studies were begun at Harvard, Berkeley, and Minnesota, as well as at the Fels Institute in Ohio. The large scale longitudinal studies were supplemented by short-term longitudinal studies (lasting a couple of years) and experimental longitudinal studies, the most important carried out by Myrtle McGraw, whom you shall meet momentarily (Cairns & Cairns, 2006).

The Formation of SRCD and Child Development

The creation of research centers, the funding of a national coordinating committee (the CCD), the provision of scholarships and fellowships to train developmental psychologists, and the launching of a series of important longitudinal studies were not quite enough to create a vibrant subfield within psychology. The last step was the formation of a scientific society (interdisciplinary to reflect the varied contributions of different disciplines) complete with its own scientific journal. This was accomplished in 1933, with the formation of the Society for Research in Child Development (SRCD). SRCD held its first biennial meeting in 1934. At its inception, SRCD had 125 members and the number quickly grew to 519 by 1938 (Rheingold, 1985). The organization took over the publication of the *Child Development Abstracts* from the CCD and launched its two journals, *Child Development*, for research articles and reviews, and a monograph series for longer research reports or scholarly works.

In a relatively short 15-year period, child and developmental psychology grew from a very small subfield within psychology to a large, diverse specialty with its own organizations, journals, research centers, and doctoral programs.

Arnold Gesell And Biological Maturation

The early developmental psychologists had a strong functionalist orientation, which placed them out of step with both behaviorism and psychoanalysis. This functionalist orientation was reflected in their research and in theoretical orientations, as we shall see.

The leading researcher, theorist, and pubic spokesperson for child psychology during the inter-war period was Arnold L. Gesell (1880-1961). After working for a time as a high school teacher in Wisconsin, Gesell attended the University of Wisconsin for his undergraduate degree and Clark University for his Ph.D. At Clark he studied with G. Stanley Hall and completed his dissertation on jealousy in children and animals. After completing his Ph.D. in 1906 he worked for a short time with Lewis Terman in California, and spent a summer working with Lightner Witmer at the University of Pennsylvania. He decided to obtain an M.D. in addition to his Ph.D. After taking some preliminary course work at the University of Wisconsin he enrolled at Yale Medical school in 1911 and completed his M.D. in 1915 (Hilgard, 1987).

Gesell worked his way through medical school by founding and directing the Yale Psychology Clinic in 1911. He became a professor and director of the child development clinic when he completed his M.D. in 1915. From that time to his retirement in 1948, he trained graduate students, carried out numerous empirical studies, and wrote scholarly and popular works on child development. Much of this research was financed by the Laura Spelman Rockefeller fund (Hilgard, 1987).

Gesell was a pioneer in the study of children. He was the first to systematically use filmed observations of children (Watson had filmed infants to document and demonstrate his findings, not as a tool of observation). and used identical twins to carry out experimental studies of children. One twin would be trained to do a particular behavior while the other would serve as the control. The use of a co-twin control, as it is called, helps separate out the effects of experience from the effects of maturation during a child's development. Gesell studied both physical and cognitive development from infancy and early childhood (the toddler and pre-school years) through adolescence. (Hilgard, 1987). Based on his observations and experiments, Gesell developed norms for the typical growth and development of children, exactly the kind of information that Watson had argued was needed by parents and medical doctors (Watson & Watson, 1921).

As a theoretician, Gesell emphasized the continuity of development and the role of biological maturation, themes he stressed in his works for parents as well. And in both his empirical research and his theorizing he resisted (or ignored, depending on your point of view) the influence of both behaviorism and psychoanalysis.

The Empirical Study Of Childhood

The psychologists at the various institutes and centers carried out a variety of empirical studies using both observational and experimental methods throughout the 1920s, 30s, and 40s. These high-quality empirical studies, even more than the work of Gesell, laid the basis for the rapid growth and development of developmental psychology after World War II. Interestingly, many of these psychologists were women during a time when women were marginalized from mainstream psychological research. Two of the leading empiricists, as we can label these psychologists, were Florence Goodenough and Myrtle B. McGraw.

Florence L. Goodenough (1886-1959) received her first undergraduate degree in 1908. She received a second bachelor's degree and a master's degree in psychology from Columbia University in 1920 and 1921, respectively. While she completed her degrees at Columbia she also worked as Director of Research for the New Jersey public schools (Johnson, 2003; 2005).

From Columbia, Goodenough went to Stanford and studied with Lewis Terman. At Stanford she worked on Terman's longitudinal study of gifted children and finished her Ph.D. in 1924. She then worked a year at the Minneapolis Child Guidance Clinic and in 1925 was one of the first people hired by John Anderson, director of the just opened Institute of Child Welfare at the University of Minnesota (now re-named the Institute of Child Development). Goodenough spent the next 22 years at the Institute, where she made a number of methodological and empirical contributions, including nine textbooks and 26 scientific papers, as well as numerous popular articles and talks. She also trained a large number of graduate students (including Ruth Howard, the first African-American women to earn a Ph.D. in psychology) and served as president of SRCD in 1946-1947. Goodenough retired in 1947 at the age of 61 because of an illness that ended her productive career (Johnson, 2003; Johnson, 2005).

Goodenough's work was characterized by careful empirical research, development and use of a variety of empirical methods, and a sophisticated concept of development which was often overlooked by historians. For example, in 1926 she published her first book on the measurement of intelligence in children which included the Goodenough Draw-A-Person Test (Goodenough, 1926). A few years later she developed IQ tests for pre-school age children (Goodenough, Foster, & Van Wagenen, 1932). She also developed the techniques of observational sampling (Goodenough, 1928) and the use of careful observations by parents of their own children, a technique she used to great success in her study of children's anger (Goodenough, 1931).

Goodenough, like the other empiricists, had a strong developmental orientation that looked at the interaction of biological factors and environmental factors over the course of the lifespan. This orientation is expressed cogently in the opening paragraph of the preface to her textbook on developmental psychology entitled simply *Developmental Psychology* (Goodenough, 1945) and is used as the epigraph for this chapter. Goodenough's insistence that sound understanding be based on knowledge of the beginnings, developmental course, and the causes of development is reflected in the structure and content of the text. Goodenough begins with two chapters on the scope of psychology and its methods. She then includes five chapters on the biological basis of development, including genetics, pre-natal development, and the neonate, along with chapters on motivation and learning. These are followed by chapters on language, cognition, perception, and socio-emotional development from infancy through middle childhood. Then came chapters on adolescence, the college years, adulthood (both social relations and work), and old age. Near the end of the text she has chapters on mental illness, mental retardation, and delinquency and crime. Finally, she ends her book with chapters on child rearing, happiness and efficiency in adulthood, and the uses and limits of science to improve human life (Goodenough, 1945).

What strikes the contemporary psychologist reading Goodenough's text is first how much more factual information we now know and second how thoroughly modern is her outlook and approach. She avoids strict biological reductionism and environmental reductionism and attempts to integrate both biological and environmental causes into an understanding of the course of development. So while she did not espouse a theory per se, she did show considerable theoretical sophistication in addition to her brilliant empirical innovations.

The second great empiricist from the 1920s, 30s, and 40s was Myrtle B. McGraw (1899-1988). McGraw received her Ph.D. from Columbia University where her doctoral dissertation (McGraw, 1931) compared Caucasian and African-American infants to test claims that racial differences were due to inherited differences in physical structure or intelligence. Using a comprehensive battery of developmental tests she found no evidence for the frequent claims of biological inferiority of African-Americans. Instead she found that the white infants had slightly higher scores on some tests and black infants had slightly higher scores on other tests, including some very complex ones. She also found extensive overlap in the distributions and wide variability within each group. She argued, on the basis of her results, that average or normative differences based on cross-sectional studies did not capture the true nature of development. Only longitudinal studies that took account of or measured environmental differences could reveal the developmental course. This position

shows its environment

put her in opposition to Gesell and his normative studies and maturationist theory (Bergenn, Dalton, & Litsitt, 1994).

McGraw's dissertation was the preface to a larger body of work that challenged both the maturationist and behaviorist orthodoxies of her time. Combining naturalistic observation and experimentation, she explored the interaction of biology and experience in development. Her first major work was a study of identical twin infants in which she tried to stimulate development in one twin while using the other as a control, a co-twin study (McGraw, 1935). McGraw worked collaboratively with a number of psychologists in New York, including J.B. Watson, Robert S. Woodworth, E.L. Thorndike, and John Dewey. She also collaborated with the neurobiologist George Coghill. Her work was supported by the Rockefeller Foundation (Bergenn, Dalton, & Litsitt, 1994).

McGraw's ideas were often misrepresented in the press and in psychology textbooks. Her work supported a complex interactionist position: both biology and experience are necessary for the emergence of behaviors. This position stood in opposition to the behaviorist position of Watson and Skinner and the maturationist position of Gesell. McGraw used the concept of critical period from embryology, the idea that experience can have a particular and potent impact on development at certain crucial stages (Bergenn, Dalton, & Litsitt, 1994).

McGraw's path-breaking early studies were followed by a series of detailed studies on selected infant behaviors such as locomotion (McGraw, 1943). On the basis of these studies, McGraw concluded that the rate and timing of cortical growth explained the pattern of development and that, in turn, cortical growth was shaped by experiential inputs. Studies of motor behavior and development declined during the late 1940s and 1950s and did not revive until the 1960s rebirth of developmental psychology, when McGraw's work was to prove influential and was to help build a foundation for a psychobiological approach to development (Bergenn, Dalton, & Litsitt, 1994).

The rapid empirical advance and dynamic character of the field was reflected by the publication of a handbook for researchers in 1931 with a revised edition in 1933 (Murchison, 1931; Murchison, 1933). The Murchison handbooks were wide-ranging and its release as a second edition only two years after the first edition was published is one indication of the explosive growth in the field. This growth was not just a consequence of the research, institutions, and training funded mostly by Rockefeller money, but also from the stimulus of Gestalt research and immigration.

Gestalt Studies Of Child Psychology

Kurt Koffka introduced American psychologists to the Gestalt study of children's cognitive development in his *Growth of the Mind: An introduction to child psychology* (Koffka, 1924/1959). But Koffka was neither the only nor even the most important Gestalt theorist to study children. That distinction belongs to Kurt Lewin. Lewin first appeared on the American scene with two papers in 1931, both of which dealt with the need to study individual children in their concrete total situation as opposed to the study of group averages, in an effort to understand the essence of a group. He likened his approach to that of Galileo and likened the approach based on comparisons of average behavior to that of Aristotle (Lewin, 1931a; Lewin, 1931b).

After fleeing the Nazis, he found permanent work at the Iowa Child Study station, which was then under the direction of Robert R. Sears. While at Iowa Lewin carried out a series of path-breaking studies, relevant to both child and social psychology, including studies of levels of aspiration in children (Lewin, Dembo, Festinger, & Sears, 1944), the effects of leadership style on children's group processes (Lewin, Lippitt, & White, 1939), and frustration and aggression (Barker, Dembo, & Lewin, 1941).

Lewin's theory and empirical research was stimulating to both developmental and social psychology (we return to his contributions to social psychology in the next chapter). But as the war progressed, Lewin turned his attention increasingly toward action research, group dynamics, and social psychology. His presence remained strong within developmental psychology because of the work of his former students such as Roger Barker, who went on to develop Lewinian ideas in the form of ecological psychology, the study of the psychological environment and its effects on individuals, and Marian Radke Yarrow (Cairns & Cairns, 2006).

The Nadir Of Child Psychology

Robert R. Sears, himself a leader in child and developmental psychology,

he spent time carrying out anthropological studies on American Indian reservations.

Erikson developed his theory relatively late in his life. His theory is a modification of Freud's psychoanalytic theory that takes into consideration data from anthropology and psychology and views development as occurring over the entire lifespan. While he was productive his entire career and widely respected as a clinician and researcher, his first major work describing eight stages of personality development over the lifespan, was presented in *Childhood and Society* (Erikson, 1950) when he was 46. Each stage in Erikson's theory revolves around an issue or crisis that pre-occupies the individual. For example the first stage is the crisis of trust vs. mistrust, where the major psychological issue is the formation of a trusting relationship with a caregiver during infancy. The major crisis of the teen years is identity vs. role confusion, where the major psychological issue is the formation of your identity. His second major work was a psychobiography of Martin Luther (Erikson, 1958), a study that examined the psychological development and personality of the founder of Protestantism. Five years later, when he was 59, he published an expanded second edition of *Childhood and Society* (Erikson, 1963). Erikson returned to the issue of identity in his third major work *Identity, Youth, and Crisis* (Erikson, 1968) and in his fourth major work, a psychobiography of Gandhi (Erikson, 1969).

Erikson contributed a lifespan theory of personality development that synthesized findings from psychology and anthropology with psychoanalytic theory. As with social learning theory, it was yet another medium by which psychoanalysis shaped non-psychoanalytic psychology. Erikson also provided a framework and a set of empirical problems (such as the nature of identity and identity formation, the importance of the first relationship, and so on) that have inspired researchers for 50 years.

Piaget And The Cognitive Revolution In Child Psychology

The contributions of Jean Piaget (1896-1980) to the cognitive revolution have been described in Chapter 10. To briefly summarize his contributions: Piaget's career can be roughly divided into four overlapping phases. In the first phase during the 1920s and 1930s he studied language development, egocentrism, children's thinking and their conceptions of reality, causality, and morality. In his second phase during the 1930s he studied infancy and the child's relationship to physical objects, such as the famous conservation tasks. He refined his notions of cognitive structure and stages during this phase as well. In his third phase, beginning in the late 1930s and extending into the early 1970s, he studied thinking about logic, mathematics, and scientific concepts, and developed his mature theory of genetic (*i.e.*, developmental) epistemology. In the fourth phase, from the early 1970s to his death, he examined cognitive functions, exploring strategies used by children, the effects of training on cognitive development, and the development of understanding (Beilin, 1994).

When Piaget's work was reintroduced into the U.S. in the early 1960s, it had an electrifying effect on developmental psychology. Developmental psychologists returned to the study of thinking, memory, language, and problem-solving with new hypotheses to test and new ways of testing them. Soon the approaches from information processing were also introduced and the two different ways of looking at cognition fed off of each other, as developmental psychologists examined the cognitive abilities of infants through the elderly. This dynamic period in cognitive research, occurring from the mid-1960s through the mid-1990s, has been described as a re-emergence (not a revolution) by some historians of developmental psychology (Cairns & Cairns, 2006) because of the traditional interest in these subjects in the field. Whatever the descriptor used, revolution or re-emergence, the effect was tonic. By the 1970s and 1980s, the emphasis on cognition also influenced the thinking about social and personality development, leading to the dynamic research programs in the area of social cognition (including knowledge of self and others, knowledge of morality, emotions, and social relations) and a revision in social leaning theory (Bandura, 1986) into a social cognitive theory.

Attachment: The Work Of John Bowlby And Mary Ainsworth

Psychoanalysis continued to exert a strong influence on developmental psychology in the post-World War II period. In addition to social learning theory and Erikson's psychosocial theory, a third strand of work influenced by psychoanalysis, attachment theory, shaped the study of social and emotional development. Attachment theory examines the emotional attachments formed between infants and caregivers, variations in those attachments, and the consequences of those attachments. Attachment theory was developed collectively by researchers based primarily in the English-speaking world. Without a doubt the two major figures in the development of attachment theory are John Bowlby and Mary Ainsworth.

John E.J. Bowlby (1907-1990) was educated at Cambridge, graduating with his undergraduate degree in 1928. He taught for a year in a school for children with psychological problems, and then returned to Cambridge to complete his medical degree, specializing in child psychiatry. While in medical school, Bowlby also studied psychoanalysis at the British Psychoanalytic Institute, where he was supervised by Melanie Klein. From early in his training at the Institute, Bowlby rejected the then current emphasis on children's fantasies and instead sought to empirically examine the actual relationships between children and parents. This orientation put him at odds with the psychoanalytic establishment in Great Britain (Bretherton, 1994).

World War II interrupted Bowlby's new career as a child psychiatrist. He served as an officer in the British Army charged with researching issues related to officer selection. This experience, in which he worked with researchers from the Tavistock Clinic in London, provided him with additional training in statistics and research methods. By the end of the war, Bowlby was one of the most skilled empirical researchers within psychoanalysis (Bretherton, 1994). After the war, Bowlby was hired by the Tavistock Clinic to head their children's department. It was at the Tavistock Clinic that Bowlby, working with a gifted and collegial group of researchers, developed the theory of attachment and made a number of other important contributions to clinical practice and public policy.

Bowlby had a keen interest in family interaction and the effect those interactions had on children. This interest in real relationships and their real consequences prompted Bowlby to publish a paper (Bowlby, 1949) describing how he would interview parents about the parents' childhood in front of their children. This paper is often considered the first published work on family therapy, now a very important part of clinical psychology (Bretherton, 1994). Another important early contribution was a paper commissioned by the World Health Organization (WHO) on the psychological health of homeless children, a significant problem in post-war Europe and Asia (Bowlby, 1951), in which Bowlby summarized much of the empirical research on the effects of separation or loss of parents. The paper was translated into 14 languages and hundreds of thousands of copies were sold (Bretherton, 1994). The 1951 monograph is still worth reading. Elegantly written and carefully thought through, it is a synthesis of what was known at the time on maternal deprivation. It pointed to a number of empirical facts that cried out for explanation, such as how can maternal deprivation be so damaging to the child. Bowlby's efforts to provide a theory that could explain the consequences of maternal deprivation became the focus of his research for the next 40 years.

Bowlby, like Piaget, worked collaboratively with other talented researchers. (A contributing factor in both Piaget's and Bowlby's scientific achievement was their ability to work cooperatively with others over decades of collaboration). One of the first of Bowlby's talented collaborators was James Robertson (1911-1988), who had originally worked as a caretaker in Anna Freud's orphanage during World War II. Anna Freud required all of her staff to be trained as observers. When Robertson joined Bowlby he was already a skilled observer. He wanted to move beyond observation to directly intervene to improve the lives of children. Robertson wanted to document in a way that could be easily communicated to larger audiences the plight of his young charges. He hit upon the idea of using film. His first film, which helped change public perception, was made in 1952 with Bowlby's aid (Robertson, 1952). Entitled *A two-year old goes to hospital,* the film followed a single child and documented her emotional reactions. Robertson went on to make other films about attachment and separation, as well as carry out basic research with Bowlby and others on separation and loss in children.

Perhaps the most important of Bowlby's collaborators was Mary D. Ainsworth (1913-1999). Ainswoth was born in the U.S. She was educated in Canada, receiving her B.A. in 1935, her M.A. in 1936, and her Ph.D. in 1939, all from the University of Toronto. Her dissertation examined the ideas of her advisor on security and personality development. Ainsworth's early career as a clinical psychologist was interrupted by World War II. In 1942 she joined the Canadian Women's Army Corps, where she worked on personnel selection. During the war Ainsworth had developed her research skills to a great extent. She rose to

- interconnected to each other   438
- affect of WWII

who was able to use experiments to develop and refine concepts and theories about perception. A wonderful illustration of this is her work with her graduate student, and later collaborator, Richard Walk. Together with Walk, Eleanor Gibson developed the famous visual cliff as an experimental apparatus to test perceptual development in infants and animals (E.J. Gibson & Walk, 1960). Gibson and Walk tested human infants and the young of other species, showing that the ability to perceive depth emerges early and does not seem to be a consequence of reinforcement and punishment. Again, we learn to pick up information that is already in the world and we do not add things to a generally impoverished stimulus, a point they had made earlier in an experiment on the effects of prolonged exposure on discrimination learning in rats (E.J. Gibson & Walk, 1956).

Eleanor Gibson continued to carry out path-breaking research and refine the ecological theory of perception in the 70s and 80s. In 1975 she published a synthesis of her work as well as the work of others on reading (E.J. Gibson & Levin, 1975), effectively founding the study of the psychology of reading. She also was able to set up her own infant lab at Cornell in 1975, where she began a series of studies with her graduate students. After her husband's death in 1979 she continued to refine their theory, especially the concepts of affordances and the idea of perceptual invariants. Based solely on her own work, Eleanor Gibson can be considered the most significant figure in the study of perceptual development in the last 100 years. Taken together with her husband, what Helmholtz was to perception in the 19th century, the Gibsons were to perception in the 20th.

The dramatic rebirth of developmental (primarily child) psychology in the 1950s and 1960s was driven by careful and beautifully crafted experiments as well as the mid-range theories such as social learning theory, Piaget's cognitive developmental theory, attachment theory, Erikson's psychosocial theory, and the Gibsons' ecological approach to perception.

Child Psychology Becomes Developmental Psychology: The 1960s and 70s

While the study of adolescence and adult development, as well as the study of gerontology, became established early in the century by the functionalist psychologists, developmental psychologists during the boom times of the 1920s and 1930s focused mostly on child psychology; that was, after all, where the money was. With the theoretical and empirical rebirth of the field in the 1950s and 60s came a substantial increase in the number of researchers interested in adult development and aging. This increasing interest in turn transformed developmental psychology from a psychology of children and adolescence into a true psychology of development across the lifespan.

Psychologists established the institutional infrastructure for the expansion of the study of adult development and aging shortly after World War II. The American Psychological Association established a division on maturity and old age in 1945. The National Institute of Health established a unit dedicated to gerontology in 1946. And in 1953 the National Institute of Mental Health (NIMH) established a section on aging. The APA and NIMH together organized a major scientific conference on the psychological aspects of aging in 1955. The proceedings of this conference were edited by John E. Anderson (the director of the University of Minnesota's Institute of Child Development) and were published in 1956 (Riegel, 1977).

Numerical analysis of published papers in psychological gerontology showed steady growth in the 1920s, 30s, and 40s with exponential growth occurring after 1950 (Riegle, 1977) [See figure 11.1]. This substantial growth trailed the exponential growth in child psychology that had occurred in the 1920s by approximately 30 years (Birren & Schroots, 2001).

The renaissance in research on adult development and aging embedded in a lifespan developmental perspective during the 1950s was not the work of a single person, but the product of an interconnected group of researchers that formed a kind of invisible (or not so invisible) college. Of this group, four researchers played leading roles: Robert Havighurst, Bernice Neugarten, James Birren, and K. Warner Schaie.

Robert J. Havighurst (1900-1991) received his B.A. from Ohio Wesleyan and his Ph.D. in physical chemistry from Ohio State. He worked as a chemistry professor at the University of Wisconsin publishing papers on atomic structure until 1928 when he decided to shift his career toward adult education and development. In 1940 he took a position in developmental psychology at the University of Chicago where he worked closely for many years with Bernice Neugarten. He published extensively in the area of education and developed a theory of lifespan development based on the concepts of developmental task, an idea also proposed by Erik Erikson. While Erikson focused much of his research on identity and youth, Havighurst's work covered the entire life-span, with particular focus on early and middle adulthood, as well as the transition to retirement (Havighurst, Munnichs, Neugarten, & Thomae, 1969).

Another prominent member of this group was Bernice Neugarten (1916-2001) who received her BA in 1936 in English and French literature and her MA in 1937 in educational psychology from the University of Chicago. She married in 1940 and finished her Ph.D. in 1943, receiving the first Ph.D. in human development awarded by the University of Chicago. The topic of her dissertation was the influence of social class on children's friendships. She then took seven years off to raise her family, joining the faculty of the University of Chicago in 1950 (at the age of 35) as a part-time adjunct faculty member. She became a tenure-track associate professor in 1960 (Hogan & Iaccino, 1997).

Neugarten had received a broad education at Chicago, where she was influenced by anthropology and sociology as much as by psychology. Her focus on adult development and aging developed out of her own experience and partly by chance. While a graduate student she worked with Robert Havighurst on a study of middle-aged people in Kansas City. Around this time she was also asked to teach a new course at the University of Chicago on maturity and old age. To prepare herself for the course she studied everything available on personality development in adulthood, especially the work of Erikson. As her own thinking developed she changed the name of the course to "Adult Development and Aging" (Hogan & Iaccino, 1997).

[handwritten margin note: think of development as for children]

After becoming a tenure-track professor, she quickly achieved the rank of full professor in 1964, served as the director of the graduate program in adult development and aging, and supervised numerous Ph.D. dissertations. In addition to her work with Robert Havighurst (Havighurst & Neugarten, 1955; Havighurst & Neugarten, 1962), she carried out path-breaking research in a number of areas such as adult personality development (Neugarten, 1964) and public policy toward the elderly (Neugarten, 1982).

A contemporary of Neugarten, James E. Birren (1918-) played a key role in the flowering of gerontology as both a researcher and administrator. He received his Ph.D. from Northwestern University and worked for the Naval

Medical Research Center during World War II. In 1947 he joined the U.S. Public Health Service as a researcher in the Gerontology Unit and in 1948 was a founding member of the Gerontology Society of America. In 1950 he joined NIMH, where he created the section on aging. Since 1950 he has held a number of other prominent roles within gerontology, including the editor of the *Handbook on the Psychology of Aging.* Birren's work initially focused on cognitive development.

The youngest of the four members of the invisible college is K. Warner Schaie (1928-). Schaie received his B.A. from the University of California-Berkeley in 1952 and his Ph.D. from the University of Washington in 1956. He is most famous for launching the Seattle Longitudinal Study of cognitive development, has held several academic posts, and has also been a co-editor with Birren of *The Handbook on the Psychology of Aging.* Schaie, like the other three, has been enormously productive, with over 250 scientific articles and books.

While Havighurst, Neugarten, Birren and Schaie were the first generation to examine adult development within a lifespan perspective after the initial interest in the topic in the early 1900s, a second generation of researchers that came of age in the early 1960s also played prominent roles in researching adult development and transforming child psychology into developmental psychology. This second generation includes John Nesselroade and Paul Baltes among their most influential members.

John R. Nesselroade (1936-) received his B.Sc. from Marietta College in 1961 and his Ph.D. from the University of Illinois in 1965. Nesselroade developed considerable expertise in multivariate analysis and focused his research on personality development, an important and neglected area within adult development and aging. He also was a key proponent in the 1970s of the return to a true lifespan developmental psychology, integrating child psychology, adult development, and gerontology again into a unified discipline. Another key proponent of the lifespan developmental approach was Paul B. Baltes (1939-). Baltes was born in Germany and received his undergraduate degree in 1963 and his Ph.D. in 1967 from the University of Saarbrücken (Germany). He also spent a year as an exchange student at the University of Nebraska. After earning his Ph.D., Baltes worked for 13 years in the U.S., first at West Virginia University and later at Pennsylvania State University, before returning to Germany to work at the prestigious Max-Planck Institute. Baltes has focused much of his research on cognitive development, especially the development of wisdom in adults and the elderly. Like Nesselroade, he takes a sophisticated multivariate approach to development across the life-span.

The shift toward a true lifespan developmental psychology was also fueled by the continuation of the early longitudinal studies launched in the 1920s.

The Return of Biology: The 1980s and 1990s

The mid-level theories that animated research in the 1950s, 60s, and 70s, specifically social learning theory, Piaget's theory, Erikson's theory of psychosocial development, Gibson's theory of perceptual development, and the theory of attachment all assumed that biology played a role in development but tended to give short shrift to the biological components of development as a subject of research and theory. This neglect changed in the 1980s and 1990s as a consequence of work in behavioral genetics.

One of the pioneers in the field of behavioral genetics within developmental psychology was Sandra Scarr (1936-). Scarr received her B.A. from Vassar College in 1959, worked for a short time as a social worker, and then started graduate school in psychology at Harvard University in 1961 where she encountered considerable sexism. She graduated Harvard with her Ph.D. in 1965 with a specialization in behavioral genetics, the study of genetic influences on psychological characteristics such as intelligence and personality. Scarr faced considerable difficulty finding full-time work because she was married and had a child, but eventually she secured a full-time position at the University of Pennsylvania. In 1971 she moved to the University of Minnesota where she worked until 1977. In 1977 she moved to Yale, and then in 1983 she moved again to the University of Virginia, where she worked until she left academia to become the C.E.O. of Kindercare Learning Centers, a national chain of daycare centers (O'Connell, 2001).

Scarr's studies in the 1960s focused on the intellectual aptitude and school achievement of identical and fraternal twins, in which she discovered that intellectual development was heavily influenced by genetic factors and that black children showed less of a genetic influence and more of an environmental influence on their test scores than did white children. After moving to the University of Minnesota she collaborated with Richard Weinberg (Scarr & Weinberg, 1976) on a study of transracial adopted children (children of one race adopted by parents of a different race). Scarr and Weinberg (1976) discovered that the influence of the family environment wanes after childhood, that environmental influences have a positive effect on the adopted children's intellectual abilities, and that genetic factors also play a considerable role. In addition to her pioneering work on genetic and familial influences on intellectual abilities, Scarr carried out pioneering studies of the effects of stimulation on prematurely born infants, wrote psychology and developmental psychology textbooks (Scarr, 1987; Scarr, Weinberg, & Levin, 1986) and books for mass audiences. She also served as president of the American Psychological Society, which later changed its name to the Association for Psychological Science (O'Connell, 2001).

In addition to her empirical contributions, Scarr has made a number of conceptual contributions. Perhaps her most important one is the notion of types of genotype-environment interactions. She argued (Scarr & McCartney, 1983) that genotype-environment interactions can be passive (the environment shapes children with particular genetic characteristics), active (the child seeks and works to create a particular environment), or evocative (particular genetic characteristics can provoke certain environmental responses).

Soon other researchers were following the path that Scarr had paved. Chief among these were Robert Plomin and a group at the University of Minnesota that included Thomas Bouchard Jr. and David Lykken.

Robert Plomin (1948-)received his B.A. in psychology from DePaul University in 1970 and his Ph.D. in psychology in 1974 from the University of Texas at Austin. The University of Texas and the University of Minnesota were at the time emerging as the two leading centers for the study of behavioral genetics. After graduation Plomin worked at the University of Colorado at Boulder until 1986 and then at Pennsylvania State University until 1994, when he took a position at King's College London. Plomen has studied elderly twins reared apart and elderly twins reared together to examine the genetics of aging. He researched genetic and environmental factors that make siblings in the same family different, and he has introduced important fundamental concepts into psychology, such as the concept of the non-shared familial environment.

He also authored a leading psychological textbook on behavioral genetics (Plomen, 2004) and has written for a mass audience (Dunn & Plomen, 1990).

Plomen (Plomen & Daniels, 1987) argued that much of the environmental effects on a child's development (and the behavioral geneticists have shown that these environmental effects are substantial) are not due to the common or shared environment of children within the same family, but to environmental influences unique to each child. Thus the non-shared environment, the child's unique experiences inside and outside of the family, are very important in development. Plomen and others have demonstrated empirically (*e.g.*, Sulloway, 1996) that non-shared environmental influences account for the fact that biologically related siblings are often very different.

A third group of researchers that influenced the return of biological influences on developmental psychology was centered at the University of Minnesota. This group, which included Thomas Bouchard Jr. and David Lykken (1928-2006), carried out a set of related studies, including a study of twins reared apart. They have shown that genetic factors not only influence intellectual abilities but a range of other psychological characteristics such as basic personality characteristics (Bouchard, 1994), happiness (Lykken & Tellegen, 1996), and even how religious, politically conservative, or orderly a person is (Bouchard, Lykken, McGue, Segal, & Tellegen, 1990).

The work of developmental psychologists working in the area of behavioral genetics has generated considerable interest, and sometimes opposition, among the general public. In 1979, for instance, "Fire Bouchard" could still be seen on the walls of a University of Minnesota building. The work has also begun to transform developmental psychology. Using basic research designs pioneered by Francis Galton, developmental psychologists explored with increasing sophistication the relative contributions of nature and nurture. Along with other work in evolution psychology and neuroscience during the 1980s and 1990s, behavioral genetics contributed to a return of the field to biology.

The Impact Of Developmental Psychology

Developmental psychology was born out of society's concern for children, was weaned on foundation grants, and came of age with the mid-level theories of the 1950s, 60s, and 70s. Throughout its history, the field has been strongly tied to practical concerns, such as parenting, and philosophical concerns, such as the role of nature-vs- nurture in human development.

Without a doubt, the assumptions about development and the research questions have been shaped by broader cultural assumptions. This is perhaps most clearly seen in the impact that cultural assumptions have had on child-rearing research (Hulbert, 2003). But it is also the case that developmental psychology has changed and reshaped those cultural assumptions. Again, this is clearly illustrated in the area of childrearing, where empirical studies and theories have continually reshaped how we raise and care for our children, a process that is still going on around us (Rankin, 2005).

The research has also addressed substantial philosophical questions: How do we come to perceive the world? What is the relative impact of our genes and our environment? How does our cognition change over time? How can we maximize our cognitive development? What is the nature of love? And how do we best love our children? These questions, once the purview of philosophers and their speculations, are now the property of developmental psychologists who, true to their empiricist heritage, seek empirical answers.

Goodenough, F.L. (1926). *Measurement of intelligence by drawing.* Yonkers-On-Hudson, NY: World Book Comp.

Goodenough, F.L. (1928). Measuring behavior traits by means of repeated short samples. *Journal of Juvenile Research, 12,* 230-235.

Goodenough, F.L. (1931). *Anger in young children.* Minneapolis, MN: University of Minnesota Press.

Goodenough, F.L. (1945). *Developmental psychology*, (2nd ed.). New York, NY: Appleton-Century-Crofts.

Goodenough, F.L., Foster, J.C., & Van Wagenen, M.J. (1932). *The Minnesota Preschool Test: Manual of instructions. Forms A and B.* Minneapolis, MN: Educational Testing Bureau.

Grusec, J.E. (1994). Social learning theory and developmental psychology: The legacies of Robert R. Sears and Albert Bandura. . In R.D. Parke, P.A. Ornstein, J.J. Rieser, & C. Sahn-Waxler (Eds.) *A century of developmental psychology*, pp. 473-497. Washington, DC: American Psychological Association.

Hartup, W.W., Johnson, A., & Weinberg, R.A. (2002). The Institute of Child Development: Pioneering in science and application. In W.W. Hartup & R.A. Weinberg (Eds.) *Child psychology in retrospect and prospect: In celebration of the 75th anniversary of the Institute of Child Development. The Minnesota Symposia on Child Psychology* (Vol. 32), pp. 227-258.

Havighurst, R.J., Munnichs, J.M.A., Neugarten, B.L., & Thomae, H. (1969). *Adjustment to retirement: A cross-national study.*

Havighurst, R.J., & Neugarten, B.L. (1955). *American Indian and White children: A sociopsychological investigation.* Chicago, IL: University of Chicago Press.

Havighurst, R.J., & Neugarten, B.L. (1962). *Society and education.* Boston, MA:

Allyn & Bacon.

Hilgard, E. R. (1987). *Psychology in America: A historical survey*. San Diego, CA: Harcourt Brace Jovanovich.

Hogan, J.D., & Iaccino, W. (1997). In Sheehy, N., Chapman, A.J., & Conroy W.A., Eds. (1997). *Biographical dictionary of psychology*, pp. 423-424. London: Rout-ledge.

Hulbert, A. (2003). *Raising America: Experts, parents, and a century of advice* about *children*. New York, NY: Alfred A. Knopf.

Johnson, A. (2003). Florence Goodenough and child study in the 1930s: The question of mothers as researchers. Paper presented at the annual meeting of Cheiron: The International Society for the History of the Behavioral and Social Sciences, University of New Hampshire, Durham, NH.

Johnson, A. (2005). Florence Goodenough: Child development pioneer and in-novative women scientist. Poster presentation at the Biennial Meeting of SRCD, Atlanta, GA, April 6.

Jones, M.C. (1924). A laboratory study of fear: The case of Peter. *Journal of Genetic Psychology, 31*, 308-315.

Karen, R. (1998). *Becoming attached: First relationships and how they shape our capacity to love.* New York, NY: Oxford University Press.

Koffka, K. (1924/1959). *The growth of the mind: An introduction to child* psych-*ology*. Paterson, NJ: Littlefield, Adams, & Comp.

Kovach, J. (1997). Ainsworth, Mary Dinsmore (Slater). In N. Sheehy A.J. Chap-man, & W.A. Conroy (Eds.) *Biographical dictionary of psychology*. London: Rout-ledge, pp. 3-4.

Lewin, K. (1931a). Conflict Between aristotelian and galileian modes of thought in psychology. *Journal of Genetic Psychology, 5*, 141-177.

Lewin, K. (1931b). Environmental forces in child behavior and development. In C. Murchison (Ed.), *A handbook of child psychology* (2nd ed.), pp. 918-970. New York, NY: John Wiley & Sons.

Lewin, K., Dembo, T., Festinger, L., & Sears, P. (1944). Level of aspiration. In J.M. Hunt (Ed.) *Handbook of personality and the behavior disorders* (Vol. 1), pp. 333-378. New York, NY: Ronald Press.

Lewin, K., Lippitt, R., & White, R. (1939). Patterns of aggressive behavior in experimentally created "social climates." *Journal of Social Psychology, 10*, 271-299.

Lykken, D. T., & Tellegen, A. (1996). Happiness is a stochastic phenomenon. *Psychological Science, 7*, 186-189.

McGraw, M.B. (1931). A comparative study of a group of southern White and Negro infants. *Genetic Psychology Monographs, 10*, 1-105.

McGraw, M.B. (1935). *Growth: A study of Johnny and Jimmy*. New York, NY: Appleton-Century-Crofts.

McGraw, M.B. (1943). *The neuromuscular maturation of the human infant*. New York, NY: Columbia University Press.

Miller, N.E., & Dollard, J. (1941). *Social learning and imitation*. New Haven, CT: Yale University Press.

Murchison, C. (Ed.). (1931) *A handbook of child psychology*. Worcester, MA: Clark University Press.

Murchison, C. (Ed.). (1933) *A handbook of child psychology* (2nd. ed.). Worcester,

MA: Clark University Press.

Neugarten, B.L. (1964). *Personality in middle and late life.* Chicago, IL: University of Chicago Press.

Neugarten, B.L., ed. (1982). *Age or need: Public policies for older people.* Sage Publications.

O'Connell, A.N. (2001). *Models of achievement: Reflections of eminent women in Psychology, Vol. 3.* London: Erlbaum.

Pick Jr., H.L. (1994). Eleanor J. Gibson: Learning to perceive and perceiving to learn. In R.D. Parke, P.A. Ornstein, J.J. Rieser, & C. Sahn-Waxler (Eds.) *A century of developmental psychology*, pp. 527-544. Washington, DC: American Psychological Association.

Plomin, R. (2004). *Nature and nurture: An introduction to human behavioral genetics.* Belmont, CA: Wadsworth Publishing.

Plomin, R., & Daniels, D. (1987). Why are children in the same family so different from one another? *Behavioral and Brain Sciences, 10,* 1-60.

Rankin, J.L. (2005). *Parenting experts: Their advice, the research, and getting it right.* Westport, CN: Praeger.

Rheingold, H. L (1985). The first twenty-five years of the Society for Research in Child Development. In A.B. Smuts & J.W. Hagen (Eds.) *History and research in child development.* Monographs of the Society for Research in Child Development, Serial No. 211, Vol. 50, Nos. 4-5, pp.126-140.

Rich Harris, J. (1998). *The Nurture assumption: Why children turn out the way they do.* New York: The Free Press.

Riegel, K.F. (1977). History of psychological gerontology. In J.E. Birren & K.W.

CHAPTER 12: SOCIAL PSYCHOLOGY AND PERSONALITY PSYCHOLOGY

A business man once stated 'there is nothing as practical as a good theory.'

KURT LEWIN (1943), P. 118.

There can be little doubt that the most important single influence on the development of social psychology came from outside the system itself. I am referring, of course, to the Second World War and the political upheavals in Europe that preceded it. If I were required to name one person who has had the greatest impact upon the field, it would have to be Adolph Hitler.

DORWIN CARTWRIGHT (1979), P. 84.

Both social psychology and personality psychology emerged early within the New Psychology as areas of interest, if not yet full-fledged subfields. By the 1920s, the two fields became closely linked, and remain so to this day.

The first social psychological experimental study is usually attributed to Triplett (1898), who studied the effects of the presence of other people on behavior, what is now called social facilitation. James Mark Baldwin also contributed to social psychology with a primarily developmental study (Baldwin, 1897). The most prominent social psychologist among the early American and European psychologists was William McDougall whose *An Introduction* to *Social Psychology* (1908/1921) went through many editions. The work is, if you will forgive a bit of understatement, light on empirical evidence. McDougall's approach was based heavily on the concept of social instincts and he sought to develop a biological approach to social psychology (Hilgard, 1987). The key word in the title is "introduction." McDougall felt that to understand the behavior of groups you must first understand the behavior of individuals. And the basis for understanding individual behavior was an understanding of human instinct (Innis, 2003). It was after laying the foundation for an instinctual theory of human behavior that McDougall focused on explicitly social psychological questions in *The Group Mind* (McDougall, 1920). McDougall's work and reputation were drowned in the rising tide of behaviorism (he called Watson an insane behaviorist and himself a sane behaviorist, *cf.* Watson & McDougall, 1929). McDougall also suffered merciless public attacks by the *New York Times* and other prominent mass media (Jones, 1987). McDougall's approach to social psychology was soon eclipsed by other approaches that were both more empirical and had a different theoretical orientation.

Prior to World War I, both William James and Sigmund Freud had addressed questions of personality. James used the word "personality" in his masterpiece *Principles of Psychology* only when discussing multiple personalities, but he did talk a great deal about the self and character, the latter term to be replaced in the 1920s by the more neutral and seemingly objective term personality (Hilgard, 1987). James' work was developed and expanded upon by his student Mary Whiton Calkins (1863-1930). Calkins' work did not have a lasting influence on the field, in part because she shifted her interests to philosophy, and in part because of the hostility and isolation she experienced from such leaders as E.B. Titchener and J.B. Watson.

Freud's ideas about the structure of personality, as well as the ideas of Jung and Adler, also were introduced into the U.S. prior to World War I, especially during Freud's 1909 visit to the U.S. These ideas too were to have an indirect influence on the emergence of personality psychology as a field, but before World War I, the influence was slight.

The study of personality emerged as a distinct subfield within psychology after World War I. From its very inception, the psychology of personality was closely connected to two other fields within the broader discipline: social psychology and clinical psychology. This connection was so close that at one point in the 1970s when personality psychology was experiencing its own crisis of confidence similar to that in social psychology (known in the field as "the decade of doubt"), a reviewer noted that personality psychology can be spelled one of two ways: c-l-i-n-i-c-a-l or s-o-c-i-a-l (Sechrest, 1976).

Historically, personality psychology has had a triple emphasis: an emphasis on the whole person, an emphasis on motivation, and an emphasis on individual differences (McAdams, 1997). This triple emphasis has in turn connected personality psychology to areas other than clinical and social, such as industrial psychology and psychometrics. These connections have been long the core of behaviorism and remained a behaviorist for his entire life (F. Allport, 1978). Floyd Allport's embrace of materialism and his anti-religious attitudes were fundamental differences between him and his brother Gordon. Floyd Allport's embrace of materialism and his criticism of religion were also very public. In a 1930 article in *Harper's Magazine*, then as now an important mass magazine, Floyd Allport described "Christian" as a "slogan of intolerable slavery of the spirit" (F. Allport, 1930, p. 365).

The behaviorist approach to social psychology did not go unchallenged from the Jamesian counterculture. In addition to the work of Gordon Allport (described later in this chapter), the two leading figures within social psychology's Jamesian counter- culture were Gardner Murphy (1895-1979) and Lois Barclay Murphy (1902-2003).

Gardner Murphy received his A.B. from Yale in 1916, began graduate work at Harvard, and then served in the U.S. military in World War I. After the war, he finished his Ph.D. at Columbia in 1923. He worked as a lecturer in psychology at Columbia from 1921 to 1925 while also holding a fellowship at Harvard from 1922 to 1925—he would commute between New York and Boston to carry out his responsibilities. Murphy, like James, believed in extrasensory perception and carried out research on paranormal phenomena; he went on to write a book on parapsychology and was president of the American Society for Psychical Research (Hilgard, 1987).

Gardner Murphy became ill in 1925 and gave up his Harvard fellowship. He worked as an instructor at Columbia from 1925 to 1929 and as an assistant professor from 1929 to 1940. In spite of being a semi-invalid, Murphy was enormously productive in this period, writing a number of important books in the history of psychology (G. Murphy, 1929), personality theory (G. Murphy & Jensen, 1932), and introductory psychology texts (G. Murphy, 1933; G. Murphy, 1935). He also directed Columbia University's program in social psychology, producing a number of outstanding Ph.D.s, including Rensis Likert, Muzafer Sherif, and Theodore Newcomb (Hilgard, 1987).

Gardner Murphy's most important work during this time was a social psychology text which he co-authored with his wife Lois Barclay Murphy (G. Murphy & L.B. Murphy, 1931). Their *Experimental Social Psychology* described both experimental studies and descriptive studies, including many from sociology.

In the second edition which they co-authored with Theodore Newcomb, who later went on to have a long and distinguished career, they added extensive material on the measurement of personality and attitudes (G. Murphy, L.B. Murphy, & Newcomb, 1937).

In 1940 Gardner Murphy took a position as full professor at the College of the City of New York where he did not have graduate students but he did teach undergraduate honors students. Gardner Murphy's advancement at Columbia had been painfully slow, in spite of his enormous productivity and his influence within the fields of social and personality psychology. The Murphys emphasized the notion of the developing person in the social world and rejected the materialism and reductionism of behaviorism. The tension between the behaviorist culture and the Jamesian counterculture within social psychology was to prove fruitful for the next two decades.

Descriptive and Experimental Social Psychology in the 1920s and 30s

With the publication of Floyd Allport's classic text in 1924 social psychology began a period of rapid growth similar to the growth exhibited by developmental psychology in the mid-1920s through the late 1930s. An illustration of that growth was the publication of a handbook on social psychology, edited by Carl Murchison, in 1935 (Murchison, 1935). Murchison, as you may recall, also edited the handbooks of child psychology produced in the 1930s.

Much of the early interest focused on the definition and measurement of attitudes. Rensis Likert (1932), in his doctoral dissertation under Gardner Murphy, developed an alterative approach to Thurstone's for the measurement of attitudes. Likert asked subjects to respond to different items along a five or seven point scale ranging from strongly agree to strongly disagree and then examined the item-total correlations (how well an item correlated with the total score). Those items that correlated well with the total were kept; those items that were not highly correlated were discarded. Through a process of successive pilot studies and refinement, an attitude scale could be developed. Likert's approach was to prove enormously useful to researchers, governments, and businesses in the coming decades.

By 1935, most theoretical debates concerning attitudes and opinions were resolved when Gordon Allport, Floyd's younger brother, published his chapter on attitudes in the Murchison handbook (G. Allport, 1935). Why the intense interest in attitudes by social psychologists in the 1920s and 1930s? Both political changes and technological changes fueled the interest. Politically, a new politics emerged during World War I based on the management of public opinion. In order to promote public support for the war, President Wilson established the Committee on Public Information (CPI), also known as the Creel Commission after its chair, George Creel (1876-1953). Creel had worked as a reporter and publisher before being appointed by President Wilson to chair the committee, which was created by Executive Order 2594 on April 13, 1917 and abolished by executive order on June 30, 1919 after the war ended. The committee was led by Creel as the chair, along with Secretary of State Robert Lansing, Secretary of War Lindley M. Garrison, and Secretary of the Navy Josephus Daniels. The CPI was divided into some 20 divisions and bureaus, specializing in newspapers, magazines, posters, and film. In addition to employing many talented writers and cartoonists, the CPI had 75,000 volunteers called "the Four-Minute Men" who gave pro-war speeches around the country. An estimated 755,190 speeches were given reaching millions of Americans (Creel, 1920).

Among the talented young people who worked for the CPI were two that later played an important role in politics and psychology: Walter Lippmann (1889-1974) and Edward Bernays (1891-1995). Bernays was the nephew of Sigmund Freud and went on to be the father of the public relations industry. Lippman became a prominent journalist and political theorist. Shortly after the war he wrote *Public Opinion* (Lippmann, 1922/2004). Coining the term "public opinion," Lippmann argued that knowledgeable policy elites could mold mass opinion. Effective manipulation required accurate measurement of attitudes and opinions. Enter social psychology.

The need to measure and manipulate attitudes and opinions intensified with the social unrest generated by the Great Depression and the need of politicians to win office. Public opinion polls originated in the U.S. around the time of the U.S. Civil War. Newspapers and magazines would conduct the polls, which were often inaccurate. Later, newspapers tried to overcome the inaccuracies by surveying large numbers of people. In the 1928, the influential *Literary Digest* poll predicted Hoover's presidential victory (the poll was only 4% off of

Hoover's final percentage) by surveying a large number of people. In 1932 the Digest repeated its success by predicting Franklin D. Roosevelt's coming 2% off of Roosevelt's final percentage of the popular vote. Expecting to duplicate its past success, the *Literary Digest* surveyed 10 million people for the 1936 election. The *Digest* predicted that Alf Landon would beat the controversial Roosevelt 57% to 43%. This time the *Digest* was way off.

Researchers such as the young George Gallup (1901-1984), who after receiving his Ph.D. in journalism (the title of his 1928 Ph.D. dissertation was *A New Technique for Objective Methods for Measuring Reader Interest in Newspapers*) taught journalism on short term appointments at Iowa, Drake, and Northwestern University, used a different methodology from the *Digest*, with substantially different predictions. In 1932, Gallup joined the advertising agency Young and Rubicam. At Young and Rubicam, Gallup conducted public opinion polls for the agency's clients and pioneered market research, an enterprise long advocated by advertising guru (and founder of behaviorism) John B. Watson. Gallup used the new methods of attitude and opinion measurement, paying special attention to sampling and survey construction, developed by social psychologists. In 1936, Gallup surveyed only 50,000 (one half of one percent of the *Literary Digest* sample) and successfully predicted the Roosevelt landslide. The embarrassment of the failed predictions helped doom the *Literary Digest*: In 1938 it merged with *Time Magazine*, a weekly that had been founded in 1923.

Gallup was not the only social scientist conducting scientific polls for the rich and powerful in 1936. Hadley Cantril (1906-1969) was also carrying out scientific polls, except Cantril's were not made public. Cantril is sometimes mistakenly referred to as a sociologist for his extensive contributions to the public opinion survey but, in fact, he was a social psychologist. Cantril began graduate school at Dartmouth under Gordon Allport. When Gordon Allport returned to Harvard in 1930 (Gordon Allport taught at Dartmouth from 1924 to 1930), Cantril went with him, completing his Ph.D. at Harvard. In 1935 Cantril and Allport published a pathbreaking study of the psychology of radio (Cantril & Allport, 1935). Commercial radio began in 1922 when the first commercial radio station, KDKA in Pittsburgh, started broadcasting. By 1935, over 70% of American homes had radios (many businesses also had them as well). The rate at which the new technology of radio permeated everyday life was faster than that of the desktop computer in the last decades of the 20th century. Because of the development of radio networks, as many as 20 million people could be listening to the same program at the same time on any given night. Cantril and Allport (1935) set out to map the "new mental world created by radio" (p. vii). The study was to be a model for later psychology studies of media effects, as well as a call to social psychologists to study real world problems that mattered to society (Pandora, 1998).

While the publication of a pathbreaking study at the age of 29 is impressive enough for a young social psychologist, the next year Cantril began a long term relationship with President Roosevelt. Cantril conducted private polls for the White House, analyzed the data, and advised the president on media strategy. Cantril and his polls became Roosevelt's "secret weapon that loosened the bonds previously preventing the executive branch from becoming the leadership vehicle" which Roosevelt desired (Eisinger & Brown, 1998).

Cantril had a long and productive career as a social psychologist who studied real world problems that had real world import. After the mass panic following the Orson Wells radio broadcast of H.G. Wells' *War of the Worlds* in 1939, Cantril treated the event as an experiment of nature and carried out a fascinating study of the power of mass media and the psychological reactions to it using a variety of kinds of interview data and unobtrusive measures such as newspaper reports and police reports (Cantril, 1940). He also studied the psychology of social movements (Cantril, 1941), religion (Cantril & Sherif, 1938), and the measurement of values (Cantril & Allport, 1933).

The desire to study real world problems of real import drove the organization of the Society for the Psychological Study of Social Issues (SPSSI) in 1936, the main vehicle for the Jamesian counter culture in the face of the behaviorist behemoth. The counter culture was especially strong in social psychology. So while much of academic psychology during the 1920s and 1930s turned to studying animals (mostly rats) in laboratories, social psychologists were studying religion, the effects of mass media, political movements, conflict, discrimination, propaganda, conflict resolution, and many other problems using both experimental methods and descriptive (primarily surveys and questionnaires) methods.

In the mid-1930s, the Gestalt psychologist Kurt Lewin (1890-1947) exploded on the scene of American psychology like a supernova. His impact was felt especially in social psychology (we have already examined his impact on cognitive psychology and developmental psychology in Chapters 10 and 11 respectively).

Lewin was born in Prussia, an area now part of Poland, in 1890 into a successful middle-class Jewish family. The family moved to Berlin when he was a teenager and he completed the Gymnasium in Berlin before entering the university to study medicine. Shortly after starting college Lewin joined the socialist movement and organized classes for working women and men. Lewin started college at the University of Freiburg but only stayed for one semester. He then transferred to the University of Munich, again staying only one semester. At the end of his first year, he returned to Berlin to study at the University of Berlin. While in college, Lewin also changed his program of study from medicine to biology, and then to psychology, where he studied with Carl Stumpf for his Ph.D. His doctorate was almost complete when World War I began and he was drafted into the German military. He served from 1914 to 1918, entering as a private and leaving with the rank of lieutenant. Lewin served most of the war on the German Western Front, in France where he was injured. Lewin's younger brother was killed during the war. For his courage on the battlefield Lewin was awarded the Iron Cross, the German military's highest medal for bravery. During the war he was also able to complete his Ph.D., which was awarded to him in 1916, to publish two scientific articles, and to marry (Marrow, 1969).

The immediate post-war period plunged Germany into civil war and revolution as the German Parliament, meeting in the town of Weimer (hence the appellation "Weimer Republic") tried to establish a democratic government. The socialists split with the more radical wing forming the German Communist Party, led by Rosa Luxemberg and Karl Liebknecht. The revolution soon broke out, centered in Berlin and Munich. The mainstream of the socialist party sided with the democratic government; meanwhile the revolution was put down by paramilitary death squads organized by conservative political groups and former military officers. Luxemberg and Liebknecht were kidnapped, tortured, and killed. The revolution collapsed by mid-1920 (Haffner, 1986).

Little is known of Lewin's life during this period, although it appears he sided with the mainstream of the socialist party. His experience before, during, and immediately after the war did seem to give him a life-long interest in social justice issues, a theme of his work for the rest of his life, as we shall see. By 1921 Lewin had secured a position as a privatdozent at the University of Berlin's Psychological Institute. Lewin was a second generation Gestalt psychologist and he differed in several ways from the three founders. Like the founders, Wertheimer, Koffka, and Köhler, he had broad interests which included a deep interest in philosophy and natural science. Unlike the founders, he was less interested in perception and cognition (although here too he shared an interest in these subfields) and more interested in social psychology, personality, and motivation. Because of these interests, Lewin is sometimes described as a "hot" Gestaltist compared to the founders, who were "cold" Gestaltists (Jones, 1985).

Soon after he began as a privatdozent he established a reputation as a stimulating teacher and passionate researcher. He attracted talented graduate students, many of whom were women and Jewish. Because Lewin treated all of his students with respect, he was an especially sought after professor by those who felt some form of discrimination. Among his first graduate students (in 1924) were Bluma Ziegarnik (whom we met in Chapter 10), and Tamara Dembo. Lewin loved to continue class discussions at the local cafés. He also worked long hours and this placed a strain on his marriage, which ended in divorce. Lewin remarried in 1929. During this time Lewin's reputation started to spread internationally and he was invited by Lewis Terman to spend six months as a visiting professor at Stanford University. Lewin's reputation was based on his work with American graduate students in Berlin and on the appearance of translations of some of his work. One of his first significant articles published in English appeared in the 1931 Murchison *Handbook of Child Psychology* (Lewin, 1931a), an article that proposed new approaches to the study of child development. Also in 1931, Lewin published a theoretical article laying out his philosophy of psychology, which he presented in terms of Aristotelian vs. Galilean modes of thought (Lewin, 1931b).

On his way to Stanford in 1932, Lewin stopped in England to visit with Sir Frederick Bartlett and to lecture. After crossing the Atlantic, Lewin stayed at

Columbia University, where he met Gardner Murphy. The two soon became friends and collaborators (Marrow, 1969).

During his time at Stanford, Lewin generated interest in his ideas and research studies but many students had difficulty with his English. Lewin worked hard at improving his language skills and soon mastered the language. On his way home to Germany, Lewin traveled by way of Japan where he lectured and met with former doctoral students from the Psychological Institute. Leaving Japan he traveled by railroad to Moscow, where he met his former student Bluma Ziegarnik and his friend Alexander Luria. Lewin's Russian friends warned him about the developing situation in Germany where Hitler had been made Chancellor. Lewin realized quickly that he could not stay in Germany any longer. He wired his friends Fritz and Grace Heider, looking for work in the U.S. In the meantime, he had to return to Germany to meet his wife and family. Lewin's second wife had become pregnant with their second child and she and her daughter returned to Germany via New York, arriving before Lewin (Marrow, 1969).

The situation in Germany had already worsened considerably. German doctors were not allowed to treat Jews, so Lewin's wife had difficulty finding a physician. In her home town of Sagan, where she was staying with her mother while she waited for Lewin to arrive from Russia, a Jewish doctor was beaten to death by a Nazi youth after contradicting the young man. Lewin refused to teach at a university that would not allow his children to attend college (the Nazis expelled Jewish students from all the universities in one of their early moves to grab power), and so resigned from the institute rather than be expelled from his post (Marrow, 1969).

Lewin soon received an offer to teach at Cornell on a temporary appointment in the Department of Home Economics. He and his family arrived in New York in the fall of 1933. While in New York City, Rensis Likert had lunch with Lewin. Likert later recalled that Lewin predicted that the German people would not overthrow the new dictator. Only a major war that Germany lost, Lewin predicted to Likert, would remove Hitler from power. In the fall of 1935, Lewin took a permanent position at the University of Iowa, where he carried out major work until he moved to M.I.T. in 1944 to found the Research Center for Group Dynamics. The year 1944 was one of triumph and tragedy for Lewin. In addition to moving to M.I.T. where he directed his own well-funded and well-staffed research center, he organized the Commission on Community Interrelations (C.C.I.) to study ways to deal with anti-Semitism in the U.S. and improve relations between Jews and non-Jews. In addition to serving on a number of government committees contributing research to the war effort, Lewin advised the O.S.S. on psychological warfare against Germany. Few details are known of Lewin's work for the O.S.S., the predecessor to the C.I.A. (Marrow, 1969). Lewin's professional triumphs were overshadowed by the loss of his mother, who was killed in the Nazi death camps in 1944. Lewin had spent many years trying to get his mother out of Germany, to no avail (Marrow, 1969). Lewin died in February 1947 of a heart attack. He was 57 and near the peak of his professional productivity.

In many ways, Lewin was the complete psychologist: an outstanding researcher, an outstanding theorist, and an outstanding teacher and organizational leader. His empirical contributions were easier to assimilate into American psychology than the theoretical contributions, which required an understanding of philosophy and physics to appreciate entirely. His first major book in English was a presentation of his Gestalt theory of personality, *A Dynamic Theory of Personality* (Lewin, 1935), which we shall return to later in the chapter. His second book, published the following year, laid out his topological approach to psychology (Lewin, 1936).

Lewin's most famous study, one which nicely illustrates his conceptual approach, is the study of aggression and group climate (Lewin, Lippitt, & White, 1939) which was part of a longer series of experiments on the effects of group structures and leadership styles on children's behavior (*e.g.*, Lewin & Lippitt, 1938; Lippitt, 1940). In these studies Lewin and his colleagues created particular kinds of groups by having group leaders that behaved in particular ways (authoritarian, democratic, or laissez-faire). They found, for instance, that authoritarian groups tended to scapegoat their members, and that productivity in authoritarian groups decreased dramatically as soon as the leader left.

Lewin is sometimes considered the father of social psychology, although that honor more properly belongs to Floyd Allport. While Lewin may not be the father of social psychology, he certainly was the most significant leader of the field in the last 100 years. How and why did Lewin come to exercise such an important role within social psychology? Without a doubt, Lewin was hardworking (you could say he worked himself to death) and productive, publishing over 80 articles and eight books (Marrow, 1969). He also combined elegant and creative empirical studies with a theoretical approach (field theory) that was developed out of Gestalt psychology. This theory looked beyond the individual and beyond isolated responses to complex individuals embedded in a complex social field. Lewin also combined a passion for basic research with a passion for applied research, making social psychology both scientific and socially relevant. In addition he created entire new areas of research within social psychology, such as group dynamics and action research, and he exercised leadership in the field by teaching and inspiring a gifted group of graduate students and colleagues.

But Lewin was also the right person at the right time (Steiner, 1979), coming to America at a time when the Jamesian counterculture within social psychology and personality research was ascendant. The desire for a science of psychology for society's sake (Bruner & Allport, 1940) was strong and the Topology Group that he organized included Jerome Bruner, a young graduate student under Gordon Allport (and later a leader of the Cognitive Revolution), Gardner Murphy and Lois Barcley Murphy, and "renegade" behaviorist Edward C.Tolman (Marrow, 1969). Lewin's theory also had a strong affinity to much of the work of the later functionalists, especially John Dewey. This similarity was recognized by the Jamesian counterculture early and was acknowledged by none other than Gordon Allport (Allport, 1948). Lewin's empirical work and theoretical ideas electrified the large, anti-behaviorist current within American psychology. In the process, he shaped the history of social psychology more than any other scientist.

Social Psychology Goes To War

On the eve of World War II social psychology was a small but dynamic subfield within psychology, confined geographically to major schools in urban areas on the east coast (Harvard, Yale, Columbia, Princeton) and the Midwest (University of Michigan). The lone other major outpost was the University of Iowa under the leadership of Kurt Lewin (Jones, 1998).

While World War II did not create social psychology, which had a long record of empirical and conceptual achievement in the 15 years prior to the war, the war did allow social psychologists to demonstrate the value of their empirical methods and theories to the ruling elites in the U.S. Social psychologists were deeply involved in the war effort (as were other kinds of psychologists, such as the perceptual psychologist James Gibson) in a variety of important roles.

Rensis Likert, for instance, headed a division (the Division of Intensive Surveys) of the Office of War Information, a group which carried out surveys of civilians and military personnel to aid government planners. Likert employed a large number of social psychologists, as well as other social scientists (Hilgard, 1987).

The U.S. military directly employed social psychologists to investigate propaganda, psychological warfare, troop morale, and other important issues. Some of these studies carried out by the military were later published in what is often called the American Soldier Volumes (Hovland, Lumsdaine, & Sheffield, 1949; Stouffer, Lumsdaine, Lumsdain, Williams, Smith, Janis, Star, & Cottrell, 1949a; Stouffer, Suchman, DeVinney, Star, & Williams, 1949b; Stouffer, Guttman, Suchman, Lazarfeld, Star, & Clausen, 1950). The variety of topics covered is impressive, from the seemingly trivial (which articles were preferred in *Yank* magazine; which programs troops preferred on the radio) to the obviously important (how to demobilize the troops; which types of propaganda work best with the American people). By the end of the war, over 500,000 people had taken part in the social psychological research carried out by the military (Hilgard, 1987).

The Growth Of Social Psychology After World War 2

During World War II, social psychology had demonstrated its value to the federal government, big business, and foundations concerned with social problems. The postwar period witnessed a dramatic expansion in the funding of social psychology research, as well as a geographic expansion in the universities offering courses and graduate programs in the field (Jones, 1998).

The rapid institutional and financial expansion of social psychology was also accompanied by numerous empirical advances, many of which were extensions of work carried out before or during the war. Carl Hovland

(1912-1961), who had carried out many of the studies of persuasion and propaganda during the war, continued his research on persuasion and attitude change with rigorous experimental studies (Hovland, Janis, & Kelly, 1953). Hovland was a behaviorist social psychologist at Yale where he was a protégé of Clark Hull. His experimental studies of sender characteristics, message characteristics, and recipient characteristics shifted the attention of social psychology away from attitude measurement, which had become a well-developed technology, toward persuasion and attitude change. Hovland also started a shift toward increasingly rigorous and controlled studies. From the Jamesian counter culture, Gordon Allport (G. Allport, 1954a) published his highly influential and still invaluable *The Nature of Prejudice*, a work that demonstrated the social psychological roots of prejudice and suggested ways to overcome it. The same year a new handbook of social psychology was published (Lindzey, 1954) that demonstrated the significant empirical advances the field had made since the 1935 handbook edited by Murchison (Murchison, 1935). The advances in the 1950s laid the groundwork for the enormously productive period of the 1960s and early 1970s. Much of the work in the 1950s was influenced by Gestalt psychology.

Solomon Asch And Studies In Conformity

Kurt Lewin profoundly shaped social psychology from the mid-1930s until his death. After he died, his students continued his efforts, making Lewin perhaps the most influential social psychologist of the last century. Lewin was not, however, the only Gestalt psychologist to shape social psychology. In the 1950s social psychology benefited from the contributions of an American Gestalt psychologist: Solomon Asch.

Solomon E. Asch (1907-1996) was born in Warsaw, Poland, and emigrated to the U.S. in 1920 with his family. He attended City College, graduating in 1928. He attended graduate school at Columbia University where he carried out research on children's test scores and learning. With Ph.D. in hand in 1932 he began work at Brooklyn College. Soon after he met the Gestalt psychologist Max Wertheimer, then teaching at the New School for Social Research, who exerted a major intellectual influence on Asch. Asch rejected behaviorism, the tradition he had been trained in at Columbia, and embraced Gestalt psychology. When Wertheimer died in 1943, Asch replaced him as a professor of psychology at the New School (McCauley & Rozin, 2003). In 1947 Asch moved to Swarthmore College, where he worked until 1966. Also at Swarthmore was Wolfgang Köhler. Swarthmore became the intellectual center of Gestalt Psychology in the U.S., and much of Asch's work at Swarthmore focused on social psychology. In 1966 Asch moved to Rutgers University and turned his attention to cognition, his focus for the rest of his career. He ended his career at the University of Pennsylvania, retiring in 1979 (McCauley & Rozin, 2003).

Asch's first significant contribution to social psychology was an investigation of impression formation (Asch, 1946). Asch hypothesized that the impressions we form of other people are gestalts. Asch gave his subjects a short list of traits (intelligent, skillful, industrious, warm, determined, practical, and cautious) and asked them to write a brief description of the person, and then to check off the traits that described this person from a list of 18 pairs. His subjects performed this task without any difficulty. In a comparison condition he substituted cold for warm in the stimulus list. The results were dramatic. The descriptions produced by his subjects and the traits they checked-off changed. Asch concluded that our impressions of an individual's personality is a gestalt and the meaning of a trait, such as intelligence, varies with the overall gestalt. A person with a cold intelligence is very different from one with a warm intelligence. He also concluded that even a short list of traits implies a richer, more extensive network of traits. Asch's work was an enormous stimulus to studies of impression formation and to studies of people's implicit theories of personality (McCauley & Rozin, 2003).

Asch next turned his attention to research that showed people evaluate statements on the basis of their source, not their content. A statement is evaluated positively, for instance, if it is attributed to a respected figure, and evaluated negatively if it is attributed to an unpopular person. Asch (1948) argued that people are not as irrational as the research suggested. By re-analyzing previous research and carrying out his own experiments, he showed that the individual again forms a gestalt understanding of statements based on both the content and the person making the statements. For ambiguous statements, the person uses knowledge of the speaker to interpret the meaning of the message. Again, Asch showed that the person was an active interpreter of their world and formed social gestalts (McCauley & Rozin, 2003).

Finally, in his most important contribution to social psychology, Asch examined conformity to group judgments (Asch, 1952; Asch, 1956). In the justly famous Asch paradigm, a subject enters a lab along with six other subjects for a study of perception. The subjects are shown a target line and asked to match it to one of three possible lines. Subjects report their judgments out loud to the experimenter and in order. Six of the subjects are actually confederates of the experimenter; only the seventh subject is a genuine subject. The genuine subject is placed sixth in the row of seven subjects. On seven of the 12 trials the confederates give a false answer. Asch wanted to know what the genuine subject would do when the social information contradicted the information from his or her senses. Asch found that only 20% of his subjects resisted conforming on all trials. The other 80% conformed at on at least one trial. Asch also found stable personal differences: those who conformed on the first trial were more likely to conform on later trials. Those who resisted on the first trial were more likely to resist on later trials. Asch also found that his subjects conformed for two different reasons: some thought that the group must be right while others, the majority, simply did not want to stick out. Finally, the overall rate of conformity across all subjects and all experimental trials was 33%. The tendency to not want to stick out may have been heightened in Asch's studies by the fact that the groups were made up of people who knew each other and in some cases were friends. While many social psychologists interpreted Asch's results as evidence of the irrational and sheep-like character of human beings, Asch viewed the results as positive. The overall rate of conforming was only 33% and the tendency to conform fosters group cooperation and cohesion (McCauley & Rozin, 2003).

In addition to his empirical contributions, Asch wrote an influential textbook on social psychology (Asch, 1952) that thoughtfully criticized behaviorist and psychoanalytic approaches to social psychology, accepted that genetics must play a role in social behavior, and argued for the importance of the social world in understanding human beings. He also argued for experimental methods that were rigorous but did not strip the complexity of the real social world out of the laboratory. His studies of conformity were examples of this rigorous experimental approach to behavior in a complex social world

(McCauley & Rozin, 2003) and became a model for many subsequent social psychological research studies.

Leon Festinger And Cognitive Dissonance

Leon Festinger (1919-1989), one of Lewin's many influential students, introduced the theory of cognitive dissonance in the mid-1950s, shifting the attention of social psychologists back toward the cognitive underpinnings of social behavior. Festinger took his B.S. at City College in New York in 1939 and his Ph.D. under Lewin in 1942 at the University of Iowa. From 1943 to 1945 Festinger worked with the Committee on Selection and Training of Aircraft Pilots. When Lewin moved to M.I.T. in 1945 to establish the Research Center for Group Dynamics, Festinger joined him. When the center moved to the University of Michigan, Festinger followed, but soon moved to the University of Minnesota in 1951. He moved again in 1955 to Stanford University where he stayed until 1989. Festinger's early work focused on interpersonal communication and decision-making in small groups. His overall perspective was shaped by both Gestalt Psychology and Lewin's interest in group dynamics (Sheehy, Chapman, & Conroy, 1997a).

Festinger's first major theoretical contribution was a theory of social comparison, in which he proposed that people make sense of themselves by comparing themselves to others. Individuals, Festinger suggested, have a bias toward upward comparisons (comparing themselves to people who are slightly better) and a bias toward comparing themselves to similar others (Festinger, 1954).

While at the University of Minnesota, Festinger carried out an observational study of a religious cult that believed that the world was going to end and aliens would come to rescue the faithful. Infiltrating the cult while posing as true believers, Festinger and his co-researchers documented the reactions of the cult members when their predicted end of the world failed to materialize: the cult members believed that their faith had saved the world and they began a campaign to recruit more members (Festinger, Riecken, & Schachter, 1956).

While Festinger's study of the cult was both illuminating and clever, it was the broader theoretical concept that explained the cult's behavior that was of real interest to him. He presented this explanation in his next book, *The Theory of Cognitive Dissonance* (Festinger, 1957). The theory is elegant in its simplicity. An attitude, belief, or action can be relevant or irrelevant to one another. If they are relevant to one another, they can be either consonant (meaning compatible with one another) or dissonant (meaning incompatible with one another). The state of holding dissonant attitudes, beliefs, or actions creates discomfort and an urge to reduce that dissonance, especially when the beliefs or attitudes are important to the person. There are several ways to reduce dissonance: changing attitudes, changing behaviors, or de-emphasizing the importance of a previous significant belief. Since behaviors, especially behaviors that have already been carried out publicly, are hard to change, individuals often alter their attitudes and beliefs to reduce dissonance.

Festinger followed up the presentation of his theory with a clever experiment (Festinger & Carlsmith, 1959) showing that subjects that carried out a very boring task for little reward came to believe that the task was interesting. The impact of Festinger's two empirical studies (the participant observation of the religious cult and his experimental study of cognitive dissonance) along with his theory generated considerable interest in the 1960s. Numerous studies of the phenomenon were carried out. While a number of empirical and theoretical problems emerged with the theory, it had a significant impact on social psychology by shifting the focus of social psychologists to cognitive processes that lay at the root of social behavior. Festinger spent much of the 1960s studying cognitive dissonance. In the 1970s and 1980s his attention shifted to the study of perception (Sheehy, Chapman, & Conroy, 1997a).

Asch and Festinger were not the only Gestalt psychologists to shape social psychology in the postwar period. Fritz Heider (1896-1988) was born in Vienna and received his Ph.D. at the Karl-Franzens University in Graz. He then studied in Berlin at the Psychology Institute with Köhler, Wertheimer, and Lewin. Heider moved to the U.S. and worked at Smith College (where he taught Eleanor Jack, later Eleanor Gibson, and was a colleague of both Kurt Koffka and James Gibson). Heider helped his friend Kurt Lewin come to the U.S. and along with Grace Heider (Fritz's wife and collaborator) translated Lewin's early work into English for publication in the U.S. In 1947, Heider moved to Kansas University at the invitation of another Lewinian (as followers of Lewin were called) Roger Barker (Sheehy, Chapman, & Conroy, 1997b). In 1958, Heider published his most important work, *The Psychology of Interpersonal Relations* (Heider, 1958). Heider's work helped intensify the interest in cognitive processes, especially attributions, within social psychology.

A short chapter on the history of social psychology cannot do justice to the influence and dominance of the Lewinians during the 1950s and 1960s. In addition to Festinger, Alex Bavelas, Morton Deutsch, Doran Cartwright, John R.P. French, Harold H. Kelly, John Thibaut, Stanley Schacter, Alvin F. Zander, and Ronald Lippitt all made substantial contributions to the study of groups, conflict and cooperation, cognitive processes, and other areas within social psychology

While social psychology in the 1950s was dominated by the Lewinians, other members of the Jamesian counterculture continued to make important contributions as well. The most important member of the counterculture who remained active in research, in addition to Gordon Allport himself, was probably Muzafer Sherif (1906-1988), who received his B.A. at the International College of Turkey, an M.A. from the University of Istanbul in 1929, an M.A. from Harvard in 1932, and a Ph.D. in social psychology from Columbia in 1935 (Sheehy, Chapman, & Conroy, 1997d). Sherif was one of Gardner Murphy's students and collaborated on many research projects with Hadley Cantril, one of Gordon Allport's students. In the early 1950s Sherif and his collaborators carried out a large field experiment of intergroup conflict and cooperation (Sherif, Harvey, White, Hood, & Sherif, 1956/1961). Known as the Robber's Cave experiment for the state park near the camp where the experiment was conducted, Sherif recruited 22 boys to participate in a summer camp where he first created conditions that produced conflict and then tried to create conditions that produced cooperation.

During this period the behaviorist influence continued to shape the field as well. More and more of the studies were experimental; fewer were descriptive. And increasingly, the experimental studies were more and more rigorous. The shift from descriptive research to experimental research, paralleled by a shift from the group's influence on the individual (as seen in Sherif's work and the work of Asch) to individual variables such as cognition, took place gradually over the 1950s as social psychology expanded. The Jamesian counterculture, as represented by the Murphys and by Allport, was getting older. Their emphasis on the valuable but somewhat limited role of experimentation was lost. Lewin, a champion of experimental methods, insisted that experiments reflect the impact of the social psychological Gestalt on individual behavior. Lewin also rejected the primacy of statistical analysis as a road toward the development of theories and laws of human behavior. Lewin's students sometimes failed to understand his philosophy of science and his emphasis on the group. This was especially true of Festinger, who criticized Lewin's experimental work as sloppy (Festinger, 1953), emphasized the study of individual variables, and employed traditional statistical significance tests (MacMartin & Winston, 2000). As an interesting aside, Festinger's attack on Lewin's sloppy methods appeared in a book he edited with Daniel Katz, Floyd Allport's student and one of the leading behaviorist social psychologists.

The Golden Age of Social Psychology: The 1960s and early 1970s

The intellectual achievements and material expansion of the 1950s produced a period of almost 12 years of enormous intellectual achievements during the 1960s and early 1970s. This period has sometimes been called the Golden Age of Social Psychology, a period of productivity and self-confidence, before the field suffered an intellectual and institutional crisis in the 1970s.

The Golden Age witnessed both the material transformation of the field and its intellectual coming of age. Money flowed from government agencies, foundations, and corporations. The number of graduate students and programs multiplied to such an extent that by 1979, 90 percent of all social psychologists who had ever lived were alive and working that year (Cartwright, 1979). Another indication of the growth of the field was the appearance of new scientific journals, such as the *Journal of Personality and Social Psychology*, which began publication in 1965, and the *Journal of Experimental Social Psychology*, which also began publication in 1965.

During the Golden Age women also began to make considerable gains: their numbers in graduate programs started to increase in the 1960s and their presence as researchers and faculty members started to increase as well. Much of this increase resulted from, according to Ellen Berscheid, who is one of the early women social psychologists (she received her Ph.D. in social psychology in 1965), the support and mentoring of women by the male leaders of the field.

Many of the members of SPSSI were pro-women's rights. They treated their female graduate students with the same respect and support as they treated their male students at a time when this was, as Berscheid pointed out, neither politically correct nor popular (Berscheid, 1992). Another clear indication of the progress women made as leaders in the field was their representation as editors in the various handbooks of social psychology. In the 1968 handbooks (Lindzey & Aronson, 1968) both editors were male, only two of the 70 authors were female (approximately 3%), and none of the women were first authors of a chapter. In the 1998 handbooks (Gilbert, Fiske, & Lindzey, 1998), one of the three editors was female, 20 of the 66 authors were female (approximately 30%), and nine of the 37 first authors are women (approximately 24% of the total). In a little over 30 years, women had made substantial progress in overcoming the marginalization pervasive in earlier generations within psychology.

The breadth and depth of Golden Age social psychology is revealed through an examination of the 1968 Handbook of Social Psychology (Lindzey & Aronson, 1968) which had five volumes, a significant expansion over the 1954 handbook which only had two volumes (Lindzey, 1954). The 1968 edition devoted the first volume to theoretical perspectives, including behaviorism, psychoanalysis, Lewinian field theory, and cognitive theories. The second volume was devoted to various research methods. The third volume focused on individuals in a social context, covering such topics as attitudes and attitude change, person perception, personality, and socialization. The fourth volume focused on group phenomena, including group problem solving, leadership, communication, and collective behavior. The final volume was devoted to applied social psychology and included chapters on prejudice and ethnic relations, mass media, industrial psychology, education, economics, politics, mental health, and religion. The breadth and depth of the handbook chapters was impressive. The handbook was a tribute to the record of achievement during the approximately 44 years since the publication of Floyd Allport's *Social Psychology*.

Obedience To Authority: Exemplar Of Golden Age Research

One of the most famous and important experimental studies of the Golden

Age was carried out by Stanley Milgram (1933-1984) in the early 1960s at Yale University. In this series of experiments, Milgram asked subjects to give electric shocks to a "learner" who was actually a confederate of Milgram's, when the leaner did not respond correctly in a memory test. The experimental set-up was actually part of a deception; Milgram's true focus was on obedience to authority. Before discussing the experiments in detail, we must know a little about the experimenter and the events that prompted him to carry out the experiments.

Stanley Milgram was born in New York City, in the Bronx, of eastern European Jewish immigrants. Stanley's father was a baker. Growing up in the Great Depression and reaching adolescence during World War II, Milgram was, not surprisingly, interested in political science and international relations. He majored in political science and international relations at Queens College in New York City, which he attended on scholarship. During the summer of his junior year he toured Spain, Italy, and France on a motorized bike. He spent a month in France, where he studied French at the Sorbonne. Milgram was later to achieve fluency in French, and was often interviewed in the language on French radio and television. Milgram's father died of a heart attack during his senior year of college, a time of transition for Milgram. His interests shifted from international relations and political science to psychology. He applied and received a Ford Foundation fellowship for graduate study in psychology. His efforts to get into Harvard's graduate program failed however: Harvard rejected him for lack of preparation in psychology. He did receive an encouraging letter from Gordon Allport, who encouraged him to take summer classes in psychology and apply as a special student at Harvard. After a year of coursework at Harvard, Allport felt that Milgram would be accepted into the graduate program. This was the start of a beautiful friendship. Allport was Milgram's friend, mentor, and advisor at Harvard. While at Harvard, Milgram also studied with Jerome Bruner (he took a course on cognitive processes with Bruner) and Roger Brown, a social psychologist who was shifting his research toward linguistics. Bruner and Brown also became longtime friends and mentors to Milgram (Blass, 2004).

During Milgram's second year as a graduate student at Harvard (1954-55 was his first year as a "special student" while 1955-56 was his second year), Allport assigned him to work as a teaching assistant and later as a research assistant to Solomon Asch. Asch was spending a year at Harvard while Bruner was on sabbatical at Cambridge University. Milgram worked as Asch's research assistant for some of Asch's studies of conformity (Asch, 1956). Asch was very impressed with Milgram's work and praised him highly. Asch, along with Allport, was to exert a lasting intellectual influence on Milgram. Unlike his relationship with Allport, however, Milgram's relationship with Asch was not as amicable (Blass, 2004).

For his doctoral dissertation, Milgram proposed an ambitious cross-cultural experimental study of conformity using the Asch paradigm. This was the first cross-cultural experimental study of "national character," a topic of great interest to Allport, Brown, and others. Allport chaired the dissertation committee and Milgram spent a year and a half collecting data in Norway and France. In each country he tested subjects in five experimental conditions. He also paid close attention to ethical issues, carefully debriefing his subjects after the experiments, a practice that was highly unusual at the time (Blass, 2004).

Milgram returned from Europe with his data, but without having written up his thesis, in 1959. He initially planned on spending his last year at Harvard leisurely writing his thesis and looking for work, but near the end of the summer he received a letter from Solomon Asch, offering him a job to help Asch complete a book on conformity. Asch was now spending time at Princeton University's Institute for Advanced Study. Milgram's year at Princeton was lonely and frustrating for him. He felt exploited by Asch, who did not allow him time to write his own dissertation and who did not give Milgram any credit for his work on the book. He did manage to finish his dissertation during the last week of March, 1960. He soon had two job offers: one for a research fellowship at Bruner and Miller's new Center for Cognitive Studies; the other for an assistant professorship at Yale University. Milgram knew that to be successful at Yale, he would have to develop an important and interesting research program. He corresponded with Allport about possible research topics during the early summer of 1960. By the end of June, when he was leaving Princeton, he had informed Asch that he intended to study obedience to authority (Blass, 2004).

When Milgram arrived in New Haven in the fall of 1960, he immediately set to work developing studies of obedience. He also carried out a study of the effects of mescaline on aesthetic judgments. Milgram had experimented with drugs at Harvard (including peyote) and continued drug use at Yale. He used marijuana, amphetamines, and cocaine--the former socially and the latter two to overcome his severe writer's block, a problem he suffered from for most of his life (Blass, 2004).

Milgram wanted to carry out a study that focused on an important problem, in a rigorous laboratory setting that was simultaneously phenomenologically real to his subjects. To do this he built upon the Asch paradigm. A subject entered the lab and was told that he (in the initial conditions, all of the subjects were men) would be part of a study of the effects of punishment on learning. The subjects drew lots to see who would be a teacher and who the learner. But the drawing was rigged, and in fact the person who became the learner was a confederate of Milgram's. The learner was then hooked up to electrodes and was given an electric shock by the teacher (the real subject of the experiment) every time the learner made a mistake. The learner made mistakes on a pre-arranged schedule. The purpose of the experiment was to see how many subjects would obey the experimenter under varying conditions. Milgram varied the distance between the teacher and learner (from next to each other to in separate rooms where they could not see or hear each other, except at a pre-arranged level where the learner pounded on the wall and asked to be let out); the distance between the experimenter, who was the authority figure, and the teacher (from in the same room to in different rooms with the directions given by a tape recorder). Milgram also tested obedience in group situations, where all the subjects were confederates save one, and where the group either obeyed the experimenter or disobeyed the experimenter at a pre-determined point (Milgram, 1974).

Milgram found very high levels of obedience, a finding which surprised him and shocked most everyone else who heard about the study. His findings quickly generated controversy, as people, including many psychologists, criticized his methods or his ethics. The findings have proven invaluable both for psychology and for other fields, such as the historical study of the holocaust. Milgram quickly became a star. After three years at Yale, he was offered a job at Harvard, where he was eager to return. He started as an untenured faculty member at Harvard in July 1963, but controversy dogged him there. While he shifted his research focus away from obedience, he was considered too controversial to be given tenure. Disappointed, he left Harvard in 1967 to take a full professorship in psychology at the Graduate Center of the City University of New York (CUNY). While his salary nearly doubled in his new job, he was sad to leave Harvard (Blass, 2004).

Milgram's study is not just the most well-known of the Golden Age experiments, it is also prototypical. The study involved deception, employed rigorous operational definitions, and dealt with a basic social process: obedience to authority. It also had relevance to current social issues (in this instance, an explanation for the Nazi holocaust) and revealed surprising and unexpected facts about human nature. The study was clearly influenced by the work of Gestalt theorists. (Asch influenced the experimental design and Lewin's field theory influenced Milgram's explanation in terms of psychological distance from authority to subject and subject to victim.)

In spite of his fall from Harvard, Milgram established himself as a leading social psychologist. One indication of his status was his co-authorship of a chapter in the 1968 edition of the *Handbook of Social Psychology* (Milgram & Toch, 1968) on collective behavior. Before his death of a heart attack in 1984 (at the age of 51), he also directed and produced several films (including *On Obedience* in 1965, a documentary of his experiments showing actual footage of some of the experimental conditions, and *The City and the Self* in 1972); pioneered the study of the cognitive maps of urban areas (Milgram, Greenwald, Kessler, McKenna, & Waters,1972); developed the study of the social psychology of urban environments (Milgram, 1970); and explored normative behavior in urban environments (Milgram & Sabini, 1978). In addition, he edited a series of his studies and essays into a textbook presenting a coherent approach to social psychology (Milgram, 1977) and co-authored a monograph containing field experiments of television and antisocial behavior (Milgram & Shotland, 1973).

Milgram was a gifted experimentalist who rejected theory. His rejection of theory resulted in criticism, especially from behavioristic social psychologists who felt that all studies should be based on theory (Blass, 2004). Milgram's position as a leader within psychology was also limited by some of his own professional missteps. Milgram had difficulty writing for scientific publications. Instead of publishing his brilliant doctoral dissertation in a psychology journal, he published it in *Scientific American* (Milgram, 1961), a prestigious outlet but not as significant as a peer-reviewed psychology journal. The studies of obedience to authority were published in four psychology journals (Milgram 1963; Milgram, 1964; Milgram, 1965a; Milgram, 1965b) but the complete description of all of his studies did not appear until 1974, when he published a book- length description of his experiments along with his conceptual analysis (Milgram, 1974).

Milgram mismanaged his career in other ways as well. He developed an innovative research technique for assessing opinions on controversial topics. The technique, known as the lost letter technique, was first presented in the *Public Opinion Quarterly,* a scientific journal read by pollsters and sociologists (Milgram, Mann, & Harter, 1965) and then in a popular magazine, *Psychology Today* (Milgram, 1969). He also carried out several studies on the small world problem using an innovative descriptive method based on chain letters. These studies, too, he first presented in *Psychology Today* (Milgram, 1967) and only later did he publish them in scientific journals (Korte & Milgram, 1970; Travers & Milgram, 1969). Writing for popular magazines and non-psychology journals is a way to exercise leadership in the field of psychology, but it is not a substitute for publishing research in scholarly journals within the field.

Milgram's professional missteps, however, were not the main reason for his fall from Harvard and his lack of recognition as a leading social psychologist. The main reason was the counter-intuitive findings about human nature that Milgram's obedience studies revealed. Many had difficulty accepting the message. Instead, they tried to kill the messenger.

Six Degrees Of Separation

Stanley Milgram has had a greater impact on popular culture than any other social psychologist. His obedience studies have inspired a murder mystery (*Dying by Degrees* by Eileen Coughlan), a rock song (*We Do What We are Told (Milgram's 37)* by Peter Gabriel), at least four plays (*The Dogs of Pavlov* by Dannie Abse, *Tolliver's Trick* by Anthony Cardinale, *Mosaic* by Daphne Hull, and *One more volt* by John P. Lavin), and two full length movies, one in English (*The Tenth*

Level starring William Shatner as Milgram) and one in French (*I ...comme Icare* starring Yves Montand). Milgram would no doubt be pleased with this, as he was both a lover of film and theater and he saw an affinity between the arts and sciences. Milgram stated that "good experiments, like good drama, embody verities" (Blass, 2004, p. 263).

The obedience studies were not the only experiments to influence popular culture. His study of the small world problem, the fact that we seem to meet people who know people we know more often than expected by chance, led to his discovery that in an infinite population that is structured, a finite number of people link us to everyone else in the population. In his studies, Milgram found that on average in the U.S., we are linked to everyone else by six degrees of separation (Korte & Milgram, 1970; Travers & Milgram, 1969).

The notion of six degrees of separation was incorporated into the 1990 play by John Guare entitled, fittingly enough, *Six Degrees of Separation*. In 1993 the play was turned into a movie starring Will Smith and Donald Sutherland (Blass, 2004). The notion of six degrees of separation has also inspired a game, Six Degrees of Kevin Bacon. The purpose of the game is to connect any actor to Kevin Bacon through actors that have been in movies together.

Milgram's influence on popular culture is just one facet of his influence: outside of psychology he has also influenced the study of human evil, historical studies of the holocaust, work in mathematics on the small world problem and network structures, and in sociology. Milgram's legacy is rich and widespread.

The Crisis Of Confidence And The End Of The Golden Age

Beginning in the late 1960s and extending through the 1970s, social psychology was convulsed with self-criticism, a period that soon received the label "the crisis in social psychology." In some ways reflecting the social unrest in the broader society in the late 1960s and early 70s, the crisis consisted of a series of critiques or attacks on certain aspects of social psychology.

It is typical in science for scientists to criticize one or more aspect of the content and concepts in a field. What distinguished the crisis of confidence from the normal process of criticism was the extent and vehemence of the criticisms. There are at least four different strands in the crisis: the lack of ethics, the lack of theoretical progress, the lack of external validity, and the lack of science for society's sake. The criticisms of a lack of ethics started with Milgram's studies on obedience and continued until the 1973 APA ethical guidelines were adopted. The lack of theoretical progress, a criticism raised by researchers much influenced by Thomas Kuhn's notion of paradigms, seems to have subsided by the late 1970s without any resolution. At its most extreme form, these criticisms questioned the very possibility of a science of social psychology. Some of the lack of theoretical progress was attributed to the experimental situations themselves, which were deemed artificial. These artificial situations were not thought to produce results that were valid in the real world (hence lacking in external validity). Finally, the field was criticized for having abandoned the idea of science for society's sake advocated by Allport and the Jamesian counter culture and by Kurt Lewin and his followers. The majority of social psychologists seemed to have ignored these criticisms, although a number of changes were made. In addition to adopting ethical standards, social psychologists increasingly turned their attention to applied areas (in part a consequence of declining funds for pure research) and again devoted efforts to descriptive studies, similar to those carried out in the 1930s and 1940s.

Social Psychology Goes Cognitive: The 1970s to the Present

Historically, social psychology had a long interest in cognitive variables, such as attitudes and opinions. This interest was strengthened throughout the 1950s with the study of cognitive dissonance and attributions. Social psychological research indirectly contributed to the cognitive revolution but not significantly. When the cognitive revolution swept through psychology, it was embraced by social psychologists more readily than by others. By 1979, the vast majority of work in social psychology focused on cognitive processes or the outcome of cognitive processes (Cartwright, 1979). This included work in social judgments, identity, persuasion, stereotyping, and social comparison, as well as many of the other traditional areas of concern.

The emphasis on cognition was partly a result of necessity. Cognitive studies can be done relatively inexpensively, with computers, paper, and pencils. With the declining support, more expensive or advanced equipment was often beyond the reach of social psychologists without a generous source of funds.

But social psychologists also, it seems, made lemonade out of lemons. In response to the criticism during the crisis of confidence, and the lack of money for basic research, they turned their attention increasingly toward areas of applied social psychology, such as health behavior and organizational psychology, where they had some opportunity for funding while simultaneously helping to solve real world problems.

The final historical transformation that occurred in the early 1970s involved the intellectual status and centrality of social psychology. During the behaviorist heyday prior to World War II, social psychology was a marginalized sub-field. After the Golden Age, social psychology was considered a central or core part of the discipline, and continues to be considered a core subfield. A result of the success within social psychology, this also appears to be a consequence of the rise of the cognitive metatheory and the shift within social psychology to a focus on the individual, and not the group or the relationship of the individual to the group.

The Return of Biology to Social Psychology: The 1990s

A funny thing happened to social psychology, something wholly unexpected by most social psychologists in the 1970s or early 1980s: social psychology began to turn (or return) to biology. Reflecting the rise of the biological metatheory, major handbooks and graduate textbooks within Social Psychology included chapters on evolutionary social psychology (Archer, 1996; Buss & Kenrick, 1998). This return to biology was totally unexpected as late as 1979, when Cartwright noted that McDougall's biologically based social psychology never had a chance in the U.S. because of our cultural assumptions about the modifiability of human nature (Cartwright, 1979).

With the increased funding likely for neuroscientific studies of social behavior, the return to biology is likely to continue. So far, only some of the traditional topics of social psychology (aggression, interpersonal attraction, cooperation) have proven amenable to a biological approach. We must wait to see what the future holds. In any event, the cognitive metatheory and the biological metatheory are not incompatible. Both share a focus on the individual and on intra-individual determinants of behavior. While the cognitive metatheory investigates proximate causes of behavior, the biological metatheory focuses on both proximate and distal causes. The two metatheories could productively coexist for a long time.

The Creation of Personality Psychology Between World War 1 and 2

As with social psychology, personality psychology was a clear area of interest before World War I. With the involvement of psychologists in World War I, the emergence of personality psychology as a distinct subfield got a push.

The first personality test developed by psychologists was created during World War I by Robert S. Woodworth (Woodworth, 1919). Woodworth developed a scale, known as the Personal Data Sheet, to distinguish soldiers who would be susceptible to "shell shock" and those soldiers who would be less susceptible. Woodworth collected a long list of symptoms from case histories of shell shock victims and neurotics. Using this list, he developed a list of 116 simple yes or no questions that would distinguish shell shocked cases from normal soldiers. This test (of neuroticism, as it was later termed) became the first empirically validated personality test (Winter & Barenbaum, 1999). A single test, however, does not a subfield make.

The conditions for the creation of a new subfield within psychology after World War I were fertile. While the child study movement flourished (see Chapter 11), a parallel social movement, the mental hygiene movement, emphasized the development of moral and civil virtues through character development. At the same time, mental testing was experiencing its first successes. The ability to measure intelligence led psychologists to look at the possibility of measuring other kinds of individual differences, such as attitudes, opinions, and values. Finally, the prevalence of materialistic and behavioristic approaches to human beings, specifically Freudianism and Behaviorism, provoked a backlash among thoughtful people who wanted to preserve the uniqueness of the individual and the dignity of the person. This backlash was a driving force behind the development of the Jamesian counterculture in the 1920s and 1930s (Pandora, 1997), as well as an impetus for the development of personality psychology (Nicholson, 2003).

Gordon Allport: The Father Of Personality Psychology

Gordon Allport (1897-1967) was not just an influential social psychologist and historian of social psychology, he was also the father of personality psychology. Allport was born in Indiana and grew up near Cleveland, where his parents had moved when he was very young. Gordon was the fourth son in a very religious and socially engaged family. His father was a doctor and businessman. His mother was involved in a large number of social causes. For the members of the Allport family, service to others was an important part of their religious beliefs. After graduating from high school, Gordon followed his brother to Harvard University. Allport received his A.B. from Harvard in 1919, the year his older brother and mentor Floyd Allport received his Ph.D. But the two brothers were very different—Floyd was a "man's man" who loathed Christianity, was an early behaviorist, and was an unapologetic materialist. Gordon was interested in ethics at Harvard and was deeply influenced by James Ford of the Department of Social Ethics at Harvard. While an undergraduate Gordon Allport worked extensively as a volunteer social worker and explored different forms of Christianity (Hilgard, 1987; Nicholson, 2003).

After graduating from Harvard, Gordon spent a year teaching at a private Christian college in Constantinople (present day Istanbul). The experience of teaching and working in a large urban area in a Moslem country and his travels in Europe during his year abroad had a significant impact on Allport. While returning from Constantinople at the end of his year teaching, he visited Freud. When Allport tried to describe a child he had witnessed on the train to discuss the child's behavior with him, Freud said "and the little boy was you." This was the start of Allport's lifelong interest in and rejection of psychoanalysis. Allport later became a strong critic of what he termed psychoanalytic excesses (Nicholson, 2003).

Returning to Harvard to study for his Ph.D., Allport studied with his brother Floyd, William McDougall, and Herbert Langfeld. Gordon Allport soon gravitated toward the study of personality, reflecting both his concern for character development and the uniqueness of the individual. His first published research, carried out with his brother, was an effort to measure several personality traits (F. Allport & G. Allport, 1921). In his second published scholarly article, Allport argued for the significance of personality as a topic of study within psychology (G. Allport, 1921). Finally, in his 1922 Ph.D. dissertation, Allport attempted a behaviorist analysis of personality traits and also linked the study of personality to work in social work and diagnosis. Allport selected two traits: ascendance-submission and extroversion-introversion. These traits were relevant, Allport felt, to adjustment to modern industrial life and to the understanding of social conflicts (G. Allport, 1922; Nicholson, 2003). It is significant both that Allport never tried to publish his thesis and that his work was not perceived as "scientific" by leaders in the field such as Titchener (Nicholson, 2003), who responded with silence to Allport's presentation of his work at a scholarly conference in 1921.

After earning his Ph.D., Allport received a one year post-doctoral fellowship to study in Europe, a fellowship that was later renewed for a second year. He had impressed all of his teachers at Harvard with both his character (hardworking, urbane, and socially skilled) and his intellectual abilities. At first, Allport seemed unsure about continuing in psychology, was unimpressed with many of the initial lectures he attended in Germany, and seemed to be searching for a spiritual direction which he did not find in behaviorism. He did attend lectures by Stumpf, Wertheimer, and Köhler, which impressed him. He also spent a great deal of time absorbing the culture in Europe by attending operas and plays, visiting cathedrals, and making friends (Nicholson, 2003).

Allport became more serious about his scholarly pursuits in spring of 1923. He moved from Berlin to Hamburg to study with William Stern (1871-1938). Stern, a student of Ebbinghaus, is most known for his work in applied psychology and mental testing (Stern invented the concept of IQ based on Binet's work). But by the 1920s Stern was interested in personality and the measurement of personality traits. In his dissertation, Allport had criticized Stern's approach as reductionistic when, in fact, Stern opposed reductionism. Upon arriving in Hamburg, Allport rented a room from Stern and the two developed a close relationship. Stern was especially interested in developing a psychology that protected individuality in the face of growing mechanization and conformity of modern life. Allport and Stern's interests coincided greatly and Allport later described his experience working and living with the older Stern as a second intellectual dawn. Stern, who himself was greatly influenced by William James, argued for a broad, philosophically grounded non-mechanistic science of psychology. Stern and other German psychologists had a very strong impact on Allport. He began in 1923 to systematically re-read William James'

Varieties of Religious Experience and he rejected behaviorism for good. He also embraced Anglo-Catholicism as his religious faith (Nicholson, 2003).

In the second year of his fellowship, Allport moved to Cambridge to continue his studies. His time in Cambridge was darkened by the news that his father had died in September 1923. Compared to the U.S. and Germany, British psychology was underdeveloped and lacked vigor, in Allport's view. Allport studied with Sir Frederick Bartlett and with one of the leaders of mental testing, Charles Spearman. Allport also enjoyed the cultural attractions of England and was confirmed in the Church of England, formalizing his religious commitments (Nicholson, 2003).

Allport returned to the U.S. to take a sabbatical replacement position at Harvard in the Department of Social Ethics in the fall of 1924. He began teaching a course on personality that was soon cross-listed with the psychology department. In spite of his success as a teacher and rising scholar, Allport felt limited at Harvard by the strong behaviorist tendencies there and his position in a somewhat marginal department, the Department of Social Ethics, which was finally abolished in 1931. When an opening in the Harvard Psychology Department became available, Allport had the strong backing of McDougall (himself somewhat of an outcast at Harvard) but was opposed by Boring, who wanted a "real" experimental psychologist to join the department. Allport found other employment at Dartmouth College, where he was offered a tenure track position as an assistant professor (he had only been a lecturer at Harvard) and the chance to work with graduate students. Allport had recently married and was happy to have greater financial stability for his new wife and soon-to-be family (Nicholson, 2003).

The Allports arrived at Dartmouth in the fall of 1926, the start of an enormously productive period in Allport's career during which he helped to create the sub-field of personality psychology and made contributions to social psychology. In 1927 he published a presentation of his concept of traits as a basis for the understanding of personality (G. Allport, 1927) and in 1928 he published a test of ascendance-submission, a trait measured by a psychometric test (G. Allport, 1928). In 1929 he published a detailed study of an individual, introducing the idea that personality must be studied both with psychometric tests of individual differences (the nomothetic approach) and a detailed study of individual uniqueness (the ideographic approach). The complementary role of nomothetic and ideographic approaches was borrowed from Münsterberg and Stern and was central to Allport's subsequent approach to personality.

In 1930, after four productive years at Dartmouth, the Allports returned to Cambridge where Gordon Allport took a position at Harvard, replacing William McDougall. McDougall left Harvard in 1928, tired of his marginal status, to head the new psychology department at Duke University. The Harvard search committee offered the job initially to Lashley, hoping to strengthen its role as a center of behaviorism. Lashley declined. Gestalt psychologists Kurt Koffka and Wolfgang Köhler were considered but rejected by the pro-behaviorist elements in the department. Finally, Allport emerged as a consensus candidate. He was a rising star who would fill McDougall's slot as a social psychologist and also had a significant record in the emerging area of personality and personality measurement. The clincher for many on Harvard's faculty was that Allport was perceived as a reasonable person who would work with all factions in the department (Nicholson, 2003).

Allport was offered the position for the academic year 1929 but declined, citing salary and lack of a tenure track position. Allport was also getting offers from other universities. Harvard came back with another offer, with a much higher salary and job security. Allport accepted, and started in 1930, remaining at Harvard for the rest of his career. He brought with him some of his graduate students and an ambitious agenda for teaching, research, and publication. He soon joined the editorial board of *Psychological Bulletin* (Nicholson, 2003).

At Harvard, Allport developed psychometric tests of values as part of his approach to understanding personality (Vernon & Allport, 1931; Cantril & Allport, 1933). He also continued to argue for the valuable but limited role of experimental approaches to personality (these included psychometric measures of personality) and the need to complement these methods with ideographic studies (Allport, 1933). A clear indication of Allport's success in forging a new subfield out of social psychology was the publication of a new journal devoted to personality psychology, entitled *Character and Personality*, in 1932-1933. McDougall wrote the lead article in the first issue and Allport was an important contributor. Adler and Jung were also among the international list of contributors (McAdams, 1997).

The subfield was clearly born in 1937 with the publication of Allport's masterpiece, *Personality: A Psychological Interpretation* (Allport, 1937). Allport carefully presented all the various theories and research up to that time, giving them both sympathetic and critical treatment. He also presented in detail his own complete theory of personality. The combination of scholarly and balanced survey with the presentation of his own theory made Allport's text both an instantaneous success and the most influential book on personality in U.S. history. The text became the basis for many graduate and undergraduate courses in the new field of personality. Personality became a standard part of many college curriculums (McAdams, 1997).

Allport's approach to personality was one of several possible ones that could have come into existence. In the same year that Allport published his masterpiece, Ross Stagner published a competing text, *Psychology of Personality* (Stagner, 1937). Allport and Stagner were friends and when they met at the 1937 APA convention Stagner predicted great things for Allport's text. While both books sold well, it was indeed Allport's work that shaped the field. What is interesting about Stagner's approach, essentially a road not taken by the emerging field, was that it was both more behavioristic and more politically radical. Stagner emphasized the social determinants of personality, devoting almost half of his book to that topic. In contrast, Allport's work was acontextual and did not explore the social roots of personality, a shortcoming that seemed odd to Stagner (Stagner, 1938) given that both he and Allport were members of SPSSI and politically left-wing. Stagner's politics were shaped by the Great Depression. Receiving his Ph.D. in 1932, he had a one-year fellowship followed by a year of unemployment. In 1932 he secured a job at the University of Akron (Nicholson, 2003). Reviewing the book at the 1937 APA convention, Allport noted that the approach taken by the two authors was completely different (Nicholson, 2003).

The reasons for these differences are two-fold. First, Allport resisted any approach that would diminish the apparent personal freedom of the individual. In the social conflicts of the Great Depression, Allport was particularly vigilant in defending the idea that humans were free. Second, Allport adopted a rhetorical style of moderation, appearing to be the reasonable middle position between different "extremist" positions. This "moderate" and "balanced" style was to be an especially persuasive rhetorical strategy in light of the claims of the reductionisms of behaviorism, psychoanalysis, and socialism. This rhetorical strategy was made even more effective by Allport's careful scholarship —he could fairly present and criticize competing positions like few other scholars (Nicholson, 2003).

Allport used the notion of psychological traits organized into a meaningful and, to each person, unique gestalt as the basis of his theory. At the most general level, personality can be described in terms of cardinal traits, an individual's overarching passions or emotions. Below cardinal traits are central traits, the general traits one uses in a letter of recommendation or describing a person, such as introversion vs. extroversion, emotional stability vs. emotional volatility, and so on. Central traits are few in number but fairly pervasive. Finally, individuals have secondary traits which are specific and narrow dispositions that are aroused by very specific situations. In addition to understanding traits, you must also understand, according to Allport, an individual's values and the situations they find themselves in, as both values and situations shape behavior in conjunction with personality (Allport, 1937; Hilgard, 1987). Traits can be measured nomothetically with psychometric tests but individuals must be understood by combining this knowledge from psychometric tests with an ideographic approach that specifies the pattern of an individual's traits, the individual's unique whole.

After the publication of *Personality,* Allport was the acknowledged leader of the Jamesian counterculture. He was elected president of the APA in 1939 and president of the SPSSI in 1944. In addition to shaping psychology through his work in personality psychology and social psychology, and through his service to the APA and the SPSSI, Allport exercised influence through his teaching. In 1963 he was given two bound volumes of the writings of 55 of his former Ph.D. students, with the inscription: "From his students—in appreciation of his respect for their individuality." Allport had practiced what he preached, a respect for and nurturance of the uniqueness of every individual person. In the process, he had nurtured 55 successful scholars in the field of psychology, including leading psychologists in cognitive psychology, social psychology, and personality psychology, such as Harvey Cantril, Jerome Bruner, and Stanley

Milgram, among many others (Hilgard, 1987).

Henry Murray And The Psychoanalytic Influence

Allport's chief intellectual ally at Harvard against the behaviorists and hardcore experimentalists was Henry A. Murray(1893-1988). Murray was a physician and since 1928 the head of the Harvard Psychology Clinic. An enormously popular teacher, he was also a devout Jungian with a broad knowledge of psychoanalytic theory. Murray was also a caustic and unrelenting critic of American psychology, a discipline he felt contributed little to the understanding of human nature and did little to alleviate the suffering of real people (Nicholson, 2003). Needless to say, Murray was a thorn in the side of the department.

Murray's position became threatened (he held a three-year renewable contract since 1928) when Karl Lashley was finally lured to Harvard to chair the psychology department in the mid-1930s. Along with Lashley's appointment came an increased emphasis from the Harvard administration on scholarly productivity that was rigorously experimental. Even Boring's quantitative studies of perception and psychophysics were not considered rigorous enough by Lashley. Murray was considered an out and out embarrassment (Nicholson, 2003).

Lashley wanted to purge the department of all dubious and unscientific elements: this meant first and foremost getting rid of Murray. The president of Harvard formed a committee to determine whether Murray should stay or go. The committee consisted of six faculty: Allport, Boring, and Lashley from the psychology department, and three from outside of the department. Allport soon became Murray's leading defender on the committee. Allport supported Murray based on his teaching, contributions to the psychology clinic, and because of his broad intellectual and multidisciplinary interests. In short, Allport was defending a unique individual against an effort to impose homogeneity on the department. Allport also had his own self-interest in mind. While Allport had enormous respect among more rigorously-oriented psychologists for his careful psychometric work, he was clearly next on Lashley's list of unscientific (read: non-behaviorist) psychologists that had to go (Nicholson, 2003). Allport eventually prevailed and Murray stayed at Harvard. But the department was permanently divided from that point on, in spite of efforts by Boring to forge a cohesive department (Nicholson, 2003).

Murray's primary contribution to personality psychology was to inject a strong current of psychoanalysis into the subfield. In 1935 he developed a projective test for personality research and clinical diagnosis called the Thematic Apperception Test (TAT), a test that is still used today (Morgan & Murray, 1935). Murray argued for a clinical psychology based on psychoanalysis and through his teaching and publications influenced many American psychotherapists and personality psychologists. He sought to investigate psychoanalytic concepts using empirical methods, a significant advance over the approach of Freud and his followers. Finally, Murray emphasized case studies of individuals and an alternative personality psychology which he termed personology. The basic concepts of personology are laid out in Murray's *Explorations in Personality* (Murray, 1938).

The first basic concept in personology is need. Murray argued that humans are motivated by approximately 20 different needs, such as the need for achievement, the need for affiliation, and the need for dominance. Each need is a force that organizes and drives behavior. The second basic concept in personology is press. Individuals with various needs are faced with situations that are either opportunities or obstacles to the fulfillment of their needs. These situations are environmental press. A thema, the third basic concept in personology, is a reoccurring need-press interaction. And a unity-thema, the fourth basic concept of personology, is a dominant pattern of needs and press which organizes much of a person's life (like cardinal traits in Allports theory). While Murray was a Jungian, he had a broad knowledge of Freudian psychoanalysis and he used it as the foundation for his own unique theory of personality (McAdams, 1997). Some parts of Murray's theory, such as the concept of need for achievement, were to be very influential in the 1950s and 1960s.

Kurt Lewin's Gestalt Theory Of Personality

Kurt Lewin had turned his attention to personality and motivation early in his time at the University of Berlin. He approached the topic by developing a gestalt theory of personality, arguing, like Allport and Murray, that behavior is always a product of the situation and the person. He called his gestalt theory of personality-within-a-social-context field theory and he tested the theory with experimental studies of motivation. Most of the nearly 20 studies carried out to test the theory were done as doctoral dissertations by Lewin's students. Lewin always bubbled over with ideas and most of the experiments were the product of Lewin's discussions with his students. Lewin always gave his students credit for the work, but the theory was clearly his (Marrow, 1969).

Lewin often thought in terms of diagrams and mathematical relationships using concepts from physics. He expressed the relationship of social environment and personality to behavior in the formula $B=f(p,e)$, meaning behavior is always a function of the person and the psychological environment. The person, including his or her needs and goals, and the psychological environment make up the life space. Behavior occurs in the life space, the total psychological environment experienced by the person. Behavior is not a product of the past or future, but of the forces in the life space at the present moment (Marrow, 1969; Lewin, 1935). Modern students of psychology who are not familiar with field theories of physics, which was a source of inspiration for Lewin, find Lewin's theory difficult to understand in its details. What is perhaps most important historically is that the theory inspired Lewin and his students to carry out unique and revealing experiments on motivation. The first of these, which was discussed in Chapter 10, was by Bluma Zeigarnik and the now well-known Zeigarnik Effect. Her study was the first of several efforts to test Lewin's theory. Lewin argued that the intention to carry out a task creates a system of psychological tensions and that the need to release the tension sustains goal related activity. When the task is complete, the tension is released and no longer shapes behavior (including, in this case, memory). Ziegarnik found a strong tendency in her subjects to recall interrupted tasks, supporting Lewin's theoretical idea that reaching a goal releases the psychological tensions in a life space (Marrow, 1969).

Another of the experimental tests of Lewin's theory was carried out by Maria Ovsiankina (1898-1993). Ovsiankina investigated whether interrupted tasks are spontaneously resumed. She found that they did indeed tend to be resumed, again supporting Lewin's theory that tension will continue to exist until the goal is achieved (Marrow, 1969).

Lewin's theory suggested the importance of goal achievement as a motive force in human behavior. This in turn raised the question of how and why people set the goals that they set for themselves. Lewin's students named this level of aspiration: whether you aspire to easy goals or to difficult goals, and why. People who set easy goals have a low level of aspiration. People who set difficult goals have a high level of aspiration. Lewin's students examined this question by looking at the effects of success or failure on an individual's decision to raise or lower their level of aspiration (Marrow, 1969).

Lewin and his students also examined emotions as important motivating forces within the life space. The empirical study of emotions had generally been neglected by American and European psychologists. Lewin's student Tamara Dembo (1902-1993) carried out the most important work in this area by examining anger and why frustration caused anger in some situations but not others. Dembo found that anger is more likely to occur if the person cannot escape the psychological field when progress toward a goal is blocked. In addition, the more intensely a need is felt (even if it is trivial), the more likely anger is to occur. Anger was not the only emotion studied in the life space. Anitra Karsten (1902-1988) studied the impact of satiation. Karsten found that repeating the same activities led to a decreased desire to perform the activities, to the point where subjects refused to continue (Marrow, 1969). The above are just a sample of the experimental studies of motive forces within the life space that shaped behavior.

Lewin's theory of personality and his descriptions of the studies of the Berlin studies of his students were published in English in *A Dynamic Theory of Personality* (Lewin, 1935). Lewin had pioneered the experimental study of motivation, an approach that fit well with the emerging field of personality psychology in the U.S. Lewin's strong emphasis on understanding the person in her or his psychological environment tied personality psychology to social psychology even more closely than did Allport's work.

Karen Horney And The Neurotic Personality

Karen Horney (1885-1952) was perhaps the most influential neo-analytic theorist in the U.S. (see Chapter 5 for more on Horney). She came to the U.S. in 1932 and settled in Chicago where she directed the Chicago Psychoanalytic Institute. While there she published *The Neurotic Personality of Our Time* (Horney, 1937), which introduced her views that society shapes personality and that social factors are crucial to the formation of both healthy and neurotic personalities.

By 1940, the basic orientation of personality psychology had been established; the triple focus on the whole person, motivation, and individual differences in personality. Careful measurement of individual differences, experimental studies of motivation, and in-depth case studies all contributed to increased understanding of the person. Allport and Lewin had also firmly tied the subfield to social psychology while Murray and Horney tied the subfield to clinical psychology. These connections had existed from the very earliest developments in the field. The work of Allport, Lewin, Murray, and Horney strengthened these connections and made them an essential part of personality psychology.

Personality Psychology Goes To War

At the time the U.S. entered World War II, Lewin's interests had already shifted away from personality and developmental toward social psychology. He actively supported the war through his work with the OSS, but this work did not deal directly with personality psychology, as we saw in Chapter 11 (see also Marrow, 1969). Horney was not involved in the war but continued her clinical practice and teaching in New York, where she had moved in 1941 to head the American Institute of Psychoanalysis (Hilgard, 1987). Allport worked as a social psychologist investigating problems of rumor and morale (Hilgard, 1987). Only Murray played a key role in the war effort qua personality psychologist. Murray served full-time in the OSS where he developed screening tests for applicants and operatives who were to be sent behind enemy lines as spies and where he monitored military experiments on brainwashing. The screening tests were not paper and pencil affairs but real situations that tested the applicants' ability to stand up to forced interrogations (meaning torture), to lie, and to be a leader under pressure (Chase, 2000). While Murray was the most senior personality psychologist to work in the war effort, a number of younger personality psychologists also participated as officers or researchers.

Outside of the war effort other work continued as well. At the University of Minnesota, the Minnesota Multiphasic Personality Inventory (MMPI) was developed through an empirical process similar to the one used by Woodworth. A large pool of items was tested on groups with various kinds of neuroses, as well as on normal people: the items that distinguished normal personalities from nine distinct neurotic personalities were incorporated into a single scale. The MMPI was to prove enormously useful to clinical psychologists and personality researchers, as were the other comprehensive personality tests that were soon to be developed (Hilgard, 1987). To this day the MMPI remains one of the most frequently administered psychological tests.

As the war ended, personality psychology shifted directions. The shift was reflected in the main scientific journal, *Character and Personality*, which changed its name to the *Journal of Personality*. With the new name came a new editorial policy. Instead of publishing a wide variety of case studies, theoretical articles, and nomothetic studies, the journal was going to give preference to experimental investigations (Zener, 1945). As universities expanded with the returning GIs and the GI Bill of Rights, the number of personality psychologists increased as did the number of faculty positions at major universities. At the same time this expansion and shift in emphasis occurred, a large influx of money flowed to some researchers in personality psychology, most of it coming from military or government grants. Gone were the days when Allport and his students carried out fascinating and wide-ranging studies on a shoestring budget. Big science had arrived to personality psychology, just as it had to other subfields within psychology. As we have seen before in cognitive, developmental, and social psychology: money talks.

The 1950s and 60s: Advances and Decline in Personality Psychology

Viewed historically, the 1950s and 1960s were a period of simultaneous advances and significant decline for personality psychology. In terms of advances, a number of new measures of personality were developed, new models of personality were proposed, and a large number of nomothetic studies were carried out, as we shall see shortly. But the field also retreated from its emphasis on the whole person, interest in broad models of motivation declined, and empirical methods became more restricted and narrowly defined. Personality psychology as a whole seemed to flounder. While social psychology was experiencing the Golden Age, personality psychology was losing its identity as a separate subfield within psychology (McAdams, 1997). This decline eventually brought personality psychology to a decade of doubt almost at the same time that social psychology experienced its crisis of confidence. Before we can discuss the decade of doubt, we need a taste of the empirical advances that occurred in the 1950s and 1960s.

Considerable advances in trait measurement took place. The California Personality Inventory (Gough, 1957) and the Sixteen Personality Factory Questionnaire (Cattell, 1957) were both developed and found widespread use. Many of the advances in trait measurement resulted from the use of factor analysis, a technique developed in the area of mental testing.

One of the leaders in using factor analysis within personality was Raymond B. Cattell (no relation to James McKeen Cattell), an English psychologist who received his Ph.D. with Spearman (whom you shall meet in Chapter 14). Raymond Cattell (1905-1998) came to the U.S. in 1937, and after having several jobs became a research professor at the University of Illinois in 1944. Factor analysis takes a large number of items and allows a researcher to identity groups or clusters of items, called factors or components, that tend to measure the same construct. Cattell's factor analyis of a large group of items measuring personality characteristics produced sixteen unique factors or components that could be used to describe every individual (Hilgard, 1987). Other personality psychologists, making different decisions and using somewhat different sets of items, found three factors (Eysenck, 1952). The discrepancy was not to be resolved for three decades.

Another advance came with the intense empirical study of selected concepts from the earlier broad theories of personality. One of the most intensely studied of the selected concepts was Murray's need for achievement. The leading researcher in this area was David McClelland (1917-1998) who, along with his colleagues, produced hundreds of studies on the need to achieve (e.g., McClelland, 1961; McClelland, Atkinson, Clark, & Lowell, 1953). At the same time that McClelland gave lip service to the whole person (McClelland, 1951), he saw the future of personality psychology as the intensive empirical study of key constructs (McAdams, 1997).

Personality Psychology, LSD, and the Unabomber

In 1942, the director of the Office of Strategic Services (OSS), General William "Wild Bill" Donovan launched an effort to develop a "truth drug," which was considered a crucial weapon in the war. Research efforts soon focused on marijuana. The OSS started giving a highly potent, clear marijuana extract to unknowing victims. The experiments did not prove particularly successful so the search was expanded. When the U.S. learned of Nazi experiments at the Dachau concentration camp with mescaline, the U.S. government recruited hundreds (the best estimate is 600 doctors and scientists) of former Nazis to continue their studies in the U.S. Efforts were expanded beyond the search for a truth serum to the study of mind control technologies, specifically drugs, hypnosis, and torture. When the CIA replaced the OSS in 1945 the mind control programs were consolidated under a single program codenamed BLUEBIRD (Lee & Shlain, 1985).

Murray was deeply involved in the OSS research projects, although details of his specific involvements with the truth drug research are unknown. What is well established is that the CIA funded research with a variety of drugs, including LSD and psilocybin (the magic mushroom) at several U.S. universities. Much of the money went to Murray and his students at Harvard and many psychology graduate students participated in the studies, including Stanley Milgram (see Chapter 11).

In 1953 CIA Director Allen Dulles, the architect of the covert operation that overthrew the democratically elected liberal government of Guatemala in 1954, launched a new psychological warfare initiative called MK-ULTRA that was to investigate a variety of chemical and psychological weapons. CIA official Richard Helms was placed in charge and a major focus of research was the effects of LSD and other "mind control" drugs. Some of the research projects were carried out in conjunction with the U.S. military and included two "safe houses" in San Francisco where the CIA paid prostitutes to lure men to the houses and give them LSD. The men were then observed by CIA operatives behind one-way mirrors. The San Francisco safe houses functioned from 1955 to 1963. In addition, U.S. troops (both officers and enlisted men) were given LSD and other drugs to see how they would function in combat. These Army tests involved troops at Fort Bragg (North Carolina), Fort McClellan (Alabama) and at other U.S. bases. In addition, the CIA experimented on prisoners at various federal penitentiaries and drug rehabilitation centers (Lee & Shlain, 1985).

The CIA channeled considerable monies to psychologists and psychiatrists to carry out drug research. Some of the money was given to foundations which acted as covers for the CIA. One such foundation which channeled CIA money (in addition to using its own funds) was the Macy Foundation (Lee & Shlain, 1985) which helped fund the cognitive revolution.

Enter clinical and personality psychologist Timothy Leary(1920-1996). From 1954 to 1959 Leary had worked as director of clinical research at the Kaiser Foundation in Oakland, California. He successfully developed a personality test that was used in prisons and the military. As a promising young researcher, he was lured to Harvard in 1959 as an instructor. With Murray's strong support (Murray went so far as to take LSD as one of Leary's subjects), Leary began experimenting with LSD on students and prisoners. His experiments on prisoners were unconventional, however, as Leary did not force the drug on the prisoners but took the drug with them in a pleasant relaxed atmosphere. The results seemed to be positive and Leary and his associates began preaching the value of the drug as a mind-enhancing substance, going so far as to distribute it to artists, musicians, and writers in New York City and Boston. Leary's unconventional experiments soon incurred the wrath of both the Harvard faculty and the U.S. government, which did not want the drug to become an uncontrolled recreational substance. After several clashes at Harvard faculty meetings, Leary was fired. He went on to preach the value of LSD as a mind-enhancing drug and became the "high priest" of the psychedelic movement, eventually landing in prison where he had to take the very personality test he had developed (Lee & Shlain, 1985).

Meanwhile, back at Harvard, Murray was continuing experiments originally begun with the OSS. He received a grant from the Rockefeller Foundation for a study of "multiform assessment of personality development." The study involved undergraduate "volunteers" (there was no informed consent or debriefing and many participants felt coerced into participating) who after writing about their hopes, fears, and beliefs, were placed in a brightly lit room in front of a one-way mirror with physiological monitoring devices attached to them (so the observers could record levels of physiological arousal) while they were verbally assaulted and belittled. Murray was essentially subjecting them to psychological torture to see how bright young people with various personalities could withstand torture (Chase, 2000).

Among the undergraduate subjects in the experiment was Theodore Kacznski (1942-), a gifted math major from Chicago. Kacznski had started at Harvard in 1958 at the age of 16. At the time all Harvard students were required to have a psychological evaluation before attending and Kacznski's file shows that he was shy but exceedingly stable and well adjusted. This was not the case after he left Harvard in 1962, however. After getting a Ph.D. in mathematics from the University of Michigan in 1967, Kacznski worked for a short time as a mathematics professor at the University of California before dropping out of society in 1971 and moving to Montana. Kacznski had developed an anti-science philosophy and turned to terrorism as a tool to fight science. Becoming known as the Unabomber (because he sent bombs to scientists at universities, including psychologists), he sent his first mail bomb in 1978. His 16th bomb exploded in April of 1995, killing the president of the California Forestry Association. His anti-science manifesto was published by the *Washington Post* and the *New York Times* in 1995. Kaczinski was arrested in 1996 by the FBI and tried and sentenced in 1998. He is now serving a life sentence with no possibility of parole. His defense lawyers, against his wishes, sought to portray him as insane in order to save his life (Chase, 2000).

danger of Psych

The responsibility of Murray and his study in multiform personality assessment for the development of the Unabomber has been ignored. The case and its multiple connections to military and CIA drug testing raise ethical issues far beyond those raised by Milgram's study or addressed in the APA code of ethics. What is, and should be, the relationship between psychology and the powerful institutions in our society? What are the moral obligations of the scientist? The CIA and military researchers felt that what they were doing was morally right—that they were the good guys fighting evil. This was a sentiment shared by Murray, who felt he was contributing to the fight against world evil. Recall that the U.S. was involved in the Cold War at the time and political repression in the U.S., under the name of McCarthyism, was widespread. How does the scientist know what is morally right? What ~~is the responsibility~~ of the psychologist for his or her research? Finally, does torture itself create the terrorists against whom torture is supposed to defend us? Think about these questions when you consider the connections between LSD, the sixties, and the Unabomber.

Another important development in the 1950s and 1960s was the emergence of social learning theories of personality. These theories had their genesis in a seminar held at Yale University in the fall of 1937 under the direction of Clark Hull. Five of the seminar participants: the sociologist John Dollard and the experimental psychologists Neal Miller, Hobart Mower, Robert Sears, and Leonard Doob, had all been trained in psychoanalysis or had been psychoanalyzed. Miller and Dollard proposed a strategy for synthesizing and testing psychoanalysis and learning theory. Freud's concepts would be taken one at a time, cast in learning theory form, and empirically tested (Lemov, 2005). The first two major products of this approach were the publication of *Frustration and Aggression* (Dollard, Doob, Miller, Mower, & Sears, 1939), followed by *Social Learning and Imitation* (Miller & Dollard, 1941). The war slowed progress as the participants became involved in the war effort and graduate training virtually ceased. After the war the approach was applied to personality and clinical psychology in *Personality and Psychotherapy* (Dollard & Miller, 1950). With this recasting of psychoanalysis in behavioristic terms, behaviorism now had a strong presence within personality psychology.

The Yale group was not the only one to develop a learning theory of personality. At Ohio State University Julian Rotter (1916-) developed a learning theory of personality that incorporated individuals' expectations and beliefs. Rotter had received his undergraduate degree in chemistry from Brooklyn College in 1937, an M.A. in psychology from the University of Iowa in 1938, and a Ph.D. in psychology in 1941 from Indiana University. During the war he worked as a military psychologist and when the war ended he joined the faculty at Ohio State. Rotter's interests focused on both clinical and personality psychology. His general theory of social learning was presented in *Social Learning and Clinical Psychology* (Rotter, 1954). Rotter argued that there are important individual differences in people's beliefs or expectancies about themselves and the world, and these differences in expectancies influence how people react to events in their environment. Rotter advanced this idea further with the development of the Rotter Internal-External Locus of Control scale (Rotter, 1966), an important measuring tool for individual differences in expectancies. This scale precipitated numerous studies on locus of control and further scale development. Rotter forcefully introduced cognitive variables into the study of personality.

The emphasis on cognition as an important element in personality was advanced further with Albert Bandura and Richard Walters' *Social Learning and Personality Development* (Bandura & Walters, 1963). They emphasized the role of observational learning (in addition to classical and operant conditioning) and of cognitive processes such as attention and retention.

Much of the work in the 1950s and 1960s rejected the broad theories of Allport, Murray, and Lewin and instead focused on behavioristic approaches to personality, trait measurement, or in-depth empirical study of well-defined (but decontextualized) constructs such as need for achievement (McAdams, 1997). An exception to this rule was the work of Abraham Maslow. Maslow had been trained as a learning theorist and primatologist. After taking a position in New York City he came under the influence of Gestalt psychologist Max Wertheimer at the New School. Maslow came to question the materialism inherent in both psychoanalysis and learning theories of personality, and the emphasis on biological needs to the neglect of other needs, such as the need for beauty, love, and ultimately self-actualization (Maslow, 1954). Wertheimer was to be a model of the self-actualized person in Maslow's writings. Maslow's work helped launch the third force (opposed to both behaviorism and psychoanalysis) within clinical psychology during the 1960s and 1970s. This movement was also referred to as humanistic psychology. The third force psychologists included clinical psychologist Carl Rogers, whom we shall meet in Chapter 13. The humanistic movement can be viewed as a new counterculture that emerged in the post-World War II period, replacing to a certain extent the Jamesian counterculture that had flourished in the 1920s and 1930s.

Personality's Decade Of Doubt: 1968-1978

The decline within personality psychology did not go unnoticed by key researchers in the field. Starting in 1968 three important critiques of personality psychology appeared, generating considerable discussion and a debate in what is sometimes referred to as the decade of doubt. Ultimately scholars achieved a degree of empirical and theoretical resolution.

The decade of doubt started with the publication of *Personality and Assessment* by Walter Mischel (Mischel, 1968). Mischel, who was born in Vienna, received his B.A. from New York University in 1951, his M.A. from CUNY in 1953, and his Ph.D. from Ohio State University in 1956. Mischel was a student of Julian Rotter and studied under Rotter when he developed his social learning theory of personality and clinical psychology. Mischel spent two years at the University of Colorado and four years at Harvard before taking a permanent position at Stanford University in 1962, where he was to spend the next 21 years before returning to New York to teach at Columbia University.

Mischel published *Personality and Assessment* when he was only 38. In the book Mischel extensively reviewed studies that correlated measures of trait characteristics with trait relevant behaviors. In his review he found that few trait measures correlated with behaviors higher than r=.30 and many hovered around r=.20. While measures of intellectual ability showed considerable stability across situations, trait measures of personality did not. Traits, Mischel concluded, explained little of human behavior; behavior seemed more powerfully determined by situational factors.

Mishcel's critique was very influential but it was soon followed by others. Carlson (1971) asked the question "Where is the Person in Personality Research?" in the provocative title of a *Psychological Bulletin* article. Carlson reviewed 226 articles published in the 1960s from two major personality journals. She found that virtually no attention was given to the organization of personality, to the stability of personality, to sexuality, power, friendship, or love. These important areas were sacrificed to "norms of convenience and methodological orthodoxy" (Carlson, 1971, p. 207). An even more pessimistic critique (and the least influential) was published by Fiske (1974), who argued that personality constructs are inherently ambiguous and could not form the basis for a true science.

Mischel's critique generated the person-situation debate. Interestingly, the debate was carried on in the terms set by Mischel, that is, mostly as an empirical issue. New studies were carried out to determine the predictive power of traits and situations and to study the consistency of behavior across time and situations (McAdams, 1997). Conceptual and methodological advances were also made as personality psychologists grappled with the issues raised by Mischel.

One of the first responses in the person-situation debate was by Endler and Magnusson (1976), who argued that the person and situation always interact and both must be considered when predicting behavior. Their position was a return to the interactionist position of Allport, Murray, and Lewin. A second response came from personality psychologist Seymour Epstein (Epstein, 1979; Epstein, 1984). Using psychometric theory, Epstein argued that a single behavioral act is not a good measure of behavior across many situations. A single behavioral act is like a single test item, which is always composed of two components: a true score and error. Measures of traits, Epstein showed, have far greater predictive power for aggregates of behaviors in similar situations than they do for a single behavior. As Epstein showed, traits can predict behaviors for most of the people much of the time (Epstein, 1979).

Mischel suggested a possible solution by stressing the importance of cognitive variables as a predictor of behaviors (Mischel, 1973) as part of the cognitive social learning theory advanced by Bandura, a colleague of Mischel's at Stanford. By understanding how individuals tend to think about situations, Mischel argued, one can better predict their behavior across situations. The study of attributional styles, also called explanatory styles, became an important part of personality psychology after the decade of doubt (McAdams, 1997). Finally, Bem and Allen (1974) proposed that the influence of traits on behavior is shaped by moderator variables--whether or not a trait is considered relevant to a situation, salient, or important for the person, while determining how predictive the trait will be of behavior in a given situation. For instance, if a trait is not considered relevant by a person, that judgment will decrease the predictive power of the trait. Empirical work by Synder (1983), who studied self-monitoring, demonstrated that moderator variables modify the predictive power of traits.

While Mischel's critique generated the most debate, Carlson's critique also had an impact. Personality psychologists embraced a broader array of methods, including ideographic studies and longitudinal studies of personality. Interest in the whole person was reflected in a resurgence of interest in the self and the self-concept (McAdams, 1997). Personality psychologists also became more interactionist in their thinking and research designs; they had profited from the person-situation debate (Kenrick & Funder, 1988).

Personality's Renewed Confidence and Growth: The 1980s and 1990s

The field of personality psychology emerged from the decade of doubt with an increased theoretical and methodological sophistication. In some ways, the field had returned to the original vision of Allport, with a plurality of methods, a concern with the whole person, with individual differences, and with motivation. In addition to the traditional concerns expressed in the 1930s, personality psychologists added a strong interest in cognition as a component of personality and an interest in the biological basis of personality. These new interests reflected broader changes in the field, specifically, the cognitive revolution and the neuroscientific revolution.

In addition to the new interest in cognition and biology, old questions seemed to be resolved. The debates on the trait structure of personality were resolved when new factor analyses converged on five main traits (which can be considered the central traits in Allport's theory). While the names of the traits vary from researcher to researcher, the five are essentially the same and are known as the big five (McCrae & Costa, 1987). These traits are (1) openness to experience (O), (2) conscientiousness-undirectedness (C), (3) extraversion-introversion (E), (4) agreeableness-antagonism (A), and (5) neuroticism(N). The acronym for the big five is OCEAN.

The influence of the cognitive revolution on personality psychology was indirect, coming through the work of cognitive social learning theorists who explored the stable strategies that individuals employ in managing their social relationships. Foremost in this area of research was Nancy Cantor who, following Mischel, explored cognitive strategies (Cantor & Kihlstrom, 1985; Cantor, 1990; Cantor & Zirkel, 1990). A more forceful indirect influence came from work in social psychology on attribution (Weiner, 1990). Attribution researchers found stable patterns of attribution (called attributional or explanatory style) that along with traits and situational variables predicted behavior. The work on attributional style owed much to the work of social psychologists, as well as to work following Rotter's locus of control construct.

The influence of the neuroscientific revolution is also still indirect, but growing. The first significant inroad of the biological approach to personality came with the discovery that the big five personality traits are all partially biologically based, accounting for the high degree of similarity in the personalities of identical twins reared apart (see Segal, 1999, for a review).

At the end of the 1990s, personality psychology seemed to have returned to its roots, but with a richer (both conceptually and empirically) understanding of the original ideas of Allport and the other founders. Still central to personality psychology was an emphasis on the whole person, on individual differences in personality, and on motivation. In addition, concerns with the role of cognition, biological influences, and temporal and situation stability of personality were added. While nomothetic methods still dominate (as they did in the 1920s and 1930s also), personality psychology employs a wide array of descriptive methods as well, including an ideographic approach that complements the predominant nomothetic approach.

The Place Of Social And Personality Psychology In The Modern World

Allport envisioned the study of personality as a defense of the uniqueness and spirituality of the individual. His broad conception of personality psychology was not enough, however, to withstand the pressures of positivism and behaviorism in the 1950s and 1960s when personality psychology, like the rest of psychology, became big science. It was only when the field returned to its roots, after making new empirical and conceptual advances, after the decade of doubt that the subfield experience renewed vigor. In spite of this renewed vigor, personality psychology remains somewhat marginalized, being out of step with the materialism of much of mainstream psychology.

For a time in the 1970s, it appeared that personality psychology would disappear into clinical and social psychology. The links to these two important subfields within psychology still may threaten the existence of personality, but the links also could guarantee the continued dynamic growth of the subfield. Clinicians need to understand unique human beings while social psychology is built on the assumption that the individual is the fundamental building block of their specialty. Whether the field will continue to make progress, and whether it is indeed a defense against the homogenizing influences of modern life, is yet to be seen.

Personality psychology has received varying degrees of financial support over the years from government, especially the military and intelligence apparatus. This support has not coincided with substantial progress in the field, either empirically or conceptually. It has resulted in some flagrant and unethical abuses of individuals. Personality psychologists appear to do best when they cannot sell their souls, but instead ply their craft with modest means. Does this generalization apply to all of psychology? Perhaps it is too early, historically, to make that judgment.

Themes And Patterns

Now that we have surveyed the history of perception and physiological psychology, cognitive psychology, developmental psychology, and social psychology, several patterns have emerged. First and foremost, it should be clear the leading psychologists who have shaped the field often move from one subfield to another during their career. Furthermore, researchers within each subfield use the empirical results and theories from other subfields in their own work: developmental psychologists borrowed from cognitive psychologists (and vice versa), social psychologists borrowed from cognitive psychologists (and vice versa), and so forth. Finally, the boundaries between the subfields are fuzzy and porous. The fact that the boundaries between subfields are fuzzy and porous does not, however, mean that all fields are equally connected to one another. Some fields are more closely tied together than others. As we shall see in the next chapter, social psychology has historically been closely tied to the study of personality. The study of personality, in turn, has been closely tied to clinical psychology, a topic we explore in the next chapter.

Historically, the intellectual leaders of the field have all been hardworking and productive, they have all studied with teachers who were themselves gifted and hardworking members of the field. In addition, the intellectual leaders of the field were intelligent, they had broad interests, and they typically were effective writers or speakers. But these characteristics could also describe many of the individuals who were not the intellectual leaders of the field as well. Beyond these shared characteristics, however, they all exercised leadership in the field through four basic mechanisms: scholarly productivity and quality, teaching and mentoring, organizational leadership and editorship, and mass communication.

Leadership is exercised through scholarly productivity and quality. The intellectual leaders of the field often produce between 100 and 200 books and articles over the course of their careers. These books and articles are on average of high quality, with a number playing pivotal roles in the development of the field, becoming, in essence, classics that changed history.

Leadership is also exercised through the teaching and mentoring of graduate students and post-doctoral fellows, and in some cases of undergraduates who go on to graduate school. The relationship between the student and the teacher is two-way: the students often work as collaborators and bring fresh ideas to the table, while the teacher nurtures and inspires individuals who will spread the teacher's influence either directly or indirectly. The role of teaching is clear when psychologists are denied access to graduate students, as in the case of the Gestalt psychologists or in the case of psychologists at primarily undergraduate institutions: their ability to exercise leadership in the field diminishes.

Leadership is also exercised through organizational service, such as service as chair of a department or as an officer of a major organization such as SPSSI or APA. These roles can also interfere with your research and teaching, so there are tradeoffs involved for the individual. An especially important form of organizational service is to work as an editor for a journal or scholarly book. Organizational service does not seem to be as significant as scholarship and teaching as a mechanism for scientific leadership.

Finally, leadership is often exercised by communicating with the broader public, especially through the publication of undergraduate textbooks, popular books, and articles written for a broader audience. These books do not often have the same impact as scholarly publications, but they do exert both a direct influence on the discipline and an indirect influence on the discipline as mediated through an educated public.

On a broader level, the field is also shaped by forces outside of its boundaries. The successive transformation of American psychology from a behaviorist metatheory to a cognitive metatheory to finally a biological (including both evolutionary factors and neurological factors) metatheory across broad swaths of psychology is not an accident. These changes correspond to both changes in the public perception of what a science of psychology should be and changes in funding. To understanding much of the history of psychology, it is important to follow the money that flows to research and training.

Specific events also play a role in the history of the field. Both World War I and World War II led to the growth and legitimacy of various areas of the field. The Great Depression and the rise of Fascism created conditions for the survival and growth of the Jamesian counterculture which, without the social dislocation of the 1930s, would most likely have been obliterated by behaviorism. The rise of the Nazis in Germany, leading to the mass exodus of German and Austrian psychologists, transformed American social psychology and prepared the ground for the cognitive revolution. The social turmoil generated in the late 1960s and early 1970s called into question the legitimacy of science, especially of psychology, and created the conditions for the crisis of confidence that descended upon social psychology almost immediately after the field had made incredible scientific breakthroughs.

In the midst of the internal and external dynamics shaping the field, psychology's intellectual leaders are both the right people at the right time, both shaped by fate and shapers of fate. They make history, but not under conditions of their own choosing and not always in the way that they would wish it to be.

References

Allport, F.H. (1919a). Behavior and experiment in social psychology. *Journal of Abnormal Psychology*, 14, 297-306.

Allport, F.H. (1919b). The social influence: An experimental study of effects of the group upon   individual mental processes. Unpublished doctoral dissertation, Harvard University.

Allport, F. H. (1924a). *Social psychology*. Boston, MA: Houghton Mifflin.

Allport, F.H. (1924b). The group fallacy in relation to social science. *American Journal of Sociology*, 29, 688-703.

Allport, F.H. (1930). The religion of a scientist. *Harper's, 160*, 352-366.

Allport, F.H. (1933). *Institutional behavior*. Chapel Hill, NC: University of North Carolina Press.

Allport, F.H. (1974). Floyd H. Allport. In G. Lindzey (Ed.), *A history of psychology in autobiography*, Vol. 6. Engelwood Cliffs, NJ: Prentice-Hall.

Allport, F.H., & Allport, G.W. (1921). Personality traits: Their classification and measurement. *Journal of Abnormal and Social Psychology, 16*, 6-40.

Allport, G.W. (1921). Personality and character. *Psychological Bulletin, 18*, 441-455.

Allport, G.W. (1922). *An experimental study of the traits of personality with application to the problems of social diagnosis*. Unpublished doctoral dissertation, Harvard University.

Allport, G.W. (1927). Concepts of trait and personality. *Psychological Bulletin, 24*, 284-293.

Allport, G.W. (1928). A test for ascendance-submission. *Journal of Abnormal and Social Psychology, 23,* 118-136.

Allport, G.W.(1929). The study of personality by the intuitive method: An experiment in teaching from *The Locomotive God. Journal of Abnormal and Social Psychology, 24,* 14-27.

Allport, G.W. (1933). The study of personality by the experimental method. *Character and Personality, 1,* 259-264.

Allport, G.W. (1935). Attitudes. In C. Murchison (Ed.), *A handbook of social psychology.* Worcester, MA: Clark University Press.

Allport, G.W. (1937). *Personality: A psychological interpretation.* New York, NY: Holt.

Allport, G.W. (1948). Foreword. In K. Lewin *Resolving social conflicts: Selected papers of Kurt Lewin,* ed. By G.W. Lewin. New York, NY: Harper & Row.

Allport, G.W. (1954a). The nature of prejudice. Reading, MA: Addison-Wesley.

Allport, G.W. (1954b). The historical background of modern social psychology. In G. Lindzey (Ed.), *The handbook of Social Psychology,* (Vol. 1, pp. 3-56). Cambridge, MA: Addison-Wesley.

Asch, S.E. (1946). Forming impressions of personality. *Journal of Abnormal and Social Psychology, 41,* 258-290.

Asch, S.E. (1948). The doctrine of suggestion, prestige, and imitation in social psychology. *Psychological Review, 55,* 250-276.

Asch, S.E. (1952). *Social psychology.* New York, NY: Prentice-Hall.

Asch, S.E. (1956). Studies of independence and conformity, I. A minority of one against a unanimous majority. *Psychological Monographs, 70*, 1-70.

Baldwin, J.M. (1897). *Social and ethical interpretations in mental development: A study in social psychology.* New York, NY: Macmillan.

Bandura, A.L., & Walters, R.H. (1963). *Social learning and personality* development. New York, NY: Holt, Rinehart & Winston.

Bem, D.J., & Allen, A. (1974). On predicting some of the people some of the time: The search for cross-situational consistencies in behavior. *Psychological Review, 81*, 506-520.

Berscheid, E. (1992). A glance back at a quarter century of social psychology. *Journal of Personality and Social Psychology, 63*(4), 525-533.

Blass, T. (2004). *The man who shocked the world: The life and legacy of Stanley Milgram.* New York, NY: Basic Books.

Bruner, J.S., & Allport, G.W. (1940). Fifty years of change within American psychology. *Psychological Bulletin, 37*, 757-776.

Cantor, N. (1990). From thought to behavior: "Having" and "doing" in the study of personality and cognition. *American Psychologist, 45*, 735-750.

Cantor, N, & Kihlstrom, J.F. (1985). Social intelligence: The basis of personality. *Review of Personality and Social Psychology, 6*, 15-34.

Cantor, N., & Zirkel, S. (1990). Personality, cognition, and purposive behavior. In L. Pervin (Ed.), *Handbook of personality: Theory and research* (pp. 135-164). New York, NY: Guilford Press.

Cantril, H. (1940). *The invasion From Mars.* Princeton, NJ: Princeton University Press.

Cantril, H. (1941). *The psychology of social movements.* New York, NY: Wiley.

Cantril, H., & Allport, G.W. (1933). Recent applications of the study of values. *Journal of Abnormal and Social Psychology, 28,* 259-273.

Cantril, H., & Allport, G.W. (1935). *The psychology of radio.* New York, NY: Harper.

Cantril, H., & Sherif, M. (1938). The kingdom of Father Divine. *Journal of Abnormal and Social Psychology, 33,* 147-167.

Carlson, R. (1971). Where is the person in personality research? *Psychological Bulletin, 75,* 203-219.

Cartwright, D. (1979). Contemporary social psychology in historical perspective. *Social Psychology Quarterly,* 42(1), 82-93.

Cattell, R.B. (1946). *Description and measurement of personality.* New York, NY: World Book.

Cattell, R.B. (1950). *Personality: A systematic, theoretical, and factual study.* New York, NY: McGraw-Hill.

Cattell, R.B. (1957). *Personality and motivation structure and measurement.* New York, NY: World Book.

Chase, A. (2000, June). Harvard and the making of the Unabomber. *The Atlantic Monthly,* pp. 41-63.

Creel, G. (1920). *How we advertised America.* New York, NY: Harper & Brothers.

Dollard, J., Doob, L.W., Miller, N.E., Mower, O.H., & Sears, R.R. (1939). *Frustration and aggression.* New Haven, CT: Yale University Press.

Dollard, J., & Miller, N.E. (1950). *Personality and psychotherapy: An analysis in terms of learning, thinking, and culture.* New York, NY: McGraw-Hill.

Eisinger, R.M., & Brown, J. (1998). Polling as a means toward presidential autonomy: Emil Hurja, Hadley Cantril, and the Roosevelt Administration. *International Journal of Public Opinion Research, 10*(3), 237-256.

Endler, N.S., & Magnusson, D. (1976). Toward an interactional psychology of personality. *Psychological Bulletin, 83,* 956-974.

Epstein, S. (1973). The stability of behavior: 1. On predicting most of the people much of the time. *Journal of Personality and Social Psychology, 77,* 1097-1126.

Epstein, S. (1984). The stability of behavior across time and situations. In R.A. Zucker, J. Aronoff, & A.I. Rabin (Eds.), *Personality and the prediction of behavior* (pp. 209-268). New York, NY: Academic Press.

Eysenck, H. J. (1952). *The scientific study of personality.* London, Great Britain: Routledge & Kegan Paul.

Festinger, L. (1953). Laboratory experiments. In L. Festinger & D. Katz (Eds.), *Research methods in the behavioral sciences,* pp. 136-172. New York, NY: Holt, Rinehart & Winston.

Festinger, L. (1954). A theory of social comparison processes. *Human Relations, 7,* 117-140.

Festinger, L. (1957). *A theory of cognitive dissonance.* Evanston, IL: Row, Peterson.

Festinger, L., & Carlsmith, J.M. (1959). Cognitive consequences of forced compliance. *Journal of Abnormal and Social Psychology, 58,* 203-210.

Festinger, L., Riecken, H.W., & Schachter, S. (1956). *When prophecy fails: A social and psychological study of a modern group that predicted the end of the world.* Minneapolis, MN: University of Minnesota Press.

Fiske, D.W. (1974). The limits of the conventional science of personality. *Journal of Personality, 42*, 1-11.

Gilbert, D.T., Fiske, S.T., & Lindzey, G. (1998). *The handbook of social psychology* (4th ed.), Vols. 1 & 2. Boston, MA: McGraw-Hill.

Gough, H.G. (1957). *California Psychological Inventory: Manual.* Palo Alto, CA: ConsultingPsychologists Press.

Graumann, C.F. (1996). Introduction to history of social psychology. In M. Hewstone, W. Stroebe, & G.M. Stephenson (Eds.), *Introduction to social psychology: A European perspective* (2nd ed.), pp. 3-23. Cambridge, MA: Blackwell.

Haffner, S. (1986). *Failure of a revolution: Germany, 1918-1919.* Chicago, IL: Banner Press.

Hathaway, S.R., & McKinley, J.C. (1943). *MMPI Manual.* New York, NY: Psychological Corporation.

Heider, F. (1958). *The psychology of interpersonal relations.* New York, NY: Wiley.

Hilgard, E.R. (1987). *Psychology in America: A historical survey.* San Diego, CA: Harcourt Brace Jovanovich.

Horney, K. (1937). *The neurotic personality of our time.* New York, NY: Norton.

Hovland, C.I., Janis, I. L., & Kelly, H.H. (1953). *Communication and persuasion: Psychological studies of opinion change.* New Haven, CT: Yale University Press.

Hovland, C.I., Lumsdaine, A.A., & Sheffield, F.D. (1949). *Experiments in mass communication* (Studies in Social Psychology in World War II, Vol. 3). Princeton, NJ: Princeton University Press.

Innis, N.K. (2003). William McDougall: "A major tragedy"? In *Portraits of pioneers in psychology*, Vol. 5, edited by G.A. Kimble & M. Wertheimer, pp.91-108. Washington, DC: American Psychological Association & Mahwah, NJ: Lawence Erlbaum.

Jones, E. E. (1985). History of social psychology. In G.A. Kimble & K. Schlesinger (Eds.), *Topics in the history of psychology*, Vol. 2, pp. 371-407. Hillsdale, NJ: Lawrence Erlbaum.

Jones, E.E. (1998). Major developments in five decades of social psychology. In D.T. Gilbert, S.T. Fiske, & G. Lindzey (Eds.), *The handbook of social psychology*, Vol. 1 (4th ed.), pp. 3-57. Boston, MA: McGraw-Hill.

Jones, R.A. (1987). Psychology, history, and the press. The case of William McDougall and the *New York Times*. *American Psychologist, 42*, 931-940.

Katz, D., & Allport, F.H. (1931). *Student attitudes: A report of the Syracuse University reaction study*. Syracuse, NY: Craftsman Press.

Kenrick, D.T., & Funder, D.C. (1988). Profiting from controversy: Lessons from the person-situation debate. *American Psychologist, 43*, 23-34.

Korte, C., & Milgram, S. (1970). Acquaintance networks between racial groups: Application of the small world method. *Journal of Personality and Social Psychology, 5*, 101-108.

Lee, M.A., & Shlain, B. (1985). *Acid dreams: The CIA, LSD, and the sixties rebellion*. New York, NY: Grove Press.

Lemov, R. (2005). *World as laboratory: Experiments with mice, mazes, and men.*

New York, NY: Hill and Wang.

Lewin, K. (1931a). Environmental forces in child behavior and development. In C. Murchison (Ed.), *A handbook of child psychology*. Worcester, MA: Clark University Press.

Lewin, K. (1931b). The conflict between aristotelian and galilean modes of thought in contemporary psychology. *Journal of Genetic Psychology, 5*, 141-177.

Lewin, K. (1935). *A dynamic theory of personality*. New York, NY: McGraw-Hill.

Lewin, K. (1936). *Principles of topological psychology*. New York, NY: McGraw-Hill.

Lewin, K. (1943). Psychology and the process of group living. *The Journal of Social Psychology, SPSSI Bulletin, 17*, 113-131.

Lewin, K., & Lippitt, R. (1938). An experimental approach to the study of autocracy and democracy: A preliminary note. *Sociometry, 1*, 292-300.

Lewin, K., Lippitt, R., & White, R.K. (1939). Patterns of aggressive behavior in experimentally created "social climates." *Journal of Social Psychology, 10*, 271-299.

Likert, R. (1932). A technique for the measurement of attitudes. *Archives of Psychology* (No. 140).

Lindzey, G. (Ed.), (1954). *The handbook of social psychology*. Cambridge, MA: Addison-Wesley.

Lindzey, G., & Aronson, E. (Eds.), (1968). *The handbook of social psychology*, 2nd ed. Reading, MA: Addison-Wesley.

Lippitt, R. (1940). An experimental study of the effects of democratic and authoritarian group atmospheres. *University of Iowa Studies in Child Welfare, 16,* 45-195.

Lippman, W. (1922/2004). *Public opinion.* Mineola, NY: Dover Publications. Originally published in New York, NY: Harcourt Brace & Comp.

MacMartin, C., & Winston, A.S. (2000). The rhetoric of experimental social psychology, 1930-1960: From caution to enthusiasm. *Journal of the History of the Behavioral Sciences,* 36(4), 349-364.

Marrow, A.J. (1969). *The practical theorist: The life and work of Kurt Lewin.* New York, NY: Basic Books.

Maslow, A.H. (1954). *Motivation and personality.* New York, NY: Harper.

McAdams, D.P. (1997). A conceptual history of personality psychology. In R. Hogans, J. Johnson, & S. Briggs (Eds.), *Handbook of personality psychology.* San Diego, CA:
Academic Press.

McCauley, C., & Rozin, P. (2003). Solomon Asch: Scientist and humanist. In G. A. Kimble & M. Wertheimer (Eds.), *Portraits of pioneers in psychology,* Vol. 5. Mahwah, NJ: Lawrence Erlbaum and Washington, D.C.: American Psychological Association.

McClelland, D.C. (1951). *Personality.* New York, NY: Holt, Rinehart & Winston.

McClelland, D.C. (1961). *The achieving society.* New York, NY: Van Nostrand.

McClelland, D.C., Atkinson, J.W., Clark, R.A., & Lowell, E.L. (1953). *The achievement motive.* New York, NY: Appleton-Century-Crofts.

McCrae, R.R., & Costa, P.T., Jr. (1987). Validation of the five factor model of personality across instruments and observers. *Journal of Personality and Social Psychology, 52,* 81-90.

McDougall, W. (1908/1921). *An Introduction to social psychology,* 14th ed. Boston, MA: John W. Luce & Comp.

McDougall, W. (1920). *The group mind.* Cambridge, England: Cambridge University Press.

Milgram, S. (1961, December). Nationality and conformity. *Scientific American,* pp. 45-51.

Milgram, S. (1963). Behavioral study of obedience. *Journal of Abnormal and Social Psychology, 67,* 371-378.

Milgram, S. (1964). Group pressure and action against a person. *Journal of Abnormal and Social Psychology, 69,* 137-143.

Milgram, S. (1965a). Liberating effects of group pressure. *Journal of Personality and Social Psychology, 1,* 127-134.

Milgram, S. (1965b). Some conditions of obedience and disobedience to authority. *Human Relations, 18,* 57-76.

Milgram, S. (1967, May). The small-world problem. *Psychology Today,* 1, 60-67.

Milgram, S. (1969, June). The lost-letter technique. *Psychology Today,* pp. 30-33, 66, 68.

Milgram, S. (1970). The experience of living in cities. *Science,* 167, 1461-1468.

Milgram, S. (1974). *Obedience to authority: An experimental view.* New York, NY: Harper & Row.

Milgram, S. (1977). *The individual in a social world: Essays and experiments.* Reading, MA: Addison-Wesley.

Milgram, S., Greenwald, J., Kessler, S., McKenna, W., & Waters, J. (1972, March-April). A psychological map of New York City. *American Scientist,* pp. 194-200.

Milgram, S., Mann, L., & Harter, S. (1965). The lost-letter technique: A tool of social research. *Public Opinion Quarterly, 29,* 437-438.

Milgram, S., & Sabini, J. (1978). On maintaining urban norms: A field experiment in the subway. In A. Baum, J.E. Singer, and S. Valins (Eds.), *Advances in environmental psychology,* Vol. 1, pp. 31-40. Hillsdale, NJ: Lawrence Erlbaum.

Milgram, S., & Shotland,R.L. (1973). *Television and antisocial behavior: Field experiments.* New York, NY: Academic Press.

Milgram, S., & Toch, H. (1969). Collective behavior: Crowds and social movements. In G.Lindzey & E. Aronson (Eds.), *The handbook of social psychology* (2nd ed., Vol. 4, pp. 507-610). Reading, MA: Addison-Wesley.

Miller, N.E., & Dollard, J. (1941). *Social learning and imitation.* New Haven, CT: Yale University Press.

Mischel, W. (1968). *Personality and assessment.* New York, NY: Wiley.

Mischel, W. (1973). Toward a cognitive social learning reconceptualization of personality.*Psychological Review, 80,* 730-755.

Morgan, C.D., & Murray, H.A. (1935). A method for investigating fantasies: The Thematic Apperception Test. *Archives of Neurology and Psychiatry, 34,* 289-306.

Murchison, C. (Ed.). (1935). *Handbook of social psychology.* Worcester, MA: Clark University Press.

Murphy, G. (1929). *Historical introduction to modern psychology*. New York, NY: Harcourt Brace.

Murphy, G. (1933). *General psychology*. New York, NY: Harper.

Murphy, G. (1935). *A briefer general psychology*. New York, NY: Harper.

Murphy, G., & Jensen, F. (1932). *Approaches to personality*. New York, NY: Coward-McCann.

Murphy, G., & Murphy, L.B. (1931). *Experimental social psychology*. New York, NY: Harper.

Murphy, G., Murphy, L.B., & Newcomb, T.M. (1937). *Experimental social psychology*, (rev. ed.). New York, NY: Harper.

Murray, H.A. (1938). *Explorations in personality*. New York, NY: Oxford University Press.

Nicholson, I.A.M. (2003). *Inventing personality: Gordon Allport and the science of selfhood*. Washington, DC: American Psychological Association.

Pandora, K. (1997). *Rebels within the ranks: Psychologists' critique of scientific authority and democratic realities in New Deal America*. New York, NY: Cambridge University Press.

Pandora, K. (1998). "Mapping the new mental world created by radio": Media messages, cultural politics, and Cantril and Allport's 'The psychology of radio.' *Journal of Social Issues*.

Rotter, J. B. (1954). *Social learning and clinical psychology*. Englewood Cliffs, NJ: Prentice Hall.

Rotter, J.B. (1966). Generalized expectancies for internal versus external control of reinforcement. *Psychological Monographs, 80*(Whole No. 609).

Sahakian, W.S. (1982). *History and systems of social psychology* (2nd ed.). Washington, DC: Hemisphere.

Sechrest, L. (1976). Personality. *Annual Review of Psychology*, 27, 1-27.

Segal, N.L. (1999). *Entwined lives: Twins and what they tell us about human behavior.* New York, NY: Dutton.

Sheehy, N., Chapman, A.J., & Conroy, W.A. (1997a). Festinger, Leon. In *Biographical dictionary of psychology,* pp. 192-193. London, England, and New York, NY: Routledge.

Sheehy, N., Chapman, A.J., & Conroy, W.A. (1997b). Heider, Fritz. In *Biographical dictionary of psychology,* pp. 261-262. London, England, and New York, NY: Routledge.

Sheehy, N., Chapman, A.J., & Conroy, W.A. (1997c). Latane, Bibb. In *Biographical dictionary of psychology,* pp. 348-349. London, England, and New York, NY: Routledge.

Sheehy, N., Chapman, A.J., & Conroy, W.A. (1997d). Sherif, Muzafer. In *Biographical dictionary of psychology,* pp. 520-521. London, England, and New York, NY: Routledge.

Sherif, M., Harvey, O.J., White, B., Hood, W., & Sherif, C. (1956/1961). *Intergroup conflict and cooperation: The Robbers' Cave experiment.* Norman, OK: Institute of Group Relations, University of Oklahoma.

Stagner, R. (1937). *Psychology of personality.* New York, NY: McGraw-Hill.

Stagner, R. (1938). Review of the book *Personality: A psychological interpretation.*

Journal of Applied Psychology, 22, 219-221.

Steiner, I.D. (1979). Social psychology. In E. Hearst (Ed.) *The first century of experimental psychology*, pp. 513-558. Hillsdale, NJ: Lawrence Elrbaum.

Stouffer, S.A., Guttman, L. Suchman, E.A., Lazarsfeld, P.F., Star, S.A., & Clausen, J.A. (1950). *Measurement and prediction* (Studies in Social Psychology in World War II, Vol. 4). Princeton, NJ: Princeton University Press.

Stouffer, S.A., Lumsdaine, A.A., Lumsdaine, M.H., Williams, R.B., Jr., Smith, M.B., Janis, I.L. Star, S.A., & Cottrell, L.S., Jr. (1949a). *The American soldier: Combat and it aftermath*. (Studies in Social Psychology in World War II, Vol. 2). Princeton, NJ: Princeton University Press.

Stouffer, S.A., Suchman, E.A., DeVinney, L.S., Star, S.A., & Williams, R.B., Jr. (1949b). *The American soldier: Adjustment during army life*. (Studies in Social Psychology in World War II, Vol. 1). Princeton, NJ: Princeton University Press.

Synder, M. (1983). The influence of individuals on situations: Implications for understanding the links between personality and social behavior. *Journal of Personality, 51*, 497-516.

Thomas, W.I., & Znaniecki, F. (1918). *The Polish peasant in America*, Vol. 1. Boston, MA: Badger.

Thurstone, L.L. (1928). Attitudes can be measured. *American Journal of Sociology, 19*, 441-453.

Thurstone, L.L., & Chave, E.J. (1929). *The measurement of values*. Chicago, IL: University of Chicago Press.

Travers, J., & Milgram, S. (1969). An experimental study of the small world problem. *Sociometry, 32*, 425-443.

Triplett, N. (1898). The dynamogenic factors in pacemaking and competition. *American Journal of Psychology, 9*, 507-533.

Vernon, P., & Allport, G. (1931). A test for personal values. *Journal of Abnormal and Social Psychology, 26*, 231-248.

Watson, J.B. (1925). *Behaviorism.* New York, NY: Norton.

Weiner, B. (1990). Attribution in personality psychology. In L. Pervin (Ed.), *Handbook of personality: Theory and research* (pp. 465-485). New York, NY: Guilford Press.

Winter, D.G., & Barenbaum, N.B. (1999). History of modern personality theory and research. In L.A. Pervin & O.P. John (Eds.), *Handbook of personality: Theory and research* (2nd ed.). New York, NY: Guilford Press.

Woodworth, R.S. (1919). Examination of emotional fitness for warfare. *Psychological Bulletin, 15*, 59-60.

Zener, K. (1945). A note concerning editorial reorientation. *Journal of Personality, 14*, 1-2.

CHAPTER 13: CLINICAL PSYCHOLOGY AND PSYCHOTHERAPY

· ethics · mental health · empirical support · stigma

But in the final analysis, the progress of clinical psychology, as of every other science, will be determined by the value and amount of its contribution to the advance of the human race. (Witmer, 1907, p. 4).

Indeed, the split between the research and practice wings of psychology has grown so wide that many psychologists now speak glumly of the "scientist-practitioner gap," although that is like saying there is an "Arab-Israeli gap" in the Middle East. It is a war, involving deeply held beliefs, political passions, views of human nature and the nature of knowledge, and—as all wars ultimately do—money and livelihoods. (Tavris, 2003, p. B7).

Clinical psychology is the largest subfield within what is known as applied psychology. Applied psychology includes all of those areas of psychology devoted to the application of psychological knowledge to the solution of real world problems. Other areas of applied psychology include the development of tests and measurements for schools and businesses, school psychology, forensic psychology, and industrial and organizational psychology, among many other applied fields. Applied psychology developed early in the history of the field. Functionalists were very concerned with applying what they learned to practical problems. But until World War II, most psychologists were basic psychologists, with only a minority working in applied settings.

Clinical psychology is not just the largest subfield within applied psychology, it is the largest subfield within psychology as a whole. There are presently more clinical psychologists than all other types of psychologists combined. While clinical is only one subfield among many, it is the one in which most students are interested, and the one in which most practicing psychologists specialize.

The history of clinical psychology, which includes the history of psychotherapy, is a complex one. On the one hand, clinical psychology was shaped not just by psychology in general and personality psychology in particular.

It was strongly influenced by both psychiatry and psychoanalysis. Furthermore, psychotherapy, the psychological techniques used by therapists to help their clients, is not just the product of clinical psychology, but of psychiatry, psychoanalysis, social work, and non-scientific self-help movements such as the Emmanuel Movement. In light of this complexity, the history of clinical psychology and psychotherapy can and must be told together.

Clinical psychology has another distinction—it is a profession. A profession is a highly skilled occupation whose members enjoy considerable autonomy in the control of their work and enjoy status and prestige in society. Traditionally, there were three professions: medicine, law, and college teaching. In the late 19th century other fields developed as professions, including accounting and engineering. In the post-World War II period clinical psychology also developed into a profession.

Professions are shaped by economic forces. Among these economic forces are market share and market size, the efforts to exclude competition, certification of members qualified to practice the profession, and some restrictions in the number of members. These economic factors, as you will see, have played an important role in the history of clinical psychology as a profession, just as economic factors played an important role in the history of the science of psychology based in the universities.

Until recently most clinical psychologists in the world lived and practiced in the United States. It is only in the last 50 years that clinical psychology has spread throughout the world, providing services that had formerly been provided only by psychiatrists and psychoanalysts.

History Of Clinical Psychology Before World War 2

Lightner Witmer (1867-1956) founded the subfield of clinical psychology in 1896 at the University of Pennsylvania. Clinical psychology, as conceived by Witmer and other psychologists, was based on the testing and diagnosis of individuals with problems, followed by training and education. Treatment and therapy were considered the job of the medical doctor. Psychology clinics were based in universities and medical schools and by 1914 there were 19 such clinics in the U.S. (Reisman, 1991).

The early clinical psychologists were eager to avoid conflicts with the more prestigious medical profession who tended to attack psychology for perceived encroachments on the medical profession. In 1917, for instance, the New York Psychiatrical Society, a leading organization of psychiatrists in the U.S., wrote the American Psychological Association to protest the use of psychologists in the testing of the mentally retarded and in diagnosis and treatment of abnormal emotional conditions. The psychiatrists viewed these as medical problems beyond the abilities of clinical psychologists (Reisman, 1991). This was just an early example of a long and hostile relationship between an established profession and an emerging one that competed for market share.

The clinicians and other applied psychologists were also concerned about the neglect of their interests by the American Psychological Association. In 1918 only 15 of the 375 members of the APA listed clinical as their primary subfield and only 16 of the 375 worked outside of the universities (Reisman, 1991). The dissatisfaction of those with clinical and applied interests led briefly in 1917 to the formation of the American Association of Clinical Psychologists (AACP). The AACP merged into the APA in 1919 when the APA created a separate division of clinical psychology, the first such separate division in the organization (Reisman, 1991).

Clinical psychology continued its slow and steady growth throughout the 1920s and 1930s, but it was primarily confined to testing, diagnosis, and training. A notable university clinic opened at Harvard in 1926, the Harvard Psychological Clinic. The clinic was set up by Morton Prince (1854-1929) as a separate entity from the psychology department at the suggestion of E.G. Boring. Henry Murray succeeded Prince as director of the clinic (Reisman, 1991).

Two other forces shaped clinical psychology during the first four decades of the 20th century: the mental hygiene movement and psychoanalysis. The story of the mental hygiene movement and its founder, Clifford W. Beers (1876-1943), is itself inspiring. Beers graduated from Yale University and suffered an emotional breakdown at the age of 24. He attempted suicide by leaping from a fourth floor window, but landed on soft ground and was not killed. He continued to be very depressed for the next year and was committed to a mental hospital in Connecticut. After approximately a year in the mental hospital he entered a manic phase, writing voluminously about his experience and the experience of the other patients in the hospital. A physician at the hospital confiscated his writing materials and put Beers in a straight jacket in a padded cell for 21 days and nights. He was soon transferred to another hospital in Connecticut and was released in 1903. Upon his release he was determined to write a book about his experience and to organize a movement that would work to prevent mental illness and alleviate the abuses found in mental hospitals. After leaving the hospital, Beers married, became a businessman, and wrote a draft of his autobiography. He took this draft to William James in 1906. James, ever tolerant of other people and their ideas, took the time to carefully read the manuscript and was impressed. James wrote a letter of support for the book and started to interest other leading psychologists and psychiatrists in the manuscript. Among the people James introduced to Beers was Adolf Meyer (1866-1950), the leading psychiatrist in the U.S. and a professor at Johns Hopkins University. Meyers, who helped introduce psychoanalysis to the U.S., wanted to increase public awareness of mental illness and secure greater public funding for treatment and research. The relationship between Beers and Meyers was to be mutually beneficial (Reisman, 1991).

Beers published his autobiography describing his experiences as a mental patient in *The Mind that Found Itself* (Beers, 1908). At the same time, he founded the mental hygiene society (the name mental hygiene was suggested to him by Meyer) in Connecticut to educate the public about mental illness and promote the prevention and treatment of mental illness. The following year, in 1909, Beers organized the National Committee for Mental Hygiene. The committee soon received financial support from private foundations (Reisman, 1991) and eventually changed its name to the National Committee for Mental Health. The movement is often called the mental health movement, using the later appellation. The movement promoted awareness of mental illness by gathering statistics on frequency and types of mental illness, publicizing the treatment of the mentally ill, and supporting research and treatment. The movement was to be a crucial force in the development of clinical psychology and in the development of social work (Trattner, 1999).

The second major force shaping clinical psychology during the first four decades of the 20th century was psychoanalysis. Prior to 1908 William James organized a group of psychologists and physicians into a reading group that studied Freud's works in German. In 1908 G. Stanley Hall at Clark University

536

also started teaching a course on Freud and invited Freud to speak at the 1909 Clark University conference. Also in 1908 A.A. Brill began the first psychoanalytic practice in the U.S. in New York City and the first description of Freudian psychotherapy was published in the *Journal of Abnormal Psychology* (Scott, 1908-1909). The next year, when Freud visited the U.S., Brill also published the first English translation of Freud's early work on hysteria. The British follower of Freud and later a member of Freud's Committee, Ernest Jones, was made an editorial board member of the *Journal of Abnormal Psychology* in 1910. From 1910 onward, psychoanalysis was to have a steady and significant influence on American psychology, especially clinical psychology.

Freud and his followers soon monopolized the treatment of the many kinds of mental illness that did not require long-term treatment in mental institutions. These forms of mental illness include most of what we now call neurosis, as well as simple problems in living. Prior to 1900 these neuroses and problems in living were treated by doctors at health spas, using a variety of treatments such as rest, hot baths, massage, diet, and enemas. By the end of the 1800s, Freud and a small group of doctors (mostly spa doctors and neurologists) developed psychotherapy based on the talking cure used by Pinel and hypnotherapy used by French physicians. Freud's techniques, the most systematic and well-articulated, soon became the dominant form of psychotherapy, used even by physicians who were not formal psychoanalysts (Shorter, 1997).

Not content with their influence in psychology and neurology, Freud and his followers began an effort to take over psychiatry. This was done by insisting, especially in the U.S., that all psychoanalysts also be trained in psychiatry and that psychoanalytic training be restricted to medical doctors (this was later opposed by Freud who argued for lay analysts—one of the few occasions where Freud's followers opposed, and won over, the master). The Freudians also extended their theories to more extreme forms of mental illness such as schizophrenia and autism. In public, Freud doubted that psychoanalysis could be extended to severe mental illness, but in private he was very supportive of all efforts to apply his theories to the kind of extreme cases that were normally treated by psychiatrists in mental hospitals (Shorter, 1997).

By the 1930s training in psychoanalysis had become rigid and dogmatic. Psychoanalytically trained psychiatrists or psychoanalysts dominated most

departments of psychiatry at major universities and they held many of the major positions as editors of journals or officers in the American Psychiatric Association. Psychiatrists, especially the psychoanalysts among them, did everything they could to exclude social workers and psychologists from treating the mentally ill or providing psychotherapy (Shorter, 1997).

The small number of clinical psychologists who practiced in the 1920s, 1930s, and early 1940s struggled to carve out a place for clinical psychology in the provision of psychotherapy, not just the testing of individuals. A leader and representative figure of this group was Carl Rogers, who paved the way for the post-World War II growth of clinical psychology.

Carl R. Rogers (1902-1987) is best known for his leadership of the humanistic psychology movement in the 1960s and 1970s. Along with Abraham Maslow, Rogers was the premier leader of a second psychological counterculture in the second half of the 20th century. But Rogers was an important clinical psychologist decades before he became a leader of the humanistic psychology movement; he made significant contributions in the 1930s and 1940s.

Rogers was born into a hardworking Midwestern family. His father ran a farm and was an engineer trained at the University of Wisconsin. In addition to the farm, his father ran an engineering firm. Rogers read extensively as a child, did very well in school, and worked on the farm. He started at the University of Wisconsin in agriculture but his interests soon shifted to history. Rogers' family was very religious and he was very active in a Christian student group affiliated with the YMCA. While a student he was selected for a Christian delegation to China and spent six months in China and the Far East under the sponsorship of the World Student Christian Federation. After returning, he was hospitalized for an intestinal ulcer for six months. As a result of his trip and illness, Rogers took five years to graduate instead of four, completing his history degree in 1924 (Rogers, 1967a).

Shortly after graduating, Rogers married and moved to New York City, where he began studies at the Union Theological Seminary. The liberal protestant seminary played an important role in the psychological counterculture —Lois Barclay Murphy was a student there (she and Gardner Murphy were married in 1926) as was Theodore Newcomb, the social psychologist who also worked with the Murphy's. Newcomb was a friend and classmate of Rogers at the seminary. Rogers was exposed to pastoral counseling at the seminary and he found his true calling: psychotherapy. After two years at the seminary he transferred across the street to Columbia University where he studied for his Ph.D. At the time, there was no real program in clinical psychology at Columbia, so Rogers had to create his own. He took a course in clinical psychology with Leta Hollingworth, an early leader in clinical and applied psychology. Under Hollingworth's supervision, Rogers did his first work in child clinical psychology. Rogers also received a fellowship to work at the newly formed Institute of Child Guidance (funded by the Commonwealth Fund), where he was trained in psychotherapy as practiced by Freud and learned about the work of Alfred Adler, who lectured at the Institute. Rogers' clinical training was very different from his academic work at Columbia, which was strongly influenced by E.L. Thorndike and Robert S. Woodworth. For his doctoral dissertation, Rogers developed and validated a test of personality adjustment for children (Rogers, 1931). The test proved very valuable to clinicians and was used for over three decades (Rogers, 1967a).

Rogers knew from early in his graduate training at Columbia University that he wanted to practice clinical psychology. Unlike many of his fellow Ph.D.s, he sought employment as a full-time clinician. He was hired to work in the Rochester Child Study Department, which later was renamed the Rochester (New York) Child Guidance Center, where he worked with troubled children, many of whom were referred to the center by the court system. Rogers soon rose to the position of clinic director, one of the few psychologists to actually direct a clinic in the U.S. Most clinics were directed by psychiatrists who sought to limit the role of clinical psychologists to testing. Indeed, in 1937 and 1938, when the Child Study Department was being enlarged and transformed into the Rochester Child Guidance Clinic, psychiatrists made an unsuccessful attempt to oust Rogers from the directorship, arguing that since psychiatrists were in charge of almost all similar clinics in the U.S., a psychiatrist should also be in charge of the Rochester clinic (Rogers, 1967a; Reisman, 1991).

In addition to directing the Rochester clinic, Rogers taught summer classes at Columbia in clinical psychology, and carried out psychotherapy with children and their parents. The therapy was called the treatment interview, in part to avoid confrontation with psychiatrists and psychoanalysts, who had a virtual monopoly on psychotherapy. During his Rochester years, Rogers also worked with social workers and remained active in the APA, although he felt very alienated from the APA due to its emphasis on behaviorism during the 1930s (Rogers, 1967a).

Rogers was concerned from early in his career with finding empirical evidence of effective treatment, an attitude that put him at odds with psychoanalysts who resisted empirical studies of psychotherapy. Rogers also adopted an eclectic approach, using a variety of techniques. He was especially influenced by Otto Rank's will therapy, which emphasized the present and the future and not the past, and the work of Fredrick Allen (1890-1964), a psychiatrist who directed the Philadelphia Child Guidance Clinic (Reisman, 1991). Allen, who was also influenced by Rank, had bachelor's and master's degrees in psychology as well as an M.D. Allen emphasized that the child psychotherapist must respect and accept children as they were, a concept Rogers later extended to adults and termed unconditional positive regard (Allen, 1934; Allen, 1940).

Rogers synthesized these various eclectic elements and his experience with children into a coherent approach to child clinical psychology in his first book, *The Clinical Treatment of the Problem Child* (Rogers, 1939a). The book represented a major advance in child clinical psychology and brought Rogers to the attention of leading academic psychologists. Rogers also carried out early studies of the effectiveness of various treatments with children (Rogers, 1937) and made thoughtful recommendations on the characteristics and training of clinical psychologists (Rogers, 1939b). In 1940 he was offered a position at Ohio State University as a full professor of clinical psychology. His work in clinical psychology was so impressive that Rogers started at the top of the academic ladder. Rogers now had the opportunity to carry out more extensive research in clinical psychology and to train graduate students as clinicians.

In his new job he was able to articulate a process approach to therapy, looking at what therapists actually did in therapy that was associated with positive outcomes (Rogers, 1940). As part of this approach, Rogers made audiotapes of all sessions conducted with selected clients (he called them clients to avoid conflict with the psychoanalysts) and analyzed the tapes, looking at what was predictive of positive outcomes for the client. He soon presented his first formal and worked out approach to therapy, which included the first published verbatim record of a series of psychotherapy sessions (Rogers, 1942). This was the first highly developed theory of psychotherapy that was not based on the work of Freud or his followers or apostates, and that had empirical evidence for the recommended techniques—a major achievement.

On the eve of World War II and the rapid expansion of clinical psychology, Rogers was the leading clinical psychologist in the U.S. and the developer of an approach to psychotherapy that rivaled that of psychoanalysis. He continued as the leader in the field throughout the war years and into the 1950s. He served as president of the American Association of Applied Psychologists (AAAP) in 1944-1945. The AAAP had been formed in 1937 when clinical psychologists, school psychologists, and other professional psychologists left the APA which, the applied psychologists felt, was not addressing their needs. As president of the AAAP, Rogers negotiated with the APA to create a single unified organization with different divisions. He was elected president of the newly reorganized APA in 1946. Also in 1945, Rogers moved to the University of Chicago where he founded and led the university's counseling center from 1945 to 1957, where he extended his work to counseling of normal young people. While at the University of Chicago he renamed his approach client-centered therapy (Rogers, 1946) and refined it based on empirical studies (Rogers, 1951). He also examined personality change during therapy (Rogers & Dymond, 1954) and did empirical studies of the conditions necessary for effective therapy (Rogers, 1957) and he continued research on the process of therapy (Rogers, 1958). At the University of Chicago, Rogers had to fight a sustained battle against the psychiatrists who were adamantly opposed to his clinic and tried to shut it down (Shorter, 1997). In 1957 he left the University of Chicago for the University of Wisconsin, but his interests were turning to education, personality psychology, and philosophy. He emerged as the leader of humanistic psychology, the so-called third force in psychology in the 1960s, but this is getting a little ahead of our story.

Carl Rogers was the right person at the right time. On the eve of the dramatic expansion of clinical psychology in 1942 he had already established himself as the leading and most creative clinical psychologist in the country, with a unique, non-psychoanalytic approach to psychotherapy. By emphasizing the process of psychotherapy, the characteristics of effective therapists, and the importance of empirical studies of the process of therapy and the outcomes of therapy, he created a distinct and empirically grounded approach to psychotherapy. Clinical psychologists were well positioned at the start of World War II to make valuable contributions to the care of veterans.

World War 2 And The Growth Of Clinical Psychology

By 1945 clinical psychology had experienced twenty years of steady growth. In 1918, only 4% of the members of APA had interests in clinical psychology. By 1945, 53% of the members of the APA expressed interest in clinical psychology. Many of these were full-time clinicians (Reisman, 1991). The number of psychologists in the U.S. was still small, perhaps 2,000 to 3,000 (based on the combined membership of the APA and the AAAP and assuming no overlap of membership). Of these, over 1,700 had served in the war (Reisman, 1991).

Psychologists contributed to a number of areas during the war, as described in previous chapters, but a significant number served as clinical psychologists during the war to supplement the work of psychiatrists who were even fewer in number than the psychologists.

Working with the U.S. government, psychologists also prepared for the post-war period. On the one hand, psychologists sought to reunify the profession to meet the challenges and opportunities of the post-war period. This resulted in the reorganization of the APA in 1944 and the merger of the AAAP and the APA into a single APA in the same year. The new organization had a divisional structure that reflected the diverse nature of applied and basic psychology, with 19 different divisions and a provision for the addition or deletion of new divisions in the future as the field changed. The newly reorganized APA also published a new flagship journal with scholarly articles of broad interest, entitled *American Psychologist* (Hilgard, 1987).

On the other hand, psychologists responded to the anticipated need for additional clinical psychologists. The government asked the APA to develop a plan for the training of additional clinicians to meet the anticipated need. The APA decided to train clinicians within existing university graduate programs and to accredit graduate programs that met quality standards of training. Thus began the system of APA clinical accreditation which is still very important.

In fact, an APA-approved graduate program and internship remain important elements of a competitive job application for today's clinical psychology graduates. The federal government hired only clinicians from accredited programs, a strong incentive to study in such programs (Hilgard, 1987). The APA adopted a model of training that emphasized training as a scientist and researcher as well as a clinician, sometimes called the Boulder model after a 1949 conference in Boulder, Colorado that specified the model in detail. Graduate students were to complete a four-year program that included a doctoral dissertation based on original research and a one-year supervised clinical internship before the Ph.D. was granted (Hilgard, 1987).

Psychiatric Casualties

Over 16 million men and women served in the U.S. military during World War II. At the end of the war many of them needed vocational counseling or psychotherapy for war-related emotional problems and a significant number, around 44,000, required extensive care for war-induced mental illnesses in VA hospitals. A need for post-war mental health services is an inevitable outcome of war over the last 100 years. The VA placed clinical psychologists on par with psychiatrists and gave the clinical psychologists equal pay and comparable responsibilities to the psychiatrists. Clinical psychologists working at VA hospitals also carried out research and supervised clinical internships for clinical graduate students. The emotionally disturbed and mentally ill military veterans were known as psychiatric casualties and their numbers equaled or exceeded the number of physical casualties from the war (Reisman 1991). In a pattern that was to be repeated in the Korean War, the Vietnam War, the Persian Gulf War, and now the Iraq and Afghanistan Wars, the number of veterans needing some form of therapy was very large and fueled the continued demand for clinical psychologists.

Universities and the APA responded quickly to the increased demand for clinical psychologists. In 1947, 22 universities had APA-accredited graduate programs in clinical psychology, enrolling a total of 210 graduate students. By 1949, there were 42 accredited programs with many more graduate students and more qualified applicants than the universities could accommodate (Reisman, 1991).

In addition to the demand for clinical psychology created by the need to treat the psychiatric casualties in the VA hospitals, the National Institute of Mental Health (NIMH), created by the National Mental Health Act of 1946, fueled the growth of clinical psychology. As part of the National Institutes of Health, the NIMH funded research at universities and community centers and provided fellowships to support graduate study in psychology. Together, the VA and NIMH propelled the massive growth of clinical psychology in the 1950s and beyond (Hilgard, 1987). The growth in clinical psychology was not merely an increase in the number of people working as psychotherapists or receiving psychotherapy; the growth in clinical psychology also witnessed the development of new therapies and dramatic increases in the empirical study of psychotherapy.

New Therapies: Behavioral Therapy And Rational-Emotive Therapy

Two distinct and relatively new forms of psychotherapy emerged in the 1950s to supplement client-centered therapy. These two forms of therapy made clinical psychologists even more competitive with psychiatrists and psychoanalysts. Most clinicians were trained in an eclectic approach, following a practice that was encouraged by Rogers. They were trained in different approaches to psychotherapy and encouraged to use what seemed to work best for their patients. Against this backdrop of eclecticism, two new forms of therapy were developed. The first new form of psychotherapy was behavior therapy, the second was rational-emotive therapy.

Behavior therapy had its roots in the emphasis of the early clinical psychologists, such as Witmer, on clinical psychology as education and learning, and in the work of Mary Cover Jones. Jones, working with John B. Watson as mentor, showed that children can "unlearn" a phobia using principles of classical conditioning (Jones, 1924).

Efforts in the 1930s to develop behavior therapy (Dunlap, 1932; Mower & Mower, 1938) were not very successful. However, Joseph Wolpe (1915-1997), a clinical psychologist originally from South Africa, developed a number of successful techniques based on classical conditioning, including systematic desensitization of phobias (Wolpe, 1958). Wolpe later extended his behavioral therapy to a wide variety of problems such as smoking, weight loss, assertiveness, and shyness (Wolpe & Lazarus, 1966). Other researchers using operant conditioning also developed useful behavioral techniques in the 1960s, such as token economies, that proved very useful in the treatment of autistic children and schizophrenics (Ayllon & Azrin, 1968). Behavior therapy, originally developed in the 1950s, experienced steady growth and development in the1960s and 1970s as a consequence of the application of classical and operant conditioning, and modeling to new problems, and as a consequence of the use of N=1 experiments and other research designs to test and evaluate these behavioral techniques.

The second new therapy that emerged in the 1950s was developed by Albert Ellis (1913-2007) and was called by Ellis rational-emotive therapy (Ellis, 1958). Ellis was born in Pittsburgh and received his B.A. from City College in New York and his M.A. and Ph.D. from Columbia University in 1934 and 1943, respectively. Ellis was also trained in psychoanalysis and practiced psychoanalysis from 1947 to 1953. In addition, he was a prominent expert on sex and marriage and published a number of popular books in that area. He found psychoanalysis to be ineffective and was disturbed by the lack of empirical evidence showing that psychoanalysis worked, so he developed his own approach emphasizing that to change people's neurotic behavior, the therapist had to change their irrational and neurotic beliefs and thinking patterns. He started his own institute for clinical training and research (the Institute for Rational-Emotive Therapy) and was its executive director, as well as a popular author and therapist (Sheehy, Chapman, & Conway, 1997a). Ellis was criticized extensively by psychoanalysts and psychoanalytically-oriented psychiatrists in the 1950s while clinical psychologists began to learn his methods and subject them to empirical investigation, a development that Ellis welcomed. In the mid-to-late 1960s, empirical evidence had accumulated to support many of his techniques, such as the use of homework by patients and the disputation of clients' irrational or neurotic beliefs.

Empirical Criticism: The Work Of Eysenck And Meehl

With the expansion of clinical psychology as a profession also came the expansion of basic research into clinical psychology. This is most clearly seen in the dramatic rise in studies of the effectiveness of psychotherapy and studies of the process of psychotherapy. Until 1931, there were no outcome studies. Between 1931 and 1945 there was an average of two published studies per year, and after 1945 the number of studies increased geometrically, with almost 160 studies carried out between 1966 and 1970, an average of 32 studies per year.

Outcome and process studies are difficult to do because it is difficult to standardize a treatment process while remaining sensitive to the unique needs and responses of an individual client. As more and more such studies started to appear, researchers in clinical psychology shifted to broader questions, such as whether psychotherapy really works. One of the first to ask these broader questions was Hans J. Eysenck (1916-1997). Eysenck was born in Berlin but was a naturalized British citizen. He moved to England in 1934 to attend college and was educated at the University of London where he received his B.A. in 1938 and his Ph.D. in 1940. Both of Eysenck's parents, who had remained in Germany, were killed in the Nazi concentration camps. After receiving his Ph.D. under the direction of Sir Cyril Burt (whom you shall meet in Chapter 14), Eysenck had difficulty finding a job because of anti-German prejudice, although Eysenck hated Hitler and the Nazis. He eventually found work at the Maudsley Hospital, the premier psychiatric hospital in Britain, where he became director of the psychology department from 1946 to 1983. He also secured a joint appointment at the University of London, first as a reader from 1950 to 1954 (a low academic rank in the British university system) and later as a professor from 1954 to 1983. Eysenck was enormously productive, authoring or editing over 60 books and over 600 scientific articles or chapters. Much of his work was devoted to personality measurement and theory, and he did important work that resolved the controversy over the structure of personality and led to the five factor model of personality. He also developed and validated a number of personality tests, argued for a genetic component of basic personality traits, and wrote a series of books for the general public on psychology (Terry, 1997).

In addition to his many contributions to personality psychology, Eysenck made two important contributions to clinical psychology. He was one of the first to address empirically the question of whether psychotherapy works. Based on a review of controlled studies of outcomes of Freudian psychotherapy, Eysenck found Freudian psychotherapy no more effective in helping people than no treatment at all (Eysenck, 1952). Eysenck's conclusion provoked a hailstorm of criticism (some of it personal) from psychoanalysts. Eysenck's paper also forced psychotherapists to consider the effectiveness of every form of therapy. Second, Eysenck was a leader in the development of behavior therapy and was especially concerned with empirical studies of the effectiveness of behavior therapy techniques. His work in this area had a considerable impact in Britain where he was considered the father of British clinical psychology, and in the U.S. (Terry, 1997).

Another researcher to ask broad empirical questions about clinical psychology was Paul E. Meehl (1920-2003). Meehl was born in Minneapolis, Minnesota and earned his B.A. and Ph.D. from the University of Minnesota in 1941 and 1945, respectively. Meehl became interested in psychology by reading Freud as a high school student and as an undergraduate was an honor student who studied with B.F. Skinner. He started as an instructor at the University of Minnesota in 1944 (before completing his Ph.D.) and was a full professor by 1952. Meehl was a genuine polymath—an expert in many things. Over the course of his career he published over 180 scientific books and papers, making contributions to psychology, law, psychiatry, political science, and philosophy, and at various times in his career held faculty positions in law, psychiatry, neurology, and philosophy (Smetanka, 2003).

Meehl made a number of important contributions to clinical psychology during the 1950s. In addition to his work on the MMPI as a tool for clinicians (Hathaway & Meehl, 1951), Meehl studied the diagnostic skills of clinical psychologists. In a little book that provoked controversy for years afterwards (and is still valuable to read), Meehl showed in a series of studies that simple psychometric tests did better than experienced clinicians at diagnosing mental illness and predicting which treatments would work best for a client (Meehl, 1954). He went on to show how an accurate diagnosis required not just an accurate test, but knowledge of the base-rate of a mental illness to judge the likelihood that a person with a particular score on a test actually had a mental illness. This is an application of Bayes Theorem in statistics to medicine and clinical psychology (Meehl & Rosen, 1955). Meehl argued, quite provocatively for his time, for the need for a good clinical cookbook—essentially empirically validated tools to diagnose mental illness, along with therapeutic techniques

that have been empirically evaluated and demonstrated to work for particular kinds of mental illness (Meehl, 1956). Finally, Meehl showed that not only are clinical psychologists and psychiatrists poor diagnosticians who do not understand how to think about the results of effective tests, they tend to ignore the test results most of the time (Meehl, 1960). All four contributions created a firestorm among clinicians and are still debated today, but also earned him a place as one of the leading clinical researchers in the U.S. Finally, Meehl was one of the first prominent clinical psychologists to argue, in his presidential address to the APA (after being elected to that post in 1962 at the age of 42) that schizophrenia had a biological basis (Meehl, 1962). This argument further antagonized psychoanalysts and psychiatrists who argued that schizophrenia was caused by poor mothering in infancy and early childhood.

Meehl made many other contributions to psychology over his career, including the use of statistics in psychological research (Meehl, 1967; Meehl, 1978), learning theory, and psychometrics (MacCorquedale & Meehl, 1948; Cronbach & Meehl, 1955). Meehl also was a kind and gentle teacher who encouraged his students to think deeply about psychology. In his writing he was clear and forceful. In person, he was engaging and encouraging. When his students would ask a stupid or ignorant question, he would turn the question into something insightful and brilliant, make the student feel like the question was theirs, and then try to answer the question with the student. (I can attest to this personally because I was a student in two of Meehl's graduate seminars and Meehl was a member of my dissertation committee.) Colleagues took to calling this way of answering silly or stupid questions "Meehl errors" (Smetanka, 2003). He also had a small clinical practice where he used a combination of psychoanalytic, behavioral, and rational-emotive techniques with his clients (Sheehy, Chapman, & Conroy, 1997b).

In addition to his emphasis on the importance of empirical research in clinical psychology, Meehl was distinct in his approach in two ways. First, the psychoanalytically-oriented therapists and the therapists influenced by Carl Rogers ignored and neglected diagnosis while Meehl emphasized the importance of diagnosis. Second, both psychoanalytically-oriented therapists and therapists influenced by Rogers neglected the precise description and symptoms of mental illness, something which Meehl emphasized. While Meehl believed that psychotherapy could help people with bad habits or problems in living, he also believed that mental illness, such as schizophrenia and major depression, are real and exist in nature. Effective treatment of real mental illness requires accurate diagnosis and knowledge of the characteristics of those illnesses. Much of his later work focused on the classification of mental illness (Meehl, 1995).

The 1960s and 1970s: Controversy and Achievement

Throughout the 1960s and 1970s clinical psychology faced its own internal problems, in some ways akin to the crisis of confidence in social psychology and the decade of doubt in personality psychology. The 1960s and 1970s were also a period of achievement for clinical psychology, in spite of and partly because of the internal problems and dissensions.

The 1960s began in the United States with the birth of the antipsychiatry movement, which can be dated to the publication of Thomas Szasz's article in *American Psychologist* on mental illness as a socially constructed myth (Szasz, 1960), followed the next year by a full-length book on the same theme entitled *The Myth of Mental Illness* (Szasz, 1961). Szasz had been born in Hungary and was trained in Chicago as a psychoanalyst. He developed an historical and socio-cultural critique of mental illness as a myth created by society to control and regulate deviants. The same year that Szasz's book was published, sociologist Irving Goffman published a highly critical empirical study of mental hospitals (Goffman, 1961) that showed them to be degrading and controlling institutions. The following year, 1962, Ken Kesey, who had taken a creative writing course at Stanford and had participated as a volunteer in government-run LSD experiments, published *One Flew over the Cuckoo's Nest* (Kesey, 1962). The novel was based on his experiences as an orderly at a Veteran's Administration hospital in California and illustrated Goffman's claim for the dehumanizing and controlling character of the mental health system. The cumulative impact of these three books and the many articles published by Szasz created widespread hostility towards psychiatry in general. The hostility was also directed toward psychotherapy, given that the general public at the time had (and still to this day has) difficulty distinguishing psychiatrists from psychologists and often think that all psychologists are clinical psychologists. Lost was Szasz' claim that psychotherapy could help people who had problems in living.

The antipsychiatry movement gained substantial support among intellectuals and the general public in the mid-1960s and 1970s. The work of Michel Foucault, originally published in French in 1961, was translated and published in English in 1965 (Foucault, 1965) as *Madness and Civilization*. Foucault argued that insanity was a social invention of the 18th century in a book that persuaded many of the truth of his claim. In 1970, Szasz published a comparative study of the mental health movement and The Inquisition, making a similar historical argument (Szasz, 1970). In 1973, Rosenhan, a professor of psychology and law at Stanford University, published an empirical demonstration of the social definition of mental illness. In what was one of the most widely read studies from the 1970s, Rosenhan sent normal, emotionally healthy people to mental hospitals with the complaint that they heard voices in their head saying "hollow," "empty," and "thud." The eight pseudopatients, as Rosenhan referred to them, immediately ceased complaining of hearing voices upon being admitted. All were diagnosed as being schizophrenic and were later released with a diagnosis of schizophrenia in remission. During their stay in the mental hospitals, the pseudopatients' normal behavior was interpreted as symptoms of their schizophrenia (Rosenhan, 1973). Rosenhan's research study was published in the prestigious journal *Science* (*Science*, as you will recall, was founded and edited for many years by psychologist James McKeen Cattell). The antipsychiatry movement reached the public in 1975 with a film based on Kesey's novel. The movie *One Flew Over the Cuckoo's Nest*, staring Jack Nicholson, won five Oscars and was a big money-maker for United Artists studio, who produced the movie (Shorter, 1997).

While mental health professionals were being portrayed as brutal, controlling monsters, and mental illness was portrayed as a social construction or myth, clinical psychologists reacted by embracing a view of psychology as humanistic and positive. The humanistic psychology movement was also called the third force in psychology because it rejected the materialism of both behaviorism and psychoanalysis while emphasizing the positive in human beings, the potential for growth and transcendence, and the dignity and worth of the person. The main leader and organizer of humanistic psychology was Abraham Maslow (1908-1970). After the publication of his book on personality (Maslow, 1954), he organized a group of correspondents to discuss issues raised in his book. The group met several times in the late 1950s and in 1961 began publishing the *Journal of Humanistic Psychology*. In 1963 Maslow and his colleagues organized the American Association of Humanistic Psychology. In 1972 the association became a division of the APA, the Division of Humanistic Psychology (Hilgard, 1987).

Maslow was the leading humanistic psychologist within basic psychology. He was a highly respected researcher who had received his Ph.D. under Harry Harlow at the University of Wisconsin studying primate behavior, and had done a post-doctoral fellowship with E.L. Thorndike at Columbia. After finishing, he took a job at Brandeis University in New York and was influenced by the Gestalt psychologist Max Wertheimer, who was teaching at the New School in New York. Maslow attended Wertheimer's courses early in his time at Brandeis and used Wertheimer as a model of a self-actualized person. Maslow was highly respected for his work in personality and motivation carried out in the 1950s. In a relatively short time in the late 1950s and early 1960s he produced important works on the psychology of religion, on peak-experiences, self-actualized personalities (those people who are extremely emotional healthy and completed), and emotional maturity (Maslow, 1962; Maslow, 1964). His death from a heart attack at the age of 62 deprived the movement of its primary academic leader. The other two prominent leaders of the movement were the clinical psychologists Rollo May and Carl Rogers. May had edited a volume on existential psychology (May, 1961) and written a popular books on existentialism and psychology (May, 1953; May, 1969). He was a respected clinician and a skilled writer.

The third leader of the humanistic psychology movement was Carl Rogers. Rogers moved from the University of Chicago to the University of Wisconsin in 1957. At Wisconsin Rogers carried out a large study of the effectiveness of client-centered therapy with schizophrenics (1967b); the techniques of client-centered therapy had only minimal effects with schizophrenics. While at Wisconsin, Rogers also wrote his first explicitly humanistic book, *On Becoming a Person* (Rogers, 1961), a collection of previous and revised articles. Rogers' attention increasingly shifted away from individual therapy and counseling toward education and group therapy. He became a leading proponent (and facilitator) of encounter groups—groups for normal individuals designed to break down social barriers and promote emotional health and development. Encounter groups, under a variety of names, were very popular and common during the 1960s and 1970s (Hilgard, 1987). Many humanistic psychologists were involved in promoting and facilitating these groups.

Humanistic psychologists had few adherents within academic psychology. Most humanistic psychologists were clinicians. From a sociological perspective, humanistic psychology served as a defense against the antipsychiatry movement and as a means to distinguish the humanists as the "good guys" against the psychiatrists, psychoanalysts, and behaviorists, who were the "bad guys" in the minds of many. Humanistic psychology also provided a second counterculture within psychology, a counterculture that opposed the materialism of behaviorism and psychoanalysis, and emphasized the positive aspects of human nature. A number of the surviving members of the original Jamesian counterculture became supporters of this new counterculture, including Gardner Murphy and Hadley Cantril. Cantril joined the editorial board of the *Journal of Humanistic Psychology* shortly after the journal began publication (Hilgard, 1987). It is interesting that the humanists generally avoided the cognitive revolution that was sweeping through psychology in the 1960. This was not so of the empirical researchers within universities who studied clinical psychology. Much of the progress within clinical psychology came from these empirical researchers, and they paid close attention to the cognitive revolution.

The Cognitive Revolution Comes To Clinical Psychology

The empirical researchers situated in university settings were deeply influenced by the cognitive revolution. The two primary achievements of these researchers during the 1960s and 1970s were first, the empirical validation of the effectiveness of various kinds of psychotherapy though the use of outcome studies and meta-analytic syntheses of these studies and second, the development of new, highly effective therapies for depression and anxiety disorders, known as cognitive-behavioral therapy.

Following the argument of Carl Rogers that the processes and outcomes of psychotherapy can be studied empirically and experimentally, clinical psychologists increasingly used empirical studies of therapies: investigating therapist characteristics, client characteristics (such as the kind of problem they were experiencing and their motivation to change), the process of therapy, and the outcomes of therapy. They increasingly used experimental designs where treatment groups were compared with no-treatment control groups and placebo control groups as well. At the same time, debate raged over the proper way to statistically analyze and synthesize the data from these studies, part of the statistical significance test controversy. As clinical researchers became increasingly sophisticated in their use of statistics, they turned to a new form of synthesizing research findings: meta-analysis. The first major meta-analysis of psychotherapy outcomes was published in 1977 and others soon followed (Smith & Glass, 1977). These syntheses of hundreds and hundreds of studies showed that psychotherapy was indeed an effective treatment for certain problems. The meta-analyses also started to address the issue of which factors produce success with which patients and which problems.

The second achievement of this period was the development of cognitive behavior therapy (sometimes called cognitive therapy). The primary researcher behind cognitive behavior therapy is Aaron T. Beck (1921-). Beck, who is called Tim by his friends and colleagues, was born in Providence, Rhode Island, and received his bachelor's degree from Brown University and his M.D. from Yale in 1946. Beck worked in several VA hospitals after finishing medical school where he became interested in research on the effectiveness of psychotherapy. Beck joined the Department of Psychiatry at the University of Pennsylvania in 1954, where he has remained to this day. At the beginning of his time at the University of Pennsylvania, Beck carried out studies of psychoanalysis and depression. When research showed that the psychoanalytic treatment of depression was not effective, he started searching for more effective treatments. Beck soon developed an approach that emphasized the thinking processes of the depressed patient and how to change those patterns of thinking (Beck, 1963; Beck, 1967), an approach similar to Ellis' Rational-Emotive Therapy. The difference between the two approaches (which both men acknowledged are slight at a joint presentation at the 2000 APA convention) is that Beck carried out a series of outcome studies to demonstrate the effectiveness of the approach and to modify the techniques based on the empirical studies. In addition, Beck began by focusing on a treatment for a single mental illness, depression. He later expanded this work to anxiety disorders (Beck, 1976), personality disorders (Beck, Freeman, & Davis, 2003), and anger and violence (Beck, 1999). In addition to his development of cognitive-behavioral therapy and its empirical validation, Beck developed and validated a number of tests for diagnosing various types of mental illnesses. The most famous and widely used of these tests is the Beck Depression Inventory, but he also developed the Beck Anxiety Inventory and the Beck Hopelessness Scale, also very useful to clinicians.

Beck received the Lasker Award in 2006, the highest award given to a physician in the United States. Even though he was trained as a psychiatrist and neurologist, and has worked for over 50 years at the University of Pennsylvania Medical School, he is perhaps the most important scientific leader in clinical psychology in the 20th century next to Carl Rogers. Beck also acknowledges the many contributions of behavioral therapy in his books and scholarly publications (*e.g.*, Beck, 1970), as well as the work of Albert Ellis, whom he has called a "major pioneer in the field of psychotherapy, a David who went out to slay Goliath" (Beck, 2003).

Two limitations of the empirical validation of psychotherapy became apparent in the 1960s and 1970s and must be mentioned so that we can place the achievement of the empirical researchers in perspective. First, therapies multiplied far faster than they could be empirically validated and were often adopted by clinicians and became popular before there was any real evidence of their effectiveness. So by the 1970s, there were over 130 types of psychotherapy. Most were not standardized and many clinicians employed a variety of therapeutic types. The situation, in fact, was called the therapeutic jungle by some observers (Hale, 1995).

There are several illustrative examples of the therapeutic jungle and the rise and popularization of empirically untested forms of therapy. One of the most tragic involved Carl Rogers. Rogers became an early and enthusiastic proponent of encounter groups and spent a large amount of his time in the 1960s and 1970s running such groups or training others to run them. Rogers' approach was the most conservative, stressing the honest expression of positive and negative emotions. Other approaches included 24 (or more) hours of non-stop meetings, screaming (Primal Scream therapy), beating pillows, sexual fondling and touching, meeting in the nude, and holding in one's urine (Reisman, 1991). In the mid-1970s substantial evidence had accumulated that many people were harmed by these groups. The rate of psychiatric casualties ranged from 1% to 47%, depending on the type of encounter group experience, with an 8% casualty rate across all groups (Hartley, Roback, & Abramowitz, 1976). In addition to the harmful effects, there was little evidence that most of these groups produced any positive effects. By the end of the 1970s, the clinical enthusiasm for encounter groups had died down and a more sober approach to group therapy predominated (Reisman, 1991). However, these techniques can still be found in use around the world.

Two other examples involve Gestalt Therapy (not related in any way to Gestalt psychology) developed by Fritz Perls (Perls, 1969) and Transactional Analysis (TA), associated with Eric Berne (Berne, 1964) and Thomas Harris (Harris, 1967). Perls was originally a psychoanalyst who become a guru-like figure who conducted Gestalt therapy group sessions using a "hot seat," where one member of the group was challenged and interrogated by the group about their feelings (Perls, 1969). Eric Berne was also trained as a psychoanalyst and presented a therapy based on the idea that personality is made up of a parent, an adult, and a child (read superego, ego, and id), and that much of behavior is based on different kinds of games that are played between these three components of personality and between people. People behaved in particular ways in order to compel others to behave in particular ways (Berne, 1964). Berne's book was a bestseller and sold well through the 1990s. Berne's book was followed by another bestseller on TA, *I'm OK, You're OK* (Harris, 1967). Harris emphasized emotional acceptance of self and others, in addition to the importance of strokes (read reinforcement) for happiness. Harris' book also became a bestseller. Soon, TA was practiced by a number of clinicians who had trained in the techniques in order to meet the demands of clients for TA. The popularity and widespread use of Encounter Groups, Gestalt Therapy, and TA all occurred in the absence of any evidence that they worked.

A second limitation which will put the achievements of the empirical researchers into perspective is that when research showed that a therapy was not effective, the evidence seemed to have little impact on the behavior of clinicians who continued to promote and use particular techniques. The once popular but ineffective therapies lingered, as new and untested therapies rose in popularity.

By the end of the 1970s, clinical psychology was a field and a profession rife with contradiction. On the one hand, clinicians had made many significant advances, both scientifically and professionally. On the other hand, the profession seemed out of control, suggesting that the antipsychiatry movement may indeed have been right. The contradictions were to deepen in the 1980s.

The 1970s and 80s: The Return of the Biological Approach

While the antipsychiatry movement, humanistic psychology, the empirical validation of psychotherapy, and the development of new forms of therapy during the 1960s and 1970s took center stage, three significant changes were taking place off stage in clinical psychology. These changes became increasingly prominent in the late 1970s and dominated clinical psychology during the 1980s. These changes included the transformation of graduate training in clinical psychology, the rise of a system of diagnosis and categorization of mental illness, and the chemical revolution.

The number of jobs for psychologists in colleges and universities did not increase significantly in the mid-1970s, when the post-World War II growth of universities slowed. The demand for clinical psychologists continued to increase however, and it was difficult for colleges and universities to keep pace with the demand. For instance, the number of APA-accredited programs in clinical psychology increased from 70 in 1969 to approximately 100 ten years later (Reisman, 1991). Since the 1960s, clinicians and graduate students in clinical psychology had expressed some dissatisfaction with the nature of graduate training, feeling that too much emphasis was placed on developing research skills and too little on developing clinical skills (Thelen & Ewing, 1970). As a remedy for this imbalance in clinical programs, some psychologists recommended an alternative to the Boulder model of the scientist-practitioner: that of the professional school model, similar to law schools, medical schools, and dental schools. The University of Illinois began such a program in 1968 and it appeared very promising (Peterson, 1971). The development of the University of Illinois program was soon followed by the founding of

PSY D.

the first independent graduate school of psychology in 1969, The California School of Professional Psychology, which offered a six-year Ph.D. program in clinical psychology designed to produce skilled psychotherapists (Reisman, 1991). During the 1960s and 1970s, interest in the professional school model of graduate training grew slowly; there were still only two such programs in existence in 1978. By 1980, however, the number of such programs had skyrocketed to 21. Some were associated with long-established universities, such as Rutgers or Denver University, and others were independent, such as the California School of Professional Psychology and the Chicago School of Professional Psychology (Reisman, 1991). In addition, some of the programs granted the traditional Ph.D. and others granted the Psy.D. (the Doctorate of Psychology), a graduate degree comparable in many ways to a J.D. for lawyers or an M.D. for physicians. These programs graduate larger numbers of clinical psychologists than the traditional programs. With each passing year, more and more clinicians are being trained in professional programs (McNett, 1982).

At the same time that a growing number of clinical psychologists were being trained in professional programs, two developments reasserted the biological model of mental illness into clinical psychology and psychiatry: the development of a standardized system for classifying mental illnesses, the Diagnostic and Statistical Manuals, and the increasing use of drug therapies for mental illness.

The Diagnostic And Statistical Manuals

Psychoanalysis went into sharp decline in the 1970s. With this general decline also came a decline in the influence of psychoanalysis over psychiatry (Hale, 1995; Shorter, 1997). A new generation of psychiatrists had developed in the 1950s and 1960s that chafed under the yoke of the psychoanalytic establishment. This generation of psychiatrists, many of whom were researchers, was disturbed by the lack of empirical support for psychoanalysis and by the gap between psychoanalysis and medicine. This younger generation embraced a biological approach to psychiatry. The chemical revolution and the collapse of psychoanalysis favored their approach (Shorter, 1997).

The U.S. government, insurance companies, and the medical profession all sought to standardize the system of naming diseases, called nosology, during the 20th century. The first nosology of psychiatric illnesses was published in 1918 by the American Medico-Psychological Association. The National Committee for Mental Hygiene worked with the association in the development of the nosology. A revised nosology was published in 1933 as part of a comprehensive nosology for all illnesses, both mental and physical (Shorter, 1997).

The nosology for mental illness was revised again by the American Psychiatric Association in 1952. The *Diagnostic and Statistical Manual of Mental Disorders* soon became known as *DSM-I*, the "I" indicating that it was the first edition. *DSM-I* was revised in 1968 and was subsequently known as *DSM II*. Both *DSM-I* and *DSM-II* were heavily influenced by psychoanalysis and the committees that developed them were dominated by Freudians. The nosology embodied the empirically unsubstantiated psychoanalytic explanation of the cause and symptoms of mental illness (Shorter, 1997). Not only were *DSM-I* and *DSM-II* unsupported by empirical research, they were generally ignored by practicing psychoanalysts, psychiatrists, and clinical psychologists, except for those working in the VA system, who were required to provide a diagnosis based on the *DSM* for government records and treatment.

As psychoanalysis collapsed, the new generation of psychiatrists moved to revise the outdated and non-empirical nosology of DSM-II. A leader in this effort was Robert L. Spitzer (1932-), a professor of psychiatry at Columbia University. Spitzer had been a strong defender of psychiatry against the antipsychiatry movement as well as a strong advocate of biological psychology. He published an attack on Rosenhan's study of "being sane in insane places" (Spitzer, 1975) and became the head of the American Psychiatric Association committee in charge of revising the *DSM-II*. Spitzer had received his M.D. from New York University and trained as a psychoanalyst at Columbia University. In the late 1950s he abandoned psychoanalysis as scientifically groundless and sought to develop precise descriptions of mental illness, on the assumption that mental illness was real and that it could be diagnosed and classified like physical illness (Shorter, 1997).

The American Psychiatric Association organized a committee to revise the *DSM* in 1973, a scant five years after the publication of *DSM-II*. In 1974 Spitzer became the leader of the committee to revise the *DSM*, which was made up overwhelmingly by biological psychiatrists. A third of the committee had trained at Washington University in St. Louis, a center for biological psychiatry at the time and the vast majority had carried out scientific research on the biological basis of mental illness (Shorter, 1997). To a far greater extent than the first two editions of the *DSM*, *DSM-III* was based on empirical evidence for various forms of mental illness and on extensive clinical trials involving over 500 psychiatrists and 12,000 patients. *DSM-III*, finally published in 1980, was both longer and more detailed than the previous two editions, containing long lists of diagnostic criteria for each disorder (Shorter, 1997).

Insurance companies, which increasingly paid for psychotherapy through third party payments, were a driving force behind the adoption of the *DSM-III*. The companies required hospitals and therapists in private practice (clinical psychologists, psychiatrists, and social workers) to provide a DSM diagnosis before they would pay for treatment. The amount of treatment for which they would pay also depended on the diagnosis. The *DSM* soon swept through clinical psychology and psychiatry, becoming the diagnostic bible of the mental health profession. By the 1990s, *DSM-III* or its later revisions had been translated into over 20 languages and was used around the world (Shorter, 1997). The success of *DSM-III* resulted both from the demands of powerful institutions such as insurance companies and governments for a detailed nosology of mental illness, but also from the superior empirical content and development of *DSM-III*. Its publication also marked the death of psychoanalysis within psychiatry.

During the development of *DSM-III* and after its publication, controversy swirled around it. Aside from the criticism directed at the *DSM* from psychoanalysts, the *DSM* was criticized on three grounds: first, that some of the disease entities were not well supported by research; second, that some of the disease entities reflected cultural, gender, class, or racial bias; and the third, that political pressures influenced the inclusion or exclusion of certain disease entities. We shall return to these criticisms below.

DSM-III was revised at more or less regular intervals to take into account new research and in an effort to increase the reliability of the diagnostic criteria. Table 13.1 shows the dates of the revisions, as well as the number of disease entities listed in the manual. As can be seen, the number of disease entities continued to expand throughout the 1980s and 1990s, from 265 in *DSM-III* to

297 in *DSM IV*, published in 1994. The expansion in the number of disease entities also gave rise to criticism of the entire nosology (Shorter, 1997).

Table 13.1

The Evolution of DSM

Date	Edition	Number of Disease Entities
1968	*DSM-II*	180
1980	*DSM-III*	265
1987	*DSM-III R*	292
1994	*DSM-IV*	297
2000	*DSM-IV-TR*	

stigma

The development and widespread adoption of the *DSM* was an important element in the rise (again) of the biological approach to mental illness. Another important element in the rise of the biological approach was the steady rise in the number of drugs that were developed and used to treat mental illness, a development that constituted a veritable chemical revolution. Together with the development of profession schools for clinical psychology and the *DSM*, the chemical revolution is the third major transformation in clinical psychology and psychotherapy during the 1970s and 1980s.

The Chemical Revolution

The discovery and use of drugs for the treatment of mental illness began shortly after World War II with the use of LSD in research on psychological warfare and psychosis. LSD was developed by the Sandoz Company in 1938 as a stimulant for circulation. The drug was not effective so it was stored at Sandoz until 1943, when Albert Hoffman took the drug off the storeroom shelf for further tests. Accidentally absorbing a trace though his skin on April 16, he experienced a feeling of intoxication with vivid perceptions and emotions. On April 19th he intentionally ingested 250 micrograms and experienced an intense "trip" during which he thought he was going crazy. As the symptoms lessened, Hoffman became engrossed in his altered state of consciousness. The next morning he felt fine. Hoffman and Sandoz realized immediately the drug could be used to study the brain and the relationship of brain chemistry to mental illness (Lee & Shlain, 1985).

LSD was soon used in research by two diverse but sometimes connected groups: the CIA and psychiatrists. The CIA examined LSD as a potential truth serum and biological weapon. Psychiatrists used it to experimentally induce states similar to schizophrenia. The experimental study of mental illness and brain chemistry was carried out with both humans and animals. Many of the humans were tested illegally against their wishes, either in CIA facilities (see Chapter 12) or in federal prisons and hospitals (Lee & Shlain, 1985).

Some psychiatrists started to use LSD as an adjunct to psychoanalysis in the early 1950s. Two approaches to LSD therapy arose. In Europe, the psycholytic approach used small doses of LSD given in repeated sessions to facilitate the process of psychoanalysis by allegedly lowering psychological defenses and facilitating access to repressed memories (a topic that will be addressed again later in this chapter). The first clinic using psycholytic therapy in Europe was open in England in 1953. Similar clinics were soon open throughout Europe (Lee & Shlain, 1985).

In the U.S. and Canada, the psychedelic approach used very high doses of LSD to help the patient achieve a mystical experience and reorganize their consciousness. This form of therapy soon became very popular with the wealthy and famous. In 1959, the famed film star of the 1950s Cary Grant praised LSD, which he used in therapy, in an article in the widely-read magazine *Look* (Berquist, 1959). The prominent Republicans and owners of Time-Life publishing Henry Luce and his wife Clare Boothe Luce both used LSD as part of therapy. Henry once claimed he talked to God while using LSD on a golf course (Lee & Shlain, 1985). Psychiatrists were soon using LSD in experimental treatments for a variety of problems, including juvenile delinquency, drug addiction, and anxiety disorders (Lee & Shlain, 1985). In 1954 British researcher John Gaddum proposed that LSD produced hallucinations by blocking the neurotransmitter serotonin. This was the first theory of mental illness based on brain chemistry and was to inspire numerous studies of brain chemistry and mental illness (Valenstein, 1998).

Pharmaceutical companies realized quickly the potential value in developing drugs for mental illness and the discovery of LSD produced increased drug company research. A pattern quickly developed in which the drug companies, lured by the promise of profit, would develop drugs for various mental illnesses. Since they did not know how the drugs actually affected the brain (something we still do not have precise knowledge of), they would test the drugs for a variety of possible uses. Effective drugs would then be marketed broadly and often claims of their effectiveness would be exaggerated. As the harmful side effects or limitation of the drug became known, the use would be restricted to those areas where it was most effective given its side effects and limitations. Often, however, a new drug would have been developed and marketed as a replacement for the earlier drug and the cycle would repeat itself.

While LSD was the precursor to the chemical revolution, the first real successes with drugs were Chlorpromazine (known also by its trade name Thorazine) and Lithium. Chlorpromazine ushered in the chemical revolution. Originally tested as a drug that would facilitate recovery from surgery, French physicians experimented with chlorpromazine using mental patients in 1952. They found it to be effective in calming agitated patients suffering from mania or schizophrenia, making them much easier to manage in mental hospitals. The drug appeared to alleviate psychotic symptoms and make the patient passive and indifferent, while also producing some side effects such as symptoms similar to Parkinson's Disease, called tardive dyskinesia. As an aside, Chlorpromazine was also tested as a potential medicine for Parkinson's (Valenstein, 1998). Within a few short years, chlorpromazine was used in mental institutions throughout Europe and North America.

Lithium was also discovered as a psycho-pharmaceutical in the late 1940s by medical researchers, not by pharmaceutical companies. Lithium was easy to synthesize and not profitable for the companies to produce, so there was little interest in the drug and relatively little research on it. Lithium is toxic and early research showed that it could result in death if the physician prescribed too large a dose. Early reports also suggested it could be effective for the treatment of manic-depressive disorders. A Dutch psychiatrist, working on his own and using the first double-blind placebo control group in drug studies found that lithium was highly effective (over 80% success rate) for mania and manic-depression. He published his results in 1959. Also during the 1950s, psychiatrists developed methods for monitoring levels of lithium in the blood and used smaller doses of lithium to avoid the problem of toxicity. In 1970, the drug was finally licensed by the FDA in the U.S. after overwhelming evidence of its effectiveness was published. Also in 1970, several drug companies were persuaded to produce the drug for commercial sale (Valenstein, 1998). The drug was not aggressively promoted by the pharmaceutical companies because it was not very profitable and had a limited market (the number of manic-depressives or bipolar depression is relatively small compared to other forms of mental illness).

A flood of psycho-pharmaceuticals now started to flow from drug company labs. The next major breakthrough occurred in 1955 when Meprobamate (marketed under the trade names Miltown and Equanol) was discovered to reduce anxiety and "tranquilize" anxious and unhappy individuals. Miltown soon became a household word with sales over $100 million per year. The drug soon replaced barbiturates, which had been used for anxiety and were highly addictive. The pharmaceutical companies' claim that Miltown was not addictive, a claim that was often made about new drugs, later proved false. The drug companies' pattern of claiming non-addictive properties for new drugs began in 1898 when Bayer claimed that its heroin based cough medicine was not addictive (Valenstein, 1998).

Table 13. 2

Milestones in the Chemical Revolution

Date	Drug [trade name]	Use
1943	LSD	Experimental Psychosis
1952	Chlorpromazine [thorazine]	Schizophrenia
1955	Lithium*	Bi-polar Depression
1957	Meprobamate [Miltown, Equanol] [Ritalin] Haloperidol [Haldol]	Tranquilizers ADHD Schizophrenia
1958	Imipramine [Tofranil]**	Depression
1960	Chlordiaespoxide [Librium]***	Sedatives
1963	Diazepam [Valium]	Sedatives
1981	[Xanax]	Panic
1987	Fluoxetine [Prozac]	Depression
1989	Clozaril	Schizophrenia

Lithium was first used in 1952 but not used in the U.S. until 1960

** *The first tricyclic, which now includes a large class of medicines*

*** *The first "benzos," which also now includes a large number of drugs*

The introduction of Miltown was followed two years later, in 1957, by the introduction of haloperidol (known by its trade name Haldol), an antipsychotic with fewer side-effects than chlorpromazine, and Ritalin, a stimulant used to treat ADHD. By 1995, 2.5 million school children were prescribed Ritalin, or approximately one out of every 25 school children (Valenstein, 1998). Soon after the introduction of both Ritalin and Haldol, Tofranil was introduced for depression in 1958. Trofranil was the first tricyclic antidepressant, and other tricyclics soon followed (Valenstein, 1998).

The introduction of the tricyclics was soon followed by the introduction of another new class of drugs, the benzodiazepines, or "benzos" in 1960. The benzos were used as an anti-anxiety drug and soon replaced Miltown, which in addition to being addictive, produced drowsiness. The first benzo introduced to the market was Librium in 1960, followed in 1963 by Valium. The benzos soon had an enormous market. By 1975, approximately 100 million prescriptions for benzos were filled in the U.S. and 15% of the adult population had used them. Valium and Librium, along with the more recent anti-anxiety drug Xanax (introduced in 1980) are still widely used in the U.S. (Valenstein, 1998).

Another milestone in the history of the chemical revolution occurred in 1987 with the introduction of fluoxetine (trade named Prozac), the first of the anti-depressants in the selective serotonin re-uptake inhibitors (SSRIs) class. Prozac, and the many other anti-depressants now in this class of drugs, have fewer side effects than the tricyclics and have been show to work better for some patients who do not respond well to the tricyclics. As with the other drugs produced by the pharmaceutical companies, Prozac was aggressively marketed and off-label use, such as prescribing it to teen-agers, was encouraged (Valenstein, 1998).

Finally, in 1989 a new class of antipsychotic drugs was introduced to compete with the older antipsychotics. The first of this new class of drugs was Clozaril and they were collectively referred to as "atypicals" because they did not produce the typical side effects of the earlier antipsychotic drugs. Other atypicals were introduced in the 1990s, including Risperdal in 1994 and Zyprexa in 1996. Clozaril was found to produce a life-threatening blood disorder and was soon replaced by the newer atypicals. As is par for the course, the drug companies minimized the potential and actual side-effects and encouraged off-label use, including urging doctors to use the drugs for Alzheimer's, anxiety, impulse-control, depression, and bipolar depression. By the beginning of the 21st century, the antipsychotics had become the fourth most prescribed class of drugs, behind cholesterol lowering drugs, ulcer medication, and anti-depressants (Goode, 2003).

The chemical revolution had paradoxical effects on psychiatry and clinical psychology. The rise of medication for mental illness shifted the practice of psychiatry away from psychotherapy toward diagnosis and dispensation of medicines. This also led to a decline in the number of medical students entering the specialty. From 1984 to 1994, for instance, the percentage of medical students specializing in psychiatry declined from 3.5% to 2% (Shorter, 1997). At the same time, primary care physicians, such as general practitioners, pediatricians, and internists, increasingly gave out medicine for mental illness. By 1984, over 70% of people who received medication for mental disorders were cared for by primary care physicians who had little or no training in diagnosing and treating mental illness (Valenstein, 1998). Since the decline in the number of psychiatrists in the U.S from 1984 to 1994, the number of people receiving medication for mental illness from their primary care physicians has probably increased.

The effects of the chemical revolution on clinical psychology were both beneficial and harmful. The use of medication by itself helps on average 30% of individuals in double-blind placebo-control studies. While pharmaceutical companies often exaggerate the effectiveness rates and minimize dangers and side effects, a 30% effectiveness rate is impressive by medical standards. The effectiveness of psychotherapy alone for a variety of mental disorders is somewhat higher, but the highest rates of success are found when psychotherapy is combined with some drug treatment. The chemical revolution, along with empirically validated forms of therapy, have given clinical psychologists powerful tools to help their clients, an enormous benefit to clinical psychology. Harmful effects stem from the promulgation of biological theories of mental illness that minimize both the environmental factors in mental illness and the value of therapy. The biological theories are promoted by pharmaceutical companies and their marketing campaigns targeted both at doctors and at consumers, and sometimes by insurance companies who view medication as a cheaper alternative to, and substitute for, therapy (Valenstein, 1998).

The 1980s and 90s: Continuing Growth, Continuing Problems

The 1980s and 1990s witnessed the increased autonomy and growth of clinical psychology as a profession. In 1985 psychologists filed a class-action lawsuit against the American Psychoanalytic Association, which had restricted psychoanalytic training to M.D.s. The psychologists argued that the prohibition against non-M.D.s violated anti-trust laws because it represented a monopoly. In their settlement in 1988, the psychoanalysts agreed to open their training institutes to non-M.D.s. Soon after, psychologists and social workers enrolled in these training institutes in large numbers (Shorter, 1997). Of course, many would argue that being trained in an ineffective form of therapy does not constitute progress. The fact that social workers and clinical psychologists were accepted as the professional equals of medical doctors was, however, considered progress.

Another advance for clinical psychology was securing the right to receive third-party payments. Third-party payments come from insurance companies or health maintenance organizations (HMOs). Prior to 1980, psychiatrists could receive third-party payments but social workers and clinical psychologists could not. When social workers and clinical psychologists won the right to receive third-party payments for providing psychotherapy (a right they won through lawsuits), they achieved a measure of professional equality with psychiatrists (Stone, 1981).

This increased autonomy and status was soon counter-balanced by another important development. Beginning around 1990, managed care came to increasingly dominate the mental healthcare field. Managed care systems, including HMOs, insurance plans that use networks of healthcare providers, or government-run plans such as Medicare and Medicaid, seek to influence the quality and cost of healthcare (Bobbitt, 2006). Note that managed care can be either public or private, for profit or non-profit. The defining feature is the effort to manage the care given to patients and to influence cost and quality.

The continued growth of psychology as a profession was also reflected in the composition and leadership of the APA. By the 1980s over half of the members of the APA were clinical psychologists. Five of the 10 APA presidents during the 1980s were clinicians. The tensions between those who viewed psychology as a science and those who viewed psychology as a profession came to a head, with a plan to reorganize the APA so that the interests of researchers (who felt neglected and ignored by the professionals) would be safeguarded. The plan was submitted to the APA membership in 1988 and was rejected by the professional majority, whereupon many researchers walked out of the organization to form a group dedicated to psychology as a science. This group, the American Psychological Society (APS), held its founding convention in 1989 and began publishing its own scientific journal, *Psychological Science*. The APS later changed its name to the Association for Psychological Science. The leadership of the APA did not seem concerned with the split for two reasons. First, both organizations are open to all psychologists and many researchers remained in the APA or are members of both organizations. Second, the APA owns and publishes all of the major psychological journals, save *Psychological Science*, that are essential to the operation of psychology as a science. Since the APS was formed, both organizations have cooperated on issues that concern both researchers and professionals (Reisman, 1991).

The disagreements between the researchers and practitioners were not just organizational. A number of disagreements developed over issues of substance and fact that caused what many researchers felt to be a gap between the science of clinical psychology and the practice of clinical psychology. One development that illustrated the gap or split between scientist and practitioner in psychology was the controversy over recovered memory therapy (RMT) and reports of sexual abuse, satanic ritual abuse, and alien abductions in the 1980s and 1990s. But the controversy over the recovered memory therapy was not the only conflict between scientists and practitioners in the 1980s and 1990s. In fact, the conflict was so extensive it has been called a war by some psychologists (Tavris, 2003).

The War Between Scientists And Practitioners Within Clinical Psychology

The 1980s and 1990s witnessed a new kind of antipsychiatry movement that was not so much directed at psychiatry (although some of it was) as the practice of psychotherapy by clinical psychologists, psychiatrists, and social workers. This war between scientists and practitioners involved four main issues: first, the criticism of harmful therapy techniques such as RMT; second, the criticisms of the *DSMs* and diagnostic bias; third, criticisms of the biological model of mental illness; and fourth, debates over clinical intuition-based therapy versus evidence-based therapies.

In the 1980s, a series of high profile sexual abuse trials involving day care workers captured the attention of the U.S. public. At the same time, the number of sexual abuse allegations against parents and teachers, based on formerly-repressed but recovered memories, started to climb dramatically. Two problems never before encountered by therapists also grabbed the public's attention: reports of Satan worshipers abusing and sacrificing children, and reports of alien abductions. What united these disparate developments was the use by therapists of various therapeutic techniques to recover memories that were alleged to be repressed in the unconscious, collectively referred to as recovered memory therapy (Tavris, 2003).

RMT is based on two concepts that researchers argued were empirically false: the first was that memories for traumatic events could be repressed (not in conscious memory) and simultaneously perfectly preserved in the unconscious; the second was that the therapist, with the use of hypnosis, guided imagery, and other techniques, could bring these memories to consciousness. Researchers, on the other hand, argued first that memory did not work the way the recovered memory therapists believed, and second that the techniques used by therapists created false memories. [Detailed accounts of these conflicts can be found in Ofshe and Watters (1994), Loftus and Ketcham (1994), and Dawes (2001)]. Hundreds of parents and day care workers were convicted and many thousands of families were hurt by allegations that parents had sexually abused their children. The emotions in the debate were intense, with therapists and their clients attacking (verbally) researchers for their immorality. Families that had been hurt by the allegations, along with former clients who later retracted their allegations, formed the False Memory Syndrome Foundation. Successful lawsuits for malpractice (arguing that the therapist hurt the client by using RMT) and the reversal by higher courts of the convictions of many of the people put in prison on the basis of RMT (and the absence of any other kind of evidence) led to the decline in RMT. While the therapy declined, there are still many therapists who use RMT and claim it to be effective. What is worse, researchers argue, is that as one harmful therapy based on empirically false concepts declines, others rise up to replace them. The therapy that have been most strongly criticized in the late 1990s is re-birthing therapy which resulted in the death of a child in Colorado (Tavris, 2003).

While the use of harmful therapy techniques, particularly RMT with its concomitant sexual abuse cases, alien abductions, and satanic ritual abuse, received the most public attention, it was not the only issue that scientists and practitioners fought over. A second issue was clinical diagnosis and bias. Many of these criticisms were directed at the *DSM*, the process used to develop it, and certain mental illnesses contained within it. One of the problems confronted by the developers of *DSM-III* was the low reliability and imprecision of the diagnostic categories. In everyday language, one clinician would diagnose a person with one disorder and another clinician would diagnosis the same person with a very different disorder. This is like going to several doctors with an ailment and having the first tell you that you have a cold, the second that you have cancer, and the third that you need a heart transplant. The developers of *DSM-III* sought to improve reliability by using detailed diagnostic criteria and testing those criteria. They claimed considerable success in improving diagnostic reliability. Unfortunately, it was just that—a claim unsupported by their own evidence. Careful review of the reliability studies showed only modest improvement in reliability. The diagnostic criteria were still not precise enough to meet generally accepted standards (Kirk & Kutchins, 1992).

The reliability problem was compounded by the way that the *DSM-III* was developed. A small group made up of mostly psychiatrists reviewed the evidence for the inclusion of different mental illnesses in the manual. Sometimes, ailments that had little empirical evidence of actually existing (other than in the minds of the clinicians) were included, such as Self-Defeating Personality Disorder (SDPD) and Premenstrual Dysphoric Disorder (PMDD) in *DSM-III R*. In other cases, "illnesses" were included, such as PTSD, or excluded, such as homosexuality, on the basis of political pressure and compromise in order to get the manual approved. The empirical question of what is and is not a mental illness was simply not addressed (Caplan, 1995; Caplan & Cosgrove, 2004; Kutchins & Kirk, 1997). The result of political negotiations and the failure to use evidence to determine what is and is not a mental illness produced a dramatic expansion in the number of mental illnesses from 180 mental illnesses in *DSM-II* to 292 mental illnesses in *DSM-III R*. The expansion in the number of mental illnesses slowed in *DSM-IV* when the committee adopted a policy that any new disorders had to have empirical evidence supporting their existence in order to be included (the rule requiring empirical evidence does not apply to mental illnesses already included in the manual). Most of the diagnostic categories in the *DSM* are likely real disorders, but the *DSM* is itself a flawed and imperfect nosology. Efforts to improve the nosology continue.

The third issue in the war between researchers and practitioners involves criticism of the biological model of mental illness, especially biological psychiatry. The major criticisms do not apply to researchers in the area of the biological basis of mental illness so much as what we may call vulgar biological psychiatry, the idea often promoted by drug company advertising and believed by a number of consumers that mental illness is the consequence of a chemical imbalance in the brain and that a particular drug will remedy that imbalance. Indeed, the leading critic of vulgar biological psychiatry is Elliot S. Valenstein, himself a leading brain researcher and neuroscientist, as well as an historian of psychology and psychiatry. Valenstein (1998) is a strong advocate of the biopsychosocial approach to the study of the brain. He is not only interested in brain chemistry, neurophysiology, and neuroanatomy, but in how experience and the environment shape the brain. He carefully argues that simple theories of chemical imbalances in the brain are not supported by evidence and that neuroscientists have a great deal to learn yet about the brain and mental illness. His anger is directed, primarily, to "Big Pharma," the large pharmaceutical companies that promote simplistic ideas about the brain and mental illness while exaggerating drug benefits and underplaying drug dangers. Valenstein's views are shared by many neuroscientists and psychologists. The Surgeon General's report on mental illness (U.S. Public Health Service, 1999) points out how little we know of the biological causes of mental illness, going so far as to state that "the precise cause (etiology) of most mental disorders is not known" (p. 49). Others have criticized the corrupting power of Big Pharma to shape prescription practices (Wazana, 2000) and its powerful marketing campaigns (Healy, 2002).

The criticisms of Valenstein and others who embrace the biopsychosocial approach to mental illness fare less well against the positions of biological psychiatry itself, which does not make simplistic claims about brain chemistry and mental illness. Instead the biological psychiatrists pursue a three prong strategy: basic research on the brain and mental illness; careful diagnosis and description of mental illness; and research and development of better medications for mental illness. These medications not only improve people's lives, but provide additional research tools for exploring the brain and mental illness (Shorter, 1997)

The fourth major issue in the war between scientists and practitioners is over the use of evidence-based practices (EBP), that is, therapists must apply empirically supported principles in their treatments (Levant, 2005). Closely related (but not identical) to the notion of EBP is the idea of empirically-supported treatments (EST) and empirically-based treatments (EBT). Empirically-supported treatments are those that are shown to be effective in carefully controlled experimental trials while empirically-based treatments are those whose components have been shown to be effectively through empirical research (Kendall & Beidas, 2007). While EBP has been endorsed by the APA, the use of EST is more controversial. Clinicians argue that cookbook type approaches (if the client suffers from x, treat them with y), subverts the process of therapy and ignores the fact that therapy is an art, not a science, and that the art depends on the clinical judgment of the therapists. These arguments go back over 40 years to Meehl's demonstration of the superiority of actuarial prediction over clinical judgments and the need for "a good cookbook." Both EBP and EST remained highly controversial within the APA during the 1990s. Clinicians feared both a loss of control over their work and a debasement of psychotherapy. For the clinicians the villains in this scenario were managed care (most managed care organizations are strong advocates of EBP and EST) and researchers who are critical of clinical psychologists. These villains have been called the "psychotherapy police" (Glenn, 2003). At the end of the 20th century, EBP had been making considerable headway within clinical psychology, but still faced opposition.

The Struggle For Prescription Rights

In the 1970s the APA Board of Directors appointed a committee to study the question of seeking prescription rights (the right to write a prescription) for clinical psychologists. The committee recommended that clinical psychologists not seek prescription rights, but the issue returned in the 1980s when U.S. Senator Daniel Inouye of Hawaii urged psychologists to seek prescription rights to improve the availability of high-quality mental health care. (Hawaii, as many other states, suffered from a severe shortage of psychiatrists.) Soon leaders of the APA took up the issue. In 1989, the APA Board of Professional Affairs strongly supported research on prescription rights for clinical psychologists and the development of model curricula to train clinical psychologists in the use of drugs. The leadership of the APA voted to form a task force to develop recommendations on this issue soon after, and the task force issued their report in 1992 (Fox & Sammons, 1998).

The task force argued that clinical psychologists with training in psychopharmacology and with prescription rights had the potential to dramatically improve mental health care. In 1995 the APA formally endorsed prescription rights for appropriately trained clinical psychologists and called for the development of model state-enabling legislation and model training programs. The following year the APA adopted a model bill and training program, and in 1997 authorized the development of a professional examination for prescription rights. By 1998, seven states had prescription privilege legislation pending (Fox & Sammons, 1998). Debate over these bills has often been intense, with psychiatrists battling psychiatrists and clinical psychologists battling research psychologists. In 2002, New Mexico became the first state to pass legislation to permit appropriately trained clinical psychologists to prescribe medications for mental illness.

The battle over prescription rights entails issues of effective mental health care as well as issues of professional power and market share. If clinical psychologists gain prescription rights, they will have triumphed completely over the psychoanalysts and psychiatrists and will be able to compete against primary care physicians for the treatment of mental illness. Given the nature of the professions, this kind of struggle is bound to continue.

Themes And Patterns

Clinical psychology has grown since 1918 when only 15 members of the APA were clinicians (and most of these were in university clinics), to the end of the 20th century when over 55,000 clinicians were practicing. In the course of this 82-year time span, clinical psychology has been transformed from a specialty within scientific psychology to a large and dynamic profession. The forces that shape this profession are different from the forces that shape the science, with a consequent gap between researchers and practitioners. The forces that have historically shaped the profession of psychology include competition with other professions, market share and market size for mental health care, and, increasingly, economic factors such as third party payments and managed care.

Beyond these historical forces and the war between researchers and practitioners lay issues of the cultural embeddedness of clinical psychology. Clinical psychology is highly individualistic, focusing on helping the person adapt to the world and to be happy. These are preeminently American values and increasingly western values. The cultural embeddedness of clinical psychology and psychotherapy has been questioned by some (Cushman, 1995) while others have questioned the moral values implicit in the profession, values that emphasize healing the wounded but not preventing them from getting hurt in the first place, values that maintain the status quo but do not challenge it (Prilleltensky, 1994). Given how the profession has benefited from war and committed its own share of abuses, these broader cultural and moral questions are also part of the history of clinical psychology.

References

Allen, F.W. (1934). Therapeutic work with children. *American Journal of Ortho-psychiatry, 4*, 193-202.

Allen, F.W. (1940). Otto Rank. *American Journal of Orthopsychiatry, 10*, 186-187.

Ayllon, T., & Azrin, N.H. (1968). *The token economy: A motivational system for therapy and rehabilitation.* New York, NY: Appleton-Century-Crofts.

Baker, R.A. (Ed.). (1998). *Child sexual abuse and false memory syndrome.* Amherst, NY: Prometheus Books.

Beck, A.T. (1963). Thinking and depression. *Archives of General Psychiatry, 9*, 324-333.

Beck, A.T. (1967). *Depression: Clinical, experimental, and theoretical aspects.* New York, NY: Harper & Row.

Beck, A.T. (1970). Cognitive therapy: Nature and relation to behavior therapy. *Behavior Therapy, 1*, 184-200.

Beck, A.T. (1976). *Cognitive therapy and the emotional disorders.* New York, NY: International Universities Press.

Beck, A.T. (1999). *Prisoners of hate: The cognitive basis of anger, hostility, and violence.* New York, NY: HarperCollins.

Beck, A.T. (2003). Getting it right—Legend Aaron Beck in conversation with Frank Farley. Toronto, Canada: American Psychological Association 111th Convention, August 7.

Beck, A.T., Freeman, A., & Davis, D.D. (2003). *Cognitive therapy of personality disorders.* New York, NY: Guilford Press.

Beers, C.W. (1908). *The mind that found itself.* New York, NY: Longmans, Green.

Berne, E. (1964). *Games people play: The psychology of human relationships.* New York, NY: Grove Press.

Berquist, L (1959). The curious story behind the new Cary Grant. *Look,* September 1, pp. 57-59.

Bobbitt, B.L. (2006). The importance of professional psychology: A view from managed care. *Professional Psychology: Research and Practice, 37*(6), 590-597.

Caplan, P.J. (1995). *They say you're crazy: How the world's most powerful psychiatrists decide who's normal.* Reading, MA: Addison-Wesley.

Caplan, P.J., & Cosgrove, L. (Eds.). (2004). *Bias in psychiatric diagnosis.* Lanham, MD: Rowman & Littlefield.

Cronbach, L.J., & Meehl, P.E. (1955). Construct validity in psychological tests. *Psychological Bulletin, 52,* 281-302.

Cushman, P. (1995). *Constructing the self, constructing America: A cultural history of psychotherapy.* Reading, MA: Addison-Wesley.

Dawes, R.M. (1994). *House of cards: Psychology and psychotherapy built on myth.* New York, NY: The Free Press.

Dawes, R.M. (2001). *Everyday irrationality: How pseudo-scientists, lunatics, and the rest of us systematically fail to think rationally.* Boulder, CO: Westview Press.

Dunlap, K. (1932). *Habits: Their making and unmaking.* New York, NY: Liveright.

Ellis, A. (1958). Rational psychotherapy. *Journal of General Psychology, 59,* 35-49.

Eysenck, H.J.(1952). The effects of psychotherapy: An evaluation. *Journal of Consulting Psychology, 16*, 319-324.

Foucault, M. (1965). *Madness and civilization: A history of insanity in the age of reason.* Translated by Richard Howard. New York, NY: Pantheon.

Fox, R.E., & Sammons, M.T. (1998). A history of prescription privileges. *APA Monitor,* September, Vol. 29(9).

Glenn, D. (2003). Nightmare scenarios: Some scholars say that science can make psychotherapy more effective, while many clinicians insist that therapy is more art than science. *Chronicle of Higher Education,* October 24, Vol. 50(9), p. A14.

Goffman, E. (1961). *Asylums: Essays on the social situation of mental patients and other inmates.* New York, NY: Doubleday.

Goode, E. (2003). Leading drugs for psychosis come under new scrutiny. *New York Times,* May 20, pp. A1, A25.

Hale, N.G., Jr. (1995). *The rise and crisis of psychoanalysis in the United States: Freud and the Americans, 1917-1985.* New York, NY: Oxford University Press.

Harris, T.A. (1967). *I'm OK—you're OK: A practical guide to transactional analysis.* New York, NY: Harper.

Hartley, D., Roback, H.D., & Abramowitz, S.I. (1976). Deterioration effects in encounter groups. *American Psychologist, 31*, 247-255.

Healy, D. (2002). *The creation of psychopharmacology.* Cambridge, MA: Harvard University Press.

Hilgard, E.R. (1987). *Psychology in America: A historical survey.* San Diego, CA:

Harcourt Brace Jovanovich.

Jones, M.C. (1924). A laboratory study of fear: The case of Peter. *Journal of Genetic Psychology, 31*, 308-315.

Kesey, K. (1962). *One flew over the cuckoo's nest.* New York, NY: Viking Press.

Kirk, S.A., & Kutchins, H. (1992). *The selling of DSM: The rhetoric of science in psychiatry.* New York, NY: Aldine de Gruyter.

Kutchins, H., & Kirk, S.A. (1997). *Making us crazy: DSM, the psychiatric bible and the creation of mental disorders.* New York, NY: The Free Press.

Lee, M.A., & Shlain, B. (1985). *Acid dreams: The CIA, LSD, and the sixties rebellion.* New York: Grove Press.

Loftus, E. F., & Ketcham, K. (1994). *The myth of repressed memory.* New York, NY: St. Martin's Press.

MacCorquodale, K., & Meehl, P.E. (1948). On a distinction between hypothetical constructs and intervening variables. *Psychological Review, 55*, 95-107.

Maslow, A. H. (1954). *Motivation and personality.* New York, NY: Harper.

Maslow, A.H. (1962). *Toward a psychology of being.* Princeton, NJ: Van Nostrand.

Maslow, A.H. (1964). *Religions, values, and peak-experiences.* Columbus, OH: Ohio State University Press.

May, R. (1953). *Man's search for himself.* New York, NY: Norton.

May, R. (Ed.). (1961). *Existential psychology.* New York, NY: Random House.

May, R. (1969). *Love and will.* New York, NY: Norton.

McNett, I. (1982, January). Psy.D fills demand for practitioners. *APA Monitor, 13,* 10-11.

Meehl, P.E. (1954). *Clinical versus statistical prediction.* Minneapolis, MN: University of Minnesota Press.

Meehl, P.E. (1956). Wanted—a good cookbook. *American Psychologist, 11,* 263-272.

Meehl, P.E. (1960). The cognitive activity of the clinician. *American Psychologist, 15,* 19-27.

Meehl, P.E. (1962). Schizotaxia, schizotypy, schizophrenia. *American Psychologist, 17,* 827-838.

Meehl, P.E. (1967). Theory testing in psychology and physics: A methodological paradox. *Philosophy of Science, 34,* 103-115.

Meehl, P.E. (1978). Theoretical risks and tabular asterisks: Sir Karl, Sir Ronald, and the slow progress of soft psychology. *Journal of Consulting and Clinical Psychology, 46,* 806-834.

Meehl, P.E. (1995). Bootstraps taxometrics. *American Psychologist, 50,* 266-275.

Meehl, P.E., & Rosen, A. (1955). Antecedent probability and the efficiency of psychometric signs, patterns, or cutting scores. *Psychological Bulletin 52,* 194-216.

Mower, O.H., & Mower, W.M. (1938). Enuresis: A method for its study and treatment. *American Journal of Orthopsychiatry, 8,* 436-459.

Ofshe, R., & Watters, E. (1994). *Making monsters: False memories, psychotherapy, and sexual hysteria.* Berkeley and Los Angeles, CA: University of California

Press.

Perls, F.S. (1969). *Gestalt therapy verbatim*. New York, NY: Bantam.

Peterson, D.R. (1971). Status of the Doctor of Psychology program, 1970. *Professional Psychology, 2*, 271-275.

Prilleltensky, I. (1994). *The morals and politics of Psychology: Psychological discourse and the status quo*. New York, NY: State University of New York Press.

Reisman, J.M. (1991). *A history of clinical psychology*, 2nd ed. New York, NY: Brunner-Routledge.

Rogers, C.R. (1931). *Measuring personality adjustments in children nine to thirteen*. New York, NY: Columbia University Teacher's College.

Rogers, C.R. (1939a). *The clinical treatment of the problem child*. Boston, MA: Houghton Mifflin.

Rogers, C.R. (1939b). Needed emphasis in the training of clinical psychologists. *Journal of Consulting Psychology, 3*, 141-143.

Rogers, C.R. (1940). The process of therapy. *Journal of Consulting Psychology, 4*, 161-164.

Rogers, C.R. (1942). *Counseling and psychotherapy*. New York, NY: Houghton Mifflin.

Rogers, C.R. (1946). Significant aspects of client-centered therapy. *American Psychologist, 1*, 415-422.

Rogers, C.R. (1951). *Client-centered therapy*. Boston, MA: Houghton Mifflin.

Rogers, C.R. (1957). The necessary and sufficient conditions of therapeutic personality change. *Journal of Consulting Psychology, 21*, 95-103.

Rogers, C.R. (1958). A process conception of psychotherapy. *American Psychologist, 13*, 142-149.

Rogers, C.R. (1961). *On becoming a person.* Boston, MA: Houghton Mifflin.

Rogers, C.R. (1967a). Carl R. Rogers. In E.G. Boring & G. Lindzey (Eds.), *A history of psychology in autobiography*, Vol. V, pp. 341-384.

Rogers, C.R. (1967b). *The therapeutic relationship and its impact: A study psychotherapy with schizophrenics.* Madison, WI: University of Wisconsin Press.

Rogers, C.R., & Dymond, R.F. (1954). *Psychotherapy and personality change.* Chicago, IL: University of Chicago Press.

Rosenhan, D.L. (1973). On being sane in insane places. *Science*, 179(4070), 250-258.

Scott, W.D. (1908-1909). An interpretation of the psychoanalytic method in psychotherapy with a report of a case so treated. *Journal of Abnormal Psychology, 3*, 371-377.

Sheehy, N., Chapman, A.J., & Conroy, W.A. (1997a). Ellis, Albert. In N. Sheehy, A.J. Chapman, & W.A. Conroy (Eds.), *Biographical dictionary of psychology*, pp. 163-165. New York, NY: Routledge.

Sheehy, N., Chapman, A.J., & Conroy, W.A. (1997b). Meehl, Paul Everett. In N. Sheehy, A.J. Chapman, & W.A. Conroy (Eds.), *Biographical dictionary of psychology*, pp. 388-389. New York, NY: Routledge.

Shorter, E. (1997). *A history of psychiatry: From the era of the asylum to the age of prozac.* New York, NY: John Wiley & Sons.

Smetanka, M.J. (2003). Paul Meehl, innovator and 'U' professor, dies. *Minneapolis Star Tribune*, p. B6, February 18.

Smith, M.L., & Glass, G.V. (1977). Meta-analysis of psychotherapy outcome studies. *American Psychologist, 32*, 752-760.

Spitzer, R.L. (1975). On pseudoscience in science, logic in remission, and psychiatric diagnosis: A critique of Rosenhan's "On being sane in insane places." *Journal of Abnormal Psychology, 84*, 442-452.

Stone, A. A. (1981). Recent developments in law and psychiatry. In S. Arieti & H.K. Brodie (Eds.), *American handbook of psychiatry* (Vol. 7). New York, NY: Basic Books.

Szasz, T.S. (1960). The myth of mental illness. *American Psychologist, 15*, 113-118.

Szasz, T.S. (1961). *The myth of mental illness: Foundations of a theory of personal conduct.* New York, NY: Hoeber-Harper.

Szasz, T.S. (1970). *The manufacture of madness: A comparative study of the inquisition and the mental health movement.* New York, NY: Harper & Row.

Tavris, C. (2003). Mind games: Psychological warfare between therapists and scientists. *The Chronicle of Higher Education*, p. B7, February 28.

Terry, W.S. (1997). Eysenck, Hans Jurgen. In N. Sheehy, A.J. Chapman, & W.A. Conroy (Eds.), *Biographical dictionary of psychology*, pp. 176-179. New York, NY: Routledge.

Thelen, M.H., & Ewing, D.R. (1970). Roles, functions, and training in clinical psychology: A survey of academic clinicians. *American Psychologist, 25*, 550-554.

Trattner, W.I. (1999). *From poor law to welfare state: A history of social welfare in America*, 6th ed. New York, NY: The Free Press.

U.S. Public Health Service (1999). *Mental health: The Surgeon General's report.*

Valenstein, E.S. (1998). *Blaming the brain: The truth about drugs and mental health.* New York, NY: The Free Press.

Wazana, A. (2000). Physcians and the pharmaceutical industry: Is a gift ever just a gift? *Journal of the American Medical Association, 283*, 373-380.

Witmer, L. (1907). Clinical psychology. *Psychological Clinic, 1*, 1-9.

Wolpe, J. (1958). *Psychotherapy by reciprocal inhibition.* Stanford, CA: Stanford University Press.

Wolpe, J., & Lazarus, A.A. (1966). *Behavior therapy techniques: A guide to the treatment of neuroses.* New York, NY: Pergamon.

Wright, L. (1995). *Remembering Satan.* New York, NY: Vintage.

CHAPTER 14: APPLIED PSYCHOLOGY

The Many Faces Of Applied Psychology

Applied psychology encompasses every subfield of psychology in which basic psychological knowledge, theories, and methods are applied to real world problems. The largest area of applied psychology is clinical psychology, which in fact is so large that most people equate the entire field with just this one area within applied psychology. But there are many areas of applied psychology including psychological testing (technically termed psychometrics), school psychology, organizational psychology, industrial psychology, forensic psychology, and health psychology.

All areas of applied psychology draw from basic psychology. Clinical, for example, draws from social psychology, personality psychology, and basic research in psychopathology and treatment effectiveness. Historically, as an area of applied psychology grows, it has becomes professionalized. Again, the model is clinical psychology, where the professionals greatly outnumber the scientists.

Because applied psychology is so diverse, this chapter will only examine the history of two applied areas: psychometrics, or the history of psychological tests and measurement, and school psychology. After clinical and counseling psychology, school psychology is the largest single subfield of psychology and the most professionalized; it plays an important role within the U.S. education system. Psychometrics is one of the smallest of the applied psychology fields, but also one that has been historically important to psychology and society. It is included here because of its historical importance,, and will be presented first because it antedates school psychology.

The Rise Of Psychological Testing

Psychological testing began early in the history of modern psychology and is linked with three early pioneers: Francis Galton, James McKeen Cattell, and Alfred Binet. Galton and Cattell, who coined the term mental tests (Cattell,

1890), focused on the measurement of highly specific mental and physical abilities. In the process, Galton developed the scatterplot in 1877 graphically represent bivariate data and, along with his student Karl Pearson, the correlation coefficient in 1884. Cattell and Galton were interested in both a theoretical question—what the relative influence of biological factors vs. environmental factors is in human behavior (what Galton termed nature vs. nurture), and in practical problems (Hilgard, 1987).

One of the first practical problems Cattell tackled was predicting success in college. Cattell and his student Livingston Farrand tested 100 first year college students at Columbia University, measuring a variety of specific mental and physical abilities, and correlated the results with grades in college. The study entailed an enormous amount of work, as correlations had to be computed with pencil and paper—there were no adding machines available to them, let alone calculators or computers. They found few correlations greater than what you would expect from chance, with the exception of class attendance, which correlated positively with class grade, a very disappointing finding (Cattell & Farrand, 1896).

Alfred Binet's approach was different in two respects. First, Binet sought to measure global and somewhat ill-defined concepts such as intelligence, as opposed to highly specific mental and physical abilities. Second, Binet was interested only in practical questions, such as how to predict which children should be placed in special schools, and not in the theoretical question of nature vs. nurture, which he did not believe could be addressed using tests that inevitably confound biological and environmental factors (Hilgard, 1987). In his approach, Binet was following pioneering work by Hugo Münsterberg (1891). Binet's first efforts (Binet & Henri, 1894) at measuring global intelligence were successful, and Ebbinghaus, who had carried out the first experimental studies on memory, supported Binet's approach with his own empirical work on sentence completion tasks and school success (Ebbinghaus, 1897). Reflecting the strong interest in this problem, the APA organized a special session on the topic of mental testing at its 1897 meeting. A consensus soon emerged among psychologists that the global measurement of somewhat ill-defined psychological concepts was more useful than a focus on highly specific physical and mental tests (Baldwin, Cattell, & Jastrow, 1898).

Stanford-Binet, and Goddard were also deeply involved in the committee. The result of their work was the development of two tests: the Army Alpha test for those who could read and write English, and the Army Beta test for illiterates and non-native speakers of English. The tests were designed to be administered in groups. Development of the tests was completed in September and between that date and January 1919, when the war ended, over 1.75 million soldiers took the tests. The Alpha and Beta tests brought psychologists and psychological testing to the attention of the American public (Hilgard, 1987).

The public attention was both a benefit and a curse. Schools, colleges, and businesses had a new and increased interest in psychological testing in particular and psychology in general. This interest also resulted in the first major public controversy involving psychology—a conflict over the purported anti-democratic assumptions and uses of the tests. The controversy began with a serious of six articles in the liberal intellectual magazine *The New Republic*, authored by Walter Lippmann. Lippmann, who had worked with Creel on propaganda during the war (see Chapter 12), argued that the tests did not measure anything related to real life and could not properly be called intelligence. Lippmann also argued that the psychologists who constructed the tests held extreme hereditarian views that were anti-democratic and racist (Lippmann, 1922).

While Lippmann's articles were for the educated public, critics within psychology also attacked the tests. First, psychologists who embraced the behaviorist position were strongly anti-hereditarian in outlook and rejected the notion that intelligence was biologically determined. Second, psychologists who viewed themselves as defenders of democracy argued that intelligence could be raised by education and was the consequence of the environment (Bagley, 1922).

Terman was one of the first to respond to these criticisms. Addressing Bagley, he (Terman, 1922a) argued that individual differences in intelligence do not undermine democracy (differences in physical or mental characteristics do not entail differences in individual rights) and that education can improve the skills and abilities of all people (a position held strongly by Goddard as well, who was a champion of special education for the mentally retarded). Addressing Lippmann, he (Terman, 1922b) argued that Lippman made a number of factual errors and that most psychologists felt that both environment and heredity influenced the scores on tests.

Lippman continued his attack, directing his criticism toward the work of the British psychologists Cyril Burt (Lippmann, 1923), and this time E.G. Boring (Boring, 1923a) responded with an effort to provide an operational definition of intelligence (intelligence is what intelligence tests measure) and point out that much more research needed to be conducted with the tests before definitive conclusions could be reached. In essence, Boring tried to de-politicize the debate and take it out of the public domain.

The efforts of Terman and Boring were undercut by a minority of psychologists who held extreme and racist views. In 1923, Carl C. Brigham (1890-1943) published *A Study of American Intelligence* (Brigham, 1923), in which he summarized the results of the Army Alpha and Beta tests and compared average scores by nationality. Brigham argued that certain groups were inferior to others and that the results supported the doctrine of Nordic superiority and the need for eugenics. The book soon became a favorite among racists. [Brigham later repudiated his study and its conclusions, in the face of data that showed that differences in group averages were due to differences in language proficiency and environments (Brigham, 1930)].

Yerkes, who had earlier edited the book summarizing the research with the army tests (Yerkes, 1921), wrote a positive introduction to Brigham's book and also published his own views in the mainstream media (Yerkes, 1923) in which he favored restrictive immigration policies in. This is an historical irony, as Yerkes advocated the extreme behaviorist position of Watson yet also argued that differences in IQ were due to biological differences, not environmental differences. The fact that he would make a claim inconsistent with his basic position and in the absence of relevant data shows how racism can distort the thinking of even intelligent people. The battle over nature vs. nurture and the meaning of the IQ tests could not be contained. It raged within and without psychology.

Within psychology, the response to Brigham and Yerkes' position was harsh. Boring (Boring, 1923b) published an unfavorable review, focusing on the inadequacy of the data. Other harsh reviews were published by Percy Davidson of Stanford (Davidson, 1923), Kimball Young (Young, 1923), who published his review in the prestigious journal *Science* (edited by James McKeen Cattell), and others (e.g., Hexter & Myerson, 1924). Only one reviewer within psychology was positive (Pinter, 1923) and another, by Floyd Allport, was mixed (Allport, 1924). Terman devoted his APA presidential address to the question of IQ testing. In spite of his personal preference for restrictive immigration laws, he argued that whether the tests reflect primarily the influence of the environment or of heredity was a question that could not be answered at the time given the data at hand (Terman, 1924). Terman went on to chair a committee to review all available data on the role of nature and nurture in intellectual development. This review (Terman, 1928) concluded that both heredity and environment play a role in intelligence, that intelligence is not fixed, and that while heredity may fix a range of scores, the environment can add or subtract from the hereditary endowment. The research questions to be addressed included the potency of various kinds of environments. This consensus position received positive reviews (Whipple, 1928). While psychologists achieved consensus, the debate dropped from public view, although the extreme claims of Brigham and others still circulated and became part of what was to be called scientific racism for the next several decades.

Psychology, Eugenics, And The Holocaust

The history of most nations is filled with racism and wrongdoing, and the United States is no exception. In 1924 the U.S. adopted a law, the Immigration Act of 1924 which established strict racial quotas. These quotas kept out Jews and Eastern Europeans and prevented millions of Jews from fleeing to the U.S. during the Nazi rise to power. Indirectly, then, millions died because of the act.

At the same time that the Immigration Act of 1924 was passed, eugenics laws were being adopted in the U.S. Eugenics, the selective breeding of human beings to improve our species, was first proposed by Francis Galton, one of the forefathers of modern psychology. Eugenics laws were adopted in many states. These laws employed forced sterilization of men and women found unfit. The first such law was adopted in 1907 by the state of Indiana. In 1927, the U.S. Supreme Court upheld eugenics laws in the Buck v. Bell decision. The decision, written by Justice Oliver Wendell Holmes Jr. (who had been a member of the Metaphysical Club, along with C.S. Pierce and William James), found that the sterilization of the genetically unfit was for the greater good of humanity.

In all, 33 U.S. states passed forced sterilization laws. These states forcibly sterilized 65,000 Americans. The sterilizations were not performed by psychologists of course (medical doctors performed the operations) but the psychologists did develop and sometimes administer the tests used to determine who was to be sterilized. Other countries followed the U.S. example and passed forced sterilization laws, including Canada, Denmark, Finland, Japan, Norway, and Nazi Germany.

An important justification for these laws was the scientific racism that pervaded North American and Europe. Scientific racism has little science in it—it is a justification of racism or racist beliefs on the basis of partial or pseudo-scientific claims. Lippmann's aim in attacking intelligence testing was to attack what he believed was a form of scientific racism that undermined democracy. When scientific racism emerged again in the late 1960s and 1970s historians revisited the question of the connection between psychology, scientific racism, the immigration act of 1924, and the eugenics movement.

The biologist Stephen Jay Gould (Gould, 1981) and the historian Allan Chase (Chase, 1977) hold psychologists partly responsible for both the immigration act and the eugenics movement, especially Carl Brigham and his book *A study of American intelligence* (Brigham, 1923).

Let us examine both issues separately, beginning with the Immigration Act of 1924. While Brigham's book was very popular among racists and he did testify in congress in support of the bill (the only psychologist to do so), an examination of the legislative record shows that Brigham's work in particular, and psychologists' work in general, had no real effect at all on the passage of the bill. The data presented by Brigham were not referenced by members of the committee and were not discussed in the debate in congress, except on a few occasions when it was severely criticized. The main issues in the debate had to do with protecting jobs and promoting profits through low-wage immigrant labor. In short, the correlation between the publication of data on IQ and the passage of the immigration act does not entail causation (Snyderman & Herrstein, 1983). Psychology is not to blame for the Immigration Act and its horrific consequences—the deaths of millions of innocents during World War II. Racism is.

Not to blame, but certainly played a role

college admissions examinations, specifically the Scholastic Aptitude Test (SAT), the American College Testing (ACT) exam, the Law School Aptitude Test (LSAT), and the Medical College Aptitude Test (MCAT). The people behind standardized college admissions testing were not psychologists, but two administrators at Harvard University: James Bryant Conant, the president of Harvard, and Henry Chauncey, a Harvard dean. To understand the actions of these academic administrators and their peers at other colleges, we must backtrack to the 1920s and 1930s.

Working at Princeton after World War I, C.C. Brigham turned his attention to testing undergraduates with a modified Army Alpha test. By 1926 he had modified the multiple choice test into the SAT. Brigham was especially concerned with the test's reliability (the stability of an individual's score over time) and its predictive validity (its power to statistically predict how well a student would do in college). In order to refine the test further, in 1926 he persuaded Princeton, Yale, and West Point to administer the test. He also administered the test to over 8,000 high school students who were also taking a series of essay examinations sponsored by the College Board. He continued testing high school students and first year college students into the 1930s, seeking to refine the tests and increase their predictive validity. He also rejected the notion that the tests measured native intelligence and adopted Thurstone's concept of breaking the test into two subscales, one verbal and one quantitative. The SAT proved easier to administer than the essay examinations used by many colleges and was more reliable. Brigham was also able to increase the predictive validity of the tests from a correlation of .20 (the correlation between the essays and the first year college grades) to almost .50. At the same time he strongly objected to all assumptions about what the tests measured—he had come a long way since his first book and publicly repudiated it in 1930 (Lemann, 1999).

In 1933 James Bryant Conant (1893-1978), a distinguished chemist, became president of Harvard University. Conant succeeded Abbott Lawrence Lowell, who served as Harvard president from 1909 to 1933. Lowell, in turn, had succeeded Charles William Eliot. Lowell had been installed at Harvard in part to put a stop to the revolutionary changes brought about by Eliot at Harvard. While he could not reverse most of those changes, he did his best to stop subsequent change. When Conant took over, he was most deeply disturbed by the character of the Harvard undergraduates. Like most of the Ivy League schools, Harvard maintained quotas against talented Catholic and Jewish students (the exact quotas were not publicized at the Ivy League schools except at Yale, when the president revealed that no more than 13% of the student body could be Catholic and Jewish). In addition, Harvard drew its students mostly from a small number of expensive private New England preparatory schools, excluding working class and middle class students as well as Catholics, Jews, Blacks, and Hispanics. As a consequence, the typical Harvard man during the early 1930s, the depths of the Great Depression, lived with servants, played sports, and did very little work. Most of these students came from wealthy or well off New England protestant families and were descendants of the traditional upper-crust (Lemann, 1999).

affirmative action [handwritten margin note]

Conant was upset not only by the lack of academic purpose and interest among the undergraduates, but by the nature of the traditional elite. He felt that the elite had failed to govern the country (hence the Great Depression) and had to be replaced in order for the country to survive. To replace an elite based on inherited wealth, Conant envisioned an elite based on intellectual ability. He started modestly by transforming Harvard's scholarship program, which included athletic scholarships and a very small scholarship program for poor students who had to maintain a minimum GPA. Conant abolished the athletic scholarships and proposed a four-year, full scholarship (covering tuition, room, and board) given to students of high ability from across the entire U.S. The mechanism for selecting these students was to be the SAT. The program began in January 1934, when Conant instructed his dean Henry Chauncey to select 10 young men from the Midwest using grades, letters of recommendation, and SAT scores. When these 10 young men graduated in the class of 1938, eight of them were elected to Phi Beta Kappa, the national honor society. By 1937, the SAT was given at 150 sites across the U.S. to 2,005 students competing for the scholarships. Conant's experiment proved enormously successful and he proposed a national testing agency and the use of intellectual talent as the primary basis for college admissions (Lemann, 1999). In addition to this successful merit based scholarship program, he opened Harvard Law School and Harvard Medical School to women.

At this point, Conant's efforts to transform American undergraduate education and, in turn, the American ruling class, ran into opposition from the creator of the SAT: Carl Brigham. Brigham argued that de facto national standardized tests, which was what Conant was proposing, had many dangers. In particular, Brigham worried that national testing would harm critical research into the nature of the tests and lead to uses of testing that were not justified by research. In spite of Brigham's criticisms, the use of the SAT by colleges continued to grow (at the start of World War II, around 20,000 high school students took the test each year). In January 1943, Brigham died at the age of 52. The chief opposition to Conant's plan to transform higher education was now removed (Lemann, 1999).

Conant moved quickly on two fronts, the first intellectual and the second organizational. Intellectually he set out the basis for a new ruling class based on ability in an article in the *Atlantic Monthly* in May 1943 and entitled "Wanted: American Radicals." The new American radicals, according to Conant, wanted equality of opportunity and would wield an axe against inherited privilege. Conant drew upon Jefferson and others (such as Ralph Waldo Emerson, the philosopher and writer who was a friend of the James family) to justify replacing the old aristocracy of inherited wealth with a natural aristocracy of ability. In the late 1950s, this system was to be named the "meritocracy." The name itself taken from a science fiction novel that was critical of the use of standardized testing in England (Lemann, 1999).

Organizationally, Conant moved to create a quasi-national testing organization, a difficult task that required substantial negotiation. Conant was finally successful when on January 1, 1948, the Educational Testing Service (ETS) opened in Princeton. Conant was chairman of the board and Henry Chauncey, his former dean who had administered the scholarship program and worked with the military testing recruits during World War II, became president. The new organization controlled the SAT, and the Graduate Record Exam (GRE) which had been developed by a rival testing organization, the American Council on Education, and the old College Board essay exams. In a short time, ETS also developed the LSAT and began developing the MCAT. ETS expanded slowly at first, developing tests for draft deferments during the Korean War, and then more quickly. In 1957 over 500,000 took the SAT, and the number continued to grow. Soon after, in 1959, a second major national testing organization emerged (this one centered originally in Iowa): American College Testing, or the ACT. Soon the ACT exam was to be the SAT's leading, or rather only, rival, as it remains to this day (Lemann, 1999). Since the 1950s, standardized testing has become an essential component of college admissions throughout the United States. Conant's dream of transforming the undergraduate student body has been partially realized, and the student body of 2000 differed widely from the student body of 1930. Whether or not Conant succeeded in replacing the old ruling class based on wealth with a new meritocracy is an open question. Some doubt that he was successful (Lemann, 1999) but data from the 1990s (discussed below) suggest otherwise.

The Refinement Of Psychometrics

The 1950s and 1960s saw the refinement of psychometrics as a well-established, albeit small, subfield within psychology and the continued growth of testing as a profession. The two leaders in the subfield during this period were Joy Paul Guilford (1897-1987) and Anne Anastasi (1908-2001).

Guilford was interested in individual differences from early in his college career. He graduated with a BA from the University of Nebraska in 1922 and a Ph.D. from Cornell in 1926. He was influenced by Spearman's work and especially by the work of Thurstone on multiple factor analysis and measurement. He published a graduate textbook on psychometrics in 1936 (Guilford, 1936) and a college textbook on statistics and measurement (Guilford, 1942). Both textbooks were reprinted and served as basic texts in the field for several decades. During World War II he served as the director of aviation research for the Army air corps, which later became the U.S. Air Force (Sheehy, Chapman, & Conroy, 1997a).

Guilford took a broad view of intellectual abilities and intelligence and sought to measure intellectual abilities, such as creativity and divergent thinking, that were not measured on traditional tests (Guilford, 1940; Guilford, 1950; Guilford, 1957; Guilford, 1959a). He also extended and refined the measurement of personality (Guilford, 1959b) and developed a model of intelligence that emphasized cognitive processes (Guilford, 1967). For his many contributions he was elected president of the APA in 1950. He remained active as a researcher and participated in the cognitive revolution into his 80s (see for instance, Guilford, 1980; Guilford, 1982).

The other major leader within psychometrics during the 1950s and 1960s was Anne Anastasi. Anastasi spent most of her life in New York City, where she was born, educated, and worked. She attended Barnard College and graduated in 1928. Originally a mathematics major, she switched her field to psychology after reading Spearman's work. She then attended Columbia University, where she received her Ph.D. in 1930. She met and fell in love with another Ph.D. student in psychology at Columbia, John Porter Foley. In 1933, they married. In 1934, at the age of 26, she developed cancer. She recovered but was not able to have children as a result of the treatment (Cooper, 1997). She devoted her time to teaching and research after that, working first at Barnard College and later at Fordham University until the end of her career.

Anastasi wrote two popular and highly influential textbooks, the first on differential psychology (Anastasi, 1937) and the second on psychometrics (Anastasi, 1954), both of which went through multiple editions. Like Guilford, she applied psychometric techniques to a number of problems such as sex differences (Anastasi, 1981) and was interested in the processes underlying intellectual abilities and traits (Anastasi, 1958), arguing that while both biological factors and environmental factors shape abilities, the important question is "how?" For her many contributions as a teacher and researcher, she was elected president of the APA in 1971 and received the APA's Thorndike Medal in 1983 (Cooper, 1997).

The Cognitive Revolution Comes To Psychometrics

The cognitive revolution that swept through psychology in the 1960s and 1970s also affected psychometrics. David McClelland advanced the idea that psychometricians should be testing for competence rather than intelligence (McClelland, 1973), while several cognitive psychologists proposed that cognitive psychology could be used to study the component processes that underlie the individual differences in IQ tests (Estes, 1974; Hunt, Frost, & Lunneborg, 1973). A series of conference papers (Resnick, 1976) further advanced this merger of cognitive psychology and psychometrics.

The merger of a cognitive approach to the study of the processes underlying intellectual abilities with the psychometric study of intellectual abilities soon produced two major revisionist theories of intelligence, one proposed by Robert J. Sternberg (1949-), and the other by Howard E. Gardner (1943-).

Sternberg was born in New Jersey and suffered from severe test anxiety as a child. He overcame the anxiety in the sixth grade when the school psychologist sent him back to the fifth grade class to retake the fifth grade test, apparently because he was not considered bright enough to take the test with the sixth graders. This was the start of a life-long interest in intelligence testing for Sternberg. In the seventh grade he developed an IQ test and read a text by Terman on the Stanford-Binet. He then practiced giving the verbal items of the test to some of his classmates, for which he got in trouble. In the 10th grade, Sternberg, with the support of his biology teacher, designed and carried out a study of a new biology curriculum and compared it to the standard curriculum. At this point, Sternberg was on his way as a researcher. In the summer after 10th grade he studied (experimentally) the effects of distraction on test performance. Before graduating from high school he also developed a physics aptitude test. The test correlated r=.65 with grades in physics and was used by the school as an admissions test for advanced physics classes (Sternberg, 2002).

Sternberg received his B.A. from Yale University in 1972 and his Ph.D. from Stanford in 1975. While a Yale undergraduate, he published two research articles on undergraduate admissions, marking the beginning of a very productive research career (Sternberg, 2002). At Stanford he studied with one of the leading cognitive psychologists of the day, Gordon Bower. After graduating from Stanford, Sternberg returned to Yale as an assistant professor and has remained there to the present (Sheehy, Chapman, & Conroy, 1997b). In 1977 he presented his componential theory of intelligence along with research supporting the theory (Sternberg, 1977a; Sternberg, 1977b;). The basic notion of the theory is that intelligence consists of a series of underlying components that combine to determine performance on intellectual tasks. These underlying components fall into three categories: metacomponents that monitor and plan problem solving; performance components which execute plans and processes; and knowledge-acquisition components, which guide the learning and development of new skills and knowledge.

Sternberg's research using the componential approach to intelligence led him to propose a new model of intelligence which he called the triarchic theory of intelligence. According the the tirarchic theory, intelligence is made up of three aspects (Sternberg, 1984). Since proposing the triarchic theory Sternberg has focused much of his research on developing and teaching intellectual skills (Sternberg, 1986a). He has also made contributions to the study of creativity (Sternberg, 1999) and love (Sternberg, 1986b; Sternberg, 1995).

At approximately the same time that Sternberg introduced his triarchic theory of intelligence, Howard E. Gardner introduced a theory of multiple intelligences (Gardner, 1983). Gardner was born and raised in Scranton, Pennsylvania. He became an accomplished pianist and considered a career as a composer or musician. He started working as a piano teacher at the age of 15, a part-time job he continued through college and part of graduate school. He attended Harvard, graduating in 1965, and went on to graduate school there, completing his Ph.D. in 1971. At Harvard, Gardner studied with Jerome Bruner and Erik Erikson, as well as Gordon Allport, Henry Murray, and David McClelland, among others (Gardner, 2002). Gardner also had a deep interest in reading and writing from an early age and started writing books as a graduate student. Before receiving his doctorate, he co-authored a social psychology textbook (Grossack & Gardner, 1970) and drafts of two other books which he published during his postdoctoral fellowship (Gardner, 1973a; Gardner, 1973b).

After completing his Ph.D., Gardner did a three-year postdoctoral fellowship at Boston University School of Medicine researching brain-damaged patients. At the same time, he worked as co-director of Harvard's Project Zero, a study of cognition in artists. Gardner continued as co-director of the project from 1972 to 1995 (Nucci, 1997). Gardner's many contributions to various subfields of psychology resulted in his being awarded a MacArthur Prize, the so-called genius prize, in 1981.

Gardner's studies of brain damage (e.g., Gardner, 1975), his studies of neurophysiology resulting in over 60 published research articles in this area (Gardner, 2002), and his interests in developmental psychology and creativity (Gardner, 1980), led him to propose his theory of multiple intelligences (Gardner, 1983). Part of Gardner's theory was popularized by his Harvard graduate school classmate, Daniel Goleman, under the label EQ or emotional intelligence (Goleman, 1995).

Gardner (1983) initially proposed seven distinct kinds of intelligence based on neurophysiological studies, traditional psychometric data, and case studies of child prodigies, savants, and highly creative people. These seven kinds of intelligence are: 1) linguistic; 2) logical-mathematical; 3) spatial; 4) bodily-kinesthetic; 5) musical; 6) interpersonal; and 7) intrapersonal. Interpersonal intelligence (being intelligent about others) and intrapersonal intelligence (being smart about yourself) were lumped together by Goleman as EQ or emotional intelligence (Goleman, 1995). Later, Gardner added an eighth type of intelligence: naturalistic intelligence (Gardner, 1999)

Sternberg and other cognitive psychologists transformed psychometrics by incorporating the experimental study of cognitive processes into the subfield. Gardner has had a major impact by incorporating neurophysiological data into theories of intelligence, as well as the descriptive study of gifted artists, scientists, and leaders. Gardner's theory of multiple intelligences, while very popular and influential at present, is controversial and lacks substantial empirical support beyond the work carried out by Gardner himself (Sternberg, 1991; Waterhouse, 2006a; Waterhouse, 2006b).

Like many of the historical leaders in psychology, Gardner has been and continues to be enormously productive, having authored over 20 books and 400 articles by the age of 53 (Nucci, 1997). In addition to his major contributions to psychometrics, he has made substantial contributions to education (Gardner, 1991), the study of creativity (Gardner, 1993), and the history of psychology (Gardner, 1985).

While Sternberg, Gardner, and others were transforming psychometrics and our ideas about intelligence during the 1970s and 1980s, traditional ideas about intelligence and intelligence testing were again generating widespread controversy. The controversy began in 1969 with an article in the *Harvard Educational Review* by Arthur Jensen (1923-). In the article, he (Jensen, 1969) argued that the mean IQ difference between whites and blacks in the U.S. (which averages 15 points) was partly due to genetic differences between races. The article provoked widespread criticism from within psychology including a statement by SPSSI and an issue of the *Harvard Educational Review* devoted to critical responses from scientists (Hilgard, 1987). The article also occurred in the political context of an intense struggle for civil rights by minorities and with his future colleague at Columbia, Robert S. Woodworth, showed that this was not true (Thorndike & Woodworth, 1901). Thorndike used empirical and experimental methods to tackle two problems—the measurement of learning and the improvement of classroom instruction (Hilgard, 1987). Among Thorndike's many achievements were his arithmetic textbooks (Thorndike, 1917), his word book for teachers containing the 10,000 most common and important words to teach children (Thorndike, 1921), his early textbook on educational psychology for teachers and educators (Thorndike, 1903), and, what was to become a standard work in the area, his three-volume work on educational psychology that became the model for subsequent texts in the field (Thorndike, 1913a; Thorndike, 1913b, Thorndike, 1914). This is all in addition to his contributions to psychometrics (Thorndike, 1904).

From the 1920s to the 1950s, educational psychology shifted somewhat toward counseling and mental health and away from the early emphasis on brain physiology and sensation. The emphasis on learning, the psychology of particular topics, and on tests and measurement remained unchanged throughout these decades (Hilgard, 1987).

The other parent of school psychology was clinical psychology. Early clinical psychology in the U.S. was based in university clinics, many serving schools or communities. Witmer's clinic, founded at the University of Pennsylvania, served school children in Philadelphia starting in 1896. Another important early clinic was started by the Chicago school board, at the urging of Dewey, in 1900. In the next two decades clinics serving school children spread to many cities. By 1914 there were 70 recognized psychological clinics in the U.S., 20 of which were in schools (French, 1990).

The term "school psychologist" was first used by William Stern (the student of Ebbinghaus who invented the idea of IQ and had a profound influence on Gordon Allport) in 1910 and appeared in English in a translation of Stern's work in 1911. The term referred to a psychologist working within a school doing testing, diagnosis, and treatment, and use of the term soon spread among psychologists. Whipple, a translator of Stern's work, used it in *The Journal of Educational Psychology* in 1913 in an editorial announcing Cyril Burt's appointment as a psychologist to the London schools. Witmer used the same term in *The Psychological Clinic,* also announcing Burt's appointment later in 1913. The first American with the title of school psychologist (for the state of Connecticut) was Arnold Gesell, who held that position from 1915 to 1922. In 1923, an article on "the school psychologist" appeared in *The Psychological Clinic* (Fagan & Delugach, 1984). Thus by the mid-1920s, school psychology was recognized as a distinct, albeit small, specialty within clinical psychology.

School psychology continued to grow slowly through the 1930s and 1940s. The first major college textbook on the topic was published in 1930 and in the 1945 reorganization of the APA, a Division of School Psychologists was created (Fagan, 1986). Another important milestone in the development of the profession of school psychology was the Thayer Conference, named for the Thayer Hotel in West Point, New York where it was held in 1954. Like the Boulder Conference which created a model for clinical training, the Thayer Conference set standards for training, functioning, and certification of school psychologists. The Boulder Conference, focused as it was on clinical psychology for adults, and the Thayer Conference, focused on the provision of various psychological services to school-age children, marked the clear professional separation of clinical and school psychology (French, 1990). MONAYYY

Federal money for education increased dramatically in the late 1950s and early 1960s as the U.S. engaged in a space race with the Soviet Union as part of the Cold War. Funding for science and math education, libraries, and counseling increased. School psychology also benefited and grew substantially. Reflecting this growth was the publication of a journal in 1963 devoted strictly to school psychology, followed by several additional journals in the 1960s, and the organization of the National Association of School Psychologists (NASP) in 1969. NASP is professionally separate from organizations for special education and guidance counseling, although some school psychologists are also members of the APA (French, 1990). The APA and NASP sometimes clash but often cooperate on the development of licensing standards, program accreditation, and public policy regarding school psychology. huge development from 1903-1990

By the 1990s, school psychologists were an important part of almost all school districts in the United States. The role of the school psychologist had changed little since the 1950s when it was codified at the Thayer Conference. The duties of the school psychologist remain essentially testing and interpretation of test results, identification of exceptional children and development of

keiten und ihreAnwendung bei Schulkindern. *Zietschrift fur Psychologie, 13*, 401-459.

Estes, W.K. (1974). Learning theory and intelligence. *American Psychologist, 29*, 740-749.

Faber, D. (1997). Terman, Lewis Madison. In N. Sheehy, A.J. Chapman, & W. A. Conroy (Eds.), *Biographical dictionary of psychology*, 563-564. London, UK: Routledge.

Fagan, T.K. (1986). The evolving literature of school psychology. *School Psychology Review, 15*(3), 430-440.

Fagan, T.K., & Delugach,, F.J. (1984). Literary origings of the term "school psychologist." *School Psychology Review, 13*(2), 216-220.

Fancher, R.E. (1987). Henry Goddard and the Kallikak family photographs: Conscious skuldrugger or "whig history"? *American Psychologist, 42*(6), 585-590.

Flynn, J.R. (1984). The mean IQ of Americans: Massive gains 1932 to 1978. *Psychological Bulletin, 95,* 29-51.

Flynn, J.R. (1987). Massive IQ gains in 14 nations: What IQ tests really measure. *Psychological Bulletin, 101,* 171-191.

French, J.L. (1990). History of school psychology. In T.G. Gutkin & C.R. Reynolds (Eds.), *Handbook of school psychology*, pp. 3-20. New York, NY: John Wiley & Sons.

Gardner, H. (1973a). *The arts and human intelligence: A psychological study of the artistic process*. New York, NY: John Wiley.

Gardner, H. (1973b). *The quest for mind: Piaget, Levi-Strauss and the structuralist movement*. New York, NY: Alfred Knopf.

Gardner, H. (1975). *The shattered mind: The person after brain damage.* New York, NY: Knopf.

Gardner, H. (1980). *Artful scribbles: The significance of children's drawings.* New York, NY: Basic Books.

Gardner, H. (1983). *Frames of mind: The theory of multiple intelligences.* New York, NY: Basic Books.

Gardner, H. (1985). *The mind's new science: A history of the cognitive revolution.* New York, NY: Basic Books.

Gardner, H. (1991). *The unschooled mind: How children think and how schools should teach.* New York, NY: Basic Books.

Gardner, H. (1993). *Creating minds: An anatomy of creativity as seen through the lives of Freud, Einstein, Picasso, Stravinsky, Eliot, Graham, and Gandhi.* New York, NY: Basic Books.

Gardner, H. (1999). *Intelligence reframed: Multiple intelligences for the 21st century.* New York, NY: Basic Books.

Gardner, H. (2002). My way. In R.J. Sternberg (Ed.), *Psychologists defying the crowd: Stories of those who battled the establishment and won,* pp. 79-88. Washington, DC: American Psychological Association.

Goddard, H.H. (1908). The Binet and Simon tests of intellectual capacity. *Training School Bulletin, 5*(10), 3-9.

Goddard, H.H. (1910). A measuring scale for intelligence. *Training School Bulletin, 6,* 146-155.

Goddard, H.H. (1912). *The Kallikak family: A study in the heredity of feeble-*

mindedness. New York, NY: Macmillan.

Goddard, H.H. (1914). *Feeblemindedness: Its causes and consequences.* New York, NY: Macmillan.

Goleman, D. (1995). *Emotional intelligence: Why it can matter more than IQ.* New York, NY: Bantum Books.

Goodenough, F.L. (1940). New evidence on environmental influences on intelligence. In G.D. Stoddard (Chr.), *Intelligence: Its nature and nurture.* (39th Yearbook of the National Society for the Study of Education, Pt. 1). Bloomington, IL: Public School Publishing.

Gould, S.J. (1981). *The mismeasure of man.* New York, NY: Norton.

Grossack, M., & Gardner, H. (1970). *Man and men: Social psychology as social science.* Scranton, PA: International Textbook.

Guilford, J.P. (1936). *Psychometric methods.* New York, NY: McGraw-Hill.

Guilford, J.P. (1940). Human abilities. *Psychological Review, 47,* 367-394.

Guilford, J.P. (1942). *Fundamental statistics in psychology and education.* New York, NY: McGraw-Hill.

Guilford, J.P. (1950). Creativity. *American Psychologist, 5,* 444-454.

Guilford, J.P. (1957). Creative abilities in the arts. *Psychological Review, 64,* 110-118.

Guilford, J.P. (1959a). Three faces of intellect. *American Psychologist, 14,* 469-479.

Guilford, J.P. (1959b). *Personality.* New York, NY: McGraw-Hill.

Guilford, J.P. (1967). *The nature of human intelligence.* New York, NY: McGraw-Hill.

Guilford, J.P. (1980). Cognitive styles: What are they? *Educational and Psychological Measurement, 40,* 715-735.

Guilford, J.P. (1982). Cognitive psychology's ambiguities: Some suggested remedies. *Psychological Review, 89,* 48-59.

Hearnshaw, L.S. (1981). *Cyril Burt: Psychologist.* New York, NY: Random House/ Vintage Books.

Hernstein, R.J. (1971). IQ. *Atlantic Monthly, 228,* 43-64.

Hernstein, R.J. (1973). *IQ in the meritocracy.* Boston, MA: Atlantic Monthly Press.

Herrnstein, R.J., & Murray, C. (1994). *The bell curve: Intelligence and class structure in American life.* New York, NY: Free Press.

Herszenhorn, D.M. (2006). As test-taking grows, test-makers grow rarer. *New York Times,* May 5, pp. A1, A19.

Hexter, M.B., & Myerson, A. (1924). 13.77 versus 12.05: A study in probable error. *Mental Hygiene, 8,* 69-82.

Hilgard, E.R. (1987). *Psychology in America: A historical survey.* San Diego, CA: Harcourt Brace Jovanovich.

Huey, E.B. (1910). The Binet scale for measuring intelligence and retardation. *Journal of Educational Psychology, 1,* 435-444.

Hunt, E.B, Frost, N., & Lunneborg, C. (1973). Individual differences in cognition: A new approach to intelligence. In G.H. Bower (Ed.), *The psychology of learning and motivation* (Vol. 7). New York, NY: Academic Press.

James, W. (1899/1962). *Talks to teachers on psychology and to students on some of life's ideals*. Mineola, NY: Dover Publications. Originally published by Henry Holt and Company.

Jensen, A.R. (1969). How much can we boost IQ and scholastic achievement? *Harvard Educational Review, 39*, 1-123.

Joynson, R.B. (1989). *The Burt affair*. London, UK, and New York, NY: Routledge.

Kamin, L.J. (1974). *The science and politics of IQ*. Potomac, MD: Lawrence Erlbaum.

Kevles, D. (1985). *In the name of eugenics*. New York: Alfred A. Knopf.

Lemann, N. (1999). *The big test: The secret history of the American meritocracy.* New York, NY: Farrar, Straus and Giroux.

Lippmann, W. (1922). The mental age of Americans, etc. *New Republic, 32,* 213-215, 246-248, 275-277, 297-298, 328-380; *33,* 9-11, 145-146.

Lippmann, W. (1923). Mr. Burt and the intelligence tests, etc. *New Republic, 34,* 263-264, 295-296, 322-323.

Loehlin, J.C., Lindzey, G., & Spuhler, J.N. (1975). *Race differences in intelligence.* San Francisco, CA: Freeman.

Mackintosh, N.J. (Ed.). (1995). *Cyril Burt: Fraud or framed.* Oxford, UK: Oxford University Press.

Marks, D.F. (1997). Thurstone, Louis Leon. In N. Sheehy, A.J. Chapman, & W. A. Conroy (Eds.), *Biographical dictionary of psychology*, 571-572. London, UK: Routledge.

McClelland, D.C. (1973). Testing for competence rather than "intelligence." *American Psychologist, 28*, 1-14.

McNemar, Q. (1940). A critical examination of the University of Iowa studies of environmental influences upon IQ. *Psychological Bulletin, 37*, 63-92.

Münsterberg, H. (1891). Zur indivudal Psychologie. *Centralblatt fur Nervenheikunde und Psychiatrie, 14*, 196ff.

Neisser, U. (Ed.). (1986). *The school achievement of minority children: New Perspectives.* Hillsdale, NJ: Lawrence Erlbaum.

Neisser, U. (Ed.). (1998). *The rising curve: Long-term gains in IQ and related measures.* Washington, DC: American Psychological Association.

Neisser, U., Boodoo, G., Bouchard, T.J., Jr., Boykin, A.W., Brody, N., Ceci, S.J., Halpern, D.F., Loehlin, J.C., Perloff, R., Sternberg, R. J., & Urbina, S. (1996). Intelligence: Knowns and unknowns. *American Psychologist, 51*, 77-101.

Nucci, L.P. (1997). Gardner, Howard Earl. In N. Sheehy, A.J. Chapman, & W.A. Conroy (Eds.), *Biographical dictionary of psychology*, pp 222-223. London, UK: Routledge.

Pinter, R. (1923). Review of *A study of American intelligence. Journal of Educational Psychology, 13*, 184-185.

Resnick, L.B. (1976). *The nature of intelligence.* Hillsdale, NJ: Lawrence Erlbaum.

Sharp, S.E. (1899). Individual psychology: A study in psychological method. *American Journal of Psychology, 10*, 329-391. 539-540.

Sheehy, N., Chapman, A.J., & Conroy, W.A. (1997a). Guilford, Joy Paul. In N. Sheehy, A.J. Chapman, & W.A. Conroy (Eds.), *Biographical dictionary of psych-*

ology, pp. London, UK: Routledge.

Sheehy, N., Chapman, A.J., & Conroy, W.A. (1997b). Sternberg, Robert J. In N. Sheehy, A.J. Chapman, & W.A. Conroy (Eds.), *Biographical dictionary of psychology*, pp. 539-540. London, UK: Routledge.

Snyderman, M., & Herrnstein, R.J. (1983). Intelligence tests and the Immigration Act of 1924. *American Psychologist, 38*(9), 986-995.

Spearman, C.E. (1904). General intelligence objectively determined and measured. *American Journal of Psychology, 15*, 201-293.

Spearman, C.E. (1914). The theory of two factors. *Psychological Review, 21*, 101-115.

Sternberg, R.J. (1977a). Component processes in analogical reasoning. *Psychological Review, 84*, 353-378.

Sternberg, R.J. (1977b). The nature of mental abilities. *American Psychologist, 34*, 214-220.

Sternberg, R.J. (1984). *Beyond IQ: A triarchic theory of intelligence*. New York, NY: Cambridge University Press.

Sternberg, R.J. (1986a). *Intelligence applied: Understanding and increasing your intellectual skills*. New York, NY: Harcourt, Brace and Jovanovich.

Sternberg, R.J. (1986b). A triangular theory of love. *Psychological Review, 93*, 119-135.

Sternberg, R.J. (1991). Death, taxes, and bad intelligence tests. *Intelligence, 15*(3), 257-270.

Sternberg, R.J. (1995). Love as a story. *Journal of Social and Personal Relation-*

ships, 12, 541-546.

Sternberg, R.J. (1999). A propulsion theory of types of creative contributions. *Review of General Psychology, 3,* 83-100.

Sternberg, R.J. (2002). It all started with those darn IQ tests: Half a career spent defying the crowd. In R.J. Sternberg (Ed.), *Psychologists defying the crowd: Stories of those who battled the establishment and won,* pp. 257-270. Washington, DC: American Psychological Association.

Stoddard, G.D., & Wellman, B.L. (1940). Environment and the IQ. In G.D. Stoddard (Chr.), *Intelligence: Its nature and nurture.* (39th Yearbook of the National Society for the Study of Education, Pt. 1). Bloomington, IL: Public School Publishing.

Terman, L.M. (1906). Genius and stupidity: A study of some of the intellectual processes of seven "bright" and seven "stupid" boys. *Pedagogical Seminary, 13,* 307-373.

Terman, L.M. (1911). The Binet-Simon scale for measuring intelligence: Impressions gained by its application upon four hundred non-selected children. *Psychological Clinic, 5,* 199-206.

Terman, L.M. (1916). *The measurement of intelligence.* Boston, MA: Houghton Mifflin.

Terman, L.M. (1922a). The psychological determinist, or democracy and the IQ. *Journal of Educational Research, 6,* 57-62.

Terman, L.M. (1922b). The great conspiracy, or the impulse imperious of intelligence testers, psychoanalyzed and exposed by Mr. Lippmann. *New Republic, 33,* 116-120.

Terman, L.M. (1924). The mental test as a psychological method. *Psychological*

Review, 31, 93-117.

Terman, L.M. (Chr.). (1928). Nature and nurture: Their influence on intelligence (27th Yearbook of the National Society for the Study of Education, Pts. 1-2). Bloomington, IN: Public School Publishing.

Terman, L.M. (1938). *Psychological factors in marital happiness*. New York, NY: McGraw-Hill.

Terman, L.M., & Childs, H.G.(1912). A tentative revision and extension of the Binet-Simon measuring scale of intelligence. *Journal of Educational Psychology, 3*, 61-74.

Terman, L.M., Kelly, T.L., & Ruch, G.M. (1923) *Stanford Achievement Test*. Yonkers, NY: World Book.

Terman, L.M., & Miles, C.C. (1936). *Sex and personality: Studies in masculinity and femininity*. New York, NY: McGraw-Hill.

Thorndike, E.L. (1903). *Educational psychology*. New York, NY: Teachers College.

Thorndike, E.L. (1904). *Introduction to the theory of mental and social measurements.* New York, NY: Science Press.

Thorndike, E.L. (1913a). *Educational psychology: Vol. 1. The original nature of man.* New York, NY: Teachers College.

Thorndike, E.L. (1913b). *Educational psychology: Vol. 2. The psychology of learning.* New York, NY: Teachers College.

Thorndike, E.L. (1914). *Educational psychology: Vol. 3. Mental work and fatigue, and individual differences and their causes..* New York, NY: Teachers College.

Thorndike, E.L. (1917). *The Thorndike arithmetics* (Books 1-3). New York, NY:

Rand McNally.

Thorndike, E.L. (1921). *The teacher's word book.* New York, NY: Teachers College.

Thorndike, E.L., Lay, W., & Dean, P.R. (1909). The relation of accuracy in sensory discrimination to general intelligence. *American Journal of Psychology, 20,* 364-369.

Thorndike, E.L., & Woodward, R.S. (1901). The influence of one mental function upon the efficiency of other functions. *Psychological Review, 8,* 247-261, 384-395, 553-564.

Thurstone, L.L. (1924a). *Psychological examination for high school graduates and college freshman.* Washington, DC: American Council on Education.

Thurstone, L.L. (1924b). *The fundamentals of statistics.* New York, NY: Macmillan.

Thurstone, L.L. (1925). A method of scaling psychological and educational tests. *Journal of Educational Psychology, 16,* 433-451.

Thurstone, L.L. (1927). A law of comparative judgment. *Psychological Review, 34,* 273-286.

Thurstone, L.L. (1928). Attitudes can be measured. *American Journal of Sociology, 19,* 441-453.

Thurstone, L.L. (1931). Multiple factor analysis. *Psychological Review, 38,* 406-427.

Thurstone, L.L. (1934). The vectors of mind. *Psychological Review, 41,* 1-32.

Thurstone, L.L. (1935). *Vectors of the mind.* Chicago, IL: University of Chicago

Press.

Thurstone, L.L. (1938). *Primary mental abilities*. Chicago, IL: University of Chicago Press.

Thurstone, L.L. (1947). *Multiple factor analysis*. Chicago, IL: University of Chicago Press.

Thurstone, L.L, & Chave, E.J. (1929). *The measurement of attitudes*. Chicago, IL: University of Chicago Press.

Thurstone, L.L., & Thurstone, T.G. (1930). A neurotic inventory. *Journal of Social Psychology, 1*, 3-30.

Waterhouse, L. (2006a). Multiple intelligence, the Mozart effect, and emotional intelligence: A critical review. *Educational Psychologist, 41*(4), 207-225.

Waterhouse, L. (2006b). Inadequate evidence for multiple intelligences, Mozart effect, and emotional intelligence theories. *Educational Psychologist, 41*(4), 247-255.

Wechsler, D. (1939). *The measurement of adult intelligence*. Baltimore, MD: Williams & Wilkins.

Wechsler, D. (1949). *Wechsler Intelligence Scale for Children*. New York, NY: Psychological Corporation.

Wissler, C. (1901). The correlation of mental and physical tests. *Psychological Review, Monograph Supplement, 3*(6).

Whipple, F.M. (1910). *Manual of mental and physical tests* (Vols. 1-2). Baltimore, MD: Warwich & York.

Whipple, G.M. (1928). Editorial impressions of the contribution to knowledge of the 27th Yearbook. *Journal of Educational Psychology, 19,* 392.

Woodworth, R.S. (1941). *Heredity and environment: A critical survey of recently published material on twins and foster children.* New York, NY: Social Science Research Council (Bulletin No. 47).

Yerkes, R.M. (Ed.). (1921). *Psychological examining in the U.S. Army.* Memoirs of the National Academy of Sciences, No. 15.

Yerkes, R.M. (1923). Testing the human mind. *Atlantic Monthly, 121,* 358-370.

Young, K. (1923). Review of *A study of American intelligence. Science, 57,* 666-670.

Zenderland, L. (1998). *Measuring minds: Henry Herbert Goddard and the origins of American intelligence testing.* Cambridge, United Kingdom: Cambridge University Press.

Zuckerman, H. (1977). Deviant behavior and social control in science. In E. Sagarin (Ed.), *Deviance and social change,* pp. 87-138. Beverly Hills, CA: Sage Publications.

CHAPTER 15: EXAMINING OUR PAST, FINDING OUR PRESENT

When a field formally undertakes an examination of its past, it is often a way of finding its present. The search for history accomplishes, intentionally or not, two related goals. On the one hand, the past is constructed to legitimize the present by giving it a history, grounding some current practices and understandings in a tradition, leading from the past that seems to point to the present. The present is then seen as an extension of the fundamental insights of that past. On the other hand, finding a history can be a way of relegating figures of potentially contemporary relevance to "history" and, hence, outside of the domain of current interests. In both of these senses, finding one's history is really a way of constructing oneself in the present. (Glick, 1994, p. 291).

History is too often limited to the stories we tell about the past either, as Joseph Glick observed, to legitimize the present or marginalize parts of our past. But there is another use of history, history in the sense of an accurate description of the people, events, and forces that shaped the past. We may discover history so we can find our present. That is the aim of this text and it is now time to sum up what we have found out about our present moment.

Common Themes

In the first chapter I highlighted five themes that run through the historical narrative. These themes were:
1) Everything is connected to everything else;
2) Psychology is shaped by the broader society and culture;
3) Psychology shapes the broader society and culture;
4) Psychology is an eminently practical field;
5) Psychological "truth" must be carefully proven.
Let us review each theme in turn.

That everything is connected to everything else does not mean that everything is equally connected. Some connections are closer than others. Still, it is surprising how closely connected psychology is to the developments in biology, in philosophy, and in politics and the arts. Broad cultural changes, such as the materialism and despair following World War I, or specific political events, such as the rise of Hitler and the holocaust, shape psychology. So too does the rise and decline of government support for education and research, and the impact that wars have on the field. In some cases, the connections are intimate, such as the discovery by Milgram of six degrees of separation and the play and movie that was inspired by his work.

Psychology is shaped by the broader social and cultural environment. Psychologists and their research are shaped by the broader context. In this sense, there is no pure isolated science or scientist.

On the other hand, psychology has shaped both broad cultural and social trends (such as child rearing, advertising, and education), as well as created specific features of modern life, such as educational tests and particular words (e.g., IQ, moron).

The impact of psychology illustrates how even (or especially) the basic research that psychologists carry out have practical consequences and benefits. While the benefits may not be obvious at first, they emerge in due time.

Finally, because psychology is shaped by the social and political culture, and because it is useful (and easy to misuse or abuse), we must be very critical of its truth-claims. Perhaps the most powerful aspect of modern psychology is its evolving research methods, a kind of mitigated skepticism that has slowly, sometimes painfully so, modified our understanding of human nature. The history of psychology is littered with examples of injustice carried out in the name of science, just as it has produced brilliant discoveries and practical nuggets.

Four Futures

The best way to look into the future is to extrapolate from the past and the present. There are four contemporary developments that may prove significant in the history of the field: evolutionary psychology, positive psychology, neuroscience, and cognitive science. Let us first survey these current developments, four possible futures, if you will, and then turn to the broader question of the future of psychology in light of its past.

In the past 20 years evolutionary psychology has emerged and gained widespread attention, both within the field and in the broader public. Evolutionary psychology incorporates evolutionary theory and Darwinian ideas along with psychological research methods into the study of behavior. Three indicators that evolutionary psychology has emerged as a specific subfield are that there are now college textbooks in evolutionary psychology (*e.g.*, Buss, 2004), evolutionary psychology is taught at the graduate and undergraduate level in some universities, and there are mass market books on the topic (e.g., Wright, 1994).

Evolutionary psychology, as all parts of psychology, must be understood in historical context. In this case, evolutionary psychology can be seen as part of the continuing effort to absorb evolution into our understanding of humans (and other animals). The first effort at absorbing evolutionary theory was the founding of the New Psychology in the United States. Functionalism itself, as much of the work of James and other American psychologists, was an effort to wrestle with Darwin and his work. In addition, the subfield of comparative psychology, described in Chapter 4, was a direct response to Darwin and his work.

The effort to absorb Darwin's work, and that of subsequent evolutionary biologists, has been ongoing in all areas of psychology. Psychoanalysis, in the sense of the theory of unconscious instincts, was a second attempt.

Relatively recently two knowledgeable observers of contemporary psychology have noted that the history of the assimilation of Darwin's work has been the history of the failure to fully assimilate his work (Charlesworth, 1992; Ghiselin, 1986). Evolutionary psychology is the latest effort to more fully assimilate the revolutionary ideas of Darwin and his fellow biologists. Whether or not evolutionary psychology will succeed is still an open question. The fact that Darwin, the theory of evolution, and modern biology will continue to have a powerful impact on psychology is beyond doubt.

A second current development is positive psychology which examines positive emotions and character, and the institutions that foster and support positive human characteristics. Positive psychology is thought of as a corrective to present-day work that focuses too often on the negative, the sick, and the defective in human life (Seligman & Csikzentmihalyi, 2000). While positive psychologists trace their lineage back to Allport's conception of personality and the humanistic psychologists, positive psychologists differ from the humanists in two important respects; one scientific, the other sociological.

Scientifically, the humanists carried out little rigorous empirical research (with the exception of Maslow and a few others). The positive psychologists have applied rigorous methods to a broad range of problems, such as excellence, savoring, and happiness. Their research productivity and quality is impressive and they appear to be making steady empirical progress (cf. Seligman, Steen, Park, & Peterson, 2005).

Sociologically, humanistic psychology, the so-called third force, was situated in the profession of clinical psychology. Positive psychology seems situated in the research centers of major universities, especially in the subfields of social and personality psychology. The success of their empirical research programs, and their location in research centers of personality and social psychology suggests that positive psychology will be an important part of future psychology (although only history will show whether it gets assimilated into personality and social psychology or whether it becomes a separate subfield).

Two other developments may represent the splitting-off of parts of psychology and their merger into two new sciences. I speak here of Neuroscience (described in Chapter 9) and Cognitive Science (described in Chapter 10). Both of these fields overlap extensively with modern psychology. Whatever the fate of these two fields (and both are thriving at the moment), a psychology without a neurophysiological basis and an interest in cognition is almost unimaginable. A more likely development will be the study of neurophysiology and cognition in more than one field, just as social psychology is now studied within both psychology and sociology.

If I was to be so foolish as to make a prediction about the future, I would predict that all four current developments will be important for the next 30 years. But then, such predictions are dangerous for an historian.

The Future Of Psychology

Psychology has shaped the social order, just as it is shaped by that order. While nothing lasts forever, and science developed and then disappeared twice before its present incarnation, given psychology's centrality to modern life and its global extent, it will be around for a while. Will it become a science in the sense that physics and biology are sciences? That is yet to be determined. The future is to be made.

References

Buss, D.M. (2004). *Evolutionary psychology: The new science of the mind* (2nd ed.). Boston, MA: Allyn & Bacon.

Charlesworth, W.R. (1992). Charles Darwin and developmental psychology: Past and present. *Developmental Psychology, 28*, 5-16.

Ghiselin, M.T. (1986). The assimilation of darwinism in developmental psychology. *Human Development, 29*, 12-21.

Pickren, W.E., & Dewsbury, D.A. (eds.). (2002). *Evolving perspectives on the history of psychology*. Washington, DC: American Psychological Association.

Seligman, M.E.P., & Csikszentmihalyi, M. (2000). Positive psychology: An introduction. *American Psychologist, 55*(1), 5-14.

Seligman, M.E.P., Steen, T.A., Park, N., & Peterson, C. (2005). Positive psychology progress: Empirical validation of interventions. *American Psychologist, 60*(5), 410-421.

Wright, R. (1994). *The moral animal: Evolutionary psychology and everyday life*. New York: Vintage Books.

ABOUT THE AUTHOR

Michael G. Livingston

Michael G. Livingston fell in love with the history of psychology in 1976 when, as a second semester senior at the University of Michigan, he took his first seminar in the history of the field. After a three year hiatus from college, during which he served in the Peace Corps and continued to cultivate his passion for history and for psychology, he began graduate studies at the University of Minnesota´s Institute of Child Development where his professors graciously allowed him to take one of his four preliminary exams in the philosophy and history of psychology. Livingston eventually earned his Ph.D. in Child Psychology and, after a few part time jobs as a contingent faculty member, began teaching full time at the College of St. Benedict/St. John´s University in Minnesota in 1985.

One of the first courses he was assigned to teach was history of psychology, a course he has taught on a regular basis since 1986. Students taking the history of psychology course often had little interest in the content of the course. History was a required capstone taken at the end of their undergraduate major. Over the years, Livingston tried many texts and experimented with many active learning strategies with the goal of fostering in his students an interest in the history of the field and an appreciation for how the field has evolved within the broader social context. Eventually, he started writing and then using his own history text in these courses, modifying the text in response to student feedback.

In addition to the History of Psychology course, he regularly teaches Developmental Psychology, Research Methods in Psychology, the Psychology of Emotions, and a seminar on Freud and Psychoanalysis. He also has directed five study abroad programs, two in Spain and three in Chile, and taught his university´s first year writing and speaking seminar. He has won Saint John´s University teacher of distinction award in 2003, the Minnesota Psychological Association´s undergraduate teacher of the year award in 2005, and the Robert E. Sloan award from the Minnesota Association of University Professors for his contributions to academic freedom and the professoriate in 2007.

Made in the USA
Monee, IL
13 February 2021